THE Java™ Tutorial
Fourth Edition

A Short Course on the Basics

The Java™ Series

Ken Arnold, James Gosling, David Holmes
The Java™ Programming Language, Fourth Edition

Joshua Bloch
Effective Java™ Programming Language Guide

Stephanie Bodoff, Dale Green, Kim Haase, Eric Jendrock
The J2EE™ Tutorial, Second Edition

Mary Campione, Kathy Walrath, Alison Huml
The Java™ Tutorial, Third Edition: A Short Course on the Basics

Mary Campione, Kathy Walrath, Alison Huml, The Tutorial Team
The Java™ Tutorial Continued: The Rest of the JDK™

Patrick Chan
The Java™ Developers Almanac 1.4, Volume 1

Patrick Chan
The Java™ Developers Almanac 1.4, Volume 2

Patrick Chan, Rosanna Lee
The Java™ Class Libraries, Second Edition, Volume 2: java.applet, java.awt, java.beans

Patrick Chan, Rosanna Lee, Doug Kramer
The Java™ Class Libraries, Second Edition, Volume 1: Supplement for the Java™ 2 Platform, Standard Edition, v1.2

Kirk Chen, Li Gong
Programming Open Service Gateways with Java™ Embedded Server

Zhiqun Chen
Java Card™ Technology for Smart Cards: Architecture and Programmer's Guide

Maydene Fisher, Jon Ellis, Jonathan Bruce
JDBC™ API Tutorial and Reference, Third Edition

Eric Freeman, Susanne Hupfer, Ken Arnold
JavaSpaces™ Principles, Patterns, and Practice

Li Gong, Gary Ellison, Mary Dageforde
Inside Java™ 2 Platform Security, Second Edition: Architecture, API Design, and Implementation

James Gosling, Bill Joy, Guy Steele, Gilad Bracha
The Java™ Language Specification, Third Edition

Mark Hapner, Rich Burridge, Rahul Sharma, Joseph Fialli, Kim Haase
Java™ Message Service API Tutorial and Reference: Messaging for the J2EE™ Platform

Jonni Kanerva
The Java™ FAQ

Doug Lea
Concurrent Programming in Java™, Second Edition: Design Principles and Patterns

Rosanna Lee, Scott Seligman
JNDI API Tutorial and Reference: Building Directory-Enabled Java™ Applications

Sheng Liang
The Java™ Native Interface: Programmer's Guide and Specification

Tim Lindholm, Frank Yellin
The Java™ Virtual Machine Specification, Second Edition

Roger Riggs, Antero Taivalsaari, Jim Van Peursem, Jyri Huopaniemi, Mark Patel, Aleksi Uotila
Programming Wireless Devices with the Java™ 2 Platform, Micro Edition, Second Edition

Rahul Sharma, Beth Stearns, Tony Ng
J2EE™ Connector Architecture and Enterprise Application Integration

Inderjeet Singh, Beth Stearns, Mark Johnson, Enterprise Team
Designing Enterprise Applications with the J2EE™ Platform, Second Edition

Inderjeet Singh, Sean Brydon, Greg Murray, Vijay Ramachandran, Thierry Violleau, Beth Stearns
Designing Web Services with the J2EE™ 1.4 Platform: JAX-RPC, SOAP, and XML Technologies

Sun Microsystems, Inc.
Java™ Look and Feel Design Guidelines: Advanced Topics

Kathy Walrath, Mary Campione, Alison Huml, Sharon Zakhour
The JFC Swing Tutorial, Second Edition: A Guide to Constructing GUIs

Steve Wilson, Jeff Kesselman
Java™ Platform Performance: Strategies and Tactics

THE Java™ Tutorial
Fourth Edition

A Short Course on the Basics

Sharon Zakhour
Scott Hommel
Jacob Royal
Isaac Rabinovitch
Tom Risser
Mark Hoeber

ADDISON-WESLEY

Upper Saddle River, NJ • Boston • Indianapolis • San Francisco
New York • Toronto • Montreal • London • Munich • Paris • Madrid
Capetown • Sydney • Tokyo • Singapore • Mexico City

The publisher offers excellent discounts on this book when ordered in quantity for bulk purchases or special sales, which may include electronic versions and/or custom covers and content particular to your business, training goals, marketing focus, and branding interests. For more information, please contact:

U.S. Corporate and Government Sales
(800) 382–3419
corpsales@pearsontechgroup.com

For sales outside the United States please contact:

International Sales
international@pearsoned.com

This Book Is Safari Enabled

The Safari® Enabled icon on the cover of your favorite technology book means the book is available through Safari Bookshelf. When you buy this book, you get free access to the online edition for 45 days.

Safari Bookshelf is an electronic reference library that lets you easily search thousands of technical books, find code samples, download chapters, and access technical information whenever and wherever you need it.

To gain 45-day Safari Enabled access to this book:

- Go to http://www.awprofessional.com/safarienabled
- Complete the brief registration form
- Enter the coupon code S1KU-LBNJ-GNTJ-WAJT-PZJV

If you have difficulty registering on Safari Bookshelf or accessing the online edition, please e-mail customer-service@safaribooksonline.com.

Visit us on the Web: www.awprofessional.com

Library of Congress Cataloging-in-Publication Data

The Java tutorial : a short course on the basics / Sharon Zakhour... [et al.]. -- 4th ed.
p. cm.
Previous ed: The Java tutorial / by Mary Campione.
Includes index.
ISBN 0-321-33420-5 (pbk. : alk. paper)
1. Java (Computer program language) I. Zakhour, Sharon. II. Campione, Mary. Java tutorial.

QA76.73.J38C365 2006
005.13'3--dc22 2006028544

Pearson Education, Inc.
Rights and Contracts Department
75 Arlington Street, Suite 300
Boston, MA 02116
Fax: (617) 848-7047

ISBN 0-321-33420-5
Text printed in the United States on recycled paper at RR Donnelley in Crawfordsville, Indiana.
First printing, October 2006

Contents

Foreword

IT is with some pleasure that I write this foreword to the new edition of the *Java Tutorial*.

One of the distinguishing characteristics of the Java platform has been the quality of its documentation. This has included the tutorials, as well as the detailed documentation of the APIs by means of JavaDoc, and the many books published in the Java series. One could argue that the quality of the documentation resources has been every bit as important to the widespread adoption of the Java platform as the quality of the language and libraries themselves. Indeed, they are all of a piece, and each deserves recognition and credit for the qualities it manifests.

Millions of developers spend their professional lives enveloped in the ecosystem engendered by the Java platform. There are myriad standards, APIs and tools. There is so much to learn! What's more, the amount of information you need to know keeps on growing. While this growth is something we software professionals should all be thankful for, it is an ongoing challenge for developers. I hope this tutorial will make it easier to meet this challenge and obtain competence and even mastery of the Java platform.

Whether you become a truly "competent programmer," as Edsger Dijkstra put it many years ago, is up to you; but if you don't, it cannot be blamed on the lack of a good Java tutorial. A number of dedicated professionals have done their best to see to that.

I hope this new edition meets and even exceeds the high standards set by its predecessors. Ultimately, it is you, the reader, who must be the judge. I expect you will not be disappointed.

Gilad Bracha
Los Altos, California
June 2006

Preface

SINCE the release of the original Java Development Kit in May of 1995, the engineering team at Sun Microsystems has been hard at work improving and enhancing the Java platform. The publication of this edition coincides with the release of Version 6 of the Java Platform Standard Edition (Java SE) and reflects the API of that release.

This edition introduces new features added to the Java platform since the publication of the third edition (under release 1.3), such as a chapter on Generics and information on annotations. There are new chapters on Java Web Start, The Platform Environment, and Regular Expressions. Most chapters, such as Concurrency (formerly Threads), I/O, Object-Oriented Programming Concepts, and Language Basics, have been completely rewritten. Collections has been brought out of the appendix and into its own chapter. A new appendix contains information on how to prepare for the Java Programming Language Certification exam.

All of the material has been thoroughly reviewed by members of engineering to ensure that the information is accurate and up to date.

Like the previous editions, this book is based on the online tutorial hosted at Sun Microsystems' Web site:

```
http://java.sun.com/docs/books/tutorial/
```

The information in this book is—often referred to as "the core tutorial" or "the basics"—that are required by most beginning to intermediate programmers. Once you have mastered the material in this book, you can explore the rest of the Java platform on the Web site.

As always, our goal is to create an easy-to-read practical programmer's guide with lots of examples to help people learn to program.

Who Should Read This Book?

This book is geared towards both novice and experienced programmers.

- *New programmers* can benefit most from reading the book from beginning to end, including the step by step instructions for compiling and running your first program in Getting Started (page 1).
- *Programmers experienced with procedural languages* such as C++ may wish to start with the material on object-oriented concepts and features of the Java programming language.
- *Experienced programmers* may want to jump feet first into more advanced topics, such as generics, concurrency, or Java Web Start.

This book contains information to address the learning needs of programmers with various levels of experience.

How to Use This Book

This book is designed so you can read it straight through or skip around from topic to topic. The information is presented in a logical order, and forward references are avoided wherever possible.

The examples in this tutorial are compiled against the 6.0 release. *You need to download this release in order to compile and run most examples.*

The accompanying CD contains the content of this book (including examples, and solutions and answers to the questions and exercises), as well as the online-only Java SE tutorials, an early 6.0 release of the Java SE Development Kit (JDK), and the corresponding API specification and guide documentation.

You will see footnotes like the following:

```
docs/api/java/lang/Class.html
```

and

```
tutorial/deployment/applet/examples/TalkServer.java
```

The highest level of the CD contains `docs` and `tutorial` directories, so those footnotes can be located on the CD as specified. To locate the latest pages online, prepend `http://java.sun.com/javase/6/` to the `docs` footnotes and `http://java.sun.com/docs/books/` to the `tutorial` footnotes:

http://java.sun.com/javase/6/docs/api/java/lang/Class.html

http://java.sun.com/docs/books/tutorial/deployment/applet/examples/TalkServer.java

The chapters in this book can be found on the CD at the following locations:

Chapter	Location
1. Getting Started	tutorial/getStarted
2. Object-Oriented Programming Concepts	tutorial/java/concepts
3. Language Basics	tutorial/java/nutsandbolts
4. Classes and Objects	tutorial/java/javaOO
5. Interfaces and Inheritance	tutorial/java/IandI
6. Generics	tutorial/java/generics
7. Packages	tutorial/java/package
8. Numbers and Strings	tutorial/java/data
9. Exceptions	tutorial/essential/exceptions
10. Basic I/O	tutorial/essential/io
11. Collections	tutorial/collections
12. Concurrency	tutorial/essential/concurrency
13. Regular Expressions	tutorial/essential/regex
14. The Platform Environment	tutorial/essential/environment
15. Swing	tutorial/ui
16. Packaging Programs in JAR Files	tutorial/deployment/jar
17. Java Web Start	tutorial/deployment/webstart
18. Applets	tutorial/deployment/applet

We welcome feedback on this edition. Please use the Tutorial feedback form:

http://developers.sun.com/contact/tutorial_feedback.jsp

Acknowledgments

Many Internet readers have helped us maintain and improve the quality of the tutorial by sending us email and cheerfully pointing out typos, broken links, and areas of the tutorial that caused confusion or could benefit from rewriting.

Many current and former members of the Java Software engineering and documentation teams have given us counsel, answered our many questions, reviewed our material, and even made contributions to it. The list is long, but we would particularly like to note the contributions of Eric Armstrong, David Bristor, Martin Buchholz, Mandy Chung, Iris Garcia Clark, Margarita Fischer, Amy Fowler, Andy Herrick, Shannon Hickey, David Holmes, Jim Holmlund, Patrick Keegan, Peter Korn, Masayoshi Okutsu, Scott Seligman, Xueming Shen, Sundar Sivasubramanian, Pete Soper, Scott Violet, and Kathy Walrath. We are also grateful for the talented writers and programmers at Sun who have contributed to the online tutorial as guest authors.

We want to thank our former colleague, Joshua Bloch, the original author of the Collections chapter who made the time to provide us with updated information. Thanks also to our external reviewers and longtime supporters, Doug Lea and Brian Goetz.

Debra Scott, our manager, gave us encouragement and the support necessary to do our work — and bring it in on time.

Our program managers, Mary Lautner and Ian Hardie, tracked schedules, ran interference, and provided comic relief.

Illustrators Michael Quillman and Dwayne Wolff created the professional graphics, quickly and efficiently.

We also thank the members of the SQE team who have provided valuable feedback.

Finally, thanks to the managers in Java SE for allowing their engineers and illustrators time to devote to this effort, and particularly: Uday Dhanikonda, Frances Ho, James Hsieh, Janet Koenig, and Keith Yarwood.

About the Authors

Sharon Zakhour, the Tutorial team lead, has worked at Sun as a senior technical writer for seven years. She contributed to *The JFC Swing Tutorial, Second Edition*, and has worked with the Swing and AWT teams for several years. She graduated from UC Berkeley with a B.A. in Computer Science and has worked as a programmer, developer support engineer, and technical writer for more than twenty years.

Scott Hommel is a technical writer on staff at Sun Microsystems, where he documents the Java Platform, Standard Edition. Since 1999, he has contributed to every major release of the JDK, mostly in the form of API spec clarifications and core release documentation. He currently works from home in the green mountains of Killington, Vermont.

Jacob Royal has a master's degree in IT and an MBA in Information Systems. He has authored administrator's guides, API references, programmer's guides and has identified new tools and developed code and writing standards for various companies including Lucent Technologies and Autodesk. He also contributes to the JSR APT specification and the Java deployment guides at Sun.

Isaac Rabinovitch is a freelance technical writer. He has authored user's manuals, programmer's guides, administrator's manuals, API references, release notes, and support documentation at Sun, Borland, SGI, and many other companies. He is fond of technical trivia, and has been playing with computers for longer than he cares to think about.

Thomas Risser was educated in physics at Harvard (B.A.) and the University of California at Berkeley (Ph.D.). He has been a technical writer in the computer industry for fifteen years.

Mark Hoeber is a former senior technical writer at Sun Microsystems. He has worked as a technical writer for twelve years, focusing on documentation for software developers and system administrators. In addition, Mark has worked on implementing content management systems for technical writing teams.

1

Getting Started

The Java Technology Phenomenon

Talk about Java technology seems to be everywhere, but what exactly is it? The following sections explain how Java technology is both a programming language and a platform, and provide an overview of what this technology can do for you.

About the Java Technology

Java technology is both a programming language and a platform.

The Java Programming Language

The Java programming language is a high-level language that can be characterized by all of the following buzzwords:

- Simple
- Architecture neutral
- Object oriented
- Portable
- Distributed
- High performance

- Multithreaded
- Robust
- Dynamic
- Secure

Each of the preceding buzzwords is explained in *The Java Language Environment*,[1] a white paper written by James Gosling and Henry McGilton.

In the Java programming language, all source code is first written in plain text files ending with the `.java` extension. Those source files are then compiled into `.class` files by the `javac` compiler. A `.class` file does not contain code that is native to your processor; it instead contains *bytecodes*—the machine language of the Java Virtual Machine (Java VM).[2] The `java` launcher tool then runs your application with an instance of the Java Virtual Machine (Figure 1.1).

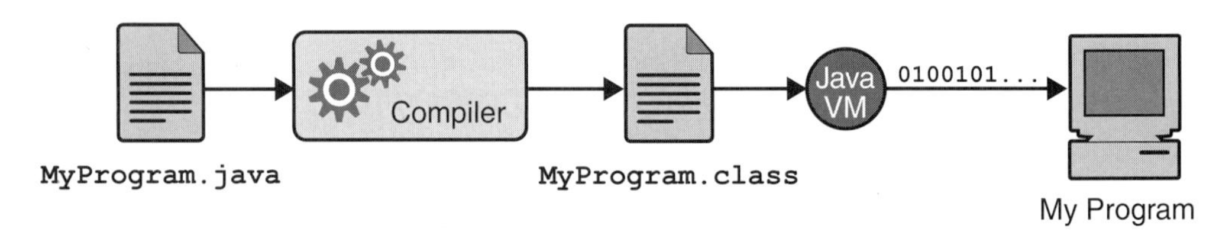

Figure 1.1 Compiling and running an application.

Because the Java VM is available on many different operating systems, the same `.class` files are capable of running on Microsoft Windows, the Solaris Operating System (Solaris OS), Linux, or Mac OS. Some virtual machines, such as the Java HotSpot virtual machine,[3] perform additional steps at runtime to give your application a performance boost. This includes various tasks such as finding performance bottlenecks and recompiling (to native code) frequently used sections of code (Figure 1.2).

1. `http://java.sun.com/docs/white/langenv/`
2. The terms "Java Virtual Machine" and "JVM" mean a Virtual Machine for the Java platform.
3. `http://java.sun.com/javase/technology/hotspot.jsp`

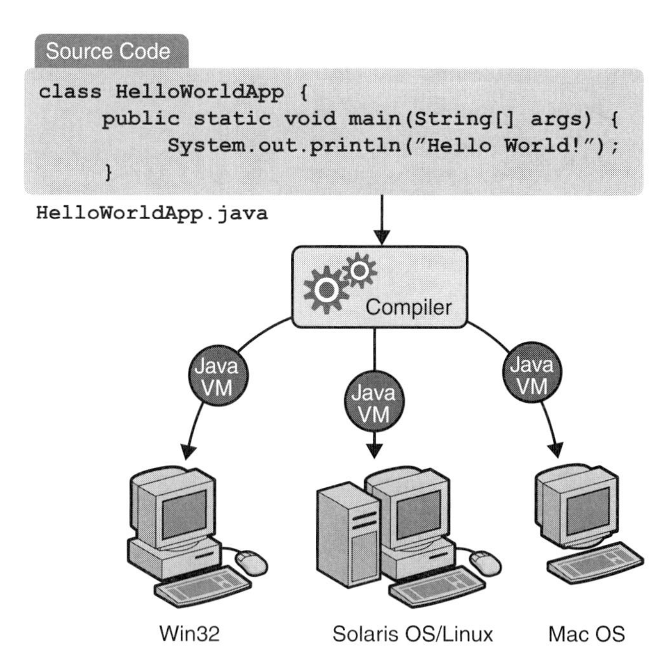

Figure 1.2 Through the Java VM, the same application is capable of running on multiple platforms.

The Java Platform

A *platform* is the hardware or software environment in which a program runs. We've already mentioned some of the most popular platforms like Microsoft Windows, Linux, Solaris OS, and Mac OS. Most platforms can be described as a combination of the operating system and underlying hardware. The Java platform differs from most other platforms in that it's a software-only platform that runs on top of other hardware-based platforms.

The Java platform has two components:

- The *Java Virtual Machine*
- The *Java Application Programming Interface* (API)

You've already been introduced to the Java Virtual Machine; it's the base for the Java platform and is ported onto various hardware-based platforms (Figure 1.3).

The API is a large collection of ready-made software components that provide many useful capabilities. It is grouped into libraries of related classes and interfaces; these libraries are known as *packages*. The next section highlights some of the functionality provided by the API.

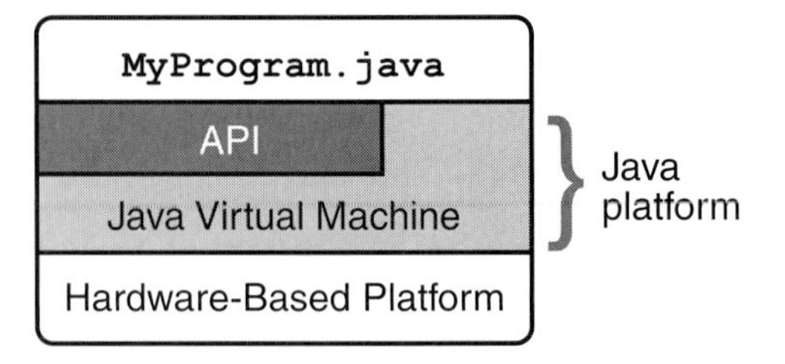

Figure 1.3 The API and Java Virtual Machine insulate the program from the underlying hardware.

As a platform-independent environment, the Java platform can be a bit slower than native code. However, advances in compiler and virtual machine technologies are bringing performance close to that of native code without threatening portability.

What Can Java Technology Do?

The general-purpose, high-level Java programming language is a powerful software platform. Every full implementation of the Java platform gives you the following features:

Development Tools The development tools provide everything you'll need for compiling, running, monitoring, debugging, and documenting your applications. As a new developer, the main tools you'll be using are the `javac` compiler, the `java` launcher, and the `javadoc` documentation tool.

Application Programming Interface (API) The API provides the core functionality of the Java programming language. It offers a wide array of useful classes ready for use in your own applications. The core API is very large; to get an overview of what it contains, consult the Java SE Development Kit 6 (JDK 6) documentation.[4]

Deployment Technologies The JDK software provides standard mechanisms such as the Java Web Start software and Java Plug-In software for deploying your applications to end users.

User Interface Toolkits The Swing and Java 2D toolkits make it possible to create sophisticated Graphical User Interfaces (GUIs).

4. `docs/index.html`

Integration Libraries Integration libraries such as the Java IDL API, JDBC API, Java Naming and Directory Interface ("J.N.D.I.") API, Java RMI, and Java Remote Method Invocation over Internet Inter-ORB Protocol Technology (Java RMI-IIOP Technology) enable database access and manipulation of remote objects.

How Will Java Technology Change My Life?

We can't promise you fame, fortune, or even a job if you learn the Java programming language. Still, it is likely to make your programs better and requires less effort than other languages. We believe that Java technology will help you do the following:

Get started quickly Although the Java programming language is a powerful object-oriented language, it's easy to learn, especially for programmers already familiar with C or C++.

Write less code Comparisons of program metrics (class counts, method counts, and so on) suggest that a program written in the Java programming language can be four times smaller than the same program written in C++.

Write better code The Java programming language encourages good coding practices, and automatic garbage collection helps you avoid memory leaks. Its object orientation, its JavaBeans component architecture, and its wide-ranging, easily extendible API let you reuse existing, tested code and introduce fewer bugs.

Develop programs more quickly The Java programming language is simpler than C++, and as such, your development time could be up to twice as fast when writing in it. Your programs will also require fewer lines of code.

Avoid platform dependencies You can keep your program portable by avoiding the use of libraries written in other languages.

Write once, run anywhere Because applications written in the Java programming language are compiled into machine-independent bytecodes, they run consistently on any Java platform.

Distribute software more easily With Java Web Start software, users will be able to launch your applications with a single click of the mouse. An automatic version check at startup ensures that users are always up to date with the latest version of your software. If an update is available, the Java Web Start software will automatically update their installation.

The "Hello World!" Application

The following sections provide detailed instructions for compiling and running a simple "Hello World!" application. The first section provides information on getting started with the NetBeans IDE, an integrated development environment that greatly simplifies the software development process. The remaining sections provide platform-specific instructions for getting started without an integrated development environment.

"Hello World!" for the NetBeans IDE

It's time to write your first application! These detailed instructions are for users of the NetBeans IDE. The NetBeans IDE runs on the Java platform, which means that you can use it with any operating system for which there is a JDK 6 available. These operating systems include Microsoft Windows, Solaris OS, Linux, and Mac OS X.

If you prefer to follow the tutorial *without* using an IDE, see (depending on your platform) "Hello World!" for Microsoft Windows (page 14) or "Hello World!" for Solaris OS and Linux (page 19) to get started.

A Checklist

To write your first program, you'll need:

1. **The Java SE Development Kit 6 (JDK 6)**
2. **The NetBeans IDE**

   You can download a bundle of the JDK and NetBeans IDE.[5] Bundle installers are available for the Microsoft Windows, Solaris OS, and Linux operating systems.

   You can also download and install the JDK and the IDE separately. Separate downloads of the JDK are available at:

   `http://java.sun.com/javase/6/download.jsp`

   (Make sure you download the **JDK**, *not* the JRE.)

   Separate downloads of the NetBeans IDE are available at:

   `http://www.netbeans.org/downloads/`

5. `http://java.sun.com/javase/6/download.jsp`

Note: The screen captures shown in this section reflect NetBeans IDE 5.0 running on JDK 6. At the time of this writing, 5.0 was the most current IDE version number. By the time you read this a newer IDE version may be available, but the workflow demonstrated here should remain the same.

Creating Your First Application

Your first application, `HelloWorldApp`, will simply display the greeting "Hello World!". To create this program, you will:

- **Create an IDE project.** When you create an IDE project, you create an environment in which to build and run your applications. Using IDE projects eliminates configuration issues normally associated with the `javac` compiler and `java` launcher tools. You can build or run your application by choosing a single menu item within the IDE.
- **Add code to the generated source file.** A source file contains code, written in the Java programming language, that you and other programmers can understand. As part of creating an IDE project, a skeleton source file will be automatically generated. You will then modify the source file to add the "Hello World!" message.
- **Compile the source file into a `.class` file.** The IDE invokes the Java programming language *compiler* (`javac`), which takes your source file and translates its text into instructions that the Java virtual machine can understand. The instructions contained within this file are known as *bytecodes.*
- **Run the program.** The IDE invokes the Java application *launcher tool* (`java`), which uses the Java virtual machine to run your application.

Create an IDE Project

To create an IDE project:

1. Launch the NetBeans IDE.
   - On Microsoft Windows systems, you can use the NetBeans IDE item in the Start menu.
   - On Solaris OS and Linux systems, you execute the IDE launcher script by navigating to the IDE's `bin` directory and typing `./netbeans`.
   - On Mac OS X systems, click the NetBeans IDE application icon.
2. In the NetBeans IDE, choose **File | New Project** (Figure 1.4).

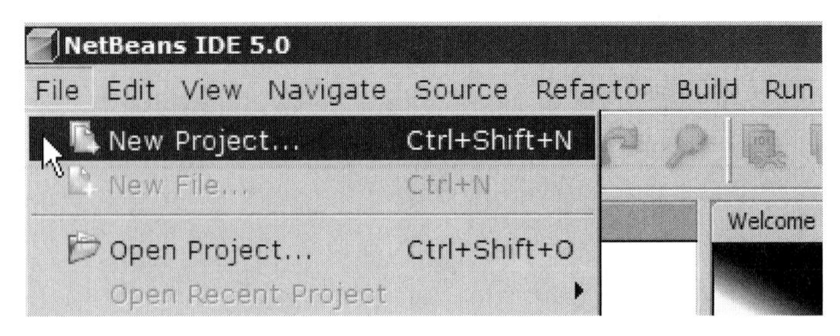

Figure 1.4 NetBeans IDE with the **File | New Project** menu item selected.

3. In the **New Project** wizard, expand the **General** category and select **Java Application** (Figure 1.5).

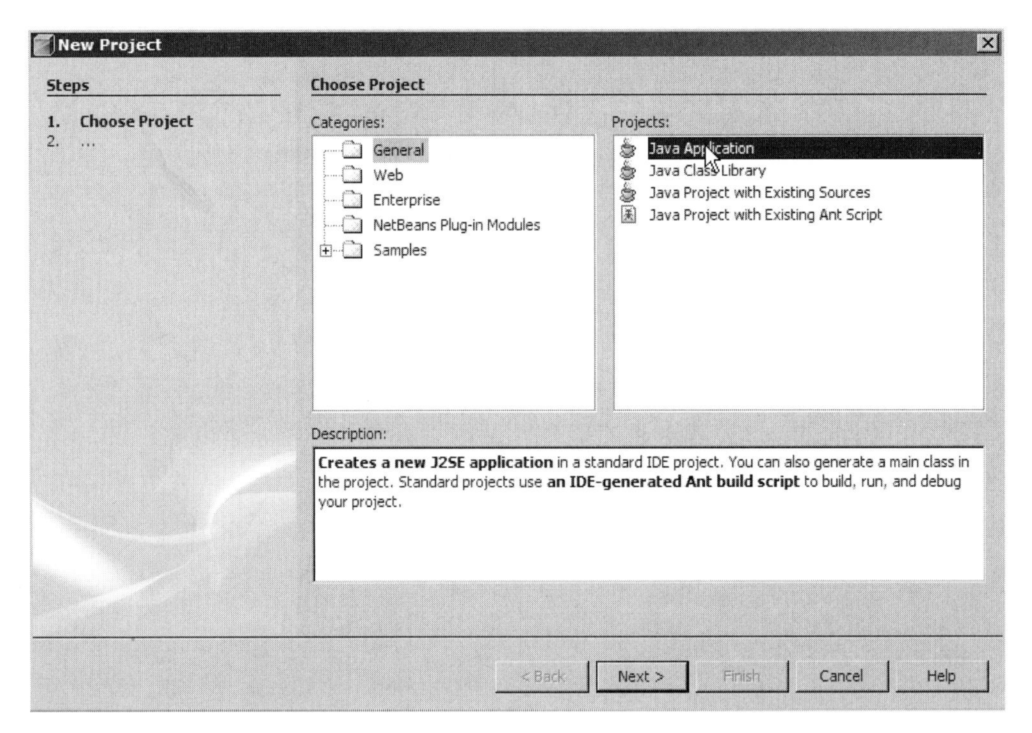

Figure 1.5 NetBeans IDE, New Project wizard, **Choose Project** page.

4. In the **Name and Location** page of the wizard, do the following (Figure 1.6):
   - In the **Project Name** field, type `Hello World App`.
   - In the **Create Main Class** field, type `helloworldapp.HelloWorldApp`.
   - Leave the **Set as Main Project** checkbox selected.
5. Click **Finish**.

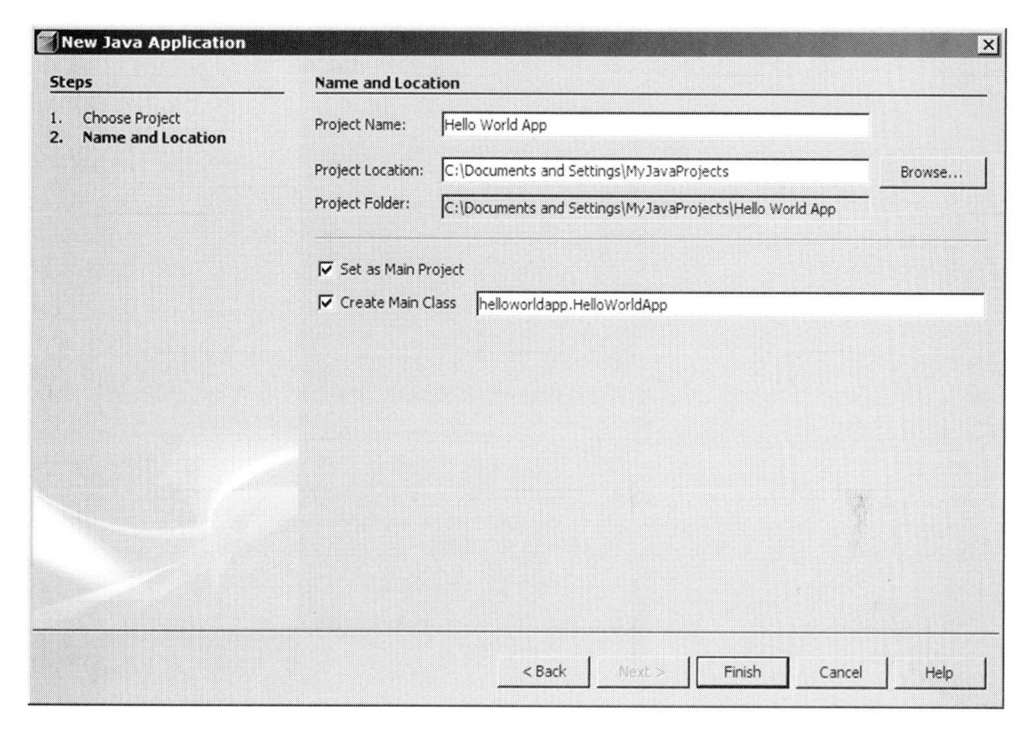

Figure 1.6 NetBeans IDE, New Project wizard, **Name and Location** page.

The project is created and opened in the IDE. You should see the following components:

- The **Projects** window, which contains a tree view of the components of the project, including source files, libraries that your code depends on, and so on.
- The **Source Editor** window with a file called `HelloWorldApp` open.
- The **Navigator** window, which you can use to quickly navigate between elements within the selected class (Figure 1.7).

Add Code to the Generated Source File

Because you have left the **Create Main Class** checkbox selected in the **New Project** wizard, the IDE has created a skeleton class for you. You can add the "Hello World!" message to the skeleton code by replacing the line:

```
// TODO code application logic here
```

with the line:

```
System.out.println("Hello World!"); // Display the string.
```

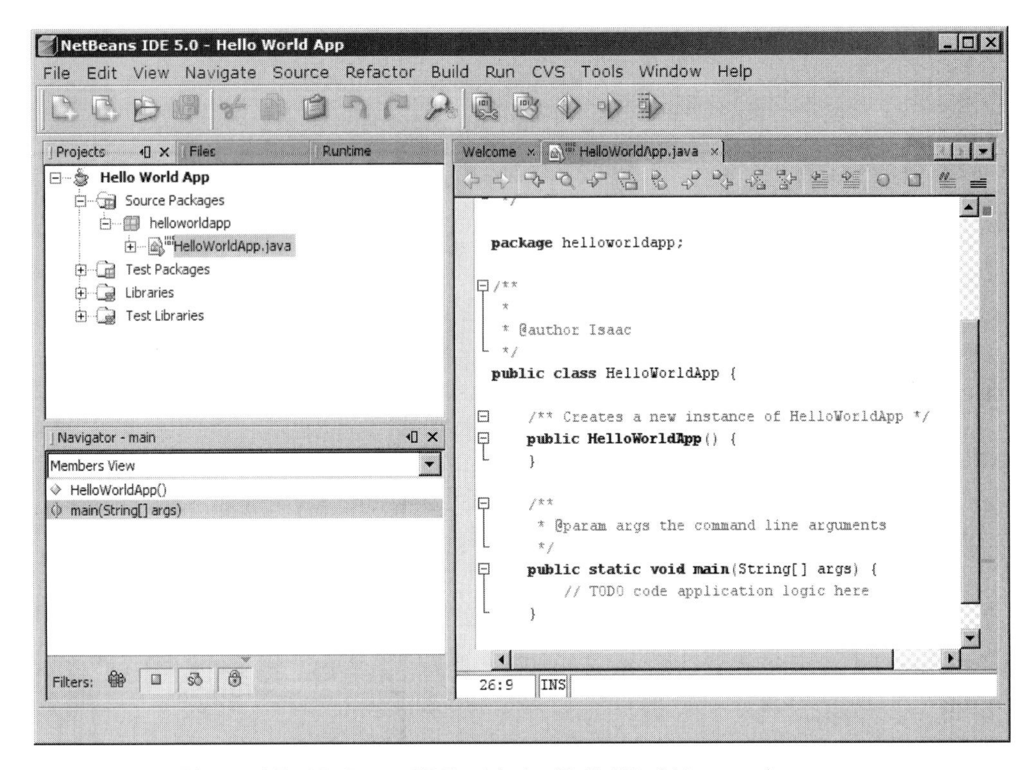

Figure 1.7 NetBeans IDE with the HelloWorldApp project open.

Optionally, replace these four lines of generated code

```
/**
 *
 * @author
 */
```

with these lines:

```
/**
 * The HelloWorldApp class implements an application that
 * simply prints "Hello World!" to standard output.
 */
```

These four lines are a code comment and do not affect how the program runs. Later sections of this tutorial explain the use and format of code comments.

Be Careful When You Type: Type all code, commands, and file names exactly as shown. Both the compiler (`javac`) and launcher (`java`) are *case-sensitive*, so you must capitalize consistently. In other words, `HelloWorldApp` is not equivalent to `helloworldapp`.

Save the change by choosing **File | Save**.

The file should look something like the following:

```
/*
 * HelloWorldApp.java
 *
 * Created on February 5, 2006, 6:43 PM
 *
 * To change this template, choose Tools | Template Manager
 * and open the template in the editor.
 */

package helloworldapp;

/**
 * The HelloWorldApp class implements an application that
 * simply prints "Hello World!" to standard output.
 */
public class HelloWorldApp {

  /** Creates a new instance of HelloWorldApp */
  public HelloWorldApp() {
  }

  /**
   * @param args the command line arguments
   */
  public static void main(String[] args) {
    System.out.println("Hello World!"); // Display the string.
  }

}
```

Compile the Source File into a .class File

To compile your source file, choose **Build | Build Main Project** from the IDE's main menu.

The **Output** window opens and displays output similar to what you see in Figure 1.8.

Figure 1.8 Output window showing results of building the HelloWorld project.

If the build output concludes with the statement `BUILD SUCCESSFUL`, congratulations! You have successfully compiled your program!

If the build output concludes with the statement `BUILD FAILED`, you probably have a syntax error in your code. Errors are reported in the **Output** window as hyper-linked text. You double-click such a hyper-link to navigate to the source of an error. You can then fix the error and once again choose **Build | Build Main Project**.

When you build the project, the bytecode file `HelloWorldApp.class` is generated. You can see where the new file is generated by opening the **Files** window and expanding the `Hello World App/build/classes/helloworldapp` node as shown in Figure 1.9.

Figure 1.9 Files window, showing the generated `.class` file.

Now that you have built the project, you can run your program.

Run the Program

From the IDE's menu bar, choose **Run | Run Main Project**.

Figure 1.10 shows what you should now see.

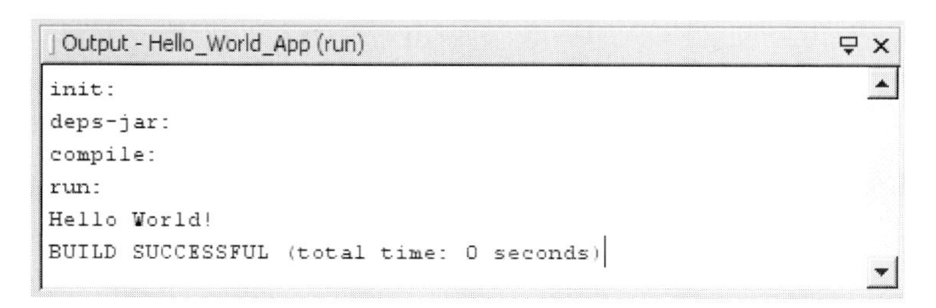

Figure 1.10 The program prints "Hello World!" to the **Output** window (along with other output from the build script).

Congratulations! Your program works!

Continuing the Tutorial with the NetBeans IDE

The section "A Closer Look at the "Hello World!" Application" on page 24 will explain the code in this simple application. Although the rest of the tutorial does not give specific instructions about using the NetBeans IDE, you can easily use the IDE to write and run the sample code. The following are some tips on using the IDE and explanations of some IDE behavior that you are likely to see:

- Once you have created a project in the IDE, you can add files to the project using the **New File** wizard. Choose **File | New File**, and then select a template in the wizard, such as the **Empty Java File** template.
- You can compile and run an individual file (as opposed to a whole project) using the IDE's **Compile File** (F9) and **Run File** (Shift-F6) commands. If you use the Run Main Project command, the IDE will run the file that the IDE associates as the main class of the main project. Therefore, if you create an additional class in your `HelloWorldApp` project and then try to run that file with the **Run Main Project** command, the IDE will run the `HelloWorldApp` file instead.
- You might want to create separate IDE projects for sample applications that include more than one source file.
- As you are typing in the IDE, a code completion box might periodically appear. You can either ignore the code completion box and keep typing, or you can select one of the suggested expressions. If you would prefer not to have the code completion box automatically appear, you can turn off the feature. Choose **Tools | Options**, click the **Editor** tab, and clear the **Auto Popup Completion Window** checkbox.
- If you try to rename the node for a source file in the **Projects** window, the IDE prompts you with the **Rename** dialog box to lead you through the options of renaming the class and the updating of code that refers to that class. Click **Next** to display the **Refactoring** window, which contains a tree view of changes to be made. Then click **Do Refactoring** to apply the changes. This sequence of clicks might seem

unnecessary if you have just a single class in your project, but it is very useful when your changes affect other parts of your code in larger projects.

- For a more thorough guide to the features of the NetBeans IDE, see the NetBeans IDE Docs and Support page[6] or explore the documentation available from the IDE's Help menu.

"Hello World!" for Microsoft Windows

It's time to write your first application! The following instructions are for users of Windows XP Professional, Windows XP Home, Windows Server 2003, Windows 2000 Professional, and Windows Vista. Instructions for Solaris OS and Linux are in the "Hello World!" for Solaris OS and Linux section (page 19).

A Checklist

To write your first program, you'll need:

1. **The Java SE Development Kit 6 (JDK 6)**

   You can download the Windows version now.[7] (Make sure you download the **JDK**, *not* the JRE.) Consult the installation instructions.[8]

2. **A text editor**

   In this example, we'll use Notepad, a simple editor included with the Windows platforms. You can easily adapt these instructions if you use a different text editor.

These two items are all you'll need to write your first application.

Creating Your First Application

Your first application, `HelloWorldApp`, will simply display the greeting "Hello World!". To create this program, you will:

- **Create a source file.** A source file contains code, written in the Java programming language, that you and other programmers can understand. You can use any text editor to create and edit source files.

- **Compile the source file into a `.class` file.** The Java programming language *compiler* (`javac`) takes your source file and translates its text into instructions that the Java virtual machine can understand. The instructions contained within this file are known as *bytecodes*.

---

6. `http://www.netbeans.org/kb/`
7. `http://java.sun.com/javase/6/download.jsp`
8. `http://java.sun.com/javase/6/webnotes/install/`

- **Run the program.** The Java application *launcher tool* (`java`) uses the Java virtual machine to run your application.

Create a Source File

To create a source file, you have two options:

- You can save the file `HelloWorldApp.java`[9] on your computer and avoid a lot of typing. Then, you can go straight to the Compile the Source File into a `.class` File section (page 16).
- Or, you can use the following (longer) instructions.

First, start your editor. You can launch the Notepad editor from the **Start** menu by selecting **Programs > Accessories > Notepad**. In a new document, type in the following code:

```
/**
 * The HelloWorldApp class implements an application that
 * simply prints "Hello World!" to standard output.
 */
class HelloWorldApp {
  public static void main(String[] args) {
    System.out.println("Hello World!"); // Display the string.
  }
}
```

Be Careful When You Type: Type all code, commands, and file names exactly as shown. Both the compiler (`javac`) and launcher (`java`) are *case-sensitive*, so you must capitalize consistently. In other words, `HelloWorldApp` is not equivalent to `helloworldapp`.

Save the code in a file with the name `HelloWorldApp.java`. To do this in Notepad, first choose the **File > Save As** menu item. Then, in the **Save As** dialog box:

1. Using the **Save in** combo box, specify the folder (directory) where you'll save your file. In this example, the directory is `java` on the `C` drive.
2. In the **File name** text field, type `"HelloWorldApp.java"`, including the quotation marks.
3. From the **Save as type** combo box, choose **Text Documents (*.txt)**.
4. In the **Encoding** combo box, leave the encoding as ANSI.

---

9. `tutorial/getStarted/application/examples/HelloWorldApp.java`

When you're finished, the dialog box should look like Figure 1.11.

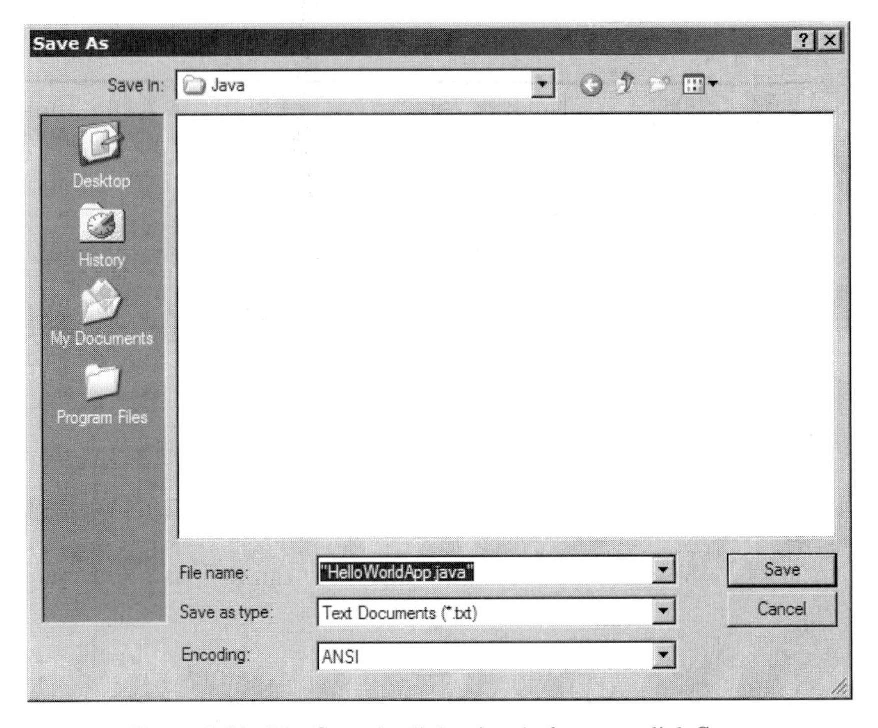

Figure 1.11 The **Save As** dialog just before you click **Save**.

Now click **Save**, and exit Notepad.

Compile the Source File into a .class File

Bring up a shell, or "command," window. You can do this from the **Start** menu by choosing **Command Prompt** (Windows XP), or by choosing **Run . . .** and then entering `cmd`. The shell window should look similar to Figure 1.12.

The prompt shows your *current directory*. When you bring up the prompt, your current directory is usually your home directory for Windows XP (as shown in Figure 1.12).

```
Command Prompt
Microsoft Windows XP [Version 5.1.2600]
(C) Copyright 1985-2001 Microsoft Corp.

C:\>
```

Figure 1.12 A shell window.

To compile your source file, change your current directory to the directory where your file is located. For example, if your source directory is `java` on the `C` drive, type the following command at the prompt and press **Enter**:

```
cd C:\java
```

Now the prompt should change to `C:\java>`.

Note: To change to a directory on a different drive, you must type an extra command: the name of the drive. For example, to change to the `java` directory on the `D` drive, you must enter `D:`, as shown in Figure 1.13.

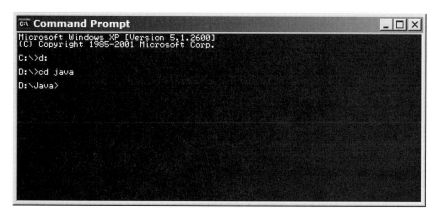

Figure 1.13 Changing directory on an alternate drive.

If you enter `dir` at the prompt, you should see your source file, as Figure 1.14 shows.

```
Command Prompt
Microsoft Windows XP [Version 5.1.2600]
(C) Copyright 1985-2001 Microsoft Corp.

C:\>d:

D:\>cd java

D:\Java>dir
 Volume in drive D is Second Partition
 Volume Serial Number is CCC5-CD80

 Directory of D:\Java

07/10/2006  10:38 PM    <DIR>          .
07/10/2006  10:38 PM    <DIR>          ..
07/10/2006  10:28 PM               286 HelloWorldApp.java
               1 File(s)            286 bytes
               2 Dir(s)   1,298,436,096 bytes free

D:\Java>
```

Figure 1.14 Directory listing showing the `.java` source file.

Now you are ready to compile. At the prompt, type the following command and press **Enter**.

```
javac HelloWorldApp.java
```

The compiler has generated a bytecode file, `HelloWorldApp.class`. At the prompt, type `dir` to see the new file that was generated, as shown in Figure 1.15.

```
Command Prompt
 Directory of D:\Java

07/10/2006  10:38 PM    <DIR>          .
07/10/2006  10:38 PM    <DIR>          ..
07/10/2006  10:28 PM               286 HelloWorldApp.java
               1 File(s)            286 bytes
               2 Dir(s)   1,298,436,096 bytes free

D:\Java>javac HelloWorldApp.java

D:\Java>dir
 Volume in drive D is Second Partition
 Volume Serial Number is CCC5-CD80

 Directory of D:\Java

07/10/2006  10:44 PM    <DIR>          .
07/10/2006  10:44 PM    <DIR>          ..
07/10/2006  10:44 PM               432 HelloWorldApp.class
07/10/2006  10:28 PM               286 HelloWorldApp.java
               2 File(s)            718 bytes
               2 Dir(s)   1,298,436,096 bytes free

D:\Java>
```

Figure 1.15 Directory listing showing the generated `.class` file.

Now that you have a `.class` file, you can run your program.

Run the Program

In the same directory, enter the following command at the prompt:

```
java HelloWorldApp
```

Figure 1.16 shows what you should now see.

```
Command Prompt
07/10/2006  10:38 PM    <DIR>          ..
07/10/2006  10:28 PM               286 HelloWorldApp.java
               1 File(s)            286 bytes
               2 Dir(s)   1,298,436,096 bytes free

D:\Java>javac HelloWorldApp.java

D:\Java>dir
 Volume in drive D is Second Partition
 Volume Serial Number is CCC5-CD80

 Directory of D:\Java

07/10/2006  10:44 PM    <DIR>          .
07/10/2006  10:44 PM    <DIR>          ..
07/10/2006  10:44 PM               432 HelloWorldApp.class
07/10/2006  10:28 PM               286 HelloWorldApp.java
               2 File(s)            718 bytes
               2 Dir(s)   1,298,436,096 bytes free

D:\Java>java HelloWorldApp
Hello World!

D:\Java>
```

Figure 1.16 The program prints "Hello World!" to the screen.

Congratulations! Your program works!

"Hello World!" for Solaris OS and Linux

It's time to write your first application! These detailed instructions are for users of Solaris OS and Linux. Instructions for Microsoft Windows are in the "Hello World!" for Microsoft Windows section (page 14).

A Checklist

To write your first program, you'll need:

1. **The Java SE Development Kit 6 (JDK 6)**

   You can download the Solaris OS or Linux version now.[10] (Make sure you download the **JDK**, *not* the JRE.) Consult the installation instructions.[11]

2. **A text editor**

   In this example, we'll use Pico, an editor available for many UNIX-based platforms. You can easily adapt these instructions if you use a different text editor, such as `vi` or `emacs`.

These two items are all you'll need to write your first application.

---

10. `http://java.sun.com/javase/6/download.jsp`

11. `http://java.sun.com/javase/6/webnotes/install/`

Creating Your First Application

Your first application, `HelloWorldApp`, will simply display the greeting "Hello world!". To create this program, you will:

- **Create a source file.** A source file contains code, written in the Java programming language, that you and other programmers can understand. You can use any text editor to create and edit source files.
- **Compile the source file into a `.class` file.** The Java programming language *compiler* (`javac`) takes your source file and translates its text into instructions that the Java virtual machine can understand. The instructions contained within this `.class` file are known as *bytecodes*.
- **Run the program.** The Java application *launcher tool* (`java`) uses the Java virtual machine to run your application.

Create a Source File

To create a source file, you have two options:

- You can save the file `HelloWorldApp.java`[12] on your computer and avoid a lot of typing. Then, you can go straight to the Compile the Source File into a `.class` File section (page 22).
- Or, you can use the following (longer) instructions.

First, open a shell, or "terminal," window (Figure 1.17).

Figure 1.17 A new terminal window.

12. `tutorial/getStarted/application/examples/HelloWorldApp.java`

When you first bring up the prompt, your *current directory* will usually be your *home directory*. You can change your current directory to your home directory at any time by typing `cd` at the prompt and then pressing **Return**.

The source files you create should be kept in a separate directory. You can create a directory by using the command `mkdir`. For example, to create the directory `java` in your home directory, use the following commands:

```
cd
mkdir java
```

To change your current directory to this new directory, you then enter:

```
cd java
```

Now you can start creating your source file.

Start the Pico editor by typing `pico` at the prompt and pressing **Return**. If the system responds with the message `pico: command not found`, then Pico is most likely unavailable. Consult your system administrator for more information, or use another editor.

When you start Pico, it'll display a new, blank *buffer*. This is the area in which you will type your code.

Type the following code into the new buffer:

```
/**
 * The HelloWorldApp class implements an application that
 * simply prints "Hello World!" to standard output.
 */
class HelloWorldApp {
  public static void main(String[] args) {
    System.out.println("Hello World!"); // Display the string.
  }
}
```

Be Careful When You Type: Type all code, commands, and file names exactly as shown. Both the compiler (`javac`) and launcher (`java`) are *case-sensitive*, so you must capitalize consistently. In other words, `HelloWorldApp` is not equivalent to `helloworldapp`.

Save the code in a file with the name `HelloWorldApp.java`. In the Pico editor, you do this by typing **Ctrl-O** and then, at the bottom where you see the prompt `File Name to write:`, entering the directory in which you wish to create the file, followed by `HelloWorldApp.java`. For example, if you wish to save

`HelloWorldApp.java` in the directory `/home/jdoe/java`, then you type `/home/jdoe/java/HelloWorldApp.java` and press **Return**.

You can type **Ctrl-X** to exit Pico.

Compile the Source File into a .class File

Bring up another shell window. To compile your source file, change your current directory to the directory where your file is located. For example, if your source directory is `/home/jdoe/java`, type the following command at the prompt and press **Return**:

```
cd /home/jdoe/java
```

If you enter `pwd` at the prompt, you should see the current directory, which in this example has been changed to `/home/jdoe/java`.

If you enter `ls` at the prompt, you should see your file (Figure 1.18).

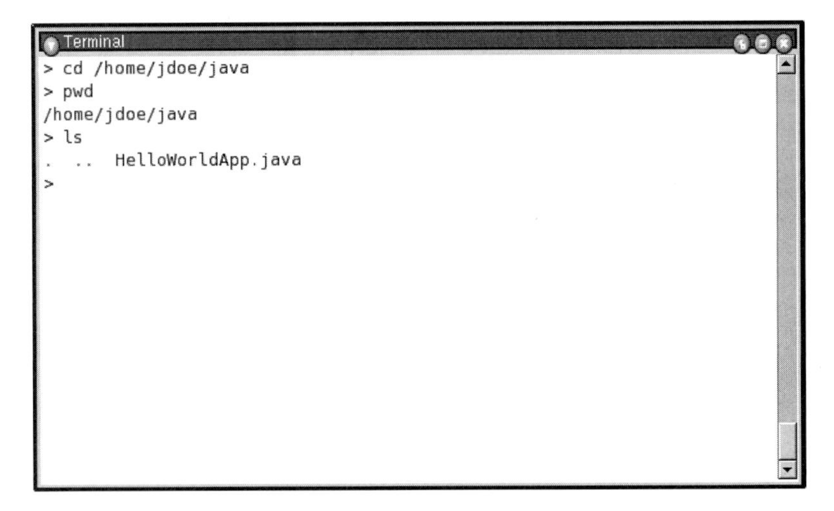

Figure 1.18 Results of the `ls` command, showing the `.java` source file.

Now are ready to compile the source file. At the prompt, type the following command and press **Return**.

```
javac HelloWorldApp.java
```

The compiler has generated a bytecode file, `HelloWorldApp.class`. At the prompt, type `ls` to see the new file that was generated: Figure 1.19.

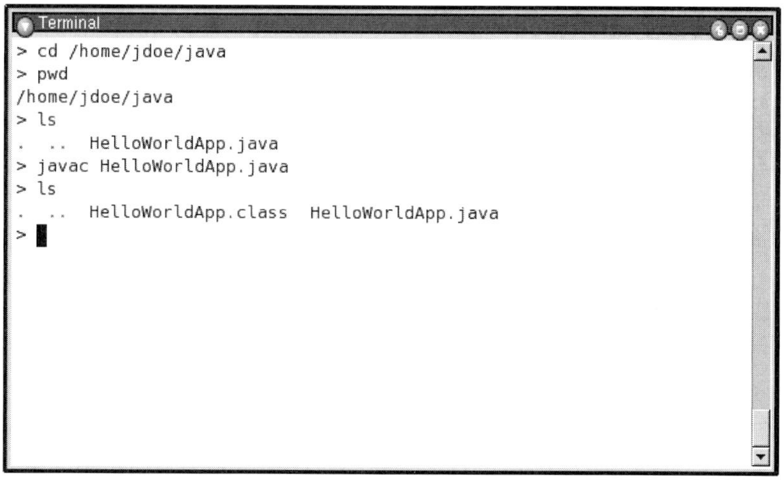

```
Terminal
> cd /home/jdoe/java
> pwd
/home/jdoe/java
> ls
.  ..  HelloWorldApp.java
> javac HelloWorldApp.java
> ls
.  ..  HelloWorldApp.class  HelloWorldApp.java
>
```

Figure 1.19 Results of the `ls` command, showing the generated `.class` file.

Now that you have a `.class` file, you can run your program.

Run the Program

In the same directory, enter at the prompt:

```
java HelloWorldApp
```

Figure 1.20 shows what you should now see.

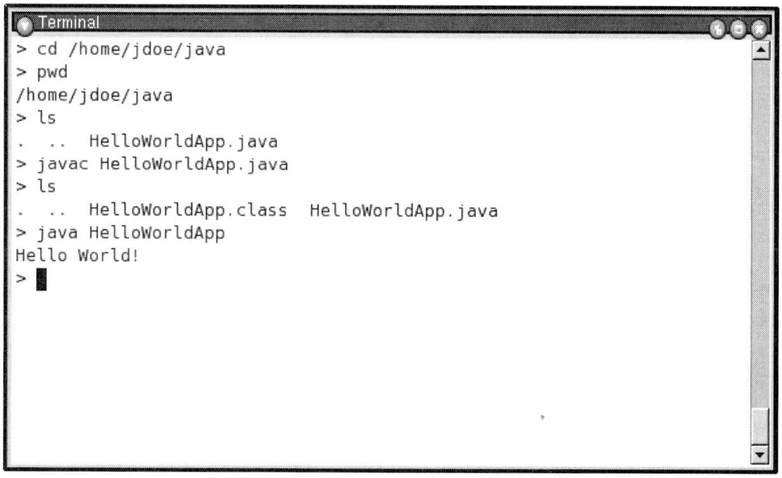

```
Terminal
> cd /home/jdoe/java
> pwd
/home/jdoe/java
> ls
.  ..  HelloWorldApp.java
> javac HelloWorldApp.java
> ls
.  ..  HelloWorldApp.class  HelloWorldApp.java
> java HelloWorldApp
Hello World!
>
```

Figure 1.20 The output prints "Hello World!" to the screen.

Congratulations! Your program works!

A Closer Look at the "Hello World!" Application

Now that you've seen the "Hello World!" application (and perhaps even compiled and run it), you might be wondering how it works. Here again is its code:

```
/**
 * The HelloWorldApp class implements an application that
 * simply prints "Hello World!" to standard output.
 */
class HelloWorldApp {
  public static void main(String[] args) {
    System.out.println("Hello World!"); // Display the string.
  }
}
```

The "Hello World!" application consists of three primary components: source code comments, the `HelloWorldApp` class definition, and the `main` method. The following explanation will provide you with a basic understanding of of the code, but the deeper implications will only become apparent after you've finished reading the subsequent chapters.

Source Code Comments

The following bold text defines the *comments* of the "Hello World!" application:

```
/**
 * The HelloWorldApp class implements an application that
 * simply prints "Hello World!" to standard output.
 */
class HelloWorldApp {
  public static void main(String[] args) {
    System.out.println("Hello World!"); // Display the string.
  }
}
```

Comments are ignored by the compiler but are useful to other programmers. The Java programming language supports three kinds of comments:

`/* text */` The compiler ignores everything from `/*` to `*/`.

`/** documentation */` This indicates a documentation comment (*doc comment*, for short). The compiler ignores this kind of comment, just like it ignores comments that use `/*` and `*/`. The `javadoc` tool uses doc comments when preparing automatically generated documentation. For more information on `javadoc`, see the Javadoc tool documentation.[13]

`// text` The compiler ignores everything from `//` to the end of the line.

The HelloWorldApp Class Definition

The following bold text begins the class definition block for the "Hello World!" application:

```
/**
 * The HelloWorldApp class implements an application that
 * simply prints "Hello World!" to standard output.
 */
class HelloWorldApp {
  public static void main(String[] args) {
    System.out.println("Hello World!"); // Display the string.
  }
}
```

As shown above, the most basic form of a class definition is:

```
class name {
  ...
}
```

The keyword `class` begins the class definition for a class named `name`, and the code for each class appears between the opening and closing curly braces marked in bold above. Chapter 2 provides an overview of classes in general, and Chapter 4 discusses classes in detail. For now it is enough to know that every application begins with a class definition.

The main Method

The following bold text begins the definition of the `main` method:

13. `docs/guide/javadoc/index.html`

```
/**
 * The HelloWorldApp class implements an application that
 * simply prints "Hello World!" to standard output.
 */
class HelloWorldApp {
  public static void main(String[] args) {
    System.out.println("Hello World!"); // Display the string.
  }
}
```

In the Java programming language, every application must contain a `main` method whose signature is:

```
public static void main(String[] args)
```

The modifiers `public` and `static` can be written in either order (`public static` or `static public`), but the convention is to use `public static` as shown above. You can name the argument anything you want, but most programmers choose "args" or "argv."

The `main` method is similar to the `main` function in C and C++; it's the entry point for your application and will subsequently invoke all the other methods required by your program.

The `main` method accepts a single argument: an array of elements of type `String`.

```
public static void main(String[] args)
```

This array is the mechanism through which the runtime system passes information to your application. Each string in the array is called a *command-line argument*. Command-line arguments let users affect the operation of the application without recompiling it. For example, a sorting program might allow the user to specify that the data be sorted in descending order with this command-line argument:

```
-descending
```

The "Hello World!" application ignores its command-line arguments, but you should be aware of the fact that such arguments do exist.

Finally, the line:

```
System.out.println("Hello World!");
```

uses the `System` class from the API to print the "Hello World!" message to standard output.

Common Problems (and Their Solutions)

Compiler Problems

Common Error Messages on Microsoft Windows Systems

'javac' is not recognized as an internal or external command, operable program or batch file

If you receive this error, Windows cannot find the compiler (javac).

Here's one way to tell Windows where to find javac. Suppose you installed the JDK in C:\jdk6. At the prompt you would type the following command and press Enter:

```
C:\jdk6\bin\javac HelloWorldApp.java
```

If you choose this option, you'll have to precede your javac and java commands with C:\jdk6\bin\ each time you compile or run a program. To avoid this extra typing, consult the Update the PATH variable section[14] in the JDK 6 installation instructions.

Common Error Messages on UNIX Systems

javac: Command not found

If you receive this error, UNIX cannot find the compiler, javac.

Here's one way to tell UNIX where to find javac. Suppose you installed the JDK in /usr/local/jdk6. At the prompt you would type the following command and press Return:

```
/usr/local/jdk6/javac HelloWorldApp.java
```

Note: If you choose this option, each time you compile or run a program, you'll have to precede your javac and java commands with /usr/local/jdk6/. To avoid this extra typing, you could add this information to your PATH variable. The steps for doing so will vary depending on which shell you are currently running.

Syntax Errors (All Platforms)

If you mistype part of a program, the compiler may issue a *syntax* error. The message usually displays the type of the error, the line number where the error was detected, the

14. http://java.sun.com/javase/6/webnotes/install/jdk/install-windows.html

code on that line, and the position of the error within the code. Here's an error caused by omitting a semicolon (;) at the end of a statement:

```
testing.java:14: ';' expected.
System.out.println("Input has " + count + " chars.")
                                                    ^
1 error
```

Sometimes the compiler can't guess your intent and prints a confusing error message or multiple error messages if the error cascades over several lines. For example, the following code snippet omits a semicolon (;) from the bold line:

```
while (System.in.read() != -1)
    count++
System.out.println("Input has " + count + " chars.");
```

When processing this code, the compiler issues two error messages:

```
testing.java:13: Invalid type expression.
        count++
             ^
testing.java:14: Invalid declaration.
    System.out.println("Input has " + count + " chars.");
                      ^
2 errors
```

The compiler issues two error messages because after it processes count++, the compiler's state indicates that it's in the middle of an expression. Without the semicolon, the compiler has no way of knowing that the statement is complete.

If you see any compiler errors, then your program did not successfully compile and the compiler did not create a .class file. Carefully verify the program, fix any errors that you detect, and try again.

Semantic Errors

In addition to verifying that your program is syntactically correct, the compiler checks for other basic correctness. For example, the compiler warns you each time you use a variable that has not been initialized:

```
testing.java:13: Variable count may not have been initialized.
        count++
        ^
testing.java:14: Variable count may not have been initialized.
    System.out.println("Input has " + count + " chars.");
                                      ^
2 errors
```

Again, your program did not successfully compile, and the compiler did not create a `.class` file. Fix the error and try again.

Runtime Problems

Error Messages on Microsoft Windows Systems

`Exception in thread "main" java.lang.NoClassDefFoundError: HelloWorldApp`

If you receive this error, `java` cannot find your bytecode file, `HelloWorldApp.class`.

One of the places `java` tries to find your `.class` file is your current directory. So if your `.class` file is in `C:\java`, you should change your current directory to that. To change your directory, type the following command at the prompt and press Enter:

```
cd c:\java
```

The prompt should change to `C:\java>`. If you enter `dir` at the prompt, you should see your `.java` and `.class` files. Now enter `java HelloWorldApp` again.

`CLASSPATH` If you still have problems, you might have to change your `CLASSPATH` variable. To see if this is necessary, try clobbering the classpath with the following command:

```
set CLASSPATH=
```

Now enter `java HelloWorldApp` again. If the program works now, you'll have to change your `CLASSPATH` variable. To set this variable, consult the Update the PATH variable section in the JDK 6 installation instructions. The `CLASSPATH` variable is set in the same manner.

Error Messages on UNIX Systems

`Exception in thread "main" java.lang.NoClassDefFoundError: HelloWorldApp`

If you receive this error, `java` cannot find your bytecode file, `HelloWorldApp.class`.

One of the places `java` tries to find your bytecode file is your current directory. So, for example, if your bytecode file is in `/home/jdoe/java`, you should change your current directory to that. To change your directory, type the following command at the prompt and press Return:

```
cd /home/jdoe/java
```

If you enter `pwd` at the prompt, you should see `/home/jdoe/java`. If you enter `ls` at the prompt, you should see your `.java` and `.class` files. Now enter `java HelloWorldApp` again.

If you still have problems, you might have to change your `CLASSPATH` environment variable. To see if this is necessary, try clobbering the classpath with the following command.

```
unset CLASSPATH
```

Now enter `java HelloWorldApp` again. If the program works now, you'll have to change your `CLASSPATH` variable in the same manner as the `PATH` variable.

A common error of beginner programmers is to try and run the `java` launcher on the `.class` file that was created by the compiler. For example, if you try to run your program with `java HelloWorldApp.class` instead of `java HelloWorldApp`, you'll see this error message:

```
Exception in thread "main" java.lang.NoClassDefFoundError:
HelloWorldApp/class
```

The argument is the *name of the class* that you want to use, *not* the filename.

The main Method Is Not Defined

The Java Virtual Machine requires that the class you execute with it have a `main` method at which to begin execution of your application. The A Closer Look at the "Hello World!" Application section (page 24) discusses the `main` method in detail. If you are missing this method, you'll see the following error at runtime:

```
Exception in thread "main" java.lang.NoSuchMethodError: main
```

Questions and Exercises: Getting Started

Questions

1. When you compile a program written in the Java programming language, the compiler converts the human-readable source file into platform-independent code that a Java Virtual Machine can understand. What is this platform-independent code called?
2. Which of the following is *not* a valid comment?

a. `/** comment */`

b. `/* comment */`

c. `/* comment`

d. `// comment`

3. What is the first thing you should check if at runtime you see the following error?

```
Exception in thread "main" java.lang.NoClassDefFoundError:
HelloWorldApp.java
```

4. The signature for the main method must contain the keywords `public` and `static`. Does the order of these two keywords matter?

5. The main method accepts a single parameter. By convention, what is this parameter's name?

Exercises

1. Change the `HelloWorldApp.java` program so that it displays `Hola Mundo!` instead of `Hello World!`.

2. Here is a slightly modified version of `HelloWorldApp`:

```
// HelloWorldApp2.java

// INTENTIONALLY UNCOMPILABLE!

/**
 * The HelloWorldApp class implements an application that
 * simply prints "Hello World!" to standard output.
 */
class HelloWorldApp2 {
  public static void main(String[] args) {
    System.out.println("Hello World!); // Display the string.
  }
}
```

The program has an error. Fix the error so that the program successfully compiles and runs. What was the error?

Answers

You can find answers to these Questions and Exercises at:

```
tutorial/getStarted/QandE/answers.html
```

2

Object-Oriented Programming Concepts

IF you've never used an object-oriented programming language before, you'll need to learn a few basic concepts before you can begin writing any code. This chapter will introduce you to objects, classes, inheritance, interfaces, and packages. Each discussion focuses on how these concepts relate to the real world while simultaneously providing an introducion to the syntax of the Java programming language.

What Is an Object?

Objects are key to understanding *object-oriented* technology. Look around right now and you'll find many examples of real-world objects: your dog, your desk, your television set, your bicycle.

Real-world objects share two characteristics: They all have *state* and *behavior*. Dogs have state (name, color, breed, hungry) and behavior (barking, fetching, wagging tail). Bicycles also have state (current gear, current pedal cadence, current speed) and behavior (changing gear, changing pedal cadence, applying brakes). Identifying the state and behavior for real-world objects is a great way to begin thinking in terms of object-oriented programming.

Take a minute right now to observe the real-world objects that are in your immediate area. For each object that you see, ask yourself two questions: "What possible states can this object be in?" and "What possible behavior can this object perform?" Make sure to write down your observations. As you do, you'll notice that real-world objects vary in complexity; your desktop lamp may have only two possible states (on and off) and two possible behaviors (turn on, turn off) but your desktop radio might have additional states (on, off, current volume, current station) and behavior (turn on, turn off, increase volume, decrease volume, seek, scan, and tune). You may also notice that some objects, in turn, will also contain other objects. These real-world observations all translate into the world of object-oriented programming.

Software objects (Figure 2.1) are conceptually similar to real-world objects: they too consist of state and related behavior. An object stores its state in *fields* (variables in some programming languages) and exposes its behavior through *methods* (functions in some programming languages). Methods operate on an object's internal state and serve as the primary mechanism for object-to-object communication. Hiding internal state and requiring all interaction to be performed through an object's methods is known as *data encapsulation* a fundamental principle of object-oriented programming.

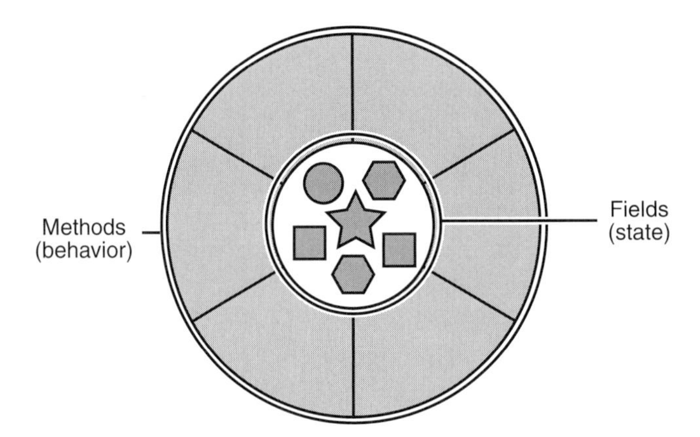

Figure 2.1 A software object.

Consider a bicycle (Figure 2.2). By attributing state (current speed, current pedal cadence, and current gear) and providing methods for changing that state, the object remains in control of how the outside world is allowed to use it. For example, if the bicycle only has 6 gears, a method to change gears could reject any value that is less than 1 or greater than 6.

Bundling code into individual software objects provides a number of benefits, including:

Modularity The source code for an object can be written and maintained independently of the source code for other objects. Once created, an object can be easily passed around inside the system.

Information-hiding By interacting only with an object's methods, the details of its internal implementation remain hidden from the outside world.

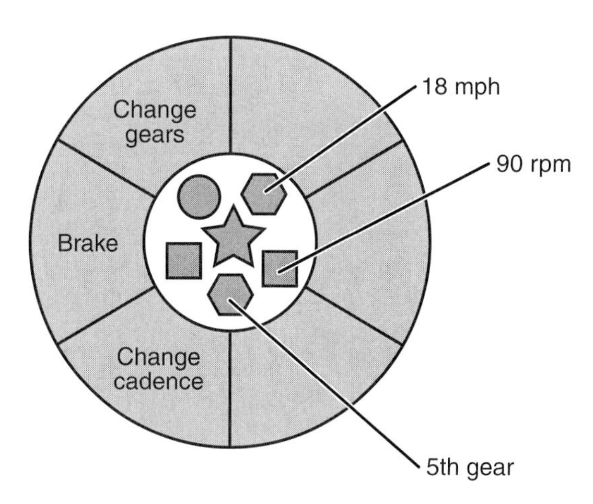

Figure 2.2 A bicycle modeled as a software object.

Code re-use If an object already exists (perhaps written by another software developer), you can use that object in your program. This allows specialists to implement/test/debug complex, task-specific objects, which you can then trust to run in your own code.

Pluggability and debugging ease If a particular object turns out to be problematic, you can simply remove it from your application and plug in a different object as its replacement. This is analogous to fixing mechanical problems in the real world. If a bolt breaks, you replace *it*, not the entire machine.

What Is a Class?

In the real world, you'll often find many individual objects all of the same kind. There may be thousands of other bicycles in existence, all of the same make and model. Each bicycle was built from the same set of blueprints and therefore contains the same components. In object-oriented terms, we say that your bicycle is an *instance* of the *class of objects* known as bicycles. A *class* is the blueprint from which individual objects are created.

The following `Bicycle`[1] class is one possible implementation of a bicycle:

1. `tutorial/java/concepts/examples/Bicycle.java`

```
class Bicycle {

  int cadence = 0;
  int speed = 0;
  int gear = 1;

  void changeCadence(int newValue) {
    cadence = newValue;
  }

  void changeGear(int newValue) {
    gear = newValue;
  }

  void speedUp(int increment) {
    speed = speed + increment;
  }

  void applyBrakes(int decrement) {
    speed = speed - decrement;
  }

  void printStates() {
    System.out.println("cadence:"+cadence+"
                         speed:"+speed+" gear:"+gear);
  }
}
```

The syntax of the Java programming language will look new to you, but the design of this class is based on the previous discussion of bicycle objects. The fields `cadence`, `speed`, and `gear` represent the object's state, and the methods (`changeCadence`, `changeGear`, `speedUp`, etc.) define its interaction with the outside world.

You may have noticed that the `Bicycle` class does not contain a `main` method. That's because it's not a complete application; it's just the blueprint for bicycles that might be *used* in an application. The responsibility of creating and using new `Bicycle` objects belongs to some other class in your application.

Here's a `BicycleDemo`[2] class that creates two separate `Bicycle` objects and invokes their methods:

2. `tutorial/java/concepts/examples/BicycleDemo.java`

```
class BicycleDemo {
  public static void main(String[] args) {

    // Create two different Bicycle objects
    Bicycle bike1 = new Bicycle();
    Bicycle bike2 = new Bicycle();

    // Invoke methods on those objects
    bike1.changeCadence(50);
    bike1.speedUp(10);
    bike1.changeGear(2);
    bike1.printStates();

    bike2.changeCadence(50);
    bike2.speedUp(10);
    bike2.changeGear(2);
    bike2.changeCadence(40);
    bike2.speedUp(10);
    bike2.changeGear(3);
    bike2.printStates();
  }
}
```

The output of this test prints the ending pedal cadence, speed, and gear for the two bicycles:

```
cadence:50 speed:10 gear:2
cadence:40 speed:20 gear:3
```

What Is Inheritance?

Different kinds of objects often have a certain amount in common with each other. Mountain bikes, road bikes, and tandem bikes, for example, all share the characteristics of bicycles (current speed, current pedal cadence, current gear). Yet each also defines additional features that make them different: tandem bicycles have two seats and two sets of handlebars; road bikes have drop handlebars; some mountain bikes have an additional chain ring, giving them a lower gear ratio.

Object-oriented programming allows classes to *inherit* commonly used state and behavior from other classes. In this example, `Bicycle` now becomes the *superclass* of `MountainBike`, `RoadBike`, and `TandemBike`. In the Java programming language, each class is allowed to have one direct superclass, and each superclass has the potential for an unlimited number of *subclasses* (Figure 2.3).

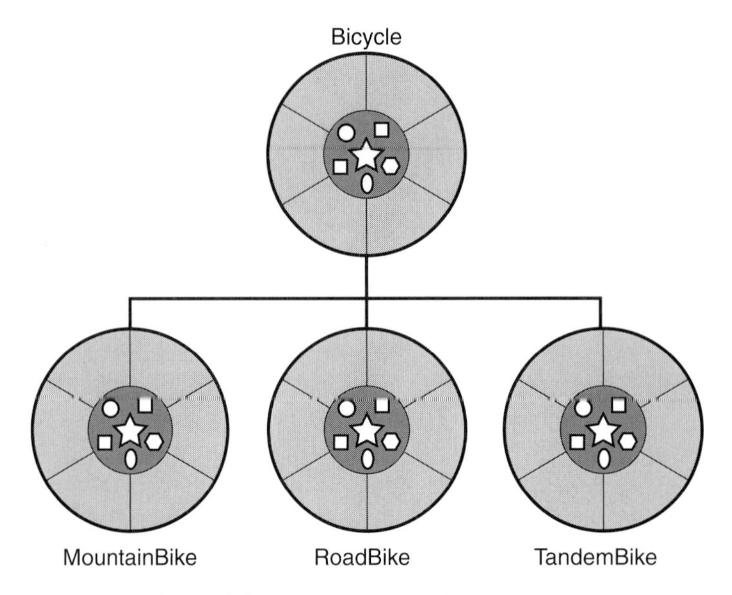

Figure 2.3 A hierarchy of bicycle classes.

The syntax for creating a subclass is simple. At the beginning of your class declaration, use the `extends` keyword, followed by the name of the class to inherit from:

```
class MountainBike extends Bicycle {

  // new fields and methods defining a mountain bike
  // would go here

}
```

This gives `MountainBike` all the same fields and methods as `Bicycle`, yet allows its code to focus exclusively on the features that make it unique. This makes code for your subclasses easy to read. However, you must take care to properly document the state and behavior that each superclass defines, since that code will not appear in the source file of each subclass.

What Is an Interface?

As you've already learned, objects define their interaction with the outside world through the methods that they expose. Methods form the object's *interface* with the outside world; the buttons on the front of your television set, for example, are the interface between you and the electrical wiring on the other side of its plastic casing. You press the "power" button to turn the television on and off.

In its most common form, an interface is a group of related methods with empty bodies. A bicycle's behavior, if specified as an interface, might appear as follows:

```
interface Bicycle {

  void changeCadence(int newValue);

  void changeGear(int newValue);

  void speedUp(int increment);

  void applyBrakes(int decrement);
}
```

To implement this interface, the name of your class would change (to `ACMEBicycle`, for example), and you'd use the `implements` keyword in the class declaration:

```
class ACMEBicycle implements Bicycle {

  // remainder of this class implemented as before

}
```

Implementing an interface allows a class to become more formal about the behavior it promises to provide. Interfaces form a contract between the class and the outside world, and this contract is enforced at build time by the compiler. If your class claims to implement an interface, all methods defined by that interface must appear in its source code before the class will successfully compile.

What Is a Package?

A package is a namespace that organizes a set of related classes and interfaces. Conceptually you can think of packages as being similar to different folders on your computer. You might keep HTML pages in one folder, images in another, and scripts or applications in yet another. Because software written in the Java programming language can be composed of hundreds or *thousands* of individual classes, it makes sense to keep things organized by placing related classes and interfaces into packages.

The Java platform provides an enormous class library (a set of packages) suitable for use in your own applications. As you learned in Chapter 1, this library is known as the "Application Programming Interface," or "API" for short. Its packages represent the tasks most commonly associated with general-purpose programming. For example, a `String` object contains state and behavior for character strings; a `File` object allows a programmer to easily create, delete, inspect, compare, or modify a file on the filesystem; a `Socket` object allows for the creation and use of network sockets; various GUI objects control buttons and checkboxes and anything else related to graphical user interfaces. There are literally thousands of classes to choose from. This allows you, the programmer, to focus on the design of your particular application, rather than the infrastructure required to make it work.

The Java Platform API Specification[3] contains the complete listing for all packages, interfaces, classes, fields, and methods supplied by the Java Platform 6, Standard Edition. Load the page in your browser and bookmark it. As a programmer, it will become your single most important piece of reference documentation.

Questions and Exercises: Object-Oriented Programming Concepts

Questions

1. Real-world objects contain ___ and ___.
2. A software object's state is stored in ___.
3. A software object's behavior is exposed through ___.
4. Hiding internal data from the outside world and accessing it only through publicly exposed methods is known as data ___.
5. A blueprint for a software object is called a ___.
6. Common behavior can be defined in a ___ and inherited into a ___ using the ___ keyword.
7. A collection of methods with no implementation is called an ___.
8. A namespace that organizes classes and interfaces by functionality is called a ___.
9. The term API stands for ___?

Exercises

1. Create new classes for each real-world object that you observed at the beginning of this trail. Refer to the Bicycle class if you forget the required syntax.
2. For each new class that you've created above, create an interface that defines its behavior, then require your class to implement it. Omit one or two methods and try compiling. What does the error look like?

3. `docs/api/index.html`

Answers

You can find answers to these Questions and Exercises at:

```
tutorial/java/concepts/QandE/answers.html
```

3

Language Basics

Variables

As you learned in the previous chapter, an object stores its state in *fields*.

```
int cadence = 0;
int speed = 0;
int gear = 1;
```

The What Is an Object? section (page 33) introduced you to fields, but you probably still have a few questions, such as: What are the rules and conventions for naming a field? Besides `int`, what other data types are there? Do fields have to be initialized when they are declared? Are fields assigned a default value if they are not explicitly initialized? We'll explore the answers to such questions in this chapter, but before we do, there are a few technical distinctions you must first become aware of. In the Java programming language, the terms "field" and "variable" are both used; this is a common source of confusion among new developers, since both often seem to refer to the same thing.

The Java programming language defines the following kinds of variables:

Instance Variables (Non-Static Fields) Technically speaking, objects store their individual state in "non-static fields," that is, fields declared without the `static` keyword. Non-static fields are also known as *instance variables* because their values are unique to each *instance* of a class (to each object, in other words); the `currentSpeed` of one bicycle is independent from the `currentSpeed` of another.

Class Variables (Static Fields) A *class variable* is any field declared with the `static` modifier; this tells the compiler that there is exactly one copy of this variable in existence, regardless of how many times the class has been instantiated. A field defining the number of gears for a particular kind of bicycle could be marked as `static` since conceptually the same number of gears will apply to all instances. The code `static int numGears = 6;` would create such a static field. Additionally, the keyword `final` could be added to indicate that the number of gears will never change.

Local Variables Similar to how an object stores its state in fields, a method will often store its temporary state in *local variables*. The syntax for declaring a local variable is similar to declaring a field (for example, `int count = 0;`). There is no special keyword designating a variable as local; that determination comes entirely from the location in which the variable is declared—which is between the opening and closing braces of a method. As such, local variables are only visible to the methods in which they are declared; they are not accessible from the rest of the class.

Parameters You've already seen examples of parameters, both in the `Bicycle` class and in the `main` method of the "Hello World!" application. Recall that the signature for the `main` method is `public static void main(String[] args)`. Here, the `args` variable is the parameter to this method. The important thing to remember is that parameters are always classified as "variables," not "fields." This applies to other parameter-accepting constructs as well (such as constructors and exception handlers) that you'll learn about later in the tutorial.

Having said that, the remainder of this tutorial uses the following general guidelines when discussing fields and variables. If we are talking about "fields in general" (excluding local variables and parameters), we may simply say "fields." If the discussion applies to "all of the above," we may simply say "variables." If the context calls for a distinction, we will use specific terms (static field, local variable, etc.) as appropriate. You may also occasionally see the term "member" used as well. A type's fields, methods, and nested types are collectively called its *members*.

Naming

Every programming language has its own set of rules and conventions for the kinds of names that you're allowed to use, and the Java programming language is no different. The rules and conventions for naming your variables can be summarized as follows:

- Variable names are case sensitive. A variable's name can be any legal identifier—an unlimited-length sequence of Unicode letters and digits, beginning with a letter, the dollar sign, "`$`", or the underscore character, "`_`". The convention, however, is to always begin your variable names with a letter, not "`$`" or "`_`". Additionally, the dollar sign character, by convention, is never used at all. You may find some situations were auto-generated names will contain the dollar sign, but your variable names should always avoid using it. A similar convention exists for the underscore character; while it's technically legal to begin your variable's name with "_", this practice is discouraged. White space is not permitted.

- Subsequent characters may be letters, digits, dollar signs, or underscore characters. Conventions (and common sense) apply to this rule as well. When choosing a name for your variables, use full words instead of cryptic abbreviations. Doing so will make your code easier to read and understand. In many cases it will also make your code self-documenting; fields named `cadence`, `speed`, and `gear`, for example, are much more intuitive than abbreviated versions, such as `s`, `c`, and `g`. Also keep in mind that the name you choose must not be a keyword or reserved word. See Appendix A, "Java Language Keywords" on page 603.
- If the name you choose consists of only one word, spell that word in all lowercase letters. If it consists of more than one word, capitalize the first letter of each subsequent word. The names `gearRatio` and `currentGear` are prime examples of this convention. If your variable stores a constant value, such as `static final int NUM_GEARS = 6`, the convention changes slightly, capitalizing every letter and separating subsequent words with the underscore character. By convention, the underscore character is never used elsewhere.

Primitive Data Types

The Java programming language is strongly typed, which means that all variables must first be declared before they can be used. This involves stating the variable's type and name, as you've already seen:

```
int gear = 1;
```

Doing so tells your program that a field named "gear" exists, holds numerical data, and has an initial value of "1". A variable's data type determines the values it may contain, plus the operations that may be performed on it. In addition to `int`, the Java programming language supports seven other *primitive data types*. A primitive type is predefined by the language and is named by a reserved keyword. Primitive values do not share state with other primitive values. The eight primitive data types supported by the Java programming language are:

byte The `byte` data type is an 8-bit signed two's complement integer. It has a minimum value of –128 and a maximum value of 127 (inclusive). The `byte` data type can be useful for saving memory in large arrays, where the memory savings actually matters. You'll learn about arrays on page 49. They can also be used in place of `int`, where their limits help to clarify your code; the fact that a variable's range is limited can serve as a form of documentation.

short The `short` data type is a 16-bit signed two's complement integer. It has a minimum value of –32,768 and a maximum value of 32,767 (inclusive). As with `byte`, the same guidelines apply: you can use a `short` to save memory in large arrays, in situations where the memory savings actually matters.

int The `int` data type is a 32-bit signed two's complement integer. It has a minimum value of –2,147,483,648 and a maximum value of 2,147,483,647 (inclusive). For integral values, this data type is generally the default choice unless there is a reason (like the above) to choose something else. This data type will most likely be large enough for the numbers your program will use, but if you need a wider range of values, use `long` instead.

long The `long` data type is a 64-bit signed two's complement integer. It has a minimum value of –9,223,372,036,854,775,808 and a maximum value of 9,223,372,036,854,775,807 (inclusive). Use this data type when you need a range of values wider than those provided by `int`.

float The `float` data type is a single-precision 32-bit IEEE 754 floating point. Its range of values is beyond the scope of this discussion, but is specified in section 4.2.3 of the Java Language Specification.[1] As with the recommendations for `byte` and `short`, use a `float` (instead of `double`) if you need to save memory in large arrays of floating point numbers. This data type should never be used for precise values, such as currency. For that, you will need to use the `java.math.BigDecimal` class instead.[2] Chapter 8 covers `BigDecimal` and other useful classes provided by the Java platform.

double The `double` data type is a double-precision 64-bit IEEE 754 floating point. Its range of values is beyond the scope of this discussion, but is specified in section 4.2.3 of the Java Language Specification. For decimal values, this data type is generally the default choice. As mentioned above, this data type should never be used for precise values, such as currency.

boolean The `boolean` data type has only two possible values: `true` and `false`. Use this data type for simple flags that track true/false conditions. This data type represents one bit of information, but its "size" isn't something that's precisely defined.

char The `char` data type is a single 16-bit Unicode character. It has a minimum value of `'\u0000'` (or 0) and a maximum value of `'\uffff'` (or 65,535 inclusive).

---

1. `docs/books/jls/third_edition/html/typesValues.html`
2. `docs/api/java/math/BigDecimal.html`

In addition to the eight primitive data types listed above, the Java programming language also provides special support for character strings via the `java.lang.String` class.[3] Enclosing your character string within double quotes will automatically create a new `String` object; for example, `String s = "this is a string";`. `String` objects are *immutable*, which means that once created, their values cannot be changed. The `String` class is not technically a primitive data type, but considering the special support given to it by the language, you'll probably tend to think of it as such. You'll learn more about the `String` class in Chapter 8.

Default Values

It's not always necessary to assign a value when a field is declared. Fields that are declared but not initialized will be set to a resonable default by the compiler. Generally speaking, this default will be zero or `null`, depending on the data type. Relying on such default values, however, is generally considered bad programming style.

Table 3.1 summarizes the default values for the above data types.

Table 3.1 Data Types and Their Default Values

Data Type	Default Value (for fields)
byte	`0`
short	`0`
int	`0`
long	`0L`
float	`0.0f`
double	`0.0d`
char	`'\u0000'`
`String` (or any object)	`null`
boolean	`false`

Local variables are slightly different; the compiler never assigns a default value to an uninitialized local variable. If you cannot initialize your local variable where it is declared, make sure to assign it a value before you attempt to use it. Accessing an uninitialized local variable will result in a compile-time error.

3. `docs/api/java/lang/String.html`

Literals

You may have noticed that the `new` keyword isn't used when initializing a variable of a primitive type. Primitive types are special data types built into the language; they are not objects created from a class. A *literal* is the source code representation of a fixed value; literals are represented directly in your code without requiring computation. As shown below, it's possible to assign a literal to a variable of a primitive type:

```
boolean result = true;
char capitalC = 'C';
byte b = 100;
short s = 10000;
int i = 100000;
```

The integral types (`byte`, `short`, `int`, and `long`) can be expressed using decimal, octal, or hexadecimal number systems. Decimal is the number system you already use every day; it's based on 10 digits, numbered 0 through 9. The octal number system is base 8, consisting of the digits 0 through 7. The hexadecimal system is base 16, whose digits are the numbers 0 through 9 and the letters A through F. For general-purpose programming, the decimal system is likely to be the only number system you'll ever use. However, if you need octal or hexadecimal, the following example shows the correct syntax. The prefix `0` indicates octal, whereas `0x` indicates hexadecimal.

```
int decVal = 26;    // The number 26, in decimal
int octVal = 032;   // The number 26, in octal
int hexVal = 0x1a;  // The number 26, in hexadecimal
```

The floating point types (`float` and `double`) can also be expressed using `E` or `e` (for scientific notation), `F` or `f` (32-bit float literal), and `D` or `d` (64-bit double literal; this is the default and by convention is omitted).

```
double d1 = 123.4;
double d2 = 1.234e2; // same value as d1,
                     // but in scientific notation
float f1  = 123.4f;
```

Literals of types `char` and `String` may contain any Unicode (UTF-16) characters. If your editor and file system allow it, you can use such characters directly in your code. If not, you can use a "Unicode escape" such as `'\u0108'` (capital C with circumflex) or `"S\u00ED se\u00F1or"` (Sí Señor in Spanish). Always use 'single quotes' for `char` literals and "double quotes" for `String` literals. Unicode escape sequences may be used elsewhere in a program (such as in field names, for example), not just in `char` or `String` literals.

The Java programming language also supports a few special escape sequences for `char` and `String` literals: `\b` (backspace), `\t` (tab), `\n` (line feed), `\f` (form feed), `\r` (carriage return), `\"` (double quote), `\'` (single quote), and `\\` (backslash).

There's also a special `null` literal that can be used as a value for any reference type. `null` may be assigned to any variable, except variables of primitive types. There's little you can do with a `null` value beyond testing for its presence. Therefore, `null` is often used in programs as a marker to indicate that some object is unavailable.

Finally, there's also a special kind of literal called a *class literal*, formed by taking a type name and appending "`.class`"; for example, `String.class`. This refers to the object (of type `Class`) that represents the type itself.

Arrays

An *array* is a container object that holds a fixed number of values of a single type. The length of an array is established when the array is created. After creation, its length is fixed. You've seen an example of arrays already, in the `main` method of the "Hello World!" application. This section discusses arrays in greater detail.

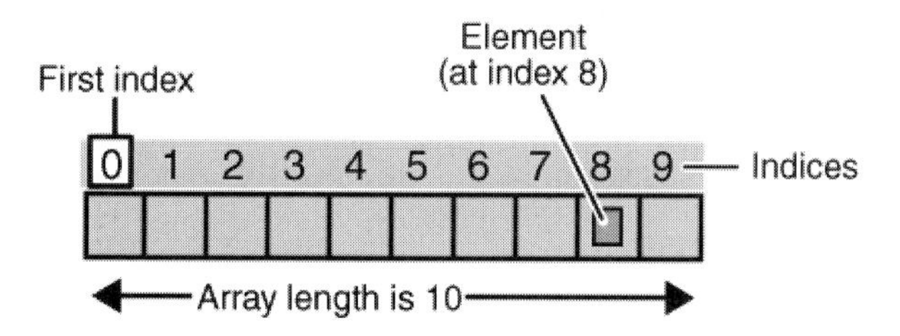

Figure 3.1 An array of ten elements.

Each item in an array is called an *element*, and each element is accessed by its numerical *index*. As shown in Figure 3.1, numbering begins with 0. The 9th element, for example, would therefore be accessed at index 8.

The following program, `ArrayDemo`,[4] creates an array of integers, puts some values in it, and prints each value to standard output.

4. `tutorial/java/nutsandbolts/examples/ArrayDemo.java`

```
class ArrayDemo {
  public static void main(String[] args) {
    int[] anArray;          // declares an array of integers

    anArray = new int[10];  // allocates memory for 10 integers

    anArray[0] = 100; // initialize first element
    anArray[1] = 200; // initialize second element
    anArray[2] = 300; // etc.
    anArray[3] = 400;
    anArray[4] = 500;
    anArray[5] = 600;
    anArray[6] = 700;
    anArray[7] = 800;
    anArray[8] = 900;
    anArray[9] = 1000;

    System.out.println("Element at index 0: " + anArray[0]);
    System.out.println("Element at index 1: " + anArray[1]);
    System.out.println("Element at index 2: " + anArray[2]);
    System.out.println("Element at index 3: " + anArray[3]);
    System.out.println("Element at index 4: " + anArray[4]);
    System.out.println("Element at index 5: " + anArray[5]);
    System.out.println("Element at index 6: " + anArray[6]);
    System.out.println("Element at index 7: " + anArray[7]);
    System.out.println("Element at index 8: " + anArray[8]);
    System.out.println("Element at index 9: " + anArray[9]);
  }
}
```

The output from this program is:

```
Element at index 0: 100
Element at index 1: 200
Element at index 2: 300
Element at index 3: 400
Element at index 4: 500
Element at index 5: 600
Element at index 6: 700
Element at index 7: 800
Element at index 8: 900
Element at index 9: 1000
```

In a real-world programming situation, you'd probably use one of the supported *looping constructs* to iterate through each element of the array, rather than write each line individually as shown above. However, this example clearly illustrates the array syntax. You'll learn about the various looping constructs (`for`, `while`, and `do-while`) in the Control Flow Statements section (page 69).

Declaring a Variable to Refer to an Array

The above program declares `anArray` with the following line of code:

```
int[] anArray;          // declares an array of integers
```

Like declarations for variables of other types, an array declaration has two components: the array's type and the array's name. An array's type is written as *type*`[]`, where *type* is the data type of the contained elements; the square brackets are special symbols indicating that this variable holds an array. The size of the array is not part of its type (which is why the brackets are empty). An array's name can be anything you want, provided that it follows the rules and conventions as previously discussed in the Naming section (page 44). As with variables of other types, the declaration does not actually create an array—it simply tells the compiler that this variable will hold an array of the specified type.

Similarly, you can declare arrays of other types:

```
byte[] anArrayOfBytes;
short[] anArrayOfShorts;
long[] anArrayOfLongs;
float[] anArrayOfFloats;
double[] anArrayOfDoubles;
boolean[] anArrayOfBooleans;
char[] anArrayOfChars;
String[] anArrayOfStrings;
```

You can also place the square brackets after the array's name:

```
float anArrayOfFloats[]; // this form is discouraged
```

However, convention discourages this form; the brackets identify the array type and should appear with the type designation.

Creating, Initializing, and Accessing an Array

One way to create an array is with the `new` operator. The next statement in the `ArrayDemo` program allocates an array with enough memory for ten integer elements and assigns the array to the `anArray` variable.

```
anArray = new int[10];  // create an array of integers
```

If this statement were missing, the compiler would print an error like the following, and compilation would fail:

```
ArrayDemo.java:4: Variable anArray may
                    not have been initialized.
```

The next few lines assign values to each element of the array:

```
anArray[0] = 100; // initialize first element
anArray[1] = 200; // initialize second element
anArray[2] = 300; // etc.
```

Each array element is accessed by its numerical index:

```
System.out.println("Element 1 at index 0: " + anArray[0]);
System.out.println("Element 2 at index 1: " + anArray[1]);
System.out.println("Element 3 at index 2: " + anArray[2]);
```

Alternatively, you can use the shortcut syntax to create and initialize an array:

```
int[] anArray = {100, 200, 300, 400, 500,
                 600, 700, 800, 900, 1000};
```

Here the length of the array is determined by the number of values provided between { and }.

You can also declare an array of arrays (also known as a *multidimensional* array) by using two or more sets of square brackets, such as `String[][] names`. Each element, therefore, must be accessed by a corresponding number of index values.

In the Java programming language, a multidimensional array is simply an array whose components are themselves arrays. This is unlike arrays in C or Fortran. A consequence of this is that the rows are allowed to vary in length, as shown in the following `MultiDimArrayDemo`[5] program:

```
class MultiDimArrayDemo {
  public static void main(String[] args) {
    String[][] names = {{"Mr. ", "Mrs. ", "Ms. "},
                        {"Smith", "Jones"}};
    System.out.println(names[0][0] + names[1][0]); // Mr. Smith
    System.out.println(names[0][2] + names[1][1]); // Ms. Jones
  }
}
```

The output from this program is:

```
Mr. Smith
Ms. Jones
```

5. `tutorial/java/nutsandbolts/examples/MultiDimArrayDemo.java`

Finally, you can use the built-in `length` property to determine the size of any array. The code

```
System.out.println(anArray.length);
```

will print the array's size to standard output.

Copying Arrays

The `System` class has an `arraycopy` method that you can use to efficiently copy data from one array into another:

```
public static void arraycopy(Object src,
                             int srcPos,
                             Object dest,
                             int destPos,
                             int length)
```

The two `Object` arguments specify the array to copy *from* and the array to copy *to*. The three `int` arguments specify the starting position in the source array, the starting position in the destination array, and the number of array elements to copy.

The following program, `ArrayCopyDemo`, declares an array of `char` elements, spelling the word "decaffeinated." It uses `arraycopy` to copy a subsequence of array components into a second array:

```
class ArrayCopyDemo {
  public static void main(String[] args) {
    char[] copyFrom = { 'd', 'e', 'c', 'a', 'f', 'f', 'e',
                        'i', 'n', 'a', 't', 'e', 'd' };
    char[] copyTo = new char[7];

    System.arraycopy(copyFrom, 2, copyTo, 0, 7);
    System.out.println(new String(copyTo));
  }
}
```

The output from this program is:

```
caffein
```

Summary of Variables

The Java programming language uses both "fields" and "variables" as part of its terminology. Instance variables (non-static fields) are unique to each instance of a class. Class variables (static fields) are fields declared with the `static` modifier; there is exactly one copy of a class variable, regardless of how many times the class has been instantiated. Local variables store temporary state inside a method. Parameters are variables that provide extra information to a method; both local variables and parameters are always classified as "variables" (not "fields"). When naming your fields or variables, there are rules and conventions that you should (or must) follow.

The eight primitive data types are: byte, short, int, long, float, double, boolean, and char. The `java.lang.String` class represents character strings. The compiler will assign a reasonable default value for fields of the above types; for local variables, a default value is never assigned. A literal is the source code representation of a fixed value. An array is a container object that holds a fixed number of values of a single type. The length of an array is established when the array is created. After creation, its length is fixed.

Questions and Exercises: Variables

Questions

1. The term "instance variable" is another name for ___.
2. The term "class variable" is another name for ___.
3. A local variable stores temporary state; it is declared inside a ___.
4. A variable declared within the opening and closing parentheses of a method signature is called a ____.
5. What are the eight primitive data types supported by the Java programming language?
6. Character strings are represented by the class ___.
7. An ___ is a container object that holds a fixed number of values of a single type.

Exercises

1. Create a small program that defines some fields. Try creating some illegal field names and see what kind of error the compiler produces. Use the naming rules and conventions as a guide.
2. In the program you created in Exercise 1, try leaving the fields uninitialized and print out their values. Try the same with a local variable and see what kind of compiler errors you can produce. Becoming familiar with common compiler errors will make it easier to recognize bugs in your code.

Answers

You can find answers to these Questions and Exercises at:

```
tutorial/java/nutsandbolts/QandE/answers_variables.html
```

Operators

Now that you've learned how to declare and initialize variables, you probably want to know how to *do something* with them. Learning the operators of the Java programming language is a good place to start. Operators are special symbols that perform specific operations on one, two, or three *operands*, and then return a result.

As we explore the operators of the Java programming language, it may be helpful for you to know ahead of time which operators have the highest precedence. The operators in Table 3.2 are listed according to precedence order. The closer to the top of the table an operator appears, the higher its precedence. Operators with higher precedence are

Table 3.2 Operator Precedence

Operators	Precedence
postfix	*expr*++ *expr*--
unary	++*expr* --*expr* +*expr* -*expr* ~ !
multiplicative	* / %
additive	+ -
shift	<< >> >>>
relational	< > <= >= instanceof
equality	== !=
bitwise AND	&
bitwise exclusive OR	^
bitwise inclusive OR	|
logical AND	&&
logical OR	||
ternary	? :
assignment	= += -= *= /= %= &= ^= |= <<= >>= >>>=

evaluated before operators with relatively lower precedence. Operators on the same line have equal precedence. When operators of equal precedence appear in the same expression, a rule must govern which is evaluated first. All binary operators except for the assignment operators are evaluated from left to right; assignment operators are evaluated right to left.

In general-purpose programming, certain operators tend to appear more frequently than others; for example, the assignment operator "=" is far more common than the unsigned right shift operator ">>>". With that in mind, the following discussion focuses first on the operators that you're most likely to use on a regular basis, and ends focusing on those that are less common. Each discussion is accompanied by sample code that you can compile and run. Studying its output will help enforce what you've just learned.

Assignment, Arithmetic, and Unary Operators

The Simple Assignment Operator

One of the most common operators that you'll encounter is the simple assignment operator "=". You saw this operator in the `Bicycle` class; it assigns the value on its right to the operand on its left:

```
int cadence = 0;
int speed = 0;
int gear = 1;
```

This operator can also be used on objects to assign *object references*, as discussed in Chapter 8.

The Arithmetic Operators

The Java programming language provides operators that perform addition, subtraction, multiplication, and division. There's a good chance you'll recognize them by their counterparts in basic mathematics. The only symbol that might look new to you is "%", which divides one operand by another and returns the remainder as its result.

```
+    additive operator (also used for String concatenation)
-    subtraction operator
*    multiplication operator
/    division operator
%    remainder operator
```

The following program, `ArithmeticDemo`,[6] tests the arithmetic operators.

6. `tutorial/java/nutsandbolts/examples/ArithmeticDemo.java`

```
class ArithmeticDemo {

  public static void main (String[] args){

    int result = 1 + 2; // result is now 3
    System.out.println(result);

    result = result - 1; // result is now 2
    System.out.println(result);

    result = result * 2; // result is now 4
    System.out.println(result);

    result = result / 2; // result is now 2
    System.out.println(result);

    result = result + 8; // result is now 10
    result = result % 7; // result is now 3
    System.out.println(result);

  }
}
```

You can also combine the arithmetic operators with the simple assignment operator to create *compound assignments*. For example, `x+=1;` and `x=x+1;` both increment the value of `x` by 1.

The + operator can also be used for concatenating (joining) two strings together, as shown in the following `ConcatDemo`[7] program:

```
class ConcatDemo {
  public static void main(String[] args){
    String firstString = "This is";
    String secondString = " a concatenated string.";
    String thirdString = firstString+secondString;
    System.out.println(thirdString);
  }
}
```

By the end of this program, the variable `thirdString` contains "This is a concatenated string.", which gets printed to standard output.

7. `tutorial/java/nutsandbolts/examples/ConcatDemo.java`

The Unary Operators

The unary operators require only one operand; they perform various operations such as incrementing/decrementing a value by one, negating an expression, or inverting the value of a boolean.

```
+   Unary plus operator; indicates positive value
    (numbers are positive without this, however)
-   Unary minus operator; negates an expression
++  Increment operator; increments a value by 1
--  Decrement operator; decrements a value by 1
!   Logical complement operator; inverts the value of a boolean
```

The following program, `UnaryDemo`,[8] tests the unary operators:

```
class UnaryDemo {

  public static void main(String[] args){
    int result = +1; // result is now 1
    System.out.println(result);
    result--;  // result is now 0
    System.out.println(result);
    result++; // result is now 1
    System.out.println(result);
    result = -result; // result is now -1
    System.out.println(result);
    boolean success = false;
    System.out.println(success); // false
    System.out.println(!success); // true
  }
}
```

The increment/decrement operators can be applied before (prefix) or after (postfix) the operand. The code `result++;` and `++result;` will both end in `result` being incremented by one. The only difference is that the prefix version (`++result`) evaluates to the incremented value, whereas the postfix version (`result++`) evaluates to the original value. If you are just performing a simple increment/decrement, it doesn't really matter which version you choose. But if you use this operator in part of a larger expression, the one that you choose may make a significant difference.

The following program, `PrePostDemo`, illustrates the prefix/postfix unary increment operator:

---

8. `tutorial/java/nutsandbolts/examples/UnaryDemo.java`

```
class PrePostDemo {
  public static void main(String[] args){
    int i = 3;
    i++;
    System.out.println(i);    // "4"
    ++i;
    System.out.println(i);    // "5"
    System.out.println(++i); // "6"
    System.out.println(i++); // "6"
    System.out.println(i);    // "7"
  }
}
```

Equality, Relational, and Conditional Operators

The Equality and Relational Operators

The equality and relational operators determine if one operator is greater than, less than, equal to, or not equal to another operand. The majority of these operators will probably look familiar to you as well. Keep in mind that you must use "==", not "=", when testing if two primitive values are equal.

```
==  equal to
!=  not equal to
>   greater than
>=  greater than or equal to
<   less than
<=  less than or equal to
```

The following program, `ComparisonDemo`,[9] tests the comparison operators:

```
class ComparisonDemo {

  public static void main(String[] args) {
    int value1 = 1;
    int value2 = 2;
    if(value1 == value2)
                  System.out.println("value1 == value2");
    if(value1 != value2)
                  System.out.println("value1 != value2");
    if(value1 > value2) System.out.println("value1 > value2");
    if(value1 < value2) System.out.println("value1 < value2");
    if(value1 <= value2)
               System.out.println("value1 <= value2");
  }
}
```

9. `tutorial/java/nutsandbolts/examples/ComparisonDemo.java`

```
Output:

value1 != value2
value1 < value2
value1 <= value2
```

The Conditional Operators

The && and || operators perform *Conditional-AND* and *Conditional-OR* operations on two boolean expressions. These operators exhibit "short-circuiting" behavior, which means that the second operand is evaluated only if needed.

```
&&  Conditional-AND
||  Conditional-OR
```

The following program, ConditionalDemo1,[10] tests these operators:

```
class ConditionalDemo1 {

  public static void main(String[] args){
    int value1 = 1;
    int value2 = 2;
    if((value1 == 1) && (value2 == 2))
      System.out.println("value1 is 1 AND value2 is 2");
    if((value1 == 1) || (value2 == 1))
      System.out.println("value1 is 1 OR value2 is 1");

  }
}
```

Another conditional operator is ?:, which can be thought of as shorthand for an if-then-else statement (discussed in the Control Flow Statements section, page 69). This operator is also known as the *ternary operator* because it uses three operands. In the following example, this operator should be read as: "If someCondition is true, assign the value of value1 to result. Otherwise, assign the value of value2 to result."

The following program, ConditionalDemo2,[11] tests the ?: operator:

10. tutorial/java/nutsandbolts/examples/ConditionalDemo1.java

11. tutorial/java/nutsandbolts/examples/ConditionalDemo2.java

```
class ConditionalDemo2 {

  public static void main(String[] args){
    int value1 = 1;
    int value2 = 2;
    int result;
    boolean someCondition = true;
    result = someCondition ? value1 : value2;
    System.out.println(result);
  }
}
```

Because `someCondition` is true, this program prints "1" to the screen. Use the `?:` operator instead of an `if-then-else` statement if it makes your code more readable; for example, when the expressions are compact and without side-effects (such as assignments).

The Type Comparison Operator instanceof

The `instanceof` operator compares an object to a specified type. You can use it to test if an object is an instance of a class, an instance of a subclass, or an instance of a class that implements a particular interface.

The following program, `InstanceofDemo`,[12] defines a parent class (named `Parent`), a simple interface (named `MyInterface`), and a child class (named `Child`) that inherits from the parent and implements the interface.

```
class InstanceofDemo {
  public static void main(String args[]) {
    Parent obj1 = new Parent();
    Parent obj2 = new Child();

    System.out.println("obj1 instanceof Parent: " +
                       (obj1 instanceof Parent));
    System.out.println("obj1 instanceof Child: " +
                       (obj1 instanceof Child));
    System.out.println("obj1 instanceof MyInterface: " +
                       (obj1 instanceof MyInterface));
    System.out.println("obj2 instanceof Parent: " +
                       (obj2 instanceof Parent));
    System.out.println("obj2 instanceof Child: " +
                       (obj2 instanceof Child));
    System.out.println("obj2 instanceof MyInterface: " +
                       (obj2 instanceof MyInterface));
  }
}
```

12. `tutorial/java/nutsandbolts/examples/InstanceofDemo.java`

```
class Parent{}
class Child extends Parent implements MyInterface{}
interface MyInterface{}

Output:

obj1 instanceof Parent: true
obj1 instanceof Child: false
obj1 instanceof MyInterface: false
obj2 instanceof Parent: true
obj2 instanceof Child: true
obj2 instanceof MyInterface: true
```

When using the `instanceof` operator, keep in mind that `null` is not an instance of anything.

Bitwise and Bit Shift Operators

The Java programming language also provides operators that perform bitwise and bit shift operations on integral types. The operators discussed in this section are less commonly used. Therefore, their coverage is brief; the intent is to simply make you aware that these operators exist.

The unary bitwise complement operator "~" inverts a bit pattern; it can be applied to any of the integral types, making every "0" a "1" and every "1" a "0". For example, a `byte` contains 8 bits; applying this operator to a value whose bit pattern is "00000000" would change its pattern to "11111111".

The signed left shift operator "<<" shifts a bit pattern to the left, and the signed right shift operator ">>" shifts a bit pattern to the right. The bit pattern is given by the left-hand operand, and the number of positions to shift by the right-hand operand. The unsigned right shift operator ">>>" shifts a zero into the leftmost position, while the leftmost position after ">>" depends on sign extension.

The bitwise `&` operator performs a bitwise AND operation.

The bitwise `^` operator performs a bitwise exclusive OR operation.

The bitwise `|` operator performs a bitwise inclusive OR operation.

For `&` and `|` above, the result has a 1 in each bit position for which both of the operands have a 1.

The following program, `BitDemo`,[13] uses the bitwise AND operator to print the number "2" to standard output.

---

13. `tutorial/java/nutsandbolts/examples/BitDemo.java`

```
class BitDemo {
  public static void main(String[] args) {
    int bitmask = 0x000F;
    int val = 0x2222;
    System.out.println(val & bitmask);  // prints "2"
  }
}
```

Summary of Operators

The following quick reference summarizes the operators supported by the Java programming language.

Simple Assignment Operator

```
=  simple assignment operator
```

Arithmetic Operators

```
+   additive operator (also used for String concatenation)
-   subtraction operator
*   multiplication operator
/   division operator
%   remainder operator
```

Unary Operators

```
+   Unary plus operator; indicates positive value
    (numbers are positive without this, however)
-   Unary minus operator; negates an expression
++  Increment operator; increments a value by 1
--  Decrement operator; decrements a value by 1
!   Logical complement operator; inverts the value of a boolean
```

Equality and Relational Operators

```
==  equal to
!=  not equal to
>   greater than
>=  greater than or equal to
<   less than
<=  less than or equal to
```

Conditional Operators

```
&&  Conditional-AND
||  Conditional-OR
?:  Ternary (shorthand for if-then-else statement)
```

Type Comparison Operator

```
instanceof  compares an object to a specified type
```

Bitwise and Bit Shift Operators

```
~    unary bitwise complement
<<   signed left shift
>>   signed right shift
>>>  unsigned right shift
&    bitwise AND
^    bitwise exclusive OR
|    bitwise inclusive OR
```

Questions and Exercises: Operators

Questions

1. Consider the following code snippet.

   ```
   arrayOfInts[j] > arrayOfInts[j+1]
   ```

   Which operators does the code contain?
2. Consider the following code snippet.

   ```
   int i = 10;
   int n = i++%5;
   ```

   a. What are the values of `i` and `n` after the code is executed?

   b. What are the final values of `i` and `n` if instead of using the postfix increment operator (`i++`) you use the prefix version (`++i`)?
3. To invert the value of a boolean, which operator would you use?
4. Which operator is used to compare two values, = or == ?
5. Explain the following code sample:

   ```
   result = someCondition ? value1 : value2;
   ```

Exercises

1. Change the following program to use compound assignments:

```
class ArithmeticDemo {

  public static void main (String[] args){

    int result = 1 + 2; // result is now 3
    System.out.println(result);

    result = result - 1; // result is now 2
    System.out.println(result);

    result = result * 2; // result is now 4
    System.out.println(result);

    result = result / 2; // result is now 2
    System.out.println(result);

    result = result + 8; // result is now 10
    result = result % 7; // result is now 3
    System.out.println(result);

  }
}
```

2. In the following program, explain why the value "6" is printed twice in a row:

```
class PrePostDemo {
  public static void main(String[] args){
    int i = 3;
    i++;
    System.out.println(i);   // "4"
    ++i;
    System.out.println(i);   // "5"
    System.out.println(++i); // "6"
    System.out.println(i++); // "6"
    System.out.println(i);   // "7"
  }
}
```

Answers

You can find answers to these Questions and Exercises at:

```
tutorial/java/nutsandbolts/QandE/questions_expressions.html
```

Expressions, Statements, and Blocks

Now that you understand variables and operators, it's time to learn about *expressions*, *statements*, and *blocks*. Operators may used in building expressions, which compute values; expressions are the core components of statements; statements may be grouped into blocks.

Expressions

An *expression* is a construct made up of variables, operators, and method invocations, which are constructed according to the syntax of the language, that evaluates to a single value. You've already seen examples of expressions, illustrated in bold below:

```
int cadence = 0;
anArray[0] = 100;
System.out.println("Element 1 at index 0: " + anArray[0]);

int result = 1 + 2; // result is now 3
if(value1 == value2) System.out.println("value1 == value2");
```

The data type of the value returned by an expression depends on the elements used in the expression. The expression `cadence = 0` returns an `int` because the assignment operator returns a value of the same data type as its left-hand operand; in this case, `cadence` is an `int`. As you can see from the other expressions, an expression can return other types of values as well, such as `boolean` or `String`.

The Java programming language allows you to construct compound expressions from various smaller expressions as long as the data type required by one part of the expression matches the data type of the other. Here's an example of a compound expression:

```
1 * 2 * 3
```

In this particular example, the order in which the expression is evaluated is unimportant because the result of multiplication is independent of order; the outcome is always the same, no matter in which order you apply the multiplications. However, this is not true of all expressions. For example, the following expression gives different results, depending on whether you perform the addition or the division operation first:

```
x + y / 100    // ambiguous
```

You can specify exactly how an expression will be evaluated using balanced parenthesis: `(` and `)`. For example, to make the previous expression unambiguous, you could write the following:

```
(x + y) / 100  // unambiguous, recommended
```

If you don't explicitly indicate the order for the operations to be performed, the order is determined by the precedence assigned to the operators in use within the expression. Operators that have a higher precedence get evaluated first. For example, the division operator has a higher precedence than does the addition operator. Therefore, the following two statements are equivalent:

```
x + y / 100
x + (y / 100)  // unambiguous, recommended
```

When writing compound expressions, be explicit and indicate with parentheses which operators should be evaluated first. This practice makes code easier to read and to maintain.

Statements

Statements are roughly equivalent to sentences in natural languages. A *statement* forms a complete unit of execution. The following types of expressions can be made into a statement by terminating the expression with a semicolon (;).

- Assignment expressions
- Any use of ++ or --
- Method invocations
- Object creation expressions

Such statements are called *expression statements*. Here are some examples of expression statements.

```
aValue = 8933.234;                  // assignment statement
aValue++;                           // increment statement
System.out.println("Hello World!"); // method invocation
                                    // statement
Bicycle myBike = new Bicycle();     // object creation
                                    // statement
```

In addition to expression statements, there are two other kinds of statements: *declaration statements* and *control flow statements*. A *declaration statement* declares a variable. You've seen many examples of declaration statements already:

```
double aValue = 8933.234; // declaration statement
```

Finally, *control flow statements* regulate the order in which statements get executed. You'll learn about control flow statements in the Control Flow Statements section (page 69).

Blocks

A *block* is a group of zero or more statements between balanced braces and can be used anywhere a single statement is allowed. The following example, `BlockDemo`,[14] illustrates the use of blocks:

```
class BlockDemo {
  public static void main(String[] args) {
    boolean condition = true;
    if (condition) { // begin block 1
      System.out.println("Condition is true.");
    } // end block one
    else { // begin block 2
      System.out.println("Condition is false.");
    } // end block 2
  }
}
```

Questions and Exercises: Expressions, Statements, and Blocks

Questions

1. Operators may used in building ___, which compute values.
2. Expressions are the core components of ___.
3. Statements may be grouped into ___.
4. The following code snippet is an example of a ___ expression.

   ```
   1 * 2 * 3
   ```

5. Statements are roughly equivalent to sentences in natural languages, but instead of ending with a period, a statement ends with a ___.
6. A block is a group of zero or more statements between balanced ___ and can be used anywhere a single statement is allowed.

---

14. `tutorial/java/nutsandbolts/examples/BlockDemo.java`

Exercises

Identify the following kinds of expression statements:

- `aValue = 8933.234;`
- `aValue++;`
- `System.out.println("Hello World!");`
- `Bicycle myBike = new Bicycle();`

Answers

You can find answers to these Questions and Exercises at:

```
tutorial/java/nutsandbolts/QandE/answers_expressions.html
```

Control Flow Statements

The statements inside your source files are generally executed from top to bottom, in the order that they appear. *Control flow statements*, however, break up the flow of execution by employing decision making, looping, and branching, enabling your program to *conditionally* execute particular blocks of code. This section describes the decision-making statements (`if-then`, `if-then-else`, `switch`), the looping statements (`for`, `while`, `do-while`), and the branching statements (`break`, `continue`, `return`) supported by the Java programming language.

The if-then and if-then-else Statements

The if-then Statement

The `if-then` statement is the most basic of all the control flow statements. It tells your program to execute a certain section of code *only if* a particular test evaluates to `true`. For example, the `Bicycle` class could allow the brakes to decrease the bicycle's speed *only if* the bicycle is already in motion. One possible implementation of the `applyBrakes` method could be as follows:

```
void applyBrakes(){
  if (isMoving){     // the "if" clause: bicycle must moving
    currentSpeed--; // the "then" clause:
                    // decrease current speed
  }
}
```

If this test evaluates to `false` (meaning that the bicycle is not in motion), control jumps to the end of the `if-then` statement.

In addition, the opening and closing braces are optional, provided that the "then" clause contains only one statement:

```
void applyBrakes(){
  if (isMoving) currentSpeed--; // same as above,
                                // but without braces
}
```

Deciding when to omit the braces is a matter of personal taste. Omitting them can make the code more brittle. If a second statement is later added to the "then" clause, a common mistake would be forgetting to add the newly required braces. The compiler cannot catch this sort of error; you'll just get the wrong results.

The if-then-else Statement

The `if-then-else` statement provides a secondary path of execution when an "if" clause evaluates to `false`. You could use an `if-then-else` statement in the `applyBrakes` method to take some action if the brakes are applied when the bicycle is not in motion. In this case, the action is to simply print an error message stating that the bicycle has already stopped.

```
void applyBrakes(){
  if (isMoving) {
      currentSpeed--;
  } else {
      System.err.println("The bicycle has already stopped!");
  }
}
```

The following program, `IfElseDemo`,[15] assigns a grade based on the value of a test score: an A for a score of 90% or above, a B for a score of 80% or above, and so on.

15. `tutorial/java/nutsandbolts/examples/IfElseDemo.java`

```
class IfElseDemo {
  public static void main(String[] args) {

    int testscore = 76;
    char grade;

    if (testscore >= 90) {
        grade = 'A';
    } else if (testscore >= 80) {
        grade = 'B';
    } else if (testscore >= 70) {
        grade = 'C';
    } else if (testscore >= 60) {
        grade = 'D';
    } else {
        grade = 'F';
    }
    System.out.println("Grade = " + grade);
  }
}
```

The output from the program is:

```
Grade = C
```

You may have noticed that the value of `testscore` can satisfy more than one expression in the compound statement: `76 >= 70` and `76 >= 60`. However, once a condition is satisfied, the appropriate statements are executed `(grade = 'C';)` and the remaining conditions are not evaluated.

The switch Statement

Unlike `if-then` and `if-then-else`, the `switch` statement allows for any number of possible execution paths. A `switch` works with the `byte`, `short`, `char`, and `int` primitive data types. It also works with *enumerated types* discussed in the Enum Types section (page 128) and a few special classes that "wrap" certain primitive types: `Character`,[16] `Byte`,[17] `Short`,[18] and `Integer`[19] discussed in Chapter 8.

16. `docs/api/java/lang/Character.html`

17. `docs/api/java/lang/Byte.html`

18. `docs/api/java/lang/Short.html`

19. `docs/api/java/lang/Integer.html`

The following program, `SwitchDemo`,[20] declares an `int` named `month` whose value represents a month out of the year. The program displays the name of the month, based on the value of month, using the `switch` statement.

```
class SwitchDemo {
  public static void main(String[] args) {

    int month = 8;
    switch (month) {
      case 1:  System.out.println("January"); break;
      case 2:  System.out.println("February"); break;
      case 3:  System.out.println("March"); break;
      case 4:  System.out.println("April"); break;
      case 5:  System.out.println("May"); break;
      case 6:  System.out.println("June"); break;
      case 7:  System.out.println("July"); break;
      case 8:  System.out.println("August"); break;
      case 9:  System.out.println("September"); break;
      case 10: System.out.println("October"); break;
      case 11: System.out.println("November"); break;
      case 12: System.out.println("December"); break;
      default: System.out.println("Invalid month.");break;
    }
  }
}
```

In this case, "August" is printed to standard output.

The body of a `switch` statement is known as a *switch block*. Any statement immediately contained by the `switch` block may be labeled with one or more `case` or `default` labels. The `switch` statement evaluates its expression and executes the appropriate `case`.

Of course, you could also implement the same thing with `if-then-else` statements:

```
int month = 8;
if (month == 1) {
    System.out.println("January");
} else if (month == 2) {
    System.out.println("February");
}
... // and so on
```

Deciding whether to use `if-then-else` statements or a `switch` statement is sometimes a judgment call. You can decide which one to use based on readability and other factors. An `if-then-else` statement can be used to make decisions based on ranges of values

20. `tutorial/java/nutsandbolts/examples/SwitchDemo.java`

or conditions, whereas a switch statement can make decisions based only on a single integer or enumerated value.

Another point of interest is the break statement after each case. Each break statement terminates the enclosing switch statement. Control flow continues with the first statement following the switch block. The break statements are necessary because without them, case statements fall through; that is, without an explicit break, control will flow sequentially through subsequent case statements. The following program, SwitchDemo2,[21] illustrates why it might be useful to have case statements fall through:

```
class SwitchDemo2 {
  public static void main(String[] args) {

    int month = 2;
    int year = 2000;
    int numDays = 0;

    switch (month) {
      case 1:
      case 3:
      case 5:
      case 7:
      case 8:
      case 10:
      case 12:
        numDays = 31;
        break;
      case 4:
      case 6:
      case 9:
      case 11:
        numDays = 30;
        break;
      case 2:
        if ( ((year % 4 == 0) && !(year % 100 == 0))
             || (year % 400 == 0) )
          numDays = 29;
        else
          numDays = 28;
        break;
      default:
        System.out.println("Invalid month.");
        break;
    }
    System.out.println("Number of Days = " + numDays);
  }
}
```

21. tutorial/java/nutsandbolts/examples/SwitchDemo2.java

This is the output from the program:

```
Number of Days = 29
```

Technically, the final break is not required because flow would fall out of the switch statement anyway. However, we recommend using a break so that modifying the code is easier and less error-prone. The default section handles all values that aren't explicitly handled by one of the case sections.

The while and do-while Statements

The while statement continually executes a block of statements while a particular condition is true. Its syntax can be expressed as:

```
while (expression) {
  statement(s)
}
```

The while statement evaluates *expression*, which must return a boolean value. If the expression evaluates to true, the while statement executes the *statement(s)* in the while block. The while statement continues testing the expression and executing its block until the expression evaluates to false. Using the while statement to print the values from 1 through 10 can be accomplished as in the following WhileDemo[22] program:

```
class WhileDemo {
  public static void main(String[] args){
    int count = 1;
    while (count < 11) {
      System.out.println("Count is: " + count);
      count++;
    }
  }
}
```

You can implement an infinite loop using the while statement as follows:

```
while (true){
  // your code goes here
}
```

The Java programming language also provides a do-while statement, which can be expressed as follows:

22. tutorial/java/nutsandbolts/examples/WhileDemo.java

```
do {
    statement(s)
} while (expression);
```

The difference between do-while and while is that do-while evaluates its expression at the bottom of the loop instead of the top. Therefore, the statements within the do block are always executed at least once, as shown in the following DoWhileDemo[23] program:

```
class DoWhileDemo {
  public static void main(String[] args){
    int count = 1;
    do {
        System.out.println("Count is: " + count);
        count++;
    } while (count <= 11);
  }
}
```

The for Statement

The for statement provides a compact way to iterate over a range of values. Programmers often refer to it as the "for loop" because of the way in which it repeatedly loops until a particular condition is satisfied. The general form of the for statement can be expressed as follows:

```
for (initialization; termination; increment) {
  statement(s)
}
```

When using this version of the for statement, keep in mind that:

- The *initialization* expression initializes the loop; it's executed once, as the loop begins.
- When the *termination* expression evaluates to false, the loop terminates.
- The *increment* expression is invoked after each iteration through the loop; it is perfectly acceptable for this expression to increment *or* decrement a value.

The following program, ForDemo,[24] uses the general form of the for statement to print the numbers 1 through 10 to standard output:

23. tutorial/java/nutsandbolts/examples/DoWhileDemo.java

24. tutorial/java/nutsandbolts/examples/ForDemo.java

```
class ForDemo {
  public static void main(String[] args){
    for(int i=1; i<11; i++){
      System.out.println("Count is: " + i);
    }
  }
}
```

The output of this program is:

```
Count is: 1
Count is: 2
Count is: 3
Count is: 4
Count is: 5
Count is: 6
Count is: 7
Count is: 8
Count is: 9
Count is: 10
```

Notice how the code declares a variable within the initialization expression. The scope of this variable extends from its declaration to the end of the block governed by the `for` statement, so it can be used in the termination and increment expressions as well. If the variable that controls a `for` statement is not needed outside of the loop, it's best to declare the variable in the initialization expression. The names `i`, `j`, and `k` are often used to control `for` loops; declaring them within the initialization expression limits their life span and reduces errors.

The three expressions of the `for` loop are optional; an infinite loop can be created as follows:

```
for ( ; ; ) {    // infinite loop

  // your code goes here
}
```

The `for` statement also has another form designed for iteration through collections (see Chapter 11) and arrays (see the Arrays section beginning on page 49). This form is sometimes referred to as the *enhanced for* statement, and can be used to make your loops more compact and easy to read. To demonstrate, consider the following array, which holds the numbers 1 through 10:

```
int[] numbers = {1,2,3,4,5,6,7,8,9,10};
```

The following program, `EnhancedForDemo`,[25] uses the enhanced `for` to loop through the array:

```
class EnhancedForDemo {
  public static void main(String[] args){
    int[] numbers = {1,2,3,4,5,6,7,8,9,10};
    for (int item : numbers) {
      System.out.println("Count is: " + item);
    }
  }
}
```

In this example, the variable `item` holds the current value from the numbers array. The output from this program is the same as before:

```
Count is: 1
Count is: 2
Count is: 3
Count is: 4
Count is: 5
Count is: 6
Count is: 7
Count is: 8
Count is: 9
Count is: 10
```

We recommend using this form of the `for` statement instead of the general form whenever possible.

Branching Statements

The break Statement

The `break` statement has two forms: labeled and unlabeled. You saw the unlabeled form in the previous discussion of the `switch` statement.

You can also use an unlabeled `break` to terminate a `for`, `while`, or `do-while` loop, as shown in the following `BreakDemo`[26] program:

25. `tutorial/java/nutsandbolts/examples/EnhancedForDemo.java`

26. `tutorial/java/nutsandbolts/examples/BreakDemo.java`

```
class BreakDemo {
  public static void main(String[] args) {

    int[] arrayOfInts = { 32, 87, 3, 589, 12, 1076,
                          2000, 8, 622, 127 };
    int searchfor = 12;

    int i;
    boolean foundIt = false;

    for (i = 0; i < arrayOfInts.length; i++) {
      if (arrayOfInts[i] == searchfor) {
        foundIt = true;
        break;
      }
    }

    if (foundIt) {
        System.out.println("Found " + searchfor +
                                " at index " + i);
    } else {
        System.out.println(searchfor + " not in the array");
    }
  }
}
```

This program searches for the number 12 in an array. The `break` statement, shown in boldface, terminates the `for` loop when that value is found. Control flow then transfers to the print statement at the end of the program.

This program's output is:

```
Found 12 at index 4
```

An unlabeled `break` statement terminates the innermost `switch`, `for`, `while`, or `do-while` statement, but a labeled `break` terminates an outer statement. The following program, `BreakWithLabelDemo`,[27] is similar to the previous program, but uses nested `for` loops to search for a value in a two-dimensional array. When the value is found, a labeled `break` terminates the outer `for` loop (labeled "search"):

27. `tutorial/java/nutsandbolts/examples/BreakWithLabelDemo.java`

```
class BreakWithLabelDemo {
  public static void main(String[] args) {

    int[][] arrayOfInts = { { 32, 87, 3, 589 },
                            { 12, 1076, 2000, 8 },
                            { 622, 127, 77, 955 }
                          };
    int searchfor = 12;

    int i;
    int j = 0;
    boolean foundIt = false;

  search:
    for (i = 0; i < arrayOfInts.length; i++) {
      for (j = 0; j < arrayOfInts[i].length; j++) {
        if (arrayOfInts[i][j] == searchfor) {
          foundIt = true;
          break search;
        }
      }
    }

    if (foundIt) {
        System.out.println("Found " +
                           searchfor + " at " + i + ", " + j);
    } else {
        System.out.println(searchfor + " not in the array");
    }
  }
}
```

This is the output of the program:

```
Found 12 at 1, 0
```

The `break` statement terminates the labeled statement; it does not transfer the flow of control to the label. Control flow is transferred to the statement immediately following the labeled (terminated) statement.

The continue Statement

The `continue` statement skips the current iteration of a `for`, `while`, or `do-while` loop. The unlabeled form skips to the end of the innermost loop's body and evaluates the `boolean` expression that controls the loop. The following program, `ContinueDemo`,[28]

---

28. `tutorial/java/nutsandbolts/examples/ContinueDemo.java`

steps through a `String`, counting the occurrences of the letter "p". If the current character is not a p, the `continue` statement skips the rest of the loop and proceeds to the next character. If it *is* a p, the program increments the letter count.

```
class ContinueDemo {
  public static void main(String[] args) {

    String searchMe = "peter piper picked a peck of " +
                      "pickled peppers";
    int max = searchMe.length();
    int numPs = 0;

    for (int i = 0; i < max; i++) {
      //interested only in p's
      if (searchMe.charAt(i) != 'p')
          continue;

      //process p's
      numPs++;
    }
    System.out.println("Found " + numPs +
                       " p's in the string.");
  }
}
```

Here is the output of this program:

```
Found 9 p's in the string.
```

To see this effect more clearly, try removing the `continue` statement and recompiling. When you run the program again, the count will be wrong, saying that it found 44 p's instead of 9.

A labeled `continue` statement skips the current iteration of an outer loop marked with the given label. The following example program, `ContinueWithLabelDemo`,[29] uses nested loops to search for a substring within another string. Two nested loops are required: one to iterate over the substring and one to iterate over the string being searched. The following program, `ContinueWithLabelDemo`, uses the labeled form of continue to skip an iteration in the outer loop.

29. `tutorial/java/nutsandbolts/examples/ContinueWithLabelDemo.java`

```
class ContinueWithLabelDemo {
  public static void main(String[] args) {

    String searchMe = "Look for a substring in me";
    String substring = "sub";
    boolean foundIt = false;

    int max = searchMe.length() - substring.length();

  test:
    for (int i = 0; i <= max; i++) {
      int n = substring.length();
      int j = i;
      int k = 0;
      while (n-- != 0) {
        if (searchMe.charAt(j++) != substring.charAt(k++)) {
          continue test;
        }
      }
      foundIt = true;
      break test;
    }
    System.out.println(foundIt ? "Found it" :
                                 "Didn't find it");
  }
}
```

Here is the output from this program:

```
Found it
```

The return Statement

The last of the branching statements is the `return` statement. The `return` statement exits from the current method, and control flow returns to where the method was invoked. The `return` statement has two forms: one that returns a value, and one that doesn't. To return a value, simply put the value (or an expression that calculates the value) after the `return` keyword.

```
return ++count;
```

The data type of the returmed value must match the type of the method's declared return value. When a method is declared `void`, use the form of `return` that doesn't return a value.

```
return;
```

The Calling an Object's Methods section (page 105) will cover everything you need to know about writing methods.

Summary of Control Flow Statements

The `if-then` statement is the most basic of all the control flow statements. It tells your program to execute a certain section of code *only if* a particular test evaluates to `true`.

The `if-then-else` statement provides a secondary path of execution when an "if" clause evaluates to `false`.

Unlike `if-then` and `if-then-else`, the `switch` statement allows for any number of possible execution paths.

The `while` and `do-while` statements continually execute a block of statements while a particular condition is `true`.

The difference between `do-while` and `while` is that `do-while` evaluates its expression at the bottom of the loop instead of the top. Therefore, the statements within the `do` block are always executed at least once.

The `for` statement provides a compact way to iterate over a range of values. It has two forms, one of which was designed for looping through collections and arrays.

Questions and Exercises: Control Flow Statements

Questions

1. The most basic control flow statement supported by the Java programming language is the ___ statement.
2. The ___ statement allows for any number of possible execution paths.
3. The ___ statement is similar to the `while` statement, but evaluates its expression at the ___ of the loop.
4. How do you write an infinite loop using the `for` statement?
5. How do you write an infinite loop using the `while` statement?

Exercises

1. Consider the following code snippet.

```
if (aNumber >= 0)
  if (aNumber == 0) System.out.println("first string");
else System.out.println("second string");
System.out.println("third string");
```

   a. What output do you think the code will produce if `aNumber` is 3?

   b. Write a test program containing the previous code snippet; make `aNumber` 3. What is the output of the program? Is it what you predicted? Explain why the output is what it is; in other words, what is the control flow for the code snippet?

c. Using only spaces and line breaks, reformat the code snippet to make the control flow easier to understand.

d. Use braces, { and }, to further clarify the code.

Answers

You can find answers to these Questions and Exercises at:

```
tutorial/java/nutsandbolts/QandE/answers_flow.html
```

4

Classes and Objects

WITH the knowledge you now have of the basics of the Java programming language, you can learn to write your own classes. In this chapter, you will find information about defining your own classes, including declaring member variables, methods, and constructors.

You will learn to use your classes to create objects and how to use the objects you create.

This chapter also covers nesting classes within other classes, enumerations, and annotations.

Classes

The introduction to object-oriented concepts in Chapter 2 used a bicycle class as an example, with racing bikes, mountain bikes, and tandem bikes as subclasses. Here is sample code for a possible implementation of a `Bicycle` class, to give you an overview of a class declaration. Subsequent sections of this chapter will back up and explain class declarations step by step. For the moment, don't concern yourself with the details.

```
public class Bicycle {
  // the Bicycle class has three fields
  public int cadence;
  public int gear;
  public int speed;

  // the Bicycle class has one constructor
  public Bicycle(int startCadence,
                 int startSpeed, int startGear) {
    gear = startGear;
    cadence = startCadence;
    speed = startSpeed;
  }

  // the Bicycle class has four methods
  public void setCadence(int newValue) {
    cadence = newValue;
  }

  public void setGear(int newValue) {
    gear = newValue;
  }

  public void applyBrake(int decrement) {
    speed -= decrement;
  }

  public void speedUp(int increment) {
    speed += increment;
  }
}
```

A class declaration for a `MountainBike` class that is a subclass of `Bicycle` might look like this:

```
public class MountainBike extends Bicycle {
  // the MountainBike subclass has one field
  public int seatHeight;

  // the MountainBike subclass has one constructor
  public MountainBike(int startHeight, int startCadence,
                      int startSpeed, int startGear) {
    super(startCadence, startSpeed, startGear);
    seatHeight = startHeight;
  }

  // the MountainBike subclass has one method
  public void setHeight(int newValue) {
    seatHeight = newValue;
  }
}
```

`MountainBike` inherits all the fields and methods of `Bicycle` and adds the field `seatHeight` and a method to set it (mountain bikes have seats that can be moved up and down as the terrain demands).

Declaring Classes

You've seen classes defined in the following way:

```
class MyClass {
  // field, constructor, and method declarations
}
```

This is a *class declaration*. The *class body* (the area between the braces) contains all the code that provides for the life cycle of the objects created from the class: constructors for initializing new objects, declarations for the fields that provide the state of the class and its objects, and methods to implement the behavior of the class and its objects.

The preceding class declaration is a minimal one—it contains only those components of a class declaration that are required. You can provide more information about the class, such as the name of its superclass, whether it implements any interfaces, and so on, at the start of the class declaration. For example,

```
class MyClass extends MySuperClass implements YourInterface {
  // field, constructor, and method declarations
}
```

means that `MyClass` is a subclass of `MySuperClass` and that it implements the `YourInterface` interface.

You can also add modifiers like `public` or `private` at the very beginning—so you can see that the opening line of a class declaration can become quite complicated. The modifiers `public` and `private`, which determine what other classes can access `MyClass`, are discussed later in this chapter. Chapter 5 will explain how and why you would use the `extends` and `implements` keywords in a class declaration. For the moment you do not need to worry about these extra complications.

In general, class declarations can include these components, in order:

1. Modifiers such as *public*, *private*, and a number of others that you will encounter later.
2. The class name, with the initial letter capitalized by convention.
3. The name of the class's parent (superclass), if any, preceded by the keyword *extends*. A class can only *extend* (subclass) one parent.

4. A comma-separated list of interfaces implemented by the class, if any, preceded by the keyword *implements*. A class can *implement* more than one interface.
5. The class body, surrounded by braces, `{ }`.

Declaring Member Variables

There are several kinds of variables:

- Member variables in a class—these are called *fields*.
- Variables in a method or block of code—these are called *local variables*.
- Variables in method declarations—these are called *parameters*.

The `Bicycle` class uses the following lines of code to define its fields:

```
public int cadence;
public int gear;
public int speed;
```

Field declarations are composed of three components, in order:

1. Zero or more modifiers, such as `public` or `private`.
2. The field's type.
3. The field's name.

The fields of `Bicycle` are named `cadence`, `gear`, and `speed` and are all of data type integer (`int`). The `public` keyword identifies these fields as public members, accessible by any object that can access the class.

Access Modifiers

The first (left-most) modifier used lets you control what other classes have access to a member field. For the moment, consider only `public` and `private`. Other access modifiers will be discussed later.

- `public` modifier—the field is accessible from all classes.
- `private` modifier—the field is accessible only within its own class.

In the spirit of encapsulation, it is common to make fields private. This means that they can only be *directly* accessed from the `Bicycle` class. We still need access to these values, however. This can be done *indirectly* by adding public methods that obtain the field values for us:

```
public class Bicycle {

  private int cadence;
  private int gear;
  private int speed;

  public Bicycle(int startCadence,
                 int startSpeed, int startGear) {
    gear = startGear;
    cadence = startCadence;
    speed = startSpeed;
  }

  public int getCadence() {
    return cadence;
  }

  public void setCadence(int newValue) {
    cadence = newValue;
  }

  public int getGear() {
    return gear;
  }

  public void setGear(int newValue) {
    gear = newValue;
  }

  public int getspeed() {
    return speed;
  }

  public void applyBrake(int decrement) {
    speed -= decrement;
  }

  public void speedUp(int increment) {
    speed += increment;
  }

}
```

Types

All variables must have a type. You can use primitive types such as `int`, `float`, `boolean`, etc. Or you can use reference types, such as strings, arrays, or objects.

Variable Names

All variables, whether they are fields, local variables, or parameters, follow the same naming rules and conventions that were covered in the Naming section (page 44).

In this chapter, be aware that the same naming rules and conventions are used for method and class names, except that:

- the first letter of a class name should be capitalized, and
- the first (or only) word in a method name should be a verb.

Defining Methods

Here is an example of a typical method declaration:

```
public double calculateAnswer(double wingSpan,
    int numberOfEngines, double length, double grossTons) {
  // do the calculation here
}
```

The only required elements of a method declaration are the method's return type, name, a pair of parentheses, `()`, and a body between braces, `{}`.

More generally, method declarations have six components, in order:

1. Modifiers—such as `public`, `private`, and others you will learn about later.
2. The return type—the data type of the value returned by the method, or `void` if the method does not return a value.
3. The method name—the rules for field names apply to method names as well, but the convention is a little different.
4. The parameter list in parenthesis—a comma-delimited list of input parameters, preceded by their data types, enclosed by parentheses, `()`. If there are no parameters, you must use empty parentheses.
5. An exception list—to be discussed later.
6. The method body, enclosed between braces—the method's code, including the declaration of local variables, goes here.

Modifiers, return types, and parameters will be discussed later in this chapter. Exceptions are discussed in Chapter 9.

Definition: Two of the components of a method declaration comprise the *method signature*—the method's name and the parameter types.

The signature of the method declared above is:

```
calculateAnswer(double, int, double, double)
```

Naming a Method

Although a method name can be any legal identifier, code conventions restrict method names. By convention, method names should be a verb in lowercase or a multi-word name that begins with a verb in lowercase, followed by adjectives, nouns, etc. In multi-word names, the first letter of each of the second and following words should be capitalized. Here are some examples:

```
run
runFast
getBackground
getFinalData
compareTo
setX
isEmpty
```

Typically, a method has a unique name within its class. However, a method might have the same name as other methods due to *method overloading*.

Overloading Methods

The Java programming language supports *overloading* methods, and Java can distinguish between methods with different *method signatures*. This means that methods within a class can have the same name if they have different parameter lists. (There are some qualifications to this that will be discussed in Chapter 5.)

Suppose that you have a class that can use calligraphy to draw various types of data (strings, integers, and so on) and that contains a method for drawing each data type. It is cumbersome to use a new name for each method—for example, `drawString`, `drawInteger`, `drawFloat`, and so on. In the Java programming language, you can use the same name for all the drawing methods but pass a different argument list to each method. Thus, the data drawing class might declare four methods named `draw`, each of which has a different parameter list:

```
public class DataArtist {
  ...
  public void draw(String s) {
    ...
  }
  public void draw(int i) {
    ...
  }
  public void draw(double f) {
    ...
  }
  public void draw(int i, double f) {
    ...
  }
}
```

Overloaded methods are differentiated by the number and the type of the arguments passed into the method. In the code sample, `draw(String s)` and `draw(int i)` are distinct and unique methods because they require different argument types.

You cannot declare more than one method with the same name and the same number and type of arguments, because the compiler cannot tell them apart.

The compiler does not consider return type when differentiating methods, so you cannot declare two methods with the same signature even if they have a different return type.

Note: Overloaded methods should be used sparingly, as they can make code much less readable.

Providing Constructors for Your Classes

A class contains constructors that are invoked to create objects from the class blueprint. Constructor declarations look like method declarations—except that they use the name of the class and have no return type. For example, `Bicycle` has one constructor:

```
public Bicycle(int startCadence,
               int startSpeed, int startGear) {
  gear = startGear;
  cadence = startCadence;
  speed = startSpeed;
}
```

To create a new `Bicycle` object called `myBike`, a constructor is invoked by the `new` operator:

```
Bicycle myBike = new Bicycle(30, 0, 8);
```

`new Bicycle(30, 0, 8)` creates space in memory for the object and initializes its fields.

Although `Bicycle` only has one constructor, it could have others, including a no-argument constructor:

```
public Bicycle() {
  gear = 1;
  cadence = 10;
  speed = 0;
}
```

`Bicycle yourBike = new Bicycle();` invokes the no-argument constructor to create a new `Bicycle` object called `yourBike`.

Both constructors could have been declared in `Bicycle` because they have different argument lists. As with methods, the Java platform differentiates constructors on the basis of the number of arguments in the list and their types. You cannot write two constructors that have the same number and type of arguments for the same class, because the platform would not be able to tell them apart. Doing so causes a compile-time error.

You don't have to provide any constructors for your class, but you must be careful when doing this. The compiler automatically provides a no-argument, default constructor for any class without constructors. This default constructor will invoke the no-argument constructor of the superclass. In this situation, the compiler will complain if the superclass doesn't have a no-argument constructor, so you must verify that it does. If your class has no explicit superclass, then it has an implicit superclass of `Object`, which *does* have a no-argument constructor.

You can use a superclass constructor yourself. The `MountainBike` class at the beginning of this chapter did just that. This will be discussed later, in Chapter 5.

You can use access modifiers in a constructor's declaration to control which other classes can invoke the constructor.

Note: If another class cannot invoke a `MyClass` constructor, it cannot directly create `MyClass` objects.

Passing Information to a Method or a Constructor

The declaration for a method or a constructor declares the number and the type of the arguments for that method or constructor. For example, the following is a method that computes the monthly payments for a home loan, based on the amount of the loan, the interest rate, the length of the loan (the number of periods), and the future value of the loan:

```
public double computePayment(double loanAmt,
                             double rate,
                             double futureValue,
                             int numPeriods) {
  double interest = rate / 100.0;
  double partial1 = Math.pow((1 + interest), -numPeriods);
  double denominator = (1 - partial1) / interest;
  double answer = (-loanAmt / denominator) -
                  ((futureValue * partial1) / denominator);
  return answer;
}
```

This method has four parameters: the loan amount, the interest rate, the future value and the number of periods. The first three are double-precision floating point numbers, and the fourth is an integer. The parameters are used in the method body and at runtime will take on the values of the arguments that are passed in.

Note: *Parameters* refers to the list of variables in a method declaration. *Arguments* are the actual values that are passed in when the method is invoked. When you invoke a method, the arguments used must match the declaration's parameters in type and order.

Parameter Types

You can use any data type for a parameter of a method or a constructor. This includes primitive data types, such as doubles, floats, and integers, as you saw in the `computePayment` method, and reference data types, such as objects and arrays.

Here's an example of a method that accepts an array as an argument. In this example, the method creates a new `Polygon` object and initializes it from an array of `Point` objects (assume that `Point` is a class that represents an x, y coordinate):

```
public Polygon polygonFrom(Point[] corners) {
  // method body goes here
}
```

Note: The Java programming language doesn't let you pass methods into methods. But you can pass an object into a method and then invoke the object's methods.

Arbitrary Number of Arguments

You can use a construct called *varargs* to pass an arbitrary number of values to a method. You use varargs when you don't know how many of a particular type of argument will be passed to the method. It's a shortcut to creating an array manually (the previous method could have used varargs rather than an array).

To use varargs, you follow the type of the last parameter by an ellipsis (three dots, . . .), then a space, and the parameter name. The method can then be invoked with any number of that parameter, including none.

```
public Polygon polygonFrom(Point... corners) {
  int numberOfSides = corners.length;
  double squareOfSide1, lengthOfSide1;
  squareOfSide1 =
  (corners[1].x - corners[0].x)*(corners[1].x - corners[0].x) +
  (corners[1].y - corners[0].y)*(corners[1].y - corners[0].y);
  lengthOfSide1 = Math.sqrt(squareOfSide1);
  // more method body code follows that creates
  // and returns a polygon connecting the Points
}
```

You can see that, inside the method, `corners` is treated like an array. The method can be invoked either with an array or with a sequence of arguments. The code in the method body will treat the parameter as an array in either case.

You will most commonly see varargs with the printing methods—for example, this `printf` method:

```
public PrintStream printf(String format, Object... args)
```

allows you to print an arbitrary number of objects. It can be invoked like this:

```
System.out.printf("%s: %d, %s%n", name, idnum, address);
```

or like this:

```
System.out.printf("%s: %d, %s, %s, %s%n", name,
                  idnum, address, phone, email);
```

or with yet a different number of arguments.

Parameter Names

When you declare a parameter to a method or a constructor, you provide a name for that parameter. This name is used within the method body to refer to the passed-in argument.

The name of a parameter must be unique in its scope. It cannot be the same as the name of another parameter for the same method or constructor, and it cannot be the name of a local variable within the method or constructor.

A parameter can have the same name as one of the class's fields. If this is the case, the parameter is said to *shadow* the field. Shadowing fields can make your code difficult to read and is conventionally used only within constructors and methods that set a particular field. For example, consider the following Circle class and its setOrigin method:

```
public class Circle {
  private int x, y, radius;
  public void setOrigin(int x, int y) {
    ...
  }
}
```

The Circle class has three fields: x, y, and radius. The setOrigin method has two parameters, each of which has the same name as one of the fields. Each method parameter shadows the field that shares its name. So using the simple names x or y within the body of the method refers to the parameter, *not* to the field. To access the field, you must use a qualified name. This will be discussed later in this chapter in the Using the this Keyword section (page 109).

Passing Primitive Data Type Arguments

Primitive arguments, such as an int or a double, are passed into methods *by value*. This means that any changes to the values of the parameters exist only within the scope of the method. When the method returns, the parameters are gone and any changes to them are lost. Here is an example:

```
public class PassPrimitiveByValue {

  public static void main(String[] args) {

    int x = 3;

    // invoke passMethod() with x as argument
    passMethod(x);

    // print x to see if its value has changed
    System.out.println("After invoking passMethod, x = " + x);

  }

  // change parameter in passMethod()
  public static void passMethod(int p) {
    p = 10;
  }
}
```

When you run this program, the output is:

```
After invoking passMethod, x = 3
```

Passing Reference Data Type Arguments

Reference data type parameters, such as objects, are also passed into methods *by value*. This means that when the method returns, the passed-in reference still references the same object as before. *However*, the values of the object's fields *can* be changed in the method, if they have the proper access level.

For example, consider a method in an arbitrary class that moves `Circle` objects:

```
public void moveCircle(Circle circle, int deltaX, int deltaY) {

  // code to move origin of circle to x+deltaX, y+deltaY
  circle.setX(circle.getX + deltaX);
  circle.setY(circle.getY + deltaY);

  // code to assign a new reference to circle
  circle = new Circle(0, 0);
}
```

Let the method be invoked with these arguments:

```
moveCircle(myCircle, 23, 56)
```

Inside the method, `circle` initially refers to `myCircle`. The method changes the x and y coordinates of the object that `circle` references (i.e., `myCircle`) by 23 and 56, respectively. (These changes will persist when the method returns.) Then `circle` is assigned a reference to a new `Circle` object with `x = y = 0`. This reassignment has no permanence, however, because the reference was passed in by value and cannot change. Within the method, the object pointed to by `circle` has changed, but, when the method returns, `myCircle` still references the same `Circle` object as before the method was invoked.

Objects

A typical Java program creates many objects, which, as you know, interact by invoking methods.

Through these object interactions, a program can carry out various tasks, such as implementing a GUI, running an animation, or sending and receiving information over a network. Once an object has completed the work for which it was created, its resources are recycled for use by other objects.

Here's a small program, called `CreateObjectDemo`,[1] that creates three objects: one `Point` object and two `Rectangle` objects. The `Point` and `Rectangle` classes are listed in the Initializing an Object section (page 101).

```
public class CreateObjectDemo {

  public static void main(String[] args) {

    // Declare and create a point object
    // and two rectangle objects.
    Point originOne = new Point(23, 94);
    Rectangle rectOne = new Rectangle(originOne, 100, 200);
    Rectangle rectTwo = new Rectangle(50, 100);

    // display rectOne's width, height, and area
    System.out.println("Width of rectOne: " + rectOne.width);
    System.out.println("Height of rectOne: " + rectOne.height);
    System.out.println("Area of rectOne: " +
                                rectOne.getArea());

    // set rectTwo's position
    rectTwo.origin = originOne;

    // display rectTwo's position
    System.out.println("X Position of rectTwo: " +
                                     rectTwo.origin.x);
    System.out.println("Y Position of rectTwo: " +
                                     rectTwo.origin.y);

    // move rectTwo and display its new position
    rectTwo.move(40, 72);
    System.out.println("X Position of rectTwo: " +
                                     rectTwo.origin.x);
    System.out.println("Y Position of rectTwo: " +
                                     rectTwo.origin.y);
  }
}
```

This program creates, manipulates, and displays information about various objects. Here's the output:

1. `tutorial/java/javaOO/examples/CreateObjectDemo.java`

```
Width of rectOne: 100
Height of rectOne: 200
Area of rectOne: 20000
X Position of rectTwo: 23
Y Position of rectTwo: 94
X Position of rectTwo: 40
Y Position of rectTwo: 72
```

The following three sections use the above example to describe the life cycle of an object within a program. From them, you will learn how to write code that creates and uses objects in your own programs. You will also learn how the system cleans up after an object when its life has ended.

Creating Objects

As you know, a class provides the blueprint for objects; you create an object from a class. Each of the following statements taken from the `CreateObjectDemo` program creates an object and assigns it to a variable:

```
Point originOne = new Point(23, 94);
Rectangle rectOne = new Rectangle(originOne, 100, 200);
Rectangle rectTwo = new Rectangle(50, 100);
```

The first line creates an object of the `Point` class, and the second and third lines each create an object of the `Rectangle` class.

Each of these statements has three parts (discussed in detail below):

1. **Declaration.** The code set in **bold** are all variable declarations that associate a variable name with an object type.
2. **Instantiation.** The `new` keyword is a Java operator that creates the object.
3. **Initialization.** The `new` operator is followed by invoking a constructor, which initializes the new object.

Declaring a Variable to Refer to an Object

Previously, you learned that to declare a variable, you write:

```
type name;
```

This notifies the compiler that you will use *name* to refer to data whose type is *type*. With a primitive variable, this declaration also reserves the proper amount of memory for the variable.

You can also declare a reference variable on its own line. For example:

```
Point originOne;
```

If you declare `originOne` like this, its value will be undetermined until an object is actually created and assigned to it. Simply declaring a reference variable does not create an object. For that, you need to use the `new` operator, as described in the next section. You must assign an object to `originOne` before you use it in your code. Otherwise, you will get a compiler error.

A variable in this state, which currently references no object, can be illustrated by Figure 4.1 (the variable name, `originOne`, plus a reference pointing to nothing).

Figure 4.1 `originOne` is `null`.

Instantiating a Class

The `new` operator instantiates a class by allocating memory for a new object and returning a reference to that memory. The `new` operator also invokes the object constructor.

Note: The phrase "instantiating a class" means the same thing as "creating an object." When you create an object, you are creating an "instance" of a class, therefore "instantiating" a class.

The `new` operator requires a single, postfix argument: invoking a constructor. The name of the constructor provides the name of the class to instantiate.

The `new` operator returns a reference to the object it created. This reference is usually assigned to a variable of the appropriate type, like:

```
Point originOne = new Point(23, 94);
```

The reference returned by the `new` operator does not have to be assigned to a variable. It can also be used directly in an expression. For example:

```
int height = new Rectangle().height;
```

This statement will be discussed in the next section.

Initializing an Object

Here's the code for the `Point` class:[2]

```
public class Point {
  public int x = 0;
  public int y = 0;
  // constructor
  public Point(int a, int b) {
  x = a;
  y = b;
  }
}
```

This class contains a single constructor. You can recognize a constructor because its declaration uses the same name as the class and it has no return type. The constructor in the `Point` class takes two integer arguments, as declared by the code `(int a, int b)`. The following statement provides 23 and 94 as values for those arguments:

```
Point originOne = new Point(23, 94);
```

The result of executing this statement can be illustrated by Figure 4.2.

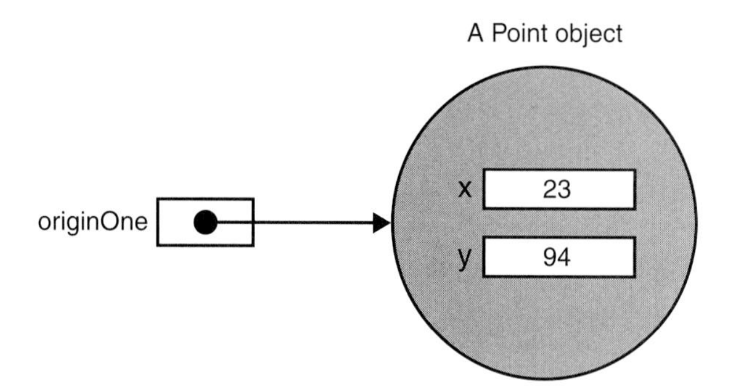

Figure 4.2 `originOne` now points to a `Point` object.

Here's the code for the `Rectangle` class,[3] which contains four constructors:

2. `tutorial/java/javaOO/examples/Point.java`

3. `tutorial/java/javaOO/examples/Rectangle.java`

```
public class Rectangle {
  public int width = 0;
  public int height = 0;
  public Point origin;

  // four constructors
  public Rectangle() {
    origin = new Point(0, 0);
  }
  public Rectangle(Point p) {
    origin = p;
  }
  public Rectangle(int w, int h) {
    origin = new Point(0, 0);
    width = w;
    height = h;
  }
  public Rectangle(Point p, int w, int h) {
    origin = p;
    width = w;
    height = h;
  }

  // a method for moving the rectangle
  public void move(int x, int y) {
    origin.x = x;
    origin.y = y;
  }

  // a method for computing the area of the rectangle
  public int getArea() {
    return width * height;
  }
}
```

Each constructor lets you provide initial values for the rectangle's size and width, using both primitive and reference types. If a class has multiple constructors, they must have different signatures. The Java compiler differentiates the constructors based on the number and the type of the arguments. When the Java compiler encounters the following code, it knows to invoke the constructor in the `Rectangle` class that requires a `Point` argument followed by two integer arguments:

```
Rectangle rectOne = new Rectangle(originOne, 100, 200);
```

This invokes one of `Rectangle`'s constructors that initializes `origin` to `originOne`. Also, the constructor sets `width` to 100 and `height` to 200. Now there are two references to the same `Point object`; an object can have multiple references to it, as shown in Figure 4.3.

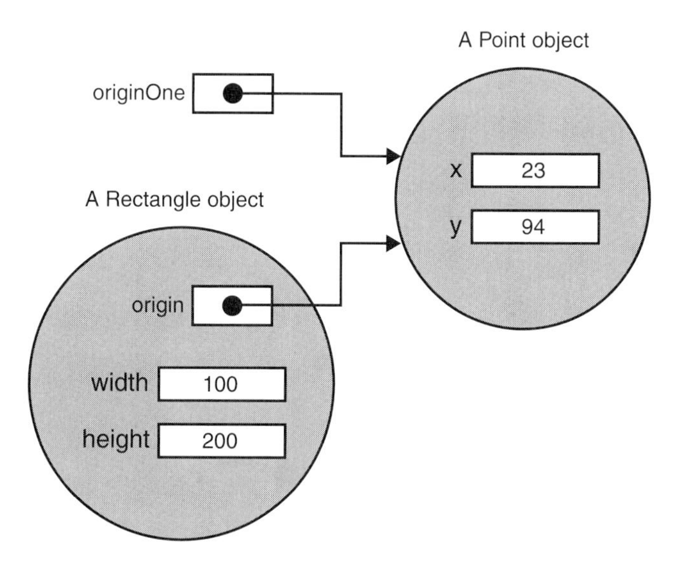

Figure 4.3 `originOne` now points to a `Point` object.

The following line of code invokes the `Rectangle` constructor that requires two integer arguments, which provide the initial values for `width` and `height`. If you inspect the code within the constructor, you will see that it creates a new `Point` object whose `x` and `y` values are initialized to 0:

```
Rectangle rectTwo = new Rectangle(50, 100);
```

The `Rectangle` constructor used in the following statement doesn't take any arguments, so it's called a *no-argument constructor*:

```
Rectangle rect = new Rectangle();
```

All classes have at least one constructor. If a class does not explicitly declare any, the Java compiler automatically provides a no-argument constructor, called the *default constructor*. This default constructor invokes the class parent's no-argument constructor, or the `Object` constructor if the class has no other parent. If the parent has no constructor (`Object` does have one), the compiler will reject the program.

Using Objects

Once you've created an object, you probably want to use it for something. You may need to use the value of one of its fields, change one of its fields, or invoke one of its methods to perform an action.

Referencing an Object's Fields

Object fields are accessed by their name. You must use a name that is unambiguous.

You may use a simple name for a field within its own class. For example, we can add a statement *within* the `Rectangle` class that prints the `width` and `height`:

```
System.out.println("Width and height are: " +
                                   width + ", " + height);
```

In this case, `width` and `height` are simple names.

Code that is outside the object's class must use an object reference or expression, followed by the dot (`.`) operator, followed by a simple field name, as in:

```
objectReference.fieldName
```

For example, the code in the `CreateObjectDemo` class is outside the code for the `Rectangle` class. So to refer to the `origin`, `width`, and `height` fields within the `Rectangle` object named `rectOne`, the `CreateObjectDemo` class must use the names `rectOne.origin`, `rectOne.width`, and `rectOne.height`, respectively. The program uses two of these names to display the `width` and the `height` of `rectOne`:

```
System.out.println("Width of rectOne: " + rectOne.width);
System.out.println("Height of rectOne: " + rectOne.height);
```

Attempting to use the simple names `width` and `height` from the code in the `CreateObjectDemo` class doesn't make sense—those fields exist only within an object—and results in a compiler error.

Later, the program uses similar code to display information about `rectTwo`. Objects of the same type have their own copy of the same instance fields. Thus, each `Rectangle` object has fields named `origin`, `width`, and `height`. When you access an instance field through an object reference, you reference that particular object's field. The two objects `rectOne` and `rectTwo` in the `CreateObjectDemo` program have different `origin`, `width`, and `height` fields.

To access a field, you can use a named reference to an object, as in the previous examples, or you can use any expression that returns an object reference. Recall that the `new` operator returns a reference to an object. So you could use the value returned from new to access a new object's fields:

```
int height = new Rectangle().height;
```

This statement creates a new `Rectangle` object and immediately gets its height. In essence, the statement calculates the default height of a `Rectangle`. Note that after this statement has been executed, the program no longer has a reference to the created

Rectangle, because the program never stored the reference anywhere. The object is unreferenced, and its resources are free to be recycled by the Java Virtual Machine.

Invoking an Object's Methods

You also use an object reference to invoke an object's method. You append the method's simple name to the object reference, with an intervening dot operator (.). Also, you provide, within enclosing parentheses, any arguments to the method. If the method does not require any arguments, use empty parentheses.

```
objectReference.methodName(argumentList);
```

or

```
objectReference.methodName();
```

The Rectangle class has two methods: getArea() to compute the rectangle's area and move() to change the rectangle's origin. Here's the CreateObjectDemo code that invokes these two methods:

```
System.out.println("Area of rectOne: " + rectOne.getArea());
...
rectTwo.move(40, 72);
```

The first statement invokes rectOne's getArea() method and displays the results. The second line moves rectTwo because the move() method assigns new values to the object's origin.x and origin.y.

As with instance fields, *objectReference* must be a reference to an object. You can use a variable name, but you also can use any expression that returns an object reference. The new operator returns an object reference, so you can use the value returned from new to invoke a new object's methods:

```
new Rectangle(100, 50).getArea()
```

The expression new Rectangle(100, 50) returns an object reference that refers to a Rectangle object. As shown, you can use the dot notation to invoke the new Rectangle's getArea() method to compute the area of the new rectangle.

Some methods, such as getArea(), return a value. For methods that return a value, you can use the method invocation in expressions. You can assign the return value to a variable, use it to make decisions, or control a loop. This code assigns the value returned by getArea() to the variable areaOfRectangle:

```
int areaOfRectangle = new Rectangle(100, 50).getArea();
```

Remember, invoking a method on a particular object is the same as sending a message to that object. In this case, the object that `getArea()` is invoked on is the rectangle returned by the constructor.

The Garbage Collector

Some object-oriented languages require that you keep track of all the objects you create and that you explicitly destroy them when they are no longer needed. Managing memory explicitly is tedious and error-prone. The Java platform allows you to create as many objects as you want (limited, of course, by what your system can handle), and you don't have to worry about destroying them. The Java runtime environment deletes objects when it determines that they are no longer being used. This process is called *garbage collection*.

An object is eligible for garbage collection when there are no more references to that object. References that are held in a variable are usually dropped when the variable goes out of scope. Or, you can explicitly drop an object reference by setting the variable to the special value `null`. Remember that a program can have multiple references to the same object; all references to an object must be dropped before the object is eligible for garbage collection.

The Java runtime environment has a garbage collector that periodically frees the memory used by objects that are no longer referenced. The garbage collector does its job automatically when it determines that the time is right.

More on Classes

This section covers more aspects of classes that depend on using object references and the `dot` operator that you learned about in the preceding sections on objects:

- Returning values from methods
- The `this` keyword
- Class vs. instance members
- Access control

Returning a Value from a Method

A method returns to the code that invoked it when it

- completes all the statements in the method,
- reaches a `return` statement, or

• throws an exception (covered later),

whichever occurs first.

You declare a method's return type in its method declaration. Within the body of the method, you use the `return` statement to return the value.

Any method declared `void` doesn't return a value. It does not need to contain a `return` statement, but it may do so. In such a case, a `return` statement can be used to branch out of a control flow block and exit the method and is simply used like this:

```
return;
```

If you try to return a value from a method that is declared `void`, you will get a compiler error.

Any method that is not declared `void` must contain a `return` statement with a corresponding return value, like this:

```
return returnValue;
```

The data type of the return value must match the method's declared return type; you can't return an integer value from a method declared to return a boolean.

The `getArea()` method in the `Rectangle` class that was discussed in the Objects section (page 97) returns an integer:

```
// a method for computing the area of the rectangle
public int getArea() {
  return width * height;
}
```

This method returns the integer that the expression `width*height` evaluates to.

The `area` method returns a primitive type. A method can also return a reference type. For example, in a program to manipulate `Bicycle` objects, we might have a method like this:

```
public Bicycle SeeWhosFastest(Bicycle myBike,
                 Bicycle yourBike, Environment env) {
  Bicycle fastest;
  // code to calculate which bike is faster, given
  // each bike's gear and cadence and given
  // the environment (terrain and wind)
  return fastest;
}
```

Returning a Class or Interface

Subclasses and interfaces will be discussed in Chapter 5. If this section confuses you, skip it and return to it after you have finished Chapter 5.

When a method uses a class name as its return type, such as `whosFastest` does, the class of the type of the returned object must be either a subclass of, or the exact class of, the return type. Suppose that you have a class hierarchy in which `ImaginaryNumber` is a subclass of `java.lang.Number`, which is in turn a subclass of `Object`, as illustrated by Figure 4.4.

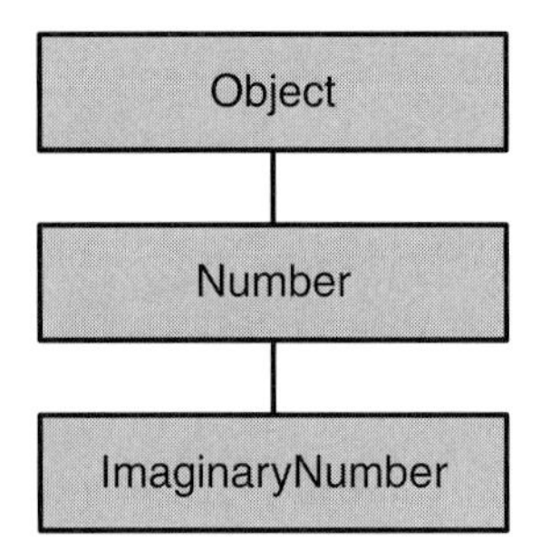

Figure 4.4 The class hierarchy for `ImaginaryNumber`.

Now suppose that you have a method declared to return a `Number`:

```
public Number returnANumber() {
   ...
}
```

The `returnANumber` method can return an `ImaginaryNumber` but not an `Object`. `ImaginaryNumber` is a `Number` because it's a subclass of `Number`. However, an `Object` is not necessarily a `Number`—it could be a `String` or another type.

You can override a method and define it to return a subclass of the original method, like this:

```
public ImaginaryNumber returnANumber() {
   ...
}
```

This technique, called *covariant return type*, means that the return type is allowed to vary in the same direction as the subclass.

Note: You also can use interface names as return types. In this case, the object returned must implement the specified interface.

Using the this Keyword

Within an instance method or a constructor, `this` is a reference to the *current object*—the object whose method or constructor is being invoked. You can refer to any member of the current object from within an instance method or a constructor by using `this`.

Using this with a Field

The most common reason for using the `this` keyword is because a field is shadowed by a method or constructor parameter.

For example, the `Point` class was written like this:

```
public class Point {
  public int x = 0;
  public int y = 0;

  // constructor
  public Point(int a, int b) {
    x = a;
    y = b;
  }
}
```

but it could have been written like this:

```
public class Point {
  public int x = 0;
  public int y = 0;

  // constructor
  public Point(int x, int y) {
    this.x = x;
    this.y = y;
  }
}
```

Each argument to the second constructor shadows one of the object's fields—inside the constructor **`x`** is a local copy of the constructor's first argument. To refer to the `Point` field **`x`**, the constructor must use **`this.x`**.

Using this with a Constructor

From within a constructor, you can also use the `this` keyword to invoke another constructor in the same class. Doing so is called an *explicit constructor invocation.* Here's another `Rectangle` class, with a different implementation from the one in the Objects section (page 97).

```
public class Rectangle {
  private int x, y;
  private int width, height;

  public Rectangle() {
    this(0, 0, 0, 0);
  }
  public Rectangle(int width, int height) {
    this(0, 0, width, height);
  }
  public Rectangle(int x, int y, int width, int height) {
    this.x = x;
    this.y = y;
    this.width = width;
    this.height = height;
  }
  ...
}
```

This class contains a set of constructors. Each constructor initializes some or all of the rectangle's member variables. The constructors provide a default value for any member variable whose initial value is not provided by an argument. For example, the no-argument constructor invokes the four-argument constructor with four 0 values and the two-argument constructor invokes the four-argument constructor with two 0 values. As before, the compiler determines which constructor to invoke, based on the number and the type of arguments.

If present, the invocation of another constructor must be the first line in the constructor.

Controlling Access to Members of a Class

Access level modifiers determine whether other classes can use a particular field or invoke a particular method. There are two levels of access control:

- At the top level—`public`, or *package-private* (no explicit modifier).
- At the member level—`public`, `private`, `protected`, or *package-private* (no explicit modifier).

A class may be declared with the modifier `public`, in which case that class is visible to all classes everywhere. If a class has no modifier (the default, also known as *package-private*), it is visible only within its own package (packages are named groups of related classes—you will learn about them in Chapter 7).

At the member level, you can also use the `public` modifier or no modifier (*package-private*) just as with top-level classes, and with the same meaning. For members, there are two additional access modifiers: `private` and `protected`. The `private` modifier specifies that the member can only be accessed in its own class. The `protected` modifier specifies that the member can only be accessed within its own package (as with *package-private*) and, in addition, by a subclass of its class in another package.

Table 4.1 shows the access to members permitted by each modifier.

Table 4.1 Access Levels

Modifier	Class	Package	Subclass	World
`public`	Y	Y	Y	Y
`protected`	Y	Y	Y	N
no modifier	Y	Y	N	N
`private`	Y	N	N	N

The first data column indicates whether the class itself has access to the member defined by the access level. As you can see, a class always has access to its own members. The second column indicates whether classes in the same package as the class (regardless of their parentage) have access to the member. The third column indicates whether subclasses of the class—declared outside this package—have access to the member. The fourth column indicates whether all classes have access to the member.

Access levels affect you in two ways. First, when you use classes that come from another source, such as the classes in the Java platform, access levels determine which members of those classes your own classes can use. Second, when you write a class, you need to decide what access level every member variable and every method in your class should have.

Let's look at a collection of classes and see how access levels affect visibility. Figure 4.5 shows the four classes in this example and how they are related.

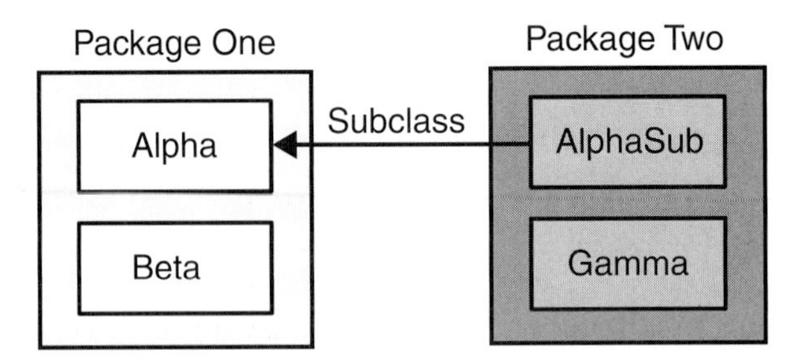

Figure 4.5 Classes and packages of the example used to illustrate access levels.

Table 4.2 shows where the members of the `Alpha` class are visible for each of the access modifiers that can be applied to them.

Table 4.2 Visibility

Modifier	Alpha	Beta	Alphasub	Gamma
`public`	Y	Y	Y	Y
`protected`	Y	Y	Y	N
no modifier	Y	Y	N	N
`private`	Y	N	N	N

Tips on Choosing an Access Level: If other programmers use your class, you want to ensure that errors from misuse cannot happen. Access levels can help you do this.

- Use the most restrictive access level that makes sense for a particular member. Use `private` unless you have a good reason not to.
- Avoid `public` fields except for constants. (Many of the examples in the tutorial use `public` fields. This may help to illustrate some points concisely, but is not recommended for production code.) Public fields tend to link you to a particular implementation and limit your flexibility in changing your code.

Understanding Instance and Class Members

In this section, we discuss the use of the `static` keyword to create fields and methods that belong to the class, rather than to an instance of the class.

Class Variables

When a number of objects are created from the same class blueprint, they each have their own distinct copies of *instance variables*. In the case of the `Bicycle` class, the instance variables are cadence, gear, and speed. Each Bicycle object has its own values for these variables, stored in different memory locations.

Sometimes, you want to have variables that are common to all objects. This is accomplished with the static modifier. Fields that have the static modifier in their declaration are called *static fields* or *class variables*. They are associated with the class, rather than with any object. Every instance of the class shares a class variable, which is in one fixed location in memory. Any object can change the value of a class variable, but class variables can also be manipulated without creating an instance of the class.

For example, suppose you want to create a number of Bicycle objects and assign each a serial number, beginning with 1 for the first object. This ID number is unique to each object and is therefore an instance variable. At the same time, you need a field to keep track of how many Bicycle objects have been created so that you know what ID to assign to the next one. Such a field is not related to any individual object, but to the class as a whole. For this you need a class variable, numberOfBicycles, as follows:

```
public class Bicycle{

  private int cadence;
  private int gear;
  private int speed;

  // add an instance variable for the object ID
  private int id;

  // add a class variable for the number
  // of Bicycle objects instantiated
  private static int numberOfBicycles = 0;
    ...
}
```

Class variables are referenced by the class name itself, as in:

```
Bicycle.numberOfBicycles
```

This makes it clear that they are class variables.

Note: You can also refer to static fields with an object reference like:

```
myBike.numberOfBicycles
```

but this is discouraged because it does not make it clear that they are class variables.

You can use the Bicycle constructor to set the id instance variable and increment the numberOfBicycles class variable:

```
public class Bicycle{

  private int cadence;
  private int gear;
  private int speed;
  private int id;
  private static int numberOfBicycles = 0;

  public Bicycle(int startCadence,
                 int startSpeed, int startGear){
    gear = startGear;
    cadence = startCadence;
    speed = startSpeed;

    // increment number of Bicycles and assign ID number
    id = ++numberOfBicycles;
  }

  // new method to return the ID instance variable
  public int getID() {
    return id;
  }
  .....
}
```

Class Methods

The Java programming language supports static methods as well as static variables. Static methods, which have the `static` modifier in their declarations, should be invoked with the class name, without the need for creating an instance of the class, as in:

```
ClassName.methodName(args)
```

Note: You can also refer to static methods with an object reference like

```
instanceName.methodName(args)
```

but this is discouraged because it does not make it clear that they are class variables.

A common use for static methods is to access static fields. For example, we could add a static method to the `Bicycle` class to access the `numberOfBicycles` static field:

```
public static int getNumberOfBicycles() {
  return numberOfBicycles;
}
```

Not all combinations of instance and class variables and methods are allowed:

- Instance methods can access instance variables and instance methods directly.
- Instance methods can access class variables and class methods directly.
- Class methods can access class variables and class methods directly.
- Class methods *cannot* access instance variables or instance methods directly—they must use an object reference. Also, class methods cannot use the `this` keyword as there is no instance for `this` to refer to.

Constants

The `static` modifier, in combination with the `final` modifier, is also used to define constants.

The `final` modifier indicates that the value of this field cannot change.

For example, the following variable declaration defines a constant named `PI`, whose value is an approximation of pi (the ratio of the circumference of a circle to its diameter):

```
static final double PI = 3.141592653589793;
```

Constants defined in this way cannot be reassigned, and it is a compile-time error if your program tries to do so. By convention, the names of constant values are spelled in uppercase letters. If the name is composed of more than one word, the words are separated by an underscore (_).

Note: If a primitive type or a string is defined as a constant and the value is known at compile time, the compiler replaces the constant name everywhere in the code with its value. This is called a *compile-time constant*. If the value of the constant in the outside world changes (for example, if it is legislated that pi actually should be 3.975), you will need to recompile any classes that use this constant to get the current value.

The Bicycle Class

After all the modifications made in this section, the `Bicycle` class is now:

```
public class Bicycle{
  private int cadence;
  private int gear;
  private int speed;
  private int id;
  private static int numberOfBicycles = 0;

  public Bicycle(int startCadence,
                 int startSpeed, int startGear) {
    gear = startGear;
    cadence = startCadence;
    speed = startSpeed;
    id = ++numberOfBicycles;
  }

  public int getID() {
    return id;
  }

  public static int getNumberOfBicycles() {
    return numberOfBicycles;
  }

  public int getCadence(){
    return cadence;
  }

  public void setCadence(int newValue){
    cadence = newValue;
  }

  public int getGear(){
  return gear;
  }

  public void setGear(int newValue){
    gear = newValue;
  }

  public int getspeed(){
    return speed;
  }

  public void applyBrake(int decrement){
    speed -= decrement;
  }

  public void speedUp(int increment){
    speed += increment;
  }
}
```

Initializing Fields

As you have seen, you can often provide an initial value for a field in its declaration:

```
public class BedAndBreakfast {
  public static int capacity = 10;  // initialize to 10
  private boolean full = false;     // initialize to false
}
```

This works well when the initialization value is available and the initialization can be put on one line. However, this form of initialization has limitations because of its simplicity. If initialization requires some logic (for example, error handling or a `for` loop to fill a complex array), simple assignment is inadequate. Instance variables can be initialized in constructors, where error handling or other logic can be used. To provide the same capability for class variables, the Java programming language includes *static initialization blocks*.

Note: It is not necessary to declare fields at the beginning of the class definition, although this is the most common practice. It is only necessary that they be declared and initialized before they are used.

Static Initialization Blocks

A *static initialization block* is a normal block of code enclosed in braces, `{ }`, and preceded by the `static` keyword. Here is an example:

```
static {
  // whatever code is needed for initialization goes here
}
```

A class can have any number of static initialization blocks, and they can appear anywhere in the class body. The runtime system guarantees that static initialization blocks are executed in the order that they appear in the source code.

There is an alternative to static blocks—you can write a private static method:

```
class Whatever {
  public static varType myVar = initializeClassVariable();
  private static varType initializeClassVariable() {
    // initialization code goes here
  }
}
```

The advantage of private static methods is that they can be reused later if you need to reinitialize the class variable.

Initializing Instance Members

Normally, you would put code to initialize an instance variable in a constructor. There are two alternatives to using a constructor to initialize instance variables: initializer blocks and final methods.

Initializer blocks for instance variables look just like static initializer blocks, but without the `static` keyword:

```
{
  // whatever code is needed for initialization goes here
}
```

The Java compiler copies initializer blocks into every constructor. Therefore, this approach can be used to share a block of code between multiple constructors.

A *final method* cannot be overridden in a subclass. This is discussed in Chapter 5. Here is an example of using a final method for initializing an instance variable:

```
class Whatever {
  private varType myVar = initializeInstanceVariable();
  protected final varType initializeInstanceVariable() {
    // initialization code goes here
  }
}
```

This is especially useful if subclasses might want to reuse the initialization method. The method is final because invoking non-final methods during instance initialization can cause problems. Joshua Bloch describes this in more detail in *Effective Java*.[4]

Summary of Creating and Using Classes and Objects

A class declaration names the class and encloses the class body between braces. The class name can be preceded by modifiers. The class body contains fields, methods, and constructors for the class. A class uses fields to contain state information and uses methods to implement behavior. Constructors that initialize a new instance of a class use the name of the class and look like methods without a return type.

You control access to classes and members in the same way: by using an access modifier such as `public` in their declaration.

You specify a class variable or a class method by using the `static` keyword in the member's declaration. A member that is not declared as `static` is implicitly an instance member. Class variables are shared by all instances of a class and can be accessed

---

4. `docs/books/effective`

through the class name as well as an instance reference. Instances of a class get their own copy of each instance variable, which must be accessed through an instance reference.

You create an object from a class by using the `new` operator and a constructor. The new operator returns a reference to the object that was created. You can assign the reference to a variable or use it directly.

Instance variables and methods that are accessible to code outside of the class that they are declared in can be referred to by using a qualified name. The qualified name of an instance variable looks like this:

```
objectReference.variableName
```

The qualified name of a method looks like this:

```
objectReference.methodName(argumentList)
```

or

```
objectReference.methodName()
```

The garbage collector automatically cleans up unused objects. An object is unused if the program holds no more references to it. You can explicitly drop a reference by setting the variable holding the reference to `null`.

Questions and Exercises: Classes

Questions

Consider the following class:

```
public class IdentifyMyParts {
  public static int x = 7;
  public int y = 3;
}
```

a. What are the class variables?

b. What are the instance variables?

c. What is the output from the following code:

```
IdentifyMyParts a = new IdentifyMyParts();
IdentifyMyParts b = new IdentifyMyParts();
a.y = 5;
b.y = 6;
IdentifyMyParts.x = 1;
b.x = 2;
System.out.println("a.y = " + a.y);
System.out.println("b.y = " + b.y);
System.out.println("IdentifyMyParts.x = " + a.x);
System.out.println("b.x = " + b.x);
```

Exercises

1. Write a class whose instances represent a single playing card from a deck of cards. Playing cards have two distinguishing properties: rank and suit. Be sure to keep your solution as you will be asked to rewrite it in the Questions and Exercises: Enum Types section (page 132).

Hint: You can use the `assert` statement to check your assignments. You write:

```
assert (boolean expression to test);
```

If the boolean expression is false, you will get an error message. For example,

```
assert toString(ACE) == "Ace";
```

should return `true`, so there will be no error message.

If you use the `assert` statement, you must run your program with the `ea` flag:

```
java -ea YourProgram.class
```

---

2. Write a class whose instances represent a **full** deck of cards. You should also keep this solution.
3. Write a small program to test your deck and card classes. The program can be as simple as creating a deck of cards and displaying its cards.

Answers

You can find answers to these Questions and Exercises at:

```
tutorial/java/javaOO/QandE/creating-answers.html
```

Questions and Exercises: Objects

Questions

1. What's wrong with the following program?

```
public class SomethingIsWrong {
  public static void main(String[] args) {
    Rectangle myRect;
    myRect.width = 40;
    myRect.height = 50;
    System.out.println("myRect's area is " + myRect.area());
  }
}
```

2. The following code creates one Point object and one Rectangle object. How many references to those objects exist after the code executes? Is either object eligible for garbage collection?

```
...
Point point = new Point(2,4);
Rectangle rectangle = new Rectangle(point, 20, 20);
point = null;
...
```

3. How does a program destroy an object that it creates?

Exercises

1. Fix the program called SomethingIsWrong shown in Question 1.
2. Given the following class, called NumberHolder,[5] write some code that creates an instance of the class, initializes its two member variables, and then displays the value of each member variable:

```
public class NumberHolder {
  public int anInt;
  public float aFloat;
}
```

Answers

You can find answers to these Questions and Exercises at:

```
tutorial/java/javaOO/QandE/objects-answers.html
```

5. tutorial/java/javaOO/QandE/NumberHolder.java

Nested Classes

The Java programming language allows you to define a class within another class. Such a class is called a *nested class*:

```
class OuterClass {
  ...
  class NestedClass {
    ...
  }
}
```

A nested class is a member of its enclosing class and, as such, has access to other members of the enclosing class, even if they are declared `private`. As a member of `OuterClass`, a nested class can be declared `private`, `public`, `protected`, or *package private*. (Recall that outer classes can only be declared `public` or *package private*.)

Terminology: Nested classes are divided into two categories: static and non-static. Nested classes that are declared `static` are simply called *static nested classes*. Non-static nested classes are called *inner classes*.

```
class OuterClass {
  ...
  static class StaticNestedClass {
    ...
  }
  class InnerClass {
    ...
  }
}
```

Why Use Nested Classes?

There are several compelling reasons for using nested classes, among them:

- It is a way of logically grouping classes that are only used in one place.
- It increases encapsulation.
- Nested classes can lead to more readable and maintainable code.

Logical grouping of classes If a class is useful to only one other class, then it is logical to embed it in that class and keep the two together. Nesting such "helper classes" makes their package more streamlined.

Increased encapsulation Consider two top-level classes, A and B, where B needs access to members of A that would otherwise be declared `private`. By hiding class B within class A, A's members can be declared `private` and B can access them. In addition, B itself can be hidden from the outside world.

More readable, maintainable code Nesting small classes within top-level classes places the code closer to where it is used.

Static Nested Classes

As with class methods and variables, a static nested class is associated with its outer class. And like static class methods, a static nested class cannot refer directly to instance variables or methods defined in its enclosing class—it can use them only through an object reference.

Note: A static nested class interacts with the instance members of its outer class (and other classes) just like any other top-level class. In effect, a static nested class is behaviorally a top-level class that has been nested in another top-level class for packaging convenience.

Static nested classes are accessed using the enclosing class name:

```
OuterClass.StaticNestedClass
```

For example, to create an object for the static nested class, use this syntax:

```
OuterClass.StaticNestedClass nestedObject =
                     new OuterClass.StaticNestedClass();
```

Inner Classes

As with instance methods and variables, an inner class is associated with an instance of its enclosing class and has direct access to that object's methods and fields. Also, because an inner class is associated with an instance, it cannot define any static members itself.

Objects that are instances of an inner class exist *within* an instance of the outer class. Consider the following classes:

```
class OuterClass {
   ...
   class InnerClass {
      ...
   }
}
```

An instance of InnerClass can exist only within an instance of OuterClass and has direct access to the methods and fields of its enclosing instance. Figure 4.6 illustrates this idea.

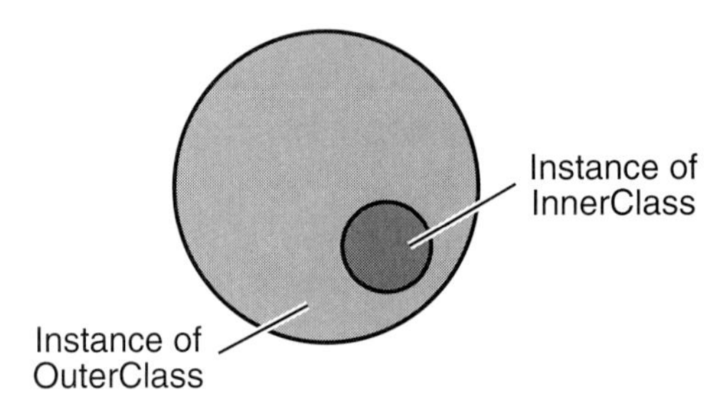

Figure 4.6 An InnerClass exists within an instance of OuterClass.

To instantiate an inner class, you must first instantiate the outer class. Then, create the inner object within the outer object with this syntax:

```
OuterClass.InnerClass innerObject =
                            outerObject.new InnerClass();
```

Additionally, there are two special kinds of inner classes: local classes and anonymous classes (also called anonymous inner classes). Both of these will be discussed briefly in the next section.

Inner Class Example

To see an inner class in use, consider a simple *stack* of integers. Stacks, which are a common data structure in programming, are well named—they are like a "stack" of dishes. When you add a dish to the stack, you put it on top; when you remove one, you remove it from the top. The acronym for this is LIFO (last in, first out). Dishes on the bottom of the stack may stay there quite a long time while the upper dishes come and go.

The `StackOfInts` class below is implemented as an array. When you add an integer (called "pushing"), it goes into the first available empty element. When you remove an integer (called "popping"), you remove the last integer in the array.

The `StackOfInts` class below (an application) consists of:

- The `StackOfInts` outer class, which includes methods to push an integer onto the stack, pop an integer off the stack, and test to see if the stack is empty.
- The `StepThrough` inner class, which is similar to a standard Java *iterator*. Iterators are used to step through a data structure and typically have methods to test for the last element, retrieve the current element, and move to the next element.
- A `main` method that instantiates a `StackOfInts` array (`stackOne`) and fills it with integers (0, 2, 4, etc.), then instantiates a `StepThrough` object (`iterator`) and uses it to print out the contents of `stackOne`.

```
public class StackOfInts {

  private int[] stack;
  private int next = 0;  // index of last item in stack + 1

  public StackOfInts(int size) {
    // create an array large enough to hold the stack
    stack = new int[size];
  }

  public void push(int on) {
    if (next < stack.length)
      stack[next++] = on;
  }
  public boolean isEmpty() {
    return (next == 0);
  }

  public int pop(){
    if (!isEmpty())
      return stack[--next]; // top item on stack
    else
      return 0;
  }

  public int getStackSize() {
    return next;
  }
```

```
  private class StepThrough {
    // start stepping through at i=0
    private int i = 0;

    // increment index
    public void increment() {
      if ( i < stack.length)
        i++;
    }

    // retrieve current element
    public int current() {
      return stack[i];
    }

    // last element on stack?
    public boolean isLast(){
      if (i == getStackSize() - 1)
        return true;
      else
        return false;
    }
  }

  public StepThrough stepThrough() {
    return new StepThrough();
  }

  public static void main(String[] args) {

    // instantiate outer class as "stackOne"
    StackOfInts stackOne = new StackOfInts(15);

    // populate stackOne
    for (int j = 0 ; j < 15 ; j++) {
      stackOne.push(2*j);
    }

    // instantiate inner class as "iterator"
    StepThrough iterator = stackOne.stepThrough();

    // print out stackOne[i], one per line
    while(!iterator.isLast()) {
      System.out.print(iterator.current() + " ");
      iterator.increment();
    }
    System.out.println();
  }
}
```

The output is:

```
0 2 4 6 8 10 12 14 16 18 20 22 24 26
```

Note that the `StepThrough` class refers directly to the `stack` instance variable of `StackOfInts`.

Inner classes are used primarily to implement helper classes like the one shown in this example. If you plan on handling user-interface events, you'll need to know about using inner classes because the event-handling mechanism makes extensive use of them.

Local and Anonymous Inner Classes

There are two additional types of inner classes. You can declare an inner class within the body of a method. Such a class is known as a *local inner class*. You can also declare an inner class within the body of a method without naming it. These classes are known as *anonymous inner classes*. You will encounter such classes in advanced Java programming.

Modifiers

You can use the same modifiers for inner classes that you use for other members of the outer class. For example, you can use the access specifiers—`private`, `public`, and `protected`—to restrict access to inner classes, just as you do to other class members.

Summary of Nested Classes

A class defined within another class is called a nested class. Like other members of a class, a nested class can be declared static or not. A nonstatic nested class is called an inner class. An instance of an inner class can exist only within an instance of its enclosing class and has access to its enclosing class's members even if they are declared private.

Table 4.3 shows the types of nested classes.

Table 4.3 Types of Nested Classes

Type	Scope	Inner
static nested class	member	no
inner [non-static] class	member	yes
local class	local	yes
anonymous class	only the point where it is defined	yes

Questions and Exercises: Nested Classes

Questions

1. The program `Problem.java`[6] doesn't compile. What do you need to do to make it compile? Why?
2. Use the Java API documentation for the `Box` class (in the `javax.swing` package) to help you answer the following questions:
   a. What static nested class does `Box` define?
   b. What inner class does `Box` define?
   c. What is the superclass of `Box`'s inner class?
   d. Which of `Box`'s nested classes can you use from any class?
   e. How do you create an instance of `Box`'s `Filler` class?

Exercises

Get the file `Class1.java`.[7] Compile and run `Class1`. What is the output?

Answers

You can find answers to these Questions and Exercises at:

```
tutorial/java/javaOO/QandE/nested-answers.html
```

Enum Types

An *enum type* is a type whose *fields* consist of a fixed set of constants. Common examples include compass directions (values of `NORTH`, `SOUTH`, `EAST`, and `WEST`) and the days of the week.

Because they are constants, the names of an enum type's fields are in uppercase letters.

In the Java programming language, you define an enum type by using the `enum` keyword. For example, you would specify a days-of-the-week enum type as:

6. `tutorial/java/javaOO/QandE/Problem.java`
7. `tutorial/java/javaOO/QandE/Class1.java`

```
public enum Day {
  SUNDAY, MONDAY, TUESDAY, WEDNESDAY,
  THURSDAY, FRIDAY, SATURDAY
}
```

You should use enum types any time you need to represent a fixed set of constants. That includes natural enum types such as the planets in our solar system and data sets where you know all possible values at compile time—for example, the choices on a menu, command line flags, and so on.

Here is some code that shows you how to use the `Day` enum defined above:

```
public class EnumTest {
  Day day;

  public EnumTest(Day day) {
    this.day = day;
  }

  public void tellItLikeItIs() {
    switch (day) {
      case MONDAY: System.out.println("Mondays are bad.");
                   break;

      case FRIDAY: System.out.println("Fridays are better.");
                   break;

      case SATURDAY:
      case SUNDAY: System.out.println("Weekends are best.");
                   break;

      default: System.out.println("Midweek days are so-so.");
               break;
    }
  }

  public static void main(String[] args) {
    EnumTest firstDay = new EnumTest(Day.MONDAY);
    firstDay.tellItLikeItIs();
    EnumTest thirdDay = new EnumTest(Day.WEDNESDAY);
    thirdDay.tellItLikeItIs();
    EnumTest fifthDay = new EnumTest(Day.FRIDAY);
    fifthDay.tellItLikeItIs();
    EnumTest sixthDay = new EnumTest(Day.SATURDAY);
    sixthDay.tellItLikeItIs();
    EnumTest seventhDay = new EnumTest(Day.SUNDAY);
    seventhDay.tellItLikeItIs();
  }
}
```

The output is:

```
Mondays are bad.
Midweek days are so-so.
Fridays are better.
Weekends are best.
Weekends are best.
```

Java programming language enum types are much more powerful than their counterparts in other languages. The `enum` declaration defines a *class* (called an *enum type*). The enum class body can include methods and other fields. The compiler automatically adds some special methods when it creates an enum. For example, they have a static `values` method that returns an array containing all of the values of the enum in the order they are declared. This method is commonly used in combination with the for-each construct to iterate over the values of an enum type. For example, this code in the `Planet` class example below iterates over all the planets in the solar system:

```
for (Planet p : Planet.values()) {
  System.out.printf("Your weight on %s is %f%n",
                    p, p.surfaceWeight(mass));
}
```

Note: *All* enums implicitly extend `java.lang.Enum`. Since Java does not support multiple inheritance, an enum cannot extend anything else.

In the following example, `Planet` is an enum type that represents the planets in the solar system. They are defined with constant mass and radius properties.

Each enum constant is declared with values for the mass and radius parameters. These values are passed to the constructor when the constant is created. Java requires that the constants be defined first, prior to any fields or methods. Also, when there are fields and methods, the list of enum constants must end with a semicolon.

Note: The constructor for an enum type must be package-private or private access. It automatically creates the constants that are defined at the beginning of the enum body. You cannot invoke an enum constructor yourself.

In addition to its properties and constructor, `Planet` has methods that allow you to retrieve the surface gravity and weight of an object on each planet. Here is a sample program that takes your weight on earth (in any unit) and calculates and prints your weight on all of the planets (in the same unit):

```
public enum Planet {
  MERCURY (3.303e+23, 2.4397e6),
  VENUS   (4.869e+24, 6.0518e6),
  EARTH   (5.976e+24, 6.37814e6),
  MARS    (6.421e+23, 3.3972e6),
  JUPITER (1.9e+27,   7.1492e7),
  SATURN  (5.688e+26, 6.0268e7),
  URANUS  (8.686e+25, 2.5559e7),
  NEPTUNE (1.024e+26, 2.4746e7),
  PLUTO   (1.27e+22,  1.137e6);

  private final double mass;   // in kilograms
  private final double radius; // in meters
  Planet(double mass, double radius) {
    this.mass = mass;
    this.radius = radius;
  }
  private double mass()   { return mass; }
  private double radius() { return radius; }

  // universal gravitational constant  (m3 kg-1 s-2)
  public static final double G = 6.67300E-11;

  double surfaceGravity() {
    return G * mass / (radius * radius);
  }
  double surfaceWeight(double otherMass) {
    return otherMass * surfaceGravity();
  }
  public static void main(String[] args) {
    double earthWeight = Double.parseDouble(args[0]);
    double mass = earthWeight/EARTH.surfaceGravity();
    for (Planet p : Planet.values())
      System.out.printf("Your weight on %s is %f%n",
                        p, p.surfaceWeight(mass));
  }
}
```

If you run `Planet.class` from the command line with an argument of 175, you get this output:

```
$ java Planet 175
Your weight on MERCURY is 66.107583
Your weight on VENUS is 158.374842
Your weight on EARTH is 175.000000
Your weight on MARS is 66.279007
Your weight on JUPITER is 442.847567
Your weight on SATURN is 186.552719
Your weight on URANUS is 158.397260
Your weight on NEPTUNE is 199.207413
Your weight on PLUTO is 11.703031
```

Questions and Exercises: Enum Types

Exercises

1. Rewrite the class `Card` that you wrote for the exercise in the Questions and Exercises: Classes section (page 119) so that it represents the rank and suit of a card with enum types.
2. Rewrite the `Deck` class.

Answers

You can find answers to these Questions and Exercises at:

```
tutorial/java/javaOO/QandE/enum-answers.html
```

Annotations

Annotations provide data about a program that is not part of the program itself. They have no direct effect on the operation of the code they annotate.

Annotations have a number of uses, among them:

Information for the compiler Annotations can be used by the compiler to detect errors or suppress warnings.

Compiler-time and deployment-time processing Software tools can process annotation information to generate code, XML files, and so forth.

Runtime processing Some annotations are available to be examined at runtime.

Annotations can be applied to a program's declarations of classes, fields, methods, and other program elements.

The annotation appears first, often (by convention) on its own line, and may include *elements* with named or unnamed values:

```
@Author(
  name = "Benjamin Franklin",
  date = "3/27/2003"
)
class MyClass() { }
```

or

```
@SuppressWarnings(value = "unchecked")
void myMethod() { }
```

If there is just one element named "value," then the name may be omitted, as in:

```
@SuppressWarnings("unchecked")
void myMethod() { }
```

Also, if an annotation has no elements, the parentheses may be omitted, as in:

```
@Override
void mySuperMethod() { }
```

Documentation

Many annotations replace what would otherwise have been comments in code.

Suppose that a software group has traditionally begun the body of every class with comments providing important information:

```
public class Generation3List extends Generation2List {

  // Author: John Doe
  // Date: 3/17/2002
  // Current revision: 6
  // Last modified: 4/12/2004
  // By: Jane Doe
  // Reviewers: Alice, Bill, Cindy

  // class code goes here

}
```

To add this same metadata with an annotation, you must first define the *annotation type*. The syntax for doing this is:

```
@interface ClassPreamble {
  String author();
  String date();
  int currentRevision() default 1;
  String lastModified() default "N/A";
  String lastModifiedBy() default "N/A";
  String[] reviewers();  // Note use of array
}
```

The annotation type definition looks somewhat like an interface definition where the keyword `interface` is preceded by the @ character (@ = "AT" as in Annotation Type). Annotation types are, in fact, a form of *interface*, which will be covered in a later chapter. For the moment, you do not need to understand interfaces.

The body of the annotation definition above contains *annotation type element* declarations, which look a lot like methods. Note that they may define optional default values.

Once the annotation type has been defined, you can use annotations of that type, with the values filled in, like this:

```
@ClassPreamble (
   author = "John Doe",
   date = "3/17/2002",
   currentRevision = 6,
   lastModified = "4/12/2004",
   lastModifiedBy = "Jane Doe"
   reviewers = {"Alice", "Bob", "Cindy"} // Note array notation
)
public class Generation3List extends Generation2List {

   // class code goes here

}
```

Note: To make the information in `@ClassPreamble` appear in Javadoc-generated documentation, you must annotate the `@ClassPreamble` definition itself with the `@Documented` annotation:

```
import java.lang.annotation.*; // import this to use @Documented

@Documented
@interface ClassPreamble {

   // Annotation element definitions

}
```

Annotations Used by the Compiler

There are three annotation types that are predefined by the language specification itself: `@Deprecated`, `@Override`, and `@SuppressWarnings`.

The `@Deprecated`[8] annotation indicates that the marked element is *deprecated* and should no longer be used. The compiler generates a warning whenever a program uses a method, class, or field with the `@Deprecated` annotation. When an element is deprecated, it should also be documented using the Javadoc `@deprecated` tag, as shown in the following example. The use of the "@" symbol in both Javadoc comments and in

8. `docs/api/java/lang/Deprecated.html`

annotations is not coincidental—they are related conceptually. Also, note that the Javadoc tag starts with a lowercase "d" and the annotation starts with an uppercase "D".

```
    // Javadoc comment follows
    /**
     * @deprecated
     * explanation of why it was deprecated
     */
    @Deprecated
    static void deprecatedMethod() { }
}
```

The `@Override`[9] annotation informs the compiler that the element is meant to override an element declared in a superclass. (Overriding methods will be discussed in Chapter 5.)

```
// mark method as a superclass method
// that has been overridden
@Override
int overriddenMethod() { }
```

While it's not required to use this annotation when overriding a method, it helps to prevent errors. If a method marked with `@Override` fails to correctly override a method in one of its superclasses, the compiler generates an error.

The `@SuppressWarnings`[10] annotation tells the compiler to suppress specific warnings that it would otherwise generate. In the example below, a deprecated method is used and the compiler would normally generate a warning. In this case, however, the annotation causes the warning to be suppressed.

```
// use a deprecated method and tell
// compiler not to generate a warning
@SuppressWarnings("deprecation")
void useDeprecatedMethod() {
  objectOne.deprecatedMethod(); // deprecation warning
                                // suppressed
}
```

Every compiler warning belongs to a category. The Java Language Specification lists two categories: "deprecation" and "unchecked." The "unchecked" warning can occur

9. `docs/api/java/lang/Override.html`

10. `docs/api/java/lang/SuppressWarnings.html`

when interfacing with legacy code written before the advent of generics (discussed in Chapter 6). To suppress more than one category of warnings, use the following syntax:

```
@SuppressWarnings({"unchecked", "deprecation"})
```

Annotation Processing

The more advanced uses of annotations include writing an *annotation processor* that can read a Java program and take actions based on its annotations. It might, for example, generate auxiliary source code, relieving the programmer of having to create boilerplate code that always follows predictable patterns. To facilitate this task, release 5.0 of the JDK includes an annotation processing tool, called `apt`. In release 6 of the JDK, the functionality of `apt` is a standard part of the Java compiler.

To make annotation information available at runtime, the annotation type itself must be annotated with `@Retention(RetentionPolicy.RUNTIME)`, as follows:

```
import java.lang.annotation.*;

@Retention(RetentionPolicy.RUNTIME)
@interface AnnotationForRuntime {

  // Elements that give information
  // for runtime processing

}
```

Questions and Exercises: Annotations

Questions

1. What is wrong with the following interface?

```
public interface House {
  @Deprecated
  void open();
  void openFrontDoor();
  void openBackDoor();
}
```

2. Compile this program:

```
interface Closable {
  void close();
}

class File implements Closable {
  @Override
  public void close() {
    // ... close this file...
  }
}
```

What happens? Can you explain why?

3. Consider this implementation of the `House` interface, shown in Question 1:

```
public class MyHouse implements House {
  public void open() {}
  public void openFrontDoor() {}
  public void openBackDoor() {}
}
```

If you compile this program, the compiler complains that `open` has been deprecated (in the interface). What can you do to get rid of that warning?

Answers

You can find answers to these Questions and Exercises at:

```
tutorial/java/javaOO/QandE/annotations-answers.html
```

5

Interfaces and Inheritance

YOU saw an example of implementing an interface in the previous chapter. You can read more about interfaces here—what they are for, why you might want to write one, and how to write one.

This chapter also describes the way in which you can derive one class from another, that is, how a *subclass* can inherit fields and methods from a *superclass*. You will learn that all classes are derived from the `Object` class, and how to modify the methods that a subclass inherits from superclasses. This chapter also covers interface-like *abstract* classes.

Interfaces

There are a number of situations in software engineering when it is important for disparate groups of programmers to agree to a "contract" that spells out how their software interacts. Each group should be able to write their code without any knowledge of how the other group's code is written. Generally speaking, *interfaces* are such contracts.

For example, imagine a futuristic society where computer-controlled robotic cars transport passengers through city streets without a human operator. Automobile manufacturers write software (Java, of course) that operates the automobile—stop, start, accelerate, turn left, and so forth. Another industrial group, electronic guidance instrument manufacturers, make computer systems that receive GPS (Global Positioning Satellite) position data and wireless transmission of traffic conditions and use that information to drive the car.

The auto manufacturers must publish an industry-standard interface that spells out in detail what methods can be invoked to make the car move (any car, from any manufacturer). The guidance manufacturers can then write software that invokes the methods described in the interface to command the car. Neither industrial group needs to know *how* the other group's software is implemented. In fact, each group considers its software highly proprietary and reserves the right to modify it at any time, as long as it continues to adhere to the published interface.

Interfaces in Java

In the Java programming language, an *interface* is a reference type, similar to a class, that can contain *only* constants, method signatures, and nested types. There are no method bodies. Interfaces cannot be instantiated—they can only be *implemented* by classes or *extended* by other interfaces. (Extension is discussed later in this chapter.)

Defining an interface is similar to creating a new class:

```
public interface OperateCar {

  // constant declarations, if any

  // method signatures
  int turn(Direction direction, // An enum with values
                                // RIGHT, LEFT
  double radius, double startSpeed, double endSpeed);
  int changeLanes(Direction direction,
                  double startSpeed, double endSpeed);
  int signalTurn(Direction direction, boolean signalOn);
  int getRadarFront(double distanceToCar, double speedOfCar);
  int getRadarRear(double distanceToCar, double speedOfCar);
    ...
  // more method signatures
}
```

Note that the method signatures have no braces and are terminated with a semicolon.

To use an interface, you write a class that *implements* the interface. When an instantiable class implements an interface, it provides a method body for each of the methods declared in the interface. For example,

```
public class OperateBMW760i implements OperateCar {

  // the OperateCar method signatures, with implementation --
  // for example:
  int signalTurn(Direction direction, boolean signalOn) {
    //code to turn BMW's LEFT turn indicator lights on
    //code to turn BMW's LEFT turn indicator lights off
    //code to turn BMW's RIGHT turn indicator lights on
    //code to turn BMW's RIGHT turn indicator lights off
  }

  // other members, as needed -- for example, helper classes
  // not visible to clients of the interface

}
```

In the robotic car example above, it is the automobile manufacturers who will implement the interface. Chevrolet's implementation will be substantially different from that of Toyota, of course, but both manufacturers will adhere to the same interface. The guidance manufacturers, who are the clients of the interface, will build systems that use GPS data on a car's location, digital street maps, and traffic data to drive the car. In so doing, the guidance systems will invoke the interface methods: turn, change lanes, brake, accelerate, and so forth.

Interfaces as APIs

The robotic car example shows an interface being used as an industry standard *Application Programming Interface (API)*. APIs are also common in commercial software products. Typically, a company sells a software package that contains complex methods that another company wants to use in its own software product. An example would be a package of digital image processing methods that are sold to companies making end-user graphics programs. The image processing company writes its classes to implement an interface, which it makes public to its customers. The graphics company then invokes the image processing methods using the signatures and return types defined in the interface. While the image processing company's API is made public (to its customers), its implementation of the API is kept as a closely guarded secret—in fact, it may revise the implementation at a later date as long as it continues to implement the original interface that its customers have relied on.

Interfaces and Multiple Inheritance

Interfaces have another very important role in the Java programming language. Interfaces are not part of the class hierarchy, although they work in combination with classes. The Java programming language does not permit multiple inheritance (inheritance is discussed later in this chapter), but interfaces provide an alternative.

In Java, a class can inherit from only one class but it can implement more than one interface. Therefore, objects can have multiple types: the type of their own class and the types of all the interfaces that they implement. This means that if a variable is declared to be the type of an interface, its value can reference any object that is instantiated from any class that implements the interface. This is discussed later in the Using an Interface as a Type section (page 145).

Defining an Interface

An interface declaration consists of modifiers, the keyword `interface`, the interface name, a comma-separated list of parent interfaces (if any), and the interface body. For example:

```
public interface GroupedInterface extends Interface1,
                                    Interface2, Interface3 {

  // constant declarations
  double E = 2.718282;  // base of natural logarithms

  // method signatures
  void doSomething (int i, double x);
  int doSomethingElse(String s);

}
```

The `public` access specifier indicates that the interface can be used by any class in any package. If you do not specify that the interface is public, your interface will be accessible only to classes defined in the same package as the interface.

An interface can extend other interfaces, just as a class can extend or subclass another class. However, whereas a class can extend only one other class, an interface can extend any number of interfaces. The interface declaration includes a comma-separated list of all the interfaces that it extends.

The Interface Body

The interface body contains method declarations for all the methods included in the interface. A method declaration within an interface is followed by a semicolon, but no braces, because an interface does not provide implementations for the methods declared within it. All methods declared in an interface are implicitly `public`, so the public modifier can be omitted.

An interface can contain constant declarations in addition to method declarations. All constant values defined in an interface are implicitly `public`, `static`, and `final`. Once again, these modifiers can be omitted.

Implementing an Interface

To declare a class that implements an interface, you include an `implements` clause in the class declaration. Your class can implement more than one interface, so the `implements` keyword is followed by a comma-separated list of the interfaces implemented by the class.

By convention, the `implements` clause follows the `extends` clause, if there is one.

A Sample Interface, Relatable

Consider an interface that defines how to compare the size of objects.

```
public interface Relatable {

  // this (object calling isLargerThan) and
  // other must be instances of the same class
  // returns 1, 0, -1 if this is greater
  // than, equal to, or less than other
  public int isLargerThan(Relatable other);

}
```

If you want to be able to compare the size of similar objects, no matter what they are, the class that instantiates them should implement `Relatable`.

Any class can implement `Relatable` if there is some way to compare the relative "size" of objects instantiated from the class. For strings, it could be number of characters; for books, it could be number of pages; for students, it could be weight; and so forth. For planar geometric objects, area would be a good choice (see the `RectanglePlus` class that follows), while volume would work for three-dimensional geometric objects. All such classes can implement the `isLargerThan()` method.

If you know that a class implements `Relatable`, then you know that you can compare the size of the objects instantiated from that class.

Implementing the Relatable Interface

Here is the `Rectangle` class that was presented in the Creating Objects section (page 99), rewritten to implement `Relatable`:

```
public class RectanglePlus implements Relatable {
  public int width = 0;
  public int height = 0;
  public Point origin;

  // four constructors
  public RectanglePlus() {
    origin = new Point(0, 0);
  }
  public RectanglePlus(Point p) {
    origin = p;
  }
  public RectanglePlus(int w, int h) {
    origin = new Point(0, 0);
    width = w;
    height = h;
  }
  public RectanglePlus(Point p, int w, int h) {
    origin = p;
    width = w;
    height = h;
  }

  // a method for moving the rectangle
  public void move(int x, int y) {
    origin.x = x;
    origin.y = y;
  }

  // a method for computing the area of the rectangle
  public int getArea() {
    return width * height;
  }

  // a method to implement Relatable
  public int isLargerThan(Relatable other) {
    RectanglePlus otherRect = (RectanglePlus)other;
    if (this.getArea() < otherRect.getArea())
      return -1;
    else if (this.getArea() > otherRect.getArea())
      return 1;
    else
      return 0;
  }
}
```

Because `RectanglePlus` implements `Relatable`, the size of any two `RectanglePlus` objects can be compared.

Using an Interface as a Type

When you define a new interface, you are defining a new reference data type. You can use interface names anywhere you can use any other data type name. If you define a reference variable whose type is an interface, any object you assign to it *must* be an instance of a class that implements the interface.

As an example, here is a method for finding the largest object in a pair of objects, for *any* objects that are instantiated from a class that implements `Relatable`:

```
public Object findLargest(Object object1, Object object2) {
  Relatable obj1 = (Relatable)object1;
  Relatable obj2 = (Relatable)object2;
  if ( (obj1).isLargerThan(obj2)) > 0)
    return object1;
  else
    return object2;
}
```

By casting `object1` to a `Relatable` type, it can invoke the `isLargerThan` method.

If you make a point of implementing `Relatable` in a wide variety of classes, the objects instantiated from *any* of those classes can be compared with the `findLargest()` method—provided that both objects are of the same class. Similarly, they can all be compared with the following methods:

```
public Object findSmallest(Object object1, Object object2) {
  Relatable obj1 = (Relatable)object1;
  Relatable obj2 = (Relatable)object2;
  if ( (obj1).isLargerThan(obj2)) < 0)
    return object1;
  else
    return object2;
}

public boolean isEqual(Object object1, Object object2) {
  Relatable obj1 = (Relatable)object1;
  Relatable obj2 = (Relatable)object2;
  if ( (obj1).isLargerThan(obj2)) == 0)
    return true;
  else
    return false;
}
```

These methods work for any "relatable" objects, no matter what their class inheritance is. When they implement `Relatable`, they can be of both their own class (or superclass) type and a `Relatable` type. This gives them some of the advantages of multiple inheritance, where they can have behavior from both a superclass and an interface.

Rewriting Interfaces

Consider an interface that you have developed called `DoIt`:

```
public interface DoIt {
  void doSomething(int i, double x);
  int doSomethingElse(String s);
}
```

Suppose that, at a later time, you want to add a third method to `DoIt`, so that the interface now becomes:

```
public interface DoIt {
  void doSomething(int i, double x);
  int doSomethingElse(String s);
  boolean didItWork(int i, double x, String s);
}
```

If you make this change, all classes that implement the old `DoIt` interface will break because they don't implement the interface anymore. Programmers relying on this interface will protest loudly.

Try to anticipate all uses for your interface and to specify it completely from the beginning. Given that this is often impossible, you may need to create more interfaces later. For example, you could create a `DoItPlus` interface that extends `DoIt`:

```
public interface DoItPlus extends DoIt {

  boolean didItWork(int i, double x, String s);

}
```

Now users of your code can choose to continue to use the old interface or to upgrade to the new interface.

Summary of Interfaces

An interface defines a protocol of communication between two objects.

An interface declaration contains signatures, but no implementations, for a set of methods, and might also contain constant definitions.

A class that implements an interface must implement all the methods declared in the interface.

An interface name can be used anywhere a type can be used.

Questions and Exercises: Interfaces

Questions

1. What methods would a class that implements the `java.lang.CharSequence`[1] interface have to implement?
2. What is wrong with the following interface?

```
public interface SomethingIsWrong {
  void aMethod(int aValue){
    System.out.println("Hi Mom");
  }
}
```

3. Fix the interface in Question 2.
4. Is the following interface valid?

```
public interface Marker {
}
```

Exercises

1. Write a class that implements the `CharSequence` interface found in the `java.lang` package. Select one of the sentences from this book to use as the data. Write a small `main` method to test your class; make sure to call all four methods.
2. Suppose you have written a time server that periodically notifies its clients of the current date and time. Write an interface the server could use to enforce a particular protocol on its clients.

Answers

You can find answers to these Questions and Exercises at:

```
tutorial/java/IandI/QandE/interfaces-answers.html
```

Inheritance

In the preceding chapters, you have seen *inheritance* mentioned several times. In the Java language, classes can be *derived* from other classes, thereby *inheriting* fields and methods from those classes.

1. `docs/api/java/lang/CharSequence.html`

Definitions: A class that is derived from another class is called a *subclass* (also a *derived class*, *extended class*, or *child class*). The class from which the subclass is derived is called a *superclass* (also a *base class* or a *parent class*).

Excepting `Object`, which has no superclass, every class has one and only one direct superclass (single inheritance). In the absence of any other explicit superclass, every class is implicitly a subclass of `Object`.

Classes can be derived from classes that are derived from classes that are derived from classes, and so on, and ultimately derived from the topmost class, `Object`. Such a class is said to be *descended* from all the classes in the inheritance chain stretching back to `Object`.

The idea of inheritance is simple but powerful: When you want to create a new class and there is already a class that includes some of the code that you want, you can derive your new class from the existing class. In doing this, you can reuse the fields and methods of the existing class without having to write (and debug!) them yourself.

A subclass inherits all of the *public* and *protected* members (fields, methods, and nested classes) of its superclass no matter what package the subclass is in. If the subclass is in the same package as its parent, it also inherits the *package-private* members of the superclass. Constructors are not members, so they are not inherited by subclasses, but the constructor of the superclass can be invoked from the subclass.

The Java Platform Class Hierarchy

The `Object` class,[2] defined in the `java.lang` package, defines and implements behavior common to all classes—including the ones that you write. In the Java platform, many classes derive directly from `Object`, other classes derive from some of those classes, and so on, forming a hierarchy of classes (Figure 5.1).

At the top of the hierarchy, `Object` is the most general of all classes. Classes near the bottom of the hierarchy provide more specialized behavior.

An Example of Inheritance

Here is the sample code for a possible implementation of a `Bicycle` class that was presented in Chapter 4:

2. `docs/api/java/lang/Object.html`

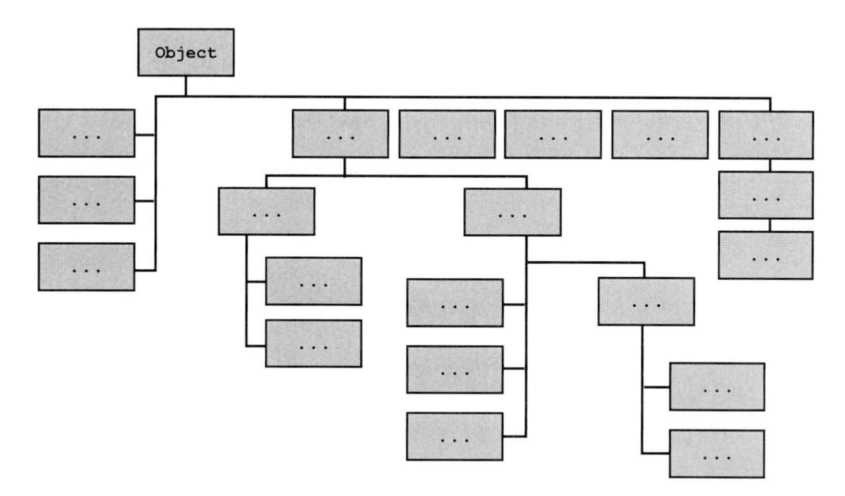

Figure 5.1 All classes in the Java platform are descendants of `Object`.

```
public class Bicycle {

  // the Bicycle class has three fields
  public int cadence;
  public int gear;
  public int speed;

  // the Bicycle class has one constructor
  public Bicycle(int startCadence,
                 int startSpeed, int startGear) {
    gear = startGear;
    cadence = startCadence;
    speed = startSpeed;
  }

  // the Bicycle class has four methods
  public void setCadence(int newValue) {
    cadence = newValue;
  }

  public void setGear(int newValue) {
    gear = newValue;
  }

  public void applyBrake(int decrement) {
    speed -= decrement;
  }

  public void speedUp(int increment) {
    speed += increment;
  }
}
```

A class declaration for a MountainBike class that is a subclass of Bicycle might look like this:

```
public class MountainBike extends Bicycle {

  // the MountainBike subclass adds one field
  public int seatHeight;

  // the MountainBike subclass has one constructor

  public MountainBike(int startHeight, int startCadence,
                                int startSpeed, int startGear) {
    super(startCadence, startSpeed, startGear);
    seatHeight = startHeight;
  }

  // the MountainBike subclass adds one method
  public void setHeight(int newValue) {
    seatHeight = newValue;
  }
}
```

MountainBike inherits all the fields and methods of Bicycle and adds the field seatHeight and a method to set it. Except for the constructor, it is as if you had written a new MountainBike class entirely from scratch, with four fields and five methods. However, you didn't have to do all the work. This would be especially valuable if the methods in the Bicycle class were complex and had taken substantial time to debug.

What You Can Do in a Subclass

A subclass inherits all of the *public* and *protected* members of its parent, no matter what package the subclass is in. If the subclass is in the same package as its parent, it also inherits the *package-private* members of the parent. You can use the inherited members as is, replace them, hide them, or supplement them with new members:

- The inherited fields can be used directly, just like any other fields.
- You can declare a field in the subclass with the same name as the one in the superclass, thus *hiding* it (not recommended).
- You can declare new fields in the subclass that are not in the superclass.
- The inherited methods can be used directly as they are.
- You can write a new *instance* method in the subclass that has the same signature as the one in the superclass, thus *overriding* it.
- You can write a new *static* method in the subclass that has the same signature as the one in the superclass, thus *hiding* it.

- You can declare new methods in the subclass that are not in the superclass.
- You can write a subclass constructor that invokes the constructor of the superclass, either implicitly or by using the keyword `super`.

The following sections in this chapter will expand on these topics.

Private Members in a Superclass

A subclass does not inherit the `private` members of its parent class. However, if the superclass has public or protected methods for accessing its private fields, these can also be used by the subclass.

A nested class has access to all the private members of its enclosing class—both fields and methods. Therefore, a public or protected nested class inherited by a subclass has indirect access to all of the private members of the superclass.

Casting Objects

We have seen that an object is of the data type of the class from which it was instantiated. For example, if we write:

```
public MountainBike myBike = new MountainBike();
```

then `myBike` is of type `MountainBike`.

`MountainBike` is descended from `Bicycle` and `Object`. Therefore, a `MountainBike` is a `Bicycle` and is also an `Object`, and it can be used wherever `Bicycle` or `Object` objects are called for.

The reverse is not necessarily true: a `Bicycle` *may be* a `MountainBike`, but it isn't necessarily. Similarly, an `Object` *may be* a `Bicycle` or a `MountainBike`, but it isn't necessarily.

Casting shows the use of an object of one type in place of another type, among the objects permitted by inheritance and implementations. For example, if we write:

```
Object obj = new MountainBike();
```

then `obj` is both an `Object` and a `Mountainbike` (until such time as `obj` is assigned another object that is *not* a `Mountainbike`). This is called *implicit casting*.

If, on the other hand, we write:

```
MountainBike myBike = obj;
```

we would get a compile-time error because `obj` is not known to the compiler to be a `MountainBike`. However, we can *tell* the compiler that we promise to assign a `MountainBike` to `obj` by *explicit casting*:

```
MountainBike myBike = (MountainBike)obj;
```

This cast inserts a runtime check that `obj` is assigned a `MountainBike` so that the compiler can safely assume that `obj` is a `MountainBike`. If `obj` is not a `Mountainbike` at runtime, an exception will be thrown.

Note: You can make a logical test as to the type of a particular object using the `instanceof` operator. This can save you from a runtime error owing to an improper cast. For example:

```
if (obj instanceof MountainBike) {
   MountainBike myBike = (MountainBike)obj;
}
```

Here the `instanceof` operator verifies that `obj` refers to a `MountainBike` so that we can make the cast with knowledge that there will be no runtime exception thrown.

Overriding and Hiding Methods

Instance Methods

An instance method in a subclass with the same signature (name, plus the number and the type of its parameters) and return type as an instance method in the superclass *overrides* the superclass's method.

The ability of a subclass to override a method allows a class to inherit from a superclass whose behavior is "close enough" and then to modify behavior as needed. The overriding method has the same name, number and type of parameters, and return type as the method it overrides. An overriding method can also return a subtype of the type returned by the overridden method. This is called a *covariant return type*.

When overriding a method, you might want to use the `@Override` annotation that instructs the compiler that you intend to override a method in the superclass. If, for some reason, the compiler detects that the method does not exist in one of the superclasses, it will generate an error. For more information on `@Override`, see the Annotations section (page 132).

Class Methods

If a subclass defines a class method with the same signature as a class method in the superclass, the method in the subclass *hides* the one in the superclass.

The distinction between hiding and overriding has important implications. The version of the overridden method that gets invoked is the one in the subclass. The version of the hidden method that gets invoked depends on whether it is invoked from the superclass or the subclass. Let's look at an example that contains two classes. The first is `Animal`, which contains one instance method and one class method:

```
public class Animal {
  public static void testClassMethod() {
    System.out.println("The class method in Animal.");
  }
  public void testInstanceMethod() {
    System.out.println("The instance method in Animal.");
  }
}
```

The second class, a subclass of `Animal`, is called `Cat`:

```
public class Cat extends Animal {
  public static void testClassMethod() {
    System.out.println("The class method in Cat.");
  }
  public void testInstanceMethod() {
    System.out.println("The instance method in Cat.");
  }

  public static void main(String[] args) {
    Cat myCat = new Cat();
    Animal myAnimal = myCat;
    Animal.testClassMethod();
    myAnimal.testInstanceMethod();
  }
}
```

The `Cat` class overrides the instance method in `Animal` and hides the class method in `Animal`. The `main` method in this class creates an instance of `Cat` and calls `testClassMethod()` on the class and `testInstanceMethod()` on the instance.

The output from this program is as follows:

```
The class method in Animal.
The instance method in Cat.
```

As promised, the version of the hidden method that gets invoked is the one in the superclass, and the version of the overridden method that gets invoked is the one in the subclass.

Modifiers

The access specifier for an overriding method can allow more, but not less, access than the overridden method. For example, a protected instance method in the superclass can be made public, but not private, in the subclass.

You will get a compile-time error if you attempt to change an instance method in the superclass to a class method in the subclass, and vice versa.

Summary

Table 5.1 summarizes what happens when you define a method with the same signature as a method in a superclass.

Table 5.1 Defining a Method with the Same Signature as a Superclass's Method

	Superclass Instance Method	**Superclass Static Method**
Subclass Instance Method	Overrides	Generates a compile-time error
Subclass Static Method	Generates a compile-time error	Hides

Note: In a subclass, you can overload the methods inherited from the superclass. Such overloaded methods neither hide nor override the superclass methods—they are new methods, unique to the subclass.

Hiding Fields

Within a class, a field that has the same name as a field in the superclass hides the superclass's field, even if their types are different. Within the subclass, the field in the superclass cannot be referenced by its simple name. Instead, the field must be accessed through `super`, which is covered in the next section. Generally speaking, we don't recommend hiding fields as it makes code difficult to read.

Using the Keyword super

Accessing Superclass Members

If your method overrides one of its superclass's methods, you can invoke the overridden method through the use of the keyword `super`. You can also use `super` to refer to a hidden field (although hiding fields is discouraged). Consider this class, `Superclass`:

```
public class Superclass {

  public void printMethod() {
    System.out.println("Printed in Superclass.");
  }
}
```

Here is a subclass, called `Subclass`, that overrides `printMethod()`:

```
public class Subclass extends Superclass {

  public void printMethod() {
    //overrides printMethod in Superclass
    super.printMethod();
    System.out.println("Printed in Subclass");
  }
  public static void main(String[] args) {

  Subclass s = new Subclass();
  s.printMethod();
  }

}
```

Within `Subclass`, the simple name `printMethod()` refers to the one declared in `Subclass`, which overrides the one in `Superclass`. So, to refer to `printMethod()` inherited from `Superclass`, `Subclass` must use a qualified name, using `super` as shown. Compiling and executing `Subclass` prints the following:

```
Printed in Superclass.
Printed in Subclass
```

Subclass Constructors

The following example illustrates how to use the `super` keyword to invoke a superclass's constructor. Recall from the `Bicycle` example (in the Inheritance section, page 147) that `MountainBike` is a subclass of `Bicycle`. Here is the `MountainBike` (subclass) constructor that calls the superclass constructor and then adds initialization code of its own:

```
public MountainBike(int startHeight, int startCadence,
                    int startSpeed, int startGear) {
  super(startCadence, startSpeed, startGear);
  seatHeight = startHeight;
}
```

Invocation of a superclass constructor must be the first line in the subclass constructor.

The syntax for calling a superclass constructor is:

```
super();
```

or

```
super(parameter list);
```

With `super()`, the superclass no-argument constructor is called. With `super(parameter list)`, the superclass constructor with a matching parameter list is called.

Note: If a constructor does not explicitly invoke a superclass constructor, the Java compiler automatically inserts a call to the no-argument constructor of the superclass. If the superclass does not have a no-argument constructor, you will get a compile-time error. `Object` *does* have such a constructor, so if `Object` is the only superclass, there is no problem.

If a subclass constructor invokes a constructor of its superclass, either explicitly or implicitly, you might think that there will be a whole chain of constructors called, all the way back to the constructor of `Object`. In fact, this is the case. It is called *constructor chaining*, and you need to be aware of it when there is a long line of class descent.

Object as a Superclass

The `Object` class, in the `java.lang` package, sits at the top of the class hierarchy tree. Every class is a descendant, direct or indirect, of the `Object` class. Every class you use or write inherits the instance methods of `Object`. You need not use any of these methods, but, if you choose to do so, you may need to override them with code that is specific to your class. The methods inherited from `Object` that are discussed in this section are:

`protected Object clone() throws CloneNotSupportedException` Creates and returns a copy of this object.

`public boolean equals(Object obj)` Indicates whether some other object is "equal to" this one.

`protected void finalize() throws Throwable` Called by the garbage collector on an object when garbage collection determines that there are no more references to the object.

`public final Class getClass()` Returns the runtime class of an object.

`public int hashCode()` Returns a hash code value for the object.

`public String toString()` Returns a string representation of the object.

The `notify`, `notifyAll`, and `wait` methods of `Object` all play a part in synchronizing the activities of independently running threads in a program, which is discussed in Chapter 12 and won't be covered here. There are five of these methods:

- `public final void notify()`
- `public final void notifyAll()`
- `public final void wait()`
- `public final void wait(long timeout)`
- `public final void wait(long timeout, int nanos)`

Note: There are some subtle aspects to a number of these methods, especially the `clone` method. You can get information on the correct usage of these methods in the book *Effective Java*[3] by Josh Bloch.

The clone() Method

If a class, or one of its superclasses, implements the `Cloneable` interface, you can use the `clone()` method to create a copy from an existing object. To create a clone, you write:

```
aCloneableObject.clone();
```

`Object`'s implementation of this method checks to see whether the object on which `clone()` was invoked implements the `Cloneable` interface. If the object does not, the method throws a `CloneNotSupportedException` exception. Exception handling will be covered in Chapter 9. For the moment, you need to know that `clone()` must be declared as:

```
protected Object clone() throws CloneNotSupportedException
```

or

```
public Object clone() throws CloneNotSupportedException
```

if you are going to write a `clone()` method to override the one in `Object`.

If the object on which `clone()` was invoked does implement the `Cloneable` interface, `Object`'s implementation of the `clone()` method creates an object of the same class as the original object and initializes the new object's member variables to have the same values as the original object's corresponding member variables.

---

3. `docs/books/effective`

The simplest way to make your class cloneable is to add `implements Cloneable` to your class's declaration. Then your objects can invoke the `clone()` method.

For some classes, the default behavior of `Object`'s `clone()` method works just fine. If, however, an object contains a reference to an external object, say `ObjExternal`, you may need to override `clone()` to get correct behavior. Otherwise, a change in `ObjExternal` made by one object will be visible in its clone also. This means that the original object and its clone are not independent—to decouple them, you must override `clone()` so that it clones the object *and* `ObjExternal`. Then the original object references `ObjExternal` and the clone references a clone of `ObjExternal`, so that the object and its clone are truly independent.

The equals() Method

The `equals()` method compares two objects for equality and returns `true` if they are equal. The `equals()` method provided in the `Object` class uses the identity operator (==) to determine whether two objects are equal. For primitive data types, this gives the correct result. For objects, however, it does not. The `equals()` method provided by `Object` tests whether the object *references* are equal—that is, if the objects compared are the exact same object.

To test whether two objects are equal in the sense of *equivalency* (containing the same information), you must override the `equals()` method. Here is an example of a `Book` class that overrides `equals()`:

```
public class Book {
  ...
  public boolean equals(Object obj) {
    if (obj instanceof Book)
      return ISBN.equals((Book)obj.getISBN());
    else
      return false;
  }
}
```

Consider this code that tests two instances of the `Book` class for equality:

```
Book firstBook  = new Book("0201914670");
  // Swing Tutorial, 2nd edition
Book secondBook = new Book("0201914670");
if (firstBook.equals(secondBook)) {
  System.out.println("objects are equal");
}
else {
  System.out.println("objects are not equal");
}
```

This program displays `objects are equal` even though `firstBook` and `secondBook` reference two distinct objects. They are considered equal because the objects compared contain the same ISBN.

You should always override the `equals()` method if the identity operator is not appropriate for your class.

Note: If you override `equals()`, you must override `hashCode()` as well.

The finalize() Method

The `Object` class provides a callback method, `finalize()`, that *may be* invoked on an object when it becomes garbage. `Object`'s implementation of `finalize()` does nothing—you can override `finalize()` to do cleanup, such as freeing resources.

The `finalize()` method *may be* called automatically by the system, but when it is called, or even if it is called, is uncertain. Therefore, you should not rely on this method to do your cleanup for you. For example, if you don't close file descriptors in your code after performing I/O and you expect `finalize()` to close them for you, you may run out of file descriptors.

The getClass() Method

You cannot override `getClass`.

The `getClass()` method returns a `Class` object, which has methods you can use to get information about the class, such as its name (`getSimpleName()`), its superclass (`getSuperclass()`), and the interfaces it implements (`getInterfaces()`). For example, the following method gets and displays the class name of an object:

```
void printClassName(Object obj) {
  System.out.println("The object's class is "
                      obj.getClass().getSimpleName());
}
```

The `Class` class,[4] in the `java.lang` package, has a large number of methods (more than fifty). For example, you can test to see if the class is an annotation (`isAnnotation()`), an interface (`isInterface()`), or an enumeration (`isEnum()`). You can see what the object's fields are (`getFields()`) or what its methods are (`getMethods()`), and so on.

---

4. `docs/api/java/lang/Class.html`

The hashCode() Method

The value returned by `hashCode()` is the object's hash code, which is the object's memory address in hexadecimal.

By definition, if two objects are equal, their hash code *must also* be equal. If you override the `equals()` method, you change the way two objects are equated and `Object`'s implementation of `hashCode()` is no longer valid. Therefore, if you override the `equals()` method, you must also override the `hashCode()` method as well.

The toString() Method

You should always consider overriding the `toString()` method in your classes.

The `Object`'s `toString()` method returns a `String` representation of the object, which is very useful for debugging. The `String` representation for an object depends entirely on the object, which is why you need to override `toString()` in your classes.

You can use `toString()` along with `System.out.println()` to display a text representation of an object, such as an instance of `Book`:

```
System.out.println(firstBook.toString());
```

which would, for a properly overridden `toString()` method, print something useful, like this:

```
ISBN: 0201914670; The JFC Swing Tutorial; A Guide to
                                Constructing GUIs, 2nd Edition
```

Writing Final Classes and Methods

You can declare some or all of a class's methods *final*. You use the `final` keyword in a method declaration to indicate that the method cannot be overridden by subclasses. The `Object` class does this—a number of its methods are `final`.

You might wish to make a method final if it has an implementation that should not be changed and it is critical to the consistent state of the object. For example, you might want to make the `getFirstPlayer` method in this `ChessAlgorithm` class final:

```
class ChessAlgorithm {
  enum ChessPlayer { WHITE, BLACK }
  ...
  final ChessPlayer getFirstPlayer() {
    return ChessPlayer.WHITE;
  }
  ...
}
```

Methods called from constructors should generally be declared final. If a constructor calls a non-final method, a subclass may redefine that method with surprising or undesirable results.

Note that you can also declare an entire class final—this prevents the class from being subclassed. This is particularly useful, for example, when creating an immutable class like the `String` class.

Abstract Methods and Classes

An *abstract class* is a class that is declared `abstract`—it may or may not include abstract methods. Abstract classes cannot be instantiated, but they can be subclassed.

An *abstract method* is a method that is declared without an implementation (without braces, and followed by a semicolon), like this:

```
abstract void moveTo(double deltaX, double deltaY);
```

If a class includes abstract methods, the class itself *must* be declared `abstract`, as in:

```
public abstract class GraphicObject {
  // declare fields
  // declare non-abstract methods
  abstract void draw();
}
```

When an abstract class is subclassed, the subclass usually provides implementations for all of the abstract methods in its parent class. However, if it does not, the subclass must also be declared `abstract`.

Note: All of the methods in an *interface*, see the Interfaces section (page 139), are *implicitly* abstract, so the `abstract` modifier is not used with interface methods (it could be—it's just not necessary).

Abstract Classes versus Interfaces

Unlike interfaces, abstract classes can contain fields that are not `static` and `final`, and they can contain implemented methods. Such abstract classes are similar to interfaces, except that they provide a partial implementation, leaving it to subclasses to complete the implementation. If an abstract class contains *only* abstract method declarations, it should be declared as an interface instead.

Multiple interfaces can be implemented by classes anywhere in the class hierarchy, whether or not they are related to one another in any way. Think of `Comparable` or `Cloneable`, for example.

By comparison, abstract classes are most commonly subclassed to share pieces of implementation. A single abstract class is subclassed by similar classes that have a lot in common (the implemented parts of the abstract class), but also have some differences (the abstract methods).

An Abstract Class Example

In an object-oriented drawing application, you can draw circles, rectangles, lines, Bezier curves, and many other graphic objects. These objects all have certain states (for example: position, orientation, line color, fill color) and behaviors (for example: moveTo, rotate, resize, draw) in common. Some of these states and behaviors are the same for all graphic objects—for example: position, fill color, and moveTo. Others require different implementations—for example, resize or draw. All `GraphicObjects` must know how to draw or resize themselves; they just differ in how they do it.

This is a perfect situation for an abstract superclass. You can take advantage of the similarities and declare all the graphic objects to inherit from the same abstract parent object—for example, `GraphicObject`, as shown in Figure 5.2.

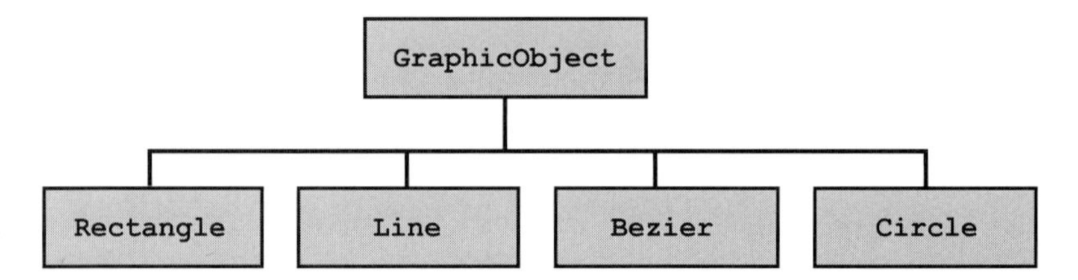

Figure 5.2 Classes `Rectangle`, `Line`, `Bezier`, and `Circle` inherit from `GraphicObject`.

First, you declare an abstract class, `GraphicObject`, to provide member variables and methods that are wholly shared by all subclasses, such as the current position and the `moveTo` method. `GraphicObject` also declares abstract methods for methods, such as `draw` or `resize`, that need to be implemented by all subclasses but must be implemented in different ways. The `GraphicObject` class can look something like this:

```
abstract class GraphicObject {
  int x, y;
  ...
  void moveTo(int newX, int newY) {
    ...
  }
  abstract void draw();
  abstract void resize();
}
```

Each non-abstract subclass of `GraphicObject`, such as `Circle` and `Rectangle`, must provide implementations for the `draw` and `resize` methods:

```
class Circle extends GraphicObject {
  void draw() {
    ...
  }
  void resize() {
    ...
  }
}
class Rectangle extends GraphicObject {
  void draw() {
    ...
  }
  void resize() {
    ...
  }
}
```

When an Abstract Class Implements an Interface

In the Interfaces section (page 139), it was noted that a class that implements an interface must implement *all* of the interface's methods. It is possible, however, to define a class that does not implement all of the interface methods, provided that the class is declared to be `abstract`. For example,

```
abstract class X implements Y {
  // implements all but one method of Y
}

class XX extends X {
  // implements the remaining method in Y
}
```

In this case, class `X` must be `abstract` because it does not fully implement `Y`, but class `XX` does, in fact, implement `Y`.

Class Members

An abstract class may have `static` fields and `static` methods. You can use these static members with a class reference—for example, `AbstractClass.StaticMethod()`—as you would with any other class.

Summary of Inheritance

Except for the `Object` class, a class has exactly one direct superclass. A class inherits fields and methods from all its superclasses, whether direct or indirect. A subclass can override methods that it inherits, or it can hide fields or methods that it inherits. (Note that hiding fields is generally bad programming practice.)

Table 5.1 in the Overriding and Hiding Methods section (page 152) shows the effect of declaring a method with the same signature as a method in the superclass.

The `Object` class is the top of the class hierarchy. All classes are descendants from this class and inherit methods from it. Useful methods inherited from `Object` include `toString()`, `equals()`, `clone()`, and `getClass()`.

You can prevent a class from being subclassed by using the `final` keyword in the class's declaration. Similarly, you can prevent a method from being overridden by subclasses by declaring it as a final method.

An abstract class can only be subclassed; it cannot be instantiated. An abstract class can contain abstract methods—methods that are declared but not implemented. Subclasses then provide the implementations for the abstract methods.

Questions and Exercises: Inheritance

Questions

1. Consider the following two classes:

```
public class ClassA {
  public void methodOne(int i) {
  }
  public void methodTwo(int i) {
  }
  public static void methodThree(int i) {
  }
  public static void methodFour(int i) {
  }
}

public class ClassB extends ClassA {
  public static void methodOne(int i) {
  }
  public void methodTwo(int i) {
  }
  public void methodThree(int i) {
  }
  public static void methodFour(int i) {
  }
}
```

a. Which method overrides a method in the superclass?

b. Which method hides a method in the superclass?

c. What do the other methods do?

2. Consider the `Card`,[5] `Deck`,[6] and `DisplayDeck`[7] classes you wrote in Questions and Exercises: Classes (page 119). What `Object` methods should each of these classes override?

Exercises

Write the implementations for the methods that you answered in question 2.

Answers

You can find answers to these Questions and Exercises at:

`tutorial/java/IandI/QandE/inherit-answers.html`

---

5. `tutorial/java/IandI/QandE/Card.java`
6. `tutorial/java/IandI/QandE/Deck.java`
7. `tutorial/java/IandI/QandE/DisplayDeck.java`

6

Generics

Introduction

In any nontrivial software project, bugs are simply a fact of life. Careful planning, programming, and testing can help reduce their pervasiveness, but somehow, somewhere, they'll always find a way to creep into your code. This becomes especially apparent as new features are introduced and your code base grows in size and complexity.

Fortunately, some bugs are easier to detect than others. Compile-time bugs, for example, tell you immediately that something is wrong; you can use the compiler's error messages to figure out what the problem is and fix it, right then and there. Runtime bugs, however, can be much more problematic; they don't always surface immediately, and when they do, it may be at a point in time that's far removed from the actual cause of the problem.

Generics add stability to your code by making more of your bugs detectable at compile time. Some programmers choose to learn generics by studying the Java Collections Framework; after all, generics *are* heavily used by those classes. However, since we haven't yet covered collections, this chapter will focus primarily on simple "collections-like" examples that we'll design from scratch. This hands-on approach will teach you the necessary syntax and terminology while demonstrating the various kinds of problems that generics were designed to solve.

A Simple Box Class

Let's begin by designing a nongeneric `Box` class that operates on objects of any type. It need only provide two methods: `add`, which adds an object to the box, and `get`, which retrieves it:

```
public class Box {

  private Object object;

  public void add(Object object) {
    this.object = object;
  }

  public Object get() {
    return object;
  }
}
```

Since its methods accept or return `Object`, you're free to pass in whatever you want, provided that it's not one of the primitive types. However, should you need to restrict the contained type to something specific (like `Integer`), your only option would be to specify the requirement in documentation (or in this case, a comment), which of course the compiler knows nothing about:[1]

```
public class BoxDemo1 {

  public static void main(String[] args) {

    // ONLY place Integer objects into this box!
    Box integerBox = new Box();

    integerBox.add(new Integer(10));
    Integer someInteger = (Integer)integerBox.get();
    System.out.println(someInteger);
  }
}
```

The `BoxDemo1` program creates an `Integer` object, passes it to `add`, then assigns that same object to `someInteger` by the return value of `get`. It then prints the object's value (10) to standard output. We know that the cast from `Object` to `Integer` is correct because we've honored the "contract" specified in the comment. But remember, the compiler knows nothing about this—it just trusts that our cast is correct. Furthermore,

1. `tutorial/java/generics/examples/BoxDemo1.java`

it will do nothing to prevent a careless programmer from passing in an object of the wrong type, such as `String`:[2]

```
public class BoxDemo2 {

  public static void main(String[] args) {

    // ONLY place Integer objects into this box!
    Box integerBox = new Box();

    // Imagine this is one part of a large application
    // modified by one programmer.
    integerBox.add("10"); // note how the type is now String

    // ... and this is another, perhaps written
    // by a different programmer
    Integer someInteger = (Integer)integerBox.get();
    System.out.println(someInteger);
  }
}
```

Here we've stored the number 10 as a `String`, which could be the case when, say, a GUI collects input from the user. However, the existing cast from `Object` to `Integer` has mistakenly been overlooked. This is clearly a bug, but because the code still compiles, you wouldn't know anything is wrong until runtime, when the application crashes with a `ClassCastException`:

```
Exception in thread "main"
  java.lang.ClassCastException:
    java.lang.String cannot be cast to java.lang.Integer
    at BoxDemo2.main(BoxDemo2.java:6)
```

If the `Box` class had been designed with generics in mind, this mistake would have been caught by the compiler, instead of crashing the application at runtime.

Generic Types

Let's update our `Box` class to use generics. We'll first create a *generic type declaration* by changing the code "`public class Box`" to "`public class Box<T>`"; this introduces one *type variable*, named `T`, that can be used anywhere inside the class. This same technique can be applied to interfaces as well. There's nothing particularly complex about this concept. In fact, it's quite similar to what you already know about variables

2. `tutorial/java/generics/examples/BoxDemo2.java`

in general. Just think of `T` as a special kind of variable, whose "value" will be whatever type you pass in; this can be any class type, any interface type, or even another type variable. It just can't be any of the primitive data types. In this context, we also say that `T` is a *formal type parameter* of the `Box` class:

```
/**
 * Generic version of the Box class.
 */
public class Box<T> {

  private T t; // T stands for "Type"

  public void add(T t) {
    this.t = t;
  }

  public T get() {
    return t;
  }
}
```

As you can see, we've replaced all occurrences of `Object` with `T`. To reference this generic class from within your own code, you must perform a *generic type invocation*, which replaces `T` with some concrete value, such as `Integer`:

```
Box<Integer> integerBox;
```

You can think of a generic type invocation as being similar to an ordinary method invocation, but instead of passing an argument to a method, you're passing a *type argument*—`Integer` in this case—to the `Box` class itself. Like any other variable declaration, this code does not actually create a new `Box` object. It simply declares that `integerBox` will hold a reference to a "`Box` of `Integer`," which is how `Box<Integer>` is read.

An invocation of a generic type is generally known as a *parameterized type*. To instantiate this class, use the `new` keyword, as usual, but place `<Integer>` between the class name and the parenthesis:

```
integerBox = new Box<Integer>();
```

Or, you can put the entire statement on one line, such as:

```
Box<Integer> integerBox = new Box<Integer>();
```

Once integerBox is initialized, you're free to invoke its get method without providing a cast, as in BoxDemo3:[3]

```
public class BoxDemo3 {

  public static void main(String[] args) {
    Box<Integer> integerBox = new Box<Integer>();
    integerBox.add(new Integer(10));
    Integer someInteger = integerBox.get(); // no cast!
    System.out.println(someInteger);
  }
}
```

Furthermore, if you try adding an incompatible type to the box, such as String, compilation will fail, alerting you to what previously would have been a runtime bug:

```
BoxDemo3.java:5: add(java.lang.Integer)
                    in Box<java.lang.Integer>
cannot be applied to (java.lang.String)
    integerBox.add("10");
              ^
1 error
```

It's important to understand that type variables are not actually types themselves. In the above examples, you won't find T.java or T.class anywhere on the filesystem. Furthermore, T is not a part of the Box class name. In fact during compilation, all generic information will be removed entirely, leaving only Box.class on the filesystem. We'll discuss this later in the Type Erasure section (page 178).

Also note that a generic type may have multiple type parameters, but each parameter must be unique within its declaring class or interface. A declaration of Box<T,T>, for example, would generate an error on the second occurrence of T, but Box<T,U>, however, would be allowed.

Type Parameter Conventions

By convention, type parameters are single, uppercase letters. This stands in sharp contrast to the variable naming conventions (see the Naming section, page 44) that you already know about, and with good reason: Without this convention, it would be difficult to tell the difference between a type variable and an ordinary class or interface name.

The most commonly used type parameter names are:

E Element (used extensively by the Java Collections Framework)

3. tutorial/java/generics/examples/BoxDemo3.java

K Key

N Number

T Typc

V Value

S, U, V, etc. 2nd, 3rd, 4th types

You'll see these names used throughout the Java SE API and the rest of this tutorial.

Generic Methods and Constructors

Type parameters can also be declared within method and constructor signatures to create *generic methods* and *generic constructors*. This is similar to declaring a generic type, but the type parameter's scope is limited to the method or constructor in which it's declared:

```
/**
 * This version introduces a generic method.
 */
public class Box<T> {

  private T t;

  public void add(T t) {
    this.t = t;
  }

  public T get() {
    return t;
  }

  public <U> void inspect(U u){
    System.out.println("T: " + t.getClass().getName());
    System.out.println("U: " + u.getClass().getName());
  }

  public static void main(String[] args) {
    Box<Integer> integerBox = new Box<Integer>();
    integerBox.add(new Integer(10));
    integerBox.inspect("some text");
  }
}
```

Here we've added one generic method, named `inspect`, that defines one type parameter, named `U`. This method accepts an object and prints its type to standard output. For comparison, it also prints out the type of `T`. For convenience, this class now also has a `main` method so that it can be run as an application.

The output from this program is:

```
T: java.lang.Integer
U: java.lang.String
```

By passing in different types, the output will change accordingly.

A more realistic use of generic methods might be something like the following, which defines a static method that stuffs references to a single item into multiple boxes:

```
public static <U> void fillBoxes(U u, List<Box<U>> boxes) {
  for (Box<U> box : boxes) {
    box.add(u);
  }
}
```

To use this method, your code would look something like the following:

```
Crayon red = ...;
List<Box<Crayon>> crayonBoxes = ...;
```

The complete syntax for invoking this method is:

```
Box.<Crayon>fillBoxes(red, crayonBoxes);
```

Here we've explicitly provided the type to be used as `U`, but more often than not, this can be left out and the compiler will infer the type that's needed:

```
Box.fillBoxes(red, crayonBoxes); // compiler infers that
                                 // U is Crayon
```

This feature, known as *type inference*, allows you to invoke a generic method as you would an ordinary method, without specifying a type between angle brackets.

Bounded Type Parameters

There may be times when you'll want to restrict the kinds of types that are allowed to be passed to a type parameter. For example, a method that operates on numbers might only want to accept instances of `Number` or its subclasses. This is what *bounded type parameters* are for.

To declare a bounded type parameter, list the type parameter's name, followed by the `extends` keyword, followed by its *upper bound*, which in this example is `Number`. Note that, in this context, extends is used in a general sense to mean either "extends" (as in classes) or "implements" (as in interfaces):

```
/**
 * This version introduces a bounded type parameter.
 */
public class Box<T> {

  private T t;

  public void add(T t) {
    this.t = t;
  }

  public T get() {
    return t;
  }

  public <U extends Number> void inspect(U u){
    System.out.println("T: " + t.getClass().getName());
    System.out.println("U: " + u.getClass().getName());
  }

  public static void main(String[] args) {
    Box<Integer> integerBox = new Box<Integer>();
    integerBox.add(new Integer(10));
    integerBox.inspect("some text"); // error: this is
                                     // still String!
  }
}
```

By modifying our generic method to include this bounded type parameter, compilation will now fail, since our invocation of inspect still includes a String:

```
Box.java:21: <U>inspect(U) in Box<java.lang.Integer> cannot
  be applied to (java.lang.String)
                        integerBox.inspect("10");
                                  ^
1 error
```

To specify additional interfaces that must be implemented, use the & character, as in:

```
<U extends Number & MyInterface>
```

Subtyping

As you already know, it's possible to assign an object of one type to an object of another type provided that the types are compatible. For example, you can assign an Integer to an Object, since Object is one of Integer's supertypes:

```
Object someObject = new Object();
Integer someInteger = new Integer(10);
someObject = someInteger; // OK
```

In object-oriented terminology, this is called an "is a" relationship. Since an Integer *is a* kind of Object, the assignment is allowed. But Integer is also a kind of Number, so the following code is valid as well:

```
public void someMethod(Number n){
  // method body omitted
}

someMethod(new Integer(10));  // OK
someMethod(new Double(10.1)); // OK
```

The same is also true with generics. You can perform a generic type invocation, passing Number as its type argument, and any subsequent invocation of add will be allowed if the argument is compatible with Number:

```
Box<Number> box = new Box<Number>();
box.add(new Integer(10));  // OK
box.add(new Double(10.1)); // OK
```

Now consider the following method:

```
public void boxTest(Box<Number> n){
  // method body omitted
}
```

What type of argument does it accept? By looking at its signature, we can see that it accepts a single argument whose type is Box<Number>. But what exactly does that mean? Are you allowed to pass in Box<Integer> or Box<Double>, as you might expect? Surprisingly, the answer is "no," because Box<Integer> and Box<Double> are not subtypes of Box<Number>.

Understanding why becomes much easier if you think of tangible objects—things you can actually picture—such as a cage:

```
// A cage is a collection of things, with bars to keep them in.
interface Cage<E> extends Collection<E>;
```

Note: The `Collection` interface is the root interface of the *collection hierarchy*; it represents a group of objects. Since a cage would be used for holding a collection of objects (the animals), it makes sense to include it in this example.

A lion is a kind of animal, so `Lion` would be a subtype of `Animal`:

```
interface Lion extends Animal {}
Lion king = ...;
```

Where we need some animal, we're free to provide a lion:

```
Animal a = king;
```

A lion can of course be put into a lion cage:

```
Cage<Lion> lionCage = ...;
lionCage.add(king);
```

and a butterfly into a butterfly cage:

```
interface Butterfly extends Animal {}
Butterfly monarch = ...;
Cage<Butterfly> butterflyCage = ...;
butterflyCage.add(monarch);
```

But what about an "animal cage"? English is ambiguous, so to be precise let's assume we're talking about an "all-animal cage":

```
Cage<Animal> animalCage = ...;
```

This is a cage designed to hold all kinds of animals, mixed together. It must have bars strong enough to hold in the lions and spaced closely enough to hold in the butterflies. Such a cage might not even be feasible to build, but if it is, then:

```
animalCage.add(king);
animalCage.add(monarch);
```

Since a lion is a kind of animal (`Lion` is a subtype of `Animal`), the question then becomes, "Is a lion cage a kind of animal cage? Is `Cage<Lion>` a subtype of `Cage<Animal>`?" By the above definition of animal cage, the answer must be "no." This is surprising! But it makes perfect sense when you think about it: A lion cage cannot be assumed to keep in butterflies, and a butterfly cage cannot be assumed to hold in lions. Therefore, neither cage can be considered an "all-animal" cage:

```
animalCage = lionCage;        // compile-time error
animalCage = butterflyCage;   // compile-time error
```

Without generics, the animals could be placed into the wrong kinds of cages, where it would be possible for them to escape.

Wildcards

Earlier we mentioned that English is ambiguous. The phrase "animal cage" can reasonably mean "all-animal cage," but it also suggests an entirely different concept: a cage designed not for *any* kind of animal, but rather for *some* kind of animal whose type is unknown. In generics, an unknown type is represented by the *wildcard* character "?".

To specify a cage capable of holding *some* kind of animal:

```
Cage<? extends Animal> someCage = ...;
```

Read "`? extends Animal`" as "an unknown type that is a subtype of `Animal`, possibly `Animal` itself," which boils down to "some kind of animal." This is an example of a *bounded wildcard*, where `Animal` forms the *upper bound* of the expected type. If you're asked for a cage that simply holds *some* kind of animal, you're free to provide a lion cage *or* a butterfly cage.

Note: It's also possible to specify a *lower bound* by using the `super` keyword instead of `extends`. The code `<? super Animal>`, therefore, would be read as "an unknown type that is a supertype of `Animal`, possibly `Animal` itself." You can also specify an unknown type with an *unbounded wilcard*, which simply looks like `<?>`. An unbounded wildcard is essentially the same as saying `<? extends Object>`.

While `Cage<Lion>` and `Cage<Butterfly>` are not subtypes of `Cage<Animal>`, they are in fact subtypes of `Cage<? extends Animal>`:

```
someCage = lionCage;        // OK
someCage = butterflyCage;   // OK
```

So now the question becomes, "Can you add butterflies and lions directly to `someCage`?" As you can probably guess, the answer to this question is "no":

```
someCage.add(king);       // compiler-time error
someCage.add(monarch);    // compiler-time error
```

If `someCage` is a butterfly cage, it would hold butterflies just fine, but the lions would be able to break free. If it's a lion cage, then all would be well with the lions, but the butterflies would fly away. So if you can't put anything at all into `someCage`, is it useless? No, because you can still read its contents:

```
void feedAnimals(Cage<? extends Animal> someCage) {
  for (Animal a : someCage)
    a.feedMe();
}
```

Therefore, you could house your animals in their individual cages, as shown earlier, and invoke this method first for the lions and then for the butterflies:

```
feedAnimals(lionCage);
feedAnimals(butterflyCage);
```

Or, you could choose to combine your animals in the all-animal cage instead:

```
feedAnimals(animalCage);
```

Type Erasure

When a generic type is instantiated, the compiler translates those types by a technique called *type erasure*—a process where the compiler removes all information related to type parameters and type arguments within a class or method. Type erasure enables Java applications that use generics to maintain binary compatibility with Java libraries and applications that were created before generics.

For instance, `Box<String>` is translated to type `Box`, which is called the *raw type*—a raw type is a generic class or interface name without any type arguments. This means that you can't find out what type of `Object` a generic class is using at runtime. The following operations are not possible:

```
public class MyClass<E> {
  public static void myMethod(Object item) {
    if (item instanceof E) {  // Compiler error
      ...
    }
    E item2 = new E();         // Compiler error
    E[] iArray = new E[10];    // Compiler error
    E obj = (E)new Object();   // Unchecked cast warning
  }
}
```

The operations shown in bold are meaningless at runtime because the compiler removes all information about the actual type argument (represented by the type parameter `E`) at compile time.

Type erasure exists so that new code may continue to interface with legacy code. Using a raw type for any other reason is considered bad programming practice and should be avoided whenever possible.

When mixing legacy code with generic code, you may encounter warning messages similar to the following:

```
Note: WarningDemo.java uses unchecked or unsafe operations.
Note: Recompile with -Xlint:unchecked for details.
```

This can happen when using an older API that operates on raw types, as shown in the following `WarningDemo`[4] program:

```
public class WarningDemo {
  public static void main(String[] args){
    Box<Integer> bi;
    bi = createBox();
  }

  /**
   * Pretend that this method is part of an old library,
   * written before generics. It returns
   * Box instead of Box<T>.
   */
  static Box createBox(){
    return new Box();
  }
}
```

Recompiling with `-Xlint:unchecked` reveals the following additional information:

```
WarningDemo.java:4: warning: [unchecked] unchecked conversion
found   : Box
required: Box<java.lang.Integer>
        bi = createBox();
                      ^
1 warning
```

Summary of Generics

This chapter described the following problem: We have a `Box` class, written to be generally useful so that it deals with `Objects`. We need an instance that takes only `Integers`. The comments say that only `Integers` go in, so the programmer knows this

4. `tutorial/java/generics/examples/WarningDemo.java`

(or should know it), but the compiler doesn't know it. This means that the compiler can't catch someone erroneously adding a `String`. When we read the value and cast it to an `Integer` we'll get an exception, but that's not ideal since the exception may be far removed from the bug in both space and time:

1. Debugging may be difficult, as the point in the code where the exception is thrown may be far removed from the point in the code where the error is located.
2. It's always better to catch bugs when compiling than when running.

Specifically, you learned that generic type declarations can include one or more type parameters; you supply one type argument for each type parameter when you use the generic type. You also learned that type parameters can be used to define generic methods and constructors. Bounded type parameters limit the kinds of types that can be passed into a type parameter; they can specify an upper bound only. Wildcards represent unknown types, and they can specify an upper or lower bound. During compilation, type erasure removes all generic information from a generic class or interface, leaving behind only its raw type. It is possible for generic code and legacy code to interact, but in many cases the compiler will emit a warning telling you to recompile with special flags for more details.

For additional information, see "Generics" by Gilad Bracha.[5]

Questions and Exercises: Generics

Questions

Consider the following classes:

```
public class AnimalHouse<E> {
  private E animal;
  public void setAnimal(E x) {
    animal = x;
  }
  public E getAnimal() {
    return animal;
  }
}

public class Animal{
}
```

5. tutorial/extra/generics/index.html

```
public class Cat extends Animal {
}

public class Dog extends Animal {
}
```

For the following code snippets, identify whether the code:

1. fails to compile,
2. compiles with a warning,
3. generates an error at runtime, or
4. none of the above (compiles and runs without problem).

a. `AnimalHouse<Animal> house = new AnimalHouse<Cat>();`

b. `AnimalHouse<Dog> house = new AnimalHouse<Animal>();`

c.
```
AnimalHouse<?> house = new AnimalHouse<Cat>();
house.setAnimal(new Cat());
```

d.
```
AnimalHouse house = new AnimalHouse();
house.setAnimal(new Dog());
```

Exercises

Design a class that acts as a library for the following kinds of media: book, video, and newspaper. Provide one version of the class that uses generics and one that does not. Feel free to use any additional APIs for storing and retrieving the media.

Answers

You can find answers to these Questions and Exercises at:

```
tutorial/java/generics/QandE/generics-answers.html
```

7

Packages

THIS chapter explains how to bundle classes and interfaces into packages, how to use classes that are in packages, and how to arrange your file system so that the compiler can find your source files.

Creating and Using Packages

To make types easier to find and use, to avoid naming conflicts, and to control access, programmers bundle groups of related types into packages.

Definition: A *package* is a grouping of related types providing access protection and name space management. Note that *types* refers to classes, interfaces, enumerations, and annotation types. Enumerations and annotation types are special kinds of classes and interfaces, respectively, so *types* are often referred to in this chapter simply as *classes and interfaces*.

The types that are part of the Java platform are members of various packages that bundle classes by function: Fundamental classes are in `java.lang`, classes for reading and writing (input and output) are in `java.io`, and so on. You can put your types in packages too.

Suppose you write a group of classes that represent graphic objects, such as circles, rectangles, lines, and points. You also write an interface, `Draggable`, that classes implement if they can be dragged with the mouse:

```
//in the Draggable.java file
public interface Draggable {
   ...
}

//in the Graphic.java file
public abstract class Graphic {
   ...
}

//in the Circle.java file
public class Circle extends Graphic implements Draggable {
   ...
}

//in the Rectangle.java file
public class Rectangle extends Graphic implements Draggable {
   ...
}

//in the Point.java file
public class Point extends Graphic implements Draggable {
   ...
}

//in the Line.java file
public class Line extends Graphic implements Draggable {
   ...
}
```

You should bundle these classes and the interface in a package for several reasons, including the following:

- You and other programmers can easily determine that these types are related.
- You and other programmers know where to find types that can provide graphics-related functions.
- The names of your types won't conflict with the type names in other packages because the package creates a new namespace.
- You can allow types within the package to have unrestricted access to one another yet still restrict access for types outside the package.

Creating a Package

To create a package, you choose a name for the package (naming conventions are discussed in the next section) and put a `package` statement with that name at the top of *every source file* that contains the types (classes, interfaces, enumerations, and annotation types) that you want to include in the package.

The `package` statement (for example, `package graphics;`) must be the first line in the source file. There can be only one `package` statement in each source file, and it applies to all types in the file.

Note: If you put multiple types in a single source file, only one can be `public`, and it must have the same name as the source file. For example, you can define `public class Circle` in the file `Circle.java`, define `public interface Draggable` in the file `Draggable.java`, define `public enum Day` in the file `Day.java`, and so forth.

You can include non-public types in the same file as a public type (this is strongly discouraged, unless the non-public types are small and closely related to the public type), but only the public type will be accessible from outside of the package. All the top-level, non-public types will be *package-private*.

If you put the graphics interface and classes listed in the preceding section in a package called `graphics`, you would need six source files, like this:

```
// in the Draggable.java file
package graphics;
public interface Draggable {
   . . .
}

// in the Graphic.java file
package graphics;
public abstract class Graphic {
   . . .
}

// in the Circle.java file
package graphics;
public class Circle extends Graphic implements Draggable {
   . . .
}

// in the Rectangle.java file
package graphics;
public class Rectangle extends Graphic implements Draggable {
   . . .
}

// in the Point.java file
package graphics;
public class Point extends Graphic implements Draggable {
   . . .
}
```

```
// in the Line.java file
package graphics;
public class Line extends Graphic implements Draggable {
   . . .
}
```

If you do not use a `package` statement, your type ends up in an unnamed package. Generally speaking, an unnamed package is only for small or temporary applications or when you are just beginning the development process. Otherwise, classes and interfaces belong in named packages.

Naming a Package

With programmers worldwide writing classes and interfaces using the Java programming language, it is likely that many programmers will use the same name for different types. In fact, the previous example does just that: It defines a `Rectangle` class when there is already a `Rectangle` class in the `java.awt` package. Still, the compiler allows both classes to have the same name if they are in different packages. The fully qualified name of each `Rectangle` class includes the package name. That is, the fully qualified name of the `Rectangle` class in the `graphics` package is `graphics.Rectangle`, and the fully qualified name of the `Rectangle` class in the `java.awt` package is `java.awt.Rectangle`.

This works well unless two independent programmers use the same name for their packages. What prevents this problem? Convention.

Naming Conventions

Package names are written in all lowercase to avoid conflict with the names of classes or interfaces.

Companies use their reversed Internet domain name to begin their package names—for example, `com.example.orion` for a package named `orion` created by a programmer at `example.com`.

Name collisions that occur within a single company need to be handled by convention within that company, perhaps by including the region or the project name after the company name (for example, `com.company.region.package`).

Packages in the Java language itself begin with `java.` or `javax`.

In some cases, the Internet domain name may not be a valid package name. This can occur if the domain name contains a hyphen or other special character, if the package name begins with a digit or other character that is illegal to use as the beginning of a Java name, or if the package name contains a reserved Java keyword, such as "int". In this event, the suggested convention is to add an underscore (see Table 7.1).

Table 7.1 Using Tricky Domain Names as Package Names

Domain Name	Package Name Prefix
`clipart-open.org`	`org.clipart_open`
`free.fonts.int`	`int_.fonts.free`
`poetry.7days.com`	`com._7days.poetry`

Using Package Members

The types that comprise a package are known as the *package members*.

To use a `public` package member from outside its package, you must do one of the following:

- Refer to the member by its fully qualified name
- Import the package member
- Import the member's entire package

Each is appropriate for different situations, as explained in the sections that follow.

Referring to a Package Member by Its Qualified Name

So far, most of the examples in this tutorial have referred to types by their simple names, such as `Rectangle` and `StackOfInts`. You can use a package member's simple name if the code you are writing is in the same package as that member or if that member has been imported.

However, if you are trying to use a member from a different package and that package has not been imported, you must use the member's fully qualified name, which includes the package name. Here is the fully qualified name for the `Rectangle` class declared in the `graphics` package in the previous example:

```
graphics.Rectangle
```

You could use this qualified name to create an instance of `graphics.Rectangle`:

```
graphics.Rectangle myRect = new graphics.Rectangle();
```

Qualified names are all right for infrequent use. When a name is used repetitively, however, typing the name repeatedly becomes tedious and the code becomes difficult to read. As an alternative, you can *import* the member or its package and then use its simple name.

Importing a Package Member

To import a specific member into the current file, put an `import` statement at the beginning of the file before any type definitions but after the `package` statement, if there is one. Here's how you would import the `Rectangle` class from the `graphics` package created in the previous section:

```
import graphics.Rectangle;
```

Now you can refer to the `Rectangle` class by its simple name:

```
Rectangle myRectangle = new Rectangle();
```

This approach works well if you use just a few members from the `graphics` package. But if you use many types from a package, you should import the entire package.

Importing an Entire Package

To import all the types contained in a particular package, use the `import` statement with the asterisk `(*)` wildcard character:

```
import graphics.*;
```

Now you can refer to any class or interface in the `graphics` package by its simple name:

```
Circle myCircle = new Circle();
Rectangle myRectangle = new Rectangle();
```

The asterisk in the `import` statement can be used only to specify all the classes within a package, as shown here. It cannot be used to match a subset of the classes in a package. For example, the following does not match all the classes in the `graphics` package that begin with `A`:

```
import graphics.A*;      // does not work
```

Instead, it generates a compiler error. With the `import` statement, you generally import only a single package member or an entire package.

Note: Another, less common form of `import` allows you to import the public nested classes of an enclosing class. For example, if the `graphics.Rectangle` class contained useful nested classes, such as `Rectangle.DoubleWide` and `Rectangle.Square`, you could import `Rectangle` and its nested classes by using the following *two* statements:

```
import graphics.Rectangle;
import graphics.Rectangle.*;
```

Be aware that the second import statement will *not* import `Rectangle`.

Another less common form of `import`, the *static import statement*, will be discussed at the end of this section.

For convenience, the Java compiler automatically imports three entire packages for each source file: (1) the package with no name, (2) the `java.lang` package, and (3) the current package (the package for the current file).

Apparent Hierarchies of Packages

At first, packages appear to be hierarchical, but they are not. For example, the Java API includes a `java.awt` package, a `java.awt.color` package, a `java.awt.font` package, and many others that begin with `java.awt`. However, the `java.awt.color` package, the `java.awt.font` package, and other `java.awt.xxxx` packages are *not included* in the `java.awt` package. The prefix `java.awt` (the Java Abstract Window Toolkit) is used for a number of related packages to make the relationship evident, but not to show inclusion.

Importing `java.awt.*` imports all of the types in the `java.awt` package, but it *does not import* `java.awt.color`, `java.awt.font`, or any other `java.awt.xxxx` packages. If you plan to use the classes and other types in `java.awt.color` as well as those in `java.awt`, you must import both packages with all their files:

```
import java.awt.*;
import java.awt.color.*;
```

Name Ambiguities

If a member in one package shares its name with a member in another package and both packages are imported, you must refer to each member by its qualified name. For example, the `graphics` package defined a class named `Rectangle`. The `java.awt` package also contains a `Rectangle` class. If both `graphics` and `java.awt` have been imported, the following is ambiguous:

```
Rectangle rect;
```

In such a situation, you have to use the member's fully qualified name to indicate exactly which `Rectangle` class you want. For example,

```
graphics.Rectangle rect;
```

The Static Import Statement

There are situations where you need frequent access to static final fields (constants) and static methods from one or two classes. Prefixing the name of these classes over and over can result in cluttered code. The *static import* statement gives you a way to import the constants and static methods that you want to use so that you do not need to prefix the name of their class.

The `java.lang.Math` class defines the `PI` constant and many static methods, including methods for calculating sines, cosines, tangents, square roots, maxima, minima, exponents, and many more. For example,

```
public static final double PI 3.141592653589793
public static double cos(double a)
```

Ordinarily, to use these objects from another class, you prefix the class name, as follows:

```
double r = Math.cos(Math.PI * theta);
```

You can use the static import statement to import the static members of `java.lang.Math` so that you don't need to prefix the class name, `Math`. The static members of `Math` can be imported either individually:

```
import static java.lang.Math.PI;
```

or as a group:

```
import static java.lang.Math.*;
```

Once they have been imported, the static members can be used without qualification. For example, the previous code snippet would become:

```
double r = cos(PI * theta);
```

Obviously, you can write your own classes that contain constants and static methods that you use frequently, and then use the static import statement. For example,

```
import static mypackage.MyConstants.*;
```

Note: Use static import very sparingly. Overusing static import can result in code that is difficult to read and maintain, because readers of the code won't know which class defines a particular static object. Used properly, static import makes code more readable by removing class name repetition.

Managing Source and Class Files

Many implementations of the Java platform rely on hierarchical file systems to manage source and class files, although *The Java Language Specification* does not require this. The strategy is as follows.

Put the source code for a class, interface, enumeration, or annotation type in a text file whose name is the simple name of the type and whose extension is `.java`. For example:

```
// in the Rectangle.java file
package graphics;
public class Rectangle() {
   ...
}
```

Then, put the source file in a directory whose name reflects the name of the package to which the type belongs:

```
...\graphics\Rectangle.java
```

The qualified name of the package member and the path name to the file are parallel, assuming the Microsoft Windows file name separator backslash (for UNIX, use the forward slash):

class name	`graphics.Rectangle`
pathname to file	`graphics\Rectangle.java`

As you should recall, by convention a company uses its reversed Internet domain name for its package names. The Example company, whose Internet domain name is `example.com`, would precede all its package names with `com.example`. Each component of the package name corresponds to a subdirectory. So, if the Example company had a `com.example.graphics` package that contained a `Rectangle.java` source file, it would be contained in a series of subdirectories like this:

```
...\com\example\graphics\Rectangle.java
```

When you compile a source file, the compiler creates a different output file for each type defined in it. The base name of the output file is the name of the type, and its extension is `.class`. For example, if the source file is like this:

```
// in the Rectangle.java file
package com.example.graphics;
public class Rectangle{
   ...
}

class Helper{
   ...
}
```

then the compiled files will be located at:

```
<path to the parent directory of the output files>\com\
                              example\graphics\Rectangle.class
<path to the parent directory of the output files>\com\
                              example\graphics\Helper.class
```

Like the `.java` source files, the compiled `.class` files should be in a series of directories that reflect the package name. However, the path to the `.class` files does not have to be the same as the path to the `.java` source files. You can arrange your source and class directories separately, as:

```
<path_one>\sources\com\example\graphics\Rectangle.java

<path_two>\classes\com\example\graphics\Rectangle.class
```

By doing this, you can give the `classes` directory to other programmers without revealing your sources. You also need to manage source and class files in this manner so that the compiler and the Java Virtual Machine (JVM) can find all the types your program uses.

The full path to the `classes` directory, `<path_two>\classes`, is called the *class path*, and is set with the `CLASSPATH` system variable. Both the compiler and the JVM construct the path to your `.class` files by adding the package name to the class path. For example, if

```
<path_two>\classes
```

is your class path, and the package name is

```
com.example.graphics
```

then the compiler and JVM look for `.class files` in

```
<path_two>\classes\com\example\graphics.
```

A class path may include several paths, separated by a semicolon (Windows) or colon (UNIX). By default, the compiler and the JVM search the current directory and the JAR file containing the Java platform classes so that these directories are automatically in your class path.

Setting the CLASSPATH System Variable

To display the current `CLASSPATH` variable, use these commands in Windows and UNIX (Bourne shell):

```
In Windows:   C:\> set CLASSPATH
In UNIX:      % echo &#36CLASSPATH
```

To delete the current contents of the `CLASSPATH` variable, use these commands:

```
In Windows:   C:\> set CLASSPATH=
In UNIX:      % unset CLASSPATH; export CLASSPATH
```

To set the `CLASSPATH` variable, use these commands (for example):

```
In Windows:   C:\> set CLASSPATH=C:\users\george\java\classes
In UNIX:      % CLASSPATH=/home/george/java/classes;
                                                   export CLASSPATH
```

Summary of Creating and Using Packages

To create a package for a type, put a `package` statement as the first statement in the source file that contains the type (class, interface, enumeration, or annotation type).

To use a public type that's in a different package, you have three choices: (1) use the fully qualified name of the type, (2) import the type, or (3) import the entire package of which the type is a member.

The path names for a package's source and class files mirror the name of the package.

You might have to set your `CLASSPATH` so that the compiler and the JVM can find the `.class` files for your types.

Questions and Exercises: Creating and Using Packages

Questions

Assume you have written some classes. Belatedly, you decide they should be split into three packages, as listed in Table 7.2. Furthermore, assume the classes are currently in the default package (they have no `package` statements).

Table 7.2 Package Names and Class Names

Package Name	Class Name
`mygame.server`	`Server`
`mygame.shared`	`Utilities`
`mygame.client`	`Client`

1. Which line of code will you need to add to each source file to put each class in the right package?
2. To adhere to the directory structure, you will need to create some subdirectories in the development directory and put source files in the correct subdirectories. What subdirectories must you create? Which subdirectory does each source file go in?
3. Do you think you'll need to make any other changes to the source files to make them compile correctly? If so, what?

Exercises

Download the source files as listed here:

- Client: `tutorial/java/package/QandE/question/Client.java`
- Server: `tutorial/java/package/QandE/question/Server.java`
- Utilities: `tutorial/java/package/QandE/question/Utilities.java`

1. Implement the changes you proposed in questions 1 through 3 using the source files you just downloaded.
2. Compile the revised source files. (*Hint:* If you're invoking the compiler from the command line [as opposed to using a builder], invoke the compiler from the directory that contains the `mygame` directory you just created.)

Answers

You can find answers to these Questions and Exercises at:

`tutorial/java/package/QandE/packages-answers.html`

8

Numbers and Strings

Numbers

This chapter begins with a discussion of the `Number`[1] class in the `java.lang` package, its subclasses, and the situations where you would use instantiations of these classes rather than the primitive number types.

This section also presents the `PrintStream`[2] and `DecimalFormat`[3] classes, which provide methods for writing formatted numerical output.

Finally, the `Math`[4] class in `java.lang` is discussed. It contains mathematical functions to complement the operators built into the language. This class has methods for the trigonometric functions, exponential functions, and so forth.

The Numbers Classes

When working with numbers, most of the time you use the primitive types in your code. For example:

---

1. `docs/api/java/lang/Number.html`
2. `docs/api/java/io/PrintStream.html`
3. `docs/api/java/text/DecimalFormat.html`
4. `docs/api/java/lang/Math.html`

```
int i = 500;
float gpa = 3.65;
byte mask = 0xff;
```

There are, however, reasons to use objects in place of primitives, and the Java platform provides *wrapper* classes for each of the primitive data types. These classes "wrap" the primitive in an object. Often, the wrapping is done by the compiler; if you use a primitive where an object is expected, the compiler *boxes* the primitive in its wrapper class for you. Similarly, if you use a number object when a primitive is expected, the compiler *unboxes* the object for you.

Here is an example of boxing and unboxing:

```
Integer x, y;
x = 12;
y = 15;
System.out.println(x+y);
```

When `x` and `y` are assigned integer values, the compiler boxes the integers because `x` and `y` are integer objects. In the `println()` statement, `x` and `y` are unboxed so that they can be added as integers.

All of the numeric wrapper classes are subclasses of the abstract class `Number` as shown in Figure 8.1.

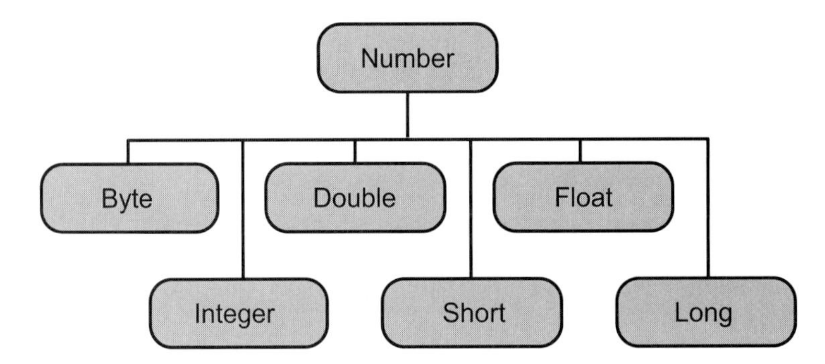

Figure 8.1 The class hierarchy of `Number`.

Note: There are four other subclasses of `Number` that are not discussed here. `BigDecimal` and `BigInteger` are used for high-precision calculations. `AtomicInteger` and `AtomicLong` are used for multi-threaded applications.

There are three reasons that you might use a `Number` object rather than a primitive:

1. as an argument of a method that expects an object (often used when manipulating collections of numbers);
2. to use constants defined by the class, such as `MIN_VALUE` and `MAX_VALUE`, that provide the upper and lower bounds of the data type;
3. to use class methods for converting values to and from other primitive types, for converting to and from strings, and for converting between number systems (decimal, octal, hexadecimal, binary).

Table 8.1 lists the instance methods that all the subclasses of the `Number` class implement.

Table 8.1 Methods Implemented by All Subclasses of `Number`

Method	Description

`byte byteValue()`
`short shortValue()`
`int intValue()`
`long longValue()`
`float floatValue()`
`double doubleValue()`
	Converts the value of this `Number` object to the primitive data type returned.

`int compareTo(Byte anotherByte)`
`int compareTo(Double anotherDouble)`
`int compareTo(Float anotherFloat)`
`int compareTo(Integer anotherInteger)`
`int compareTo(Long anotherLong)`
`int compareTo(Short anotherShort)`
	Compares this `Number` object to the argument.

`boolean equals(Object obj)`	Determines whether this number object is equal to the argument. The methods return `true` if the argument is not `null` and is an object of the same type and with the same numeric value. There are some extra requirements for `Double` and `Float` objects that are described in the Java API documentation.

Each `Number` class contains other methods that are useful for converting numbers to and from strings and for converting between number systems. Table 8.2 lists these methods in the `Integer` class. Methods for the other `Number` subclasses are similar.

Table 8.2 Conversion Methods, `Integer` Class

Method	Description
`static Integer decode(String s)`	Decodes a string into an integer. Can accept string representations of decimal, octal, or hexadecimal numbers as input.
`static int parseInt(String s)`	Returns an integer (decimal only).
`static int parseInt(String s, int radix)`	Returns an integer, given a string representation of decimal, binary, octal, or hexadecimal (`radix` equals 10, 2, 8, or 16 respectively) numbers as input.
`String toString()`	Returns a `String` object representing the value of this `Integer`.
`static String toString(int i)`	Returns a `String` object representing the specified integer.
`static Integer valueOf(int i)`	Returns an `Integer` object holding the value of the specified primitive.
`static Integer valueOf(String s)`	Returns an `Integer` object holding the value of the specified string representation.
`static Integer valueOf(String s, int radix)`	Returns an `Integer` object holding the integer value of the specified string representation, parsed with the value of radix. For example, if s = "333" and radix = 8, the method returns the base-ten integer equivalent of the octal number 333.

Formatting Numeric Print Output

Earlier you saw the use of the `print()` and `println()` methods for printing strings to standard output (`System.out`). Since all numbers can be converted to strings (as you will see later in this chapter), you can use these methods to print out an arbitrary mixture of strings and numbers. The Java programming language has other methods, however, that allow you to exercise much more control over your print output when numbers are included.

The printf() and format() Methods

The `java.io` package includes a `PrintStream` class that has two formatting methods that you can use to replace `print()` and `println()`. These methods, `format()` and `printf()`, are equivalent to one another. The familiar `System.out` that you have been using happens to be a `PrintStream` object, so you can invoke `PrintStream` methods on System.out. Thus, you can use format() or printf() anywhere in your code where you have previously been using print() or println(). For example,

```
System.out.format(.....);
```

The syntax for these two java.io.PrintStream methods is the same:

```
public PrintStream format(String format, Object... args)
```

where format is a string that specifies the formatting to be used and args is a list of the variables to be printed using that formatting. A simple example would be:

```
System.out.format("The value of the float variable is %f, " +
                  "while the value of the integer variable " +
                  "is %d, and the string is %s",
                  floatVar, intVar, stringVar);
```

The first parameter, format, is a format string specifying how the objects in the second parameter, args, are to be formatted. The format string contains plain text as well as *format specifiers*, which are special characters that format the arguments of Object... args. The notation Object... args is called *varargs*, which means that the number of arguments may vary.

Format specifiers begin with a percent sign (%) and end with a *conversion*. The conversion is a character indicating the type of argument to be formatted. In between the percent sign (%) and the conversion you can have optional flags and specifiers. There are many conversions, flags, and specifiers, which are documented in java.util.Formatter.[5]

Here is a basic example:

```
int i = 461012;
System.out.format("The value of i is: %d%n", i);
```

The %d specifies that the single variable is a decimal integer. The %n is a platform-independent newline character. The output is:

```
The value of i is: 461012
```

The printf() and format() methods are overloaded. Each has a version with the following syntax:

```
public PrintStream format(Locale l, String format,
                                                Object... args)
```

5. docs/api/java/util/Formatter.html

To print numbers in the French system (where a comma is used in place of the decimal place in the English representation of floating point numbers), for example, you would use:

```
System.out.format
  (Locale.FRANCE, "The value of the float variable is %f, " +
   "while the value of the integer variable is %d, and the " +
   "string is %s%n", floatVar, intVar, stringVar);
```

An Example

Table 8.3 lists some of the conversions and flags that are used in the sample program, `TestFormat.java`.

Table 8.3 Conversions and Flags Used in `TestPrintf.java`

Conversion	Flag	Explanation
`d`		A decimal integer.
`f`		A float.
`n`		A new line character appropriate to the platform running the application. You should always use `%n`, rather than `\n`.
`tB`		A date and time conversion—locale-specific full name of month.
`td`, `te`		A date and time conversion—2-digit day of month. `td` has leading zeroes as needed, `te` does not.
`ty`, `tY`		A date and time conversion—`ty` = 2-digit year, `tY` = 4-digit year.
`tl`		A date and time conversion—hour in 12-hour clock.
`tM`		A date and time conversion—minutes in 2 digits, with leading zeroes as necessary.
`tp`		A date and time conversion—locale-specific am/pm (lowercase).
`tm`		A date and time conversion—months in 2 digits, with leading zeroes as necessary.
`tD`		A date and time conversion—date as `%tm%td%ty`.
	`08`	Eight characters in width, with leading zeroes as necessary.
	`+`	Includes sign, whether positive or negative.
	`,`	Includes locale-specific grouping characters.
	`-`	Left justified.
	`.3`	Three places after decimal point.
	`10.3`	Ten characters in width, right justified, with three places after decimal point.

The following program shows some of the formatting that you can do with `format()`. The `java.util` package must be imported, as it contains the `Locale` and `Calendar` classes:

```
import java.util.*;

public class TestFormat {

  public static void main(String[] args) {
    long n = 461012;
    System.out.format("%d%n", n);
    System.out.format("%08d%n", n);
    System.out.format("%+8d%n", n);
    System.out.format("%,8d%n", n);
    System.out.format("%+,8d%n%n", n);

    double pi = Math.PI;
    System.out.format("%f%n", pi);
    System.out.format("%.3f%n", pi);
    System.out.format("%10.3f%n", pi);
    System.out.format("%-10.3f%n", pi);
    System.out.format(Locale.FRANCE, "%-10.4f%n%n", pi);

    Calendar c = Calendar.getInstance();
    System.out.format("%tB %te, %tY%n", c, c, c);
    System.out.format("%tl:%tM %tp%n", c, c, c);
    System.out.format("%tD%n", c);
  }
}
```

The output is:

```
461012
00461012
 +461012
 461,012
+461,012

3.141593
3.142
     3.142
3.142
3,1416

May 29, 2006
2:34 am
05/29/06
```

Note: The discussion in this section covers just the basics of the `format()` and `printf()` methods. Further detail can be found in the Formatting section (page 272).

The DecimalFormat Class

You can use the `java.text.DecimalFormat` class to control the display of leading and trailing zeros, prefixes and suffixes, grouping (thousands) separators, and the decimal separator. `DecimalFormat` offers a great deal of flexibility in the formatting of numbers, but it can make your code more complex.

The example that follows creates a `DecimalFormat` object, `myFormatter`, by passing a pattern string to the `DecimalFormat` constructor. The `format()` method, which `DecimalFormat` inherits from `NumberFormat`, is then invoked by `myFormatter`—it accepts a `double` value as an argument and returns the formatted number in a string.

Here is a sample program that illustrates the use of `DecimalFormat`:

```
import java.text.*;

public class DecimalFormatDemo {

  static public void customFormat(String pattern,
      double value ) {
    DecimalFormat myFormatter = new DecimalFormat(pattern);
    String output = myFormatter.format(value);
    System.out.println(value + "  " + pattern + "  " + output);
  }

  static public void main(String[] args) {

    customFormat("###,###.###", 123456.789);
    customFormat("###.##", 123456.789);
    customFormat("000000.000", 123.78);
    customFormat("$###,###.###", 12345.67);
  }
}
```

The output is:

```
123456.789  ###,###.###  123,456.789
123456.789  ###.##  123456.79
123.78  000000.000  000123.780
12345.67  $###,###.###  $12,345.67
```

Table 8.4 explains each line of output.

Table 8.4 DecimalFormat.java Output

Value	Pattern	Output	Explanation
123456.789	###,###.###	123,456.789	The pound sign (#) denotes a digit, the comma is a placeholder for the grouping separator, and the period is a placeholder for the decimal separator.
123456.789	###.##	123456.79	The value has three digits to the right of the decimal point, but the pattern has only two. The format method handles this by rounding up.
123.78	000000.000	000123.780	The pattern specifies leading and trailing zeros, because the 0 character is used instead of the pound sign (#).
12345.67	$###,###.###	$12,345.67	The first character in the pattern is the dollar sign ($). Note that it immediately precedes the leftmost digit in the formatted output.

Beyond Basic Arithmetic

The Java programming language supports basic arithmetic with its arithmetic operators: +, -, *, /, and %. The Math class in the java.lang package provides methods and constants for doing more advanced mathematical computations.

The methods in the Math class are all static, so you call them directly from the class, like this:

```
Math.cos(angle);
```

Note: Using the static import language feature (see the The Static Import Statement section, page 190), you don't have to write Math in front of every math function:

```
import static java.lang.Math.*;
```

This allows you to invoke the Math class methods by their simple names. For example:

```
cos(angle);
```

Constants and Basic Methods

The `Math` class includes two constants:

- `Math.E`, which is the base of natural logarithms, and
- `Math.PI`, which is the ratio of the circumference of a circle to its diameter.

The `Math` class also includes more than 40 static methods. Table 8.5 lists a number of the basic methods.

Table 8.5 Basic `Math` Methods

Method	Description

`double abs(double d)`
`float abs(float f)`
`int abs(int i)`
`long abs(long lng)`
	Returns the absolute value of the argument.

`double ceil(double d)`	Returns the smallest integer that is greater than or equal to the argument. Returned as a double.
`double floor(double d)`	Returns the largest integer that is less than or equal to the argument. Returned as a double.
`double rint(double d)`	Returns the integer that is closest in value to the argument. Returned as a double.
`long round(double d)` `int round(float f)`	Returns the closest long or int, as indicated by the method's return type, to the argument.

`double min(double arg1, double arg2)`
`float min(float arg1, float arg2)`
`int min(int arg1, int arg2)`
`long min(long arg1, long arg2)`
	Returns the smaller of the two arguments.

`double max(double arg1, double arg2)`
`float max(float arg1, float arg2)`
`int max(int arg1, int arg2)`
`long max(long arg1, long arg2)`
	Returns the larger of the two arguments.

The following program, `BasicMathDemo`,[6] illustrates how to use some of these methods:

6. `tutorial/java/data/examples/BasicMathDemo.java`

```
public class BasicMathDemo {
  public static void main(String[] args) {
    double a = -191.635;
    double b = 43.74;
    int c = 16, d = 45;

    System.out.printf("The absolute value of %.3f is %.3f%n",
                                                     a, Math.abs(a));
    System.out.printf("The ceiling of %.2f is %.0f%n",
                                                     b, Math.ceil(b));
    System.out.printf("The floor of %.2f is %.0f%n",
                                                     b, Math.floor(b));
    System.out.printf("The rint of %.2f is %.0f%n",
                                                     b, Math.rint(b));
    System.out.printf("The max of %d and %d is %d%n",
                                               c, d, Math.max(c, d));
    System.out.printf("The min of of %d and %d is %d%n",
                                               c, d, Math.min(c, d));

  }
}
```

Here's the output from this program:

```
The absolute value of -191.635 is 191.635
The ceiling of 43.74 is 44
The floor of 43.74 is 43
The rint of 43.74 is 44
The max of 16 and 45 is 45
The min of 16 and 45 is 16
```

Exponential and Logarithmic Methods

Table 8.6 lists exponential and logarithmic methods of the `Math` class.

Table 8.6 Exponential and Logarithmic Methods

Method	Description
`double exp(double d)`	Returns the base of the natural logarithms, e, to the power of the argument.
`double log(double d)`	Returns the natural logarithm of the argument.
`double pow(double base, double exponent)`	Returns the value of the first argument raised to the power of the second argument.
`double sqrt(double d)`	Returns the square root of the argument.

The following program, ExponentialDemo,[7] displays the value of e, then calls each of the methods listed in Table 8.6 on arbitrarily chosen numbers:

```
public class ExponentialDemo {

  public static void main(String[] args) {

    double x = 11.635;
    double y = 2.76;

    System.out.printf("The value of e is %.4f%n", Math.E);
    System.out.printf("exp(%.3f) is %.3f%n", x, Math.exp(x));
    System.out.printf("log(%.3f) is %.3f%n", x, Math.log(x));
    System.out.printf("pow(%.3f, %.3f) is %.3f%n",
                                       x, y, Math.pow(x, y));
    System.out.printf("sqrt(%.3f) is %.3f%n", x, Math.sqrt(x));
  }
}
```

Here's the output you'll see when you run ExponentialDemo:

```
The value of e is 2.7183
exp(11.635) is 112983.831
log(11.635) is 2.454
pow(11.635, 2.760) is 874.008
sqrt(11.635) is 3.411
```

Trigonometric Methods

The Math class also provides a collection of trigonometric functions, which are summarized in Table 8.7. The value passed into each of these methods is an angle expressed in radians. You can use the toRadians method to convert from degrees to radians.

Here's a program, TrigonometricDemo,[8] that uses each of these methods to compute various trigonometric values for a 45-degree angle:

7. tutorial/java/data/examples/ExponentialDemo.java

8. tutorial/java/data/examples/TrigonometricDemo.java

Table 8.7 Trigonometric Methods

Method	Description
`double sin(double d)`	Returns the sine of the specified double value.
`double cos(double d)`	Returns the cosine of the specified double value.
`double tan(double d)`	Returns the tangent of the specified double value.
`double asin(double d)`	Returns the arcsine of the specified double value.
`double acos(double d)`	Returns the arccosine of the specified double value.
`double atan(double d)`	Returns the arctangent of the specified double value.
`double atan2(double y, double x)`	Converts rectangular coordinates `(x, y)` to polar coordinate `(r, theta)` and returns `theta`.
`double toDegrees(double d)` `double toRadians(double d)`	Converts the argument to degrees or radians.

```
public class TrigonometricDemo {
  public static void main(String[] args) {
    double degrees = 45.0;
    double radians = Math.toRadians(degrees);

    System.out.format("The value of pi is %.4f%n", Math.PI);
    System.out.format("The sine of %.1f degrees is %.4f%n",
      degrees, Math.sin(radians));
    System.out.format("The cosine of %.1f degrees is %.4f%n",
      degrees, Math.cos(radians));
    System.out.format("The tangent of %.1f degrees is %.4f%n",
      degrees, Math.tan(radians));
    System.out.format("The arcsine of %.4f is %.4f degrees %n",
      Math.sin(radians),
      Math.toDegrees(Math.asin(Math.sin(radians))));
    System.out.format("The arccosine of %.4f is %.4f " +
      degrees %n", Math.cos(radians),
      Math.toDegrees(Math.acos(Math.cos(radians))));
    System.out.format("The arctangent of %.4f is %.4f " +
      degrees %n", Math.tan(radians),
      Math.toDegrees(Math.atan(Math.tan(radians))));

  }
}
```

The output of this program is as follows:

```
The value of pi is 3.1416
The sine of 45.0 degrees is 0.7071
The cosine of 45.0 degrees is 0.7071
The tangent of 45.0 degrees is 1.0000
The arcsine of 0.7071 is 45.0000 degrees
The arccosine of 0.7071 is 45.0000 degrees
The arctangent of 1.0000 is 45.0000 degrees
```

Random Numbers

The `random()` method returns a pseudo-randomly selected number between 0.0 and 1.0. The range includes 0.0 but not 1.0. In other words: `0.0 <= Math.random() < 1.0`. To get a number in a different range, you can perform arithmetic on the value returned by the random method. For example, to generate an integer between 1 and 10, you would write:

```
int number = (Math.random() * 10).intValue();
```

By multiplying the value by 10, the range of possible values becomes `0.0 <= number < 10.0`. The compiler boxes the primitive double, `(Math.random() * 10)`, which is then converted to a primitive in with the `intValue()` method of the `Double` class.

Using `Math.random` works well when you need to generate a single random number. If you need to generate a series of random numbers, you should create an instance of `java.util.Random` and invoke methods on that object to generate numbers.

Summary of Numbers

You use one of the wrapper classes—`Byte`, `Double`, `Float`, `Integer`, `Long`, or `Short`—to wrap a number of primitive type in an object. The Java compiler automatically wraps (boxes) primitives for you when necessary and unboxes them, again when necessary.

The `Number` classes include constants and useful class methods. The `MIN_VALUE` and `MAX_VALUE` constants contain the smallest and largest values that can be contained by an object of that type. The `byteValue`, `shortValue`, and similar methods convert one numeric type to another. The `valueOf` method converts a string to a number, and the `toString` method converts a number to a string.

To format a string containing numbers for output, you can use the `printf()` or `format()` methods in the `PrintStream` class. Alternatively, you can use the `NumberFormat` class to customize numerical formats using patterns.

The `Math` class contains a variety of class methods for performing mathematical functions, including exponential, logarithmic, and trigonometric methods. `Math` also includes basic arithmetic functions, such as absolute value and rounding, and a method, `random()`, for generating random numbers.

Questions and Exercises: Numbers

Questions

1. Use the API documentation to find the answers to the following questions:
   a. What `Integer` method can you use to convert an `int` into a string that expresses the number in hexadecimal? For example, what method converts the integer 65 into the string "41"?
   b. What `Integer` method would you use to convert a string expressed in base 5 into the equivalent `int`? For example, how would you convert the string "230" into the integer value 65? Show the code you would use to accomplish this task.
   c. What Double method can you use to detect whether a floating-point number has the special value Not a Number (`NaN`)?
2. What is the value of the following expression, and why?

```
Integer.valueOf(1).equals(Long.valueOf(1))
```

Exercises

1. Change `MaxVariablesDemo`[9] to show minimum values instead of maximum values. You can delete all code related to the variables `aChar` and `aBoolean`. What is the output?
2. Create a program that reads an unspecified number of integer arguments from the command line and adds them together. For example, suppose that you enter the following:

```
java Adder 1 3 2 10
```

   The program should display `16` and then exit. The program should display an error message if the user enters only one argument. You can base your program on `ValueOfDemo` (see the Converting Strings to Numbers section, page 216).
3. Create a program that is similar to the previous one but has the following differences:
   - Instead of reading integer arguments, it reads floating-point arguments.

9. `tutorial/java/data/QandE/MaxVariablesDemo.java`

- It displays the sum of the arguments, using exactly two digits to the right of the decimal point.

For example, suppose that you enter the following:

```
java FPAdder 1 1e2 3.0 4.754
```

The program would display `108.75`. Depending on your locale, the decimal point might be a comma (`,`) instead of a period (`.`).

Answers

You can find answers to these Questions and Exercises at:

```
tutorial/java/data/QandE/numbers-answers.html
```

Characters

Most of the time, if you are using a single character value, you will use the primitive `char` type, for example:

```
char ch = 'a';
char uniChar = '\u039A'; // Unicode for uppercase Greek
                         // omega character
char[] charArray ={ 'a', 'b', 'c', 'd', 'e' }; // an array
                                               // of chars
```

There are times, however, when you need to use a char as an object—for example, as a method argument where an object is expected. The Java programming language provides a *wrapper* class that "wraps" the `char` in a `Character` object for this purpose. An object of type `Character` contains a single field, whose type is `char`. This `Character`[10] class also offers a number of useful class (i.e., static) methods for manipulating characters.

You can create a `Character` object with the `Character` constructor:

```
Character ch = new Character('a');
```

10. `docs/api/java/lang/Character.html`

The Java compiler will also create a `Character` object for you under some circumstances. For example, if you pass a primitive `char` into a method that expects an object, the compiler automatically converts the `char` to a `Character` for you. This feature is called *autoboxing*—or *unboxing*, if the conversion goes the other way.

Here is an example of boxing:

```
Character ch = 'a'; // the primitive char 'a'
                    // is boxed into the Character object ch
```

and here is an example of both boxing and unboxing:

```
Character test(Character c) {...} // method parameter and
                                  // return type =
                                  // Character object

char c = test('x'); // primitive 'x' is boxed for method test,
                    // return is unboxed to char 'c'
```

Note: The `Character` class is immutable, so that once it is created, a `Character` object cannot be changed.

Table 8.8 lists some of the most useful methods in the `Character` class but is not exhaustive. For a complete listing of all methods in this class (there are more than fifty), refer to the `java.lang.Character` API specification.

Table 8.8 Useful Methods in the `Character` Class

Method	Description
`boolean isLetter(char ch)` `boolean isDigit(char ch)`	Determines whether the specified char value is a letter or a digit, respectively.
`boolean isWhitespace(char ch)`	Determines whether the specified char value is white space.
`boolean isUpperCase(char ch)` `boolean isLowerCase(char ch)`	Determines whether the specified char value is uppercase or lowercase, respectively.
`char toUpperCase(char ch)` `char toLowerCase(char ch)`	Returns the uppercase or lowercase form of the specified char value.
`toString(char ch)`	Returns a `String` object representing the specified character value—that is, a one-character string.

Escape Sequences

A character preceded by a backslash (\) is an *escape sequence* and has special meaning to the compiler. The newline character (\n) has been used frequently in this tutorial in `System.out.println()` statements to advance to the next line after the string is printed. Table 8.9 shows the Java escape sequences.

Table 8.9 Escape Sequences

Escape Sequence	Description
`\t`	Insert a tab in the text at this point.
`\b`	Insert a backspace in the text at this point.
`\n`	Insert a newline in the text at this point.
`\r`	Insert a carriage return in the text at this point.
`\f`	Insert a form feed in the text at this point.
`\'`	Insert a single quote character in the text at this point.
`\"`	Insert a double quote character in the text at this point.
`\\`	Insert a backslash character in the text at this point.

When an escape sequence is encountered in a print statement, the compiler interprets it accordingly. For example, if you want to put quotes within quotes you must use the escape sequence, \", on the interior quotes. To print the sentence:

```
She said "Hello!" to me.
```

you would write:

```
System.out.println("She said \"Hello!\" to me.");
```

Strings

Strings, which are widely used in Java programming, are a sequence of characters. In the Java programming language, strings are objects.

The Java platform provides the `String`[11] class to create and manipulate strings.

11. `docs/api/java/lang/String.html`

Creating Strings

The most direct way to create a string is to write:

```
String greeting = "Hello world!";
```

In this case, "Hello world!" is a *string literal*—a series of characters in your code that is enclosed in double quotes. Whenever it encounters a string literal in your code, the compiler creates a `String` object with its value—in this case, `Hello world!`.

As with any other object, you can create `String` objects by using the `new` keyword and a constructor. The `String` class has eleven constructors that allow you to provide the initial value of the string using different sources, such as an array of characters:

```
char[] helloArray = { 'h', 'e', 'l', 'l', 'o', '.'};
String helloString = new String(helloArray);
System.out.println(helloString);
```

The last line of this code snippet displays `hello`.

Note: The `String` class is immutable, so that once it is created a `String` object cannot be changed. The `String` class has a number of methods, some of which will be discussed next, that appear to modify strings. Since strings are immutable, what these methods really do is create and return a new string that contains the result of the operation.

String Length

Methods used to obtain information about an object are known as *accessor methods*. One accessor method that you can use with strings is the `length()` method, which returns the number of characters contained in the string object. After the following two lines of code have been executed, `len` equals 17:

```
String palindrome = "Dot saw I was Tod";
int len = palindrome.length();
```

A *palindrome* is a word or sentence that is symmetric—it is spelled the same forward and backward, ignoring case and punctuation. Here is a short and inefficient program to reverse a palindrome string. It invokes the `String` method `charAt(i)`, which returns the ith character in the string, counting from 0:

```
public class StringDemo {

  public static void main(String[] args) {
    String palindrome = "Dot saw I was Tod";
    int len = palindrome.length();
    char[] tempCharArray = new char[len];
    char[] charArray = new char[len];

    // put original string in an array of chars
    for (int i = 0; i < len; i++) {
      tempCharArray[i] = palindrome.charAt(i);
    }

    // reverse array of chars
    for (int j = 0; j < len; j++) {
      charArray[j] = tempCharArray[len - 1 - j];
    }

    String reversePalindrome =  new String(charArray);
    System.out.println(reversePalindrome);
  }
}
```

Running the program produces this output:

```
doT saw I was toD
```

To accomplish the string reversal, the program had to convert the string to an array of characters (first `for` loop), reverse the array into a second array (second `for` loop), and then convert back to a string. The `String` class includes a method, `getChars()`, to convert a string, or a portion of a string, into an array of characters, so we could replace the first `for` loop in the program above with:

```
palindrome.getChars(0, len - 1, tempCharArray, 0);
```

Concatenating Strings

The `String` class includes a method for concatenating two strings:

```
string1.concat(string2);
```

This returns a new string that is `string1` with `string2` added to it at the end.

You can also use the `concat()` method with string literals, as in:

```
"My name is ".concat("Rumplestiltskin");
```

Strings are more commonly concatenated with the **+** operator, as in:

```
"Hello," + " world" + "!"
```

which results in:

```
"Hello, world!"
```

The **+** operator is widely used in `print` statements. For example:

```
String string1 = "saw I was ";
System.out.println("Dot " + string1 + "Tod");
```

which prints:

```
Dot saw I was Tod
```

Such a concatenation can be a mixture of any objects. For each object that is not a `String`, its `toString()` method is called to convert it to a `String`.

Note: The Java programming language does not permit literal strings to span lines in source files, so you must use the + concatenation operator at the end of each line in a multi-line string. For example:

```
String quote = "Now is the time for all good " +
               "men to come to the aid of their country.";
```

Breaking strings between lines using the + concatenation operator is, once again, very common in `print` statements.

Creating Format Strings

You have seen the use of the `printf()` and `format()` methods to print output with formatted numbers. The `String` class has an equivalent class method, `format()`, that returns a `String` object rather than a `PrintStream` object.

Using `String`'s static `format()` method allows you to create a formatted string that you can reuse, as opposed to a one-time print statement. For example, instead of:

```
System.out.printf("The value of the float variable is " +
                  "%f, while the value of the integer " +
                      "variable is %d, and the string " +
                      "is %s", floatVar, intVar, stringVar);
```

you can write:

```
String fs;
fs = String.format("The value of the float variable is " +
                   "%f, while the value of the integer " +
                       "variable is %d, and the string " +
                       "is %s", floatVar, intVar, stringVar);
System.out.println(fs);
```

Converting Between Numbers and Strings

Converting Strings to Numbers

Frequently, a program ends up with numeric data in a string object—a value entered by the user, for example.

The `Number` subclasses that wrap primitive numeric types (`Byte`,[12] `Integer`,[13] `Double`,[14] `Float`,[15] `Long`,[16] and `Short`[17]) each provide a class method named `valueOf` that converts a string to an object of that type. Here is an example, `ValueOfDemo`,[18] that gets two strings from the command line, converts them to numbers, and performs arithmetic operations on the values:

12. `docs/api/java/lang/Byte.html`
13. `docs/api/java/lang/Integer.html`
14. `docs/api/java/lang/Double.html`
15. `docs/api/java/lang/Float.html`
16. `docs/api/java/lang/Long.html`
17. `docs/api/java/lang/Short.html`
18. `tutorial/java/data/examples/ValueOfDemo.java`

```
public class ValueOfDemo {
  public static void main(String[] args) {

    // this program requires two arguments on the command line
    if (args.length == 2) {

        // convert strings to numbers
        float a = (Float.valueOf(args[0])).floatValue();
        float b = (Float.valueOf(args[1])).floatValue();

        // do some arithmetic
        System.out.println("a + b = " + (a + b) );
        System.out.println("a - b = " + (a - b) );
        System.out.println("a * b = " + (a * b) );
        System.out.println("a / b = " + (a / b) );
        System.out.println("a % b = " + (a % b) );
    } else {
        System.out.println("This program requires " +
                           "two command-line arguments.");
    }
  }
}
```

The following is the output from the program when you use `4.5` and `87.2` for the command-line arguments:

```
a + b = 91.7
a - b = -82.7
a * b = 392.4
a / b = 0.0516055
a % b = 4.5
```

Note: Each of the `Number` subclasses that wrap primitive numeric types also provides a `parseXXX()` method (for example, `parseFloat()`) that can be used to convert strings to primitive numbers. Since a primitive type is returned instead of an object, the `parseFloat()` method is more direct than the `valueOf()` method. For example, in the `ValueOfDemo` program, we could use:

```
float a = Float.parseFloat(args[0]);
float b = Float.parseFloat(args[1]);
```

Converting Numbers to Strings

Sometimes you need to convert a number to a string because you need to operate on the value in its string form. There are several easy ways to convert a number to a string:

```
int i;
String s1 = "" + i; // Concatenate "i" with an empty string;
                    // conversion is handled for you.
```

or:

```
String s2 = String.valueOf(i);  // The valueOf class method.
```

Each of the `Number` subclasses includes a class method, `toString()`, that will convert its primitive type to a string. For example:

```
int i;
double d;
String s3 = Integer.toString(i);
String s4 = Double.toString(d);
```

The `ToStringDemo`[19] example uses the `toString` method to convert a number to a string. The program then uses some string methods to compute the number of digits before and after the decimal point:

```
public class ToStringDemo {

  public static void main(String[] args) {
    double d = 858.48;
    String s = Double.toString(d);

    int dot = s.indexOf('.');

    System.out.println(dot + " digits before decimal point.");
    System.out.println( (s.length() - dot - 1) +
                          " digits after decimal point.");
  }
}
```

The output of this program is:

```
3 digits before decimal point.
2 digits after decimal point.
```

Manipulating Characters in a String

The `String` class has a number of methods for examining the contents of strings, finding characters or substrings within a string, changing case, and other tasks.

Getting Characters and Substrings by Index

You can get the character at a particular index within a string by invoking the `charAt()` accessor method. The index of the first character is 0, while the index of the last

19. `tutorial/java/data/examples/ToStringDemo.java`

character is `length()-1`. For example, the following code gets the character at index 9 in a string:

```
String anotherPalindrome = "Niagara. O roar again!";
char aChar = anotherPalindrome.charAt(9);
```

Indices begin at 0, so the character at index 9 is "O", as illustrated in Figure 8.2.

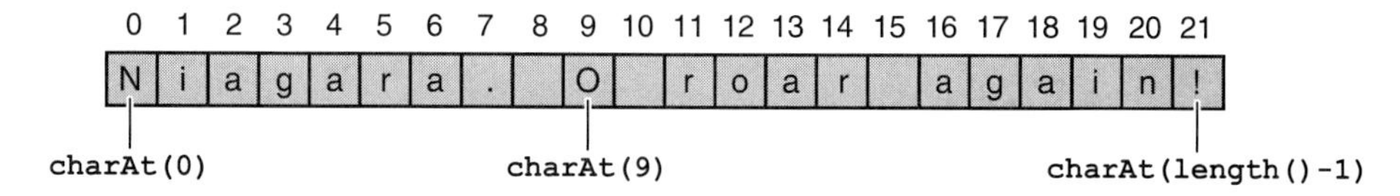

Figure 8.2 Use the `charAt` method to get a character at a particular index.

If you want to get more than one consecutive character from a string, you can use the `substring` method. The `substring` method has two versions, as shown in Table 8.10.

Table 8.10 The `substring` Methods in the `String` Class

Method	Description
`String substring(int beginIndex, int endIndex)`	Returns a new string that is a substring of this string. The first integer argument specifies the index of the first character. The second integer argument is the index of the last character + 1.
`String substring(int beginIndex)`	Returns a new string that is a substring of this string. The integer argument specifies the index of the first character. Here, the returned substring extends to the end of the original string.

The following code gets from the Niagara palindrome the substring that extends from index 11 up to, but not including, index 15, which is the word "roar" (Figure 8.3):

```
String anotherPalindrome = "Niagara. O roar again!";
String roar = anotherPalindrome.substring(11, 15);
```

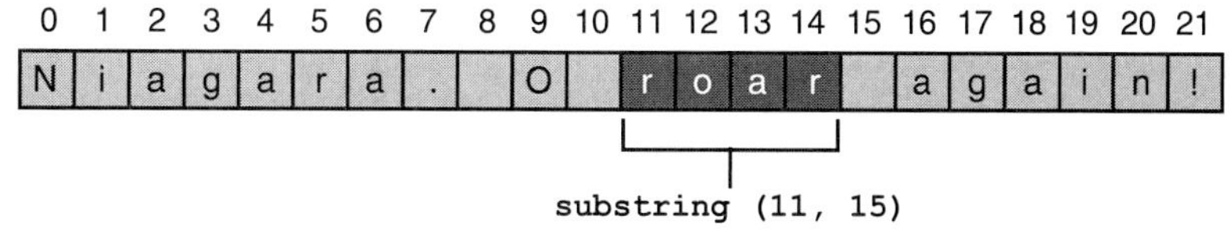

Figure 8.3 Use the `substring` method to get part of a string.

Other Methods for Manipulating Strings

Table 8.11 lists several other `String` methods for manipulating strings.

Table 8.11 Other Methods in the `String` Class for Manipulating Strings

Method	Description
`String[] split(String regex)` `String[] split(String regex, int limit)`	Searches for a match as specified by the string argument (which contains a regular expression) and splits this string into an array of strings accordingly. The optional integer argument specifies the maximum size of the returned array. Regular expressions are covered in Chapter 13.
`CharSequence subSequence(int beginIndex, int endIndex)`	Returns a new character sequence constructed from `beginIndex` index up until `endIndex` – 1.
`String trim()`	Returns a copy of this string with leading and trailing white space removed.
`String toLowerCase()` `String toUpperCase()`	Returns a copy of this string converted to lowercase or uppercase. If no conversions are necessary, these methods return the original string.

Searching for Characters and Substrings in a String

Here are some other `String` methods for finding characters or substrings within a string. The `String` class provides accessor methods that return the position within the string of a specific character or substring: `indexOf()` and `lastIndexOf()`. The `indexOf()` methods search forward from the beginning of the string, and the `lastIndexOf()` methods search backward from the end of the string. If a character or substring is not found, `indexOf()` and `lastIndexOf()` return `-1`.

The `String` class also provides a search method, `contains`, that returns true if the string contains a particular character sequence. Use this method when you only need to know that the string contains a character sequence, but the precise location isn't important.

Table 8.12 describes the various string search methods.

Note: `CharSequence` is an interface that is implemented by the `String` class. Therefore, you can use a string as an argument for the `contains()` method.

Table 8.12 The Search Methods in the `String` Class

Method	Description
`int indexOf(int ch)` `int lastIndexOf(int ch)`	Returns the index of the first (last) occurrence of the specified character.
`int indexOf(int ch, int fromIndex)` `int lastIndexOf(int ch, int fromIndex)`	Returns the index of the first (last) occurrence of the specified character, searching forward (backward) from the specified index.
`int indexOf(String str)` `int lastIndexOf(String str)`	Returns the index of the first (last) occurrence of the specified substring.
`int indexOf(String str, int fromIndex)` `int lastIndexOf(String str, int fromIndex)`	Returns the index of the first (last) occurrence of the specified substring, searching forward (backward) from the specified index.
`boolean contains(CharSequence s)`	Returns true if the string contains the specified character sequence.

Replacing Characters and Substrings into a String

The `String` class has very few methods for inserting characters or substrings into a string. In general, they are not needed: You can create a new string by concatenation of substrings you have *removed* from a string with the substring that you want to insert.

The `String` class does have four methods for *replacing* found characters or substrings, however. They are listed in Table 8.13.

Table 8.13 Methods in the `String` Class for Manipulating Strings

Method	Description
`String replace(char oldChar, char newChar)`	Returns a new string resulting from replacing all occurrences of `oldChar` in this string with `newChar`.
`String replace(CharSequence target,` `CharSequence replacement)`	Replaces each substring of this string that matches the literal target sequence with the specified literal replacement sequence.
`String replaceAll(String regex,` `String replacement)`	Replaces each substring of this string that matches the given regular expression with the given replacement.
`String replaceFirst(String regex,` `String replacement)`	Replaces the first substring of this string that matches the given regular expression with the given replacement.

An Example

The following class, `Filename`,[20] illustrates the use of `lastIndexOf()` and `substring()` to isolate different parts of a file name.

Note: The methods in the following `Filename` class don't do any error checking and assume that their argument contains a full directory path and a filename with an extension. If these methods were production code, they would verify that their arguments were properly constructed.

```
/**
 * This class assumes that the string used to initialize
 * fullPath has a directory path, filename, and extension.
 * The methods won't work if it doesn't.
 */
public class Filename {

  private String fullPath;
  private char pathSeparator, extensionSeparator;

  public Filename(String str, char sep, char ext) {
    fullPath = str;
    pathSeparator = sep;
    extensionSeparator = ext;
  }

  public String extension() {
    int dot = fullPath.lastIndexOf(extensionSeparator);
    return fullPath.substring(dot + 1);
  }

  public String filename() { // gets filename without extension
    int dot = fullPath.lastIndexOf(extensionSeparator);
    int sep = fullPath.lastIndexOf(pathSeparator);
    return fullPath.substring(sep + 1, dot);
  }

  public String path() {
    int sep = fullPath.lastIndexOf(pathSeparator);
    return fullPath.substring(0, sep);
  }
}
```

---

20. `tutorial/java/data/examples/Filename.java`

Here is a program, `FilenameDemo`,[21] that constructs a `Filename` object and calls all of its methods:

```
public class FilenameDemo {
  public static void main(String[] args) {
    final String FPATH = "/home/mem/index.html";
    Filename myHomePage = new Filename(FPATH,
                                       '/', '.');
    System.out.println("Extension = " +
                       myHomePage.extension());
    System.out.println("Filename = " +
                       myHomePage.filename());
    System.out.println("Path = " + myHomePage.path());
  }
}
```

And here's the output from the program:

```
Extension = html
Filename = index
Path = /home/mem
```

As shown in Figure 8.4, our `extension` method uses `lastIndexOf` to locate the last occurrence of the period (`.`) in the file name. Then `substring` uses the return value of `lastIndexOf` to extract the file name extension—that is, the substring from the period to the end of the string. This code assumes that the file name has a period in it; if the file name does not have a period, `lastIndexOf` returns `-1`, and the substring method throws a `StringIndexOutOfBoundsException`.

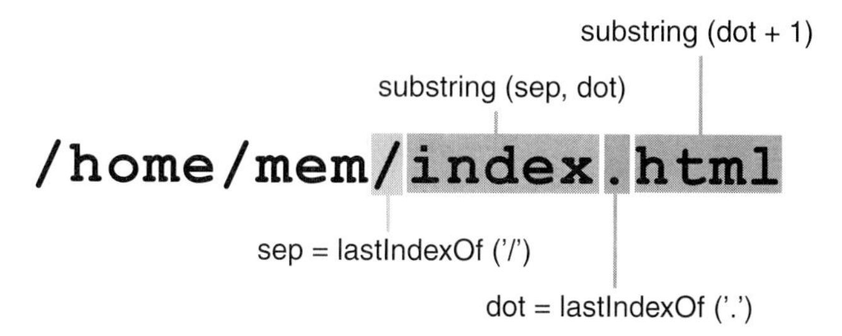

Figure 8.4 The use of `lastIndexOf` and `substring` in the `extension` method in the `Filename` class.

21. `tutorial/java/data/examples/FilenameDemo.java`

Also, notice that the extension method uses dot + 1 as the argument to substring. If the period character (.) is the last character of the string, dot + 1 is equal to the length of the string, which is one larger than the largest index into the string (because indices start at 0). This is a legal argument to substring because that method accepts an index equal to, but not greater than, the length of the string and interprets it to mean "the end of the string."

Comparing Strings and Portions of Strings

The String class has a number of methods for comparing strings and portions of strings. Table 8.14 lists these methods.

The following program, RegionMatchesDemo,[22] uses the regionMatches method to search for a string within another string:

```
public class RegionMatchesDemo {
  public static void main(String[] args) {
    String searchMe = "Green Eggs and Ham";
    String findMe = "Eggs";
    int searchMeLength = searchMe.length();
    int findMeLength = findMe.length();
    boolean foundIt = false;
    for (int i = 0; i <=
         (searchMeLength - findMeLength); i++) {
      if (searchMe.regionMatches(i, findMe, 0, findMeLength)) {
        foundIt = true;
        System.out.println(searchMe.substring(i,
                                        i + findMeLength));
        break;
      }
    }

    if (!foundIt) System.out.println("No match found.");
  }
}
```

The output from this program is Eggs.

The program steps through the string referred to by searchMe one character at a time. For each character, the program calls the regionMatches method to determine whether the substring beginning with the current character matches the string the program is looking for.

22. tutorial/java/data/examples/RegionMatchesDemo.java

Table 8.14 Methods for Comparing Strings

Method	Description
`boolean endsWith(String suffix)` `boolean startsWith(String prefix)`	Returns `true` if this string ends with or begins with the substring specified as an argument to the method.
`boolean startsWith(String prefix, int offset)`	Considers the string beginning at the index `offset`, and returns `true` if it begins with the substring specified as an argument.
`int compareTo(String anotherString)`	Compares two strings lexicographically. Returns an integer indicating whether this string is greater than (result is > 0), equal to (result is = 0), or less than (result is < 0) the argument.
`int compareToIgnoreCase(String str)`	Compares two strings lexicographically, ignoring differences in case. Returns an integer indicating whether this string is greater than (result is > 0), equal to (result is = 0), or less than (result is < 0) the argument.
`boolean equals(Object anObject)`	Returns `true` if and only if the argument is a `String` object that represents the same sequence of characters as this object.
`boolean equalsIgnoreCase(String anotherString)`	Returns `true` if and only if the argument is a `String` object that represents the same sequence of characters as this object, ignoring differences in case.
`boolean regionMatches(int toffset, String other, int ooffset, int len)`	Tests whether the specified region of this string matches the specified region of the String argument. Region is of length `len` and begins at the index `toffset` for this string and `ooffset` for the other string.
`boolean regionMatches(boolean ignoreCase, int toffset, String other, int ooffset, int len)`	Tests whether the specified region of this string matches the specified region of the String argument. Region is of length `len` and begins at the index `toffset` for this string and `ooffset` for the other string. The boolean argument indicates whether case should be ignored; if true, case is ignored when comparing characters.
`boolean matches(String regex)`	Tests whether this string matches the specified regular expression. Regular expressions are discussed in Chapter 13.

The StringBuilder Class

`StringBuilder`[23] objects are like `String` objects, except that they can be modified. Internally, these objects are treated like variable-length arrays that contain a sequence of characters. At any point, the length and content of the sequence can be changed through method invocations.

Strings should always be used unless string builders offer an advantage in terms of simpler code (see the sample program at the end of this section) or better performance. For example, if you need to concatenate a large number of strings, appending to a `StringBuilder` object is more efficient.

Length and Capacity

The `StringBuilder` class, like the `String` class, has a `length()` method that returns the length of the character sequence in the builder.

Unlike strings, every string builder also has a *capacity*, the number of character spaces that have been allocated. The capacity, which is returned by the `capacity()` method, is always greater than or equal to the length (usually greater than) and will automatically expand as necessary to accommodate additions to the string builder (Table 8.15).

Table 8.15 `StringBuilder` Constructors

Constructor	Description
`StringBuilder()`	Creates an empty string builder with a capacity of 16 (16 empty elements).
`StringBuilder(CharSequence cs)`	Constructs a string builder containing the same characters as the specified `CharSequence`, plus an extra 16 empty elements trailing the `CharSequence`.
`StringBuilder(int initCapacity)`	Creates an empty string builder with the specified initial capacity.
`StringBuilder(String s)`	Creates a string builder whose value is initialized by the specified string, plus an extra 16 empty elements trailing the string.

For example, the following code:

```
StringBuilder sb = new StringBuilder(); // creates empty
                                        // builder, capacity 16
sb.append("Greetings"); // adds 9 character string at beginning
```

23. `docs/api/java/lang/StringBuilder.html`

will produce a string builder with a length of 9 and a capacity of 16, as shown in Figure 8.5.

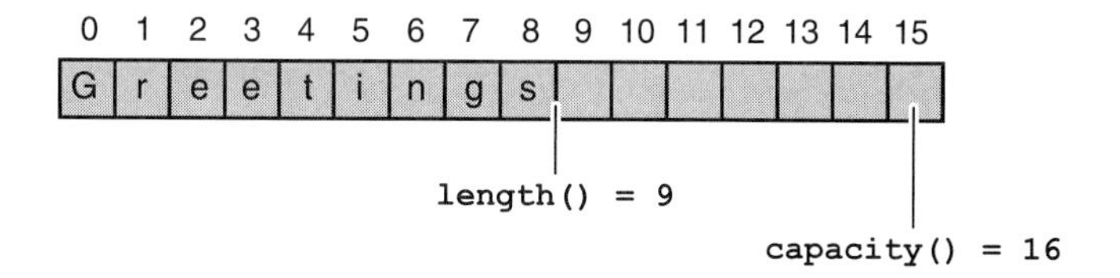

Figure 8.5 A string builder's length is the number of characters it contains; a string builder's capacity is the number of character spaces that have been allocated.

The `StringBuilder` class has some methods related to length and capacity that the `String` class does not have; see Table 8.16.

Table 8.16 Length and Capacity Methods

Constructor	Description
`void setLength(int newLength)`	Sets the length of the character sequence. If `newLength` is less than `length()`, the last characters in the character sequence are truncated. If `newLength` is greater than `length()` (`newLength - length()`), null characters are added at the end of the character sequence.
`void ensureCapacity(int minCapacity)`	Ensures that the capacity is at least equal to the specified minimum.

A number of operations (for example, `append()`, `insert()`, or `setLength()`) can increase the length of the character sequence in the string builder so that the resultant `length()` would be greater than the current `capacity()`. When this happens, the capacity is automatically increased.

StringBuilder Operations

The principal operations on a `StringBuilder` that are not available in `String` are the `append()` and `insert()` methods, which are overloaded so as to accept data of any type. Each converts its argument to a string and then appends or inserts the characters of that string to the character sequence in the string builder. The `append()` method always adds these characters at the end of the existing character sequence, while the `insert()` method adds the characters at a specified point.

Table 8.17 lists a number of the methods of the `StringBuilder` class.

Table 8.17 Various `StringBuilder` Methods

Constructor	Description

`StringBuilder append(boolean b)`
`StringBuilder append(char c)`
`StringBuilder append(char[] str)`
`StringBuilder append(char[] str, int offset, int len)`
`StringBuilder append(double d)`
`StringBuilder append(float f)`
`StringBuilder append(int i)`
`StringBuilder append(long lng)`
`StringBuilder append(Object obj)`
`StringBuilder append(String s)`
	Appends the argument to this string builder. The data is converted to a string before the append operation takes place.

`StringBuilder delete(int start, int end)` `StringBuilder deleteCharAt(int index)`	Deletes the specified character(s) in this string builder.

`StringBuilder insert(int offset, boolean b)`
`StringBuilder insert(int offset, char c)`
`StringBuilder insert(int offset, char[] str)`
`StringBuilder insert(int index, char[] str, int offset, int len)`
`StringBuilder insert(int offset, double d)`
`StringBuilder insert(int offset, float f)`
`StringBuilder insert(int offset, int i)`
`StringBuilder insert(int offset, long lng)`
`StringBuilder insert(int offset, Object obj)`
`StringBuilder insert(int offset, String s)`
	Inserts the second argument into the string builder. The first integer argument indicates the index before which the data is to be inserted. The data is converted to a string before the insert operation takes place.

`StringBuilder replace(int start, int end, String s)` `void setCharAt(int index, char c)`	Replaces the specified character(s) in this string builder.
`StringBuilder reverse()`	Reverses the sequence of characters in this string builder.
`String toString()`	Returns a string that contains the character sequence in the builder.

Note: You can use any `String` method on a `StringBuilder` object by first converting the string builder to a string with the `toString()` method of the `StringBuilder` class. Then convert the string back into a string builder using the `StringBuilder(String str)` constructor.

An Example

The `StringDemo` program that was listed in the Strings section (page 212) is an example of a program that would be more efficient if a `StringBuilder` were used instead of a `String`.

`StringDemo` reversed a palindrome. Here, once again, is its listing:

```
public class StringDemo {
  public static void main(String[] args) {
    String palindrome = "Dot saw I was Tod";
    int len = palindrome.length();
    char[] tempCharArray = new char[len];
    char[] charArray = new char[len];

    // put original string in an array of chars
    for (int i = 0; i < len; i++) {
      tempCharArray[i] = palindrome.charAt(i);
    }

    // reverse array of chars
    for (int j = 0; j < len; j++) {
      charArray[j] = tempCharArray[len - 1 - j];
    }

    String reversePalindrome =  new String(charArray);
    System.out.println(reversePalindrome);
  }
}
```

Running the program produces this output:

```
doT saw I was toD
```

To accomplish the string reversal, the program converts the string to an array of characters (first `for` loop), reverses the array into a second array (second `for` loop), and then converts back to a string.

If you convert the `palindrome` string to a string builder, you can use the `reverse()` method in the `StringBuilder` class. It makes the code simpler and easier to read:

```
public class StringBuilderDemo {
  public static void main(String[] args) {
    String palindrome = "Dot saw I was Tod";

    StringBuilder sb = new StringBuilder(palindrome);

    sb.reverse();  // reverse it

    System.out.println(sb);
  }
}
```

Running this program produces the same output:

```
doT saw I was toD
```

Note that `println()` prints a string builder, as in:

```
System.out.println(sb);
```

because `sb.toString()` is called implicitly, as it is with any other object in a `println()` invocation.

Note: There is also a `StringBuffer` class that is *exactly* the same as the `StringBuilder` class, except that it is thread-safe by virtue of having its methods synchronized. Threads will be discussed in Chapter 12.

Summary of Characters and Strings

Most of the time, if you are using a single character value, you will use the primitive `char` type. There are times, however, when you need to use a char as an object—for example, as a method argument where an object is expected. The Java programming language provides a *wrapper* class that "wraps" the `char` in a `Character` object for this purpose. An object of type `Character` contains a single field whose type is `char`. This `Character` class also offers a number of useful class (i.e., static) methods for manipulating characters.

Strings are a sequence of characters and are widely used in Java programming. In the Java programming language, strings are objects. The `String` class has over 60 methods and 13 constructors.

Most commonly, you create a string with a statement like:

```
String s = "Hello world!";
```

rather than using one of the `String` constructors.

The `String` class has many methods to find and retrieve substrings; these can then be easily reassembled into new strings using the **+** concatenation operator.

The `String` class also includes a number of utility methods, among them `split()`, `toLowerCase()`, `toUpperCase()`, and `valueOf()`. The latter method is indispensable in converting user input strings to numbers. The `Number` subclasses also have methods for converting strings to numbers and vice versa.

In addition to the `String` class, there is also a `StringBuilder` class. Working with `StringBuilder` objects can sometimes be more efficient than working with strings. The `StringBuilder` class offers a few methods that can be useful for strings, among them `reverse()`. In general, however, the `String` class has a wider variety of methods.

A string can be converted to a string builder using a `StringBuilder` constructor. A string builder can be converted to a string with the `toString()` method.

Questions and Exercises: Characters and Strings

Questions

1. What is the initial capacity of the following string builder?

```
StringBuilder sb = new StringBuilder("Able was I " +
                                     "ere I saw Elba.");
```

2. Consider the following string:

```
String hannah = "Did Hannah see bees? Hannah did.";
```

   a. What is the value displayed by the expression `hannah.length()`?

   b. What is the value returned by the method called `hannah.charAt(12)`?

   c. Write an expression that refers to the letter `b` in the string referred to by `hannah`.

3. How long is the string returned by the following expression? What is the string?

```
"Was it a car or a cat I saw?".substring(9, 12)
```

4. In the following program, called `ComputeResult.java`,[24] what is the value of `result` after each numbered line executes?

```
public class ComputeResult {
  public static void main(String[] args) {
    String original = "software";
    StringBuilder result = new StringBuilder("hi");
    int index = original.indexOf('a');

/*1*/  result.setCharAt(0, original.charAt(0));
/*2*/  result.setCharAt(1,
         original.charAt(original.length()-1));
/*3*/  result.insert(1, original.charAt(4));
/*4*/  result.append(original.substring(1,4));
/*5*/  result.insert(3, (original.substring(index, index+2)
                                                + " "));

    System.out.println(result);
  }
}
```

24. `tutorial/java/data/QandE/ComputeResult.java`

Exercises

1. Show two ways to concatenate the following two strings together to get the string `"Hi, mom."`:

```
String hi = "Hi, ";
String mom = "mom.";
```

2. Write a program that computes your initials from your full name and displays them.
3. An anagram is a word or a phrase made by transposing the letters of another word or phrase; for example, "parliament" is an anagram of "partial men," and "software" is an anagram of "swear oft." Write a program that figures out whether one string is an anagram of another string. The program should ignore white space and punctuation.

Answers

You can find answers to these Questions and Exercises at:

`tutorial/java/data/QandE/characters-answers.html`

You can also create *chained* exceptions. For more information, see the Chained Exceptions section (page 249).

The throw Statement

All methods use the `throw` statement to throw an exception. The `throw` statement requires a single argument: a throwable object. Throwable objects are instances of any subclass of the `Throwable` class. Here's an example of a `throw` statement:

```
throw someThrowableObject;
```

Let's look at the `throw` statement in context. The following `pop` method is taken from a class that implements a common stack object. The method removes the top element from the stack and returns the object:

```
public Object pop() {
  Object obj;

  if (size == 0) {
    throw new EmptyStackException();
  }

  obj = objectAt(size - 1);
  setObjectAt(size - 1, null);
  size--;
  return obj;
}
```

The `pop` method checks to see whether any elements are on the stack. If the stack is empty (its size is equal to `0`), `pop` instantiates a new `EmptyStackException` object (a member of `java.util`) and throws it. The Creating Exception Classes section (page 250) explains how to create your own exception classes. For now, all you need to remember is that you can throw only objects that inherit from the `java.lang.Throwable` class.

Note that the declaration of the `pop` method does not contain a `throws` clause. `EmptyStackException` is a not a checked exception, so `pop` is not required to state that it might occur.

Throwable Class and Its Subclasses

The objects that inherit from the `Throwable` class include direct descendants (objects that inherit directly from the `Throwable` class) and indirect descendants (objects that inherit from children or grandchildren of the `Throwable` class). Figure 9.3 illustrates the class hierarchy of the `Throwable` class and its most significant subclasses. As you can see, `Throwable` has two direct descendants: `Error`[3] and `Exception`.[4]

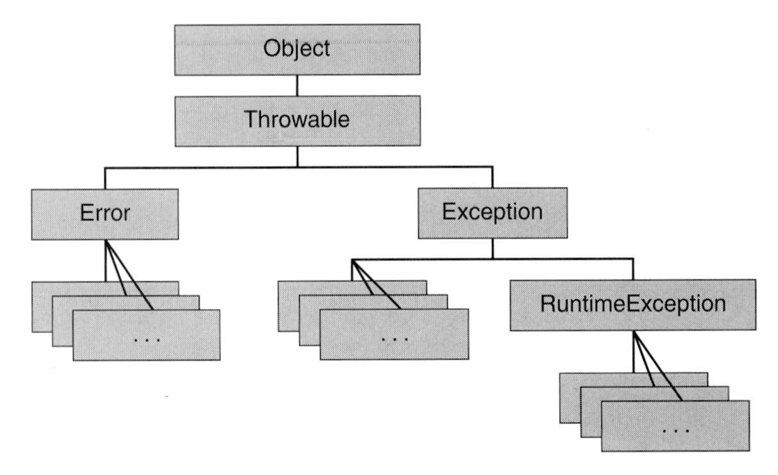

Figure 9.3 The `Throwable` class.

Error Class

When a dynamic linking failure or other hard failure in the Java virtual machine occurs, the virtual machine throws an `Error`. Simple programs typically do *not* catch or throw `Errors`.

Exception Class

Most programs throw and catch objects that derive from the `Exception` class. An `Exception` indicates that a problem occurred, but it is not a serious system problem. Most programs you write will throw and catch `Exceptions` as opposed to `Errors`.

The Java platform defines the many descendants of the `Exception` class. These descendants indicate various types of exceptions that can occur. For example, `IllegalAccessException` signals that a particular method could not be found, and `NegativeArraySizeException` indicates that a program attempted to create an array with a negative size.

One `Exception` subclass, `RuntimeException`, is reserved for exceptions that indicate incorrect use of an API. An example of a runtime exception is `NullPointerException`, which occurs when a method tries to access a member of an

3. `docs/api/java/lang/Error.html`

4. `docs/api/java/lang/Exception.html`

object through a `null` reference. The Unchecked Exceptions—The Controversy section (page 252) discusses why most applications shouldn't throw runtime exceptions or subclass `RuntimeException`.

Chained Exceptions

An application often responds to an exception by throwing another exception. In effect, the first exception *causes* the second exception. It can be very helpful to know when one exception causes another. *Chained exceptions* help the programmer do this.

The following are the methods and constructors in `Throwable` that support chained exceptions:

```
Throwable getCause()
Throwable initCause(Throwable)
Throwable(String, Throwable)
Throwable(Throwable)
```

The `Throwable` argument to `initCause` and the `Throwable` constructors is the exception that caused the current exception. `getCause` returns the exception that caused the current exception, and `initCause` returns the current exception.

The following example shows how to use a chained exception:

```
try {

} catch (IOException e) {
    throw new SampleException("Other IOException", e);
}
```

In this example, when an `IOException` is caught, a new `SampleException` exception is created with the original cause attached and the chain of exceptions is thrown up to the next higher-level exception handler.

Accessing Stack Trace Information

Now let's suppose that the higher-level exception handler wants to dump the stack trace in its own format.

Definition: A *stack trace* provides information on the execution history of the current thread and lists the names of the classes and methods that were called at the point when the exception occurred. A stack trace is a useful debugging tool that you'll normally take advantage of when an exception has been thrown.

The following code shows how to call the getStackTrace method on the exception object:

```
catch (Exception cause) {
  StackTraceElement elements[] = cause.getStackTrace();
  for (int i = 0, n = elements.length; i < n; i++) {
    System.err.println(elements[i].getFileName() + ":" +
                       elements[i].getLineNumber() +
                       ">> " +
                       elements[i].getMethodName() + "()");
  }
}
```

Logging API

The next code snippet logs where an exception occurred from within the catch block. However, rather than manually parsing the stack trace and sending the output to System.err(), it sends the output to a file using the logging facility in the java.util.logging[5] package:

```
try {
    Handler handler = new FileHandler("OutFile.log");
    Logger.getLogger("").addHandler(handler);

} catch (IOException e) {
    Logger logger = Logger.getLogger("package.name");
    StackTraceElement elements[] = e.getStackTrace();
    for (int i = 0; n = elements.length; i < n; i++) {
      logger.log(Level.WARNING, elements[i].getMethodName());
    }
}
```

Creating Exception Classes

When faced with choosing the type of exception to throw, you can either use one written by someone else—the Java platform provides a lot of exception classes you can use—or you can write one of your own. You should write your own exception classes if you answer yes to any of the following questions; otherwise, you can probably use someone else's:

- Do you need an exception type that isn't represented by those in the Java platform?
- Would it help users if they could differentiate your exceptions from those thrown by classes written by other vendors?

5. docs/api/java/util/logging/package-summary.html

- Does your code throw more than one related exception?
- If you use someone else's exceptions, will users have access to those exceptions? A similar question is, should your package be independent and self-contained?

An Example

Suppose you are writing a linked list class. The class supports the following methods, among others:

`objectAt(int n)` Returns the object in the `n`th position in the list. Throws an exception if the argument is less than 0 or more than the number of objects currently in the list.

`firstObject()` Returns the first object in the list. Throws an exception if the list contains no objects.

`indexOf(Object o)` Searches the list for the specified `Object` and returns its position in the list. Throws an exception if the object passed into the method is not in the list.

The linked list class can throw multiple exceptions, and it would be convenient to be able to catch all exceptions thrown by the linked list with one exception handler. Also, if you plan to distribute your linked list in a package, all related code should be packaged together. Thus, the linked list should provide its own set of exception classes.

Figure 9.4 illustrates one possible class hierarchy for the exceptions thrown by the linked list.

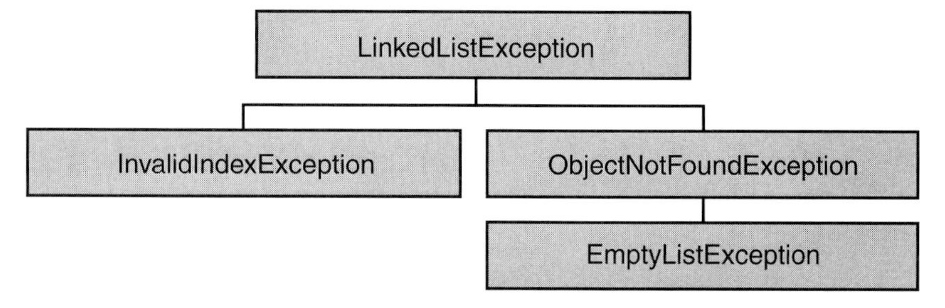

Figure 9.4 Example exception class hierarchy.

Choosing a Superclass

Any `Exception` subclass can be used as the parent class of `LinkedListException`. However, a quick perusal of those subclasses shows that they are inappropriate because they are either too specialized or completely unrelated to `LinkedListException`. Therefore, the parent class of `LinkedListException` should be `Exception`.

Most applets and applications you write will throw objects that are `Exceptions`. `Errors` are normally used for serious, hard errors in the system, such as those that prevent the JVM from running.

Note: For readable code, it's good practice to append the string `Exception` to the names of all classes that inherit (directly or indirectly) from the `Exception` class.

Unchecked Exceptions—The Controversy

Because the Java programming language does not require methods to catch or to specify unchecked exceptions (`RuntimeException`, `Error`, and their subclasses), programmers may be tempted to write code that throws only unchecked exceptions or to make all their exception subclasses inherit from `RuntimeException`. Both of these shortcuts allow programmers to write code without bothering with compiler errors and without bothering to specify or to catch any exceptions. Although this may seem convenient to the programmer, it sidesteps the intent of the Catch or Specify Requirement and can cause problems for others using your classes.

Why did the designers decide to force a method to specify all uncaught checked exceptions that can be thrown within its scope? Any `Exception` that can be thrown by a method is part of the method's public programming interface. Those who call a method must know about the exceptions that a method can throw so that they can decide what to do about them. These exceptions are as much a part of that method's programming interface as its parameters and `return` value.

The next question might be: "If it's so good to document a method's API, including the exceptions it can throw, why not specify runtime exceptions too?" Runtime exceptions represent problems that are the result of a programming problem, and as such, the API client code cannot reasonably be expected to recover from them or to handle them in any way. Such problems include arithmetic exceptions, such as dividing by zero; pointer exceptions, such as trying to access an object through a `null` reference; and indexing exceptions, such as attempting to access an array element through an index that is too large or too small.

Runtime exceptions can occur anywhere in a program, and in a typical one they can be very numerous. Having to add runtime exceptions in every method declaration would reduce a program's clarity. Thus, the compiler does not require that you catch or specify runtime exceptions (although you can).

One case where it is common practice to throw a `RuntimeException` is when the user calls a method incorrectly. For example, a method can check if one of its arguments is incorrectly `null`. If an argument is `null`, the method might throw a `NullPointerException`, which is an *unchecked* exception.

Generally speaking, do not throw a `RuntimeException` or create a subclass of `RuntimeException` simply because you don't want to be bothered with specifying the exceptions your methods can throw.

Here's the bottom line guideline: If a client can reasonably be expected to recover from an exception, make it a checked exception. If a client cannot do anything to recover from the exception, make it an unchecked exception.

Advantages of Exceptions

Now that you know what exceptions are and how to use them, it's time to learn the advantages of using exceptions in your programs.

Advantage 1: Separating Error-Handling Code from "Regular" Code

Exceptions provide the means to separate the details of what to do when something out of the ordinary happens from the main logic of a program. In traditional programming, error detection, reporting, and handling often lead to confusing spaghetti code. For example, consider the pseudocode method here that reads an entire file into memory:

```
readFile {
  open the file;
  determine its size;
  allocate that much memory;
  read the file into memory;
  close the file;
}
```

At first glance, this function seems simple enough, but it ignores all the following potential errors:

- What happens if the file can't be opened?
- What happens if the length of the file can't be determined?
- What happens if enough memory can't be allocated?
- What happens if the read fails?
- What happens if the file can't be closed?

To handle such cases, the `readFile` function must have more code to do error detection, reporting, and handling. Here is an example of what the function might look like:

```
errorCodeType readFile {
  initialize errorCode = 0;

  open the file;
  if (theFileIsOpen) {
      determine the length of the file;
      if (gotTheFileLength) {
          allocate that much memory;
          if (gotEnoughMemory) {
              read the file into memory;
              if (readFailed) {
                  errorCode = -1;
              }
          } else {
              errorCode = -2;
          }
      } else {
          errorCode = -3;
      }
      close the file;
      if (theFileDidntClose && errorCode == 0) {
          errorCode = -4;
      } else {
          errorCode = errorCode and -4;
      }
  } else {
      errorCode = -5;
  }
  return errorCode;
}
```

There's so much error detection, reporting, and returning here that the original seven lines of code are lost in the clutter. Worse yet, the logical flow of the code has also been lost, thus making it difficult to tell whether the code is doing the right thing: Is the file really being closed if the function fails to allocate enough memory? It's even more difficult to ensure that the code continues to do the right thing when you modify the method three months after writing it. Many programmers solve this problem by simply ignoring it—errors are reported when their programs crash.

Exceptions enable you to write the main flow of your code and to deal with the exceptional cases elsewhere. If the `readFile` function used exceptions instead of traditional error-management techniques, it would look more like the following:

```
readFile {
  try {
      open the file;
      determine its size;
      allocate that much memory;
      read the file into memory;
      close the file;
  } catch (fileOpenFailed) {
      doSomething;
  } catch (sizeDeterminationFailed) {
      doSomething;
  } catch (memoryAllocationFailed) {
      doSomething;
  } catch (readFailed) {
      doSomething;
  } catch (fileCloseFailed) {
      doSomething;
  }
}
```

Note that exceptions don't spare you the effort of doing the work of detecting, reporting, and handling errors, but they do help you organize the work more effectively.

Advantage 2: Propagating Errors Up the Call Stack

A second advantage of exceptions is the ability to propagate error reporting up the call stack of methods. Suppose that the `readFile` method is the fourth method in a series of nested method calls made by the main program: `method1` calls `method2`, which calls `method3`, which finally calls `readFile`:

```
method1 {
  call method2;
}

method2 {
  call method3;
}

method3 {
  call readFile;
}
```

Suppose also that `method1` is the only method interested in the errors that might occur within `readFile`. Traditional error-notification techniques force `method2` and `method3` to propagate the error codes returned by `readFile` up the call stack until the error codes finally reach `method1`—the only method that is interested in them:

```
method1 {
  errorCodeType error;
  error = call method2;
  if (error)
    doErrorProcessing;
  else
    proceed;
}

errorCodeType method2 {
  errorCodeType error;
  error = call method3;
  if (error)
    return error;
  else
    proceed;
}

errorCodeType method3 {
  errorCodeType error;
  error = call readFile;
  if (error)
    return error;
  else
    proceed;
}
```

Recall that the Java runtime environment searches backward through the call stack to find any methods that are interested in handling a particular exception. A method can duck any exceptions thrown within it, thereby allowing a method farther up the call stack to catch it. Hence, only the methods that care about errors have to worry about detecting errors:

```
method1 {
  try {
      call method2;
  } catch (exception e) {
      doErrorProcessing;
  }
}

method2 throws exception {
  call method3;
}

method3 throws exception {
  call readFile;
}
```

However, as the pseudocode shows, ducking an exception requires some effort on the part of the middleman methods. Any checked exceptions that can be thrown within a method must be specified in its `throws` clause.

Advantage 3: Grouping and Differentiating Error Types

Because all exceptions thrown within a program are objects, the grouping or categorizing of exceptions is a natural outcome of the class hierarchy. An example of a group of related exception classes in the Java platform are those defined in `java.io`—`IOException` and its descendants. `IOException` is the most general and represents any type of error that can occur when performing I/O. Its descendants represent more specific errors. For example, `FileNotFoundException` means that a file could not be located on disk.

A method can write specific handlers that can handle a very specific exception. The `FileNotFoundException` class has no descendants, so the following handler can handle only one type of exception:

```
catch (FileNotFoundException e) {
   ...
}
```

A method can catch an exception based on its group or general type by specifying any of the exception's superclasses in the `catch` statement. For example, to catch all I/O exceptions, regardless of their specific type, an exception handler specifies an `IOException` argument:

```
catch (IOException e) {
   ...
}
```

This handler will be able to catch all I/O exceptions, including `FileNotFoundException`, `EOFException`, and so on. You can find details about what occurred by querying the argument passed to the exception handler. For example, use the following to print the stack trace:

```
catch (IOException e) {
  e.printStackTrace();             // Output goes to System.err.
  e.printStackTrace(System.out); // Send trace to stdout.
}
```

You could even set up an exception handler that handles any `Exception` with the handler here:

```
catch (Exception e) {     // A (too) general exception handler
   . . .
}
```

The Exception class is close to the top of the Throwable class hierarchy. Therefore, this handler will catch many other exceptions in addition to those that the handler is intended to catch. You may want to handle exceptions this way if all you want your program to do, for example, is print out an error message for the user and then exit.

In most situations, however, you want exception handlers to be as specific as possible. The reason is that the first thing a handler must do is determine what type of exception occurred before it can decide on the best recovery strategy. In effect, by not catching specific errors, the handler must accommodate any possibility. Exception handlers that are too general can make code more error-prone by catching and handling exceptions that weren't anticipated by the programmer and for which the handler was not intended.

As noted, you can create groups of exceptions and handle exceptions in a general fashion, or you can use the specific exception type to differentiate exceptions and handle exceptions in an exact fashion.

Summary

A program can use exceptions to indicate that an error occurred. To throw an exception, use the throw statement and provide it with an exception object—a descendant of Throwable—to provide information about the specific error that occurred. A method that throws an uncaught, checked exception must include a throws clause in its declaration.

A program can catch exceptions by using a combination of the try, catch, and finally blocks:

- The try block identifies a block of code in which an exception can occur.
- The catch block identifies a block of code, known as an exception handler, that can handle a particular type of exception.
- The finally block identifies a block of code that is guaranteed to execute, and is the right place to close files, recover resources, and otherwise clean up after the code enclosed in the try block.

The try statement should contain at least one catch block or a finally block and may have multiple catch blocks.

The class of the exception object indicates the type of exception thrown. The exception object can contain further information about the error, including an error message. With exception chaining, an exception can point to the exception that caused it, which can in turn point to the exception that caused *it*, and so on.

Questions and Exercises: Exceptions

Questions

1. Is the following code legal?

```
try {

} finally {

}
```

2. What exception types can be caught by the following handler?

```
catch (Exception e) {

}
```

What is wrong with using this type of exception handler?

3. Is there anything wrong with the following exception handler as written? Will this code compile?

```
try {

} catch (Exception e) {

} catch (ArithmeticException a) {

}
```

4. Match each situation in the lettered list with an item in the numbered list:

    a. `int[] A;`
    `A[0] = 0;`

    b. The JVM starts running your program, but the JVM can't find the Java platform classes. (The Java platform classes reside in `classes.zip` or `rt.jar`.)

    c. A program is reading a stream and reaches the `end of stream` marker.

    d. Before closing the stream and after reaching the `end of stream` marker, a program tries to read the stream again.

    1. __`error`
    2. __`checked exception`

3. __`compile error`
4. __`no exception`

Exercises

1. Add a `readList` method to `ListOfNumbers.java`. This method should read in `int` values from a file, print each value, and append them to the end of the vector. You should catch all appropriate errors. You will also need a text file containing numbers to read in.
2. Modify the following `cat` method so that it will compile:

```
public static void cat(File file) {
  RandomAccessFile input = null;
  String line = null;

  try {
      input = new RandomAccessFile(named, "r");
      while ((line = input.readLine()) != null) {
        System.out.println(line);
      }
      return;
  } finally {
      if (input != null) {
        input.close();
      }
  }
}
```

Answers

You can find answers to these Questions and Exercises at:

```
tutorial/essential/exceptions/QandE/answers.html
```

10

Basic I/O

THIS chapter covers the Java platform classes used for basic I/O. It focuses primarily on *I/O streams*, a powerful concept that greatly simplifies I/O operations. The chapter also looks at serialization, which lets a program write whole objects out to streams and read them back again. Then the chapter looks at some file system operations, including random access files. Finally, it touches briefly on the advanced features of the New I/O API. Most of the classes covered are in the `java.io` package.

Security Consideration: Some I/O operations are subject to approval by the current security manager. The example programs contained in these chapters are standalone applications, which by default have no security manager. To work in an applet, most of these examples would have to be modified. See the Security Restrictions section (page 578) for information about the security restrictions placed on applets.

I/O Streams

An *I/O stream* represents an input source or an output destination. A stream can represent many different kinds of sources and destinations, including disk files, devices, other programs, and memory arrays.

Streams support many different kinds of data, including simple bytes, primitive data types, localized characters, and objects. Some streams simply pass on data; others manipulate and transform the data in useful ways.

No matter how they work internally, all streams present the same simple model to programs that use them: A stream is a sequence of data. A program uses an *input stream* to read data from a source, one item at a time (Figure 10.1).

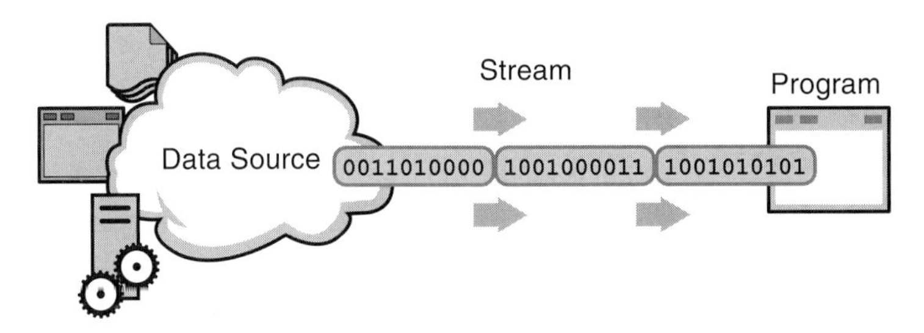

Figure 10.1 Reading information into a program.

A program uses an *output stream* to write data to a destination, one item at time (Figure 10.2).

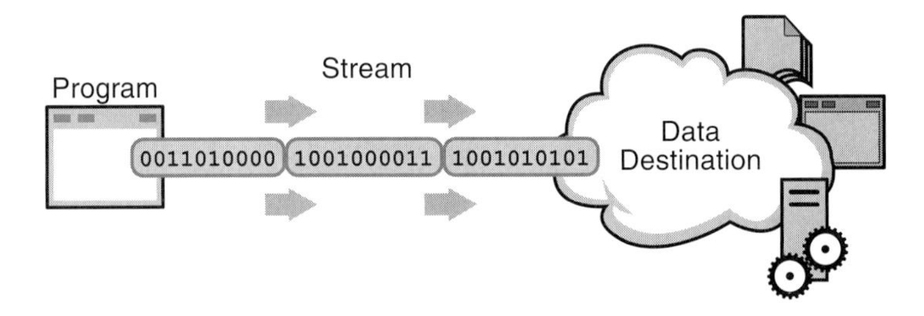

Figure 10.2 Writing information from a program.

In this chapter, we'll see streams that can handle all kinds of data, from primitive values to advanced objects.

The data source and data destination pictured in Figure 10.2 can be anything that holds, generates, or consumes data. Obviously this includes disk files, but a source or destination can also another program, a peripheral device, a network socket, or an array.

In the next section, we'll use the most basic kind of streams, byte streams, to demonstrate the common operations of stream I/O. For sample input, we'll use the example file, `xanadu.txt`,[1] which contains the following verse:

```
In Xanadu did Kubla Khan
A stately pleasure-dome decree:
Where Alph, the sacred river, ran
Through caverns measureless to man
Down to a sunless sea.
```

1. `tutorial/essential/io/examples/xanadu.txt`

Byte Streams

Programs use *byte streams* to perform input and output of 8-bit bytes. All byte stream classes are descended from `InputStream`[2] and `OutputStream`.[3]

There are many byte stream classes. To demonstrate how byte streams work, we'll focus on the file I/O byte streams, `FileInputStream`[4] and `FileOutputStream`[5]. Other kinds of byte streams are used in much the same way; they differ mainly in the way they are constructed.

Using Byte Streams

We'll explore `FileInputStream` and `FileOutputStream` by examining an example program named `CopyBytes`,[6] which uses byte streams to copy `xanadu.txt`:

```
import java.io.FileInputStream;
import java.io.FileOutputStream;
import java.io.IOException;

public class CopyBytes {

  public static void main(String[] args) throws IOException {
    FileInputStream in = null;
    FileOutputStream out = null;
    try {
        in = new FileInputStream("xanadu.txt");
        out = new FileOutputStream("outagain.txt");
        int c;
        while ((c = in.read()) != -1) {
          out.write(c);
        }
    } finally {
        if (in != null) {
          in.close();
        }
        if (out != null) {
          out.close();
        }
    }
  }
}
```

2. `docs/api/java/io/InputStream.html`
3. `docs/api/java/io/OutputStream.html`
4. `docs/api/java/io/FileInputStream.html`
5. `docs/api/java/io/FileOutputStream.html`
6. `tutorial/essential/io/examples/CopyBytes.java`

`CopyBytes` spends most of its time in a simple loop that reads the input stream and writes the output stream, one byte at a time, as shown in Figure 10.3.

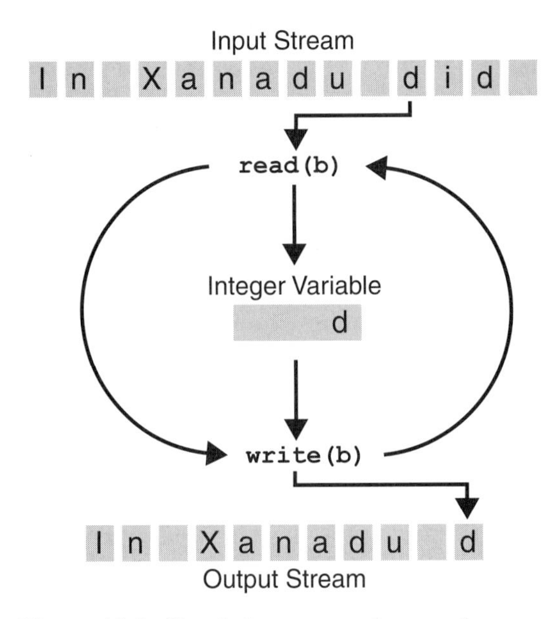

Figure 10.3 Simple byte stream input and output.

Notice that `read()` returns an `int` value. If the input is a stream of bytes, why doesn't `read()` return a `byte` value? Using an `int` as a return type allows `read()` to use `-1` to indicate that it has reached the end of the stream.

Always Close Streams

Closing a stream when it's no longer needed is very important—so important that `CopyBytes` uses a `finally` block to guarantee that both streams will be closed even if an error occurs. This practice helps avoid resource leaks.

One possible error is that `CopyBytes` was unable to open one or both files. When that happens, the stream variable corresponding to the file never changes from its initial `null` value. That's why `CopyBytes` makes sure that each stream variable contains an object reference before invoking `close`.

When Not to Use Byte Streams

`CopyBytes` seems like a normal program, but it actually represents a kind of low-level I/O that you should avoid. Since `xanadu.txt` contains character data, the best approach is to use character streams, as discussed in the next section. There are also streams for more complicated data types. Byte streams should only be used for the most primitive I/O.

So why talk about byte streams? Because all other stream types are built on byte streams.

Character Streams

The Java platform stores character values using Unicode conventions. Character stream I/O automatically translates this internal format to and from the local character set. In Western locales, the local character set is usually an 8-bit superset of ASCII.

For most applications, I/O with character streams is no more complicated than I/O with byte streams. Input and output done with stream classes automatically translates to and from the local character set. A program that uses character streams in place of byte streams automatically adapts to the local character set and is ready for internationalization—all without extra effort by the programmer.

If internationalization isn't a priority, you can simply use the character stream classes without paying much attention to character set issues. Later, if internationalization becomes a priority, your program can be adapted without extensive recoding. See the online lesson on internationalization.[7]

Using Character Streams

All character stream classes are descended from `Reader`[8] and `Writer`.[9] As with byte streams, there are character stream classes that specialize in file I/O: `FileReader`[10] and `FileWriter`.[11] The `CopyCharacters`[12] example illustrates these classes:

7. `docs/books/tutorial/i18n/index.html`
8. `docs/api/java/io/Reader.html`
9. `docs/api/java/io/Writer.html`
10. `docs/api/java/io/FileReader.html`
11. `docs/api/java/io/FileWriter.html`
12. `tutorial/essential/io/examples/CopyCharacters.java`

```
import java.io.FileReader;
import java.io.FileWriter;
import java.io.IOException;

public class CopyCharacters {

  public static void main(String[] args) throws IOException {

    FileReader inputStream = null;
    FileWriter outputStream = null;

    try {
        inputStream = new FileReader("xanadu.txt");
        outputStream = new FileWriter("characteroutput.txt");

        int c;
        while ((c = inputStream.read()) != -1) {
          outputStream.write(c);
        }
    } finally {
        if (inputStream != null) {
          inputStream.close();
        }
        if (outputStream != null) {
          outputStream.close();
        }
    }
  }

}
```

CopyCharacters is very similar to CopyBytes. The most important difference is that CopyCharacters uses FileReader and FileWriter for input and output in place of FileInputStream and FileOutputStream. Notice that both CopyBytes and CopyCharacters use an int variable to read to and write from. However, in CopyCharacters, the int variable holds a character value in its last 16 bits; in CopyBytes, the int variable holds a byte value in its last 8 bits.

Character Streams That Use Byte Streams

Character streams are often "wrappers" for byte streams. The character stream uses the byte stream to perform the physical I/O, while the character stream handles translation between characters and bytes. `FileReader`, for example, uses `FileInputStream`, while `FileWriter` uses `FileOutputStream`.

There are two general-purpose byte-to-character "bridge" streams: `InputStreamReader`[13] and `OutputStreamWriter`.[14] Use them to create character streams when there are no prepackaged character stream classes that meet your needs. For an example that creates character streams from network byte streams, refer to the online sockets lesson.[15]

Line-Oriented I/O

Character I/O usually occurs in bigger units than single characters. One common unit is the line: a string of characters with a line terminator at the end. A line terminator can be a carriage-return/line-feed sequence (`"\r\n"`), a single carriage-return (`"\r"`), or a single line-feed (`"\n"`). Supporting all possible line terminators allows programs to read text files created on any of the widely used operating systems.

Let's modify the `CopyCharacters` example to use line-oriented I/O. To do this, we have to use two classes we haven't seen before, `BufferedReader`[16] and `PrintWriter`.[17] We'll explore these classes in greater depth in the Buffered Streams (page 269) and the Formatting (page 272) sections. Right now, we're just interested in their support for line-oriented I/O.

The `CopyLines`[18] example invokes `BufferedReader.readLine` and `PrintWriter.println` to do input and output one line at a time:

---

13. `docs/api/java/io/InputStreamReader.html`
14. `docs/api/java/io/OutputStreamWriter.html`
15. `docs/books/tutorial/networking/sockets/readingWriting.html`
16. `docs/api/java/io/BufferedReader.html`
17. `docs/api/java/io/PrintWriter.html`
18. `tutorial/essential/io/examples/CopyLines.java`

```
import java.io.FileReader;
import java.io.FileWriter;
import java.io.BufferedReader;
import java.io.PrintWriter;
import java.io.IOException;

public class CopyLines {

  public static void main(String[] args) throws IOException {
    BufferedReader inputStream = null;
    PrintWriter outputStream = null;

    try {
        inputStream =
          new BufferedReader(new FileReader("xanadu.txt"));
        outputStream =
          new PrintWriter(new
                          FileWriter("characteroutput.txt"));
        String l;
        while ((l = inputStream.readLine()) != null) {
          outputStream.println(l);
        }
    } finally {
        if (inputStream != null) {
          inputStream.close();
        }
        if (outputStream != null) {
          outputStream.close();
        }
    }
  }

}
```

Invoking `readLine` returns a line of text with the line terminator removed. `CopyLines` outputs each line using `println`, which appends the line terminator for the current operating system. This might not be the same line terminator that was used in the input file.

There are many ways to structure text input and output beyond characters and lines. For more information, see the Scanning and Formatting section (page 270).

Buffered Streams

Most of the examples we've seen so far use *unbuffered* I/O. This means that each read or write request is handled directly by the underlying OS. This can make a program much less efficient, since each such request often triggers disk access, network activity, or some other operation that is relatively expensive.

To reduce this kind of overhead, the Java platform implements *buffered* I/O streams. Buffered input streams read data from a memory area known as a *buffer*; the native input API is called only when the buffer is empty. Similarly, buffered output streams write data to a buffer, and the native output API is called only when the buffer is full.

A program can convert an unbuffered stream into a buffered stream using the wrapping idiom we've used several times now, where the unbuffered stream object is passed to the constructor for a buffered stream class. Here's how you might modify the constructor invocations in the `CopyCharacters` example to use buffered I/O:

```
inputStream =
  new BufferedReader(new FileReader("xanadu.txt"));
outputStream =
  new BufferedWriter(new FileWriter("characteroutput.txt"));
```

There are four buffered stream classes used to wrap unbuffered streams: `BufferedInputStream`[19] and `BufferedOutputStream`[20] create buffered byte streams, while `BufferedReader` and `BufferedWriter`[21] create buffered character streams.

Flushing Buffered Streams

It often makes sense to write out a buffer at critical points, without waiting for it to fill. This is known as *flushing* the buffer.

Some buffered output classes support *autoflush*, specified by an optional constructor argument. When autoflush is enabled, certain key events cause the buffer to be flushed. For example, an autoflush `PrintWriter` object flushes the buffer on every invocation of `println` or `format`. See the Formatting section (page 272) for more on these methods.

To flush a stream manually, invoke its `flush` method. The `flush` method is valid on any output stream, but has no effect unless the stream is buffered.

---

19. `docs/api/java/io/BufferedInputStream.html`

20. `docs/api/java/io/BufferedOutputStream.html`

21. `docs/api/java/io/BufferedWriter.html`

Scanning and Formatting

Programming I/O often involves translating to and from the neatly formatted data humans like to work with. To assist you with these chores, the Java platform provides two APIs. The scanner API breaks input into individual tokens associated with bits of data. The formatting API assembles data into nicely formatted, human-readable form.

Scanning

Objects of type `Scanner`[22] are useful for breaking down formatted input into tokens and translating individual tokens according to their data types.

Breaking Input into Tokens

By default, a scanner uses white space to separate tokens. (White space characters include blanks, tabs, and line terminators. For the full list, refer to the documentation for `Character.isWhitespace`.[23]) To see how scanning works, let's look at `ScanXan`, a program that reads the individual words in `xanadu.txt` and prints them out, one per line:

```
import java.io.*;
import java.util.Scanner;

public class ScanXan {

  public static void main(String[] args) throws IOException {
    Scanner s = null;

    try {
      s = new Scanner(new BufferedReader(new
                      FileReader("xanadu.txt")));

      while (s.hasNext()) {
        System.out.println(s.next());
      }
    } finally {
        if (s != null) {
          s.close();
        }
    }
  }
}
```

22. `docs/api/java/util/Scanner.html`

23. `docs/api/java/lang/Character.html`

Notice that ScanXan invokes Scanner's close method when it is done with the scanner object. Even though a scanner is not a stream, you need to close it to indicate that you're done with its underlying stream.

The output of ScanXan looks like this:

```
In
Xanadu
did
Kubla
Khan
A
stately
pleasure-dome
...
```

To use a different token separator, invoke useDelimiter(), specifying a regular expression. For example, suppose you wanted the token separator to be a comma, optionally followed by white space. You would invoke:

```
s.useDelimiter(",\\s*");
```

Translating Individual Tokens

The ScanXan example treats all input tokens as simple String values. Scanner also supports tokens for all of the Java language's primitive types (except for char), as well as BigInteger and BigDecimal. Also, numeric values can use thousands separators. Thus, in a US locale, Scanner correctly reads the string "32,767" as representing an integer value.

We have to mention the locale, because thousands of separators and decimal symbols are locale specific. So, the following example would not work correctly in all locales if we didn't specify that the scanner should use the US locale. That's not something you usually have to worry about, because your input data usually comes from sources that use the same locale as you do. But this example is part of the Java Tutorial and gets distributed all over the world.

The ScanSum[24] example reads a list of double values and adds them up. Here's the source:

---

24. tutorial/essential/io/examples/ScanSum.java

```
import java.io.FileReader;
import java.io.BufferedReader;
import java.io.IOException;
import java.util.Scanner;
import java.util.Locale;

public class ScanSum {
  public static void main(String[] args) throws IOException {
    Scanner s = null;
    double sum = 0;
    try {
      s = new Scanner(new
            BufferedReader(new FileReader("usnumbers.txt")));
      s.useLocale(Locale.US);

      while (s.hasNext()) {
        if (s.hasNextDouble()) {
              sum += s.nextDouble();
          } else {
              s.next();
          }
      }
    } finally {
        s.close();
    }
    System.out.println(sum);
  }
}
```

And here's the sample input file, `usnumbers.txt`:[25]

```
8.5
32,767
3.14159
1,000,000.1
```

The output string is "`1032778.74159`". The period will be a different character in some locales, because `System.out` is a `PrintStream` object, and that class doesn't provide a way to override the default locale. We could override the locale for the whole program—or we could just use formatting, as described in the next section.

Formatting

Stream objects that implement formatting are instances of either `PrintWriter`, a character stream class, or `PrintStream`,[26] a byte stream class.

25. `tutorial/essential/io/examples/usnumbers.txt`

26. `docs/api/java/io/PrintStream.html`

Note: The only PrintStream objects you are likely to need are are System.out and System.err.[27] See the I/O from the Command Line section (page 276) for more on these objects. When you need to create a formatted output stream, instantiate PrintWriter, not PrintStream.

Like all byte and character stream objects, instances of PrintStream and PrintWriter implement a standard set of write methods for simple byte and character output. In addition, both PrintStream and PrintWriter implement the same set of methods for converting internal data into formatted output. Two levels of formatting are provided:

- print and println format individual values in a standard way.
- format formats almost any number of values based on a format string, with many options for precise formatting.

The print and println Methods

Invoking print or println outputs a single value after converting the value using the appropriate toString method. We can see this in the Root[28] example:

```
public class Root {
  public static void main(String[] args) {
    int i = 2;
    double r = Math.sqrt(i);

    System.out.print("The square root of ");
    System.out.print(i);
    System.out.print(" is ");
    System.out.print(r);
    System.out.println(".");

    i = 5;
    r = Math.sqrt(i);
    System.out.println("The square root of " +
                            i + " is " + r + ".");
  }
}
```

Here is the output of Root:

```
The square root of 2 is 1.4142135623730951.
The square root of 5 is 2.23606797749979.
```

---

27. docs/api/java/lang/System.html

28. tutorial/essential/io/examples/Root.java

The `i` and `r` variables are formatted twice: the first time using code in an overload of `print`, the second time by conversion code automatically generated by the Java compiler, which also utilizes `toString`. You can format any value this way, but you don't have much control over the results.

The format Method

The `format` method formats multiple arguments based on a *format string*. The format string consists of static text embedded with *format specifiers*; except for the format specifiers, the format string is output unchanged.

Format strings support many features. In this tutorial, we'll just cover some basics. For a complete description, see *Format String Syntax* in the API specification.[29]

The `Root2`[30] example formats two values with a single `format` invocation:

```
public class Root2 {
  public static void main(String[] args) {
    int i = 2;
    double r = Math.sqrt(i);

    System.out.format("The square root of %d is %f.%n", i, r);
  }
}
```

Here is the output:

```
The square root of 2 is 1.414214.
```

Like the three used in this example, all format specifiers begin with a `%` and end with a 1- or 2-character *conversion* that specifies the kind of formatted output being generated. The three conversions used here are:

- `d` formats an integer value as a decimal value.
- `f` formats a floating point value as a decimal value.
- `n` outputs a platform-specific line terminator.

Here are some other conversions:

- `x` formats an integer as a hexadecimal value.
- `s` formats any value as a string.
- `tB` formats an integer as a locale-specific month name.

---

29. `docs/api/java/util/Formatter.html`

30. `tutorial/essential/io/examples/Root2.java`

There are many other conversions.

Note: Except for %% and %n, all format specifiers must match an argument. If they don't, an exception is thrown.

In the Java programming language, the \n escape always generates the linefeed character (\u000A). Don't use \n unless you specifically want a linefeed character. To get the correct line separator for the local platform, use %n.

In addition to the conversion, a format specifier can contain several additional elements that further customize the formatted output. Here's an example, Format,[31] that uses every possible kind of element:

```
public class Format {
  public static void main(String[] args) {
    System.out.format("%f, %1$+020.10f %n", Math.PI);
  }
}
```

Here's the output:

```
3.141593, +00000003.1415926536
```

The additional elements are all optional.

Figure 10.4 shows how the longer specifier breaks down into elements.

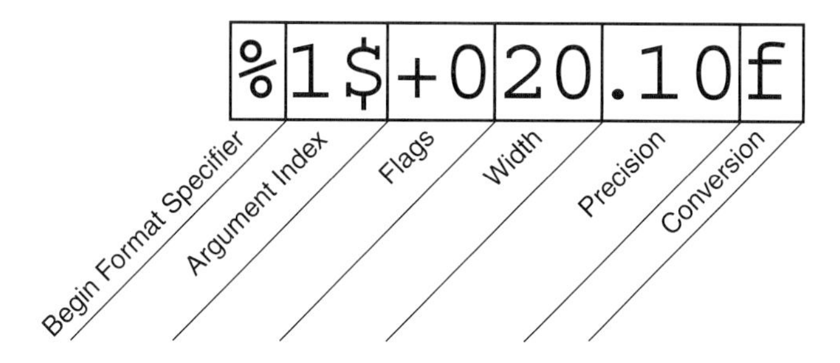

Figure 10.4 Elements of a format specifier.

31. tutorial/essential/io/examples/Format.java

The elements must appear in the order shown. Working from the right, the optional elements are:

Precision For floating point values, this is the mathematical precision of the formatted value. For `s` and other general conversions, this is the maximum width of the formatted value; the value is right-truncated if necessary.

Width The minimum width of the formatted value; the value is padded if necessary. By default the value is left-padded with blanks.

Flags Specify additional formatting options. In the `Format` example, the `+` flag specifies that the number should always be formatted with a sign, and the `0` flag specifies that `0` is the padding character. Other flags include `-` (pad on the right) and `,` (format number with locale-specific thousands separators). Note that some flags cannot be used with certain other flags or with certain conversions.

Argument Index Allows you to explicitly match a designated argument. You can also specify `<` to match the same argument as the previous specifier. Thus the example could have said:

```
System.out.format("%f, %<+020.10f %n", Math.PI);
```

I/O from the Command Line

A program is often run from the command line and interacts with the user in the command-line environment. The Java platform supports this kind of interaction in two ways: through the Standard Streams and through the Console.

Standard Streams

Standard Streams are a feature of many operating systems. By default, they read input from the keyboard and write output to the display. They also support I/O on files and between programs, but that feature is controlled by the command line interpreter, not the program.

The Java platform supports three Standard Streams: *Standard Input*, accessed through `System.in`; *Standard Output*, accessed through `System.out`; and *Standard Error*, accessed through `System.err`. These objects are defined automatically and do not need to be opened. Standard Output and Standard Error are both for output; having error output separately allows the user to divert regular output to a file and still be able to read error messages. For more information, refer to the documentation for your command-line interpreter.

You might expect the Standard Streams to be character streams, but, for historical reasons, they are byte streams. `System.out` and `System.err` are defined as `PrintStream` objects. Although it is technically a byte stream, `PrintStream` uses an internal character stream object to emulate many of the features of character streams.

By contrast, `System.in` is a byte stream with no character stream features. To use Standard Input as a character stream, wrap `System.in` in `InputStreamReader`:

```
InputStreamReader cin = new InputStreamReader(System.in);
```

The Console

A more advanced alternative to the Standard Streams is the Console. This is a single, predefined object of type `Console`[32] that has most of the features provided by the Standard Streams, and others besides. The Console is particularly useful for secure password entry. The Console object also provides input and output streams that are true character streams, through its `reader` and `writer` methods.

Before a program can use the Console, it must attempt to retrieve the Console object by invoking `System.console()`. If the Console object is available, this method returns it. If `System.console` returns `NULL`, then Console operations are not permitted, either because the OS doesn't support them or because the program was launched in a noninteractive environment.

`readPassword` The Console object supports secure password entry through its `readPassword` method. This method helps secure password entry in two ways. First, it suppresses echoing, so the password is not visible on the user's screen. Second, `readPassword` returns a character array, not a `String`, so the password can be overwritten, removing it from memory as soon as it is no longer needed.

The `Password`[33] example is a prototype program for changing a user's password. It demonstrates several `Console` methods:

32. `docs/api/java/io/Console.html`

33. `tutorial/essential/io/examples/Password.java`

```
import java.io.Console;
import java.util.Arrays;
import java.io.IOException;

public class Password {

  public static void main (String args[]) throws IOException {

    Console c = System.console();
    if (c == null) {
      System.err.println("No console.");
      System.exit(1);
    }

    String login = c.readLine("Enter your login: ");
    char [] oldPassword = c.readPassword("Enter your " +
                                          old password: ");

    if (verify(login, oldPassword)) {
      boolean noMatch;
      do {
        char [] newPassword1 =
            c.readPassword("Enter your new password: ");
        char [] newPassword2 =
            c.readPassword("Enter new password again: ");
        noMatch = ! Arrays.equals(newPassword1, newPassword2);
        if (noMatch) {
            c.format("Passwords don't match. Try again.%n");
        } else {
            change(login, newPassword1);
            c.format("Password for %s changed.%n", login);
        }
        Arrays.fill(newPassword1, ' ');
        Arrays.fill(newPassword2, ' ');
      } while (noMatch);
    }

    Arrays.fill(oldPassword, ' ');

  }

  // Dummy verify method.
  static boolean verify(String login, char[] password) {
    return true;
  }

  // Dummy change method.
  static void change(String login, char[] password) {}
}
```

`Password` follows these steps:

1. Attempt to retrieve the Console object. If the object is not available, abort.
2. Invoke `Console.readLine` to prompt for and read the user's login name.
3. Invoke `Console.readPassword` to prompt for and read the user's existing password.
4. Invoke `verify` to confirm that the user is authorized to change the password. (In this example, `verify` is a dummy method that always returns `true`.)
5. Repeat the following steps until the user enters the same password twice:
   a. Invoke `Console.readPassword` twice to prompt for and read a new password.
   b. If the user entered the same password both times, invoke `change` to change it. (Again, `change` is a dummy method.)
   c. Overwrite both passwords with blanks.
6. Overwrite the old password with blanks.

Data Streams

Data streams support binary I/O of primitive data type values (`boolean`, `char`, `byte`, `short`, `int`, `long`, `float`, and `double`) as well as `String` values. All data streams implement either the `DataInput`[34] or the `DataOutput`[35] interface. This section focuses on the most widely-used implementations of these interfaces, `DataInputStream`[36] and `DataOutputStream`.[37]

The following example demonstrates data streams by writing out a set of data records, and then reading them in again. Each record consists of three values related to an item on an invoice, as shown in Table 10.1.

34. `docs/api/java/io/DataInput.html`
35. `docs/api/java/io/DataOutput.html`
36. `docs/api/java/io/DataInputStream.html`
37. `docs/api/java/io/DataOutputStream.html`

Table 10.1 Fields in `DataStreams` Example

Order in Record	Data Type	Data Description	Output Method	Input Method	Sample Value
1	`double`	Item price	`DataOutputStream.writeDouble`	`DataInputStream.readDouble`	`19.99`
2	`int`	Unit count	`DataOutputStream.writeInt`	`DataInputStream.readInt`	`12`
3	`String`	Item description	`DataOutputStream.writeUTF`	`DataInputStream.readUTF`	`"Java T-Shirt"`

The example is a long one, so we'll present it in segments, separated by commentary. The program starts by defining some constants containing the name of the data file and the data that will be written to it:

```
public class DataStreams {
  static final String dataFile = "invoicedata";

  static final double[] prices =
    { 19.99, 9.99, 15.99, 3.99, 4.99 };
  static final int[] units = { 12, 8, 13, 29, 50 };
  static final String[] descs = { "Java T-shirt",
                                  "Java Mug",
                                  "Duke Juggling Dolls",
                                  "Java Pin",
                                  "Java Key Chain" };
```

Then `DataStreams` opens an output stream. Since a `DataOutputStream` can only be created as a wrapper for an existing byte stream object, `DataStreams` provides a buffered file output byte stream:

```
  public static void main(String[] args) throws IOException {
    DataOutputStream out = null;

    try {
      out = new DataOutputStream(new
        BufferedOutputStream(new FileOutputStream(dataFile)));
```

`DataStreams` writes out the records and closes the output stream:

```
        for (int i = 0; i < prices.length; i ++) {
          out.writeDouble(prices[i]);
          out.writeInt(units[i]);
          out.writeUTF(descs[i]);
        }
      } finally {
          out.close();
      }
```

The `writeUTF` method writes out `String` values in a modified form of UTF-8. This is a variable-width character encoding that only needs a single byte for common Western characters.

Now `DataStreams` reads the data back in again. First it must provide an input stream and variables to hold the input data. Like `DataOutputStream`, `DataInputStream` must be constructed as a wrapper for a byte stream:

```
      DataInputStream in = null;
      double total = 0.0;
      try {
        in = new DataInputStream(new
          BufferedInputStream(new FileInputStream(dataFile)));

        double price;
        int unit;
        String desc;
```

Now `DataStreams` can read each record in the stream, reporting on the data it encounters:

```
        try {
          while (true) {
            price = in.readDouble();
            unit = in.readInt();
            desc = in.readUTF();
            System.out.format("You ordered %d units of %s " +
                              "at $%.2f%n", unit, desc, price);
            total += unit * price;
          }
        } catch (EOFException e) { }
        System.out.format("For a TOTAL of: $%.2f%n", total);
      }
      finally {
        in.close();
      }
    }
  }
```

Notice that `DataStreams` detects an end-of-file condition by catching `EOFException`,[38] instead of testing for an invalid return value. All implementations of `DataInput` methods use `EOFException` instead of return values.

Also notice that each specialized `write` in `DataStreams` is exactly matched by the corresponding specialized `read`. It is up to the programmer to make sure that output types and input types are matched in this way: The input stream consists of simple binary data, with nothing to indicate the type of individual values or where they begin in the stream.

`DataStreams` uses one very bad programming technique: It uses floating point numbers to represent monetary values. In general, floating point is bad for precise values. It's particularly bad for decimal fractions, because common values (such as `0.1`) do not have a binary representation.

The correct type to use for currency values is `java.math.BigDecimal`.[39] Unfortunately, `BigDecimal` is an object type, so it won't work with data streams. However, `BigDecimal` *will* work with object streams, which are covered in the next section.

Object Streams

Just as data streams support I/O of primitive data types, object streams support I/O of objects. Most, but not all, standard classes support serialization of their objects. Those that do implement the marker interface `Serializable`.[40]

The object stream classes are `ObjectInputStream`[41] and `ObjectOutputStream`.[42] These classes implement `ObjectInput`[43] and `ObjectOutput`,[44] which are subinterfaces of `DataInput` and `DataOutput`. That means that all the primitive data I/O methods covered in the Data Streams section (page 279) are also implemented in object streams. So an object stream can contain a mixture of primitive and object values. The `ObjectStreams`[45] example illustrates this:

---

38. `docs/api/java/io/EOFException.html`
39. `docs/api/java/math/BigDecimal.html`
40. `docs/api/java/io/Serializable.html`
41. `docs/api/java/io/ObjectInputStream.html`
42. `docs/api/java/io/ObjectOutputStream.html`
43. `docs/api/java/io/ObjectInput.html`
44. `docs/api/java/io/ObjectOutput.html`
45. `tutorial/essential/io/examples/ObjectStreams.java`

```
import java.io.*;
import java.math.BigDecimal;
import java.util.Calendar;

public class ObjectStreams {

  static final String dataFile = "invoicedata";

  static final BigDecimal[] prices = {
    new BigDecimal("19.99"),
    new BigDecimal("9.99"),
    new BigDecimal("15.99"),
    new BigDecimal("3.99"),
    new BigDecimal("4.99") };

  static final int[] units = { 12, 8, 13, 29, 50 };

  static final String[] descs = {
    "Java T-shirt",
    "Java Mug",
    "Duke Juggling Dolls",
    "Java Pin",
    "Java Key Chain" };

  public static void main(String[] args)
    throws IOException, ClassNotFoundException {

    ObjectOutputStream out = null;
    try {
      out = new ObjectOutputStream(new
        BufferedOutputStream(new FileOutputStream(dataFile)));

      out.writeObject(Calendar.getInstance());
      for (int i = 0; i < prices.length; i ++) {
        out.writeObject(prices[i]);
        out.writeInt(units[i]);
        out.writeUTF(descs[i]);
      }
    } finally {
      out.close();
    }

    ObjectInputStream in = null;
    try {
      in = new ObjectInputStream(new
        BufferedInputStream(new FileInputStream(dataFile)));

      Calendar date = null;
      BigDecimal price;
      int unit;
      String desc;
```

```
            BigDecimal total = new BigDecimal(0);

            date = (Calendar) in.readObject();

            System.out.format ("On %tA, %<tB %<te, %<tY:%n", date);

            try {
                while (true) {
                    price = (BigDecimal) in.readObject();
                    unit = in.readInt();
                    desc = in.readUTF();
                    System.out.format("You ordered %d units of %s " +
                                      "at $%.2f%n", unit, desc, price);
                    total = total.add(price.multiply(new
                                                BigDecimal(unit)));
                }
            } catch (EOFException e) {}
            System.out.format("For a TOTAL of: $%.2f%n", total);
        } finally {
            in.close();
        }
    }
}
```

ObjectStreams creates the same application as DataStreams, with a couple of changes. First, prices are now BigDecimal objects. Second, a Calendar[46] object is written to the data file, indicating an invoice date.

If readObject() doesn't return the object type expected, attempting to cast it to the correct type may throw a ClassNotFoundException.[47] In this simple example, that can't happen, so we don't try to catch the exception. Instead, we notify the compiler that we're aware of the issue by adding ClassNotFoundException to the main method's throws clause.

Output and Input of Complex Objects

The writeObject and readObject methods are simple to use, but they contain some very sophisticated object management logic. This isn't important for a class like Calendar, which just encapsulates primitive values. But many objects contain references to other objects. If readObject is to reconstitute an object from a stream, it has to be able to reconstitute all of the objects the original object referred to. These additional objects might have their own references, and so on. In this situation, writeObject traverses the entire web of object references and writes all objects in that web onto the

46. docs/api/java/util/Calendar.html

47. docs/api/java/lang/ClassNotFoundException.html

stream. Thus a single invocation of writeObject can cause a large number of objects to be written to the stream.

This is demonstrated in Figure 10.5, where writeObject is invoked to write a single object named **a**. This object contains references to objects **b** and **c**, while **b** contains references to **d** and **e**. Invoking writeObject(a) writes not just **a**, but all the objects necessary to reconstitute **a**, so the other four objects in this web are written as well. When **a** is read back by readObject, the other four objects are read back also, and all the original object references are preserved.

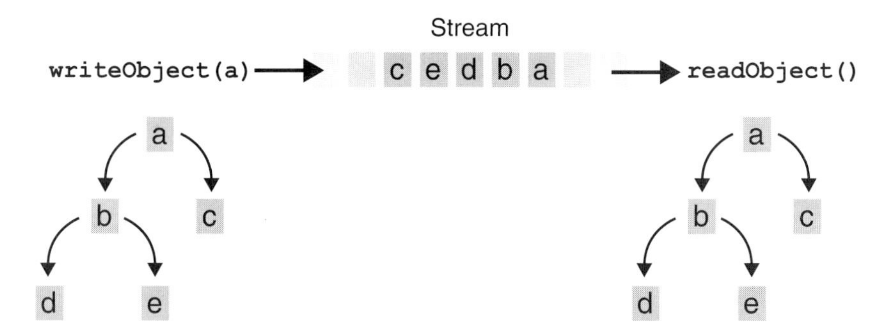

Figure 10.5 I/O of multiple referred-to objects.

You might wonder what happens if two objects on the same stream both contain references to a single object. Will they both refer to a single object when they're read back? The answer is "yes." A stream can only contain one copy of an object, though it can contain any number of references to it. Thus if you explicitly write an object to a stream twice, you're really writing only the reference twice. For example, if the following code writes an object ob twice to a stream:

```
Object ob = new Object();
out.writeObject(ob);
out.writeObject(ob);
```

each writeObject has to be matched by a readObject, so the code that reads the stream back will look something like this:

```
Object ob1 = in.readObject();
Object ob2 = in.readObject();
```

This results in two variables, ob1 and ob2, that are references to a single object.

However, if a single object is written to two different streams, it is effectively duplicated—a single program reading both streams back will see two distinct objects.

File I/O

So far, this chapter has focused on streams, which provide a simple model for reading and writing data. Streams work with a large variety of data sources and destinations, including disk files. However, streams don't support all the operations that are common with disk files. In this part of the chapter, we'll focus on non-stream file I/O. There are two topics:

- `File` is a class that helps you write platform-independent code that examines and manipulates files and directories.
- Random access files support nonsequential access to disk file data.

File Objects

The `File`[48] class makes it easier to write platform-independent code that examines and manipulates files. The name of this class is misleading: `File` instances represent file names, not files. The file corresponding to the file name might not even exist.

Why create a `File` object for a file that doesn't exist? A program can use the object to parse a file name. Also, the file can be created by passing the `File` object to the constructor of some classes, such as `FileWriter`.

If the file *does* exist, a program can examine its attributes and perform various operations on the file, such as renaming it, deleting it, or changing its permissions.

A File Has Many Names

A `File` object contains the file name string used to construct it. That string never changes throughout the lifetime of the object. A program can use the `File` object to obtain other versions of the file name, some of which may or may not be the same as the original file name string passed to the constructor.

Suppose a program creates a `File` object with the constructor invocation:

```
File a = new File("xanadu.txt");
```

The program invokes a number of methods to obtain different versions of the file name. The program is then run both on a Microsoft Windows system (in directory `c:\java\examples`) and a Solaris system (in directory `/home/cafe/java/examples`). Table 10.2 shows what the methods would return.

48. `docs/api/java/io/File.html`

Table 10.2 File Method Examples

Method Invoked	**Returns on Microsoft Windows**	**Returns on Solaris**
`a.toString()`	`xanadu.txt`	`xanadu.txt`
`a.getName()`	`xanadu.txt`	`xanadu.txt`
`a.getParent()`	`NULL`	`NULL`
`a.getAbsolutePath()`	`c:\java\examples\xanadu.txt`	`/home/cafe/java/examples/xanadu.txt`
`a.getCanonicalPath()`	`c:\java\examples\xanadu.txt`	`/home/cafe/java/examples/xanadu.txt`

Then the same program constructs a `File` object from a more complicated file name, using `File.separator` to specify the file name in a platform-independent way:

```
File b = new File(".." + File.separator + "examples" +
                         File.separator + "xanadu.txt");
```

Although `b` refers to the same file as `a`, the methods return slightly different values, as shown in Table 10.3.

Table 10.3 More File Method Examples

Method Invoked	**Returns on Microsoft Windows**	**Returns on Solaris**
`b.toString()`	`..\examples\xanadu.txt`	`../examples/xanadu.txt`
`b.getName()`	`xanadu.txt`	`xanadu.txt`
`b.getParent()`	`..\examples`	`../examples`
`b.getAbsolutePath()`	`c:\java\examples\..\examples\xanadu.txt`	`/home/cafe/java/examples/../examples/xanadu.txt`
`b.getCanonicalPath()`	`c:\java\examples\xanadu.txt`	`/home/cafe/java/examples/xanadu.txt`

Running the same program on a Linux system would give results similar to those on the Solaris system.

It's worth mentioning that `File.compareTo()` would not consider `a` and `b` to be the same. Even though they refer to the same file, the names used to construct them are different.

The FileStuff[49] example creates File objects from names passed from the command line and exercises various information methods on them. You'll find it instructive to run FileStuff on a variety of file names. Be sure to include directory names as well as the names of files that don't actually exist. Try passing FileStuff a variety of relative and absolute path names:

```
import java.io.File;
import java.io.IOException;
import static java.lang.System.out;

public class FileStuff {

  public static void main(String args[]) throws IOException {

    out.print("File system roots: ");
    for (File root : File.listRoots()) {
      out.format("%s ", root);
    }
    out.println();

    for (String fileName : args) {
      out.format("%n------%nnew File(%s)%n", fileName);
      File f = new File(fileName);
      out.format("toString(): %s%n", f);
      out.format("exists(): %b%n", f.exists());
      out.format("lastModified(): %tc%n", f.lastModified());
      out.format("isFile(): %b%n", f.isFile());
      out.format("isDirectory(): %b%n", f.isDirectory());
      out.format("isHidden(): %b%n", f.isHidden());
      out.format("canRead(): %b%n", f.canRead());
      out.format("canWrite(): %b%n", f.canWrite());
      out.format("canExecute(): %b%n", f.canExecute());
      out.format("isAbsolute(): %b%n", f.isAbsolute());
      out.format("length(): %d%n", f.length());
      out.format("getName(): %s%n", f.getName());
      out.format("getPath(): %s%n", f.getPath());
      out.format("getAbsolutePath(): %s%n",
                                f.getAbsolutePath());
      out.format("getCanonicalPath(): %s%n",
                               f.getCanonicalPath());
      out.format("getParent(): %s%n", f.getParent());
      out.format("toURI: %s%n", f.toURI());
    }
  }
}
```

49. tutorial/essential/io/examples/FileStuff.java

Manipulating Files

If a `File` object names an actual file, a program can use it to perform a number of useful operations on the file. These include passing the object to the constructor for a stream to open the file for reading or writing.

The `delete` method deletes the file immediately, while the `deleteOnExit` method deletes the file when the virtual machine terminates.

The `setLastModified` sets the modification date/time for the file. For example, to set the modification time of `xanadu.txt` to the current time, a program could do:

```
new File("xanadu.txt").setLastModified(new Date().getTime());
```

The `renameTo()` method renames the file. Note that the file name string behind the `File` object remains unchanged, so the `File` object will not refer to the renamed file.

Working with Directories

`File` has some useful methods for working with directories.

The `mkdir` method creates a directory. The `mkdirs` method does the same thing, after first creating any parent directories that don't yet exist.

The `list` and `listFiles` methods list the contents of a directory. The `list` method returns an array of `String` file names, while `listFiles` returns an array of `File` objects.

Static Methods

`File` contains some useful static methods.

The `createTempFile` method creates a new file with an unique name and returns a `File` object referring to it.

The `listRoots` returns a list of file system root names. On Microsoft Windows, this will be the root directories of mounted drives, such as `a:\` and `c:\`. On UNIX and Linux systems, this will be the root directory, `/`.

Random Access Files

Random access files permit nonsequential, or random, access to a file's contents.

Consider the archive format known as ZIP. A ZIP archive contains files and is typically compressed to save space. It also contain a directory entry at the end that indicates where the various files contained within the ZIP archive begin, as shown in Figure 10.6.

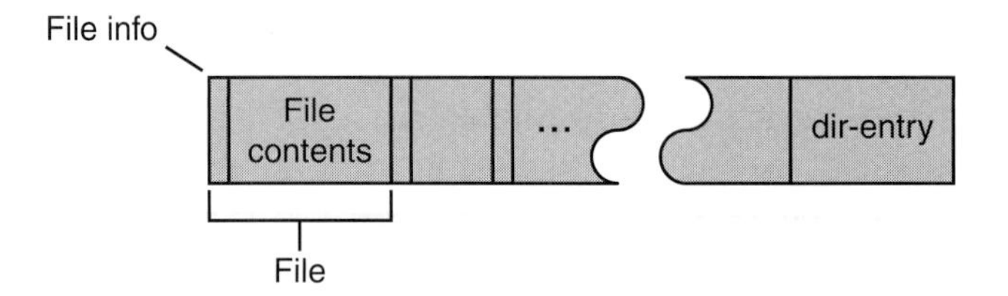

Figure 10.6 A ZIP archive.

Suppose that you want to extract a specific file from a ZIP archive. If you use a sequential access stream, you have to:

1. Open the ZIP archive.
2. Search through the ZIP archive until you locate the file you want to extract.
3. Extract the file.
4. Close the ZIP archive.

Using this procedure, on average, you'd have to read half the ZIP archive before finding the file that you want to extract. You can extract the same file from the ZIP archive more efficiently by using the seek feature of a random access file and following these steps:

1. Open the ZIP archive.
2. Seek to the directory entry and locate the entry for the file you want to extract from the ZIP archive.
3. Seek (backward) within the ZIP archive to the position of the file to extract.
4. Extract the file.
5. Close the ZIP archive.

This algorithm is more efficient because you read only the directory entry and the file that you want to extract.

The `java.io.RandomAccessFile`[50] class implements both the `DataInput` and `DataOutput` interfaces and therefore can be used for both reading and writing. `RandomAccessFile` is similar to `FileInputStream` and `FileOutputStream` in that you specify a file on the native file system to open when you create it. When you create a `RandomAccessFile`, you must indicate whether you will be just reading the file or writing to it also. (You have to be able to read a file in order to write it.) The following code creates a `RandomAccessFile` to read the file named `farrago.txt`:

```
new RandomAccessFile("xanadu.txt", "r");
```

50. `docs/api/java/io/RandomAccessFile.html`

And this one opens the same file for both reading and writing:

```
new RandomAccessFile("xanadu.txt", "rw");
```

After the file has been opened, you can use the common `read` or `write` methods defined in the `DataInput` and `DataOutput` interfaces to perform I/O on the file.

`RandomAccessFile` supports the notion of a *file pointer* (Figure 10.7). The file pointer indicates the current location in the file. When the file is first created, the file pointer is set to 0, indicating the beginning of the file. Calls to the `read` and `write` methods adjust the file pointer by the number of bytes read or written.

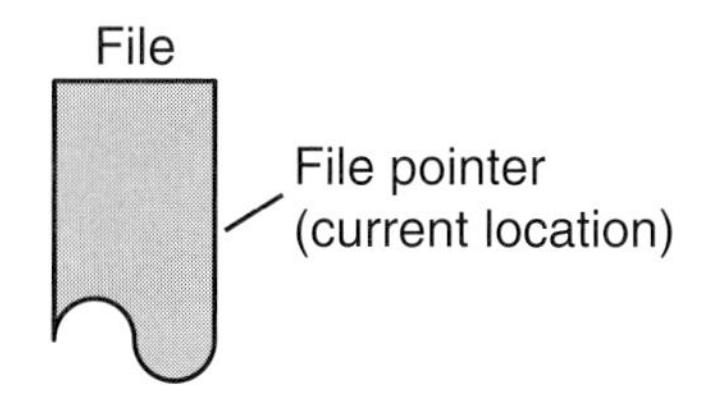

Figure 10.7 A ZIP file has the notion of a current file pointer.

In addition to the normal file I/O methods that implicitly move the file pointer when the operation occurs, `RandomAccessFile` contains three methods for explicitly manipulating the file pointer.

`int skipBytes(int)` Moves the file pointer forward the specified number of bytes.

`void seek(long)` Positions the file pointer just before the specified byte.

`long getFilePointer()` Returns the current byte location of the file pointer.

The New I/O Packages

This chapter has mostly talked about the `java.io` package. This package provides all the I/O features most programmers will ever need. The package implements basic I/O services—data streams, random access files, character translation, and buffering—with a simple and easy-to-use API.

However, some programmers of high-performance applications will need more flexibility than the `java.io` package supplies. They'll find it in the `java.nio.*` packages. These packages provide APIs for scalable I/O, fast buffered byte and character I/O, and character set conversion.

Summary

The `java.io` package contains many classes that your programs can use to read and write data. Most of the classes implement sequential access streams. The sequential access streams can be divided into two groups: those that read and write bytes, and those that read and write Unicode characters. Each sequential access stream has a speciality, such as reading from or writing to a file, filtering data as it's read or written, or serializing an object.

One class, `RandomAccessFile`, implements random input/output access to a file. An object of this type maintains a file pointer, which indicates the current location from which data will be read or to which data will be written.

Questions and Exercises: Basic I/O

Questions

1. What class would you use to read a few pieces of data that are at known positions near the end of a large file?
2. In a `format` call, what's the best way to indicate a new line?
3. How would you append data to the end of a file? Show the constructor for the class you would use and explain your answer.

Exercises

1. Implement a pair of classes, one `Reader` and one `Writer`, that count the number of times a particular character, such as `e`, is read or written. The character can be specified when the stream is created. Write a program to test your classes. You can use `xanadu.txt` as the input file.
2. The file `datafile`[51] begins with a single `long` that tells you the offset of a single `int` piece of data within the same file. Using the `RandomAccessFile` class, write a program that gets the `int` piece of data. What is the `int` data?

Answers

You can find answers to these Questions and Exercises at:

```
tutorial/essential/io/QandE/answers.html
```

51. `tutorial/essential/io/QandE/datafile`

11

Collections

THIS chapter describes the Java Collections Framework. Here you will learn what collections are and how they can make your job easier and programs better. You'll learn about the core elements—interfaces, implementations, and algorithms—that comprise the Java Collections Framework.

Introduction to Collections

A *collection*—sometimes called a container—is simply an object that groups multiple elements into a single unit. Collections are used to store, retrieve, manipulate, and communicate aggregate data. Typically, they represent data items that form a natural group, such as a poker hand (a collection of cards), a mail folder (a collection of letters), or a telephone directory (a mapping of names to phone numbers).

If you've used the Java programming language—or just about any other programming language—you're already familiar with collections. Collection implementations in earlier (pre-1.2) versions of the Java platform included `Vector`,[1] `Hashtable`,[2] and array.[3] However, those earlier versions did not contain a collections framework.

1. `docs/api/java/util/Vector.html`
2. `docs/api/java/util/Hashtable.html`
3. See the Arrays section (page 49).

What Is a Collections Framework?

A *collections framework* is a unified architecture for representing and manipulating collections. All collections frameworks contain the following:

Interfaces These are abstract data types that represent collections. Interfaces allow collections to be manipulated independently of the details of their representation. In object-oriented languages, interfaces generally form a hierarchy.

Implementations These are the concrete implementations of the collection interfaces. In essence, they are reusable data structures.

Algorithms These are the methods that perform useful computations, such as searching and sorting, on objects that implement collection interfaces. The algorithms are said to be *polymorphic*: that is, the same method can be used on many different implementations of the appropriate collection interface. In essence, algorithms are reusable functionality.

Apart from the Java Collections Framework, the best-known examples of collections frameworks are the C++ Standard Template Library (STL) and Smalltalk's collection hierarchy. Historically, collections frameworks have been quite complex, which gave them a reputation for having a steep learning curve. We believe that the Java Collections Framework breaks with this tradition, as you will learn for yourself in this chapter.

Benefits of the Java Collections Framework

Reduces Programming Effort

By providing useful data structures and algorithms, the Collections Framework frees you to concentrate on the important parts of your program rather than on the low-level "plumbing" required to make it work. By facilitating interoperability among unrelated APIs, the Java Collections Framework frees you from writing adapter objects or conversion code to connect APIs.

Increases Program Speed and Quality

This Collections Framework provides high-performance, high-quality implementations of useful data structures and algorithms. The various implementations of each interface are interchangeable, so programs can be easily tuned by switching collection implementations. Because you're freed from the drudgery of writing your own data structures, you'll have more time to devote to improving programs' quality and performance.

Allows Interoperability among Unrelated APIs

The collection interfaces are the vernacular by which APIs pass collections back and forth. If my network administration API furnishes a collection of node names and if your GUI toolkit expects a collection of column headings, our APIs will interoperate seamlessly, even though they were written independently.

Reduces Effort to Learn and to Use New APIs

Many APIs naturally take collections on input and furnish them as output. In the past, each such API had a small sub-API devoted to manipulating its collections. There was little consistency among these ad hoc collections sub-APIs, so you had to learn each one from scratch, and it was easy to make mistakes when using them. With the advent of standard collection interfaces, the problem went away.

Reduces Effort to Design New APIs

This is the flip side of the previous advantage. Designers and implementers don't have to reinvent the wheel each time they create an API that relies on collections; instead, they can use standard collection interfaces.

Fosters Software Reuse

New data structures that conform to the standard collection interfaces are by nature reusable. The same goes for new algorithms that operate on objects that implement these interfaces.

Interfaces

The *core collection interfaces* encapsulate different types of collections, which are shown in Figure 11.1. These interfaces allow collections to be manipulated independently of the details of their representation. Core collection interfaces are the foundation of the Java Collections Framework. As you can see in Figure 11.1, the core collection interfaces form a hierarchy.

A `Set` is a special kind of `Collection`, a `SortedSet` is a special kind of `Set`, and so forth. Note also that the hierarchy consists of two distinct trees—a `Map` is not a true `Collection`.

Note that all the core collection interfaces are generic. For example, this is the declaration of the `Collection` interface:

```
public interface Collection<E>...
```

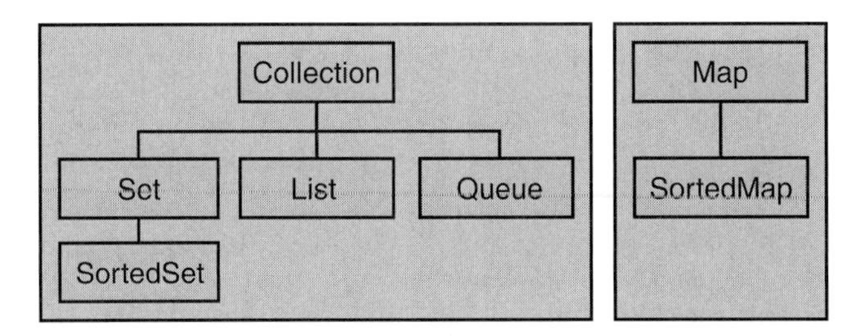

Figure 11.1 The core collection interfaces.

The `<E>` syntax tells you that the interface is generic. When you declare a `Collection` instance, you can *and should* specify the type of object contained in the collection. Specifying the type allows the compiler to verify (at compile time) that the type of object you put into the collection is correct, thus reducing errors at runtime. For information on generic types, see Chapter 6.

When you understand how to use these interfaces, you will know most of what there is to know about the Java Collections Framework. This section discusses general guidelines for effective use of the interfaces, including when to use which interface. You'll also learn programming idioms for each interface to help you get the most out of it.

To keep the number of core collection interfaces manageable, the Java platform doesn't provide separate interfaces for each variant of each collection type. (Such variants might include immutable, fixed-size, and append-only.) Instead, the modification operations in each interface are designated *optional*—a given implementation may elect not to support all operations. If an unsupported operation is invoked, a collection throws an `UnsupportedOperationException`.[4] Implementations are responsible for documenting which of the optional operations they support. All of the Java platform's general-purpose implementations support all of the optional operations.

The following list describes the core collection interfaces:

`Collection` The root of the collection hierarchy. A collection represents a group of objects known as its *elements*. The `Collection` interface is the least common denominator that all collections implement and is used to pass collections around and to manipulate them when maximum generality is desired. Some types of collections allow duplicate elements, and others do not. Some are ordered and others are unordered. The Java platform doesn't provide any direct implementations of this interface but provides implementations of more specific subinterfaces, such as `Set` and `List`. Also see The `Collection` Interface section (page 298).

4. `docs/api/java/lang/UnsupportedOperationException.html`

Set A collection that cannot contain duplicate elements. This interface models the mathematical set abstraction and is used to represent sets, such as the cards comprising a poker hand, the courses making up a student's schedule, or the processes running on a machine. See also The `Set` Interface section (page 301).

List s An ordered collection (sometimes called a *sequence*). `Lists` can contain duplicate elements. The user of a `List` generally has precise control over where in the list each element is inserted and can access elements by their integer index (position). If you've used `Vector`, you're familiar with the general flavor of `List`. Also see The `List` Interface section (page 306).

Queue A collection used to hold multiple elements prior to processing. Besides basic `Collection` operations, a `Queue` provides additional insertion, extraction, and inspection operations.

Queues typically, but do not necessarily, order elements in a FIFO (first-in, first-out) manner. Among the exceptions are priority queues, which order elements according to a supplied comparator or the elements' natural ordering. Whatever the ordering used, the head of the queue is the element that would be removed by a call to `remove` or `poll`. In a FIFO queue, all new elements are inserted at the tail of the queue. Other kinds of queues may use different placement rules. Every `Queue` implementation must specify its ordering properties. Also see The `Queue` Interface section (page 316).

Map An object that maps keys to values. A `Map` cannot contain duplicate keys; each key can map to at most one value. If you've used `Hashtable`, you're already familiar with the basics of `Map`. Also see The `Map` Interface section (page 319).

The last two core collection interfaces are merely sorted versions of `Set` and `Map`:

SortedSet A `Set` that maintains its elements in ascending order. Several additional operations are provided to take advantage of the ordering. Sorted sets are used for naturally ordered sets, such as word lists and membership rolls. Also see The `SortedSet` Interface section (page 335).

SortedMap A `Map` that maintains its mappings in ascending key order. This is the `Map` analog of `SortedSet`. Sorted maps are used for naturally ordered collections of key/value pairs, such as dictionaries and telephone directories. Also see The `SortedMap` Interface section (page 338).

To understand how the sorted interfaces maintain the order of their elements, see the Object Ordering section (page 328).

The Collection Interface

A Collection[5] represents a group of objects known as its elements. The Collection interface is used to pass around collections of objects where maximum generality is desired. For example, by convention all general-purpose collection implementations have a constructor that takes a Collection argument. This constructor, known as a *conversion constructor*, initializes the new collection to contain all of the elements in the specified collection, whatever the given collection's subinterface or implementation type. In other words, it allows you to *convert* the collection's type.

Suppose, for example, that you have a Collection<String> c, which may be a List, a Set, or another kind of Collection. This idiom creates a new ArrayList (an implementation of the List interface), initially containing all the elements in c:

```
List<String> list = new ArrayList<String>(c);
```

The following shows the Collection interface:

```
public interface Collection<E> extends Iterable<E> {
  // Basic operations
  int size();
  boolean isEmpty();
  boolean contains(Object element);
  boolean add(E element);           // optional
  boolean remove(Object element);   // optional
  Iterator<E> iterator();

  // Bulk operations
  boolean containsAll(Collection<?> c);
  boolean addAll(Collection<? extends E> c); // optional
  boolean removeAll(Collection<?> c);        // optional
  boolean retainAll(Collection<?> c);        // optional
  void clear();                              // optional

  // Array operations
  Object[] toArray();
  <T> T[] toArray(T[] a);
}
```

The interface does about what you'd expect given that a Collection represents a group of objects. The interface has methods to tell you how many elements are in the collection (size, isEmpty), to check whether a given object is in the collection (contains), to add and remove an element from the collection (add, remove), and to provide an iterator over the collection (iterator).

5. docs/api/java/util/Collection.html

The add method is defined generally enough so that it makes sense for collections that allow duplicates as well as those that don't. It guarantees that the Collection will contain the specified element after the call completes, and returns true if the Collection changes as a result of the call. Similarly, the remove method is designed to remove a single instance of the specified element from the Collection, assuming that it contains the element to start with, and to return true if the Collection was modified as a result.

Traversing Collections

There are two ways to traverse collections: (1) with the for-each construct and (2) by using Iterators.

for-each Construct

The for-each construct allows you to concisely traverse a collection or array using a for loop—see The for Statement section (page 75). The following code uses the for-each construct to print out each element of a collection on a separate line:

```
for (Object o : collection)
  System.out.println(o);
```

Iterators

An Iterator[6] is an object that enables you to traverse through a collection and to remove elements from the collection selectively, if desired. You get an Iterator for a collection by calling its iterator method. The following is the Iterator interface:

```
public interface Iterator<E> {
  boolean hasNext();
  E next();
  void remove(); // optional
}
```

The hasNext method returns true if the iteration has more elements, and the next method returns the next element in the iteration. The remove method removes the last element that was returned by next from the underlying Collection. The remove method may be called only once per call to next and throws an exception if this rule is violated.

Note that Iterator.remove is the *only* safe way to modify a collection during iteration; the behavior is unspecified if the underlying collection is modified in any other way while the iteration is in progress.

6. docs/api/java/util/Iterator.html

Use `Iterator` instead of the `for-each` construct when you need to:

- Remove the current element. The `for-each` construct hides the iterator, so you cannot call `remove`. Therefore, the `for-each` construct is not usable for filtering.
- Iterate over multiple collections in parallel.

The following method shows you how to use an `Iterator` to filter an arbitrary `Collection`—that is, traverse the collection removing specific elements:

```
static void filter(Collection<?> c) {
  for (Iterator<?> it = c.iterator(); it.hasNext(); )
    if (!cond(it.next()))
      it.remove();
}
```

This simple piece of code is polymorphic, which means that it works for *any* `Collection` regardless of implementation. This example demonstrates how easy it is to write a polymorphic algorithm using the Java Collections Framework.

Collection Interface Bulk Operations

Bulk operations perform an operation on an entire `Collection`. You could implement these shorthand operations using the basic operations, though in most cases such implementations would be less efficient. The following are the bulk operations:

`containsAll` Returns `true` if the target `Collection` contains all of the elements in the specified `Collection`.

`addAll` Adds all of the elements in the specified `Collection` to the target `Collection`.

`removeAll` Removes from the target `Collection` all of its elements that are also contained in the specified `Collection`.

`retainAll` Removes from the target `Collection` all of its elements that are *not* also contained in the specified `Collection`. That is, it retains only those elements in the target `Collection` that are also contained in the specified `Collection`.

`clear` Removes all elements from the `Collection`.

The `addAll`, `removeAll`, and `retainAll` methods all return `true` if the target `Collection` was modified in the process of executing the operation.

As a simple example of the power of bulk operations, consider the following idiom to remove *all* instances of a specified element, `e`, from a `Collection`, `c`:

```
c.removeAll(Collections.singleton(e));
```

More specifically, suppose you want to remove all of the `null` elements from a `Collection`:

```
c.removeAll(Collections.singleton(null));
```

This idiom uses `Collections.singleton`, which is a static factory method that returns an immutable `Set` containing only the specified element.

Collection Interface Array Operations

The `toArray` methods are provided as a bridge between collections and older APIs that expect arrays on input. The array operations allow the contents of a `Collection` to be translated into an array. The simple form with no arguments creates a new array of `Object`. The more complex form allows the caller to provide an array or to choose the runtime type of the output array.

For example, suppose that `c` is a `Collection`. The following snippet dumps the contents of `c` into a newly allocated array of `Object` whose length is identical to the number of elements in `c`:

```
Object[] a = c.toArray();
```

Suppose that `c` is known to contain only strings (perhaps because `c` is of type `Collection<String>`). The following snippet dumps the contents of `c` into a newly allocated array of `String` whose length is identical to the number of elements in `c`:

```
String[] a = c.toArray(new String[0]);
```

The Set Interface

A `Set`[7] is a `Collection` that cannot contain duplicate elements. It models the mathematical set abstraction. The `Set` interface contains *only* methods inherited from `Collection` and adds the restriction that duplicate elements are prohibited. `Set` also adds a stronger contract on the behavior of the `equals` and `hashCode` operations, allowing `Set` instances to be compared meaningfully even if their implementation types differ. Two `Set` instances are equal if they contain the same elements.

The following is the `Set` interface:

7. `docs/api/java/util/Set.html`

```
public interface Set<E> extends Collection<E> {
  // Basic operations
  int size();
  boolean isEmpty();
  boolean contains(Object element);
  boolean add(E element);           // optional
  boolean remove(Object element);   // optional
  Iterator<E> iterator();

  // Bulk operations
  boolean containsAll(Collection<?> c);
  boolean addAll(Collection<? extends E> c); // optional
  boolean removeAll(Collection<?> c);        // optional
  boolean retainAll(Collection<?> c);        // optional
  void clear();                              // optional

  // Array Operations
  Object[] toArray();
  <T> T[] toArray(T[] a);
}
```

The Java platform contains three general-purpose `Set` implementations: `HashSet`,[8] `TreeSet`,[9] and `LinkedHashSet`.[10] `HashSet`, which stores its elements in a hash table, is the best-performing implementation; however, it makes no guarantees concerning the order of iteration. `TreeSet`, which stores its elements in a red-black tree, orders its elements based on their values; it is substantially slower than `HashSet`. `LinkedHashSet`, which is implemented as a hash table with a linked list running through it, orders its elements based on the order in which they were inserted into the set (insertion-order). `LinkedHashSet` spares its clients from the unspecified, generally chaotic ordering provided by `HashSet` at a cost that is only slightly higher.

Here's a simple but useful `Set` idiom. Suppose you have a `Collection`, `c`, and you want to create another `Collection` containing the same elements but with all duplicates eliminated. The following one-liner does the trick:

```
Collection<Type> noDups = new HashSet<Type>(c);
```

It works by creating a `Set` (which, by definition, cannot contain a duplicate) initially containing all the elements in `c`. It uses the standard conversion constructor described in The `Collection` Interface section (page 298).

8. docs/api/java/util/HashSet.html
9. docs/api/java/util/TreeSet.html
10. docs/api/java/util/LinkedHashSet.html

Here is a minor variant of this idiom that preserves the order of the original collection while removing duplicate elements:

```
Collection<Type> noDups = new LinkedHashSet<Type>(c);
```

The following is a generic method that encapsulates the preceding idiom, returning a `Set` of the same generic type as the one passed:

```
public static <E> Set<E> removeDups(Collection<E> c) {
  return new LinkedHashSet<E>(c);
}
```

Set Interface Basic Operations

The `size` operation returns the number of elements in the `Set` (its *cardinality*). The `isEmpty` method does exactly what you think it would. The `add` method adds the specified element to the `Set` if it's not already present and returns a boolean indicating whether the element was added. Similarly, the `remove` method removes the specified element from the `Set` if it's present and returns a boolean indicating whether the element was present. The `iterator` method returns an `Iterator` over the `Set`.

The following program[11] takes the words in its argument list and prints out any duplicate words, the number of distinct words, and a list of the words with duplicates eliminated:

```
import java.util.*;

public class FindDups {
  public static void main(String[] args) {
    Set<String> s = new HashSet<String>();
    for (String a : args)
      if (!s.add(a))
        System.out.println("Duplicate detected: " + a);

    System.out.println(s.size() + " distinct words: " + s);
  }
}
```

Now run the program:

```
java FindDups i came i saw i left
```

The following output is produced:

11. `tutorial/collections/interfaces/examples/FindDups.java`

```
Duplicate detected: i
Duplicate detected: i
4 distinct words: [i, left, saw, came]
```

Note that the code always refers to the `Collection` by its interface type (`Set`) rather than by its implementation type (`HashSet`). This is a *strongly* recommended programming practice because it gives you the flexibility to change implementations merely by changing the constructor. If either of the variables used to store a collection or the parameters used to pass it around are declared to be of the `Collection`'s implementation type rather than its interface type, *all* such variables and parameters must be changed in order to change its implementation type.

Furthermore, there's no guarantee that the resulting program will work. If the program uses any nonstandard operations present in the original implementation type but not in the new one, the program will fail. Referring to collections only by their interface prevents you from using any nonstandard operations.

The implementation type of the `Set` in the preceding example is `HashSet`, which makes no guarantees as to the order of the elements in the `Set`. If you want the program to print the word list in alphabetical order, merely change the `Set`'s implementation type from `HashSet` to `TreeSet`. Making this trivial one-line change causes the command line in the previous example to generate the following output:

```
java FindDups i came i saw i left
Duplicate detected: i
Duplicate detected: i
4 distinct words: [came, i, left, saw]
```

Set Interface Bulk Operations

Bulk operations are particularly well suited to `Set`s; when applied, they perform standard set-algebraic operations. Suppose `s1` and `s2` are sets. Here's what bulk operations do:

`s1.containsAll(s2)` Returns `true` if `s2` is a **subset** of `s1`. (`s2` is a subset of `s1` if set `s1` contains all of the elements in `s2`.)

`s1.addAll(s2)` Transforms `s1` into the **union** of `s1` and `s2`. (The union of two sets is the set containing all of the elements contained in either set.)

`s1.retainAll(s2)` Transforms `s1` into the intersection of `s1` and `s2`. (The intersection of two sets is the set containing only the elements common to both sets.)

`s1.removeAll(s2)` Transforms `s1` into the (asymmetric) set difference of `s1` and `s2`. (For example, the set difference of `s1` minus `s2` is the set containing all of the elements found in `s1` but not in `s2`.)

To calculate the union, intersection, or set difference of two sets *nondestructively* (without modifying either set), the caller must copy one set before calling the appropriate bulk operation. The following are the resulting idioms:

```
Set<Type> union = new HashSet<Type>(s1);
union.addAll(s2);

Set<Type> intersection = new HashSet<Type>(s1);
intersection.retainAll(s2);

Set<Type> difference = new HashSet<Type>(s1);
difference.removeAll(s2);
```

The implementation type of the result `Set` in the preceding idioms is `HashSet`, which is, as already mentioned, the best all-around `Set` implementation in the Java platform. However, any general-purpose `Set` implementation could be substituted.

Let's revisit the `FindDups` program. Suppose you want to know which words in the argument list occur only once and which occur more than once, but you do not want any duplicates printed out repeatedly. This effect can be achieved by generating two sets—one containing every word in the argument list and the other containing only the duplicates. The words that occur only once are the set difference of these two sets, which we know how to compute. Here's how the resulting program[12] looks:

```
import java.util.*;

public class FindDups2 {
  public static void main(String[] args) {
    Set<String> uniques = new HashSet<String>();
    Set<String> dups    = new HashSet<String>();

    for (String a : args)
      if (!uniques.add(a))
        dups.add(a);

    // Destructive set-difference
    uniques.removeAll(dups);

    System.out.println("Unique words:    " + uniques);
    System.out.println("Duplicate words: " + dups);
  }
}
```

12. `tutorial/collections/interfaces/examples/FindDups2.java`

When run with the same argument list used earlier (`i came i saw i left`), the program yields the following output:

```
Unique words:    [left, saw, came]
Duplicate words: [i]
```

A less common set-algebraic operation is the *symmetric set difference*—the set of elements contained in either of two specified sets but not in both. The following code calculates the symmetric set difference of two sets nondestructively:

```
Set<Type> symmetricDiff = new HashSet<Type>(s1);
symmetricDiff.addAll(s2);
Set<Type> tmp = new HashSet<Type>(s1);
tmp.retainAll(s2));
symmetricDiff.removeAll(tmp);
```

Set Interface Array Operations

The array operations don't do anything special for `Sets` beyond what they do for any other `Collection`. These operations are described in the Collection Interface Array Operations section (page 301).

The List Interface

A `List`[13] is an ordered `Collection` (sometimes called a *sequence*). Lists may contain duplicate elements. In addition to the operations inherited from `Collection`, the `List` interface includes operations for the following:

Positional access Manipulates elements based on their numerical position in the list.

Search Searches for a specified object in the list and returns its numerical position.

Iteration Extends `Iterator` semantics to take advantage of the list's sequential nature.

Range-view Performs arbitrary *range operations* on the list.

13. `docs/api/java/util/List.html`

The List interface follows:

```
public interface List<E> extends Collection<E> {
  // Positional access
  E get(int index);
  E set(int index, E element);    // optional
  boolean add(E element);         // optional
  void add(int index, E element); // optional
  E remove(int index);            // optional
  boolean addAll(int index,
    Collection<? extends E> c);   // optional

  // Search
  int indexOf(Object o);
  int lastIndexOf(Object o);

  // Iteration
  ListIterator<E> listIterator();
  ListIterator<E> listIterator(int index);

  // Range-view
  List<E> subList(int from, int to);
}
```

The Java platform contains two general-purpose List implementations. ArrayList,[14] which is usually the better-performing implementation, and LinkedList[15] which offers better performance under certain circumstances. Also, Vector has been retrofitted to implement List.

Comparison to Vector

If you've used Vector, you're already familiar with the general basics of List. (Of course, List is an interface, while Vector is a concrete implementation.) List fixes several minor API deficiencies in Vector. Commonly used Vector operations, such as elementAt and setElementAt, have been given much shorter names. When you consider that these two operations are the List analog of square brackets for arrays, it becomes apparent that shorter names are highly desirable. Consider the following assignment statement:

```
a[i] = a[j].times(a[k]);
```

14. docs/api/java/util/ArrayList.html

15. docs/api/java/util/LinkedList.html

The `Vector` equivalent is:

```
v.setElementAt(v.elementAt(j).times(v.elementAt(k)), i);
```

The `List` equivalent is:

```
v.set(i, v.get(j).times(v.get(k)));
```

You may already have noticed that the `set` method, which replaces the `Vector` method `setElementAt`, reverses the order of the arguments so that they match the corresponding array operation. Consider the following assignment statement:

```
gift[5] = "golden rings";
```

The `Vector` equivalent is:

```
gift.setElementAt("golden rings", 5);
```

The `List` equivalent is:

```
gift.set(5, "golden rings");
```

For consistency's sake, the method `add(int, E)`, which replaces `insertElementAt(Object, int)`, also reverses the order of the arguments.

The various range operations in `Vector` (`indexOf`, `lastIndexOf`, and `setSize`) have been replaced by a single range-view operation (`subList`), which is far more powerful and consistent.

Collection Operations

The operations inherited from `Collection` all do about what you'd expect them to do, assuming you're already familiar with them. If you're not familiar with them from `Collection`, now would be a good time to read the Collection Interface Array Operations section (page 301). The `remove` operation always removes *the first* occurrence of the specified element from the list. The `add` and `addAll` operations always append the new element(s) to the *end* of the list. Thus, the following idiom concatenates one list to another:

```
list1.addAll(list2);
```

Here's a nondestructive form of this idiom, which produces a third `List` consisting of the second list appended to the first:

```
List<Type> list3 = new ArrayList<Type>(list1);
list3.addAll(list2);
```

Note that the idiom, in its nondestructive form, takes advantage of ArrayList's standard conversion constructor.

Like the Set interface, List strengthens the requirements on the equals and hashCode methods so that two List objects can be compared for logical equality without regard to their implementation classes. Two List objects are equal if they contain the same elements in the same order.

Positional Access and Search Operations

The basic *positional access* operations (get, set, add, and remove) behave just like their longer-named counterparts in Vector (elementAt, setElementAt, insertElementAt, and removeElementAt) with one noteworthy exception: The set and remove operations return the old value that is being overwritten or removed; the Vector counterparts (setElementAt and removeElementAt) return nothing (void). The *search* operations indexOf and lastIndexOf behave exactly like the identically named operations in Vector.

The addAll operation inserts all the elements of the specified Collection starting at the specified position. The elements are inserted in the order they are returned by the specified Collection's iterator. This call is the positional access analog of Collection's addAll operation.

Here's a little method to swap two indexed values in a List. It should look familiar from Programming 101:

```
public static <E> void swap(List<E> a, int i, int j) {
  E tmp = a.get(i);
  a.set(i, a.get(j));
  a.set(j, tmp);
}
```

Of course, there's one big difference. This is a polymorphic algorithm: It swaps two elements in any List, regardless of its implementation type. Here's another polymorphic algorithm that uses the preceding swap method:

```
public static void shuffle(List<?> list, Random rnd) {
  for (int i = list.size(); i > 1; i--)
    swap(list, i - 1, rnd.nextInt(i));
}
```

This algorithm, which is included in the Java platform's `Collections`[16] class, randomly permutes the specified list using the specified source of randomness. It's a bit subtle: It runs up the list from the bottom, repeatedly swapping a randomly selected element into the current position. Unlike most naive attempts at shuffling, it's *fair* (all permutations occur with equal likelihood, assuming an unbiased source of randomness) and *fast* (requiring exactly `list.size()-1` swaps). The following program uses this algorithm to print the words in its argument list in random order:

```
import java.util.*;

public class Shuffle {
  public static void main(String[] args) {
    List<String> list = new ArrayList<String>();
    for (String a : args)
      list.add(a);
    Collections.shuffle(list, new Random());
    System.out.println(list);
  }
}
```

In fact, this program can be made even shorter and faster. The `Arrays`[17] class has a static factory method called `asList`, which allows an array to be viewed as a `List`. This method does not copy the array. Changes in the `List` write through to the array and vice versa. The resulting `List` is not a general-purpose `List` implementation, because it doesn't implement the (optional) `add` and `remove` operations: Arrays are not resizable. Taking advantage of `Arrays.asList` and calling the library version of `shuffle`, which uses a default source of randomness, you get the following tiny program[18] whose behavior is identical to the previous program:

```
import java.util.*;

public class Shuffle {
  public static void main(String[] args) {
    List<String> list = Arrays.asList(args);
    Collections.shuffle(list);
    System.out.println(list);
  }
}
```

16. `docs/api/java/util/Collections.html`

17. `docs/api/java/util/Arrays.html`

18. `tutorial/collections/interfaces/examples/Shuffle.java`

Iterators

As you'd expect, the `Iterator` returned by `List`'s `iterator` operation returns the elements of the list in proper sequence. `List` also provides a richer iterator, called a `ListIterator`, which allows you to traverse the list in either direction, modify the list during iteration, and obtain the current position of the iterator. The `ListIterator` interface follows:

```
public interface ListIterator<E> extends Iterator<E> {
  boolean hasNext();
  E next();
  boolean hasPrevious();
  E previous();
  int nextIndex();
  int previousIndex();
  void remove(); // optional
  void set(E e); // optional
  void add(E e); // optional
}
```

The three methods that `ListIterator` inherits from `Iterator` (`hasNext`, `next`, and `remove`) do exactly the same thing in both interfaces. The `hasPrevious` and the `previous` operations are exact analogues of `hasNext` and `next`. The former operations refer to the element before the (implicit) cursor, whereas the latter refer to the element after the cursor. The `previous` operation moves the cursor backward, whereas `next` moves it forward.

Here's the standard idiom for iterating backward through a list:

```
for (ListIterator<Type> it = list.listIterator(list.size());
                                          it.hasPrevious(); ) {
  Type t = it.previous();
  ...
}
```

Note the argument to `listIterator` in the preceding idiom. The `List` interface has two forms of the `listIterator` method. The form with no arguments returns a `ListIterator` positioned at the beginning of the list; the form with an `int` argument returns a `ListIterator` positioned at the specified index. The index refers to the element that would be returned by an initial call to `next`. An initial call to `previous` would return the element whose index was `index-1`. In a list of length `n`, there are `n+1` valid values for `index`, from `0` to `n`, inclusive.

Intuitively speaking, the cursor is always between two elements—the one that would be returned by a call to `previous` and the one that would be returned by a call to `next`. The `n+1` valid `index` values correspond to the `n+1` gaps between elements, from the gap before the first element to the gap after the last one. Figure 11.2 shows the five possible cursor positions in a list containing four elements.

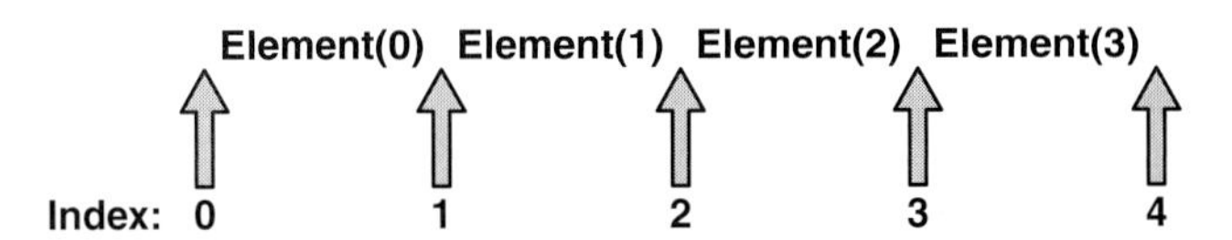

Figure 11.2 The five possible cursor positions.

Calls to `next` and `previous` can be intermixed, but you have to be a bit careful. The first call to `previous` returns the same element as the last call to `next`. Similarly, the first call to `next` after a sequence of calls to `previous` returns the same element as the last call to `previous`.

It should come as no surprise that the `nextIndex` method returns the index of the element that would be returned by a subsequent call to `next`, and `previousIndex` returns the index of the element that would be returned by a subsequent call to `previous`. These calls are typically used either to report the position where something was found or to record the position of the `ListIterator` so that another `ListIterator` with identical position can be created.

It should also come as no surprise that the number returned by `nextIndex` is always one greater than the number returned by `previousIndex`. This implies the behavior of the two boundary cases: (1) a call to `previousIndex` when the cursor is before the initial element returns `-1` and (2) a call to `nextIndex` when the cursor is after the final element returns `list.size()`. To make all this concrete, the following is a possible implementation of `List.indexOf`:

```
public int indexOf(E e) {
  for (ListIterator<E> it = listIterator(); it.hasNext(); )
    if (e == null ? it.next() == null : e.equals(it.next()))
      return it.previousIndex();
  return -1;  // Element not found
}
```

Note that the `indexOf` method returns `it.previousIndex()` even though it is traversing the list in the forward direction. The reason is that `it.nextIndex()` would return the index of the element we are about to examine, and we want to return the index of the element we just examined.

The Iterator interface provides the remove operation to remove the last element returned by next from the Collection. For ListIterator, this operation removes the last element returned by next or previous. The ListIterator interface provides two additional operations to modify the list—set and add. The set method overwrites the last element returned by next or previous with the specified element. The following polymorphic algorithm uses set to replace all occurrences of one specified value with another:

```
public static <E> void replace(List<E> list, E val, E newVal) {
  for (ListIterator<E> it = list.listIterator(); it.hasNext();)
    if (val == null ?
        it.next() == null : val.equals(it.next()))
      it.set(newVal);
}
```

The only bit of trickiness in this example is the equality test between val and it.next. You need to special-case a val value of null to prevent a NullPointerException.

The add method inserts a new element into the list immediately before the current cursor position. This method is illustrated in the following polymorphic algorithm to replace all occurrences of a specified value with the sequence of values contained in the specified list:

```
public static <E> void replace(List<E> list, E val,
                               List<? extends E> newVals) {
  for (ListIterator<E>
       it = list.listIterator(); it.hasNext(); ){
    if (val == null ?
        it.next() == null : val.equals(it.next())) {
      it.remove();
      for (E e : newVals)
        it.add(e);
    }
  }
}
```

Range-View Operation

The *range-view* operation, subList(int fromIndex, int toIndex), returns a List view of the portion of this list whose indices range from fromIndex, inclusive, to toIndex, exclusive. This *half-open range* mirrors the typical for loop:

```
for (int i = fromIndex; i < toIndex; i++) {
  ...
}
```

As the term *view* implies, the returned List is backed up by the List on which subList was called, so changes in the former are reflected in the latter.

This method eliminates the need for explicit range operations (of the sort that commonly exist for arrays). Any operation that expects a List can be used as a range operation by passing a subList view instead of a whole List. For example, the following idiom removes a range of elements from a List:

```
list.subList(fromIndex, toIndex).clear();
```

Similar idioms can be constructed to search for an element in a range:

```
int i = list.subList(fromIndex, toIndex).indexOf(o);
int j = list.subList(fromIndex, toIndex).lastIndexOf(o);
```

Note that the preceding idioms return the index of the found element in the subList, not the index in the backing List.

Any polymorphic algorithm that operates on a List, such as the replace and shuffle examples, works with the List returned by subList.

Here's a polymorphic algorithm whose implementation uses subList to deal a hand from a deck. That is, it returns a new List (the "hand") containing the specified number of elements taken from the end of the specified List (the "deck"). The elements returned in the hand are removed from the deck:

```
public static <E> List<E> dealHand(List<E> deck, int n) {
  int deckSize = deck.size();
  List<E> handView = deck.subList(deckSize - n, deckSize);
  List<E> hand = new ArrayList<E>(handView);
  handView.clear();
  return hand;
}
```

Note that this algorithm removes the hand from the *end* of the deck. For many common List implementations, such as ArrayList, the performance of removing elements from the end of the list is substantially better than that of removing elements from the beginning.

The following is a program[19] that uses the dealHand method in combination with Collections.shuffle to generate hands from a normal 52-card deck. The program takes two command-line arguments: (1) the number of hands to deal and (2) the number of cards in each hand:

19. tutorial/collections/interfaces/examples/Deal.java

```
import java.util.*;

class Deal {
  public static void main(String[] args) {
    int numHands = Integer.parseInt(args[0]);
    int cardsPerHand = Integer.parseInt(args[1]);

    // Make a normal 52-card deck.
    String[] suit = new String[]
      {"spades", "hearts", "diamonds", "clubs"};
    String[] rank = new String[]
      {"ace","2","3","4","5","6","7","8",
           "9","10","jack","queen","king"};
    List<String> deck = new ArrayList<String>();
    for (int i = 0; i < suit.length; i++)
      for (int j = 0; j < rank.length; j++)
        deck.add(rank[j] + " of " + suit[i]);

    Collections.shuffle(deck);

    for (int i=0; i < numHands; i++)
      System.out.println(dealHand(deck, cardsPerHand));
  }
}
```

Running the program produces the following output:

```
% java Deal 4 5

[8 of hearts, jack of spades, 3 of spades, 4 of spades,
                                               king of diamonds]
[4 of diamonds, ace of clubs, 6 of clubs, jack of hearts,
                                                queen of hearts]
[7 of spades, 5 of spades, 2 of diamonds, queen of diamonds,
                                                    9 of clubs]
[8 of spades, 6 of diamonds, ace of spades, 3 of hearts,
                                                  ace of hearts]
```

Although the `subList` operation is extremely powerful, some care must be exercised when using it. The semantics of the `List` returned by `subList` become undefined if elements are added to or removed from the backing `List` in any way other than via the returned `List`. Thus, it's highly recommended that you use the `List` returned by `subList` only as a transient object—to perform one or a sequence of range operations on the backing `List`. The longer you use the `subList` instance, the greater the probability that you'll compromise it by modifying the backing `List` directly or through another `subList` object. Note that it is legal to modify a sublist of a sublist and to continue using the original sublist (though not concurrently).

List Algorithms

Most polymorphic algorithms in the `Collections` class apply specifically to `List`. Having all these algorithms at your disposal makes it very easy to manipulate lists. Here's a summary of these algorithms, which are described in more detail in the Algorithms section (page 355):

`sort` Sorts a `List` using a merge sort algorithm, which provides a fast, stable sort. (A *stable sort* is one that does not reorder equal elements.)

`shuffle` Randomly permutes the elements in a `List`.

`reverse` Reverses the order of the elements in a `List`.

`rotate` Rotates all the elements in a `List` by a specified distance.

`swap` Swaps the elements at specified positions in a `List`.

`replaceAll` Replaces all occurrences of one specified value with another.

`fill` Overwrites every element in a `List` with the specified value.

`copy` Copies the source `List` into the destination `List`.

`binarySearch` Searches for an element in an ordered `List` using the binary search algorithm.

`indexOfSubList` Returns the index of the first sublist of one `List` that is equal to another.

`lastIndexOfSubList` Returns the index of the last sublist of one `List` that is equal to another.

The Queue Interface

A `Queue`[20] is a collection for holding elements prior to processing. Besides basic `Collection` operations, queues provide additional insertion, removal, and inspection operations. The `Queue` interface follows:

```
public interface Queue<E> extends Collection<E> {
  E element();
  boolean offer(E e);
  E peek();
  E poll();
  E remove();
}
```

20. `docs/api/java/util/Queue.html`

Each `Queue` method exists in two forms: (1) one throws an exception if the operation fails, and (2) the other returns a special value if the operation fails (either `null` or `false`, depending on the operation). The regular structure of the interface is illustrated in Table 11.1.

Table 11.1 Queue Interface Structure

	Throws Exception	**Returns Special Value**
Insert	`add(e)`	`offer(e)`
Remove	`remove()`	`poll()`
Examine	`element()`	`peek()`

Queues typically, but not necessarily, order elements in a FIFO (first-in, first-out) manner. Among the exceptions are priority queues, which order elements according to their values—see the Object Ordering section (page 328) for details. Whatever ordering is used, the head of the queue is the element that would be removed by a call to `remove` or `poll`. In a FIFO queue, all new elements are inserted at the tail of the queue. Other kinds of queues may use different placement rules. Every `Queue` implementation must specify its ordering properties.

It is possible for a `Queue` implementation to restrict the number of elements that it holds; such queues are known as *bounded*. Some `Queue` implementations in `java.util.concurrent` are bounded, but the implementations in `java.util` are not.

The `add` method, which `Queue` inherits from `Collection`, inserts an element unless it would violate the queue's capacity restrictions, in which case it throws `IllegalStateException`. The `offer` method, which is intended solely for use on bounded queues, differs from `add` only in that it indicates failure to insert an element by returning `false`.

The `remove` and `poll` methods both remove and return the head of the queue. Exactly which element gets removed is a function of the queue's ordering policy. The `remove` and `poll` methods differ in their behavior only when the queue is empty. Under these circumstances, `remove` throws `NoSuchElementException`, while `poll` returns `null`.

The `element` and `peek` methods return, but do not remove, the head of the queue. They differ from one another in precisely the same fashion as `remove` and `poll`: If the queue is empty, `element` throws `NoSuchElementException`, while `peek` returns `null`.

Queue implementations generally do not allow insertion of null elements. The LinkedList implementation, which was retrofitted to implement Queue, is an exception. For historical reasons, it permits null elements, but you should refrain from taking advantage of this, because null is used as a special return value by the poll and peek methods.

Queue implementations generally do not define element-based versions of the equals and hashCode methods but instead inherit the identity-based versions from Object.

The Queue interface does not define the blocking queue methods, which are common in concurrent programming. These methods, which wait for elements to appear or for space to become available, are defined in the interface java.util.concurrent.BlockingQueue,[21] which extends Queue.

In the following example program, a queue is used to implement a countdown timer. The queue is preloaded with all the integer values from a number specified on the command line to zero, in descending order. Then, the values are removed from the queue and printed at one-second intervals. The program is artificial in that it would be more natural to do the same thing without using a queue, but it illustrates the use of a queue to store elements prior to subsequent processing:

```
import java.util.*;

public class Countdown {
  public static void main(String[] args)
      throws InterruptedException {
    int time = Integer.parseInt(args[0]);
    Queue<Integer> queue = new LinkedList<Integer>();
    for (int i = time; i >= 0; i--)
      queue.add(i);
    while (!queue.isEmpty()) {
      System.out.println(queue.remove());
      Thread.sleep(1000);
    }
  }
}
```

In the following example, a priority queue is used to sort a collection of elements. Again this program is artificial in that there is no reason to use it in favor of the sort method provided in Collections, but it illustrates the behavior of priority queues:

21. docs/api/java/util/concurrent/BlockingQueue.html

```
static <E> List<E> heapSort(Collection<E> c) {
  Queue<E> queue = new PriorityQueue<E>(c);
  List<E> result = new ArrayList<E>();
  while (!queue.isEmpty())
    result.add(queue.remove());
  return result;
}
```

The Map Interface

A `Map`[22] is an object that maps keys to values. A map cannot contain duplicate keys: Each key can map to at most one value. It models the mathematical *function* abstraction. The `Map` interface follows:

```
public interface Map<K,V> {

  // Basic operations
  V put(K key, V value);
  V get(Object key);
  V remove(Object key);
  boolean containsKey(Object key);
  boolean containsValue(Object value);
  int size();
  boolean isEmpty();

  // Bulk operations
  void putAll(Map<? extends K, ? extends V> m);
  void clear();

  // Collection Views
  public Set<K> keySet();
  public Collection<V> values();
  public Set<Map.Entry<K,V>> entrySet();

  // Interface for entrySet elements
  public interface Entry {
    K getKey();
    V getValue();
    V setValue(V value);
  }
}
```

22. `docs/api/java/util/Map.html`

The Java platform contains three general-purpose `Map` implementations: `HashMap`,[23] `TreeMap`,[24] and `LinkedHashMap`.[25] Their behavior and performance are precisely analogous to `HashSet`, `TreeSet`, and `LinkedHashSet`, as described in The `Set` Interface section (page 301). Also, `Hashtable` was retrofitted to implement `Map`.

Comparison to Hashtable

If you've used `Hashtable`, you're already familiar with the general basics of `Map`. (Of course, `Map` is an interface, while `Hashtable` is a concrete implementation.) The following are the major differences:

- `Map` provides `Collection` views instead of direct support for iteration via `Enumeration` objects. `Collection` views greatly enhance the expressiveness of the interface, as discussed later in this section.
- `Map` allows you to iterate over keys, values, or key-value pairs; `Hashtable` does not provide the third option.
- `Map` provides a safe way to remove entries in the midst of iteration; `Hashtable` did not.

Finally, `Map` fixes a minor deficiency in the `Hashtable` interface. `Hashtable` has a method called `contains`, which returns `true` if the `Hashtable` contains a given *value*. Given its name, you'd expect this method to return `true` if the `Hashtable` contained a given *key*, because the key is the primary access mechanism for a `Hashtable`. The `Map` interface eliminates this source of confusion by renaming the method `containsValue`. Also, this improves the interface's consistency—`containsValue` parallels `containsKey`.

Map Interface Basic Operations

The basic operations of `Map` (`put`, `get`, `containsKey`, `containsValue`, `size`, and `isEmpty`) behave exactly like their counterparts in `Hashtable`. The following program[26] generates a frequency table of the words found in its argument list. The frequency table maps each word to the number of times it occurs in the argument list:

---

23. `docs/api/java/util/HashMap.html`

24. `docs/api/java/util/TreeMap.html`

25. `docs/api/java/util/LinkedHashMap.html`

26. `tutorial/collections/interfaces/examples/Freq.java`

```
import java.util.*;

public class Freq {
  public static void main(String[] args) {
    Map<String, Integer> m = new HashMap<String, Integer>();

    // Initialize frequency table from command line
    for (String a : args) {
      Integer freq = m.get(a);
      m.put(a, (freq == null) ? 1 : freq + 1);
    }

    System.out.println(m.size() + " distinct words:");
    System.out.println(m);
  }
}
```

The only tricky thing about this program is the second argument of the `put` statement. That argument is a conditional expression that has the effect of setting the frequency to one if the word has never been seen before or one more than its current value if the word has already been seen. Try running this program with the command:

```
java Freq if it is to be it is up to me to delegate
```

The program yields the following output:

```
8 distinct words:
{to=3, delegate=1, be=1, it=2, up=1, if=1, me=1, is=2}
```

Suppose you'd prefer to see the frequency table in alphabetical order. All you have to do is change the implementation type of the `Map` from `HashMap` to `TreeMap`. Making this four-character change causes the program to generate the following output from the same command line:

```
8 distinct words:
{be=1, delegate=1, if=1, is=2, it=2, me=1, to=3, up=1}
```

Similarly, you could make the program print the frequency table in the order the words first appear on the command line simply by changing the implementation type of the map to `LinkedHashMap`. Doing so results in the following output:

```
8 distinct words:
{if=1, it=2, is=2, to=3, be=1, up=1, me=1, delegate=1}
```

This flexibility provides a potent illustration of the power of an interface-based framework.

Like the Set and List interfaces, Map strengthens the requirements on the equals and hashCode methods so that two Map objects can be compared for logical equality without regard to their implementation types. Two Map instances are equal if they represent the same key-value mappings.

By convention, all general-purpose Map implementations provide constructors that take a Map object and initialize the new Map to contain all the key-value mappings in the specified Map. This standard Map conversion constructor is entirely analogous to the standard Collection constructor: It allows the caller to create a Map of a desired implementation type that initially contains all of the mappings in another Map, regardless of the other Map's implementation type. For example, suppose you have a Map, named m. The following one-liner creates a new HashMap initially containing all of the same key-value mappings as m:

```
Map<K, V> copy = new HashMap<K, V>(m);
```

Map Interface Bulk Operations

The clear operation does exactly what you would think it could do: It removes all the mappings from the Map. The putAll operation is the Map analogue of the Collection interface's addAll operation. In addition to its obvious use of dumping one Map into another, it has a second, more subtle use. Suppose a Map is used to represent a collection of attribute-value pairs; the putAll operation, in combination with the Map conversion constructor, provides a neat way to implement attribute map creation with default values. The following is a static factory method that demonstrates this technique:

```
static <K, V> Map<K, V> newAttributeMap(
      Map<K, V>defaults, Map<K, V> overrides) {
   Map<K, V> result = new HashMap<K, V>(defaults);
   result.putAll(overrides);
   return result;
}
```

Collection Views

The Collection view methods allow a Map to be viewed as a Collection in these three ways:

keySet The Set of keys contained in the Map.

values The Collection of values contained in the Map. This Collection is not a Set, because multiple keys can map to the same value.

entrySet The Set of key-value pairs contained in the Map. The Map interface provides a small nested interface called Map.Entry, the type of the elements in this Set.

The `Collection` views provide the *only* means to iterate over a `Map`. This example illustrates the standard idiom for iterating over the keys in a `Map` with a `for-each` construct:

```
for (KeyType key : m.keySet())
  System.out.println(key);
```

and with an `iterator`:

```
// Filter a map based on some property of its keys.
for (Iterator<Type> it = m.keySet().iterator(); it.hasNext(); )
  if (it.next().isBogus())
    it.remove();
```

The idiom for iterating over values is analogous. Following is the idiom for iterating over key-value pairs:

```
for (Map.Entry<KeyType, ValType> e : m.entrySet())
  System.out.println(e.getKey() + ": " + e.getValue());
```

At first, many people worry that these idioms may be slow because the `Map` has to create a new `Collection` instance each time a `Collection` view operation is called. Rest easy: There's no reason that a `Map` cannot always return the same object each time it is asked for a given `Collection` view. This is precisely what all the `Map` implementations in `java.util` do.

With all three `Collection` views, calling an `Iterator`'s `remove` operation removes the associated entry from the backing `Map`, assuming that the backing `Map` supports element removal to begin with. This is illustrated by the preceding filtering idiom.

With the `entrySet` view, it is also possible to change the value associated with a key by calling a `Map.Entry`'s `setValue` method during iteration (again, assuming the `Map` supports value modification to begin with). Note that these are the *only* safe ways to modify a `Map` during iteration; the behavior is unspecified if the underlying `Map` is modified in any other way while the iteration is in progress.

The `Collection` views support element removal in all its many forms—`remove`, `removeAll`, `retainAll`, and `clear` operations, as well as the `Iterator.remove` operation. (Yet again, this assumes that the backing `Map` supports element removal.)

The `Collection` views *do not* support element addition under any circumstances. It would make no sense for the `keySet` and `values` views, and it's unnecessary for the `entrySet` view, because the backing `Map`'s `put` and `putAll` methods provide the same functionality.

Fancy Uses of Collection Views: Map Algebra

When applied to the `Collection` views, bulk operations (`containsAll`, `removeAll`, and `retainAll`) are surprisingly potent tools. For starters, suppose you want to know whether one `Map` is a submap of another—that is, whether the first `Map` contains all the key-value mappings in the second. The following idiom does the trick:

```
if (m1.entrySet().containsAll(m2.entrySet())) {
    ...
}
```

Along similar lines, suppose you want to know whether two `Map` objects contain mappings for all of the same keys:

```
if (m1.keySet().equals(m2.keySet())) {
    ...
}
```

Suppose you have a `Map` that represents a collection of attribute-value pairs, and two `Sets` representing required attributes and permissible attributes. (The permissible attributes include the required attributes.) The following snippet determines whether the attribute map conforms to these constraints and prints a detailed error message if it doesn't:

```
static <K, V> boolean validate(Map<K, V> attrMap,
          Set<K> requiredAttrs, Set<K>permittedAttrs) {
  boolean valid = true;
  Set<K> attrs = attrMap.keySet();
  if (!attrs.containsAll(requiredAttrs)) {
    Set<K> missing = new HashSet<K>(requiredAttrs);
    missing.removeAll(attrs);
    System.out.println("Missing attributes: " + missing);
    valid = false;
  }
  if (!permittedAttrs.containsAll(attrs)) {
    Set<K> illegal = new HashSet<K>(attrs);
    illegal.removeAll(permittedAttrs);
    System.out.println("Illegal attributes: " + illegal);
    valid = false;
  }
  return valid;
}
```

Suppose you want to know all the keys common to two `Map` objects:

```
Set<KeyType>commonKeys = new HashSet<KeyType>(m1.keySet());
commonKeys.retainAll(m2.keySet());
```

A similar idiom gets you the common values.

All the idioms presented thus far have been nondestructive; that is, they don't modify the backing `Map`. Here are a few that do. Suppose you want to remove all of the key-value pairs that one `Map` has in common with another:

```
m1.entrySet().removeAll(m2.entrySet());
```

Suppose you want to remove from one `Map` all of the keys that have mappings in another:

```
m1.keySet().removeAll(m2.keySet());
```

What happens when you start mixing keys and values in the same bulk operation? Suppose you have a `Map`, `managers`, that maps each employee in a company to the employee's manager. We'll be deliberately vague about the types of the key and the value objects. It doesn't matter, as long as they're the same. Now suppose you want to know who all the "individual contributors" (or nonmanagers) are. The following snippet tells you exactly what you want to know:

```
Set<Employee> individualContributors =
  new HashSet<Employee>(managers.keySet());
individualContributors.removeAll(managers.values());
```

Suppose you want to fire all the employees who report directly to some manager, Simon:

```
Employee simon = ... ;
managers.values().removeAll(Collections.singleton(simon));
```

Note that this idiom makes use of `Collections.singleton`, a static factory method that returns an immutable `Set` with the single, specified element.

Once you've done this, you may have a bunch of employees whose managers no longer work for the company (if any of Simon's direct-reports were themselves managers). The following code will tell you which employees have managers who no longer work for the company.

```
Map<Employee, Employee> m =
  new HashMap<Employee, Employee>(managers);
m.values().removeAll(managers.keySet());
Set<Employee> slackers = m.keySet();
```

This example is a bit tricky. First, it makes a temporary copy of the `Map`, and it removes from the temporary copy all entries whose (manager) value is a key in the original `Map`. Remember that the original `Map` has an entry for each employee. Thus, the remaining entries in the temporary `Map` comprise all the entries from the original `Map` whose (manager) values are no longer employees. The keys in the temporary copy, then, represent precisely the employees that we're looking for.

There are many more idioms like the ones contained in this section, but it would be impractical and tedious to list them all. Once you get the hang of it, it's not that difficult to come up with the right one when you need it.

Multimaps

A *multimap* is like a `Map` but it can map each key to multiple values. The Java Collections Framework doesn't include an interface for multimaps because they aren't used all that commonly. It's a fairly simple matter to use a `Map` whose values are `List` instances as a multimap. This technique is demonstrated in the next code example, which reads a word list containing one word per line (all lowercase) and prints out all the anagram groups that meet a size criterion. An *anagram group* is a bunch of words, all of which contain exactly the same letters but in a different order. The program takes two arguments on the command line: (1) the name of the dictionary file and (2) the minimum size of anagram group to print out. Anagram groups containing fewer words than the specified minimum are not printed.

There is a standard trick for finding anagram groups: For each word in the dictionary, alphabetize the letters in the word (that is, reorder the word's letters into alphabetical order) and put an entry into a multimap, mapping the alphabetized word to the original word. For example, the word *bad* causes an entry mapping *abd* into *bad* to be put into the multimap. A moment's reflection will show that all the words to which any given key maps form an anagram group. It's a simple matter to iterate over the keys in the multimap, printing out each anagram group that meets the size constraint.

The following program[27] is a straightforward implementation of this technique:

---

27. `tutorial/collections/interfaces/examples/Anagrams.java`

```
import java.util.*;
import java.io.*;

public class Anagrams {

  public static void main(String[] args) {
    int minGroupSize = Integer.parseInt(args[1]);

    // Read words from file and put into a simulated multimap
    Map<String, List<String>> m
      = new HashMap<String, List<String>>();
    try {
      Scanner s = new Scanner(new File(args[0]));
      while (s.hasNext()) {
        String word = s.next();
        String alpha = alphabetize(word);
        List<String> l = m.get(alpha);
        if (l == null)
          m.put(alpha, l=new ArrayList<String>());
        l.add(word);
      }
    } catch (IOException e) {
        System.err.println(e);
        System.exit(1);
    }

    // Print all permutation groups above size threshold
    for (List<String> l : m.values())
      if (l.size() >= minGroupSize)
        System.out.println(l.size() + ": " + l);
  }

  private static String alphabetize(String s) {
    char[] a = s.toCharArray();
    Arrays.sort(a);
    return new String(a);
  }
}
```

Running this program on a 173,000-word dictionary file with a minimum anagram group size of eight produces the following output:

```
9: [estrin, inerts, insert, inters, niters, nitres, sinter,
                                              triens, trines]
8: [lapse, leaps, pales, peals, pleas, salep, sepal, spale]
8: [aspers, parses, passer, prases, repass, spares, sparse,
                                                      spears]
10: [least, setal, slate, stale, steal, stela, taels, tales,
                                                teals, tesla]
8: [enters, nester, renest, rentes, resent, tenser, ternes,
                                                      treens]
8: [arles, earls, lares, laser, lears, rales, reals, seral]
8: [earings, erasing, gainers, reagins, regains, reginas,
                                            searing, seringa]
8: [peris, piers, pries, prise, ripes, speir, spier, spire]
12: [apers, apres, asper, pares, parse, pears, prase, presa,
                                     rapes, reaps, spare, spear]
11: [alerts, alters, artels, estral, laster, ratels, salter,
                                 slater, staler, stelar, talers]
9: [capers, crapes, escarp, pacers, parsec, recaps, scrape,
                                              secpar, spacer]
9: [palest, palets, pastel, petals, plates, pleats, septal,
                                              staple, tepals]
9: [anestri, antsier, nastier, ratines, retains, retinas,
                                    retsina, stainer, stearin]
8: [ates, east, eats, etas, sate, seat, seta, teas]
8: [carets, cartes, caster, caters, crates, reacts, recast,
                                                      traces]
```

Many of these words seem a bit bogus, but that's not the program's fault; they're in the dictionary file[28] we used. It is derived from the Public Domain ENABLE benchmark reference word list.[29]

Object Ordering

A `List l` may be sorted as follows:

```
Collections.sort(l);
```

If the `List` consists of `String` elements, it will be sorted into alphabetical order. If it consists of `Date` elements, it will be sorted into chronological order. How does this happen? `String` and `Date` both implement the `Comparable`[30] interface. `Comparable` implementations provide a *natural ordering* for a class, which allows objects of that class to be sorted automatically. Table 11.2 summarizes some of the more important Java platform classes that implement `Comparable`.

---

28. `tutorial/collections/interfaces/examples/dictionary.txt`

29. `http://personal.riverusers.com/~thegrendel/`

30. `docs/api/java/lang/Comparable.html`

Table 11.2 Classes Implementing Comparable

Class	**Natural Ordering**
`Byte`	Signed numerical
`Character`	Unsigned numerical
`Long`	Signed numerical
`Integer`	Signed numerical
`Short`	Signed numerical
`Double`	Signed numerical
`Float`	Signed numerical
`BigInteger`	Signed numerical
`BigDecimal`	Signed numerical
`Boolean`	`Boolean.FALSE < Boolean.TRUE`
`File`	System-dependent lexicographic on path name
`String`	Lexicographic
`Date`	Chronological
`CollationKey`	Locale-specific lexicographic

If you try to sort a list, the elements of which do not implement `Comparable`, `Collections.sort(list)` will throw a `ClassCastException`.[31] Similarly, `Collections.sort(list, comparator)` will throw a `ClassCastException` if you try to sort a list whose elements cannot be compared to one another using the `comparator`. Elements that can be compared to one another are called *mutually comparable*. Although elements of different types may be mutually comparable, none of the classes listed here permit interclass comparison.

This is all you really need to know about the `Comparable` interface if you just want to sort lists of comparable elements or to create sorted collections of them. The next section will be of interest to you if you want to implement your own `Comparable` type.

Writing Your Own Comparable Types

The `Comparable` interface consists of the following method:

31. `docs/api/java/lang/ClassCastException.html`

```
public interface Comparable<T> {
  public int compareTo(T o);
}
```

The `compareTo` method compares the receiving object with the specified object and returns a negative integer, 0, or a positive integer depending on whether the receiving object is less than, equal to, or greater than the specified object. If the specified object cannot be compared to the receiving object, the method throws a `ClassCastException`.

The following class[32] representing a person's name implements `Comparable`:

```
import java.util.*;

public class Name implements Comparable<Name> {
  private final String firstName, lastName;

  public Name(String firstName, String lastName) {
    if (firstName == null || lastName == null)
      throw new NullPointerException();
    this.firstName = firstName;
    this.lastName = lastName;
  }

  public String firstName() { return firstName; }
  public String lastName()  { return lastName;  }

  public boolean equals(Object o) {
    if (!(o instanceof Name))
      return false;
    Name n = (Name)o;
    return n.firstName.equals(firstName) &&
                        n.lastName.equals(lastName);
  }
  public int hashCode() {
    return 31*firstName.hashCode() + lastName.hashCode();
  }
  public String toString() {
  return firstName + " " + lastName;
  }
  public int compareTo(Name n) {
    int lastCmp = lastName.compareTo(n.lastName);
    return (lastCmp != 0 ? lastCmp :
            firstName.compareTo(n.firstName));
  }
}
```

32. `tutorial/collections/interfaces/examples/Name.java`

To keep the preceding example short, the class is somewhat limited: It doesn't support middle names, it demands both a first and a last name, and it is not internationalized in any way. Nonetheless, it illustrates the following important points:

- `Name` objects are *immutable*. All other things being equal, immutable types are the way to go, especially for objects that will be used as elements in `Set`s or as keys in `Map`s. These collections will break if you modify their elements or keys while they're in the collection.
- The constructor checks its arguments for `null`. This ensures that all `Name` objects are well formed so that none of the other methods will ever throw a `NullPointerException`.
- The `hashCode` method is redefined. This is essential for any class that redefines the `equals` method. (Equal objects must have equal hash codes.)
- The `equals` method returns `false` if the specified object is `null` or of an inappropriate type. The `compareTo` method throws a runtime exception under these circumstances. Both of these behaviors are required by the general contracts of the respective methods.
- The `toString` method has been redefined so it prints the `Name` in human-readable form. This is always a good idea, especially for objects that are going to get put into collections. The various collection types' `toString` methods depend on the `toString` methods of their elements, keys, and values.

Since this section is about element ordering, let's talk a bit more about `Name`'s `compareTo` method. It implements the standard name-ordering algorithm, where last names take precedence over first names. This is exactly what you want in a natural ordering. It would be very confusing indeed if the natural ordering were unnatural!

Take a look at how `compareTo` is implemented, because it's quite typical. First, you compare the most significant part of the object (in this case, the last name). Often, you can just use the natural ordering of the part's type. In this case, the part is a `String` and the natural (lexicographic) ordering is exactly what's called for. If the comparison results in anything other than zero, which represents equality, you're done: You just return the result. If the most significant parts are equal, you go on to compare the next most-significant parts. In this case, there are only two parts—first name and last name. If there were more parts, you'd proceed in the obvious fashion, comparing parts until you found two that weren't equal or you were comparing the least-significant parts, at which point you'd return the result of the comparison.

Just to show that it all works, here's a program that builds a list of names and sorts them:[33]

---

33. `tutorial/collections/interfaces/examples/NameSort.java`

```
import java.util.*;

public class NameSort {
  public static void main(String[] args) {
    Name nameArray[] = {
      new Name("John", "Lennon"),
      new Name("Karl", "Marx"),
      new Name("Groucho", "Marx"),
      new Name("Oscar", "Grouch")
    };
    List<Name> names = Arrays.asList(nameArray);
    Collections.sort(names);
    System.out.println(names);
  }
}
```

If you run this program, here's what it prints:

```
[Oscar Grouch, John Lennon, Groucho Marx, Karl Marx]
```

There are four restrictions on the behavior of the `compareTo` method, which we won't go into now because they're fairly technical and boring and are better left in the API documentation. It's really important that all classes that implement `Comparable` obey these restrictions, so read the documentation for `Comparable` if you're writing a class that implements it. Attempting to sort a list of objects that violate the restrictions has undefined behavior. Technically speaking, these restrictions ensure that the natural ordering is a *total order* on the objects of a class that implements it; this is necessary to ensure that sorting is well defined.

Comparators

What if you want to sort some objects in an order other than their natural ordering? Or what if you want to sort some objects that don't implement `Comparable`? To do either of these things, you'll need to provide a `Comparator`[34]—an object that encapsulates an ordering. Like the `Comparable` interface, the `Comparator` interface consists of a single method:

```
public interface Comparator<T> {
  int compare(T o1, T o2);
}
```

The `compare` method compares its two arguments, returning a negative integer, 0, or a positive integer depending on whether the first argument is less than, equal to, or

34. `docs/api/java/util/Comparator.html`

greater than the second. If either of the arguments has an inappropriate type for the `Comparator`, the `compare` method throws a `ClassCastException`.

Much of what was said about `Comparable` applies to `Comparator` as well. Writing a `compare` method is nearly identical to writing a `compareTo` method, except that the former gets both objects passed in as arguments. The `compare` method has to obey the same four technical restrictions as `Comparable`'s `compareTo` method for the same reason—a `Comparator` must induce a total order on the objects it compares.

Suppose you have a class called `Employee`, as follows:

```
public class Employee implements Comparable<Employee> {
  public Name name()     { ... }
  public int number()    { ... }
  public Date hireDate() { ... }
  ...
}
```

Let's assume that the natural ordering of `Employee` instances is `Name` ordering (as defined in the previous example) on employee name. Unfortunately, the boss has asked for a list of employees in order of seniority. This means we have to do some work, but not much. The following program will produce the required list:

```
import java.util.*;
public class EmpSort {
  static final Comparator<Employee> SENIORITY_ORDER =
      new Comparator<Employee>() {
    public int compare(Employee e1, Employee e2) {
      return e2.hireDate().compareTo(e1.hireDate());
    }
  };

  // Employee database
  static final Collection<Employee> employees = ... ;

  public static void main(String[] args) {
    List<Employee>e = new ArrayList<Employee>(employees);
    Collections.sort(e, SENIORITY_ORDER);
    System.out.println(e);
  }
}
```

The `Comparator` in the program is reasonably straightforward. It relies on the natural ordering of `Date` applied to the values returned by the `hireDate` accessor method. Note that the `Comparator` passes the hire date of its second argument to its first rather than vice versa. The reason is that the employee who was hired most recently is the least senior; sorting in the order of hire date would put the list in reverse seniority order.

Another technique people sometimes use to achieve this effect is to maintain the argument order but to negate the result of the comparison:

```
// Don't do this!!
return -r1.hireDate().compareTo(r2.hireDate());
```

You should always use the former technique in favor of the latter because the latter is not guaranteed to work. The reason for this is that the compareTo method can return any negative int if its argument is less than the object on which it is invoked. There is one negative int that remains negative when negated, strange as it may seem:

```
-Integer.MIN_VALUE == Integer.MIN_VALUE
```

The Comparator in the preceding program works fine for sorting a List, but it does have one deficiency: It cannot be used to order a sorted collection, such as TreeSet, because it generates an ordering that is *not compatible with* equals. This means that this Comparator equates objects that the equals method does not. In particular, any two employees who were hired on the same date will compare as equal. When you're sorting a List, this doesn't matter; but when you're using the Comparator to order a sorted collection, it's fatal. If you use this Comparator to insert multiple employees hired on the same date into a TreeSet, only the first one will be added to the set; the second will be seen as a duplicate element and will be ignored.

To fix this problem, simply tweak the Comparator so that it produces an ordering that *is compatible with* equals. In other words, tweak it so that the only elements seen as equal when using compare are those that are also seen as equal when compared using equals. The way to do this is to perform a two-part comparison (as for Name), where the first part is the one we're interested in—in this case, the hire date—and the second part is an attribute that uniquely identifies the object. Here the employee number is the obvious attribute. This is the Comparator that results:

```
static final Comparator<Employee> SENIORITY_ORDER =
                              new Comparator<Employee>() {
  public int compare(Employee e1, Employee e2) {
    int dateCmp = e2.hireDate().compareTo(e1.hireDate());
    if (dateCmp != 0)
      return dateCmp;
    return (e1.number() < e2.number() ? -1 :
      (e1.number() == e2.number() ? 0 : 1));
  }
};
```

One last note: You might be tempted to replace the final return statement in the Comparator with the simpler:

```
return e1.number() - e2.number();
```

Don't do it unless you're *absolutely sure* no one will ever have a negative employee number! This trick does not work in general because the signed integer type is not big enough to represent the difference of two arbitrary signed integers. If `i` is a large positive integer and `j` is a large negative integer, `i - j` will overflow and will return a negative integer. The resulting `comparator` violates one of the four technical restrictions we keep talking about (transitivity) and produces horrible, subtle bugs. This is not a purely theoretical concern; people get burned by it.

The SortedSet Interface

A `SortedSet`[35] is a `Set` that maintains its elements in ascending order, sorted according to the elements' natural ordering or according to a `Comparator` provided at `SortedSet` creation time. In addition to the normal `Set` operations, the `SortedSet` interface provides operations for the following:

Range view Allows arbitrary range operations on the sorted set.

Endpoints Returns the first or last element in the sorted set.

`Comparator` access Returns the `Comparator`, if any, used to sort the set.

The code for the `SortedSet` interface follows:

```
public interface SortedSet<E> extends Set<E> {
  // Range-view
  SortedSet<E> subSet(E fromElement, E toElement);
  SortedSet<E> headSet(E toElement);
  SortedSet<E> tailSet(E fromElement);

  // Endpoints
  E first();
  E last();

  // Comparator access
  Comparator<? super E> comparator();
}
```

Set Operations

The operations that `SortedSet` inherits from `Set` behave identically on sorted sets and normal sets with two exceptions:

- The `Iterator` returned by the `iterator` operation traverses the sorted set in order.
- The array returned by `toArray` contains the sorted set's elements in order.

35. `docs/api/java/util/SortedSet.html`

Although the interface doesn't guarantee it, the `toString` method of the Java platform's `SortedSet` implementations returns a string containing all the elements of the sorted set, in order.

Standard Constructors

By convention, all general-purpose `Collection` implementations provide a standard conversion constructor that takes a `Collection`; `SortedSet` implementations are no exception. In `TreeSet`, this constructor creates an instance that sorts its elements according to their natural ordering. This was probably a mistake. It would have been better to check dynamically to see whether the specified collection was a `SortedSet` instance and, if so, to sort the new `TreeSet` according to the same criterion (comparator or natural ordering). Because `TreeSet` took the approach that it did, it also provides a constructor that takes a `SortedSet` and returns a new `TreeSet` containing the same elements sorted according to the same criterion. Note that it is the compile-time type of the argument, not its runtime type, that determines which of these two constructors is invoked (and whether the sorting criterion is preserved).

`SortedSet` implementations also provide, by convention, a constructor that takes a `Comparator` and returns an empty set sorted according to the specified `Comparator`. If `null` is passed to this constructor, it returns a set that sorts its elements according to their natural ordering.

Range-view Operations

The *range-view* operations are somewhat analogous to those provided by the `List` interface, but there is one big difference. Range views of a sorted set remain valid even if the backing sorted set is modified directly. This is feasible because the endpoints of a range view of a sorted set are absolute points in the element space rather than specific elements in the backing collection, as is the case for lists. A range view of a sorted set is really just a window onto whatever portion of the set lies in the designated part of the element space. Changes to the range view write back to the backing sorted set and vice versa. Thus, it's okay to use range views on sorted sets for long periods of time, unlike range views on lists.

Sorted sets provide three range-view operations. The first, `subSet`, takes two endpoints, like `subList`. Rather than indices, the endpoints are objects and must be comparable to the elements in the sorted set, using the `Set`'s `Comparator` or the natural ordering of its elements, whichever the `Set` uses to order itself. Like `subList`, the range is half open, including its low endpoint but excluding the high one.

Thus, the following line of code tells you how many words between `"doorbell"` and `"pickle"`, including `"doorbell"` but excluding `"pickle"`, are contained in a `SortedSet` of strings called `dictionary`:

```
int count = dictionary.subSet("doorbell", "pickle").size();
```

In like manner, the following one-liner removes all the elements beginning with the letter `f`:

```
dictionary.subSet("f", "g").clear();
```

A similar trick can be used to print a table telling you how many words begin with each letter:

```
for (char ch = 'a'; ch <= 'z'; ) {
  String from = String.valueOf(ch++);
  String to = String.valueOf(ch);
  System.out.println(from + ": " +
                     dictionary.subSet(from, to).size());
}
```

Suppose you want to view a *closed interval*, which contains both of its endpoints, instead of an open interval. If the element type allows for the calculation of the successor of a given value in the element space, merely request the `subSet` from `lowEndpoint` to `successor(highEndpoint)`. Although it isn't entirely obvious, the successor of a string `s` in `String`'s natural ordering is `s + "\0"`—that is, `s` with a `null` character appended.

Thus, the following one-liner tells you how many words between `"doorbell"` and `"pickle"`, including doorbell *and* pickle, are contained in the dictionary:

```
count = dictionary.subSet("doorbell", "pickle\0").size();
```

A similar technique can be used to view an *open interval*, which contains neither endpoint. The open-interval view from `lowEndpoint` to `highEndpoint` is the half-open interval from `successor(lowEndpoint)` to `highEndpoint`. Use the following to calculate the number of words between `"doorbell"` and `"pickle"`, excluding both:

```
count = dictionary.subSet("doorbell\0", "pickle").size();
```

The `SortedSet` interface contains two more range-view operations—`headSet` and `tailSet`, both of which take a single `Object` argument. The former returns a view of the initial portion of the backing `SortedSet`, up to but not including the specified object. The latter returns a view of the final portion of the backing `SortedSet`, beginning with the specified object and continuing to the end of the backing `SortedSet`. Thus, the following code allows you to view the dictionary as two disjoint `volumes` (`a-m` and `n-z`):

```
SortedSet<String> volume1 = dictionary.headSet("n");
SortedSet<String> volume2 = dictionary.tailSet("n");
```

Endpoint Operations

The SortedSet interface contains operations to return the first and last elements in the sorted set, not surprisingly called first and last. In addition to their obvious uses, last allows a workaround for a deficiency in the SortedSet interface. One thing you'd like to do with a SortedSet is to go into the interior of the Set and iterate forward or backward. It's easy enough to go forward from the interior: Just get a tailSet and iterate over it. Unfortunately, there's no easy way to go backward.

The following idiom obtains the first element that is less than a specified object o in the element space:

```
Object predecessor = ss.headSet(o).last();
```

This is a fine way to go one element backward from a point in the interior of a sorted set. It could be applied repeatedly to iterate backward, but this is very inefficient, requiring a lookup for each element returned.

Comparator Accessor

The SortedSet interface contains an accessor method called comparator that returns the Comparator used to sort the set, or null if the set is sorted according to the *natural ordering* of its elements. This method is provided so that sorted sets can be copied into new sorted sets with the same ordering. It is used by the SortedSet constructor described previously in the Standard Constructors section (page 336).

The SortedMap Interface

A SortedMap[36] is a Map that maintains its entries in ascending order, sorted according to the keys' natural ordering, or according to a Comparator provided at the time of the SortedMap creation. Natural ordering and Comparators are discussed in the Object Ordering section (page 328). The SortedMap interface provides operations for normal Map operations and for the following:

Range view Performs arbitrary range operations on the sorted map.

Endpoints Returns the first or the last key in the sorted map.

Comparator access Returns the Comparator, if any, used to sort the map.

36. docs/api/java/util/SortedMap.html

The following interface is the `Map` analog of `SortedSet`:

```
public interface SortedMap<K, V> extends Map<K, V>{
  Comparator<? super K> comparator();
  SortedMap<K, V> subMap(K fromKey, K toKey);
  SortedMap<K, V> headMap(K toKey);
  SortedMap<K, V> tailMap(K fromKey);
  K firstKey();
  K lastKey();
}
```

Map Operations

The operations `SortedMap` inherits from `Map` behave identically on sorted maps and normal maps with two exceptions:

- The `Iterator` returned by the `iterator` operation on any of the sorted map's `Collection` views traverse the collections in order.
- The arrays returned by the `Collection` views' `toArray` operations contain the keys, values, or entries in order.

Although it isn't guaranteed by the interface, the `toString` method of the `Collection` views in all the Java platform's `SortedMap` implementations returns a string containing all the elements of the view, in order.

Standard Constructors

By convention, all general-purpose `Map` implementations provide a standard conversion constructor that takes a `Map`; `SortedMap` implementations are no exception. In `TreeMap`, this constructor creates an instance that orders its entries according to their keys' natural ordering. This was probably a mistake. It would have been better to check dynamically to see whether the specified `Map` instance was a `SortedMap` and, if so, to sort the new map according to the same criterion (comparator or natural ordering). Because `TreeMap` took the approach it did, it also provides a constructor that takes a `SortedMap` and returns a new `TreeMap` containing the same mappings as the given `SortedMap`, sorted according to the same criterion. Note that it is the compile-time type of the argument, not its runtime type, that determines whether the `SortedMap` constructor is invoked in preference to the ordinary `map` constructor.

`SortedMap` implementations also provide, by convention, a constructor that takes a `Comparator` and returns an empty map sorted according to the specified `Comparator`. If `null` is passed to this constructor, it returns a `Set` that sorts its mappings according to their keys' natural ordering.

Comparison to SortedSet

Because this interface is a precise `Map` analog of `SortedSet`, all the idioms and code examples in The `SortedSet` Interface section (page 335) apply to `SortedMap` with only trivial modifications.

Summary of Interfaces

The core collection interfaces are the foundation of the Java Collections Framework.

The Java Collections Framework hierarchy consists of two distinct interface trees:

- The first tree starts with the `Collection` interface, which provides for the basic functionality used by all collections, such as `add` and `remove` methods. Its subinterfaces—`Set`, `List`, and `Queue`—provide for more specialized collections.

  The `Set` interface does not allow duplicate elements. This can be useful for storing collections such as a deck of cards or student records. The `Set` interface has a subinterface, `SortedSet`, that provides for ordering of elements in the set.

  The `List` interface provides for an ordered collection, for situations in which you need precise control over where each element is inserted. You can retrieve elements from a `List` by their exact position.

  The `Queue` interface enables additional insertion, extraction, and inspection operations. Elements in a `Queue` are typically ordered in on a FIFO basis.

- The second tree starts with the `Map` interface, which maps keys and values similar to a `Hashtable`.

  `Map`'s subinterface, `SortedMap`, maintains its key-value pairs in ascending order or in an order specified by a `Comparator`.

These interfaces allow collections to be manipulated independently of the details of their representation.

Questions and Exercises: Interfaces

Questions

1. This section mentions three ways to traverse a `List`. Describe them, and note the limitations of each.

2. Consider the four core interfaces, `Set`, `List`, `Queue`, and `Map`. For each of the following four assignments, specify which of the four core interfaces is best suited, and explain how to use it to implement the assignment:
   - Whimsical Toys Inc (WTI) needs to record the names of all its employees. Every month, an employee will be chosen at random from these records to receive a free toy.
   - WTI has decided that each new product will be named after an employee—but only first names will be used, and each name will be used only once. Prepare a list of unique first names.
   - WTI decides that it only wants to use the most popular names for its toys. Count the number of employees who have each first name.
   - WTI acquires season tickets for the local lacrosse team, to be shared by employees. Create a waiting list for this popular sport.
3. The following program is supposed to print the string "Blue." Instead, it throws an error. Why?

```
import java.util.*;

public class SortMe {
  public static void main(String args[]) {
    SortedSet<StringBuffer> s = new TreeSet<StringBuffer>();
    s.add(new StringBuffer("Red"));
    s.add(new StringBuffer("White"));
    s.add(new StringBuffer("Blue"));
    System.out.println(s.first());
  }
}
```

Exercises

1. Write a program that prints its arguments in random order. Do not make a copy of the argument array.
2. Take the `FindDups` example (page 303) and modify it to use a `SortedSet` instead of a `Set`. Specify a `Comparator` so that case is ignored when sorting and identifying set elements.
3. Write a method that takes a `List<String>` and applies `String.trim`[37] to each element. To do this, you'll need to pick one of the three iteration idioms that you described in Question 1. Two of these will not give the result you want, so be sure to write a program demonstrating that the method actually works!

---

37. `docs/api/java/lang/String.html`

Answers

You can find answers to these Questions and Exercises at:

```
tutorial/collections/interfaces/QandE/answers.html
```

Implementations

Implementations are the data objects used to store collections, which implement the interfaces described in the Interfaces section (page 295). This section describes the following kinds of implementations:

- **General-purpose implementations** are the most commonly used implementations, designed for everyday use. They are summarized in Table 11.3.
- **Special-purpose implementations** are designed for use in special situations and display nonstandard performance characteristics, usage restrictions, or behavior.
- **Concurrent implementations** are designed to support high concurrency, typically at the expense of single-threaded performance. These implementations are part of the `java.util.concurrent` package.
- **Wrapper implementations** are used in combination with other types of implementations, often the general-purpose ones, to provide added or restricted functionality.
- **Convenience implementations** are mini-implementations, typically made available via static factory methods, that provide convenient, efficient alternatives to general-purpose implementations for special collections (for example, singleton sets).
- **Abstract implementations** are skeletal implementations that facilitate the construction of custom implementations, described later in the Custom Collection Implementations section (page 360). An advanced topic, it's not particularly difficult, but relatively few people will need to do it.

Table 11.3 General-Purpose Implementations

	Implementations				
Interfaces	**Hash Table**	**Resizable Array**	**Tree**	**Linked List**	**Hash Table and Linked List**
`Set`	`HashSet`		`TreeSet`		`LinkedHashSet`
`List`		`ArrayList`		`LinkedList`	
`Queue`					
`Map`	`HashMap`		`TreeMap`		`LinkedHashMap`

As you can see from Table 11.3, the Java Collections Framework provides several general-purpose implementations of the `Set`, `List`, and `Map` interfaces. In each case, one implementation—`HashSet`, `ArrayList`, and `HashMap`—is clearly the one to use for most applications, all other things being equal. Note that the `SortedSet` and the `SortedMap` interfaces do not have rows in the table. Each of those interfaces has one implementation (`TreeSet` and `TreeMap`) and is listed in the `Set` and the `Map` rows. There are two general-purpose `Queue` implementations—`LinkedList`, which is also a `List` implementation, and `PriorityQueue`,[38] which is omitted from the table. These two implementations provide very different semantics: `LinkedList` provides FIFO semantics, while `PriorityQueue` orders its elements according to their values.

Each of the general-purpose implementations provides all optional operations contained in its interface. All permit `null` elements, keys, and values. None are synchronized (thread-safe). All have *fail-fast iterators*, which detect illegal concurrent modification during iteration and fail quickly and cleanly rather than risking arbitrary, nondeterministic behavior at an undetermined time in the future. All are `Serializable` and all support a public `clone` method.

The fact that these implementations are unsynchronized represents a break with the past: The legacy collections `Vector` and `Hashtable` are synchronized. The present approach was taken because collections are frequently used when the synchronization is of no benefit. Such uses include single-threaded use, read-only use, and use as part of a larger data object that does its own synchronization. In general, it is good API design practice not to make users pay for a feature they don't use. Furthermore, unnecessary synchronization can result in deadlock under certain circumstances.

If you need thread-safe collections, the synchronization wrappers, described in the Wrapper Implementations section (page 350), allow *any* collection to be transformed into a synchronized collection. Thus, synchronization is optional for general-purpose implementations, whereas it is mandatory for legacy implementations. Moreover, the `java.util.concurrent` package provides concurrent implementations of the `BlockingQueue` interface, which extends `Queue`, and of the `ConcurrentMap` interface, which extends `Map`. These implementations offer much higher concurrency than mere synchronized implementations.

As a rule, you should be thinking about the interfaces, *not* the implementations. That is why there are no programming examples in this section. For the most part, the choice of implementation affects only performance. The preferred style, as mentioned in the Interfaces section (page 295), is to choose an implementation when a `Collection` is created and to immediately assign the new collection to a variable of the corresponding interface type (or to pass the collection to a method expecting an argument of the

38. `docs/api/java/util/PriorityQueue.html`

interface type). In this way, the program does not become dependent on any added methods in a given implementation, leaving the programmer free to change implementations anytime that it is warranted by performance concerns or behavioral details.

The sections that follow briefly discuss the implementations. The performance of the implementations is described using words such as *constant-time*, *log*, *linear*, *n log(n)*, and *quadratic* to refer to the asymptotic upper-bound on the time complexity of performing the operation. All this is quite a mouthful, and it doesn't matter much if you don't know what it means. If you're interested in knowing more, refer to any good algorithms textbook. One thing to keep in mind is that this sort of performance metric has its limitations. Sometimes, the nominally slower implementation may be faster. When in doubt, measure the performance!

Set Implementations

The `Set` implementations are grouped into general-purpose and special-purpose implementations.

General-Purpose Set Implementations

There are three general-purpose `Set` implementations—`HashSet`, `TreeSet`, and `LinkedHashSet`. Which of these three to use is generally straightforward. `HashSet` is much faster than `TreeSet` (constant-time versus log-time for most operations) but offers no ordering guarantees. If you need to use the operations in the `SortedSet` interface, or if value-ordered iteration is required, use `TreeSet`; otherwise, use `HashSet`. It's a fair bet that you'll end up using `HashSet` most of the time.

`LinkedHashSet` is in some sense intermediate between `HashSet` and `TreeSet`. Implemented as a hash table with a linked list running through it, it provides *insertion-ordered* iteration (least recently inserted to most recently) and runs nearly as fast as `HashSet`. The `LinkedHashSet` implementation spares its clients from the unspecified, generally chaotic ordering provided by `HashSet` without incurring the increased cost associated with `TreeSet`.

One thing worth keeping in mind about `HashSet` is that iteration is linear in the sum of the number of entries and the number of buckets (the *capacity*). Thus, choosing an initial capacity that's too high can waste both space and time. On the other hand, choosing an initial capacity that's too low wastes time by copying the data structure each time it's forced to increase its capacity. If you don't specify an initial capacity, the default is 16. In the past, there was some advantage to choosing a prime number as the initial capacity. This is no longer true. Internally, the capacity is always rounded up to a power of two. The initial capacity is specified by using the `int` constructor. The following line of code allocates a `HashSet` whose initial capacity is 64:

```
Set<String> s = new HashSet<String>(64);
```

The `HashSet` class has one other tuning parameter called the *load factor*. If you care a lot about the space consumption of your `HashSet`, read the `HashSet` documentation for more information. Otherwise, just accept the default; it's almost always the right thing to do.

If you accept the default load factor but want to specify an initial capacity, pick a number that's about twice the size to which you expect the set to grow. If your guess is way off, you may waste a bit of space, time, or both, but it's unlikely to be a big problem.

`LinkedHashSet` has the same tuning parameters as `HashSet`, but iteration time is not affected by capacity. `TreeSet` has no tuning parameters.

Special-Purpose Set Implementations

There are two special-purpose `Set` implementations—`EnumSet`[39] and `CopyOnWrite-ArraySet`.[40]

`EnumSet` is a high-performance `Set` implementation for enum types. All of the members of an enum set must be of the same enum type. Internally, it is represented by a bit-vector, typically a single `long`. Enum sets support iteration over ranges of enum types. For example, given the enum declaration for the days of the week, you can iterate over the weekdays. The `EnumSet` class provides a static factory that makes it easy:

```
for (Day d : EnumSet.range(Day.MONDAY, Day.FRIDAY))
  System.out.println(d);
```

Enum sets also provide a rich, typesafe replacement for traditional bit flags:

```
EnumSet.of(Style.BOLD, Style.ITALIC)
```

`CopyOnWriteArraySet` is a `Set` implementation backed up by a copy-on-write array. All mutative operations, such as `add`, `set`, and `remove`, are implemented by making a new copy of the array; no locking is ever required. Even iteration may safely proceed concurrently with element insertion and deletion. Unlike most `Set` implementations, the `add`, `remove`, and `contains` methods require time proportional to the size of the set. This implementation is *only* appropriate for sets that are rarely modified but frequently iterated. It is well suited to maintaining event-handler lists that must prevent duplicates.

---

39. `docs/api/java/util/EnumSet.html`

40. `docs/api/java/util/concurrent/CopyOnWriteArraySet.html`

List Implementations

`List` implementations are grouped into general-purpose and special-purpose implementations.

General-Purpose List Implementations

There are two general-purpose `List` implementations—`ArrayList` and `LinkedList`. Most of the time you'll probably use `ArrayList`, which offers constant-time positional access and is just plain fast. It does not have to allocate a node object for each element in the `List`, and it can take advantage of `System.arraycopy` when it has to move multiple elements at the same time. Think of `ArrayList` as `Vector` without the synchronization overhead.

If you frequently add elements to the beginning of the `List` or iterate over the `List` to delete elements from its interior, you should consider using `LinkedList`. These operations require constant-time in a `LinkedList` and linear-time in an `ArrayList`. But you pay a big price in performance. Positional access requires linear-time in a `LinkedList` and constant-time in an `ArrayList`. Furthermore, the constant factor for `LinkedList` is much worse. If you think you want to use a `LinkedList`, measure the performance of your application with both `LinkedList` and `ArrayList` before making your choice; `ArrayList` is usually faster.

`ArrayList` has one tuning parameter—the *initial capacity*, which refers to the number of elements the `ArrayList` can hold before it has to grow. `LinkedList` has no tuning parameters and seven optional operations, one of which is `clone`. The other six are `addFirst`, `getFirst`, `removeFirst`, `addLast`, `getLast`, and `removeLast`. `LinkedList` also implements the `Queue` interface.

Special-Purpose List Implementations

`CopyOnWriteArrayList`[41] is a `List` implementation backed up by a copy-on-write array. This implementation is similar in nature to `CopyOnWriteArraySet`. No synchronization is necessary, even during iteration, and iterators are guaranteed never to throw `ConcurrentModificationException`. This implementation is well suited to maintaining event-handler lists, in which change is infrequent, and traversal is frequent and potentially time-consuming.

If you need synchronization, a `Vector` will be slightly faster than an `ArrayList` synchronized with `Collections.synchronizedList`. But `Vector` has loads of legacy

41. `docs/api/java/util/concurrent/CopyOnWriteArrayList.html`

operations, so be careful to always manipulate the `Vector` with the `List` interface or else you won't be able to replace the implementation at a later time.

If your `List` is fixed in size—that is, you'll never use `remove`, `add`, or any of the bulk operations other than `containsAll`—you have a third option that's definitely worth considering. See `Arrays.asList` in the Convenience Implementations section (page 352) for more information.

Map Implementations

`Map` implementations are grouped into general-purpose, special-purpose, and concurrent implementations.

General-Purpose Map Implementations

The three general-purpose `Map` implementations are `HashMap`, `TreeMap`, and `LinkedHashMap`. If you need `SortedMap` operations or key-ordered `Collection`-view iteration, use `TreeMap`; if you want maximum speed and don't care about iteration order, use `HashMap`; if you want near-`HashMap` performance and insertion-order iteration, use `LinkedHashMap`. In this respect, the situation for `Map` is analogous to `Set`. Likewise, everything else in The `Set` Interface section (page 301) also applies to `Map` implementations.

`LinkedHashMap` provides two capabilities that are not available with `LinkedHashSet`. When you create a `LinkedHashMap`, you can order it based on key access rather than insertion. In other words, merely looking up the value associated with a key brings that key to the end of the map. Also, `LinkedHashMap` provides the `removeEldestEntry` method, which may be overridden to impose a policy for removing stale mappings automatically when new mappings are added to the map. This makes it very easy to implement a custom cache.

For example, this override will allow the map to grow up to as many as 100 entries, and then it will delete the eldest entry each time a new entry is added, maintaining a steady state of 100 entries:

```
private static final int MAX_ENTRIES = 100;

protected boolean removeEldestEntry(Map.Entry eldest) {
  return size() > MAX_ENTRIES;
}
```

Special-Purpose Map Implementations

There are three special-purpose `Map` implementations—`EnumMap`,[42] `WeakHashMap`,[43] and `IdentityHashMap`.[44] `EnumMap`, which is internally implemented as an `array`, is a high-performance `Map` implementation for use with enum keys. This implementation combines the richness and safety of the `Map` interface with a speed approaching that of an array. If you want to map an enum to a value, you should always use an `EnumMap` rather than an array.

`WeakHashMap` is an implementation of the `Map` interface that stores only weak references to its keys. Storing only weak references allows a key-value pair to be garbage-collected when its key is no longer referenced outside of the `WeakHashMap`. This class provides the easiest way to harness the power of weak references. It is useful for implementing "registry-like" data structures, where the utility of an entry vanishes when its key is no longer reachable by any thread.

`IdentityHashMap` is an identity-based `Map` implementation based on a hash table. This class is useful for topology-preserving object graph transformations, such as serialization or deep-copying. To perform such transformations, you need to maintain an identity-based "node table" that keeps track of which objects have already been seen. Identity-based maps are also used to maintain object-to-meta-information mappings in dynamic debuggers and similar systems. Finally, identity-based maps are useful in thwarting "spoof attacks" that are a result of intentionally perverse `equals` methods because `IdentityHashMap` never invokes the `equals` method on its keys. An added benefit of this implementation is that it is fast.

Concurrent Map Implementations

The `java.util.concurrent`[45] package contains the `ConcurrentMap`[46] interface, which extends `Map` with atomic `putIfAbsent`, `remove`, and `replace` methods, and the `ConcurrentHashMap`[47] implementation of that interface.

`ConcurrentHashMap` is a highly concurrent, high-performance implementation backed up by a hash table. This implementation never blocks when performing retrievals and allows the client to select the concurrency level for updates. It is intended as a drop-in replacement for `Hashtable`: In addition to implementing `ConcurrentMap`, it supports

---

42. `docs/api/java/util/EnumMap.html`

43. `docs/api/java/util/WeakHashMap.html`

44. `docs/api/java/util/IdentityHashMap.html`

45. `docs/api/java/util/concurrent/package-summary.html`

46. `docs/api/java/util/concurrent/ConcurrentMap.html`

47. `docs/api/java/util/concurrent/ConcurrentHashMap.html`

all the legacy methods peculiar to Hashtable. Again, if you don't need the legacy operations, be careful to manipulate it with the ConcurrentMap interface.

Queue Implementations

The Queue implementations are grouped into general-purpose and concurrent implementations.

General-Purpose Queue Implementations

As mentioned in the previous section, LinkedList implements the Queue interface, providing FIFO queue operations for add, poll, and so on.

The PriorityQueue class is a priority queue based on the *heap* data structure. This queue orders elements according to an order specified at construction time, which can be the elements' natural ordering or the ordering imposed by an explicit Comparator.

The queue retrieval operations—poll, remove, peek, and element—access the element at the head of the queue. The *head of the queue* is the least element with respect to the specified ordering. If multiple elements are tied for least value, the head is one of those elements; ties are broken arbitrarily.

PriorityQueue and its iterator implement all of the optional methods of the Collection and Iterator interfaces. The iterator provided in method iterator is not guaranteed to traverse the elements of the PriorityQueue in any particular order. If you need ordered traversal, consider using Arrays.sort(pq.toArray()).

Concurrent Queue Implementations

The java.util.concurrent package contains a set of synchronized Queue interfaces and classes. BlockingQueue extends Queue with operations that wait for the queue to become nonempty when retrieving an element and for space to become available in the queue when storing an element. This interface is implemented by the following classes:

LinkedBlockingQueue[48] An optionally bounded FIFO blocking queue backed by linked nodes.

ArrayBlockingQueue[49] A bounded FIFO blocking queue backed by an array.

PriorityBlockingQueue[50] An unbounded blocking priority queue backed by a heap.

---

48. docs/api/java/util/concurrent/LinkedBlockingQueue.html

49. docs/api/java/util/concurrent/ArrayBlockingQueue.html

50. docs/api/java/util/concurrent/PriorityBlockingQueue.html

DelayQueue[51] A time-based scheduling queue backed by a heap.

SynchronousQueue[52] A simple rendezvous mechanism that uses the `BlockingQueue` interface.

Wrapper Implementations

Wrapper implementations delegate all their real work to a specified collection but add extra functionality on top of what this collection offers. For design pattern fans, this is an example of the *decorator* pattern. Although it may seem a bit exotic, it's really pretty straightforward.

These implementations are anonymous; rather than providing a public class, the library provides a static factory method. All these implementations are found in the `Collections` class, which consists solely of static methods.

Synchronization Wrappers

The synchronization wrappers add automatic synchronization (thread-safety) to an arbitrary collection. Each of the six core collection interfaces—`Collection`, `Set`, `List`, `Map`, `SortedSet`, and `SortedMap`—has one static factory method:

```
public static <T> Collection<T>
  synchronizedCollection(Collection<T> c);
public static <T> Set<T>
  synchronizedSet(Set<T> s);
public static <T> List<T>
  synchronizedList(List<T> list);
public static <K,V> Map<K,V>
  synchronizedMap(Map<K,V> m);
public static <T> SortedSet<T>
  synchronizedSortedSet(SortedSet<T> s);
public static <K,V> SortedMap<K,V>
  synchronizedSortedMap(SortedMap<K,V> m);
```

Each of these methods returns a synchronized (thread-safe) `Collection` backed up by the specified collection. To guarantee serial access, *all* access to the backing collection must be accomplished through the returned collection. The easy way to guarantee this is not to keep a reference to the backing collection. Create the synchronized collection with the following trick:

51. `docs/api/java/util/concurrent/DelayQueue.html`

52. `docs/api/java/util/concurrent/SynchronousQueue.html`

```
List<Type> list =
  Collections.synchronizedList(new ArrayList<Type>());
```

A collection created in this fashion is every bit as thread-safe as a normally synchronized collection, such as a `Vector`.

In the face of concurrent access, it is imperative that the user manually synchronize on the returned collection when iterating over it. The reason is that iteration is accomplished via multiple calls into the collection, which must be composed into a single atomic operation. The following is the idiom to iterate over a wrapper-synchronized collection:

```
Collection<Type> c =
  Collections.synchronizedCollection(myCollection);
synchronized(c) {
  for (Type e : c)
    foo(e);
}
```

If an explicit iterator is used, the `iterator` method must be called from within the `synchronized` block. Failure to follow this advice may result in nondeterministic behavior. The idiom for iterating over a `Collection` view of a synchronized `Map` is similar. It is imperative that the user synchronize on the synchronized `Map` when iterating over any of its `Collection` views rather than synchronizing on the `Collection` view itself, as shown in the following example:

```
Map<KeyType, ValType> m =
  Collections.synchronizedMap(new HashMap<KeyType, ValType>());
  ...
Set<KeyType> s = m.keySet();
  ...
synchronized(m) {  // Synchronizing on m, not s!
  while (KeyType k : s)
    foo(k);
}
```

One minor downside of using wrapper implementations is that you do not have the ability to execute any *noninterface* operations of a wrapped implementation. So, for instance, in the preceding `List` example, you cannot call `ArrayList`'s `ensureCapacity` operation on the wrapped `ArrayList`.

Unmodifiable Wrappers

Unlike synchronization wrappers, which add functionality to the wrapped collection, the unmodifiable wrappers take functionality away. In particular, they take away the ability to modify the collection by intercepting all the operations that would modify the collection and throwing an `UnsupportedOperationException`. Unmodifiable wrappers have two main uses, as follows:

- To make a collection immutable once it has been built. In this case, it's good practice not to maintain a reference to the backing collection. This absolutely guarantees immutability.
- To allow certain clients read-only access to your data structures. You keep a reference to the backing collection but hand out a reference to the wrapper. In this way, clients can look but not modify, while you maintain full access.

Like synchronization wrappers, each of the six core `Collection` interfaces has one static factory method:

```
public static <T> Collection<T>
  unmodifiableCollection(Collection<? extends T> c);
public static <T> Set<T>
  unmodifiableSet(Set<? extends T> s);
public static <T> List<T>
  unmodifiableList(List<? extends T> list);
public static <K,V> Map<K, V>
  unmodifiableMap(Map<? extends K, ? extends V> m);
public static <T> SortedSet<T>
  unmodifiableSortedSet(SortedSet<? extends T> s);
public static <K,V> SortedMap<K, V>
  unmodifiableSortedMap(SortedMap<K, ? extends V> m);
```

Checked Interface Wrappers

The `Collections.checked` *interface* wrappers are provided for use with generic collections. These implementations return a *dynamically* type-safe view of the specified collection, which throws a `ClassCastException` if a client attempts to add an element of the wrong type. The generics mechanism in the language provides compile-time (static) type-checking, but it is possible to defeat this mechanism. Dynamically type-safe views eliminate this possibility entirely.

Convenience Implementations

This section describes several mini-implementations that can be more convenient and more efficient than general-purpose implementations when you don't need their full power. All the implementations in this section are made available via static factory methods rather than `public` classes.

List View of an Array

The `Arrays.asList` method returns a `List` view of its array argument. Changes to the `List` write through to the array and vice versa. The size of the collection is that of the array and cannot be changed. If the `add` or the `remove` method is called on the `List`, an `UnsupportedOperationException` will result.

The normal use of this implementation is as a bridge between array-based and collection-based APIs. It allows you to pass an array to a method expecting a `Collection` or a `List`. However, this implementation also has another use. If you need a fixed-size `List`, it's more efficient than any general-purpose `List` implementation. This is the idiom:

```
List<String> list = Arrays.asList(new String[size]);
```

Note that a reference to the backing array is not retained.

Immutable Multiple-Copy List

Occasionally you'll need an immutable `List` consisting of multiple copies of the same element. The `Collections.nCopies` method returns such a list. This implementation has two main uses. The first is to initialize a newly created `List`; for example, suppose you want an `ArrayList` initially consisting of 1,000 `null` elements. The following incantation does the trick:

```
List<Type> list =
  new ArrayList<Type>(Collections.nCopies(1000, (Type)null);
```

Of course, the initial value of each element need not be `null`. The second main use is to grow an existing `List`. For example, suppose you want to add 69 copies of the string `"fruit bat"` to the end of a `List<String>`. It's not clear why you'd want to do such a thing, but let's just suppose you did. The following is how you'd do it:

```
lovablePets.addAll(Collections.nCopies(69, "fruit bat"));
```

By using the form of `addAll` that takes both an index and a `Collection`, you can add the new elements to the middle of a `List` instead of to the end of it.

Immutable Singleton Set

Sometimes you'll need an immutable *singleton* `Set`, which consists of a single, specified element. The `Collections.singleton` method returns such a `Set`. One use of this implementation is to remove all occurrences of a specified element from a `Collection`:

```
c.removeAll(Collections.singleton(e));
```

A related idiom removes all elements that map to a specified value from a `Map`. For example, suppose you have a `Map`—`job`—that maps people to their line of work and suppose you want to eliminate all the lawyers. The following one-liner will do the deed:

```
job.values().removeAll(Collections.singleton(LAWYER));
```

One more use of this implementation is to provide a single input value to a method that is written to accept a collection of values.

Empty Set, List, and Map Constants

The `Collections` class provides methods to return the empty `Set`, `List`, and `Map`—`emptySet`, `emptyList`, and `emptyMap`. The main use of these constants is as input to methods that take a `Collection` of values when you don't want to provide any values at all, as in this example:

```
tourist.declarePurchases(Collections.emptySet());
```

Summary of Implementations

Implementations are the data objects used to store collections, which implement the interfaces described in the Interfaces section (page 295).

The Java Collections Framework provides several general-purpose implementations of the core interfaces:

- For the `Set` interface, `HashSet` is the most commonly used implementation.
- For the `List` interface, `ArrayList` is the most commonly used implementation.
- For the `Map` interface, `HashMap` is the most commonly used implementation.
- For the `Queue` interface, `LinkedList` is the most commonly used implementation.

Each of the general-purpose implementations provides all optional operations contained in its interface.

The Java Collections Framework also provides several special-purpose implementations for situations that require nonstandard performance, usage restrictions, or other unusual behavior.

The `java.util.concurrent` package contains several collections implementations, which are thread-safe but not governed by a single exclusion lock.

The `Collections` class (as opposed to the `Collection` interface), provides static methods that operate on or return collections, which are known as wrapper implementations.

Finally, there are several Convenience implementations, which can be more efficient than general-purpose implementations when you don't need their full power. The Convenience implementations are made available through static factory methods.

Questions and Exercises: Implementations

Questions

1. You plan to write a program that uses several basic collection interfaces: `Set`, `List`, `Queue`, and `Map`. You're not sure which implementations will work best, so you decide to use general-purpose implementations until you get a better idea how your program will work in the real world. Which implementations are these?
2. If you need a `Set` implementation that provides value-ordered iteration, which class should you use?
3. Which class do you use to access wrapper implementations?

Exercises

Write a program that reads a text file, specified by the first command line argument, into a `List`. The program should then print random lines from the file, the number of lines printed to be specified by the second command line argument. Write the program so that a correctly sized collection is allocated all at once, instead of being gradually expanded as the file is read in. Hint: To determine the number of lines in the file use `java.io.File.length`[53] to obtain the size of the file, and then divide by an assumed size of an average line.

Answers

You can find answers to these Questions and Exercises at:

```
tutorial/collections/implementations/QandE/answers.html
```

Algorithms

The *polymorphic algorithms* described here are pieces of reusable functionality provided by the Java platform. All of them come from the `Collections` class, and all take the form of static methods whose first argument is the collection on which the operation is to be performed. The great majority of the algorithms provided by the Java platform operate on `List` instances, but a few of them operate on arbitrary `Collection` instances. This section briefly describes the following algorithms:

53. `docs/api/java/io/File.html`

- Sorting
- Shuffling
- Routine Data Manipulation
- Searching
- Composition
- Finding Extreme Values

Sorting

The `sort` algorithm reorders a `List` so that its elements are in ascending order according to an ordering relationship. Two forms of the operation are provided. The simple form takes a `List` and sorts it according to its elements' *natural ordering*. If you're unfamiliar with the concept of natural ordering, read the Object Ordering section (page 328).

The `sort` operation uses a slightly optimized *merge sort* algorithm that is fast and stable:

Fast It is guaranteed to run in `n log(n)` time and runs substantially faster on nearly sorted lists. Empirical tests showed it to be as fast as a highly optimized quicksort. A quicksort is generally considered to be faster than a merge sort but isn't stable and doesn't guarantee `n log(n)` performance.

Stable It doesn't reorder equal elements. This is important if you sort the same list repeatedly on different attributes. If a user of a mail program sorts the inbox by mailing date and then sorts it by sender, the user naturally expects that the now-contiguous list of messages from a given sender will (still) be sorted by mailing date. This is guaranteed only if the second sort was stable.

The following trivial program[54] prints out its arguments in lexicographic (alphabetical) order:

```
import java.util.*;

public class Sort {
  public static void main(String[] args) {
    List<String> list = Arrays.asList(args);
    Collections.sort(list);
    System.out.println(list);
  }
}
```

54. `tutorial/collections/algorithms/examples/Sort.java`

Let's run the program:

```
% java Sort i walk the line
```

The following output is produced:

```
[i, line, the, walk]
```

The program was included only to show you that algorithms really are as easy to use as they appear to be.

The second form of `sort` takes a `Comparator` in addition to a `List` and sorts the elements with the `Comparator`. Suppose you want to print out the anagram groups from our earlier example in reverse order of size—largest anagram group first. The example that follows shows you how to achieve this with the help of the second form of the `sort` method.

Recall that the anagram groups are stored as values in a `Map`, in the form of `List` instances. The revised printing code iterates through the `Map`'s values view, putting every `List` that passes the minimum-size test into a `List` of `Lists`. Then the code sorts this `List`, using a `Comparator` that expects `List` instances, and implements reverse size-ordering. Finally, the code iterates through the sorted `List`, printing its elements (the anagram groups). The following code[55] replaces the printing code at the end of the `main` method in the `Anagrams` example:

```
// Make a List of all anagram groups above size threshold.
List<List<String>> winners = new ArrayList<List<String>>();
for (List<String> l : m.values())
  if (l.size() >= minGroupSize)
    winners.add(l);

// Sort anagram groups according to size
Collections.sort(winners, new Comparator<List<String>>() {
  public int compare(List<String> o1, List<String> o2) {
    return o2.size() - o1.size();
  }});

// Print anagram groups.
for (List<String> l : winners)
  System.out.println(l.size() + ": " + l);
```

Running the program on the same dictionary as in The `Map` Interface section (page 319), with the same minimum anagram group size (eight), produces the following output:

55. `tutorial/collections/algorithms/examples/Anagrams2.java`

```
12: [apers, apres, asper, pares, parse, pears, prase, presa,
                                 rapes, reaps, spare, spear]
11: [alerts, alters, artels, estral, laster, ratels, salter,
                           slater, staler, stelar, talers]
10: [least, setal, slate, stale, steal, stela, taels, tales,
                                              teals, tesla]
9: [estrin, inerts, insert, inters, niters, nitres, sinter,
                                             triens, trines]
9: [capers, crapes, escarp, pacers, parsec, recaps, scrape,
                                             secpar, spacer]
9: [palest, palets, pastel, petals, plates, pleats, septal,
                                             staple, tepals]
9: [anestri, antsier, nastier, ratines, retains, retinas,
                                   retsina, stainer, stearin]
8: [lapse, leaps, pales, peals, pleas, salep, sepal, spale]
8: [aspers, parses, passer, prases, repass, spares, sparse,
                                                     spears]
8: [enters, nester, renest, rentes, resent, tenser, ternes,
                                                     treens]
8: [arles, earls, lares, laser, lears, rales, reals, seral]
8: [earings, erasing, gainers, reagins, regains, reginas,
                                           searing, seringa]
8: [peris, piers, pries, prise, ripes, speir, spier, spire]
8: [ates, east, eats, etas, sate, seat, seta, teas]
8: [carets, cartes, caster, caters, crates, reacts, recast,
                                                     traces]
```

Shuffling

The `shuffle` algorithm does the opposite of what `sort` does, destroying any trace of order that may have been present in a `List`. That is, this algorithm reorders the `List` based on input from a source of randomness such that all possible permutations occur with equal likelihood, assuming a fair source of randomness. This algorithm is useful in implementing games of chance. For example, it could be used to shuffle a `List` of `Card` objects representing a deck. Also, it's useful for generating test cases.

This operation has two forms: one takes a `List` and uses a default source of randomness, and the other requires the caller to provide a `Random`[56] object to use as a source of randomness. The code for this algorithm is used as an example in the Positional Access and Search Operations section (page 309).

56. `docs/api/java/util/Random.html`

Routine Data Manipulation

The `Collections` class provides five algorithms for doing routine data manipulation on `List` objects, all of which are pretty straightforward:

`reverse` Reverses the order of the elements in a `List`.

`fill` Overwrites every element in a `List` with the specified value. This operation is useful for reinitializing a `List`.

`copy` Takes two arguments, a destination `List` and a source `List`, and copies the elements of the source into the destination, overwriting its contents. The destination `List` must be at least as long as the source. If it is longer, the remaining elements in the destination `List` are unaffected.

`swap` Swaps the elements at the specified positions in a `List`.

`addAll` Adds all the specified elements to a `Collection`. The elements to be added may be specified individually or as an array.

Searching

The `binarySearch` algorithm searches for a specified element in a sorted `List`. This algorithm has two forms. The first takes a `List` and an element to search for (the "search key"). This form assumes that the `List` is sorted in ascending order according to the natural ordering of its elements. The second form takes a `Comparator` in addition to the `List` and the search key, and assumes that the `List` is sorted into ascending order according to the specified `Comparator`. The `sort` algorithm can be used to sort the `List` prior to calling `binarySearch`.

The return value is the same for both forms. If the `List` contains the search key, its index is returned. If not, the return value is `(-(insertion point) - 1)`, where the insertion point is the point at which the value would be inserted into the `List`, or the index of the first element greater than the value, or `list.size()` if all elements in the `List` are less than the specified value. This admittedly ugly formula guarantees that the return value will be `>= 0` if and only if the search key is found. It's basically a hack to combine a boolean `(found)` and an integer `(index)` into a single `int` return value.

The following idiom, usable with both forms of the `binarySearch` operation, looks for the specified search key and inserts it at the appropriate position if it's not already present:

```
int pos = Collections.binarySearch(list, key);
if (pos < 0)
  l.add(-pos-1);
```

Composition

The `frequency` and `disjoint` algorithms test some aspect of the composition of one or more `Collections`:

`frequency` Counts the number of times the specified element occurs in the specified collection.

`disjoint` Determines whether two `Collections` are disjoint; that is, whether they contain no elements in common.

Finding Extreme Values

The `min` and the `max` algorithms return, respectively, the minimum and maximum element contained in a specified `Collection`. Both of these operations come in two forms. The simple form takes only a `Collection` and returns the minimum (or maximum) element according to the elements' natural ordering. The second form takes a `Comparator` in addition to the `Collection` and returns the minimum (or maximum) element according to the specified `Comparator`.

Custom Collection Implementations

Many programmers will never need to implement their own `Collections` classes. You can go pretty far using the implementations described in the preceding sections of this chapter. However, someday you might want to write your own implementation. It is fairly easy to do this with the aid of the abstract implementations provided by the Java platform. Before we discuss *how* to write an implementation, let's discuss why you might want to write one.

Reasons to Write an Implementation

The following list illustrates the sort of custom `Collections` you might want to implement. It is not intended to be exhaustive:

Persistent All of the built-in `Collection` implementations reside in main memory and vanish when the program exits. If you want a collection that will still be present the next time the program starts, you can implement it by building a veneer over an external database. Such a collection might be concurrently accessible by multiple programs.

Application-specific This is a very broad category. One example is an unmodifiable `Map` containing real-time telemetry data. The keys could represent locations, and the values could be read from sensors at these locations in response to the `get` operation.

High-performance, special-purpose Many data structures take advantage of restricted usage to offer better performance than is possible with general-purpose implementations. For instance, consider a `List` containing long runs of identical element values. Such lists, which occur frequently in text processing, can be *run-length encoded*—runs can be represented as a single object containing the repeated element and the number of consecutive repetitions. This example is interesting because it trades off two aspects of performance: It requires less space but more time than an `ArrayList`.

High-performance, general-purpose The Java Collections Framework's designers tried to provide the best general-purpose implementations for each interface, but many, many data structures could have been used, and new ones are invented every day. Maybe you can come up with something faster!

Enhanced functionality Suppose you need an efficient bag implementation (also known as a *multiset*): a `Collection` that offers constant-time containment checks while allowing duplicate elements. It's reasonably straightforward to implement such a collection atop a `HashMap`.

Convenience You may want additional implementations that offer conveniences beyond those offered by the Java platform. For instance, you may frequently need `List` instances representing a contiguous range of `Integer`s.

Adapter Suppose you are using a legacy API that has its own ad hoc collections' API. You can write an adapter implementation that permits these collections to operate in the Java Collections Framework. An *adapter implementation* is a thin veneer that wraps objects of one type and makes them behave like objects of another type by translating operations on the latter type into operations on the former.

How to Write a Custom Implementation

Writing a custom implementation is surprisingly easy. The Java Collections Framework provides abstract implementations designed expressly to facilitate custom implementations. We'll start with the following example of an implementation of `Arrays.asList`:

```
public static <T> List<T> asList(T[] a) {
  return new MyArrayList<T>(a);
}

private static class MyArrayList<T> extends AbstractList<T> {

  private final T[] a;

  MyArrayList(T[] array) {
    a = array;
  }

  public T get(int index) {
    return a[index];
  }

  public T set(int index, T element) {
    T oldValue = a[index];
    a[index] = element;
    return oldValue;
  }

  public int size() {
    return a.length;
  }
}
```

Believe it or not, this is very close to the implementation that is contained in `java.util.Arrays`. It's that simple! You provide a constructor and the `get`, `set`, and `size` methods, and `AbstractList` does all the rest. You get the `ListIterator`, bulk operations, search operations, hash code computation, comparison, and string representation for free.

Suppose you want to make the implementation a bit faster. The API documentation for abstract implementations describes precisely how each method is implemented, so you'll know which methods to override to get the performance you want. The preceding implementation's performance is fine, but it can be improved a bit. In particular, the `toArray` method iterates over the `List`, copying one element at a time. Given the internal representation, it's a lot faster and more sensible just to clone the array:

```
public Object[] toArray() {
  return (Object[]) a.clone();
}
```

With the addition of this override and a few more like it, this implementation is exactly the one found in `java.util.Arrays`. In the interest of full disclosure, it's a bit tougher to use the other abstract implementations because you will have to write your own iterator, but it's still not that difficult.

The following list summarizes the abstract implementations:

`AbstractCollection`[57] A `Collection` that is neither a `Set` nor a `List`. At a minimum, you must provide the `iterator` and the `size` methods.

`AbstractSet`[58] A `Set`; use is identical to `AbstractCollection`.

`AbstractList`[59] A `List` backed up by a random-access data store, such as an array. At a minimum, you must provide the `positional access` methods (`get` and, optionally, `set`, `remove`, and `add`) and the `size` method. The abstract class takes care of `listIterator` (and `iterator`).

`AbstractSequentialList`[60] A `List` backed up by a sequential-access data store, such as a linked list. At a minimum, you must provide the `listIterator` and `size` methods. The abstract class takes care of the positional access methods. (This is the opposite of `AbstractList`.)

`AbstractQueue`[61] At a minimum, you must provide the `offer`, `peek`, `poll`, and `size` methods and an `iterator` supporting `remove`.

`AbstractMap`[62] A `Map`. At a minimum you must provide the `entrySet` view. This is typically implemented with the `AbstractSet` class. If the `Map` is modifiable, you must also provide the `put` method.

The process of writing a custom implementation follows:

1. Choose the appropriate abstract implementation class from the preceding list.
2. Provide implementations for all the class's abstract methods. If your custom collection is to be modifiable, you'll have to override one or more of the concrete methods as well. The API documentation for the abstract implementation class will tell you which methods to override.
3. Test and, if necessary, debug the implementation. You now have a working custom collection implementation.
4. If you're concerned about performance, read the abstract implementation class's API documentation for all the methods whose implementations you're inheriting. If any seem too slow, override them. If you override any methods, be sure to measure the performance of the method before and after the override. How much effort

---

57. `docs/api/java/util/AbstractCollection.html`

58. `docs/api/java/util/AbstractSet.html`

59. `docs/api/java/util/AbstractList.html`

60. `docs/api/java/util/AbstractSequentialList.html`

61. `docs/api/java/util/AbstractQueue.html`

62. `docs/api/java/util/AbstractMap.html`

you put into tweaking performance should be a function of how much use the implementation will get and how critical to performance its use is. (Often this step is best omitted.)

Interoperability

In this section, you'll learn about the following two aspects of interoperability:

- Compatibility: This subsection describes how collections can be made to work with older APIs that predate the addition of `Collections` to the Java platform.
- API Design: This subsection describes how to design new APIs so that they'll interoperate seamlessly with one another.

Compatibility

The Java Collections Framework was designed to ensure complete interoperability between the core collection interfaces (see the Interfaces section, page 295) and the types that were used to represent collections in the early versions of the Java platform: `Vector`, `Hashtable`, array, and `Enumeration`.[63] In this section, you'll learn how to transform old collections to the Java Collections Framework collections and vice versa.

Upward Compatibility

Suppose that you're using an API that returns legacy collections in tandem with another API that requires objects implementing the collection interfaces. To make the two APIs interoperate smoothly, you'll have to transform the legacy collections into modern collections. Luckily, the Java Collections Framework makes this easy.

Suppose the old API returns an array of objects and the new API requires a `Collection`. The Collections Framework has a convenience implementation that allows an array of objects to be viewed as a `List`. You use `Arrays.asList` to pass an array to any method requiring a `Collection` or a `List`:

```
Foo[] result = oldMethod(arg);
newMethod(Arrays.asList(result));
```

If the old API returns a `Vector` or a `Hashtable`, you have no work to do at all because `Vector` was retrofitted to implement the `List` interface and `Hashtable` was retrofitted to implement `Map`. Therefore, a `Vector` may be passed directly to any method calling for a `Collection` or a `List`:

63. `docs/api/java/util/Enumeration.html`

```
Vector result = oldMethod(arg);
newMethod(result);
```

Similarly, a `Hashtable` may be passed directly to any method calling for a `Map`:

```
Hashtable result = oldMethod(arg);
newMethod(result);
```

Less frequently, an API may return an `Enumeration` that represents a collection of objects. The `Collections.list` method translates an `Enumeration` into a `Collection`:

```
Enumeration e = oldMethod(arg);
newMethod(Collections.list(e));
```

Backward Compatibility

Suppose you're using an API that returns modern collections in tandem with another API that requires you to pass in legacy collections. To make the two APIs interoperate smoothly, you have to transform modern collections into old collections. Again, the Java Collections Framework makes this easy.

Suppose the new API returns a `Collection` and the old API requires an array of `Object`. As you're probably aware, the `Collection` interface contains a `toArray` method designed expressly for this situation:

```
Collection c = newMethod();
oldMethod(c.toArray());
```

What if the old API requires an array of `String` (or another type) instead of an array of `Object`? You just use the other form of `toArray`—the one that takes an array on input:

```
Collection c = newMethod();
oldMethod((String[]) c.toArray(new String[0]));
```

If the old API requires a `Vector`, the standard collection constructor comes in handy:

```
Collection c = newMethod();
oldMethod(new Vector(c));
```

The case where the old API requires a `Hashtable` is handled analogously:

```
Map m = newMethod();
oldMethod(new Hashtable(m));
```

Finally, what do you do if the old API requires an `Enumeration`? This case isn't common, but it does happen from time to time, and the `Collections.enumeration` method was provided to handle it. This is a static factory method that takes a `Collection` and returns an `Enumeration` over the elements of the `Collection`:

```
Collection c = newMethod();
oldMethod(Collections.enumeration(c));
```

API Design

In this short but important section, you'll learn a few simple guidelines that will allow your API to interoperate seamlessly with all other APIs that follow these guidelines. In essence, these rules define what it takes to be a good "citizen" in the world of collections.

Parameters

If your API contains a method that requires a collection on input, it is of paramount importance that you declare the relevant parameter type to be one of the collection interface types (see the Interfaces section, page 295). **Never** use an implementation (see the Implementations section, page 342) type because this defeats the purpose of an interface-based Collections Framework, which is to allow collections to be manipulated without regard to implementation details.

Further, you should always use the least-specific type that makes sense. For example, don't require a `List` (see The `List` Interface section, page 306) or a `Set` (see The `Set` Interface section, page 301) if a `Collection` (see The `Collection` Interface section, page 298) would do. It's not that you should never require a `List` or a `Set` on input; it is correct to do so if a method depends on a property of one of these interfaces. For example, many of the algorithms provided by the Java platform require a `List` on input because they depend on the fact that lists are ordered. As a general rule, however, the best types to use on input are the most general: `Collection` and `Map`.

Caution: Never define your own ad hoc `collection` class and require objects of this class on input. By doing this, you'd lose all the benefits provided by the Java Collections Framework (see the Introduction to Collections section, page 293).

Return Values

You can afford to be much more flexible with return values than with input parameters. It's fine to return an object of any type that implements or extends one of the collection interfaces. This can be one of the interfaces or a special-purpose type that extends or implements one of these interfaces.

For example, one could imagine an image-processing package, called `ImageList`, that returned objects of a new class that implements `List`. In addition to the `List` operations, `ImageList` could support any application-specific operations that seemed desirable. For example, it might provide an `indexImage` operation that returned an image containing thumbnail images of each graphic in the `ImageList`. It's critical to note that even if the API furnishes `ImageList` instances on output, it should accept arbitrary `Collection` (or perhaps `List`) instances on input.

In one sense, return values should have the opposite behavior of input parameters: It's best to return the most specific applicable collection interface rather than the most general. For example, if you're sure that you'll always return a `SortedMap`, you should give the relevant method the return type of `SortedMap` rather than `Map`. `SortedMap` instances are more time-consuming to build than ordinary `Map` instances and are also more powerful. Given that your module has already invested the time to build a `SortedMap`, it makes good sense to give the user access to its increased power. Furthermore, the user will be able to pass the returned object to methods that demand a `SortedMap`, as well as those that accept any `Map`.

Legacy APIs

There are currently plenty of APIs out there that define their own ad hoc collection types. While this is unfortunate, it's a fact of life given that there was no Collections Framework in the first two major releases of the Java platform. If you own one of these APIs, here's what you can do about it.

If possible, retrofit your legacy collection type to implement one of the standard collection interfaces. Then all the collections you return will interoperate smoothly with other collection-based APIs. If this is impossible (for example, because one or more of the preexisting type signatures conflict with the standard collection interfaces), define an *adapter class* that wraps one of your legacy collections objects, allowing it to function as a standard collection. (The `Adapter` class is an example of a *custom implementation*; see the Custom Collection Implementations section, page 360.)

Retrofit your API with new calls that follow the input guidelines to accept objects of a standard collection interface, if possible. Such calls can coexist with the calls that take the legacy collection type. If this is impossible, provide a constructor or static factory for your legacy type that takes an object of one of the standard interfaces and returns a legacy collection containing the same elements (or mappings). Either of these approaches will allow users to pass arbitrary collections into your API.

12

Concurrency

COMPUTER users take it for granted that their systems can do more than one thing at a time. They assume that they can continue to work in a word processor, while other applications download files, manage the print queue, and stream audio. Even a single application is often expected to do more than one thing at a time—for example, that streaming audio application must simultaneously read the digital audio off the network, decompress it, manage playback, and update its display. Even the word processor should always be ready to respond to keyboard and mouse events, no matter how busy it is reformatting text or updating the display. Software that can do such things is known as *concurrent* software.

The Java platform is designed from the ground up to support concurrent programming, with basic concurrency support in the Java programming language and the Java class libraries. Since version 5.0, the Java platform has also included high-level concurrency APIs. This chapter introduces the platform's basic currency support and summarizes some of the high-level APIs in the `java.util.concurrent` packages.

Processes and Threads

In concurrent programming, there are two basic units of execution: *processes* and *threads*. In the Java programming language, concurrent programming is mostly concerned with threads. However, processes are also important.

A computer system normally has many active processes and threads. This is true even in systems that only have a single execution core, and thus only have one thread actually executing at any given moment. Processing time for a single core is shared among processes and threads through an OS feature called time slicing.

It's becoming more and more common for computer systems to have multiple processors or processors with multiple execution cores. This greatly enhances a system's capacity for concurrent execution of processes and threads—but concurrency is possible even on simple systems without multiple processors or execution cores.

Processes

A process has a self-contained execution environment. A process generally has a complete, private set of basic run-time resources; in particular, each process has its own memory space.

Processes are often seen as synonymous with programs or applications. However, what the user sees as a single application may in fact be a set of cooperating processes. To facilitate communication between processes, most operating systems support *Inter Process Communication* (IPC) resources, such as pipes and sockets. IPC is used not just for communication between processes on the same system, but processes on different systems.

Most implementations of the Java virtual machine run as a single process. A Java application can create additional processes using a `ProcessBuilder` object.[1] Multiprocess applications are beyond the scope of this chapter.

Threads

Threads are sometimes called *lightweight processes*. Both processes and threads provide an execution environment, but creating a new thread requires fewer resources than creating a new process.

Threads exist within a process—every process has at least one. Threads share the process's resources, including memory and open files. This makes for efficient, but potentially problematic, communication.

Multithreaded execution is an essential feature of the Java platform. Every application has at least one thread—or several, if you count "system" threads that do things like memory management and signal handling. But from the application programmer's point of view, you start with just one thread, called the *main thread*. This thread has the ability to create additional threads, as we'll demonstrate in the next section.

---

1. `docs/api/java/lang/ProcessBuilder.html`

Thread Objects

Each thread is associated with an instance of the class `Thread`.[2] There are two basic strategies for using `Thread` objects to create a concurrent application:

- To directly control thread creation and management, simply instantiate `Thread` each time the application needs to initiate an asynchronous task.
- To abstract thread management from the rest of your application, pass the application's tasks to an *executor*.

This section documents the use of `Thread` objects. Executors are discussed with other high-level concurrency objects (page 395).

Defining and Starting a Thread

An application that creates an instance of `Thread` must provide the code that will run in that thread. There are two ways to do this:

- **Provide a `Runnable` object.** The `Runnable` interface[3] defines a single method, `run`, meant to contain the code executed in the thread. The `Runnable` object is passed to the `Thread` constructor, as in the `HelloRunnable`[4] example:

```
public class HelloRunnable implements Runnable {

  public void run() {
    System.out.println("Hello from a thread!");
  }

  public static void main(String args[]) {
    (new Thread(new HelloRunnable())).start();
  }

}
```

- **Subclass `Thread`.** The `Thread` class itself implements `Runnable`, though its `run` method does nothing. An application can subclass `Thread`, providing its own implementation of `run`, as in the `HelloThread`[5] example:

---

2. `docs/api/java/lang/Thread.html`
3. `docs/api/java/lang/Runnable.html`
4. `tutorial/essential/concurrency/example/HelloRunnable.java`
5. `tutorial/essential/concurrency/example/HelloThread.java`

```
public class HelloThread extends Thread {

  public void run() {
    System.out.println("Hello from a thread!");
  }

  public static void main(String args[]) {
    (new HelloThread()).start();
  }

}
```

Notice that both examples invoke `Thread.start` in order to start the new thread.

Which of these idioms should you use? The first idiom, which employs a `Runnable` object, is more general, because the `Runnable` object can subclass a class other than `Thread`. The second idiom is easier to use in simple applications, but is limited by the fact that your task class must be a descendant of `Thread`. This chapter focuses on the first approach, which separates the `Runnable` task from the `Thread` object that executes the task. Not only is this approach more flexible, but it is applicable to the high-level thread management APIs covered later.

The `Thread` class defines a number of methods useful for thread management. These include `static` methods, which provide information about, or affect the status of, the thread invoking the method. The other methods are invoked from other threads involved in managing the thread and `Thread` object. We'll examine some of these methods in the following sections.

Pausing Execution with sleep

`Thread.sleep` causes the current thread to suspend execution for a specified period. This is an efficient means of making processor time available to the other threads of an application or other applications that might be running on a computer system. The `sleep` method can also be used for pacing, as shown in the example that follows, and waiting for another thread with duties that are understood to have time requirements, as with the `SimpleThreads` example in a later section.

Two overloaded versions of `sleep` are provided: one that specifies the sleep time to the millisecond and one that specifies the sleep time to the nanosecond. However, these sleep times are not guaranteed to be precise, because they are limited by the facilities provided by the underlying OS. Also, the sleep period can be terminated by interrupts, as we'll see in a later section. In any case, you cannot assume that invoking `sleep` will suspend the thread for precisely the time period specified.

The `SleepMessages`[6] example uses `sleep` to print messages at four-second intervals:

```
public class SleepMessages {

  public static void main(String args[])
                      throws InterruptedException {
    String importantInfo[] = {
      "Mares eat oats",
      "Does eat oats",
      "Little lambs eat ivy",
      "A kid will eat ivy too"
    };

    for (int i = 0; i < importantInfo.length; i++) {
      // Pause for 4 seconds
      Thread.sleep(4000);
      // Print a message
      System.out.println(importantInfo[i]);
    }
  }
}
```

Notice that `main` declares that it `throws InterruptedException`. This is an exception that `sleep` throws when another thread interrupts the current thread while `sleep` is active. Since this application has not defined another thread to cause the interrupt, it doesn't bother to catch `InterruptedException`.

Interrupts

An *interrupt* is an indication to a thread that it should stop what it is doing and do something else. It's up to the programmer to decide exactly how a thread responds to an interrupt, but it is very common for the thread to terminate. This is the usage emphasized in this chapter.

A thread sends an interupt by invoking `interrupt` on the `Thread` object for the thread to be interrupted. For the interrupt mechanism to work correctly, the interrupted thread must support its own interruption.

6. `tutorial/essential/concurrency/example/SleepMessages.java`

Supporting Interruption

How does a thread support its own interruption? This depends on what it's currently doing. If the thread is frequently invoking methods that throw `InterruptedException`, it simply returns from the `run` method after it catches that exception. For example, suppose the central message loop in the `SleepMessages` example were in the `run` method of a thread's `Runnable` object. Then it might be modified as follows to support interrupts:

```
for (int i = 0; i < ImportantInfo.length; i++) {
  // Pause for 4 seconds
  try {
      Thread.sleep(4000);
  } catch (InterruptedException e) {
      // We've been interrupted: no more messages.
      return;
  }
  // Print a message
  System.out.println(ImportantInfo[i]);
}
```

Many methods that throw `InterruptedException`, such as `sleep`, are designed to cancel their current operation and return immediately when an interrupt is received.

What if a thread goes a long time without invoking a method that throws `InterruptedException`? Then it must periodically invoke `Thread.interrupted`, which returns `true` if an interrupt has been received. For example:

```
for (int i = 0; i < Inputs.length; i++) {
  heavyCrunch(inputs[i]);
  if (Thread.interrupted()) {
    // We've been interrupted: no more crunching.
    return;
  }
}
```

In this simple example, the code simply tests for the interrupt and exits the thread if one has been received. In more complex applications, it might make more sense to throw an `InterruptedException`:

```
if (Thread.interrupted()) {
  throw new InterruptedException();
}
```

This allows interrupt handling code to be centralized in a `catch` clause.

The Interrupt Status Flag

The interrupt mechanism is implemented using an internal flag known as the *interrupt status*. Invoking `Thread.interrupt` sets this flag. When a thread checks for an interrupt by invoking the static method `Thread.interrupted`, interrupt status is cleared. The non-static `Thread.isInterrupted`, which is used by one thread to query the interrupt status of another, does not change the interrupt status flag.

By convention, any method that exits by throwing an `InterruptedException` clears interrupt status when it does so. However, it's always possible that interrupt status will immediately be set again, by another thread invoking `interrupt`.

Joins

The `join` method allows one thread to wait for the completion of another. If `t` is a `Thread` object whose thread is currently executing:

```
t.join();
```

causes the current thread to pause execution until `t`'s thread terminates. Overloads of `join` allow the programmer to specify a waiting period. However, as with `sleep`, `join` is dependent on the OS for timing, so you should not assume that `join` will wait exactly as long as you specify.

Like `sleep`, `join` responds to an interrupt by exiting with an `InterruptedException`.

The SimpleThreads Example

The following example brings together some of the concepts of this section. `SimpleThreads`[7] consists of two threads. The first is the main thread that every Java application has. The main thread creates a new thread from the `Runnable` object, `MessageLoop`, and waits for it to finish. If the `MessageLoop` thread takes too long to finish, the main thread interrupts it.

The `MessageLoop` thread prints out a series of messages. If interrupted before it has printed all its messages, the `MessageLoop` thread prints a message and exits:

7. `tutorial/essential/concurrency/example/SimpleThreads.java`

```
public class SimpleThreads {

  // Display a message, preceded by the name
  // of the current thread
  static void threadMessage(String message) {
    String threadName = Thread.currentThread().getName();
    System.out.format("%s: %s%n", threadName, message);
  }

  private static class MessageLoop implements Runnable {
    public void run() {
      String importantInfo[] = {
        "Mares eat oats",
        "Does eat oats",
        "Little lambs eat ivy",
        "A kid will eat ivy too"
      };
      try {
        for (int i = 0; i < importantInfo.length; i++) {
          // Pause for 4 seconds
          Thread.sleep(4000);
          // Print a message
          threadMessage(importantInfo[i]);
        }
      } catch (InterruptedException e) {
          threadMessage("I wasn't done!");
      }
    }
  }

  public static void main(String args[])
      throws InterruptedException {

    // Delay, in milliseconds before we interrupt MessageLoop
    // thread (default one hour).
    long patience = 1000 * 60 * 60;

    // If command line argument present,
    // gives patience in seconds.
    if (args.length > 0) {
      try {
          patience = Long.parseLong(args[0]) * 1000;
      } catch (NumberFormatException e) {
          System.err.println("Argument must be an integer.");
          System.exit(1);
      }
    }
```

```
        threadMessage("Starting MessageLoop thread");
        long startTime = System.currentTimeMillis();
        Thread t = new Thread(new MessageLoop());
        t.start();

        threadMessage("Waiting for MessageLoop thread to finish");
        // loop until MessageLoop thread exits
        while (t.isAlive()) {
          threadMessage("Still waiting...");
          // Wait maximum of 1 second for MessageLoop thread to
          // finish.
          t.join(1000);
          if (((System.currentTimeMillis() - startTime) > patience)
                                                  && t.isAlive()) {
            threadMessage("Tired of waiting!");
            t.interrupt();
            // Shouldn't be long now -- wait indefinitely
            t.join();
          }

        }
        threadMessage("Finally!");
      }
    }
```

Synchronization

Threads communicate primarily by sharing access to fields and the objects reference fields refer to. This form of communication is extremely efficient, but makes two kinds of errors possible: *thread interference* and *memory consistency errors*. The tool needed to prevent these errors is *synchronization*.

Thread Interference

Consider an simple class called `Counter`:[8]

8. `tutorial/essential/concurrency/example/Counter.java`

```
class Counter {
  private int c = 0;

  public void increment() {
    c++;
  }

  public void decrement() {
    c--;
  }

  public int value() {
    return c;
  }

}
```

`Counter` is designed so that each invocation of `increment` will add 1 to `c`, and each invocation of `decrement` will subtract 1 from `c`. However, if a `Counter` object is referenced from multiple threads, interference between threads may prevent this from happening as expected.

Interference happens when two operations, running in different threads, but acting on the same data, *interleave*. This means that the two operations consist of multiple steps, and the sequences of steps overlap.

It might not seem possible for operations on instances of `Counter` to interleave, since both operations on `c` are single, simple statements. However, even simple statements can translate to multiple steps by the virtual machine. We won't examine the specific steps the virtual machine takes—it is enough to know that the single expression `c++` can be decomposed into three steps:

1. Retrieve the current value of `c`.
2. Increment the retrieved value by 1.
3. Store the incremented value back in `c`.

The expression `c--` can be decomposed the same way, except that the second step decrements instead of increments.

Suppose Thread A invokes `increment` at about the same time Thread B invokes `decrement`. If the initial value of `c` is `0`, their interleaved actions might follow this sequence:

1. Thread A: Retrieve `c`.
2. Thread B: Retrieve `c`.
3. Thread A: Increment retrieved value; result is `1`.
4. Thread B: Decrement retrieved value; result is `-1`.

5. Thread A: Store result in `c`; `c` is now `1`.
6. Thread B: Store result in `c`; `c` is now `-1`.

Thread A's result is lost, overwritten by Thread B. This particular interleaving is only one possibility. Under different circumstances it might be Thread B's result that gets lost, or there could be no error at all. Because they are unpredictable, thread interference bugs can be difficult to detect and fix.

Memory Consistency Errors

Memory consistency errors occur when different threads have inconsistent views of what should be the same data. The causes of memory consistency errors are complex and beyond the scope of this tutorial. Fortunately, the programmer does not need a detailed understanding of these causes. All that is needed is a strategy for avoiding them.

The key to avoiding memory consistency errors is understanding the *happens-before* relationship. This relationship is simply a guarantee that memory writes by one specific statement are visible to another specific statement. To see this, consider the following example. Supppose a simple `int` field is defined and initialized:

```
int counter = 0;
```

The `counter` field is shared between two threads, A and B. Suppose thread A increments `counter`:

```
counter++;
```

Then, shortly afterwords, thread B prints out `counter`:

```
System.out.println(counter);
```

If the two statements had been executed in the same thread, it would be safe to assume that the value printed out would be "1". But if the two statements are executed in separate threads, the value printed out might well be "0", because there's no guarantee that thread A's change to `counter` will be visible to thread B—unless the programmer has established a happens-before relationship between these two statements.

There are several actions that create happens-before relationships. One of them is synchronization, as we will see in the following sections.

We've already seen two actions that create happens-before relationships.

- When a statement invokes `Thread.start`, every statement that has a happens-before relationship with that statement also has a happens-before relationship with every statement executed by the new thread. The effects of the code that led up to the creation of the new thread are visible to the new thread.

- When a thread terminates and causes a `Thread.join` in another thread to return, then all the statements executed by the terminated thread have a happens-before relationship with all the statements following the successful join. The effects of the code in the thread are now visible to the thread that performed the join.

For a list of actions that create happens-before relationships, refer to the Summary page of the `java.util.concurrent` package.[9]

Synchronized Methods

The Java programming language provides two basic synchronization idioms. This section is about the more simple of the two idioms, *synchronized methods*. For the other idiom, *synchronized statements*, refer to the next section.

To make a method synchronized, simply add the `synchronized` keyword to its declaration:

```
public class SynchronizedCounter {
  private int c = 0;

  public synchronized void increment() {
    c++;
  }

  public synchronized void decrement() {
    c--;
  }

  public synchronized int value() {
    return c;
  }
}
```

If `count` is an instance of `SynchronizedCounter`,[10] then making these methods synchronized has two effects:

- First, it is not possible for two invocations of synchronized methods on the same object to interleave. When one thread is executing a synchronized method for an object, all other threads that invoke synchronized methods for the same object block (suspend execution) until the first thread is done with the object.
- Second, when a synchronized method exits, it automatically establishes a happens-before relationship with *any subsequent invocation* of a synchronized method for

9. `docs/api/java/util/concurrent/package-summary.html`

10. `tutorial/essential/concurrency/example/SynchronizedCounter.java`

the same object. This guarantees that changes to the state of the object are visible to all threads.

Note that constructors cannot be synchronized—using the `synchronized` keyword with a constructor is a syntax error. Synchronizing constructors doesn't make sense, because only the thread that creates an object should have access to it while it is being constructed.

Warning: When constructing an object that will be shared between threads, be very careful that a reference to the object does not "leak" prematurely. For example, suppose you want to maintain a `List` called `instances` containing every instance of class. You might be tempted to add the line:

```
instances.add(this);
```

to your constructor. But then other threads can use `instances` to access the object before construction of the object is complete.

Synchronized methods enable a simple strategy for preventing thread interference and memory consistency errors: If an object is visible to more than one thread, all reads or writes to that object's variables are done through `synchronized` methods. (An important exception: `final` fields, which cannot be modified after the object is constructed, can be safely read through non-synchronized methods, once the object is constructed.) This strategy is effective, but can present problems with liveness. (See the Liveness section later in this chapter.)

Intrinsic Locks and Synchronization

Synchronization is built around an internal entity known as the *intrinsic lock* or *monitor lock*. (The API specification often refers to this entity simply as a "monitor.") Intrinsic locks play a role in both aspects of synchronization: enforcing exclusive access to an object's state and establishing happens-before relationships that are essential to visibility.

Every object has an intrinsic lock associated with it. By convention, a thread that needs exclusive and consistent access to an object's fields has to *acquire* the object's intrinsic lock before accessing them and then *release* the intrinsic lock when it's done with them. A thread is said to *own* the intrinsic lock between the time it has acquired the lock and released the lock. As long as a thread owns an intrinsic lock, no other thread can acquire the same lock. The other thread will block when it attempts to acquire the lock.

When a thread releases an intrinsic lock, a happens-before relationship is established between that action and any subsequent acquisition of the same lock.

Locks In Synchronized Methods

When a thread invokes a synchronized method, it automatically acquires the intrinsic lock for that method's object and releases it when the method returns. The lock release occurs even if the return was caused by an uncaught exception.

You might wonder what happens when a static synchronized method is invoked, since a static method is associated with a class, not an object. In this case, the thread acquires the intrinsic lock for the `Class` object associated with the class. Thus access to class's static fields is controlled by a lock that's distinct from the lock for any instance of the class.

Synchronized Statements

Another way to create synchronized code is with *synchronized statements*. Unlike synchronized methods, synchronized statements must specify the object that provides the intrinsic lock:

```
public void addName(String name) {
  synchronized(this) {
    lastName = name;
    nameCount++;
  }
  nameList.add(name);
}
```

In this example, the `addName` method needs to synchronize changes to `lastName` and `nameCount`, but also needs to avoid synchronizing invocations of other objects' methods. (Invoking other objects' methods from synchronized code can create problems that are described in the Liveness section, page 384.) Without synchronized statements, there would have to be a separate, unsynchronized method for the sole purpose of invoking `nameList.add`.

Synchronized statements are also useful for improving concurrency with fine-grained synchronization. Suppose, for example, class `MsLunch` has two instance fields, `c1` and `c2`, that are never used together. All updates of these fields must be synchronized, but there's no reason to prevent an update of c1 from being interleaved with an update of c2—and doing so reduces concurrency by creating unnecessary blocking. Instead of using synchronized methods or otherwise using the lock associated with `this`, we create two objects solely to provide locks:

```
public class MsLunch {
  private long c1 = 0;
  private long c2 = 0;
  private Object lock1 = new Object();
  private Object lock2 = new Object();

  public void inc1() {
    synchronized(lock1) {
      c1++;
    }
  }

  public void inc2() {
    synchronized(lock2) {
      c2++;
    }
  }
}
```

Use this idiom with extreme care. You must be absolutely sure that it really is safe to interleave access of the affected fields.

Reentrant Synchronization

Recall that a thread cannot acquire a lock owned by another thread. But a thread *can* acquire a lock that it already owns. Allowing a thread to acquire the same lock more than once enables *reentrant synchronization*. This describes a situation where synchronized code, directly or indirectly, invokes a method that also contains synchronized code, and both sets of code use the same lock. Without reentrant synchronization, synchronized code would have to take many additional precautions to avoid having a thread cause itself to block.

Atomic Access

In programming, an *atomic* action is one that effectively happens all at once. An atomic action cannot stop in the middle: It either happens completely, or it doesn't happen at all. No side effects of an atomic action are visible until the action is complete.

We've already seen that an increment expression, such as `c++`, does not describe an atomic action. Even very simple expressions can define complex actions that can decompose into other actions. However, there are actions you can specify that are atomic:

- Reads and writes are atomic for reference variables and for most primitive variables (all types except `long` and `double`).

- Reads and writes are atomic for *all* variables declared `volatile` (*including* `long` and `double` variables).

Atomic actions cannot be interleaved, so they can be used without fear of thread interference. However, this does not eliminate all need to synchronize atomic actions, because memory consistency errors are still possible. Using `volatile` variables reduces the risk of memory consistency errors, because any write to a `volatile` variable establishes a happens-before relationship with subsequent reads of that same variable. This means that changes to a `volatile` variable are always visible to other threads. What's more, it also means that when a thread reads a `volatile` variable, it sees not just the latest change to the `volatile`, but also the side effects of the code that led up the change.

Warning: The description of `volatile` variables only applies to the Java platform 5.0 and later. Previous versions of the Java platform use slightly different semantics for `volatile` variables.

Using simple atomic variable access is more efficient than accessing these variables through synchronized code, but requires more care by the programmer to avoid memory consistency errors. Whether the extra effort is worthwhile depends on the size and complexity of the application.

Some of the classes in the `java.util.concurrent` packages provide atomic methods that do not rely on synchronization. We'll discuss them in the High-Level Concurrency Objects section (page 395).

Liveness

A concurrent application's ability to execute in a timely manner is known as its *liveness*. This section describes the most common kind of liveness problem, deadlock, and goes on to briefly describe two other liveness problems, starvation and livelock.

Deadlock

Deadlock describes a situation where two or more threads are blocked forever, waiting for each other. Here's an example.

Alphonse and Gaston are friends, and great believers in courtesy. A strict rule of courtesy is that when you bow to a friend, you must remain bowed until your friend has a chance to return the bow. Unfortunately, this rule does not account for the possibility that two friends might bow to each other at the same time. This example application, `Deadlock`,[11] models this possibility:

```
public class Deadlock {
  static class Friend {
    private final String name;
    public Friend(String name) {
      this.name = name;
    }
    public String getName() {
      return this.name;
    }
    public synchronized void bow(Friend bower) {
      System.out.format("%s: %s has bowed to me!%n",
        this.name, bower.getName());
      bower.bowBack(this);
    }
    public synchronized void bowBack(Friend bower) {
      System.out.format("%s: %s has bowed back to me!%n",
        this.name, bower.getName());
    }
  }

  public static void main(String[] args) {
    final Friend alphonse = new Friend("Alphonse");
    final Friend gaston = new Friend("Gaston");
    new Thread(new Runnable() {
      public void run() { alphonse.bow(gaston); }
    }).start();
    new Thread(new Runnable() {
      public void run() { gaston.bow(alphonse); }
    }).start();
  }
}
```

When `Deadlock` runs, it's extremely likely that both threads will block when they attempt to invoke `bowBack`. Neither block will ever end, because each thread is waiting for the other to exit `bow`.

Starvation and Livelock

Starvation and livelock are much less common a problem than deadlock, but are still problems that every designer of concurrent software is likely to encounter.

11. `tutorial/essential/concurrency/example/Deadlock.java`

Starvation

Starvation describes a situation where a thread is unable to gain regular access to shared resources and is unable to make progress. This happens when shared resources are made unavailable for long periods by "greedy" threads. For example, suppose an object provides a synchronized method that often takes a long time to return. If one thread invokes this method frequently, other threads that also need frequent synchronized access to the same object will often be blocked.

Livelock

A thread often acts in response to the action of another thread. If the other thread's action is also a response to the action of another thread, then *livelock* may result. As with deadlock, livelocked threads are unable to make further progress. However, the threads are not blocked—they are simply too busy responding to each other to resume work. This is comparable to two people attempting to pass each other in a corridor: Alphonse moves to his left to let Gaston pass, while Gaston moves to his right to let Alphonse pass. Seeing that they are still blocking each other, Alphone moves to his right, while Gaston moves to his left. They're still blocking each other, so . . .

Guarded Blocks

Threads often have to coordinate their actions. The most common coordination idiom is the *guarded block*. Such a block begins by polling a condition that must be true before the block can proceed. There are a number of steps to follow in order to do this correctly.

Suppose, for example `guardedJoy` is a method that must not proceed until a shared variable `joy` has been set by another thread. Such a method could, in theory, simply loop until the condition is satisfied, But that loop is wasteful, since it executes continuously while waiting:

```
public void guardedJoy() {
  // Simple loop guard. Wastes processor time. Don't do this!
  while(!joy) {}
  System.out.println("Joy has been achieved!");
}
```

A more efficient guard invokes `Object.wait`[12] to suspend the current thread. The invocation of `wait` does not return until another thread has issued a notification that some

12. `docs/api/java/lang/Object.html`

special event may have occurred—though not necessarily the event this thread is waiting for:

```
public synchronized void guardedJoy() {
  // This guard only loops once for each special event,
  // which may not be the event we're waiting for.
  while(!joy) {
    try {
      wait();
    } catch (InterruptedException e) {}
  }
  System.out.println("Joy and efficiency have been achieved!");
}
```

Note: Always invoke `wait` inside a loop that tests for the condition being waited for. Don't assume that the interrupt was for the particular condition you were waiting for, or that the condition is still true.

Like many methods that suspend execution, `wait` can throw `InterruptedException`. In this example, we can just ignore that exception—we only care about the value of `joy`.

Why is this version of `guardedJoy` synchronized? Suppose `d` is the object we're using to invoke `wait`. When a thread invokes `d.wait`, it must own the intrinsic lock for `d`—otherwise an error is thrown. Invoking `wait` inside a synchronized method is a simple way to acquire the intrinsic lock.

When `wait` is invoked, the thread releases the lock and suspends execution. At some future time, another thread will acquire the same lock and invoke `Object.notifyAll`, informing all threads waiting on that lock that something important has happened:

```
public synchronized void notifyJoy() {
  joy = true;
  notifyAll();
}
```

Some time after the second thread has released the lock, the first thread reacquires the lock and resumes by returning from the invocation of `wait`.

Note: There is a second notification method, `notify`, which wakes up a single thread. Because `notify` doesn't allow you to specify the thread that is woken up, it is useful only in massively parallel applications—that is, programs with a large number of threads, all doing similar chores. In such an application, you don't care which thread gets woken up.

Let's use guarded blocks to create a *Producer-Consumer* application. This kind of application shares data between two threads: the *producer* that creates the data and the *consumer* that does something with it. The two threads communicate using a shared object. Coordination is essential: The consumer thread must not attempt to retrieve the data before the producer thread has delivered it, and the producer thread must not attempt to deliver new data if the consumer hasn't retrieved the old data.

In this example, the data is a series of text messages, which are shared through an object of type `Drop`:[13]

```
public class Drop {
  // Message sent from producer to consumer.
  private String message;
  // True if consumer should wait for producer to send message,
  // false if producer should wait for consumer
  // to retrieve message.
  private boolean empty = true;

  public synchronized String take() {
    // Wait until message is available.
    while (empty) {
      try {
        wait();
      } catch (InterruptedException e) {}
    }
    // Toggle status.
    empty = true;
    // Notify producer that status has changed.
    notifyAll();
    return message;
  }

  public synchronized void put(String message) {
    // Wait until message has been retrieved.
    while (!empty) {
      try {
        wait();
      } catch (InterruptedException e) {}
    }
    // Toggle status.
    empty = false;
    // Store message.
    this.message = message;
    // Notify consumer that status has changed.
    notifyAll();
  }
}
```

13. `tutorial/essential/concurrency/example/Drop.java`

The producer thread, defined in `Producer`,[14] sends a series of familiar messages. The string "DONE" indicates that all messages have been sent. To simulate the unpredictable nature of real-world applications, the producer thread pauses for random intervals between messages:

```
import java.util.Random;

public class Producer implements Runnable {
  private Drop drop;

  public Producer(Drop drop) {
    this.drop = drop;
  }

  public void run() {
    String importantInfo[] = {
      "Mares eat oats",
      "Does eat oats",
      "Little lambs eat ivy",
      "A kid will eat ivy too"
    };
    Random random = new Random();

    for (int i = 0; i < importantInfo.length; i++) {
      drop.put(importantInfo[i]);
      try {
        Thread.sleep(random.nextInt(5000));
      } catch (InterruptedException e) {}
    }
    drop.put("DONE");
  }
}
```

The consumer thread, defined in `Consumer`,[15] simply retrieves the messages and prints them out, until it retrieves the "DONE" string. This thread also pauses for random intervals:

14. `tutorial/essential/concurrency/example/Producer.java`

15. `tutorial/essential/concurrency/example/Consumer.java`

```
import java.util.Random;

public class Consumer implements Runnable {
  private Drop drop;

  public Consumer(Drop drop) {
    this.drop = drop;
  }

  public void run() {
    Random random = new Random();
    for (String message = drop.take();
                              ! message.equals("DONE");
                                 message = drop.take()) {
      System.out.format("MESSAGE RECEIVED: %s%n", message);
      try {
        Thread.sleep(random.nextInt(5000));
      } catch (InterruptedException e) {}
    }
  }
}
```

Finally, here is the main thread, defined in `ProducerConsumerExample`,[16] that launches the producer and consumer threads:

```
public class ProducerConsumerExample {
  public static void main(String[] args) {
    Drop drop = new Drop();
    (new Thread(new Producer(drop))).start();
    (new Thread(new Consumer(drop))).start();
  }
}
```

Note: The `Drop` class was written in order to demonstrate guarded blocks. To avoid reinventing the wheel, examine the existing data structures in Chapter 11 before trying to code your own data-sharing objects. For more information, refer to the Questions and Exercises: Concurrency section (page 403).

---

16. `tutorial/essential/concurrency/example/ProducerConsumerExample.java`

Immutable Objects

An object is considered *immutable* if its state cannot change after it is constructed. Maximum reliance on immutable objects is widely accepted as a sound strategy for creating simple, reliable code.

Immutable objects are particularly useful in concurrent applications. Since they cannot change state, they cannot be corrupted by thread interference or observed in an inconsistent state.

Programmers are often reluctant to employ immutable objects, because they worry about the cost of creating a new object as opposed to updating an object in place. The impact of object creation is often overestimated and can be offset by some of the efficiencies associated with immutable objects. These include decreased overhead due to garbage collection and the elimination of code needed to protect mutable objects from corruption.

The following subsections take a class whose instances are mutable and derives a class with immutable instances from it. In so doing, they give general rules for this kind of conversion and demonstrate some of the advantages of immutable objects.

A Synchronized Class Example

The class, `SynchronizedRGB`,[17] defines objects that represent colors. Each object represents the color as three integers that stand for primary color values and a string that gives the name of the color:

```
public class SynchronizedRGB {

  // Values must be between 0 and 255.
  private int red;
  private int green;
  private int blue;
  private String name;

  private void check(int red, int green, int blue) {
    if (red < 0 || red > 255
        || green < 0 || green > 255
            || blue < 0 || blue > 255) {
      throw new IllegalArgumentException();
    }
  }
```

17. `tutorial/essential/concurrency/example/SynchronizedRGB.java`

```
    public SynchronizedRGB(int red, int green,
                           int blue, String name) {
        check(red, green, blue);
        this.red = red;
        this.green = green;
        this.blue = blue;
        this.name = name;
    }

    public void set(int red, int green, int blue, String name) {
        check(red, green, blue);
        synchronized (this) {
            this.red = red;
            this.green = green;
            this.blue = blue;
            this.name = name;
        }
    }

    public synchronized int getRGB() {
        return ((red << 16) | (green << 8) | blue);
    }

    public synchronized String getName() {
        return name;
    }

    public synchronized void invert() {
        red = 255 - red;
        green = 255 - green;
        blue = 255 - blue;
        name = "Inverse of " + name;
    }
}
```

`SynchronizedRGB` must be used carefully to avoid being seen in an inconsistent state. Suppose, for example, a thread executes the following code:

```
SynchronizedRGB color = new SynchronizedRGB(0, 0, 0,
                                            "Pitch Black");
...
int myColorInt = color.getRGB();      // Statement 1
String myColorName = color.getName(); // Statement 2
```

If another thread invokes `color.set` after Statement 1 but before Statement 2, the value of `myColorInt` won't match the value of `myColorName`. To avoid this outcome, the two statements must be bound together:

```
synchronized (color) {
  int myColorInt = color.getRGB();
  String myColorName = color.getName();
}
```

This kind of inconsistency is only possible for mutable objects—it will not be an issue for the immutable version of `SynchronizedRGB`.

A Strategy for Defining Immutable Objects

The following rules define a simple strategy for creating immutable objects. Not all classes documented as "immutable" follow these rules. This does not necessarily mean the creators of these classes were sloppy—they may have good reason for believing that instances of their classes never change after construction. However, such strategies require sophisticated analysis and are not for beginners.

1. Don't provide "setter" methods—methods that modify fields or objects referred to by fields.
2. Make all fields `final` and `private`.
3. Don't allow subclasses to override methods. The simplest way to do this is to declare the class as `final`. A more sophisticated approach is to make the constructor `private` and construct instances in factory methods.
4. If the instance fields include references to mutable objects, don't allow those objects to be changed:
   - Don't provide methods that modify the mutable objects.
   - Don't share references to the mutable objects. Never store references to external, mutable objects passed to the constructor; if necessary, create copies, and store references to the copies. Similarly, create copies of your internal mutable objects when necessary to avoid returning the originals in your methods.

Applying this strategy to `SynchronizedRGB` results in the following steps:

1. There are two setter methods in this class. The first one, `set`, arbitrarily transforms the object and has no place in an immutable version of the class. The second one, `invert`, can be adapted by having it create a new object instead of modifying the existing one.
2. All fields are already `private`; they are further qualified as `final`.
3. The class itself is declared `final`.
4. Only one field refers to an object, and that object is itself immutable. Therefore, no safeguards against changing the state of "contained" mutable objects are necessary.

After these changes, we have ImmutableRGB:[18]

```
final public class ImmutableRGB {

  // Values must be between 0 and 255.
  final private int red;
  final private int green;
  final private int blue;
  final private String name;

  private void check(int red, int green, int blue) {
    if (red < 0 || red > 255
        || green < 0 || green > 255
           || blue < 0 || blue > 255) {
      throw new IllegalArgumentException();
    }
  }

  public ImmutableRGB(int red, int green,
                      int blue, String name) {
    check(red, green, blue);
    this.red = red;
    this.green = green;
    this.blue = blue;
    this.name = name;
  }


  public int getRGB() {
    return ((red << 16) | (green << 8) | blue);
  }

  public String getName() {
    return name;
  }

  public ImmutableRGB invert() {
    return new ImmutableRGB(255 - red, 255 - green,
                            255 - blue, "Inverse of " + name);
  }
}
```

18. tutorial/essential/concurrency/example/ImmutableRGB.java

High-Level Concurrency Objects

So far, this chapter has focused on the low-level APIs that have been part of the Java platform from the very beginning. These APIs are adequate for very basic tasks, but higher-level building blocks are needed for more advanced tasks. This is especially true for massively concurrent applications that fully exploit today's multiprocessor and multi-core systems.

In this section we'll look at some of the high-level concurrency features introduced with version 5.0 of the Java platform. Most of these features are implemented in the new `java.util.concurrent` packages. There are also new concurrent data structures in the Java Collections Framework.

Lock Objects

Synchronized code relies on a simple kind of reentrant lock. This kind of lock is easy to use, but has many limitations. More sophisticated locking idioms are supported by the `java.util.concurrent.locks` package.[19] We won't examine this package in detail, but instead will focus on its most basic interface, `Lock`.[20]

`Lock` objects work very much like the implicit locks used by synchronized code. As with implicit locks, only one thread can own a `Lock` object at a time. `Lock` objects also support a `wait/notify` mechanism through their associated `Condition` objects.[21]

The biggest advantage of `Lock` objects over implicit locks is their ability to back out of an attempt to acquire a lock. The `tryLock` method backs out if the lock is not available immediately or before a timeout expires (if specified). The `lockInterruptibly` method backs out if another thread sends an interrupt before the lock is acquired.

Let's use `Lock` objects to solve the deadlock problem we saw in the Liveness section (page 384). Alphonse and Gaston have trained themselves to notice when a friend is about to bow. We model this improvement by requiring that our `Friend` objects must acquire locks for *both* participants before proceeding with the bow. Here is the source code for the improved model, `Safelock`.[22] To demonstrate the versatility of this idiom, we assume that Alphonse and Gaston are so infatuated with their newfound ability to bow safely that they can't stop bowing to each other:

---

19. `docs/api/java/util/concurrent/locks/package-summary.html`
20. `docs/api/java/util/concurrent/locks/Lock.html`
21. `docs/api/java/util/concurrent/locks/Condition.html`
22. `tutorial/essential/concurrency/example/Safelock.java`

```
import java.util.concurrent.locks.Lock;
import java.util.concurrent.locks.ReentrantLock;
import java.util.Random;

public class Safelock {
  static class Friend {
    private final String name;
    private final Lock lock = new ReentrantLock();

    public Friend(String name) {
      this.name = name;
    }

    public String getName() {
      return this.name;
    }

    public boolean impendingBow(Friend bower) {
      Boolean myLock = false;
      Boolean yourLock = false;
      try {
        myLock = lock.tryLock();
        yourLock = bower.lock.tryLock();
      } finally {
        if (! (myLock && yourLock)) {
          if (myLock) {
            lock.unlock();
          }
          if (yourLock) {
            bower.lock.unlock();
          }
        }
      }
      return myLock && yourLock;
    }

    public void bow(Friend bower) {
      if (impendingBow(bower)) {
        try {
          System.out.format("%s: %s has bowed to me!%n",
                               this.name, bower.getName());
          bower.bowBack(this);
        } finally {
          lock.unlock();
          bower.lock.unlock();
        }
      } else {
          System.out.format("%s: %s started to bow " +
            "to me, but saw that I was already " +
            "bowing to him.%n", this.name, bower.getName());
      }
    }
```

```
        public void bowBack(Friend bower) {
            System.out.format("%s: %s has bowed back to me!%n",
                              this.name, bower.getName());
        }
    }

    static class BowLoop implements Runnable {
        private Friend bower;
        private Friend bowee;

        public BowLoop(Friend bower, Friend bowee) {
            this.bower = bower;
            this.bowee = bowee;
        }

        public void run() {
            Random random = new Random();
            for (;;) {
                try {
                    Thread.sleep(random.nextInt(10));
                } catch (InterruptedException e) {}
                bowee.bow(bower);
            }
        }
    }

    public static void main(String[] args) {
        final Friend alphonse = new Friend("Alphonse");
        final Friend gaston = new Friend("Gaston");
        new Thread(new BowLoop(alphonse, gaston)).start();
        new Thread(new BowLoop(gaston, alphonse)).start();
    }
}
```

Executors

In all of the previous examples, there's a close connection between the task being done by a new thread, as defined by its `Runnable` object, and the thread itself, as defined by a `Thread` object. This works well for small applications, but in large-scale applications, it makes sense to separate thread management and creation from the rest of the application. Objects that encapsulate these functions are known as *executors*.

Executor Interfaces

The `java.util.concurrent` package defines three executor interfaces:

- `Executor`, a simple interface that supports launching new tasks.
- `ExecutorService`, a subinterface of `Executor`, which adds features that help manage the lifecycle, both of the individual tasks and of the executor itself.

- `ScheduledExecutorService`, a subinterface of `ExecutorService`, supports future and/or periodic execution of tasks.

Typically, variables that refer to executor objects are declared as one of these three interface types, not with an executor class type.

The Executor Interface

The `Executor` interface[23] provides a single method, `execute`, designed to be a drop-in replacement for a common thread-creation idiom. If `r` is a `Runnable` object and `e` is an `Executor` object, you can replace

```
(new Thread(r)).start();
```

with

```
e.execute(r);
```

However, the definition of `execute` is less specific. The low-level idiom creates a new thread and launches it immediately. Depending on the `Executor` implementation, `execute` may do the same thing, but is more likely to use an existing worker thread to run `r`, or to place `r` in a queue to wait for a worker thread to become available. (We'll describe worker threads in the Thread Pools section, page 399.)

The executor implementations in `java.util.concurrent` are designed to make full use of the more advanced `ExecutorService` and `ScheduledExecutorService` interfaces, although they also work with the base `Executor` interface.

The ExecutorService Interface

The `ExecutorService` interface[24] supplements `execute` with a similar, but more versatile `submit` method. Like `execute`, `submit` accepts `Runnable` objects, but also accepts `Callable` objects,[25] which allow the task to return a value. The `submit` method returns a `Future` object,[26] which is used to retrieve the `Callable` return value and to manage the status of both `Callable` and `Runnable` tasks.

`ExecutorService` also provides methods for submitting large collections of `Callable` objects. Finally, `ExecutorService` provides a number of methods for managing the shutdown of the executor. To support immediate shutdown, tasks should handle interrupts (see the Interrupts section, page 373) correctly.

---

23. `docs/api/java/util/concurrent/Executor.html`
24. `docs/api/java/util/concurrent/ExecutorService.html`
25. `docs/api/java/util/concurrent/Callable.html`
26. `docs/api/java/util/concurrent/Future.html`

The ScheduledExecutorService Interface

The `ScheduledExecutorService` interface[27] supplements the methods of its parent `ExecutorService` with `schedule`, which executes a `Runnable` or `Callable` task after a specified delay. In addition, the interface defines `scheduleAtFixedRate` and `scheduleWithFixedDelay`, which execute specified tasks repeatedly at defined intervals.

Thread Pools

Most of the executor implementations in `java.util.concurrent` use *thread pools*, which consist of *worker threads*. This kind of thread exists separately from the `Runnable` and `Callable` tasks it executes and is often used to execute multiple tasks.

Using worker threads minimizes the overhead due to thread creation. Thread objects use a significant amount of memory, and in a large-scale application, allocating and deallocating many thread objects creates a significant memory management overhead.

One common type of thread pool is the *fixed thread pool*. This type of pool always has a specified number of threads running; if a thread is somehow terminated while it is still in use, it is automatically replaced with a new thread. Tasks are submitted to the pool via an internal queue, which holds extra tasks whenever there are more active tasks than threads.

An important advantage of the fixed thread pool is that applications using it *degrade gracefully*. To understand this, consider a Web server application where each HTTP request is handled by a separate thread. If the application simply creates a new thread for every new HTTP request, and the system receives more requests than it can handle immediately, the application will suddenly stop responding to *all* requests when the overhead of all those threads exceed the capacity of the system. With a limit on the number of the threads that can be created, the application will not be servicing HTTP requests as quickly as they come in, but it will be servicing them as quickly as the system can sustain.

A simple way to create an executor that uses a fixed thread pool is to invoke the `newFixedThreadPool` factory method in `java.util.concurrent.Executors`.[28] This class also provides the following factory methods:

- The `newCachedThreadPool` method creates an executor with an expandable thread pool. This executor is suitable for applications that launch many short-lived tasks.

27. `docs/api/java/util/concurrent/ScheduledExecutorService.html`

28. `docs/api/java/util/concurrent/Executors.html`

- The newSingleThreadExecutor method creates an executor that executes a single task at a time.
- Several factory methods are ScheduledExecutorService versions of the above executors.

If none of the executors provided by the above factory methods meet your needs, constructing instances of java.util.concurrent.ThreadPoolExecutor[29] or java.util.concurrent.ScheduledThreadPoolExecutor[30] will give you additional options.

Concurrent Collections

The java.util.concurrent package includes a number of additions to the Java Collections Framework. These are most easily categorized by the collection interfaces provided:

- BlockingQueue[31] defines a first-in, first-out data structure that blocks or times out when you attempt to add to a full queue, or to retrieve from an empty queue.
- ConcurrentMap[32] is a subinterface of java.util.Map[33] that defines useful atomic operations. These operations remove or replace a key-value pair only if the key is present, or add a key-value pair only if the key is absent. Making these operations atomic helps avoid synchronization. The standard general-purpose implementation of ConcurrentMap is ConcurrentHashMap,[34] which is a concurrent analog of HashMap.[35]
- ConcurrentNavigableMap[36] is a subinterface of ConcurrentMap that supports approximate matches. The standard general-purpose implementation of ConcurrentNavigableMap is ConcurrentSkipListMap,[37] which is a concurrent analog of TreeMap.[38]

---

29. docs/api/java/util/concurrent/ThreadPoolExecutor.html
30. docs/api/java/util/concurrent/ScheduledThreadPoolExecutor.html
31. docs/api/java/util/concurrent/BlockingQueue.html
32. docs/api/java/util/concurrent/ConcurrentMap.html
33. docs/api/java/util/Map.html
34. docs/api/java/util/concurrent/ConcurrentHashMap.html
35. docs/api/java/util/HashMap.html
36. docs/api/java/util/concurrent/ConcurrentNavigableMap.html
37. docs/api/java/util/concurrent/ConcurrentSkipListMap.html
38. docs/api/java/util/TreeMap.html

All of these collections help avoid memory consistency errors (page 379) by defining a happens-before relationship between an operation that adds an object to the collection with subsequent operations that access or remove that object.

Atomic Variables

The `java.util.concurrent.atomic`[39] package defines classes that support atomic operations on single variables. All classes have `get` and `set` methods that work like reads and writes on `volatile` variables. That is, a `set` has a happens-before relationship with any subsequent `get` on the same variable. The atomic `compareAndSet` method also has these memory consistency features, as do the simple atomic arithmetic methods that apply to integer atomic variables.

To see how this package might be used, let's return to the `Counter` class we originally used to demonstrate thread interference:

```
class Counter {
  private int c = 0;
  public void increment() {
    c++;
  }
  public void decrement() {
    c--;
  }
  public int value() {
    return c;
  }
}
```

One way to make `Counter` safe from thread interference is to make its methods synchronized, as in `SynchronizedCounter`:

```
class SynchronizedCounter {
  private int c = 0;
  public synchronized void increment() {
    c++;
  }
  public synchronized void decrement() {
    c--;
  }
  public synchronized int value() {
    return c;
  }
}
```

39. `docs/api/java/util/concurrent/atomic/package-summary.html`

For this simple class, synchronization is an acceptable solution. But for a more complicated class, we might want to avoid the liveness impact of unnecessary synchronization. Replacing the `int` field with an `AtomicInteger` allows us to prevent thread interference without resorting to synchronization, as in `AtomicCounter`:[40]

```
import java.util.concurrent.atomic.AtomicInteger;

class AtomicCounter {
  private AtomicInteger c = new AtomicInteger(0);

  public void increment() {
    c.incrementAndGet();
  }

  public void decrement() {
    c.decrementAndGet();
  }

  public int value() {
    return c.get();
  }

}
```

For Further Reading

- *Concurrent Programming in Java: Design Principles and Pattern (2nd Edition)* by Doug Lea. A comprehensive work by a leading expert, who's also the architect of the Java platform's concurrency framework.
- *Java Concurrency in Practice* by Brian Goetz, Tim Peierls, Joshua Bloch, Joseph Bowbeer, David Holmes, and Doug Lea. A practical guide designed to be accessible to the novice.
- *Effective Java Programming Language Guide* by Joshua Bloch. Though this is a general programming guide, its chapter on threads contains essential "best practices" for concurrent programming.
- *Concurrency: State Models & Java Programs (2nd Edition)* by Jeff Magee and Jeff Kramer. An introduction to concurrent programming through a combination of modeling and practical examples.

40. `tutorial/essential/concurrency/example/AtomicCounter.java`

Questions and Exercises: Concurrency

Questions

Can you pass a `Thread` object to `Executor.execute`? Would such an invocation make sense?

Exercises

1. Compile and run `BadThreads.java`:[41]

```
public class BadThreads {

  static String message;

  private static class CorrectorThread extends Thread {

    public void run() {
      try {
        sleep(1000);
      } catch (InterruptedException e) {}
      // Key statement 1:
      message = "Mares do eat oats.";
    }
  }

  public static void main(String args[])
                         throws InterruptedException {
    (new CorrectorThread()).start();
    message = "Mares do not eat oats.";
    Thread.sleep(2000);
    // Key statement 2:
    System.out.println(message);
  }
}
```

   The application should print out "Mares do eat oats." Is it guaranteed to always do this? If not, why not? Would it help to change the parameters of the two invocations of `Sleep`? Describe two ways to change the program to enforce such a guarantee.

2. Modify the producer-consumer example in the Guarded Blocks section (page 386) to use a standard library class instead of the `Drop` class.

41. `tutorial/essential/concurrency/QandE/BadThreads.java`

Answers

You can find answers to these Questions and Exercises at:

```
tutorial/essential/concurrency/QandE/answers.html
```

13

Regular Expressions

THIS chapter explains how to use the `java.util.regex` API[1] for pattern matching with regular expressions. Although the syntax accepted by this package is similar to the Perl programming language,[2] knowledge of Perl is not a prerequisite. This chapter starts with the basics and gradually builds to cover more advanced techniques.

Introduction

What Are Regular Expressions?

Regular expressions are a way to describe a set of strings based on common characteristics shared by each string in the set. They can be used to search, edit, or manipulate text and data. You must learn a specific syntax to create regular expressions—one that goes beyond the normal syntax of the Java programming language. Regular expressions vary in complexity, but once you understand the basics of how they're constructed, you'll be able to decipher (or create) any regular expression.

This chapter teaches the regular expression syntax supported by the `java.util.regex` API and presents several working examples to illustrate how the various objects interact. In the world of regular expressions, there are many different flavors to choose from,

1. `docs/api/java/util/regex/package-summary.html`
2. `http://www.perl.com`

such as grep, Perl, Tcl, Python, PHP, and awk. The regular expression syntax in the `java.util.regex` API is most similar to that found in Perl.

How Are Regular Expressions Represented in This Package?

The `java.util.regex` package primarily consists of three classes: `Pattern`,[3] `Matcher`,[4] and `PatternSyntaxException`.[5]

- A `Pattern` object is a compiled representation of a regular expression. The `Pattern` class provides no public constructors. To create a pattern, you must first invoke one of its `public static compile` methods, which will then return a `Pattern` object. These methods accept a regular expression as the first argument; the next few pages of this chapter will teach you the required syntax.
- A `Matcher` object is the engine that interprets the pattern and performs match operations against an input string. Like the `Pattern` class, `Matcher` defines no public constructors. You obtain a `Matcher` object by invoking the `matcher` method on a `Pattern` object.
- A `PatternSyntaxException` object is an unchecked exception that indicates a syntax error in a regular expression pattern.

The last few sections of this chapter explore each class in detail. But first, you must understand how regular expressions are actually constructed. Therefore, the next section introduces a simple test harness that will be used repeatedly to explore their syntax.

Test Harness

This section defines a reusable test harness, `RegexTestHarness.java`,[6] for exploring the regular expression constructs supported by this API. The command to run this code is `java RegexTestHarness`; no command-line arguments are accepted. The application loops repeatedly, prompting the user for a regular expression and input string. Using this test harness is optional, but you may find it convenient for exploring the test cases discussed in the following pages.

---

3. `docs/api/java/util/regex/Pattern.html`
4. `docs/api/java/util/regex/Matcher.html`
5. `docs/api/java/util/regex/PatternSyntaxException.html`
6. `tutorial/essential/regex/examples/RegexTestHarness.java`

```
import java.io.Console;
import java.util.regex.Pattern;
import java.util.regex.Matcher;

public class RegexTestHarness {

  public static void main(String[] args){
    Console console = System.console();
    if (console == null) {
      System.err.println("No console.");
      System.exit(1);
    }
    while (true) {

      Pattern pattern =
      Pattern.compile(console.readLine("%nEnter your " +
                                              regex: "));

      Matcher matcher =
      pattern.matcher(console.readLine("Enter input string " +
                                            to search: "));

      boolean found = false;
      while (matcher.find()) {
        console.format("I found the text \"%s\" starting " +
                            "at index %d and ending at " +
                            "index %d.%n", matcher.group(),
                            matcher.start(), matcher.end());
        found = true;
      }
      if(!found){
        console.format("No match found.%n");
      }
    }
  }
}
```

Before continuing to the next section, save and compile this code to ensure that your development environment supports the required packages.

String Literals

The most basic form of pattern matching supported by this API is the match of a string literal. For example, if the regular expression is `foo` and the input string is `foo`, the match will succeed because the strings are identical. Try this out with the test harness:

```
Enter your regex: foo
Enter input string to search: foo
I found the text "foo" starting at index 0 and ending at index 3.
```

This match was a success. Note that while the input string is 3 characters long, the start index is 0 and the end index is 3. By convention, ranges are inclusive of the beginning index and exclusive of the end index, as shown in Figure 13.1.

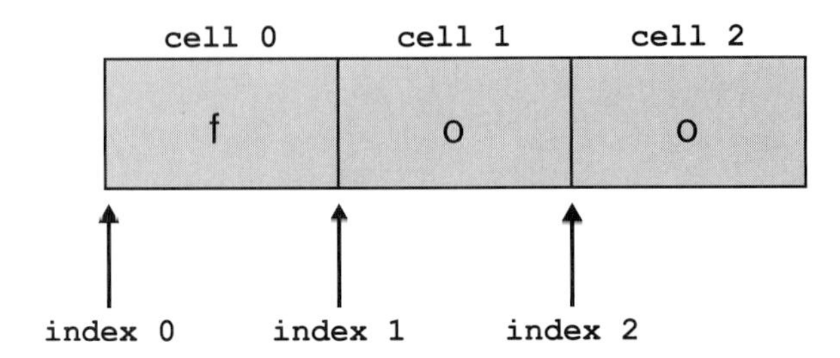

Figure 13.1 The `String` literal "foo," with numbered cells and index values.

Each character in the string resides in its own *cell*, with the index positions pointing between each cell. The string "foo" starts at index 0 and ends at index 3, even though the characters themselves only occupy cells 0, 1, and 2.

With subsequent matches, you'll notice some overlap; the start index for the next match is the same as the end index of the previous match:

```
Enter your regex: foo
Enter input string to search: foofoofoo
I found the text "foo" starting at index 0 and ending at index 3.
I found the text "foo" starting at index 3 and ending at index 6.
I found the text "foo" starting at index 6 and ending at index 9.
```

Metacharacters

This API also supports a number of special characters that affect the way a pattern is matched. Change the regular expression to `cat.` and the input string to `cats`. The output will appear as follows:

```
Enter your regex: cat.
Enter input string to search: cats
I found the text "cats" starting at index 0 and ending at index 4.
```

The match still succeeds, even though the dot (`.`) is not present in the input string. It succeeds because the dot is a *metacharacter*—a character with special meaning interpreted by the matcher. The metacharacter "." means "any character," which is why the match succeeds in this example.

The metacharacters supported by this API are: ([{\^-$|}])?*+.

Note: In certain situations the special characters listed above will *not* be treated as metacharacters. You'll encounter this as you learn more about how regular expressions are constructed. You can, however, use this list to check whether or not a specific character will ever be considered a metacharacter. For example, the characters !, @, and # never carry a special meaning.

There are two ways to force a metacharacter to be treated as an ordinary character:

- precede the metacharacter with a backslash, or
- enclose it within \Q (which starts the quote) and \E (which ends it).

When using this technique, the \Q and \E can be placed at any location within the expression, provided that the \Q comes first.

Character Classes

If you browse through the `Pattern` class specification, you'll see tables summarizing the supported regular expression constructs. Table 13.1 describes character classes.

The left-hand column specifies the regular expression constructs, while the right-hand column describes the conditions under which each construct will match.

Table 13.1 Character Classes

`[abc]`	a, b, or c (simple class)
`[^abc]`	Any character except a, b, or c (negation)
`[a-zA-Z]`	a through z, or A through Z, inclusive (range)
`[a-d[m-p]]`	a through d, or m through p: `[a-dm-p]` (union)
`[a-z&&[def]]`	d, e, or f (intersection)
`[a-z&&[^bc]]`	a through z, except for b and c: `[ad-z]` (subtraction)
`[a-z&&[^m-p]]`	a through z, and not m through p: `[a-lq-z]` (subtraction)

Note: The word "class" in the phrase "character class" does not refer to a `.class` file. In the context of regular expressions, a *character class* is a set of characters enclosed within square brackets. It specifies the characters that will successfully match a single character from a given input string.

Simple Classes

The most basic form of a character class is to simply place a set of characters side-by-side within square brackets. For example, the regular expression `[bcr]at` will match the words "bat," "cat," or "rat" because it defines a character class (accepting either "b", "c", or "r") as its first character:

```
Enter your regex: [bcr]at
Enter input string to search: bat
I found the text "bat" starting at index 0 and ending at index 3.

Enter your regex: [bcr]at
Enter input string to search: cat
I found the text "cat" starting at index 0 and ending at index 3.

Enter your regex: [bcr]at
Enter input string to search: rat
I found the text "rat" starting at index 0 and ending at index 3.

Enter your regex: [bcr]at
Enter input string to search: hat
No match found.
```

In the above examples, the overall match succeeds only when the first letter matches one of the characters defined by the character class.

Negation

To match all characters *except* those listed, insert the "^" metacharacter at the beginning of the character class. This technique is known as *negation*:

```
Enter your regex: [^bcr]at
Enter input string to search: bat
No match found.

Enter your regex: [^bcr]at
Enter input string to search: cat
No match found.

Enter your regex: [^bcr]at
Enter input string to search: rat
No match found.

Enter your regex: [^bcr]at
Enter input string to search: hat
I found the text "hat" starting at index 0 and ending at index 3.
```

The match is successful only if the first character of the input string does *not* contain any of the characters defined by the character class.

Ranges

Sometimes you'll want to define a character class that includes a range of values, such as the letters "a through h" or the numbers "1 through 5." To specify a range, simply insert the "-" metacharacter between the first and last character to be matched, such as `[1-5]` or `[a-h]`. You can also place different ranges beside each other within the class to further expand the match possibilities. For example, `[a-zA-Z]` will match any letter of the alphabet: a to z (lowercase) or A to Z (uppercase).

Here are some examples of ranges and negation:

```
Enter your regex: [a-c]
Enter input string to search: a
I found the text "a" starting at index 0 and ending at index 1.

Enter your regex: [a-c]
Enter input string to search: b
I found the text "b" starting at index 0 and ending at index 1.

Enter your regex: [a-c]
Enter input string to search: c
I found the text "c" starting at index 0 and ending at index 1.

Enter your regex: [a-c]
Enter input string to search: d
No match found.

Enter your regex: foo[1-5]
Enter input string to search: foo1
I found the text "foo1" starting at index 0 and ending at index 4.

Enter your regex: foo[1-5]
Enter input string to search: foo5
I found the text "foo5" starting at index 0 and ending at index 4.

Enter your regex: foo[1-5]
Enter input string to search: foo6
No match found.

Enter your regex: foo[^1-5]
Enter input string to search: foo1
No match found.

Enter your regex: foo[^1-5]
Enter input string to search: foo6
I found the text "foo6" starting at index 0 and ending at index 4.
```

Unions

You can also use *unions* to create a single character class comprised of two or more separate character classes. To create a union, simply nest one class inside the other, such as [0-4[6-8]]. This particular union creates a single character class that matches the numbers 0, 1, 2, 3, 4, 6, 7, and 8.

```
Enter your regex: [0-4[6-8]]
Enter input string to search: 0
I found the text "0" starting at index 0 and ending at index 1.

Enter your regex: [0-4[6-8]]
Enter input string to search: 5
No match found.

Enter your regex: [0-4[6-8]]
Enter input string to search: 6
I found the text "6" starting at index 0 and ending at index 1.

Enter your regex: [0-4[6-8]]
Enter input string to search: 8
I found the text "8" starting at index 0 and ending at index 1.

Enter your regex: [0-4[6-8]]
Enter input string to search: 9
No match found.
```

Intersections

To create a single character class matching only the characters common to all of its nested classes, use &&, as in [0-9&&[345]]. This particular intersection creates a single character class matching only the numbers common to both character classes: 3, 4, and 5:

```
Enter your regex: [0-9&&[345]]
Enter input string to search: 3
I found the text "3" starting at index 0 and ending at index 1.

Enter your regex: [0-9&&[345]]
Enter input string to search: 4
I found the text "4" starting at index 0 and ending at index 1.

Enter your regex: [0-9&&[345]]
Enter input string to search: 5
I found the text "5" starting at index 0 and ending at index 1.

Enter your regex: [0-9&&[345]]
Enter input string to search: 2
No match found.

Enter your regex: [0-9&&[345]]
Enter input string to search: 6
No match found.
```

And here's an example that shows the intersection of two ranges:

```
Enter your regex: [2-8&&[4-6]]
Enter input string to search: 3
No match found.

Enter your regex: [2-8&&[4-6]]
Enter input string to search: 4
I found the text "4" starting at index 0 and ending at index 1.

Enter your regex: [2-8&&[4-6]]
Enter input string to search: 5
I found the text "5" starting at index 0 and ending at index 1.

Enter your regex: [2-8&&[4-6]]
Enter input string to search: 6
I found the text "6" starting at index 0 and ending at index 1.

Enter your regex: [2-8&&[4-6]]
Enter input string to search: 7
No match found.
```

Subtraction

Finally, you can use *subtraction* to negate one or more nested character classes, such as `[0-9&&[^345]]`. This example creates a single character class that matches everything from 0 to 9, *except* the numbers 3, 4, and 5:

```
Enter your regex: [0-9&&[^345]]
Enter input string to search: 2
I found the text "2" starting at index 0 and ending at index 1.

Enter your regex: [0-9&&[^345]]
Enter input string to search: 3
No match found.

Enter your regex: [0-9&&[^345]]
Enter input string to search: 4
No match found.

Enter your regex: [0-9&&[^345]]
Enter input string to search: 5
No match found.

Enter your regex: [0-9&&[^345]]
Enter input string to search: 6
I found the text "6" starting at index 0 and ending at index 1.

Enter your regex: [0-9&&[^345]]
Enter input string to search: 9
I found the text "9" starting at index 0 and ending at index 1.
```

Now that we've covered how character classes are created, You may want to review Table 13.1 before continuing with the next section.

Predefined Character Classes

The `Pattern` API contains a number of useful *predefined character classes*, which offer convenient shorthands for commonly used regular expressions.

In Table 13.2, each construct in the left-hand column is shorthand for the character class in the right-hand column. For example, `\d` means a range of digits (0–9), and `\w` means a word character (any lowercase letter, any uppercase letter, the underscore character, or any digit). Use the predefined classes whenever possible. They make your code easier to read and eliminate errors introduced by malformed character classes.

Table 13.2 Predefined Character Classes

.	Any character (may or may not match line terminators)
`\d`	A digit: `[0-9]`
`\D`	A non-digit: `[^0-9]`
`\s`	A whitespace character: `[ \t\n\x0B\f\r]`
`\S`	A non-whitespace character: `[^\s]`
`\w`	A word character: `[a-zA-Z_0-9]`
`\W`	A non-word character: `[^\w]`

Constructs beginning with a backslash are called *escaped constructs*. We previewed escaped constructs in the LiteralsString Literals sectionsection (page 48) where we mentioned the use of backslash and `\Q` and `\E` for quotation. If you are using an escaped construct within a string literal, you must preceed the backslash with another backslash for the string to compile. For example:

```
private final String REGEX = "\\d"; // a single digit
```

In this example `\d` is the regular expression; the extra backslash is required for the code to compile. The test harness reads the expressions directly from the `Console`, however, so the extra backslash is unnecessary.

The following examples demonstrate the use of predefined character classes:

```
Enter your regex: .
Enter input string to search: @
I found the text "@" starting at index 0 and ending at index 1.

Enter your regex: .
Enter input string to search: 1
I found the text "1" starting at index 0 and ending at index 1.
```

```
Enter your regex: .
Enter input string to search: a
I found the text "a" starting at index 0 and ending at index 1.

Enter your regex: \d
Enter input string to search: 1
I found the text "1" starting at index 0 and ending at index 1.

Enter your regex: \d
Enter input string to search: a
No match found.

Enter your regex: \D
Enter input string to search: 1
No match found.

Enter your regex: \D
Enter input string to search: a
I found the text "a" starting at index 0 and ending at index 1.

Enter your regex: \s
Enter input string to search:
I found the text " " starting at index 0 and ending at index 1.

Enter your regex: \s
Enter input string to search: a
No match found.

Enter your regex: \S
Enter input string to search:
No match found.

Enter your regex: \S
Enter input string to search: a
I found the text "a" starting at index 0 and ending at index 1.

Enter your regex: \w
Enter input string to search: a
I found the text "a" starting at index 0 and ending at index 1.

Enter your regex: \w
Enter input string to search: !
No match found.

Enter your regex: \W
Enter input string to search: a
No match found.

Enter your regex: \W
Enter input string to search: !
I found the text "!" starting at index 0 and ending at index 1.
```

In the first three examples, the regular expression is simply . (the "dot" metacharacter) that indicates "any character." Therefore, the match is successful in all three cases (a randomly selected @ character, a digit, and a letter). The remaining examples each use a single regular expression construct from Table 13.2. You can refer to this table to figure out the logic behind each match:

- `\d` matches all digits
- `\s` matches spaces
- `\w` matches word characters

Alternatively, a capital letter means the opposite:

- `\D` matches non-digits
- `\S` matches non-spaces
- `\W` matches non-word characters

Quantifiers

Quantifiers allow you to specify the number of occurrences to match against. For convenience, the three sections of the `Pattern` API specification describing greedy, reluctant, and possessive quantifiers are presented in Table 13.3. At first glance it may appear that the quantifiers `X?`, `X??`, and `X?+` do exactly the same thing, since they all promise to match "`X`, once or not at all." There are subtle implementation differences which will be explained near the end of this section.

Table 13.3 Quantifiers

Quantifiers			
Greedy	**Reluctant**	**Possessive**	**Meaning**
`X?`	`X??`	`X?+`	`X`, once or not at all
`X*`	`X*?`	`X*+`	`X`, zero or more times
`X+`	`X+?`	`X++`	`X`, one or more times
`X{n}`	`X{n}?`	`X{n}+`	`X`, exactly `n` times
`X{n,}`	`X{n,}?`	`X{n,}+`	`X`, at least `n` times
`X{n,m}`	`X{n,m}?`	`X{n,m}+`	`X`, at least `n` but not more than `m` times

Let's start our look at greedy quantifiers by creating three different regular expressions: the letter "a" followed by either ?, *, or +. Let's see what happens when these expressions are tested against an empty input string "":

```
Enter your regex: a?
Enter input string to search:
I found the text "" starting at index 0 and ending at index 0.

Enter your regex: a*
Enter input string to search:
I found the text "" starting at index 0 and ending at index 0.

Enter your regex: a+
Enter input string to search:
No match found.
```

Zero-Length Matches

In the previous example, the match is successful in the first two cases because the expressions `a?` and `a*` both allow for zero occurrences of the letter `a`. You'll also notice that the start and end indices are both zero, which is unlike any of the examples we've seen so far. The empty input string "" has no length, so the test simply matches nothing at index 0. Matches of this sort are known as a *zero-length matches*. A zero-length match can occur in several cases: in an empty input string, at the beginning of an input string, after the last character of an input string, or in between any two characters of an input string. Zero-length matches are easily identifiable because they always start and end at the same index position.

Let's explore zero-length matches with a few more examples. Change the input string to a single letter "a" and you'll notice something interesting:

```
Enter your regex: a?
Enter input string to search: a
I found the text "a" starting at index 0 and ending at index 1.
I found the text "" starting at index 1 and ending at index 1.

Enter your regex: a*
Enter input string to search: a
I found the text "a" starting at index 0 and ending at index 1.
I found the text "" starting at index 1 and ending at index 1.

Enter your regex: a+
Enter input string to search: a
I found the text "a" starting at index 0 and ending at index 1.
```

All three quantifiers found the letter "a", but the first two also found a zero-length match at index 1; that is, after the last character of the input string. Remember, the matcher sees the character "a" as sitting in the cell between index 0 and index 1, and our test harness loops until it can no longer find a match. Depending on the quantifier used, the presence of "nothing" at the index after the last character may or may not trigger a match.

Now change the input string to the letter "a" five times in a row and you'll get the following:

```
Enter your regex: a?
Enter input string to search: aaaaa
I found the text "a" starting at index 0 and ending at index 1.
I found the text "a" starting at index 1 and ending at index 2.
I found the text "a" starting at index 2 and ending at index 3.
I found the text "a" starting at index 3 and ending at index 4.
I found the text "a" starting at index 4 and ending at index 5.
I found the text "" starting at index 5 and ending at index 5.

Enter your regex: a*
Enter input string to search: aaaaa
I found the text "aaaaa" starting at index 0 and ending at index 5.
I found the text "" starting at index 5 and ending at index 5.

Enter your regex: a+
Enter input string to search: aaaaa
I found the text "aaaaa" starting at index 0 and ending at index 5.
```

The expression `a?` finds an individual match for each character, since it matches when "a" appears zero or one times. The expression `a*` finds two separate matches: all occurrences of the letter "a" in the first match, then the zero-length match after the last character at index 5. And finally, `a+` matches all occurrences of the letter "a", ignoring the presence of "nothing" at the last index.

At this point, you might be wondering what the results would be if the first two quantifiers encounter a letter other than "a". For example, what happens if it encounters the letter "b", as in "ababaaaab"?

Let's find out:

```
Enter your regex: a?
Enter input string to search: ababaaaab
I found the text "a" starting at index 0 and ending at index 1.
I found the text "" starting at index 1 and ending at index 1.
I found the text "a" starting at index 2 and ending at index 3.
I found the text "" starting at index 3 and ending at index 3.
I found the text "a" starting at index 4 and ending at index 5.
I found the text "a" starting at index 5 and ending at index 6.
I found the text "a" starting at index 6 and ending at index 7.
I found the text "a" starting at index 7 and ending at index 8.
I found the text "" starting at index 8 and ending at index 8.
I found the text "" starting at index 9 and ending at index 9.

Enter your regex: a*
Enter input string to search: ababaaaab
I found the text "a" starting at index 0 and ending at index 1.
I found the text "" starting at index 1 and ending at index 1.
I found the text "a" starting at index 2 and ending at index 3.
I found the text "" starting at index 3 and ending at index 3.
```

```
I found the text "aaaa" starting at index 4 and ending at index 8.
I found the text "" starting at index 8 and ending at index 8.
I found the text "" starting at index 9 and ending at index 9.

Enter your regex: a+
Enter input string to search: ababaaaab
I found the text "a" starting at index 0 and ending at index 1.
I found the text "a" starting at index 2 and ending at index 3.
I found the text "aaaa" starting at index 4 and ending at index 8.
```

Even though the letter "b" appears in cells 1, 3, and 8, the output reports a zero-length match at those locations. The regular expression `a?` is not specifically looking for the letter "b"; it's merely looking for the presence (or lack thereof) of the letter "a". If the quantifier allows for a match of "a" zero times, anything in the input string that's not an "a" will show up as a zero-length match. The remaining a's are matched according to the rules discussed in the previous examples.

To match a pattern exactly *n* number of times, simply specify the number inside a set of braces:

```
Enter your regex: a{3}
Enter input string to search: aa
No match found.

Enter your regex: a{3}
Enter input string to search: aaa
I found the text "aaa" starting at index 0 and ending at index 3.

Enter your regex: a{3}
Enter input string to search: aaaa
I found the text "aaa" starting at index 0 and ending at index 3.
```

Here, the regular expression `a{3}` is searching for three occurrences of the letter "a" in a row. The first test fails because the input string does not have enough a's to match against. The second test contains exactly 3 a's in the input string, which triggers a match. The third test also triggers a match because there are exactly 3 a's at the beginning of the input string. Anything following that is irrelevant to the first match. If the pattern should appear again after that point, it would trigger subsequent matches:

```
Enter your regex: a{3}
Enter input string to search: aaaaaaaaa
I found the text "aaa" starting at index 0 and ending at index 3.
I found the text "aaa" starting at index 3 and ending at index 6.
I found the text "aaa" starting at index 6 and ending at index 9.
```

To require a pattern to appear at least *n* times, add a comma after the number:

```
Enter your regex: a{3,}
Enter input string to search: aaaaaaaaa
I found the text "aaaaaaaaa" starting at index 0 and ending at index 9.
```

With the same input string, this test finds only one match, because the 9 a's in a row satisfy the need for "at least" 3 a's.

Finally, to specify an upper limit on the number of occurrences, add a second number inside the braces:

```
Enter your regex: a{3,6}
           // find at least 3 (but no more than 6) a's in a row
Enter input string to search: aaaaaaaaa
I found the text "aaaaaa" starting at index 0 and ending at index 6.
I found the text "aaa" starting at index 6 and ending at index 9.
```

Here the first match is forced to stop at the upper limit of 6 characters. The second match includes whatever is left over, which happens to be three a's—the mimimum number of characters allowed for this match. If the input string were one character shorter, there would not be a second match since only two a's would remain.

Capturing Groups and Character Classes with Quantifiers

Until now, we've only tested quantifiers on input strings containing one character. In fact, quantifiers can only attach to one character at a time, so the regular expression `abc+` would mean "a, followed by b, followed by c one or more times." It would not mean "abc" one or more times. However, quantifiers can also attach to character classes (see the Character Classes section, page 409) and capturing groups (see the Capturing Groups section, page 422), such as `[abc]+` (a or b or c, one or more times) or `(abc)+` (the group "abc", one or more times).

Let's illustrate by specifying the group `(dog)`, three times in a row:

```
Enter your regex: (dog){3}
Enter input string to search: dogdogdogdogdogdog
I found the text "dogdogdog" starting at index 0 and ending at index 9.
I found the text "dogdogdog" starting at index 9 and ending at index 18.

Enter your regex: dog{3}
Enter input string to search: dogdogdogdogdogdog
No match found.
```

Here the first example finds three matches, since the quantifier applies to the entire capturing group. Remove the parentheses, however, and the match fails because the quantifier `{3}` now applies only to the letter "g".

Similarly, we can apply a quantifier to an entire character class:

```
Enter your regex: [abc]{3}
Enter input string to search: abccabaaaccbbbc
I found the text "abc" starting at index 0 and ending at index 3.
I found the text "cab" starting at index 3 and ending at index 6.
I found the text "aaa" starting at index 6 and ending at index 9.
I found the text "ccb" starting at index 9 and ending at index 12.
I found the text "bbc" starting at index 12 and ending at index 15.

Enter your regex: abc{3}
Enter input string to search: abccabaaaccbbbc
No match found.
```

Here the quantifier `{3}` applies to the entire character class in the first example, but only to the letter "c" in the second.

Differences among Greedy, Reluctant, and Possessive Quantifiers

There are subtle differences among greedy, reluctant, and possessive quantifiers.

Greedy quantifiers are considered "greedy" because they force the matcher to read in, or *eat*, the entire input string prior to attempting the first match. If the first match attempt (the entire input string) fails, the matcher backs off the input string by one character and tries again, repeating the process until a match is found or there are no more characters left to back off from. Depending on the quantifier used in the expression, the last thing it will try matching against is 1 or 0 characters.

The reluctant quantifiers, however, take the opposite approach: They start at the beginning of the input string, then reluctantly eat one character at a time looking for a match. The last thing they try is the entire input string.

Finally, the possessive quantifiers always eat the entire input string, trying once (and only once) for a match. Unlike the greedy quantifiers, possessive quantifiers never back off, even if doing so would allow the overall match to succeed.

To illustrate, consider the input string `xfooxxxxxxfoo`:

```
Enter your regex: .*foo  // greedy quantifier
Enter input string to search: xfooxxxxxxfoo
I found the text "xfooxxxxxxfoo" starting at index 0 and ending
                                                  at index 13.

Enter your regex: .*?foo  // reluctant quantifier
Enter input string to search: xfooxxxxxxfoo
I found the text "xfoo" starting at index 0 and ending at index 4.
I found the text "xxxxxxfoo" starting at index 4 and ending at index 13.

Enter your regex: .*+foo // possessive quantifier
Enter input string to search: xfooxxxxxxfoo
No match found.
```

The first example uses the greedy quantifier `.*` to find "anything," zero or more times, followed by the letters `"f" "o" "o"`. Because the quantifier is greedy, the `.*` portion of the expression first eats the entire input string. At this point, the overall expression cannot succeed, because the last three letters (`"f" "o" "o"`) have already been consumed. So the matcher slowly backs off one letter at a time until the rightmost occurrence of "foo" has been regurgitated, at which point the match succeeds and the search ends.

The second example, however, is reluctant, so it starts by first consuming "nothing." Because "foo" doesn't appear at the beginning of the string, it's forced to swallow the first letter (an "x"), which triggers the first match at 0 and 4. Our test harness continues the process until the input string is exhausted. It finds another match at 4 and 13.

The third example fails to find a match because the quantifier is possessive. In this case, the entire input string is consumed by `.*+`, leaving nothing left over to satisfy the "foo" at the end of the expression. Use a possessive quantifier for situations where you want to seize all of something without ever backing off; it will outperform the equivalent greedy quantifier in cases where the match is not immediately found.

Capturing Groups

Earlier we saw how quantifiers attach to one character, character class, or capturing group at a time. But until now, we have not discussed the notion of capturing groups in any detail.

Capturing groups are a way to treat multiple characters as a single unit. They are created by placing the characters to be grouped inside a set of parentheses. For example, the regular expression `(dog)` creates a single group containing the letters `"d"`, `"o"`, and `"g"`. The portion of the input string that matches the capturing group will be saved in memory for later recall via backreferences (as discussed in the Backreferences section, page 423).

Numbering

As described in the `Pattern` API, capturing groups are numbered by counting their opening parentheses from left to right. In the expression `((A)(B(C)))`, for example, there are four such groups:

1. `((A)(B(C)))`
2. `(A)`
3. `(B(C))`
4. `(C)`

To find out how many groups are present in the expression, call the `groupCount` method on a matcher object. The `groupCount` method returns an `int` showing the number of capturing groups present in the matcher's pattern. In this example, `groupCount` would return the number `4`, showing that the pattern contains 4 capturing groups.

There is also a special group, group 0, which always represents the entire expression. This group is not included in the total reported by `groupCount`. Groups beginning with `(?` are pure, *non-capturing groups* that do not capture text and do not count towards the group total. (You'll see examples of non-capturing groups later in the Methods of the `Pattern` Class section, page 425.)

It's important to understand how groups are numbered because some `Matcher` methods accept an `int` specifying a particular group number as a parameter:

`public int start(int group)` Returns the start index of the subsequence captured by the given group during the previous match operation.

`public int end(int group)` Returns the index of the last character, plus one, of the subsequence captured by the given group during the previous match operation.

`public String group(int group)` Returns the input subsequence captured by the given group during the previous match operation.

Backreferences

The section of the input string matching the capturing group(s) is saved in memory for later recall via *backreference*. A backreference is specified in the regular expression as a backslash (`\`) followed by a digit indicating the number of the group to be recalled. For example, the expression `(\d\d)` defines one capturing group matching two digits in a row, which can be recalled later in the expression via the backreference `\1`.

To match any 2 digits, followed by the exact same two digits, you would use `(\d\d)\1` as the regular expression:

```
Enter your regex: (\d\d)\1
Enter input string to search: 1212
I found the text "1212" starting at index 0 and ending at index 4.
```

If you change the last two digits, the match will fail:

```
Enter your regex: (\d\d)\1
Enter input string to search: 1234
No match found.
```

For nested capturing groups, backreferencing works in exactly the same way: Specify a backslash followed by the number of the group to be recalled.

Boundary Matchers

Until now, we've only been interested in whether or not a match is found *at some location* within a particular input string. We never cared about *where* in the string the match was taking place.

You can make your pattern matches more precise by specifying such information with *boundary matchers*. For example, maybe you're interested in finding a particular word, but only if it appears at the beginning or end of a line. Or maybe you want to know if the match is taking place on a word boundary or at the end of the previous match.

Table 13.4 lists and explains all the boundary matchers.

Table 13.4 Boundary Matchers

^	The beginning of a line
$	The end of a line
\b	A word boundary
\B	A non-word boundary
\A	The beginning of the input
\G	The end of the previous match
\Z	The end of the input but for the final terminator, if any
\z	The end of the input

The following examples demonstrate the use of boundary matchers ^ and $. As noted previously, ^ matches the beginning of a line and $ matches the end:

```
Enter your regex: ^dog$
Enter input string to search: dog
I found the text "dog" starting at index 0 and ending at index 3.

Enter your regex: ^dog$
Enter input string to search:      dog
No match found.

Enter your regex: \s*dog$
Enter input string to search:             dog
I found the text "            dog" starting at index 0 and
                                              ending at index 15.

Enter your regex: ^dog\w*
Enter input string to search: dogblahblah
I found the text "dogblahblah" starting at index 0 and
                                              ending at index 11.
```

The first example is successful because the pattern occupies the entire input string. The second example fails because the input string contains extra white space at the beginning. The third example specifies an expression that allows for unlimited white space, followed by "dog" on the end of the line. The fourth example requires "dog" to be present at the beginning of a line followed by an unlimited number of word characters.

To check if a pattern begins and ends on a word boundary (as opposed to a substring within a longer string), just use `\b` on either side; for example, `\bdog\b`:

```
Enter your regex: \bdog\b
Enter input string to search: The dog plays in the yard.
I found the text "dog" starting at index 4 and ending at index 7.

Enter your regex: \bdog\b
Enter input string to search: The doggie plays in the yard.
No match found.
```

To match the expression on a non-word boundary, use `\B` instead:

```
Enter your regex: \bdog\B
Enter input string to search: The dog plays in the yard.
No match found.

Enter your regex: \bdog\B
Enter input string to search: The doggie plays in the yard.
I found the text "dog" starting at index 4 and ending at index 7.
```

To require the match to occur only at the end of the previous match, use `\G`:

```
Enter your regex: dog
Enter input string to search: dog dog
I found the text "dog" starting at index 0 and ending at index 3.
I found the text "dog" starting at index 4 and ending at index 7.

Enter your regex: \Gdog
Enter input string to search: dog dog
I found the text "dog" starting at index 0 and ending at index 3.
```

Here the second example finds only one match, because the second occurrence of "dog" does not start at the end of the previous match.

Methods of the Pattern Class

Until now, we've only used the test harness to create `Pattern` objects in their most basic form. This section explores advanced techniques such as creating patterns with flags and using embedded flag expressions. It also explores some additional useful methods that we haven't yet discussed.

Creating a Pattern with Flags

The Pattern class defines an alternate compile method that accepts a set of flags affecting the way the pattern is matched. The flags parameter is a bit mask that may include any of the following public static fields:

Pattern.CANON_EQ Enables canonical equivalence. When this flag is specified, two characters will be considered to match if, and only if, their full canonical decompositions match. The expression "a\u030A", for example, will match the string "\u00E5" when this flag is specified. By default, matching does not take canonical equivalence into account. Specifying this flag may impose a performance penalty.

Pattern.CASE_INSENSITIVE Enables case-insensitive matching. By default, case-insensitive matching assumes that only characters in the US-ASCII charset are being matched. Unicode-aware case-insensitive matching can be enabled by specifying the UNICODE_CASE flag in conjunction with this flag. Case-insensitive matching can also be enabled via the embedded flag expression (?i). Specifying this flag may impose a slight performance penalty.

Pattern.COMMENTS Permits white space and comments in the pattern. In this mode, white space is ignored, and embedded comments starting with # are ignored until the end of a line. Comments mode can also be enabled via the embedded flag expression (?x).

Pattern.DOTALL Enables dotall mode. In dotall mode, the expression . matches any character, including a line terminator. By default this expression does not match line terminators. Dotall mode can also be enabled via the embedded flag expression (?s). (The s is a mnemonic for "single-line" mode, which is what this is called in Perl.)

Pattern.LITERAL Enables literal parsing of the pattern. When this flag is specified, the input string that specifies the pattern is treated as a sequence of literal characters. Metacharacters or escape sequences in the input sequence will be given no special meaning. The flags CASE_INSENSITIVE and UNICODE_CASE retain their impact on matching when used in conjunction with this flag. The other flags become superfluous. There is no embedded flag character for enabling literal parsing.

Pattern.MULTILINE Enables multiline mode. In multiline mode the expressions ^ and $ match just after or just before, respectively, a line terminator or the end of the input sequence. By default these expressions only match at the beginning and the end of the entire input sequence. Multiline mode can also be enabled via the embedded flag expression (?m).

Pattern.UNICODE_CASE Enables Unicode-aware case folding. When this flag is specified, then case-insensitive matching, when enabled by the CASE_INSENSITIVE flag, is done in a manner consistent with the Unicode Standard. By default, case-insensitive matching assumes that only characters in the US-ASCII charset are being matched. Unicode-aware case folding can also be enabled via the embedded flag expression `(?u)`. Specifying this flag may impose a performance penalty.

`Pattern.UNIX_LINES` Enables UNIX lines mode. In this mode, only the `'\n'` line terminator is recognized in the behavior of `.`, `^`, and `$`. UNIX lines mode can also be enabled via the embedded flag expression `(?d)`.

In the following steps we will modify the test harness, `RegexTestHarness.java`, to create a pattern with case-insensitive matching.

First, modify the code to invoke the alternate version of `compile`:

```
Pattern pattern =
Pattern.compile(console.readLine("%nEnter your regex: "),
Pattern.CASE_INSENSITIVE);
```

Then compile and run the test harness to get the following results:

```
Enter your regex: dog
Enter input string to search: DoGDOg
I found the text "DoG" starting at index 0 and ending at index 3.
I found the text "DOg" starting at index 3 and ending at index 6.
```

As you can see, the string literal "dog" matches both occurrences, regardless of case. To compile a pattern with multiple flags, separate the flags to be included using the bitwise OR operator "`|`". For clarity, the following code samples hardcode the regular expression instead of reading it from the `Console`:

```
pattern = Pattern.compile("[az]$",
            Pattern.MULTILINE | Pattern.UNIX_LINES);
```

You could also specify an `int` variable instead:

```
final int flags =
  Pattern.CASE_INSENSITIVE | Pattern.UNICODE_CASE;
Pattern pattern = Pattern.compile("aa", flags);
```

Embedded Flag Expressions

It's also possible to enable various flags using *embedded flag expressions*. Embedded flag expressions are an alternative to the two-argument version of `compile` and are specified in the regular expression itself. The following example uses the original test harness, `RegexTestHarness.java`, with the embedded flag expression `(?i)` to enable case-insensitive matching:

```
Enter your regex: (?i)foo
Enter input string to search: FOOfooFoOfoO
I found the text "FOO" starting at index 0 and ending at index 3.
I found the text "foo" starting at index 3 and ending at index 6.
I found the text "FoO" starting at index 6 and ending at index 9.
I found the text "foO" starting at index 9 and ending at index 12.
```

Once again, all matches succeed regardless of case.

The embedded flag expressions that correspond to Pattern's publicly accessible fields are presented in Table 13.5.

Table 13.5 Embedded Flag Expressions

Constant	Equivalent Embedded Flag Expression
Pattern.CANON_EQ	None
Pattern.CASE_INSENSITIVE	(?i)
Pattern.COMMENTS	(?x)
Pattern.MULTILINE	(?m)
Pattern.DOTALL	(?s)
Pattern.LITERAL	None
Pattern.UNICODE_CASE	(?u)
Pattern.UNIX_LINES	(?d)

Using the matches(String,CharSequence) Method

The Pattern class defines a convenient matches method that allows you to quickly check if a pattern is present in a given input string. As with all public static methods, you should invoke matches by its class name, such as Pattern.matches("\\d","1");. In this example, the method returns true, because the digit "1" matches the regular expression \d.

Using the split(String) Method

The split method is a great tool for gathering the text that lies on either side of the pattern that's been matched. As shown below in SplitDemo.java,[7] the split method could extract the words "one two three four five" from the string "one:two:three:four:five":

7. tutorial/essential/regex/examples/SplitDemo.java

```
import java.util.regex.Pattern;
import java.util.regex.Matcher;

public class SplitDemo {

  private static final String REGEX = ":";
  private static final String INPUT
                                  = "one:two:three:four:five";

  public static void main(String[] args) {
    Pattern p = Pattern.compile(REGEX);
    String[] items = p.split(INPUT);
    for(String s : items) {
      System.out.println(s);
    }
  }
}

OUTPUT:

one
two
three
four
five
```

For simplicity, we've matched a string literal, the colon (:) instead of a complex regular expression. Since we're still using `Pattern` and `Matcher` objects, you can use split to get the text that falls on either side of any regular expression. Here's the same example, `SplitDemo2.java`,[8] modified to split on digits instead:

```
import java.util.regex.Pattern;
import java.util.regex.Matcher;

public class SplitDemo2 {
  private static final String REGEX = "\\d";
  private static final String INPUT
                                  = "one9two4three7four1five";

  public static void main(String[] args) {
    Pattern p = Pattern.compile(REGEX);
    String[] items = p.split(INPUT)
    for(String s : items) {
      System.out.println(s);
    }
  }
}
```

8. `tutorial/essential/regex/examples/SplitDemo2.java`

```
OUTPUT:

one
two
three
four
five
```

Other Utility Methods

You may find the following methods to be of some use as well:

`public static String quote(String s)` Returns a literal pattern `String` for the specified `String`. This method produces a `String` that can be used to create a `Pattern` that would match `s` as if it were a literal pattern. Metacharacters or escape sequences in the input sequence will be given no special meaning.

`public String toString()` Returns the `String` representation of this pattern. This is the regular expression from which this pattern was compiled.

Pattern Method Equivalents in java.lang.String

Regular expression support also exists in `java.lang.String`[9] through several methods that mimic the behavior of `java.util.regex.Pattern`. For convenience, key excerpts from their API are presented below:

`public boolean matches(String regex)` Tells whether or not this string matches the given regular expression. An invocation of this method of the form `str.matches(regex)` yields exactly the same result as the expression `Pattern.matches(regex, str)`.

`public String[] split(String regex, int limit)` Splits this string around matches of the given regular expression. An invocation of this method of the form `str.split(regex, n)` yields the same result as the expression `Pattern.compile(regex).split(str, n)`.

`public String[] split(String regex)` Splits this string around matches of the given regular expression. This method works the same as if you invoked the two-argument split method with the given expression and a limit argument of zero. Trailing empty strings are not included in the resulting array.

9. `docs/api/java/util/regex/String.html`

There is also a replace method that replaces one `CharSequence` with another:

`public String replace(CharSequence target,CharSequence replacement)`
Replaces each substring of this string that matches the literal target sequence with the specified literal replacement sequence. The replacement proceeds from the beginning of the string to the end, for example, replacing "aa" with "b" in the string "aaa" will result in "ba" rather than "ab".

Methods of the Matcher Class

This section describes some additional useful methods of the `Matcher` class. For convenience, the methods listed below are grouped according to functionality.

Index Methods

Index methods provide useful index values that show precisely where the match was found in the input string:

`public int start()` Returns the start index of the previous match.

`public int start(int group)` Returns the start index of the subsequence captured by the given group during the previous match operation.

`public int end()` Returns the offset after the last character matched.

`public int end(int group)` Returns the offset after the last character of the subsequence captured by the given group during the previous match operation.

Study Methods

Study methods review the input string and return a boolean indicating whether or not the pattern is found.

`public boolean lookingAt()` Attempts to match the input sequence, starting at the beginning of the region, against the pattern.

`public boolean find()` Attempts to find the next subsequence of the input sequence that matches the pattern.

`public boolean find(int start)` Resets this matcher and then attempts to find the next subsequence of the input sequence that matches the pattern, starting at the specified index.

`public boolean matches()` Attempts to match the entire region against the pattern.

Replacement Methods

Replacement methods are useful methods for replacing text in an input string:

`public Matcher appendReplacement(StringBuffer sb, String replacement)` Implements a non-terminal append-and-replace step.

`public StringBuffer appendTail(StringBuffer sb)` Implements a terminal append-and-replace step.

`public String replaceAll(String replacement)` Replaces every subsequence of the input sequence that matches the pattern with the given replacement string.

`public String replaceFirst(String replacement)` Replaces the first subsequence of the input sequence that matches the pattern with the given replacement string.

`public static String quoteReplacement(String s)` Returns a literal replacement `String` for the specified `String`. This method produces a `String` that will work as a literal replacement `s` in the `appendReplacement` method of the `Matcher` class. The `String` produced will match the sequence of characters in `s` treated as a literal sequence. Backslashes (`\`) and dollar signs (`$`) will be given no special meaning.

Using the start and end Methods

Here's an example, `MatcherDemo.java`,[10] that counts the number of times the word "dog" appears in the input string:

10. `tutorial/essential/regex/examples/MatcherDemo.java`

```
import java.util.regex.Pattern;
import java.util.regex.Matcher;

public class MatcherDemo {

  private static final String REGEX = "\\bdog\\b";
  private static final String INPUT =
                                    "dog dog dog doggie dogg";

  public static void main(String[] args) {

    Pattern p = Pattern.compile(REGEX);
    Matcher m = p.matcher(INPUT); // get a matcher object
    int count = 0;

    while(m.find()) {
      count++;
      System.out.println("Match number "+count);
      System.out.println("start(): "+m.start());
      System.out.println("end(): "+m.end());
    }
  }
}

OUTPUT:

Match number 1
start(): 0
end(): 3
Match number 2
start(): 4
end(): 7
Match number 3
start(): 8
end(): 11
```

You can see that this example uses word boundaries to ensure that the letters "d" "o" "g" are not merely a substring in a longer word. It also gives some useful information about where in the input string the match has occurred. The `start` method returns the start index of the subsequence captured by the given group during the previous match operation, and `end` returns the index of the last character matched, plus one.

Using the matches and lookingAt Methods

The `matches` and `lookingAt` methods both attempt to match an input sequence against a pattern. The difference, however, is that `matches` requires the entire input sequence to be matched, while `lookingAt` does not. Both methods always start at the beginning of the input string. Here's the full code, `MatchesLooking.java`:[11]

```
import java.util.regex.Pattern;
import java.util.regex.Matcher;

public class MatchesLooking {

  private static final String REGEX = "foo";
  private static final String INPUT = "fooooooooooooooooo";
  private static Pattern pattern;
  private static Matcher matcher;

  public static void main(String[] args) {

    // Initialize
    pattern = Pattern.compile(REGEX);
    matcher = pattern.matcher(INPUT);

    System.out.println("Current REGEX is: "+REGEX);
    System.out.println("Current INPUT is: "+INPUT);

    System.out.println("lookingAt(): "+matcher.lookingAt());
    System.out.println("matches(): "+matcher.matches());

  }
}
```

```
Current REGEX is: foo
Current INPUT is: fooooooooooooooooo
lookingAt(): true
matches(): false
```

Using replaceFirst(String) and replaceAll(String)

The `replaceFirst` and `replaceAll` methods replace text that matches a given regular expression. As their names indicate, `replaceFirst` replaces the first occurrence, and `replaceAll` replaces all occurences. Here's the `ReplaceDemo.java`[12] code:

---

11. `tutorial/essential/regex/examples/MatchesLooking.java`

12. `tutorial/essential/regex/examples/ReplaceDemo.java`

```
import java.util.regex.Pattern;
import java.util.regex.Matcher;

public class ReplaceDemo {

  private static String REGEX = "dog";
  private static String INPUT = "The dog says meow. " +
                                 "All dogs say meow.";
  private static String REPLACE = "cat";

  public static void main(String[] args) {
    Pattern p = Pattern.compile(REGEX);
    Matcher m = p.matcher(INPUT); // get a matcher object
    INPUT = m.replaceAll(REPLACE);
    System.out.println(INPUT);
  }
}

OUTPUT: The cat says meow. All cats say meow.
```

In this first version, all occurrences of `dog` are replaced with `cat`. But why stop here? Rather than replace a simple literal like `dog`, you can replace text that matches *any* regular expression. The API for this method states that "given the regular expression `a*b`, the input `aabfooaabfooabfoob`, and the replacement string `-`, an invocation of this method on a matcher for that expression would yield the string `-foo-foo-foo-`."

Here's the `ReplaceDemo2.java`[13] code:

```
import java.util.regex.Pattern;
import java.util.regex.Matcher;

public class ReplaceDemo2 {
  private static String REGEX = "a*b";
  private static String INPUT = "aabfooaabfooabfoob";
  private static String REPLACE = "-";
  public static void main(String[] args) {
    Pattern p = Pattern.compile(REGEX);
    Matcher m = p.matcher(INPUT); // get a matcher object
    INPUT = m.replaceAll(REPLACE);
    System.out.println(INPUT);
  }
}

OUTPUT: -foo-foo-foo-
```

13. `tutorial/essential/regex/examples/ReplaceDemo2.java`

To replace only the first occurrence of the pattern, simply call `replaceFirst` instead of `replaceAll`. It accepts the same parameter.

The appendReplacement(StringBuffer,String) and appendTail(StringBuffer) Methods

The `Matcher` class also provides `appendReplacement` and `appendTail` methods for text replacement. The following example, `RegexDemo.java`,[14] uses these two methods to achieve the same effect as `replaceAll`:

```
import java.util.regex.Pattern;
import java.util.regex.Matcher;

public class RegexDemo {
  private static String REGEX = "a*b";
  private static String INPUT = "aabfooaabfooabfoob";
  private static String REPLACE = "-";
  public static void main(String[] args) {
    Pattern p = Pattern.compile(REGEX);
    Matcher m = p.matcher(INPUT); // get a matcher object
    StringBuffer sb = new StringBuffer();
    while(m.find()){
      m.appendReplacement(sb,REPLACE);
    }
    m.appendTail(sb);
    System.out.println(sb.toString());
  }
}

OUTPUT: -foo-foo-foo-
```

Matcher Method Equivalents in java.lang.String

For convenience, the `String` class mimics a couple of `Matcher` methods as well:

`public String replaceFirst(String regex, String replacement)` Replaces the first substring of this string that matches the given regular expression with the given replacement. An invocation of this method of the form `str.replaceFirst(regex, repl)` yields exactly the same result as the expression `Pattern.compile(regex).matcher(str).replaceFirst(repl)`.

14. `tutorial/essential/regex/examples/RegexDemo.java`

public String replaceAll(String regex, String replacement) Replaces each substring of this string that matches the given regular expression with the given replacement. An invocation of this method of the form *str*.replaceAll(*regex*, *repl*) yields exactly the same result as the expression Pattern.compile(*regex*).matcher(*str*).replaceAll(*repl*).

Methods of the PatternSyntaxException Class

A PatternSyntaxException is an unchecked exception that indicates a syntax error in a regular expression pattern. The PatternSyntaxException class provides the following methods to help you determine what went wrong:

public String getDescription() Retrieves the description of the error.

public int getIndex() Retrieves the error index.

public String getPattern() Retrieves the erroneous regular expression pattern.

public String getMessage() Returns a multi-line string containing the description of the syntax error and its index, the erroneous regular expression pattern, and a visual indication of the error index within the pattern.

The following source code, RegexTestHarness2.java,[15] updates our test harness to check for malformed regular expressions:

```
import java.io.Console;
import java.util.regex.Pattern;
import java.util.regex.Matcher;
import java.util.regex.PatternSyntaxException;

public class RegexTestHarness2 {

  public static void main(String[] args){

    Pattern pattern = null;
    Matcher matcher = null;

    Console console = System.console();
    if (console == null) {
      System.err.println("No console.");
      System.exit(1);
    }
```

15. tutorial/essential/regex/examples/RegexTestHarness2.java

```
      while (true) {
        try{
          pattern =
          Pattern.compile(console.readLine("%nEnter your " +
                                                   regex: "));

          matcher =
          pattern.matcher(console.readLine("Enter input " +
                                         "string to search: "));
        }
        catch(PatternSyntaxException pse){
          console.format("There is a problem with " +
                                  "the regular expression!%n");
          console.format("The pattern in question is: %s%n",
                                             pse.getPattern());
          console.format("The description is: %s%n",
                                         pse.getDescription());
          console.format("The message is: %s%n",
                                             pse.getMessage());
          console.format("The index is: %s%n",pse.getIndex());
          System.exit(0);
        }
        boolean found = false;
        while (matcher.find()) {
          console.format("I found the text \"%s\" " +
                        "starting at index %d and ending " +
                        "at index %d.%n", matcher.group(),
                               matcher.start(), matcher.end());
          found = true;
        }
        if(!found){
          console.format("No match found.%n");
        }
      }
    }
  }
```

To run this test, enter `?i)foo` as the regular expression. This mistake is a common scenario in which the programmer has forgotten the opening parenthesis in the embedded flag expression `(?i)`. Doing so will produce the following results:

```
Enter your regex: ?i)
There is a problem with the regular expression!
The pattern in question is: ?i)
The description is: Dangling meta character '?'
The message is: Dangling meta character '?' near index 0
?i)
^
The index is: 0
```

From this output, we can see that the syntax error is a dangling metacharacter (the question mark) at index 0. A missing opening parenthesis is the culprit.

Summary

In this chapter, you learned that regular expressions are a way to describe a set of strings based on common characteristics shared by each string in the set. The Java programming language supports regular expressions via the `java.util.regex` package, primarily through the `Pattern`, `Matcher`, and `PatternSyntaxException` classes.

- A `Pattern` object is a compiled representation of a regular expression. The `Pattern` class provides no public constructors. To create a pattern, you must invoke one of its `public static compile` methods, both of which will return a `Pattern` object.
- A `Matcher` object is the engine that interprets the pattern and performs match operations against an input string. Like the `Pattern` class, `Matcher` defines no public constructors. You obtain a `Matcher` object by invoking the `public matcher` method on a `Pattern` object.
- A `PatternSyntaxException` object is an unchecked exception that indicates a syntax error in a regular expression pattern.

The most basic form of pattern matching supported by this API is the match of a string literal. You can also specify metacharacters—characters that carry special meaning—that will be interpreted by the matcher.

A character class is a set of characters enclosed within square brackets. It specifies the characters that will successfully match a single character from a given input string. You can define your own character classes, or use the predefined character classes included in the API.

Quantifiers allow you to specify the number of occurrences to match against. There are three different kinds of quantifiers: greedy, reluctant, and possessive:

- Greedy quantifiers are considered "greedy" because they force the matcher to read in, or eat, the entire input string prior to attempting the first match. If the first match attempt (the entire input string) fails, the matcher backs off the input string by one character and tries again, repeating the process until a match is found or there are no more characters left to back off from. Depending on the quantifier used in the expression, the last thing it will try matching against is 1 or 0 characters.
- Reluctant quantifiers take the opposite approach: they start at the beginning of the input string, then reluctantly eat one character at a time looking for a match. The last thing they try is the entire input string.

- Possessive quantifiers always eat the entire input string, trying once (and only once) for a match. Unlike the greedy quantifiers, possessive quantifiers never back off, even if doing so would allow the overall match to succeed.

Capturing groups provide a way to treat multiple characters as a single unit. They are created by placing the characters to be grouped inside a set of parentheses, and are numbered by counting their opening parentheses from left to right. The section of the input string matching the capturing group(s) is saved in memory for later recall via a backreference. A backreference is specified in the regular expression as a backslash "\" followed by a digit indicating the number of the group to be recalled.

Boundary matchers make your matches more precise by specifying a match location within the input string. The regex API provides boundary matchers for the following locations: the beginning of a line, the end of a line, word boundaries, non-word boundaries, the beginning of the input, the end of the input, and the end of the previous match.

Finally, you explored the `Pattern`, `Matcher`, `PatternSyntaxException` classes in detail to learn about their additional functionality, including their method equivalents in `java.lang.String`.

Additional Resources

For a more precise description of the behavior of regular expression constructs, we recommend reading the book *Mastering Regular Expressions* by Jeffrey E. F. Friedl (O'Reilly, 2003).

Questions and Exercises: Regular Expressions

Questions

1. What are the three public classes in the `java.util.regex` package? Describe the purpose of each.
2. Consider the string literal `"foo"`. What is the start index? What is the end index? Explain what these numbers mean.
3. What is the difference between an ordinary character and a metacharacter? Give an example of each.
4. How do you force a metacharacter to act like an ordinary character?
5. What do you call a set of characters enclosed in square brackets? What is it for?

6. Here are three predefined character classes: `\d`, `\s`, and `\w`. Describe each one, and rewrite it using square brackets.
7. For each of `\d`, `\s`, and `\w`, write *two* simple expressions that match the *opposite* set of characters.
8. Consider the regular expression `(dog){3}`. Identify the two subexpressions. What string does the expression match?

Exercises

Use a backreference to write an expression that will match a person's name only if that person's first name and last name are the same.

Answers

You can find answers to these Questions and Exercises at:

```
tutorial/essential/regex/QandE/answers.html
```

14

The Platform Environment

AN application runs in a *platform environment*, defined by the underlying operating system, the Java virtual machine, the class libraries, and various configuration data supplied when the application is launched. This chapter describes some of the APIs an application uses to examine and configure its platform environment.

Configuration Utilities

This section describes some of the configuration utilities that help an application access its startup context.

Properties

Properties are configuration values managed as *key/value pairs*. In each pair, the key and value are both `String`[1] values. The key identifies, and is used to retrieve, the value, much as a variable name is used to retrieve the variable's value. For example, an application capable of downloading files might use a property named "download.lastDirectory" to keep track of the directory used for the last download.

To manage properties, create instances of `java.util.Properties`.[2] This class provides methods for the following:

1. `docs/api/java/lang/String.html`
2. `docs/api/java/util/Properties.html`

- loading key/value pairs into a `Properties` object from a stream,
- retrieving a value from its key,
- listing the keys and their values,
- enumerating over the keys, and
- saving the properties to a stream.

For an introduction to streams, refer to the I/O Streams section (page 261).

`Properties` extends `java.util.Hashtable`.[3] Some of the methods inherited from `Hashtable` support the following actions:

- testing to see if a particular key or value is in the `Properties` object,
- getting the current number of key/value pairs,
- removing a key and its value,
- adding a key/value pair to the `Properties` list,
- enumerating over the values or the keys,
- retrieving a value by its key, and
- finding out if the `Properties` object is empty.

Security Considerations: Access to properties is subject to approval by the current security manager. The example code segments in this section are assumed to be in standalone applications, which, by default, have no security manager. The same code in an applet may not work depending on the browser or viewer in which it is running. See `docs/books/tutorial/deployment/applet/properties.html` for information about security restrictions on applets.

The `System` class maintains a `Properties` object that defines the configuration of the current working environment. For more about these properties, see the System Properties section (page 452). The remainder of this section explains how to use properties to manage application configuration.

Properties in the Application Life Cycle

Figure 14.1 illustrates how a typical application might manage its configuration data with a `Properties` object over the course of its execution.

3. `docs/api/java/util/Hashtable.html`

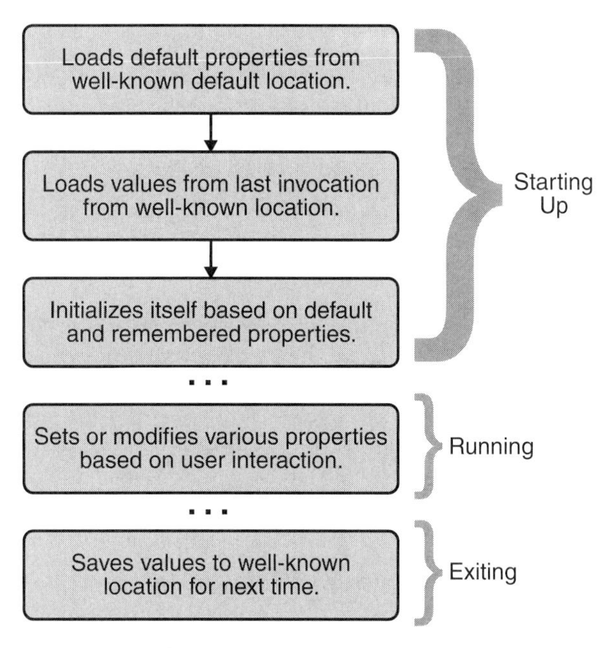

Figure 14.1 Properties roles.

Starting Up The actions given in the first three boxes occur when the application is starting up. First, the application loads the default properties from a well-known location into a `Properties` object. Normally, the default properties are stored in a file on disk along with the `.class` and other resource files for the application.

Next, the application creates another `Properties` object and loads the properties that were saved from the last time the application was run. Many applications store properties on a per-user basis, so the properties loaded in this step are usually in a specific file in a particular directory maintained by this application in the user's home directory. Finally, the application uses the default and remembered properties to initialize itself.

The key here is consistency. The application must always load and save properties to the same location so that it can find them the next time it's executed.

Running During the execution of the application, the user may change some settings, perhaps in a **Preferences** window, and the `Properties` object is updated to reflect these changes. If the user's changes are to be remembered in future sessions, they must be saved.

Exiting Upon exiting, the application saves the properties to its well-known location, to be loaded again when the application is next started up.

Setting Up the Properties Object

The following Java code performs the first two steps described in the previous section—loading the default properties and loading the remembered properties:

```
...
// create and load default properties
Properties defaultProps = new Properties();
FileInputStream in = new FileInputStream("defaultProperties");
defaultProps.load(in);
in.close();

// create application properties with default
Properties applicationProps = new Properties(defaultProps);

// now load properties from last invocation
in = new FileInputStream("appProperties");
applicationProps.load(in);
in.close();
...
```

First, the application sets up a default `Properties` object. This object contains the set of properties to use if values are not explicitly set elsewhere. Then the load method reads the default values from a file on disk named `defaultProperties`.

Next, the application uses a different constructor to create a second `Properties` object, `applicationProps`, whose default values are contained in `defaultProps`. The defaults come into play when a property is being retrieved. If the property can't be found in `applicationProps`, then its default list is searched.

Finally, the code loads a set of properties into `applicationProps` from a file named `appProperties`. The properties in this file are those that were saved from the application the last time it was invoked, as explained in the next section.

Saving Properties

The following example writes out the application properties from the previous example using `Properties.store`. The default properties don't need to be saved each time because they never change:

```
FileOutputStream out = new FileOutputStream("appProperties");
applicationProps.store(out, "---No Comment---");
out.close();
```

The `store` method needs a stream to write to, as well as a string that it uses as a comment at the top of the output.

Getting Property Information

Once the application has set up its `Properties` object, the application can query the object for information about various keys and values that it contains. An application gets information from a `Properties` object after start up so that it can initialize itself based on choices made by the user. The `Properties` class has several methods for getting property information:

`contains(Object value)`
`containsKey(Object key)`
Returns `true` if the value or the key is in the `Properties` object. `Properties` inherits these methods from `Hashtable`. Thus they accept `Object` arguments, but only `String` values should be used.

`getProperty(String key)`
`getProperty(String key, String default)`
Returns the value for the specified property. The second version provides for a default value. If the key is not found, the default is returned.

`list(PrintStream s)`
`list(PrintWriter w)`
Writes all of the properties to the specified stream or writer. This is useful for debugging.

`elements()`
`keys()`
`propertyNames()`
Returns an `Enumeration` containing the keys or values (as indicated by the method name) contained in the `Properties` object. The `keys` method only returns the keys for the object itself; the `propertyNames` method returns the keys for default properties as well.

`stringPropertyNames()`
Like `propertyNames`, but returns a `Set<String>`, and only returns names of properties where both key and value are strings. Note that the `Set` object is not backed by the `Properties` object, so changes in one do not affect the other.

`size()`
Returns the current number of key/value pairs.

Setting Properties

A user's interaction with an application during its execution may impact property settings. These changes should be reflected in the `Properties` object so that they are saved when the application exits (and calls the `store` method). The following methods change the properties in a `Properties` object:

setProperty(String key, String value) Puts the key/value pair in the Properties object.

remove(Object key) Removes the key/value pair associated with the key.

Note: Some of the methods just described are defined in Hashtable, and thus accept key and value argument types other than String. Always use Strings for keys and values, even if the method allows other types. Also, do not invoke Hashtable.set or Hastable.setAll on Properties objects; always use Properties.setProperty.

Command-Line Arguments

A Java application can accept any number of arguments from the command line. This allows the user to specify configuration information when the application is launched.

The user enters command-line arguments when invoking the application and specifies them after the name of the class to be run. For example, suppose a Java application called Sort sorts lines in a file. To sort the data in a file named friends.txt, a user would enter:

```
java Sort friends.txt
```

When an application is launched, the runtime system passes the command-line arguments to the application's main method via an array of Strings. In the previous example, the command-line arguments passed to the Sort application in an array that contains a single String: "friends.txt".

Echoing Command-Line Arguments

The Echo[4] example displays each of its command-line arguments on a line by itself:

```
public class Echo {
  public static void main (String[] args) {
    for (String s: args) {
      System.out.println(s);
    }
  }
}
```

The following example shows how a user might run Echo. User input is in italics:

---

4. tutorial/essential/environment/examples/Echo.java

```
java Echo Drink Hot Java
Drink
Hot
Java
```

Note that the application displays each word—`Drink`, `Hot`, and `Java`—on a line by itself. This is because the space character separates command-line arguments. To have `Drink`, `Hot`, and `Java` interpreted as a single argument, the user would join them by enclosing them within quotation marks:

```
java Echo "Drink Hot Java"
Drink Hot Java
```

Parsing Numeric Command-Line Arguments

If an application needs to support a numeric command-line argument, it must convert a `String` argument that represents a number, such as "34", to a numeric value. Here is a code snippet that converts a command-line argument to an `int`:

```
int firstArg;
if (args.length > 0) {
  try {
      firstArg = Integer.parseInt(args[0]);
  } catch (NumberFormatException e) {
      System.err.println("Argument must be an integer");
      System.exit(1);
  }
}
```

`parseInt` throws a `NumberFormatException` if the format of `args[0]` isn't valid. All of the `Number` classes—`Integer`, `Float`, `Double`, and so on—have `parseXXX` methods that convert a `String` representing a number to an object of their type.

Environment Variables

Many operating systems use *environment variables* to pass configuration information to applications. Like properties in the Java platform, environment variables are key/value pairs, where both the key and the value are strings. The conventions for setting and using environment variables vary between operating systems, and also between command line interpreters. To learn how to pass environment variables to applications on your system, refer to your system documentation.

Querying Environment Variables

On the Java platform, an application uses `System.getEnv` to retrieve environment variable values. Without an argument, `getEnv` returns a read-only instance of java.util.Map, where the map keys are the environment variable names, and the map values are the environment variable values. This is demonstrated in the EnvMap[5] example:

```
import java.util.Map;

public class EnvMap {
  public static void main (String[] args) {
    Map<String, String> env = System.getenv();
    for (String envName : env.keySet()) {
      System.out.format("%s=%s%n", envName, env.get(envName));
    }
  }
}
```

With a String argument, getEnv returns the value of the specified variable. If the variable is not defined, getEnv returns null. The Env[6] example uses getEnv this way to query specific environment variables, specified on the command line:

```
public class Env {
  public static void main (String[] args) {
    for (String env: args) {
      String value = System.getenv(env);
      if (value != null) {
        System.out.format("%s=%s%n", env, value);
      } else {
        System.out.format("%s is not assigned.%n", env);
      }
    }
  }
}
```

Passing Environment Variables to New Processes

When a Java application uses a ProcessBuilder[7] object to create a new process, the default set of environment variables passed to the new process is the same set provided to the application's virtual machine process. The application can change this set using ProcessBuilder.environment.

5. tutorial/essential/environment/examples/EnvMap.java

6. tutorial/essential/environment/examples/Env.java

7. docs/api/java/lang/ProcessBuilder.html

Platform Dependency Issues

There are many subtle differences between the way environment variables are implemented on different systems. For example, Windows ignores case in environment variable names, while UNIX does not. The way environment variables are used also varies. For example, Windows provides the user name in an environment variable called `USERNAME`, while UNIX implementations might provide the user name in `USER`, `LOGNAME`, or both.

To maximize portability, never refer to an environment variable when the same value is available in a system property. For example, if the operating system provides a user name, it will always be available in the system property `user.name`.

Other Configuration Utilities

Here is a summary of some other configuration utilities.

The *Preferences API* allows applications to store and retrieve configuration data in an implementation-dependent backing store. Asynchronous updates are supported, and the same set of preferences can be safely updated by multiple threads and even multiple applications. For more information, refer to the Preferences API Guide.[8]

An application deployed in a *JAR archive* uses a *manifest* to describe the contents of the archive. For more information, refer to Chapter 16.

The configuration of a *Java Web Start application* is contained in a *JNLP file*. For more information, refer to Chapter 17.

The configuration of a *Java Plug-in applet* is partially determined by the HTML tags used to embed the applet in the Web page. Depending on the applet and the browser, these tags can include `<applet>`, `<object>`, `<embed>`, and `<param>`. For more information, refer to Chapter 18.

The class `java.util.ServiceLoader`[9] provides a simple *service provider* facility. A service provider is an implementation of a *service*—a well-known set of interfaces and (usually abstract) classes. The classes in a service provider typically implement the interfaces and subclass the classes defined in the service. Service providers can be installed as extensions (see `docs/books/tutorial/ext/index.html` on the CD). Providers can also be made available by adding them to the class path or by some other platform-specific means.

8. `docs/guide/preferences/index.html`

9. `docs/api/java/util/ServiceLoader.html`

System Utilities

The `System`[10] class implements a number of system utilities. Some of these have already been covered in the Configuration Utilities section (page 443). This section covers some of the other system utilities.

Command-Line I/O Objects

`System` provides several predefined I/O objects that are useful in a Java application that is meant to be launched from the command line. These implement the Standard I/O streams provided by most operating systems and also a console object that is useful for entering passwords. For more information, refer to the I/O from the Command Line section (page 276) in Chapter 10.

System Properties

In the Properties section (page 443), we examined the way an application can use `Properties` objects to maintain its configuration. The Java platform itself uses a `Properties` object to maintain its own configuration. The `System` class maintains a `Properties` object that describes the configuration of the current working environment. System properties include information about the current user, the current version of the Java runtime, and the character used to separate components of a file path name.

Table 14.1 describes some of the most important system properties.

Security Consideration: Access to system properties can be restricted by the security manager (page 455). This is most often an issue in applets, which are prevented from reading some system properties, and from writing *any* system properties. For more on accessing system properties in applets, refer to the Getting System Properties section (page 583).

Reading System Properties

The `System` class has two methods used to read system properties: `getProperty` and `getProperties`.

The `System` class has two different versions of `getProperty`. Both retrieve the value of the property named in the argument list. The simpler of the two `getProperty`

---

10. `docs/api/java/lang/System.html`

Table 14.1 Some Important System Properties

Key	Meaning
"file.separator"	Character that separates components of a file path. This is "/" on UNIX and "\" on Windows.
"java.class.path"	Path used to find directories and JAR archives containing class files. Elements of the class path are separated by a platform-specific character specified in the path.separator property.
"java.home"	Installation directory for Java Runtime Environment (JRE)
"java.vendor"	JRE vendor name
"java.vendor.url"	JRE vender URL
"java.version"	JRE version number
"line.separator"	Sequence used by operating system to separate lines in text files
"os.arch"	Operating system architecture
"os.name"	Operating system name
"os.version"	Operating system version
"path.separator"	Path separator character used in java.class.path
"user.dir"	User working directory
"user.home"	User home directory
"user.name"	User account name

methods takes a single argument, a property key. For example, to get the value of path.separator, use the following statement:

```
System.getProperty("path.separator");
```

The getProperty method returns a string containing the value of the property. If the property does not exist, this version of getProperty returns null.

The other version of getProperty requires two String arguments: The first argument is the key to look up, and the second argument is a default value to return if the key cannot be found or if it has no value. For example, the following invocation of getProperty looks up the System property called subliminal.message. This is not a valid system property, so instead of returning null, this method returns the default value provided as a second argument: "Buy StayPuft Marshmallows!":

```
System.getProperty("subliminal.message",
                   "Buy StayPuft Marshmallows!");
```

The last method provided by the `System` class to access property values is the `getProperties` method, which returns a `Properties` object. This object contains a complete set of system property definitions.

Writing System Properties

To modify the existing set of system properties, use `System.setProperties`. This method takes a `Properties` object that has been initialized to contain the properties to be set. This method replaces the entire set of system properties with the new set represented by the `Properties` object.

Warning: Changing system properties is potentially dangerous and should be done with discretion. Many system properties are not reread after start-up and are there for informational purposes. Changing some properties may have unexpected side effects.

The next example, `PropertiesTest`,[11] creates a `Properties` object and initializes it from `myProperties.txt`:

```
subliminal.message=Buy StayPuft Marshmallows!
```

`PropertiesTest` then uses `System.setProperties` to install the new `Properties` objects as the current set of system properties:

```
import java.io.FileInputStream;
import java.util.Properties;

public class PropertiesTest {

  public static void main(String[] args) throws Exception {
    // set up new properties object
    // from file "myProperties.txt"
    FileInputStream propFile = new FileInputStream(
                                        "myProperties.txt");
    Properties p = new Properties(System.getProperties());
    p.load(propFile);

    // set the system properties
    System.setProperties(p);
    // display new properties
    System.getProperties().list(System.out);
  }
}
```

---

11. `tutorial/essential/environment/examples/PropertiesTest.java`

Note how PropertiesTest creates the Properties object, p, which is used as the argument to setProperties:

```
Properties p = new Properties(System.getProperties());
```

This statement initializes the new properties object, p, with the current set of system properties, which in the case of this small application is the set of properties initialized by the runtime system. Then the application loads additional properties into p from the file myProperties.txt and sets the system properties to p. This has the effect of adding the properties listed in myProperties.txt to the set of properties created by the runtime system at startup. Note that an application can create p without any default Properties object, like this:

```
Properties p = new Properties();
```

Also note that the value of system properties can be overwritten! For example, if myProperties.txt contains the following line, the java.vendor system property will be overwritten:

```
java.vendor=Acme Software Company
```

In general, be careful not to overwrite system properties.

The setProperties method changes the set of system properties for the current running application. These changes are not persistent. That is, changing the system properties within an application will not affect future invocations of the Java interpreter for this or any other application. The runtime system re-initializes the system properties each time its starts up. If changes to system properties are to be persistent, then the application must write the values to some file before exiting and read them in again upon startup.

The Security Manager

A *security manager* is an object that defines a security policy for an application. This policy specifies actions that are unsafe or sensitive. Any actions not allowed by the security policy cause a SecurityException[12] to be thrown. An application can also query its security manager to discover which actions are allowed.

Typically, a Web applet runs with a security manager provided by the browser or Java Plug-in. Other kinds of applications normally run without a security manager, unless the application itself defines one. If no security manager is present, the application has no security policy and acts without restrictions.

---

12. docs/api/java/lang/SecurityException.html

This section explains how an application interacts with an existing security manager. For more detailed information, including information on how to design a security manager, refer to the Security Guide.[13]

Interacting with the Security Manager

The security manager is an object of type SecurityManager;[14] to obtain a reference to this object, invoke System.getSecurityManager:

```
SecurityManager appsm = System.getSecurityManager();
```

If there is no security manager, this method returns null.

Once an application has a reference to the security manager object, it can request permission to do specific things. Many classes in the standard libraries do this. For example, System.exit, which terminates the Java virtual machine with an exit status, invokes SecurityManager.checkExit to ensure that the current thread has permission to shut down the application.

The SecurityManager class defines many other methods used to verify other kinds of operations. For example, SecurityManager.checkAccess verifies thread accesses, and SecurityManager.checkPropertyAccess verifies access to the specified property. Each operation or group of operations has its own check*XXX*() method.

In addition, the set of check*XXX*() methods represents the set of operations that are already subject to the protection of the security manager. Typically, an application does not have to directly invoke any check*XXX*() methods.

Recognizing a Security Violation

Many actions that are routine without a security manager can throw a SecurityException when run with a security manager. This is true even when invoking a method that isn't documented as throwing SecurityException. For example, consider the following code used to read a file:

```
reader = new FileReader("xanadu.txt");
```

In the absence of a security manager, this statement executes without error, provided xanadu.txt exists and is readable. But suppose this statement is inserted in a Web applet, which typically runs under a security manager that does not allow file input. The following error messages might result:

---

13. docs/guide/security/index.html

14. docs/api/java/lang/SecurityManager.html

```
appletviewer fileApplet.html
Exception in thread "AWT-EventQueue-1"
  java.security.AccessControlException: access denied
  (java.io.FilePermission characteroutput.txt write)
  ...
```

Note that the specific exception thrown in this case, `java.security.AccessControlException`,[15] is a subclass of `SecurityException`.

Miscellaneous Methods in System

This section describes some of the methods in `System` that aren't covered in the previous sections.

The `arraycopy` method efficiently copies data between arrays. For more information, refer to the Arrays section (page 49).

The `currentTimeMillis` and `nanoTime` methods are useful for measuring time intervals during execution of an application. To measure a time interval in milliseconds, invoke `currentTimeMillis` twice, at the beginning and end of the interval, and subtract the first value returned from the second. Similarly, invoking `nanoTime` twice measures an interval in nanoseconds.

Note: The accuracy of both `currentTimeMillis` and `nanoTime` is limited by the time services provided by the operating system. Do not assume that `currentTimeMillis` is accurate to the nearest millisecond or that `nanoTime` is accurate to the nearest nanosecond. Also, neither `currentTimeMillis` nor `nanoTime` should be used to determine the current time. Use a high-level method, such as `java.util.Calendar.getInstance`.[16]

The `exit` method causes the Java virtual machine to shut down, with an integer exit status specified by the argument. The exit status is available to the process that launched the application. By convention, an exit status of `0` indicates normal termination of the application, while any other value is an error code.

PATH and CLASSPATH

This section explains how to use the `PATH` and `CLASSPATH` environment variables on Microsoft Windows, Solaris, and Linux. Consult the installation instructions included

15. `docs/api/java/security/AccessControlException.html`

16. `docs/api/java/util/Calendar.html`

with your installation of the Java Development Kit (JDK) software bundle for current information.

After installing the software, the JDK directory will have the structure shown in Figure 14.2. The `bin` directory contains both the compiler and the launcher.

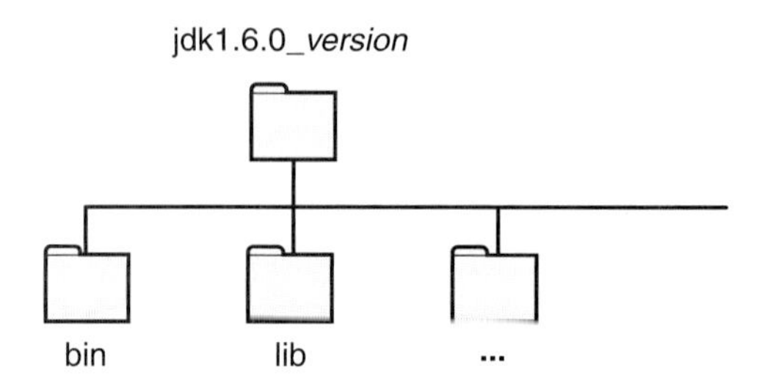

Figure 14.2 Structure of the JDK directory.

Update the PATH Variable (Microsoft Windows NT/2000/XP)

You can run Java applications just fine without setting the `PATH` variable. Or, you can optionally set it as a convenience.

Set the `PATH` variable if you want to be able to conveniently run the executables (`javac.exe`, `java.exe`, `javadoc.exe`, and so on) from any directory without having to type the full path of the command. If you do not set the `PATH` variable, you need to specify the full path to the executable every time you run it, such as:

```
C:\Program Files\Java\jdk1.6.0\bin\javac MyClass.java
```

It is useful to set the `PATH` permanently so it will persist after rebooting. To set it permanently, add the full path of the `jdk1.6.0` bin directory to the `PATH` variable. Set the `PATH` as follows.

To make a permanent change to the `CLASSPATH` variable, use the System icon in the Control Panel. The precise procedure varies depending on the version of Windows.

The `PATH` can be a series of directories separated by semicolons (`;`). Microsoft Windows looks for programs in the `PATH` directories in order, from left to right. You should have only one `bin` directory for the JDK in the path at a time (those following the first are ignored), so if one is already present you can update that particular entry.

Update the PATH Variable (Solaris and Linux)

You can run the JDK just fine without setting the `PATH` variable, or you can optionally set it as a convenience. However, you should set the path variable if you want to be able to run the executables (`javac`, `java`, `javadoc`, and so on) from any directory without having to type the full path of the command. If you do not set the `PATH` variable, you need to specify the full path to the executable every time you run it, such as:

```
% /usr/local/jdk1.6.0/bin/javac MyClass.java
```

To find out if the path is properly set, execute:

```
% java -version
```

This will print the version of the `java` tool, if it can find it. If the version is old or you get the error **java: Command not found**, then the path is not properly set.

To set the path permanently, set the path in your startup file.

For C shell (`csh`), edit the startup file (`~/.cshrc`):

```
set path=(/usr/local/jdk1.6.0/bin )
```

For `bash`, edit the startup file (`~/.bashrc`):

```
PATH=/usr/local/jdk1.6.0/bin:
export PATH
```

For `ksh`, the startup file is named by the environment variable, `ENV`. To set the path:

```
PATH=/usr/local/jdk1.6.0/bin:
export PATH
```

For `sh`, edit the profile file (`~/.profile`):

```
PATH=/usr/local/jdk1.6.0/bin:
export PATH
```

Then load the startup file and verify that the path is set by repeating the `java` command.

For C shell (`csh`):

```
% source ~/.cshrc
% java -version
```

For `ksh`, `bash`, or `sh`:

```
% . /.profile
% java -version
```

Checking the CLASSPATH Variable (All Platforms)

The `CLASSPATH` variable is one way to tell applications, including the JDK tools, where to look for user classes. (Classes that are part of the JRE, JDK platform, and extensions should be defined through other means, such as the bootstrap class path or the extensions directory.)

The preferred way to specify the class path is by using the `-cp` command line switch. This allows the `CLASSPATH` to be set individually for each application without affecting other applications. *Setting the `CLASSPATH` can be tricky and should be performed with care.*

The default value of the class path is ".", meaning that only the current directory is searched. Specifying either the `CLASSPATH` variable or the `-cp` command line switch overrides this value.

To check whether `CLASSPATH` is set on Microsoft Windows NT/2000/XP, execute the following:

```
C:> echo %CLASSPATH%
```

On Solaris or Linux, execute the following:

```
% echo $CLASSPATH
```

If `CLASSPATH` is not set you will get a **CLASSPATH: Undefined variable** error (Solaris or Linux) or simply **%CLASSPATH%** (Microsoft Windows NT/2000/XP).

To modify the `CLASSPATH`, use the same procedure you used for the `PATH` variable.

Class path wildcards allow you to include an entire directory of `.jar` files in the class path without explicitly naming them individually. For more information, including an explanation of class path wildcards and a detailed description on how to clean up the `CLASSPATH` environment variable, see `docs/books/tutorial/technotes/tools/windows/classpath.html`.

Questions and Exercises: The Platform Environment

Questions

A programmer installs a new library contained in a `.jar` file. In order to access the library from his code, he sets the CLASSPATH environment variable to point to the new

.jar file. Now he finds that he gets an error message when he tries to launch simple applications:

```
java Hello
Exception in thread "main"
  java.lang.NoClassDefFoundError: Hello
```

In this case, the Hello class is compiled into a .class file in the current directory—yet the java command can't seem to find it. What's going wrong?

Exercises

Write an application, PersistentEcho, with the following features:

1. If PersistentEcho is run with command line arguments, it prints out those arguments. It also saves the string printed out to a property, and saves the property to a file called PersistentEcho.txt.
2. If PersistentEcho is run with no command line arguments, it looks for an environment variable called PERSISTENTECHO. If that variable exists, PersistentEcho prints out its value, and also saves the value in the same way it does for command line arguments.
3. If PersistentEcho is run with no command line arguments, and the PERSISTENTECHO environment variable is not defined, it retrieves the property value from PersistentEcho.txt and prints that out.

Answers

You can find answers to these Questions and Exercises at:

```
tutorial/essential/environment/QandE/answers.html
```

15

Swing

How do you write a program in the Java programming language with a graphical user interface? The short answer is the Swing toolkit! This chapter gives you a brief overview of the graphical capabilities of the core Java platform with a special focus on Swing.

This chapter does not show how to implement these features. For a "how-to" on using the Swing toolkit, see *Creating a GUI with JFC/Swing*.[1]

A Brief Introduction to the Swing Package

This section gives you a brief introduction to the capabilities of the Java SE platform that pertain to developing programs with graphical user interfaces (GUIs). Next, it shows you a demo (sample code provided) that showcases many of these features.

The next section, Swing Features (page 470), discusses these capabilities in more detail.

What Is Swing?

To create a Java program with a graphical user interface (GUI), you'll want to learn about Swing.

1. `/tutorial/uiswing/index.html`

The Swing toolkit includes a rich set of components for building GUIs and adding interactivity to Java applications. Swing includes all the components you would expect from a modern toolkit: table controls, list controls, tree controls, buttons, and labels.

Swing is far from a simple component toolkit, however. It includes rich undo support, a highly customizable text package, integrated internationalization and accessibility support. To truly leverage the cross-platform capabilities of the Java platform, Swing supports numerous look and feels, including the ability to create your own look and feel. The ability to create a custom look and feel is made easier with Synth, a look and feel specifically designed to be customized. Swing wouldn't be a component toolkit without the basic user interface primitives such as drag and drop, event handling, customizable painting, and window management.

Swing is part of the Java Foundation Classes (JFC). The JFC also include other features important to a GUI program, such as the ability to add rich graphics functionality and the ability to create a program that can work in different languages and by users with different input devices.

Swing GUI Components

The Swing toolkit includes a rich array of components: from basic components, such as buttons and checkboxes, to rich and complex components, such as tables and text. Even deceptively simple components, such as text fields, offer sophisticated functionality, such as formatted text input or password field behavior. There are file browsers and dialogs to suit most needs, and if not, customization is possible. If none of Swing's provided components are exactly what you need, you can leverage the basic Swing component functionality to create your own.

Java 2D API

To make your application stand out; convey information visually; or add figures, images, or animation to your GUI, you'll want to use the Java 2D API. Because Swing is built on the 2D package, it's trivial to make use of 2D within Swing components. Adding images, drop shadows, compositing—it's easy with Java 2D.

Pluggable Look-and-Feel Support

Any program that uses Swing components has a choice of look and feel. The JFC classes shipped by Sun and Apple provide a look and feel that matches that of the platform. The Synth package allows you to create your own look and feel. The GTK+ look and feel makes hundreds of existing look and feels available to Swing programs.

A program can specify the look and feel of the platform it is running on, or it can specify to always use the Java look and feel, and without recompiling, it will just work. Or, you can ignore the issue and let the UI manager sort it out.

Data Transfer

Data transfer, via cut, copy, paste, and drag and drop, is essential to almost any application. Support for data transfer is built into Swing and works between Swing components within an application, between Java applications, and between Java and native applications.

Internationalization

This feature allows developers to build applications that can interact with users worldwide in their own languages and cultural conventions. Applications can be created that accept input in languages that use thousands of different characters, such as Japanese, Chinese, or Korean.

Swing's layout managers make it easy to honor a particular orientation required by the UI. For example, the UI will appear right to left in a locale where the text flows right to left. This support is automatic: You need only code the UI once and then it will work for left to right and right to left, as well as honor the appropriate size of components that change as you localize the text.

Accessibility API

People with disabilities use special software—assistive technologies—that mediates the user experience for them. Such software needs to obtain a wealth of information about the running application in order to represent it in alternate media: for a screen reader to read the screen with synthetic speech or render it via a Braille display, for a screen magnifier to track the caret and keyboard focus, for on-screen keyboards to present dynamic keyboards of the menu choices and toolbar items and dialog controls, and for voice control systems to know what the user can control with his or her voice. The accessibility API enables these assistive technologies to get the information they need and to programmatically manipulate the elements that make up the graphical user interface.

Undo Framework API

Swing's undo framework allows developers to provide support for undo and redo. Undo support is built in to Swing's text component. For other components, Swing supports an *unlimited* number of actions to undo and redo, and is easily adapted to an application. For example, you could easily enable undo to add and remove elements from a table.

Flexible Deployment Support

If you want your program to run within a browser window, you can create it as an applet and run it using Java Plug-in, which supports a variety of browsers, such as Internet Explorer, Firefox, and Safari. If you want to create a program that can be launched from a browser, you can do this with Java Web Start. Of course, your application can also run outside of browser as a standard desktop application.

For more information on deploying an application, see Chapters 17 and 18.

This chapter provides an overview of Swing capabilities, beginning with a demo that showcases many of these features. When you are ready to begin coding, the "Creating a GUI with JFC/Swing" online tutorial provides the programming techniques to take advantage of these features.

Let's examine a demo that shows many of these features.

A Swing Demo

Run the PasswordStore demo[2] for an illustration of some of Swing's rich feature set. PasswordStore allows the user to manage login information for various hosts. It also generates passwords, evaluates the effectiveness of a password, and allows you to store notes about a particular host or assign an icon to represent the host.

The following highlights some of the specific features of the PasswordStore application.[3]

Host Info

At program launch, the list of hosts is displayed in a Swing list component. Using the **View** menu, the view can be toggled between the table and the list.

In both views, the **Host/Account Filter** text field can be used to dynamically restrict the entries to those where the host or account name contains the typed string.

List View

The Swing list component can be customized to include visual data. As shown in Figure 15.1, an optional miniature icon to the left of the host name represents the host. The graphic to the right uses color and proportional fill to reflect the strength of the password (red = poor, yellow = fair, green = good). The bar changes dynamically as the user enters/modifies the password in the text field below. The user has typed the text "oo" in the filter text field, which matches two entries: Heirl**oo**m Seeds and Pacific **Zoo** Shop.

---

2. Click the `launch` button found on `tutorial/ui/overview/demo.html`.

3. The dice, flower, pill, and pocketwatch images used in the demo are courtesy of `http://www.freeimages.co.uk`. The polar bear and cubs image by Steve Amstrup and the mountain image are courtesy of `http://www.fws.gov`. The spiral galaxy image is courtesy of `http://grin.hq.nasa.gov`.

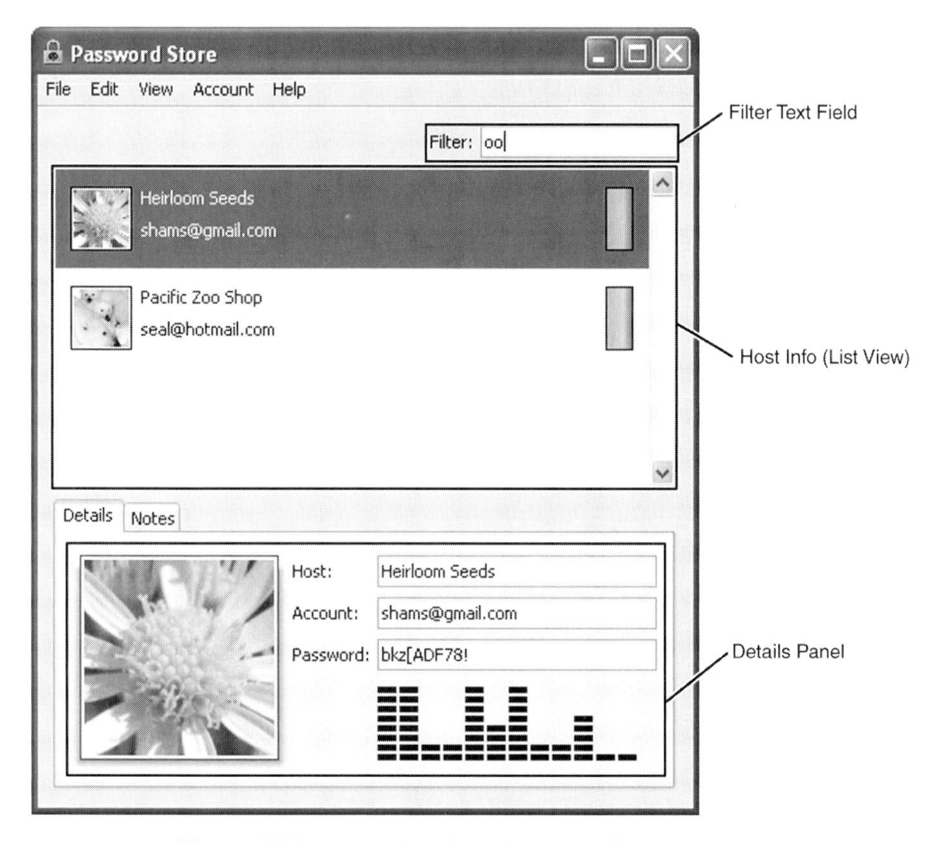

Figure 15.1 Host Info (List View) and **Filter** text field.

Table View

The Swing table component (Figure 15.2) allows the user to rearrange the columns by dragging the column header. Also, a column can be sorted by clicking the column header. If the column you click on isn't highlighted as the primary sorted column, it will become the primary sorted column in ascending order. Clicking on the primary sorted column toggles the sort order. For example, if column 1 isn't selected, clicking on it will make it the selected column and the data is sorted in ascending order. Clicking column 1 again will sort the data in descending order. Clicking on column 2 will make column 2 the primary column in ascending order.

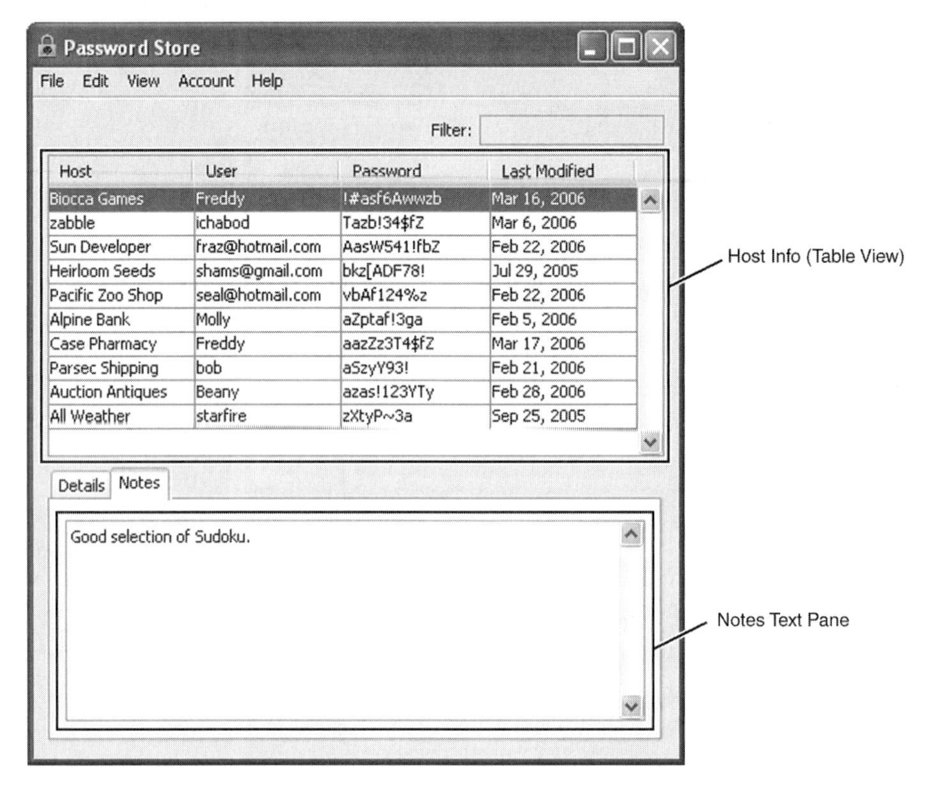

Figure 15.2 Host Info (Table View).

Details/Notes Tabbed Pane

The tabbed pane below the host info allows the user to choose between the **Details** panel and the **Notes** text pane, keeping the overall footprint of the window smaller and less overwhelming.

Details Panel

The icon area on the left can be assigned an image by either dragging an image (jpg, png, gif, or tif) to the area or by clicking the image well and bringing up a file browser.

The text fields—used to enter or modify the host name, login, and password—support cut/copy, paste, drag, drop, undo, and redo.

As the user enters or modifies the password, the 2D bar chart dynamically displays the distribution of the password. If the list view is currently displayed, the corresponding colored bar in the list also changes dynamically.

Notes Text Pane

This is the text component where the user can save notes about the selected host. If the text pane contains a URI, Swing's text component provides the ability to click on the URI and a browser window automatically opens to that location.

Wizzy 2D Graphics

PasswordStore uses customized graphics in several ways to enhance the UI: In the list view, images are used to represent each host; a colored bar, the *Strength Visualizer*, represents the effectiveness of a password; and a dynamic bar chart, the *Password Visualizer*, displays the distribution of a password. When you add an image, whether by dragging and dropping it into the image well (in the **Details** panel) or by clicking the well and bringing up the file browser, a mini-icon is automatically generated for the list view (Figure 15.3).

Note: This demo is meant to be illustrative only and not meant to be used for real analysis of passwords.

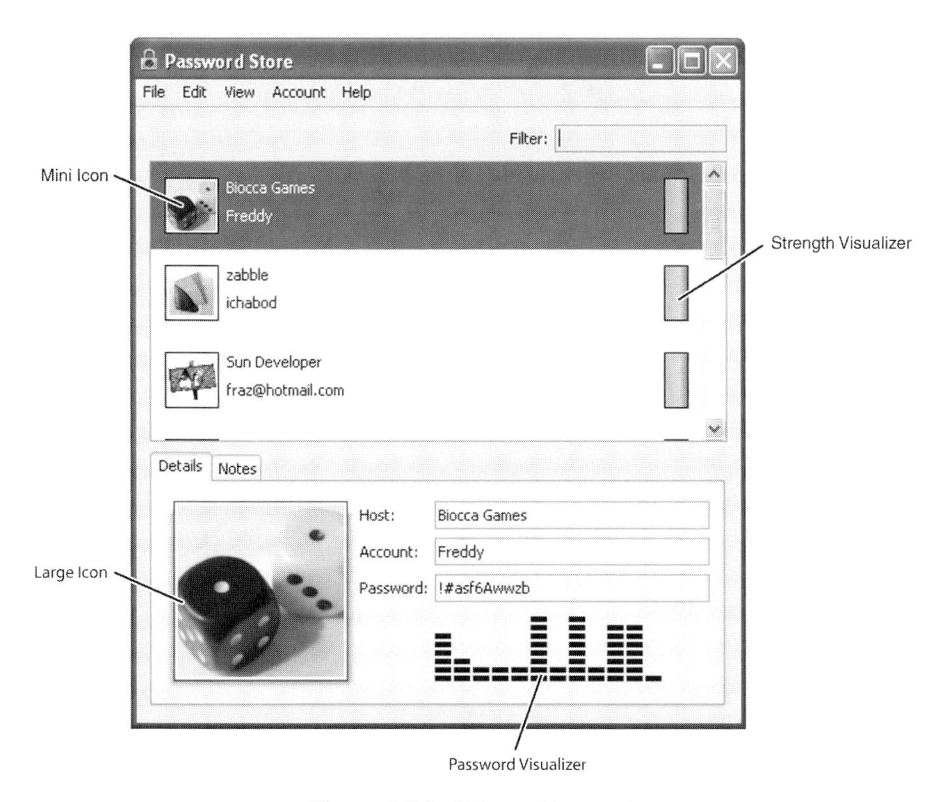

Figure 15.3 2D graphics used.

Multiple Look and Feels

This provides the ability to switch between three look and feels using the **View** menu: Java (called Metal), Motif/CDE, and the native look and feel: Windows on Microsoft Windows, Aqua on Mac OS X, and so on.

Undo and Redo

Undo and redo works on text, as you would expect, but it also works on actions. For example, you can generate a password using the **Account > Generate Password** menu, and if you don't like the new password you can undo it using **Edit > Undo** or the control-Z shortcut. Similarly, you can redo the undo using **Edit > Redo** or the control-Y shortcut.

The PasswordStore demo has a reasonable level of complexity for a small Swing application and shows a sampling of Swing's capabilities. The source code[4] is available for download, but it is outside the scope of this chapter to discuss the implementation in detail. For more information on the architecture and implementation of this application, see Scott Violet's Excellent Blog[5] on `java.net`.

> **Note:** If PasswordStore were a production application, it would most likely encrypt the password database; however, due to legal restrictions on distributing information of that nature, it is not included here.

Swing Features

PasswordStore shows some of the rich functionality of a particular Swing application. This lesson discusses the general features available to applications using the Java SE platform and, in particular, the Swing toolkit.

A Visual Guide to Swing Components

This section shows Swing components in both Java and Windows look and feel.

Basic Controls (Table 15.1)

Simple components that are used primarily to get input from the user; they may also show simple state.

4. `tutorial/ui/overview/PasswordStore-1.0-src.zip`
5. `http://weblogs.java.net/blog/zixle`

Table 15.1 Basic Controls

Name	Java Look and Feel	Windows Look and Feel
`JButton`		
`JCheckBox`		
`JComboBox`		
`JList`		
`JMenu`		
`JRadioButton`		
`JSlider`		
`JSpinner`		
`JPasswordField`		

Interactive Displays of Highly Formatted Information (Table 15.2)

These components display highly formatted information that (if you choose) can be modified by the user.

Table 15.2 Interactive Displays of Highly Formatted Information

<table>
<tr><th>Java Look and Feel</th><th>Windows Look and Feel</th></tr>
<tr><td colspan="2">JColorChooser</td></tr>
<tr><td>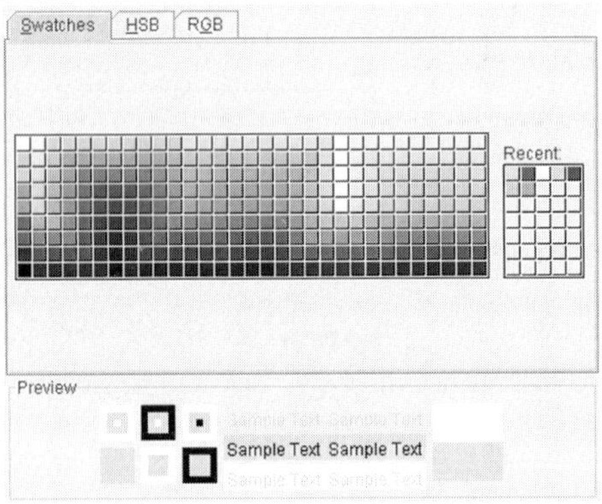
</td><td>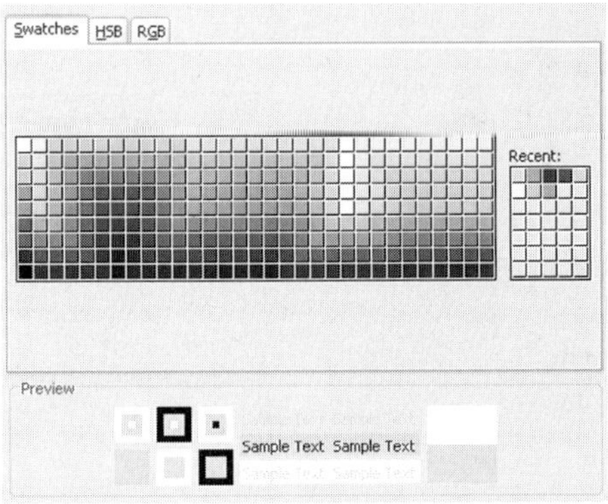
</td></tr>
<tr><td colspan="2">JEditorPane and JTextPane</td></tr>
<tr><td>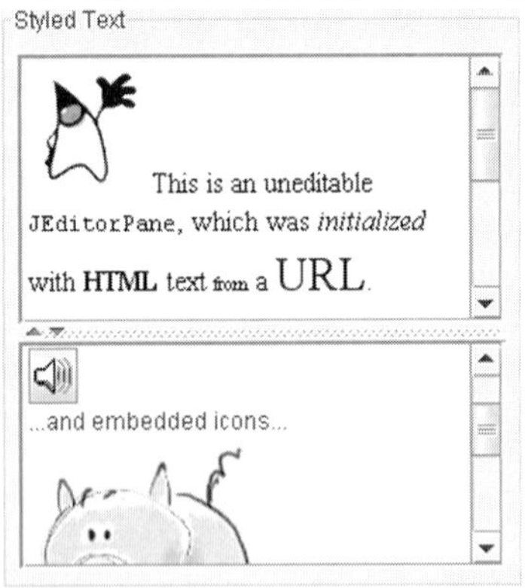
</td><td>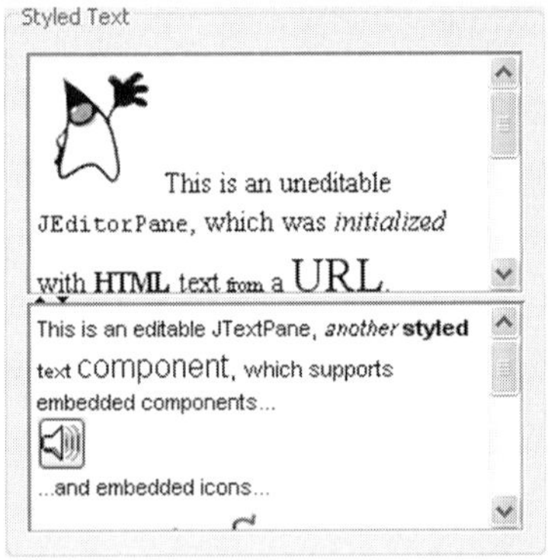
</td></tr>
</table>

(continues)

Table 15.2 Interactive Displays of Highly Formatted Information *(Continued)*

<table>
<tr><th>Java Look and Feel</th><th>Windows Look and Feel</th></tr>
<tr><td colspan="2">JFileChooser</td></tr>
<tr><td> 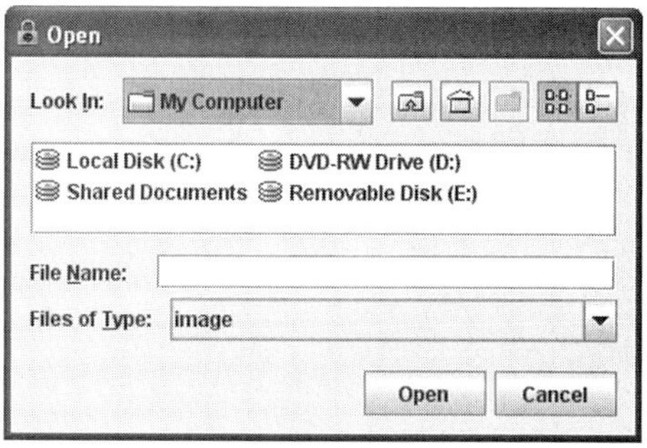Open
Look In: My Computer
Local Disk (C:) DVD-RW Drive (D:)
Shared Documents Removable Disk (E:)
File Name:
Files of Type: image
Open Cancel</td><td> 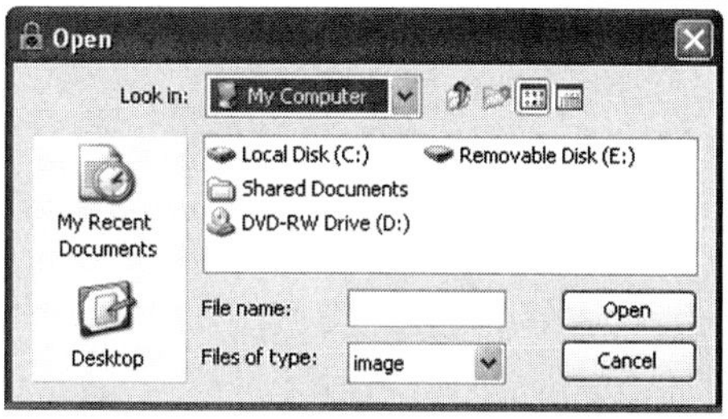Open
Look in: My Computer
Local Disk (C:) Removable Disk (E:)
Shared Documents
DVD-RW Drive (D:)
My Recent Documents
Desktop
File name: Open
Files of type: image Cancel</td></tr>
<tr><td colspan="2">JTable</td></tr>
<tr><td> 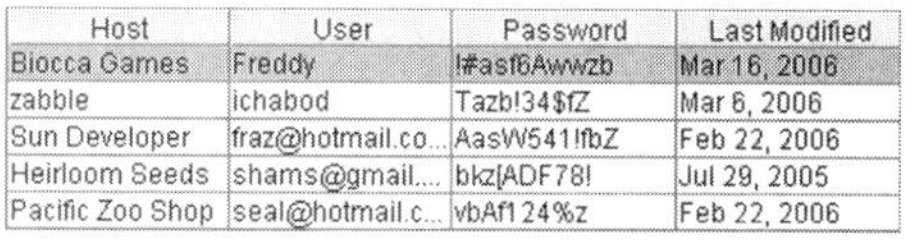Host | User | Password | Last Modified
Biocca Games | Freddy | !#asf6Awwzb | Mar 16, 2006
zabble | ichabod | Tazb!34$fZ | Mar 6, 2006
Sun Developer | fraz@hotmail.co... | AasW541!fbZ | Feb 22, 2006
Heirloom Seeds | shams@gmail.... | bkz[ADF78! | Jul 29, 2005
Pacific Zoo Shop | seal@hotmail.c... | vbAf124%z | Feb 22, 2006</td><td>Host | User | Password | Last Modified
Biocca Games | Freddy | !#asf6Awwzb | Mar 16, 2006
zabble | ichabod | Tazb!34$fZ | Mar 6, 2006
Sun Developer | fraz@hotmail.com | AasW541!fbZ | Feb 22, 2006
Heirloom Seeds | shams@gmail.com | bkz[ADF78! | Jul 29, 2005
Pacific Zoo Shop | seal@hotmail.com | vbAf124%z | Feb 22, 2006</td></tr>
<tr><td colspan="2">JTextArea</td></tr>
<tr><td> 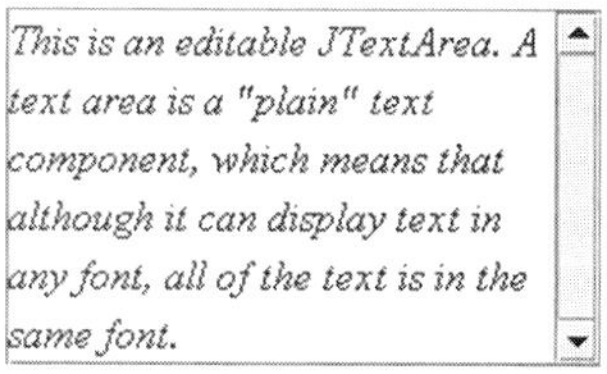This is an editable JTextArea. A text area is a "plain" text component, which means that although it can display text in any font, all of the text is in the same font.</td><td> 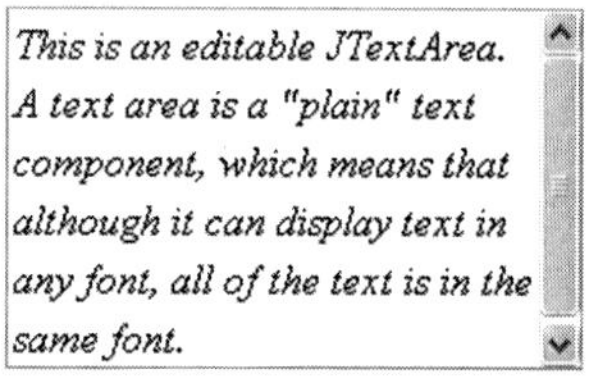This is an editable JTextArea. A text area is a "plain" text component, which means that although it can display text in any font, all of the text is in the same font.</td></tr>
<tr><td colspan="2">JTree</td></tr>
<tr><td> Mia Familia
Sharon
Maya
Muffin
Anya
Winky
Bongo</td><td> 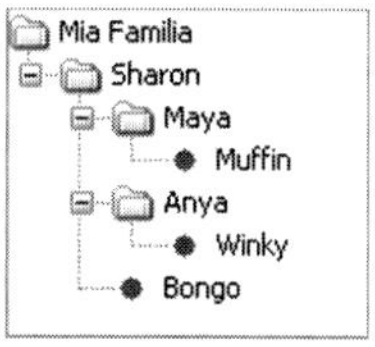Mia Familia
Sharon
Maya
Muffin
Anya
Winky
Bongo</td></tr>
</table>

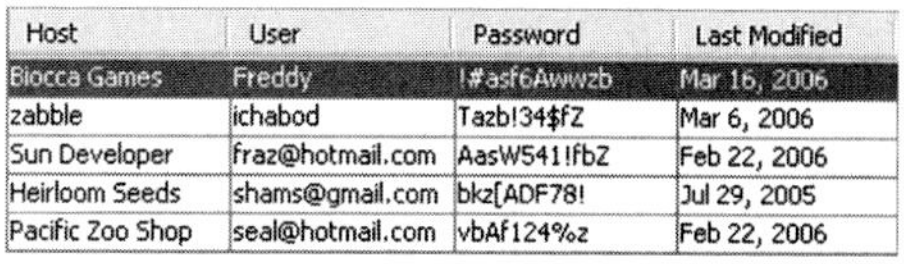

Uneditable Information Displays (Table 15.3)

These components exist solely to give the user information.

Table 15.3 Uneditable Information Displays

Name	Java Look and Feel	Windows Look and Feel
`JLabel`		
`JProgressBar`		
`JSeparator`		
`JToolTip`		

Top-Level Containers (Table 15.4)

At least one of these components must be present in any Swing application.

Table 15.4 Top-Level Containers

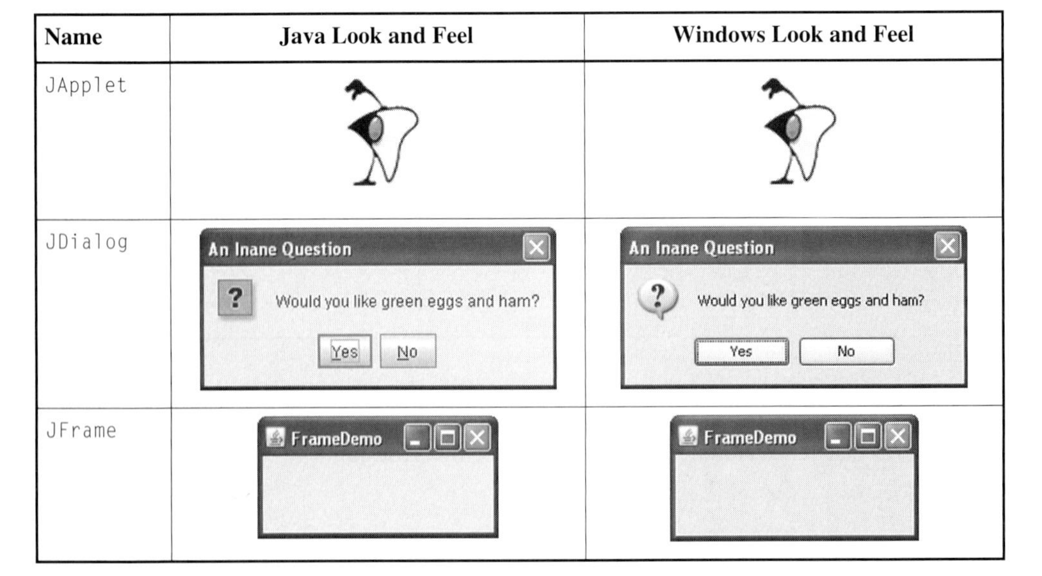

Name	Java Look and Feel	Windows Look and Feel
`JApplet`		
`JDialog`		
`JFrame`		

General-Purpose Containers (Table 15.5)

These general-purpose containers are used in most Swing applications.

Table 15.5 General-Purpose Containers

Java Look and Feel	Windows Look and Feel
JPanel	
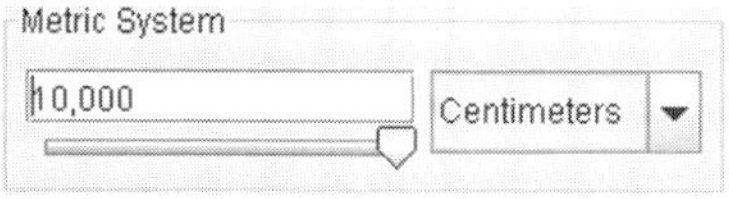 Metric System 10,000 Centimeters	 Metric System 10,000 Centimeters
JScrollPane	
JSplitPane	
 Bird.gif Cat.gif Dog.gif Rabbit.gif Pig.gif dukeWaveRed.gif kathyCosmo.gif	 Bird.gif Cat.gif Dog.gif Rabbit.gif Pig.gif dukeWaveRed.gif kathyCosmo.gif lainesTongue.gif left.gif
JTabbedPane	
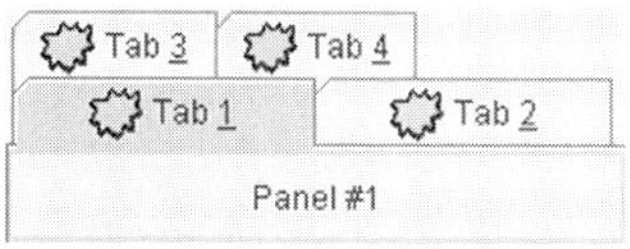 Tab 3 Tab 4 Tab 1 Tab 2 Panel #1	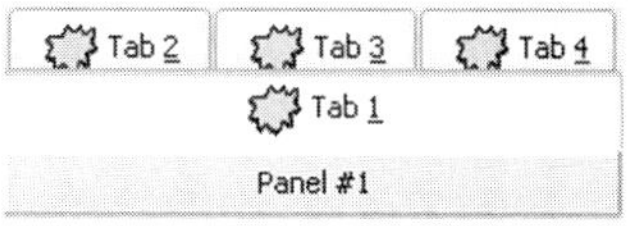 Tab 2 Tab 3 Tab 4 Tab 1 Panel #1
JToolBar	

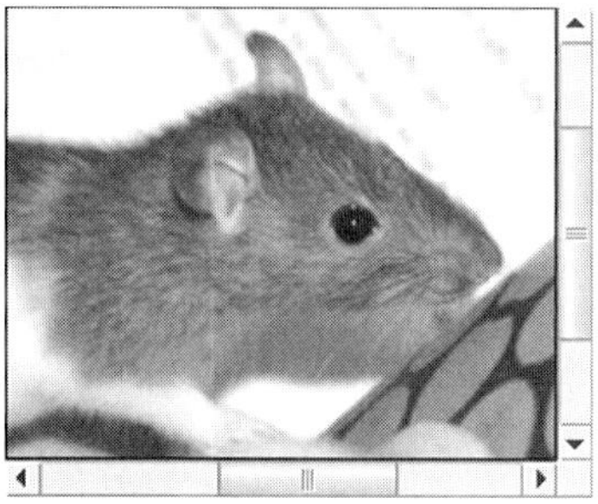

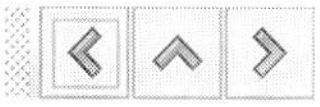

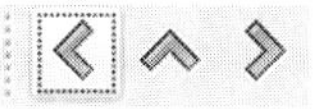

Special-Purpose Containers (Table 15.6)

These special-purpose containers play specific roles in the UI.

Table 15.6 Special-Purpose Containers

<table>
<tr><th>Java Look and Feel</th><th>Windows Look and Feel</th></tr>
<tr><td colspan="2">JInternalFrame</td></tr>
<tr><td>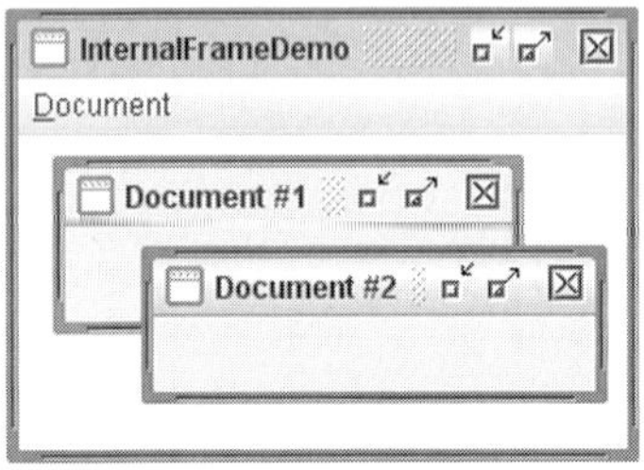
</td><td>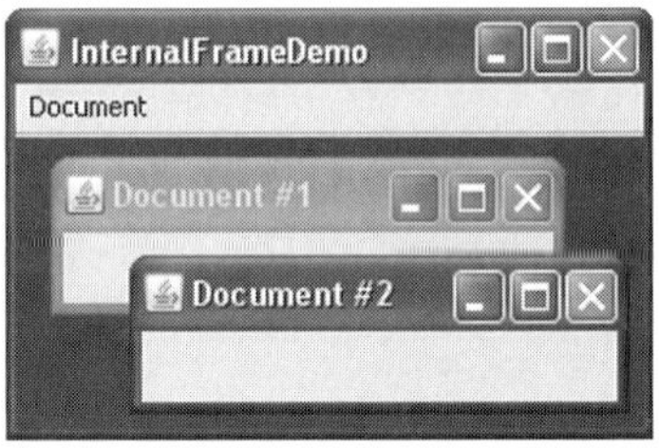
</td></tr>
<tr><td colspan="2">JLayeredPane</td></tr>
<tr><td>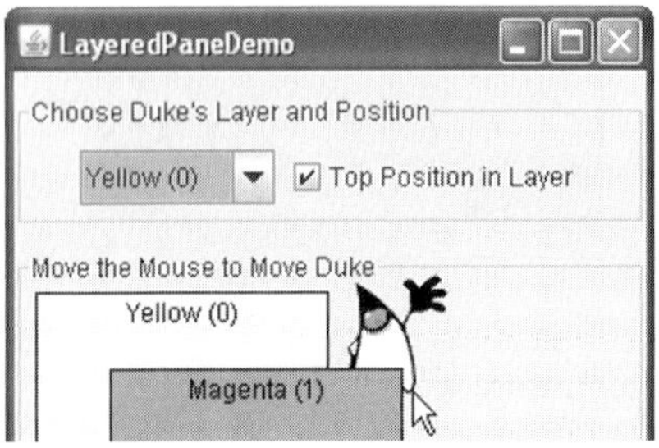
</td><td>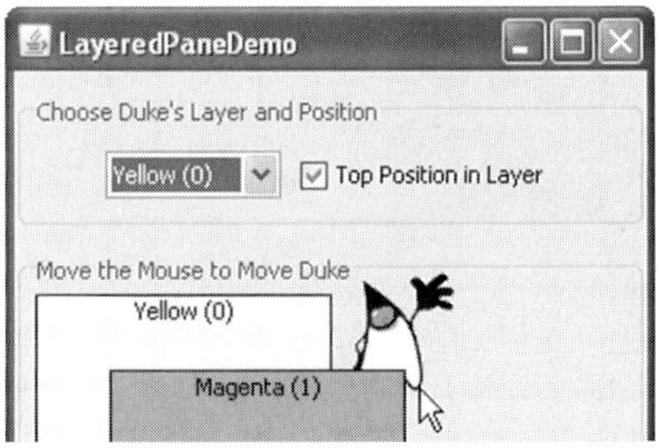
</td></tr>
<tr><td colspan="2">JRootPane</td></tr>
<tr><td>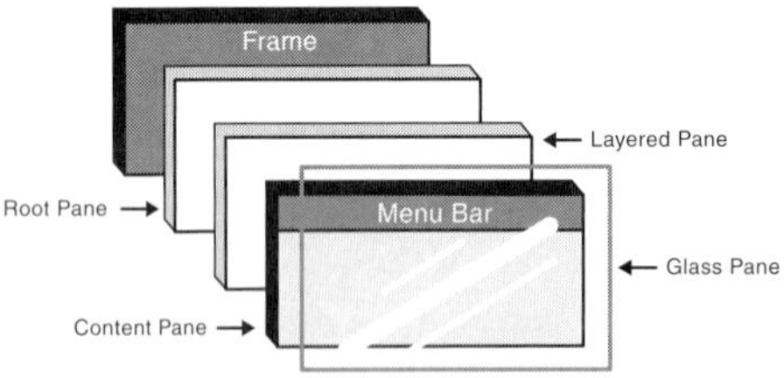
</td><td>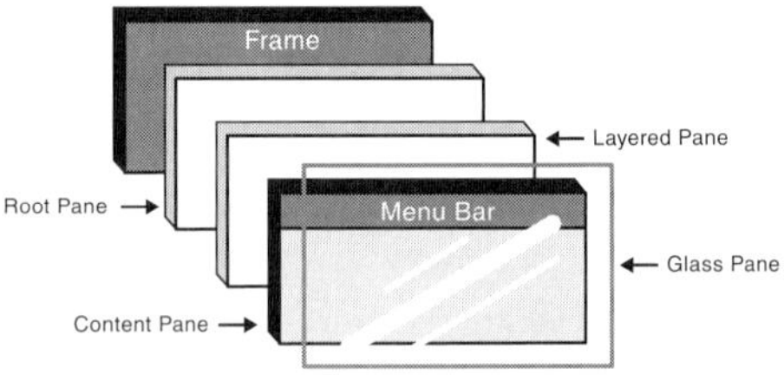
</td></tr>
</table>

Pluggable Look and Feel

The Swing toolkit allows you to decide how to configure the particular look and feel of your application. If you don't specify a look and feel, the Swing UI manager figures out which one to use. The options for setting a look and feel include:

- Leave it up to the Swing UI manager. If a particular look and feel is not specified by the program, Swing's UI manager checks whether the user has specified a preference. If that preference hasn't been specified or isn't available, the default look and feel is used. The default look and feel is determined by the supplier of the JRE. For the JRE that Sun provides, the Java look and feel (called Metal) is used. The Java look and feel works on all platforms.

- Use the look and feel of the native platform. If the application is running on a Microsoft Windows XP machine, the Windows look and feel is used. On Mac OS platforms, the Aqua look and feel is used. On UNIX platforms, such as Solaris or Linux, either the GTK+ look and feel or the CDE/Motif look and feel is used, depending on the user's desktop choice.
- Specify a particular look and feel. Swing ships with four look and feels: Java (also called Metal), Microsoft Windows, GTK+, and CDE/Motif. The GTK+ look and feel requires a theme, and there are many available for free on the Internet.
- Create your own look and feel using the Synth package.
- Use an externally provided look and feel.

As shown in Figures 15.4 to 15.8, PasswordStore offers a choice of three look and feels. The Alloy and Synthetica look and feels have been provided courtesy of Incors.[6]

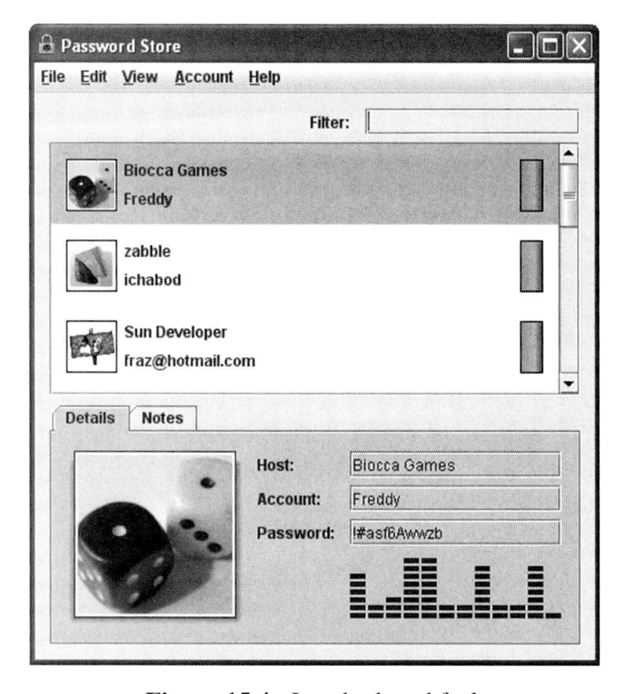

Figure 15.4 Java look and feel.

6. `http://www.incors.com/lookandfeel/`

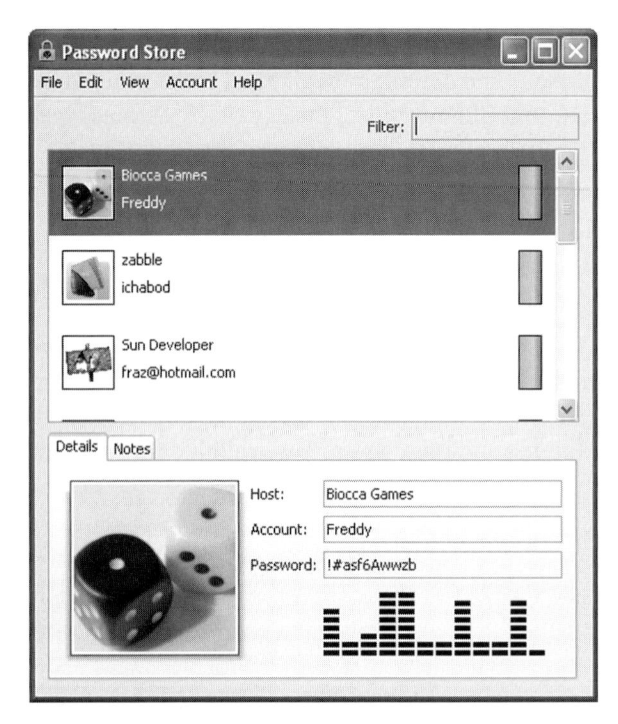

Figure 15.5 Windows look and feel.

Figure 15.6 CDE/Motif look and feel.

Figure 15.7 Default Alloy look and feel.

Figure 15.8 Synthetica look and feel.

Drag and Drop and Data Transfer

The Swing toolkit supports the ability to transfer data between components within the same Java application, between different Java applications, and between Java and native applications. Data can be transferred via a drag and drop gesture, or via the clipboard using cut, copy, and paste.

Drag and Drop

Drag-and-drop support can be easily enabled for many of Swing's components (sometimes with a single line of code). For example, it's trivial to enable drag and drop and copy and paste support for `JTable`, Swing's table component. All you need to provide is the data representing the selection and how to get your data from the clipboard—that's it!

Cut, Copy, and Paste

Most of the text-based components, such as editor pane and text field, support cut/copy and paste out of the box. Of course, menu items need to be created and "wired up" to the appropriate actions. Other components, such as list and tree, can support cut, copy, and paste with some minimal work.

PasswordStore supports data transfer in a variety of ways:

- The text in both the list and the table view supports cut, copy, and paste.
- The text fields in the **Details** panel, the **Filter** text field, and the **Notes** text pane support cut/copy, paste, and drag and drop.
- The Company icon region in the **Details** panel accepts a dropped image (jpg, png, gif, or tif).

Internationalization and Localization

Internationalization is the process of designing an application so that the user can run it using his or her cultural preferences without modifying or recompiling the code. These cultural preferences, collectively known as *locale*, include (but aren't limited to): language, currency formatting, time and date formatting, and numeric formatting.

An internationalized program is designed so that text elements, such as status messages and GUI component labels, are stored outside the source code in resource bundles and retrieved dynamically. Separating the locale-specific information from the code is what allows a program to run in different languages and with different preferences without having to recompile.

Localization is the process of translating the text to a particular language and adding any locale-specific components. When an application is localized to a language and you run the app in that locale, Swing grabs the localized strings from the resource bundle and the layout manager resizes the component accordingly.

For example, an English-speaking person writes an application following the rules of internationalization; later, that application is localized to Japanese and Spanish. When a user with the Language System Preference set to Japanese runs the application, Swing detects this. When the application appears, the menus, labels, buttons, and so on, show Japanese text, and the components are scaled accordingly. If that user then quits the program, sets the language system preference to Spanish, and re-launches the application, the application appears in Spanish, scaled according to the new character set.

Swing's layout managers understand how locale affects a UI—it is not necessary to create a new layout for each locale. For example, in a locale where text flows right to left, the layout manager will arrange components in the same orientation, if specified. *Bidi* text (mixed directional text, used by Hebrew and Arabic, for example) is supported as well.

Every program should be designed with internationalization in mind: GUI component labels, status messages, currency, date, phone, and address formats should not be hardcoded into programs. Once a program has been internationalized, a language expert can perform the actual translation at a later date without requiring any recompiling.

As Figures 15.9 and 15.10 show, PasswordStore has been localized to Japanese and Arabic.

Figure 15.9 PasswordStore in Japanese.

Figure 15.10 PasswordStore in Arabic.

Accessibility

Assistive technologies exist to enable people with permanent or temporary disabilities to use the computer. This includes a wide variety of techniques and equipment—voice interfaces, magnifiers, screen readers, closed captioning, keyboard enhancements, and so on. In many countries, including the United States, Australia, Canada, and the European Union, there are laws requiring that programs function smoothly with assistive technologies.[7]

A certain level of accessibility is built in to all Swing components, but full accessibility can be achieved by following some simple rules. For example, assign tooltips, keyboard alternatives, and textual descriptions for images, wherever possible.

The PasswordStore demo follows the rules set out for accessibility. In Figure 15.11, you can see an example of tooltip text.

7. For more information, see Sun Microsystems' Accessibility Program—Relevant Laws, `http://www.sun.com/access/background/laws.html`.

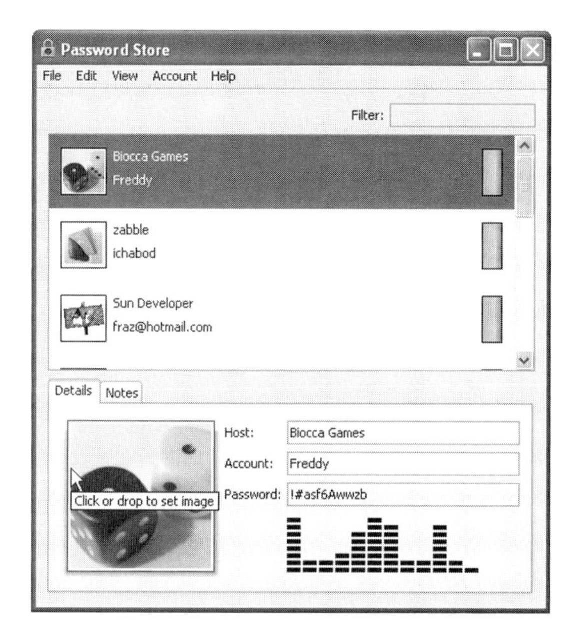

Figure 15.11 PasswordStore with a tooltip.

Integrating with the Desktop

The Desktop API,[8] introduced in version 6 of the Java Platform, Standard Edition (Java SE), enables Java applications to integrate seamlessly with the desktop. Three types of integration are supported:

- The ability to launch the host system's default browser with a specific Uniform Resource Identifier (URI).
- The ability to launch the host system's default e-mail client.
- The ability to launch applications to open, edit, or print files associated with those applications.

You can see this in the PasswordStore demo in the **Notes** text pane. Click on the link that is displayed in Figure 15.12—it opens the specified URI in the default browser.

For more information, see the *Using the Desktop API in Java SE 6* article.[9]

8. `docs/api/java/awt/Desktop.html`

9. `http://java.sun.com/developer/technicalArticles/J2SE/Desktop/mustang/desktop_api/`

Figure 15.12 Click on the URI and it opens in the default browser.

System Tray Icon Support

The desktop of some platforms, such as Microsoft Windows, includes a *system tray*, as shown in Figure 15.13.

Figure 15.13 System tray on Windows XP.

On Microsoft Windows, it is called the "Taskbar Status Area." On Gnome, the "Notification Area," and on KDE, the "System Tray." Whatever it may be called, the system tray is shared by all applications.

On platforms where it is supported, an application may insert a mini-icon, called a *tray icon*, into the system tray. This icon can be used to notify the user of a change in the application's status or a need to take a particular action. Clicking the tray icon can bring up the application window. A popup menu and a tooltip can also be attached to the tray icon.

System tray support[10] was added in version 6 of Java SE. For more information, see the *New System Tray Functionality in Java SE 6* article.[11]

Questions: Graphical User Interfaces

Questions

1. Does Swing support multiple look and feels?
2. True or False: The Java look and feel is the only look and feel that works across all platforms.
3. True or False: Swing's Undo Framework supports an unlimited number of actions to undo (and redo).
4. Can Swing's list component (JList) only display text?
5. Which Swing component provides undo support out of the box?
6. Can Java applications interact with the native desktop components?
7. Can I deploy my Swing application on the Web?

Answers

You can find answers to these Questions at:

`tutorial/ui/features/QandE/answers.html`

10. `docs/api/java/awt/SystemTray.html`
11. `http://java.sun.com/developer/technicalArticles/J2SE/Desktop/mustang/systemtray/`

16

Packaging Programs in JAR Files

THIS chapter and the two following chapters discuss deploying your Java applications and applets.

Java versions 1.4.2, 1.5.0, and 1.6.0 bundle two deployment technologies:

- Java Web Start, for deploying Java applications
- Java Plug-in, for deploying Java applets

We recommend using Java Plug-in to deploy applets when you want your application to run within a browser, or when the application is tightly integrated with Web page content.

We recommend using Java Web Start when you want your application to run stand-alone, on your users' desktops.

Java Web Start requires that applications be packed in JAR files, which is covered in this chapter.

The Java Archive (JAR) file format enables you to bundle multiple files into a single archive file. Typically a JAR file contains the class files and auxiliary resources associated with applets and applications.

The JAR file format provides many benefits:

Security You can digitally sign the contents of a JAR file. Users who recognize your signature can then optionally grant your software security privileges it wouldn't otherwise have.

Decreased download time If your applet is bundled in a JAR file, the applet's class files and associated resources can be downloaded to a browser in a single HTTP transaction without the need for opening a new connection for each file.

Compression The JAR format allows you to compress your files for efficient storage.

Packaging for extensions The extensions framework provides a means by which you can add functionality to the Java core platform, and the JAR file format defines the packaging for extensions. Java 3D[1] and JavaMail[2] are examples of extensions developed by Sun. By using the JAR file format, you can turn your software into extensions as well.

Package sealing Packages stored in JAR files can be optionally sealed so that the package can enforce version consistency. Sealing a package within a JAR file means that all classes defined in that package must be found in the same JAR file.

Package versioning A JAR file can hold data about the files it contains, such as vendor and version information.

Portability The mechanism for handling JAR files is a standard part of the Java platform's core API.

The documentation for the Java Development Kit includes information about the Jar tool:

- Java Archive (JAR) Files Guide[3]
- JAR File Specification[4]

Using JAR Files: The Basics

JAR files are packaged with the ZIP file format, so you can use them for tasks such as lossless data compression, archiving, decompression, and archive unpacking. These tasks are among the most common uses of JAR files, and you can realize many JAR file benefits using only these basic features.

1. `http://java.sun.com/products/java-media/3D`
2. `http://java.sun.com/products/javamail/`
3. `docs/technotes/guides/jar/index.html`
4. `docs/technotes/guides/jar/jar.html`

Even if you want to take advantage of advanced functionality provided by the JAR file format, such as electronic signing, you will first need to become familiar with the fundamental operations.

To perform basic tasks with JAR files, you use the Java Archive Tool provided as part of the Java Development Kit. Because the Java Archive Tool is invoked by using the `jar` command, this tutorial refers to it as "the Jar tool."

As a synopsis and preview of some of the topics to be covered in this section, Table 16.1 summarizes common JAR file operations.

Table 16.1 Common JAR File Operations

Operation	Command
To create a JAR file	`jar cf` *jar-file input-file(s)*
To view the contents of a JAR file	`jar tf` *jar-file*
To extract the contents of a JAR file	`jar xf` *jar-file*
To extract specific files from a JAR file	`jar xf` *jar-file archived-file(s)*
To run an application packaged as a JAR file (requires the `Main-class`* manifest header)	`java -jar` *app.jar*

To invoke an applet packaged as a JAR file	`<applet code=`*AppletClassName.class*
	`archive="`*JarFileName.jar*`"`
	`width=`*width* `height=`*height*`>`
	`</applet>`

* `tutorial/deployment/jar/appman.html`

This section shows you how to perform the most common JAR-file operations, with examples for each of the basic features.

The documentation for the Java Development Kit includes reference pages for the Jar tool:

- Jar tool reference for Windows platform[5]
- Jar tool reference for Solaris platform[6]

5. `docs/technotes/tools/windows/jar.html`
6. `docs/technotes/tools/solaris/jar.html`

Creating a JAR File

The basic format of the command for creating a JAR file is:

```
jar cf jar-file input-file(s)
```

The options and arguments used in this command are:

- The `c` option indicates that you want to *create* a JAR file.
- The `f` option indicates that you want the output to go to a *file* rather than to stdout.
- `jar-file` is the name that you want the resulting JAR file to have. You can use any filename for a JAR file. By convention, JAR filenames are given a `.jar` extension, though this is not required.
- The `input-file(s)` argument is a space-separated list of one or more files that you want to include in your JAR file. The `input-file(s)` argument can contain the wildcard `*` symbol. If any of the "input-files" are directories, the contents of those directories are added to the JAR archive recursively.

The `c` and `f` options can appear in either order, but there must not be any space between them.

This command will generate a compressed JAR file and place it in the current directory. The command will also generate a default manifest file for the JAR archive (see the Understanding the Default Manifest section, page 500).

Note: The metadata in the JAR file, such as the entry names, comments, and contents of the manifest, must be encoded in UTF8.

You can add any of the additional options to the `cf` options of the basic command shown in Table 16.2.

Note: When you create a JAR file, the time of creation is stored in the JAR file. Therefore, even if the contents of the JAR file do not change, when you create a JAR file multiple times, the resulting files are not exactly identical. You should be aware of this when you are using JAR files in a build environment. It is recommended that you use versioning information in the manifest file, rather than creation time, to control versions of a JAR file; see the Setting Package Version Information section (page 504).

Table 16.2 JAR Command Options

Option	Description
`v`	Produces *verbose* output on stdout while the JAR file is being built. The verbose output tells you the name of each file as it's added to the JAR file.
`0` (zero)	Indicates that you don't want the JAR file to be compressed.
`M`	Indicates that the default manifest file should not be produced.
`m`	Used to include manifest information from an existing manifest file. The format for using this option is: `jar cmf existing-manifest jar-file input-file(s)` See the Modifying a Manifest File section (page 501) for more information about this option. **Warning:** The manifest must end with a new line or carriage return. The last line will not be parsed properly if it does not end with a new line or carriage return.
`-C`	To change directories during execution of the command. See the An Example section (page 491).

An Example

Let us look at an example, a simple `TicTacToe` applet. This demo contains a bytecode class file, audio files, and images having the structure shown in Figure 16.1.

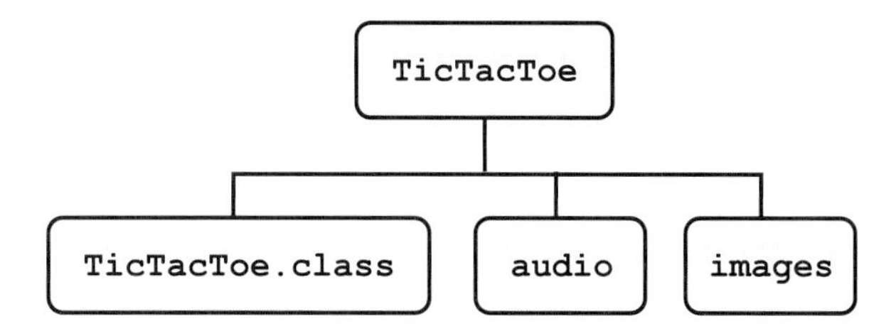

Figure 16.1 TicTacToe folder hierarchy.

The `audio` and `images` subdirectories contain sound files and GIF images used by the applet.

You can obtain all these files from *jar/examples* directory.[7] To package this demo into a single JAR file named `TicTacToe.jar`, you would run this command from inside the `TicTacToe` directory:

```
jar cvf TicTacToe.jar TicTacToe.class audio images
```

7. `tutorial/deployment/jar/examples/TicTacToe.java`

The audio and images arguments represent directories, so the Jar tool will recursively place them and their contents in the JAR file. The generated JAR file TicTacToe.jar will be placed in the current directory. Because the command used the v option for verbose output, you would see something similar to this output when you run the command:

```
adding: TicTacToe.class (in=3825) (out=2222) (deflated 41%)
adding: audio/ (in=0) (out=0) (stored 0%)
adding: audio/beep.au (in=4032) (out=3572) (deflated 11%)
adding: audio/ding.au (in=2566) (out=2055) (deflated 19%)
adding: audio/return.au (in=6558) (out=4401) (deflated 32%)
adding: audio/yahoo1.au (in=7834) (out=6985) (deflated 10%)
adding: audio/yahoo2.au (in=7463) (out=4607) (deflated 38%)
adding: images/ (in=0) (out=0) (stored 0%)
adding: images/cross.gif (in=157) (out=160) (deflated -1%)
adding: images/not.gif (in=158) (out=161) (deflated -1%)
```

You can see from this output that the JAR file TicTacToe.jar is compressed. The Jar tool compresses files by default. You can turn off the compression feature by using the 0 (zero) option, so that the command would look like:

```
jar cvf0 TicTacToe.jar TicTacToe.class audio images
```

You might want to avoid compression, for example, to increase the speed with which a JAR file could be loaded by a browser. Uncompressed JAR files can generally be loaded more quickly than compressed files because the need to decompress the files during loading is eliminated. However, there is a tradeoff in that download time over a network may be longer for larger, uncompressed files.

The Jar tool will accept arguments that use the wildcard * symbol. As long as there weren't any unwanted files in the TicTacToe directory, you could have used this alternative command to construct the JAR file:

```
jar cvf TicTacToe.jar *
```

Though the verbose output doesn't indicate it, the Jar tool automatically adds a manifest file to the JAR archive with path name META-INF/MANIFEST.MF. See the Working with Manifest Files: The Basics section (page 500) for information about manifest files.

In the previous example, the files in the archive retained their relative path names and directory structure. The Jar tool provides the -C option that you can use to create a JAR file in which the relative paths of the archived files are not preserved. It's modeled after TAR's -C option.

As an example, suppose you wanted to put audio files and gif images used by the TicTacToe demo into a JAR file, and that you wanted all the files to be on the top level, with no directory hierarchy. You could accomplish that by issuing this command from the parent directory of the `images` and `audio` directories:

```
jar cf ImageAudio.jar -C images . -C audio .
```

The `-C images` part of this command directs the Jar tool to go to the `images` directory, and the `.` following `-C images` directs the Jar tool to archive all the contents of that directory. The `-C audio .` part of the command then does the same with the `audio` directory. The resulting JAR file would have this table of contents:

```
META-INF/MANIFEST.MF
cross.gif
not.gif
beep.au
ding.au
return.au
yahoo1.au
yahoo2.au
```

By contrast, suppose that you used a command that did not employ the `-C` option:

```
jar cf ImageAudio.jar images audio
```

The resulting JAR file would have this table of contents:

```
META-INF/MANIFEST.MF
images/cross.gif
images/not.gif
audio/beep.au
audio/ding.au
audio/return.au
audio/yahoo1.au
audio/yahoo2.au
```

Viewing the Contents of a JAR File

The basic format of the command for viewing the contents of a JAR file is:

```
jar tf jar-file
```

Let's look at the options and argument used in this command:

- The `t` option indicates that you want to view the *table* of contents of the JAR file.
- The `f` option indicates that the JAR file whose contents are to be viewed is specified on the command line.

- The `jar-file` argument is the path and name of the JAR file whose contents you want to view.

The `t` and `f` options can appear in either order, but there must not be any space between them.

This command will display the JAR file's table of contents to stdout.

You can optionally add the verbose option, `v`, to produce additional information about file sizes and last-modified dates in the output.

An Example

Let's use the Jar tool to list the contents of the `TicTacToe.jar` file we created in the previous section:

```
jar tf TicTacToe.jar
```

This command displays the contents of the JAR file to stdout:

```
META-INF/MANIFEST.MF
TicTacToe.class
audio/
audio/beep.au
audio/ding.au
audio/return.au
audio/yahoo1.au
audio/yahoo2.au
images/
images/cross.gif
images/not.gif
```

The JAR file contains the `TicTacToe` class file and the audio and images directory, as expected. The output also shows that the JAR file contains a default manifest file, `META-INF/MANIFEST.MF`, which was automatically placed in the archive by the JAR tool. For more information, see the Understanding the Default Manifest section (page 500).

All pathnames are displayed with forward slashes, regardless of the platform or operating system you're using. Paths in JAR files are always relative; you'll never see a path beginning with `C:`, for example.

The JAR tool will display additional information if you use the `v` option:

```
jar tvf TicTacToe.jar
```

For example, the verbose output for the TicTacToe JAR file would look similar to this:

```
 256 Mon Apr 18 10:50:28 PDT 2005 META-INF/MANIFEST.MF
3885 Mon Apr 18 10:49:50 PDT 2005 TicTacToe.class
   0 Wed Apr 20 16:39:32 PDT 2005 audio/
4032 Wed Apr 20 16:39:32 PDT 2005 audio/beep.au
2566 Wed Apr 20 16:39:32 PDT 2005 audio/ding.au
6558 Wed Apr 20 16:39:32 PDT 2005 audio/return.au
7834 Wed Apr 20 16:39:32 PDT 2005 audio/yahoo1.au
7463 Wed Apr 20 16:39:32 PDT 2005 audio/yahoo2.au
   0 Wed Apr 20 16:39:44 PDT 2005 images/
 157 Wed Apr 20 16:39:44 PDT 2005 images/cross.gif
 158 Wed Apr 20 16:39:44 PDT 2005 images/not.gif
```

Extracting the Contents of a JAR File

The basic command to use for extracting the contents of a JAR file is:

```
jar xf jar-file [archived-file(s)]
```

Let's look at the options and arguments in this command:

- The `x` option indicates that you want to *extract* files from the JAR archive.
- The `f` option indicates that the JAR *file* from which files are to be extracted is specified on the command line, rather than through stdin.
- The `jar-file` argument is the filename (or path and filename) of the JAR file from which to extract files.
- `archived-file(s)` is an optional argument consisting of a space-separated list of the files to be extracted from the archive. If this argument is not present, the Jar tool will extract all the files in the archive.

As usual, the order in which the `x` and `f` options appear in the command doesn't matter, but there must not be a space between them.

When extracting files, the Jar tool makes copies of the desired files and writes them to the current directory, reproducing the directory structure that the files have in the archive. The original JAR file remains unchanged.

Caution: When it extracts files, the Jar tool will overwrite any existing files having the same pathname as the extracted files.

An Example

Let's extract some files from the TicTacToe JAR file we've been using in previous sections. Recall that the contents of `TicTacToe.jar` are:

```
META-INF/MANIFEST.MF
TicTacToe.class
audio/
audio/beep.au
audio/ding.au
audio/return.au
audio/yahoo1.au
audio/yahoo2.au
images/
images/cross.gif
images/not.gif
```

Suppose you want to extract the `TicTacToe` class file and the `cross.gif` image file. To do so, you can use this command:

```
jar xf TicTacToe.jar TicTacToe.class images/cross.gif
```

This command does two things:

- It places a copy of `TicTacToe.class` in the current directory.
- It creates the directory `images`, if it doesn't already exist, and places a copy of `cross.gif` within it.

The original TicTacToe JAR file remains unchanged.

As many files as desired can be extracted from the JAR file in the same way. When the command doesn't specify which files to extract, the Jar tool extracts all files in the archive. For example, you can extract all the files in the TicTacToe archive by using this command:

```
jar xf TicTacToe.jar
```

Updating a JAR File

The Jar tool provides a `u` option that you can use to update the contents of an existing JAR file by modifying its manifest or by adding files.

The basic command for adding files has this format:

```
jar uf jar-file input-file(s)
```

In this command:

- The `u` option indicates that you want to *update* an existing JAR file.
- The `f` option indicates that the JAR file to update is specified on the command line.
- `jar-file` is the existing JAR file that's to be updated.

- `input-file(s)` is a space-deliminated list of one or more files that you want to add to the Jar file.

Any files already in the archive having the same pathname as a file being added will be overwritten.

When creating a new JAR file, you can optionally use the `-C` option to indicate a change of directory. For more information, see the Creating a JAR File section (page 490).

Examples

Recall that `TicTacToe.jar` has these contents:

```
META-INF/MANIFEST.MF
TicTacToe.class
audio/
audio/beep.au
audio/ding.au
audio/return.au
audio/yahoo1.au
audio/yahoo2.au
images/
images/cross.gif
images/not.gif
```

Suppose that you want to add the file `images/new.gif` to the JAR file. You could accomplish that by issuing this command from the parent directory of the `images` directory:

```
jar uf TicTacToe.jar images/new.gif
```

The revised JAR file would have this table of contents:

```
META-INF/MANIFEST.MF
TicTacToe.class
audio/
audio/beep.au
audio/ding.au
audio/return.au
audio/yahoo1.au
audio/yahoo2.au
images/
images/cross.gif
images/not.gif
images/new.gif
```

You can use the `-C` option to “change directories” during execution of the command. For example:

```
jar uf TicTacToe.jar -C images new.gif
```

This command would change to the `images` directory before adding `new.gif` to the JAR file. The `images` directory would not be included in the pathname of `new.gif` when it's added to the archive, resulting in a table of contents that looks like this:

```
META-INF/MANIFEST.MF
TicTacToe.class
audio/
audio/beep.au
audio/ding.au
audio/return.au
audio/yahoo1.au
audio/yahoo2.au
images/
images/cross.gif
images/not.gif
new.gif
```

Running JAR-Packaged Software

Now that you've learned how to create JAR files, how do you actually run the code that you've packaged? Consider these three scenarios:

- Your JAR file contains an applet that is to be run inside a browser.
- Your JAR file contains an application that is to be invoked from the command line.
- Your JAR file contains code that you want to use as an extension.

This section will cover the first two situations. *The Extension Mechanism* by Alan Sommerer[8] covers the use of JAR files as extensions.

Applets Packaged in JAR Files

To invoke any applet from an HTML file for running inside a browser, you need to use the `APPLET` tag. For more information, see Chapter 18. If the applet is bundled as a JAR file, the only thing you need to do differently is to use the `ARCHIVE` parameter to specify the relative path to the JAR file.

As an example, let's use (again!) the TicTacToe demo applet that ships with the Java Development Kit. The `APPLET` tag in the HTML file that calls the demo looks like this:

8. `tutorial/ext/index.html`

```
<applet code=TicTacToe.class
  width=120 height=120>
</applet>
```

If the TicTacToe demo were packaged in a JAR file named `TicTacToe.jar`, you could modify the `APPLET` tag with the simple addition of an `ARCHIVE` parameter:

```
<applet code=TicTacToe.class
  archive="TicTacToe.jar"
  width=120 height=120>
</applet>
```

The `ARCHIVE` parameter specifies the relative path to the JAR file that contains `TicTacToe.class`. This example assumes that the JAR file and the HTML file are in the same directory. If they're not, you would need to include the JAR file's relative path in the `ARCHIVE` parameter's value. For example, if the JAR file was one directory below the HTML file in a directory called `applets`, the `APPLET` tag would look like this:

```
<applet code=TicTacToe.class
  archive="applets/TicTacToe.jar"
  width=120 height=120>
</applet>
```

JAR Files as Applications

You can run JAR-packaged applications with the Java interpreter. The basic command is:

```
java -jar jar-file
```

The `-jar` flag tells the interpreter that the application is packaged in the JAR file format. You can only specify one JAR file, which must contain all the application-specific code.

Before you execute this command, make sure the runtime environment has information as to which class within the JAR file is the application's entry point.

To indicate which class is the application's entry point, you must add a `Main-Class` header to the JAR file's manifest. The header takes the form:

```
Main-Class: classname
```

The header's value, `classname`, is the name of the class that's the application's entry point.

For more information, see the Setting an Application's Entry Point section (page 502).

When the `Main-Class` is set in the manifest file, you can run the application from the command line:

```
java -jar app.jar
```

Working with Manifest Files: The Basics

JAR files support a wide range of functionality, including electronic signing, version control, package sealing, and others. What gives a JAR file this versatility? The answer is the JAR file's *manifest*.

The manifest is a special file that can contain information about the files packaged in a JAR file. By tailoring this "meta" information that the manifest contains, you enable the JAR file to serve a variety of purposes.

This section will explain the contents of the manifest file and show you how to work with it, with examples for the basic features.

A specification of the manifest format is part of the online JDK documentation.

Understanding the Default Manifest

When you create a JAR file, it automatically receives a default manifest file. There can be only one manifest file in an archive, and it always has the pathname:

```
META-INF/MANIFEST.MF
```

When you create a JAR file, the default manifest file simply contains the following:

```
Manifest-Version: 1.0
Created-By: 1.6.0 (Sun Microsystems Inc.)
```

These lines show that a manifest's entries take the form of "header: value" pairs. The name of a header is separated from its value by a colon. The default manifest conforms to version 1.0 of the manifest specification and was created by the 1.6.0 version of the JDK.

The manifest can also contain information about the other files that are packaged in the archive. Exactly what file information should be recorded in the manifest depends on how you intend to use the JAR file. The default manifest makes no assumptions about what information it should record about other files.

Digest information is not included in the default manifest. To learn more about digests and signing, see the Signing and Verifying JAR Files section (page 507).

Modifying a Manifest File

You use the `m` command-line option to add custom information to the manifest during creation of a JAR file. This section describes the `m` option.

The Jar tool automatically puts a default manifest (see the Understanding the Default Manifest section, page 500) with the pathname `META-INF/MANIFEST.MF` into any JAR file you create. You can enable special JAR file functionality, such as package sealing (see the Sealing Packages Within a JAR File section, page 506), by modifying the default manifest. Typically, modifying the default manifest involves adding special-purpose *headers* to the manifest that allow the JAR file to perform a particular desired function.

To modify the manifest, you must first prepare a text file containing the information you wish to add to the manifest. You then use the Jar tool's `m` option to add the information in your file to the manifest.

Warning: The text file from which you are creating the manifest must end with a new line or carriage return. The last line will not be parsed properly if it does not end with a new line or carriage return.

The basic command has this format:

```
jar cmf jar-file manifest-addition input-file(s)
```

Let's look at the options and arguments used in this command:

- The `c` option indicates that you want to *create* a JAR file.
- The `m` option indicates that you want to *merge* information from an existing file into the manifest file of the JAR file you're creating.
- The `f` option indicates that you want the output to go to a *file* (the JAR file you're creating) rather than to standard output.
- *`manifest-addition`* is the name (or path and name) of the existing text file whose contents you want to add to the contents of JAR file's manifest.
- *`jar-file`* is the name that you want the resulting JAR file to have.
- The *`input-file(s)`* argument is a space-separated list of one or more files that you want to be placed in your JAR file.

The `m` and `f` options must be in the same order as the corresponding arguments.

Note: The contents of the manifest must be encoded in UTF-8.

The remaining subsections of this section demonstrate specific modifications you may want to make to the manifest file.

Setting an Application's Entry Point

If you have an application bundled in a JAR file, you need some way to indicate which class within the JAR file is your application's entry point. You provide this information with the `Main-Class` header in the manifest, which has the general form:

```
Main-Class: classname
```

The value *`classname`* is the name of the class that is your application's entry point.

Recall that the entry point is a class having a method with signature `public static void main(String[] args)`.

After you have set the `Main-Class` header in the manifest, you then run the JAR file using the following form of the `java` command:

```
java -jar JAR-name
```

The `main` method of the class specified in the `Main-Class` header is executed.

An Example

We want to execute the `main` method in the class `MyClass` in the package `MyPackage` when we run the JAR file.

We first create a text file named `Manifest.txt` with the following contents:

```
Main-Class: MyPackage.MyClass
```

Warning: The text file must end with a new line or carriage return. The last line will not be parsed properly if it does not end with a new line or carriage return.

We then create a JAR file named `MyJar.jar` by entering the following command:

```
jar cfm MyJar.jar Manifest.txt MyPackage/*.class
```

This creates the JAR file with a manifest with the following contents:

```
Manifest-Version: 1.0
Created-By: 1.6.0 (Sun Microsystems Inc.)
Main-Class: MyPackage.MyClass
```

When you run the JAR file with the following command, the `main` method of `MyClass` executes:

```
java -jar MyJar.jar
```

Setting an Entry Point with the JAR Tool

The `e` flag (for "entrypoint") creates or overrides the manifest's `Main-Class` attribute. It can be used while creating or updating a jar file. Use it to specify the application entry point without editing or creating the manifest file.

For example, this command creates `app.jar` where the `Main-Class` attribute value in the manifest is set to `MyApp`:

```
jar cfe app.jar MyApp MyApp.class
```

You can directly invoke this application by running the following command:

```
java -jar app.jar
```

If the entrypoint class name is in a package it may use a "." (dot) character as the delimiter. For example, if `Main.class` is in a package called `foo`, the entry point can be specified in the following ways:

```
jar -cfe Main.jar foo.Main foo/Main.class
```

Adding Classes to the JAR File's Classpath

You may need to reference classes in other JAR files from within a JAR file.

For example, in a typical situation an applet is bundled in a JAR file whose manifest references a different JAR file (or several different JAR files) that serves as a utility for the purposes of that applet.

You specify classes to include in the `Class-Path` header field in the manifest file of an applet or application. The `Class-Path` header takes the following form:

```
Class-Path: jar1-name jar2-name directory-name/jar3-name
```

By using the `Class-Path` header in the manifest, you can avoid having to specify a long `-classpath` flag when invoking Java to run your application.

Note: The `Class-Path` header points to classes or JAR files on the local network, not JAR files within the JAR file or classes accessible over Internet protocols. To load classes in JAR files within a JAR file into the class path, you must write custom code to load those classes. For example, if `MyJar.jar` contains another JAR file called `MyUtils.jar`, you cannot use the `Class-Path` header in `MyJar.jar`'s manifest to load classes in `MyUtils.jar` into the class path.

An Example

We want to load classes in `MyUtils.jar` into the class path for use in `MyJar.jar`. These two JAR files are in the same directory.

We first create a text file named `Manifest.txt` with the following contents:

```
Class-Path: MyUtils.jar
```

Warning: The text file must end with a new line or carriage return. The last line will not be parsed properly if it does not end with a new line or carriage return.

We then create a JAR file named `MyJar.jar` by entering the following command:

```
jar cfm MyJar.jar Manifest.txt MyPackage/*.class
```

This creates the JAR file with a manifest with the following contents:

```
Manifest-Version: 1.0
Class-Path: MyUtils.jar
Created-By: 1.6.0 (Sun Microsystems Inc.)
```

The classes in `MyUtils.jar` are now loaded into the class path when you run `MyJar.jar`.

Setting Package Version Information

You may need to include package version information in a JAR file's manifest. You provide this information with the headers listed in Table 16.3 in the manifest.

One set of such headers can be assigned to each package. The versioning headers should appear directly beneath the `Name` header for the package. This example shows all the versioning headers:

Table 16.3 Headers in a Manifest

Header	Definition
Name	The name of the specification.
Specification-Title	The title of the specification.
Specification-Version	The version of the specification.
Specification-Vendor	The vendor of the specification.
Implementation-Title	The title of the implementation.
Implementation-Version	The build number of the implementation.
Implementation-Vendor	The vendor of the implementation.

```
Name: java/util/
Specification-Title: Java Utility Classes
Specification-Version: 1.2
Specification-Vendor: Sun Microsystems, Inc.
Implementation-Title: java.util
Implementation-Version: build57
Implementation-Vendor: Sun Microsystems, Inc.
```

For more information about package version headers, see the Package Versioning specification.[9]

An Example

We want to include the headers in the previous example in the manifest of `MyJar.jar`.

We first create a text file named `Manifest.txt` with the following contents:

```
Name: java/util/
Specification-Title: Java Utility Classes
Specification-Version: 1.2
Specification-Vendor: Sun Microsystems, Inc.
Implementation-Title: java.util
Implementation-Version: build57
Implementation-Vendor: Sun Microsystems, Inc.
```

Warning: The text file must end with a new line or carriage return. The last line will not be parsed properly if it does not end with a new line or carriage return.

9. `docs/technotes/guides/versioning/spec/versioning2.html`

We then create a JAR file named MyJar.jar by entering the following command:

```
jar cmf MyJar.jar Manifest.txt MyPackage/*.class
```

This creates the JAR file with a manifest with the following contents:

```
Manifest-Version: 1.0
Created-By: 1.6.0 (Sun Microsystems Inc.)
Name: java/util/
Specification-Title: Java Utility Classes
Specification-Version: 1.2
Specification-Vendor: Sun Microsystems, Inc.
Implementation-Title: java.util
Implementation Version: build57
Implementation-Vendor: Sun Microsystems, Inc.
```

Sealing Packages Within a JAR File

Packages within JAR files can be optionally sealed, which means that all classes defined in that package must be archived in the same JAR file. You might want to seal a package, for example, to ensure version consistency among the classes in your software.

You seal a package in a JAR file by adding the Sealed header in the manifest, which has the general form:

```
Name: myCompany/myPackage/
Sealed: true
```

The value myCompany/myPackage/ is the name of the package to seal.

Note that the package name must end with a "/".

An Example

We want to seal two packages firstPackage and secondPackage in the JAR file MyJar.jar.

We first create a text file named Manifest.txt with the following contents:

```
Name: myCompany/firstPackage/
Sealed: true

Name: myCompany/secondPackage/
Sealed: true
```

Warning: The text file must end with a new line or carriage return. The last line will not be parsed properly if it does not end with a new line or carriage return.

We then create a JAR file named `MyJar.jar` by entering the following command:

```
jar cmf MyJar.jar Manifest.txt MyPackage/*.class
```

This creates the JAR file with a manifest with the following contents:

```
Manifest-Version: 1.0
Created-By: 1.6.0 (Sun Microsystems Inc.)
Name: myCompany/firstPackage/
Sealed: true
Name: myCompany/secondPackage/
Sealed: true
```

Sealing JAR Files

If you want to guarantee that all classes in a package come from the same code source, use JAR sealing. A sealed JAR specifies that all packages defined by that JAR are sealed unless overridden on a per-package basis.

To seal a jar file, use the `Sealed` manifest header with the value true. For example:

```
Sealed: true
```

specifies that all packages in this archive are sealed unless explicitly overridden for particular packages with the `Sealed` attribute in a manifest entry.

For further information on how to seal JAR files, see JDC TechTips.[10]

Signing and Verifying JAR Files

You can optionally sign a JAR file with your electronic "signature." Users who verify your signature can grant your JAR-bundled software security privileges that it wouldn't ordinarily have. Conversely, you can verify the signatures of signed JAR files that you want to use.

This section shows you how to use the tools provided in the Java Development Kit to sign and verify JAR files.

10. `http://java.sun.com/developer/JDCTechTips/2001/tt0130.html`

Understanding Signing and Verification

The Java platform enables you to digitally sign JAR files. You digitally sign a file for the same reason you might sign a paper document with pen and ink—to let readers know that you wrote the document, or at least that the document has your approval.

When you sign a letter, for example, everyone who recognizes your signature can confirm that you wrote the letter. Similarly, when you digitally sign a file, anyone who "recognizes" your digital signature knows that the file came from you. The process of "recognizing" electronic signatures is called *verification*.

The ability to sign and verify files is an important part of the Java platform's security architecture. Security is controlled by the security *policy* that's in force at runtime. You can configure the policy to grant security privileges to applets and to applications.

For example, you could grant permission to an applet to perform normally forbidden operations such as reading and writing local files or running local executable programs. If you have downloaded some code that's signed by a trusted entity, you can use that fact as a criterion in deciding which security permissions to assign to the code.

Once you (or your browser) have verified that an applet is from a trusted source, you can have the platform relax security restrictions to let the applet perform operations that would ordinarily be forbidden. A trusted applet can have freedoms as specified by the *policy file* in force.

The Java platform enables signing and verification by using special numbers called *public* and *private keys*. Public keys and private keys come in pairs, and they play complementary roles.

The private key is the electronic "pen" with which you can sign a file. As its name implies, your private key is known only to you so that no one else can "forge" your signature. A file signed with your private key can be verified only by the corresponding public key.

Public and private keys alone, however, aren't enough to truly verify a signature. Even if you've verified that a signed file contains a matching key pair, you still need some way to confirm that the public key actually comes from the signer that it purports to come from.

One more element, therefore, is required to make signing and verification work. That additional element is the *certificate* that the signer includes in a signed JAR file. A certificate is a digitally signed statement from a recognized *certification authority* that indicates who owns a particular public key. Certification authorities are entities (typically firms specializing in digital security) that are trusted throughout the industry to sign and issue certificates for keys and their owners. In the case of signed JAR files, the certificate indicates who owns the public key contained in the JAR file.

When you sign a JAR file, your public key is placed inside the archive along with an associated certificate so that it's easily available for use by anyone wanting to verify your signature.

To summarize digital signing:

- The signer signs the JAR file using a private key.
- The corresponding public key is placed in the JAR file, together with its certificate, so that it is available for use by anyone who wants to verify the signature.

Digests and the Signature File

When you sign a JAR file, each file in the archive is given a digest entry in the archive's manifest (see the Working with Manifest Files: The Basics section, page 500). Here's an example of what such an entry might look like:

```
Name: test/classes/ClassOne.class
SHA1-Digest: TD1GZt8G11dXY2p4olSZPc5Rj64=
```

The digest values are hashes, or encoded representations, of the contents of the files as they were at the time of signing. A file's digest will change if and only if the file itself changes.

When a JAR file is signed, a *signature* file is automatically generated and placed in the JAR file's `META-INF` directory, the same directory that contains the archive's manifest. Signature files have filenames with an `.SF` extension. Here is an example of the contents of a signature file:

```
Signature-Version: 1.0
SHA1-Digest-Manifest: h1yS+K9T7DyHtZrtI+LxvgqaMYM=
Created-By: 1.6.0 (Sun Microsystems Inc.)

Name: test/classes/ClassOne.class
SHA1-Digest: fcav7ShIG6i86xPepmitOVo4vWY=

Name: test/classes/ClassTwo.class
SHA1-Digest: xrQem9snnPhLySDiZyclMlsFdtM=

Name: test/images/ImageOne.gif
SHA1-Digest: kdHbE7kL9ZHLgK7akHttYV4XIa0=

Name: test/images/ImageTwo.gif
SHA1-Digest: mF0D5zpk68R4oaxEqoS9Q7nhm60=
```

As you can see, the signature file contains digest entries for the archive's files that look similar to the digest-value entries in the manifest. However, while the digest values in the manifest are computed from the files themselves, the digest values in the signature file are computed from the corresponding entries in the manifest. Signature files also contain a digest value for the entire manifest (see the `SHA1-Digest-Manifest` header in the previous example).

When a signed JAR file is being verified, the digests of each of its files are re-computed and compared with the digests recorded in the manifest to ensure that the contents of the JAR file haven't changed since it was signed. As an additional check, digest values for the manifest file itself are re-computed and compared against the values recorded in the signature file.

You can read additional information about signature files on the Manifest Format page of the JDK documentation.

The Signature Block File

In addition to the signature file, a *signature block* file is automatically placed in the `META-INF` directory when a JAR file is signed. Unlike the manifest file or the signature file, signature block files are not human-readable.

The signature block file contains two elements essential for verification:

- The digital signature for the JAR file that was generated with the signer's private key
- The certificate containing the signer's public key, to be used by anyone wanting to verify the signed JAR file

Signature block filenames typically will have a `.DSA` extension indicating that they were created by the default Digital Signature Algorithm. Other filename extensions are possible if keys associated with some other standard algorithm are used for signing.

Related Documentation

For additional information about keys, certificates, and certification authorities, see:

- The JDK Security Tools[11]
- X.509 Certificates[12]

For more information about the Java platform's security architecture, see this related documentation:

11. `docs/technotes/tools/`

12. `docs/technotes/guides/security/cert3.html`

- Security Features in Java SE[13]
- The Java Cryptography Extension Web site[14]
- JDK Security Documentation[15]

Signing JAR Files

You use the JAR Signing and Verification Tool to sign JAR files. You invoke the JAR Signing and Verification Tool by using the `jarsigner` command, so we'll refer to it as "Jarsigner" for short.

To sign a JAR file, you must first have a private key. Private keys and their associated public-key certificates are stored in password-protected databases called *keystores*. A keystore can hold the keys of many potential signers. Each key in the keystore can be identified by an *alias*, which is typically the name of the signer who owns the key. The key belonging to Rita Jones might have the alias "rita", for example.

The basic form of the command for signing a JAR file is:

```
jarsigner jar-file alias
```

In this command:

- `jar-file` is the pathname of the JAR file that's to be signed.
- `alias` is the alias identifying the private key that's to be used to sign the JAR file, and the key's associated certificate.

The Jarsigner tool will prompt you for the passwords for the keystore and alias.

This basic form of the command assumes that the keystore to be used is in a file named `.keystore` in your home directory. It will create signature and signature block files with names `x.SF` and `x.DSA` respectively, where `x` is the first eight letters of the alias, all converted to uppercase. This basic command will *overwrite* the original JAR file with the signed JAR file.

In practice, you may want to use this command in conjunction with one or more of the options shown in Table 16.4, which must precede the `jar-file` pathname.

13. `docs/books/tutorial/security/`
14. `http://java.sun.com/products/jce/`
15. `docs/technotes/tools/`

Table 16.4 Jarsigner Command Options

Option	Description
`-keystore` *`url`*	Specifies a keystore to be used if you don't want to use the `.keystore` default database.
`-storepass` *`password`*	Allows you to enter the keystore's password on the command line rather than be prompted for it.
`-keypass` *`password`*	Allows you to enter your alias's password on the command line rather than be prompted for it.
`-sigfile` *`file`*	Specifies the base name for the .SF and .DSA files if you don't want the base name to be taken from your alias. *file* must be composed only of uppercase letters (`A-Z`), numerals (`0-9`), hyphen ( ), and underscore (_).
`-signedjar` *`file`*	Specifies the name of the signed JAR file to be generated if you don't want the original unsigned file to be overwritten with the signed file.

Example

Let's look at a couple of examples of signing a JAR file with the Jarsigner tool. In these examples we will assume:

- Your alias is "johndoe".
- The keystore you want to use is in a file named "mykeys" in the current working directory.
- The keystore's password is "abc123".
- The password for your alias is "mypass".

Under these assumptions, you could use this command to sign a JAR file named `app.jar`:

```
jarsigner -keystore mykeys -storepass abc123
          -keypass mypass app.jar johndoe
```

Because this command doesn't make use of the `-sigfile` option, the .SF and .DSA files it creates would be named `JOHNDOE.SF` and `JOHNDOE.DSA`. Because the command doesn't use the `-signedjar` option, the resulting signed file will overwrite the original version of `app.jar`.

Let's look at what would happen if you used a different combination of options:

```
jarsigner -keystore mykeys -sigfile SIG
          -signedjar SignedApp.jar app.jar johndoe
```

This time, you would be prompted to enter the passwords for both the keystore and your alias because the passwords aren't specified on the command line. The signature and signature block files would be named `SIG.SF` and `SIG.DSA`, respectively, and the signed JAR file `SignedApp.jar` would be placed in the current directory. The original unsigned JAR file would remain unchanged.

Additional Information

Complete reference pages for the JAR Signing and Verification Tool are online at Summary of Security Tools.[16]

Verifying Signed JAR Files

Typically, verification of signed JAR files will be the responsibility of your Java Runtime Environment. Your browser will verify signed applets that it downloads. Signed applications invoked with the `-jar` option of the interpreter will be verified by the runtime environment.

However, you can verify signed JAR files yourself by using the Jarsigner tool. You might want to do this, for example, to test a signed JAR file that you've prepared.

The basic command to use for verifying a signed JAR file is:

```
jarsigner -verify jar-file
```

This command will verify the JAR file's signature and ensure that the files in the archive haven't changed since it was signed. You'll see the following message if the verification is successful:

```
jar verified.
```

If you try to verify an unsigned JAR file, the following message results:

```
jar is unsigned. (signatures missing or not parsable)
```

If the verification fails, an appropriate message is displayed. For example, if the contents of a JAR file have changed since the JAR file was signed, a message similar to the following will result if you try to verify the file:

```
jarsigner: java.lang.SecurityException: invalid SHA1
signature file digest for test/classes/Manifest.class
```

16. `docs/technotes/guides/security/SecurityToolsSummary.html`

Using JAR-Related APIs

The Java platform contains several classes for use with JAR files. Some of these APIs are:

- The `java.util.jar` package[17]
- The `java.net.JarURLConnection` class[18]
- The `java.net.URLClassLoader` class[19]

To give you an idea of the possibilities that are opened up by these new APIs, this section guides you through the inner workings of a sample application called JarRunner.

An Example—The JarRunner Application

JarRunner enables you to run an application that's bundled in a JAR file by specifying the JAR file's URL on the command line. For example, if an application called `TargetApp` were bundled in a JAR file at `http://www.xxx.yyy/TargetApp.jar`, you could run the application using this command:

```
java JarRunner http://www.xxx.yyy/TargetApp.jar
```

In order for JarRunner to work, it must be able to perform the following tasks, all of which are accomplished by using the new APIs:

- Access the remote JAR file and establish a communications link with it.
- Inspect the JAR file's manifest to see which of the classes in the archive is the main class.
- Load the classes in the JAR file.

The JarRunner application consists of two classes, `JarRunner` and `JarClassLoader`. `JarRunner` delegates most of the JAR-handling tasks to the `JarClassLoader` class. `JarClassLoader` extends the `java.net.URLClassLoader` class. You can browse the source code for the `JarRunner` and `JarClassLoader` classes before proceeding with the section:

---

17. `docs/api/java/util/jar/package-summary.html`

18. `docs/api/java/net/JarURLConnection.html`

19. `docs/api/java/net/URLClassLoader.html`

- `JarRunner.java`[20]
- `JarClassLoader.java`[21]

The JarClassLoader Class

The `JarClassLoader` class extends `java.net.URLClassLoader`. As its name implies, `URLClassLoader` is designed to be used for loading classes and resources that are accessed by searching a set of URLs. The URLs can refer either to directories or to JAR files.

In addition to subclassing `URLClassLoader`, `JarClassLoader` also makes use of features in two other new JAR-related APIs, the `java.util.jar` package and the `java.net.JarURLConnection` class. In this section, we'll look in detail at the constructor and two methods of `JarClassLoader`.

The JarClassLoader Constructor

The constructor takes an instance of `java.net.URL` as an argument. The URL passed to this constructor will be used elsewhere in `JarClassLoader` to find the JAR file from which classes are to be loaded:

```
public JarClassLoader(URL url) {
  super(new URL[] { url });
  this.url = url;
}
```

The `URL` object is passed to the constructor of the superclass, `URLClassLoader`, which takes a `URL[]` array, rather than a single `URL` instance, as an argument.

The getMainClassName Method

Once a `JarClassLoader` object is constructed with the URL of a JAR-bundled application, it's going to need a way to determine which class in the JAR file is the application's entry point. That's the job of the `getMainClassName` method:

20. `tutorial/deployment/jar/interfaces/examples/JarRunner.java`

21. `tutorial/deployment/jar/interfaces/examples/JarClassLoader.java`

```
public String getMainClassName() throws IOException {
  URL u = new URL("jar", "", url + "!/");
  JarURLConnection uc = (JarURLConnection)u.openConnection();
  Attributes attr = uc.getMainAttributes();
  return attr != null
    ? attr.getValue(Attributes.Name.MAIN_CLASS)
    : null;
}
```

You may recall from the JAR Files as Applications section (page 499) that a JAR-bundled application's entry point is specified by the `Main-Class` header of the JAR file's manifest. To understand how `getMainClassName` accesses the `Main-Class` header value, let's look at the method in detail, paying special attention to the new JAR-handling features that it uses.

The JarURLConnection Class and JAR URLs

The `getMainClassName` method uses the JAR URL format specified by the `java.net.JarURLConnection` class. The syntax for the URL of a JAR file is as in this example:

```
jar:http://www.xxx.yyy/jarfile.jar!/
```

The terminating `!/` separator indicates that the URL refers to an entire JAR file. Anything following the separator refers to specific JAR-file contents, as in this example:

```
jar:http://www.xxx.yyy/jarfile.jar!/mypackage/myclass.class
```

The first line in the `getMainClassName` method is:

```
URL u = new URL("jar", "", url + "!/");
```

This statement constructs a new `URL` object representing a JAR URL, appending the `!/` separator to the URL that was used in creating the `JarClassLoader` instance.

The java.net.JarURLConnection Class

This class represents a communications link between an application and a JAR file. It has methods for accessing the JAR file's manifest. The second line of `getMainClassName` is:

```
JarURLConnection uc = (JarURLConnection)u.openConnection();
```

In this statement, the `URL` instance created in the first line opens a `URLConnection`. The `URLConnection` instance is then cast to `JarURLConnection` so it can take advantage of `JarURLConnection`'s JAR-handling features.

Fetching Manifest Attributes: java.util.jar.Attributes

With a JarURLConnection open to a JAR file, you can access the header information in the JAR file's manifest by using the getMainAttributes method of JarURLConnection. This method returns an instance of java.util.jar.Attributes, a class that maps header names in JAR-file manifests with their associated string values. The third line in getMainClassName creates an Attributes object:

```
Attributes attr = uc.getMainAttributes();
```

To get the value of the manifest's Main-Class header, the fourth line of getMainClassName invokes the Attributes.getValue method:

```
return attr != null
  ? attr.getValue(Attributes.Name.MAIN_CLASS)
  : null;
```

The method's argument, Attributes.Name.MAIN_CLASS, specifies that it's the value of the Main-Class header that you want. (The Attributes.Name class also provides static fields such as MANIFEST_VERSION, CLASS_PATH, and SEALED for specifying other standard manifest headers.)

The invokeClass Method

We've seen how JarClassLoader can identify the main class in a JAR-bundled application. The last method to consider, JarClassLoader.invokeClass, enables that main class to be invoked to launch the JAR-bundled application:

```
public void invokeClass(String name, String[] args)
  throws ClassNotFoundException,
    NoSuchMethodException,
    InvocationTargetException
{
  Class c = loadClass(name);
  Method m = c.getMethod("main", new Class[]
                                    { args.getClass() });
  m.setAccessible(true);
  int mods = m.getModifiers();
  if (m.getReturnType() != void.class ||
    !Modifier.isStatic(mods) || !Modifier.isPublic(mods)) {
    throw new NoSuchMethodException("main");
  }
  try {
      m.invoke(null, new Object[] { args });
  } catch (IllegalAccessException e) {
  // This should not happen, as we have disabled access checks
  }
}
```

The `invokeClass` method takes two arguments: the name of the application's entry-point class and an array of string arguments to pass to the entry-point class's `main` method. First, the main class is loaded:

```
Class c = loadClass(name);
```

The `loadClass` method is inherited from `java.lang.ClassLoader`.

Once the main class is loaded, the reflection API of the `java.lang.reflect` package is used to pass the arguments to the class and launch it. You can refer to the tutorial "The Reflection API"[22] for a review of reflection.

The JarRunner Class

The JarRunner application is launched with a command of this form:

```
java JarRunner url [arguments]
```

In the previous section, we've seen how `JarClassLoader` is able to identify and load the main class of a JAR-bundled application from a given URL. To complete the JarRunner application, therefore, we need to be able to take a URL and any arguments from the command line, and pass them to an instance of `JarClassLoader`. These tasks belong to the `JarRunner` class, the entry point of the JarRunner application.

It begins by creating a `java.net.URL` object from the URL specified on the command line:

```
public static void main(String[] args) {
  if (args.length < 1) {
    usage();
  }
  URL url = null;
  try {
      url = new URL(args[0]);
  } catch (MalformedURLException e) {
      fatal("Invalid URL: " + args[0]);
  }
  ...
```

If `args.length < 1`, that means no URL was specified on the command line, so a usage message is printed. If the first command-line argument is a good URL, a new `URL` object is created to represent it.

22. `tutorial/reflect/index.html`

Next, JarRunner creates a new instance of JarClassLoader, passing to the constructor the URL that was specified on the command-line:

```
JarClassLoader cl = new JarClassLoader(url);
```

As we saw in the previous section, it's through JarClassLoader that JarRunner taps into the JAR-handling APIs.

The URL that's passed to the JarClassLoader constructor is the URL of the JAR-bundled application that you want to run. JarRunner next calls the class loader's getMainClassName method to identify the entry-point class for the application:

```
String name = null;
try {
    name = cl.getMainClassName();
} catch (IOException e) {
    System.err.println("I/O error while loading JAR file:");
    e.printStackTrace();
    System.exit(1);
}
if (name == null) {
    fatal("Specified jar file does not " +
          "contain a 'Main-Class' manifest attribute");
}
```

The key statement is highlighted in bold. The other statements are for error handling.

Once JarRunner has identified the application's entry-point class, only two steps remain: passing any arguments to the application and actually launching the application. JarRunner performs these steps with this code:

```
// Get arguments for the application
String[] newArgs = new String[args.length - 1];
System.arraycopy(args, 1, newArgs, 0, newArgs.length);
// Invoke application's main class
try {
    cl.invokeClass(name, newArgs);
} catch (ClassNotFoundException e) {
    fatal("Class not found: " + name);
} catch (NoSuchMethodException e) {
    fatal("Class does not define a 'main' method: " + name);
} catch (InvocationTargetException e) {
    e.getTargetException().printStackTrace();
    System.exit(1);
}
```

Recall that the first command-line argument was the URL of the JAR-bundled application. Any arguments to be passed to that application are therefore in element 1 and beyond in the args array. JarRunner takes those elements and creates a new array called newArgs to pass to the application (bold line above). JarRunner then passes the entry-point's class name and the new argument list to the invokeClass method of JarClassLoader. As we saw in the previous section, invokeClass will load the application's entry-point class, pass it any arguments, and launch the application.

Questions: JAR Files

Questions

1. How do you invoke an applet that is packaged as a JAR file?
2. What is the purpose of the -e option in a jar command?
3. What is the significance of the manifest in a JAR file?
4. How do you modify a JAR's manifest file?

Answers

You can find answers to these Questions at:

```
tutorial/deployment/jar/QandE/answers.html
```

17

Java Web Start

JAVA Web Start provides the power to launch full-featured applications with a single click. Users can download and launch applications, such as a complete spreadsheet program or an Internet chat client, without going through complicated installation procedures.

With Java Web Start, the user can launch a Java application by clicking a link in a Web page. The link points to a `JNLP` file, which instructs Java Web Start to download, cache, and run the application.

Java Web Start provides Java developers and users with many deployment advantages:

- With Java Web Start, you can place a single Java application on a Web server for deployment to a wide variety of platforms, including Windows 2003/Vista/2000/XP, Linux, and Solaris.
- Java Web Start supports multiple, simultaneous versions of the Java Standard Edition platform. Specific applications can request specific Java versions without conflicting with the different needs of other applications. Java Web Start automatically downloads and installs the correct version of the Java platform as necessary based on the application's needs and the user's environment.
- Users can launch a Java Web Start application independent of a Web browser. The user can be offline or unable to access the browser. Desktop shortcuts can also launch the application, providing the user with the same experience as a native application.

- Java Web Start takes advantage of the inherent security of the Java platform. By default, applications have restricted access to local disk and network resources. Users can safely run applications from sources that are not trusted.
- Applications launched with Java Web Start are cached locally, for improved performance.
- Java Web Start provides limited support for applets through its built-in applet viewer. However, this is not intended to be a full-scale applet environment, such as the one provided by Java Plug-in. Java Web Start's applet viewer has certain limitations; for example, you cannot specify class files as resources, and it does not accept policy files.

In Java version 1.4.2 and beyond, Java Web Start is installed as part of the JRE. Users do not have to install it separately or perform additional tasks to use Java Web Start applications.

This chapter is intended to get you started with Java Web Start and does not include all available documentation. For more information about Java Web Start, see the following:

- Java Web Start Guide[1]
- Java Web Start FAQ[2]
- JNLP Specification[3]
- `javax.jnlp` API Documentation[4]
- Java Web Start Developers Site[5]

Running Java Web Start Applications

Users can run Java Web Start applications in the following ways:

- Running a Java Web Start application from a browser
- Running an application from the Java Cache Viewer
- Running a Java Web Start application from the desktop

---

1. `docs/technotes/guides/javaws/developersguide/contents.html`
2. `docs/technotes/guides/javaws/developersguide/faq.html`
3. `http://jcp.org/en/jsr/detail?id=56`
4. `docs/jre/api/javaws/jnlp/index.html`
5. `http://java.sun.com/products/javawebstart/developers.html`

Note: Users of applications deployed with Java Web Start must have a compatible version of the Java Runtime Environment (JRE). The complete JDK is not required.

Running a Java Web Start Application from a Browser

You run an application with Java Web Start from a browser simply by clicking a link to the application's JNLP file, such as:

```
<a href="Notepad.jnlp">Launch Notepad Application</a>
```

Java Web Start then loads and runs the application based on instructions in the JNLP file.

Running an Application from the Java Cache Viewer

If you are using Java Version 1.6.0, you can run a Java Web Start application through the Java Cache Viewer.

When Java Web Start first loads an application, information from the application's JNLP file is stored in the local Java Cache Viewer. To launch the application again, you do not need to return to the Web page where you first launched it; you can simply open the Java Cache Viewer.

To open the Java Cache Viewer:

1. Open the Control Panel.
2. Double-click on the Java icon. The Java Control Panel opens.
3. Select the **General** tab.
4. Click **View**. The Java Cache Viewer opens.

The application is listed in the viewer as shown in Figure 17.1.

To run the application, select it and click the Run button, , or double-click the application. The application starts just as it did from the Web page.

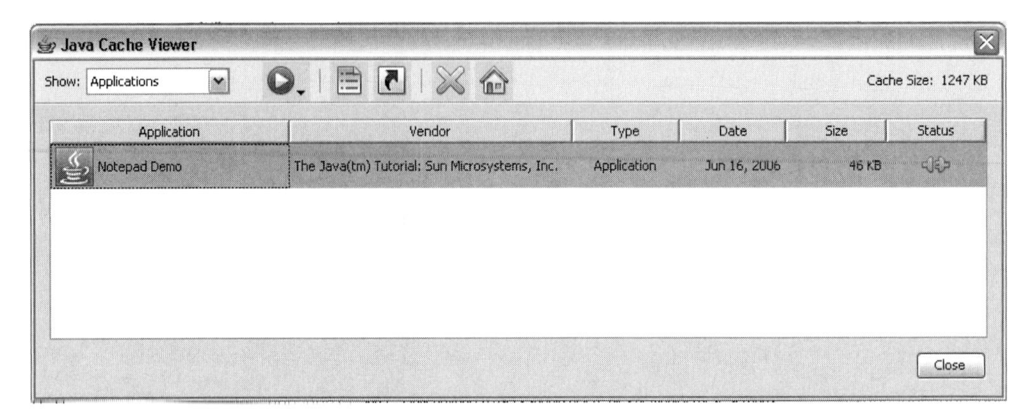

Figure 17.1 Java Cache Viewer application.

Running a Java Web Start Application from the Desktop

Through the Java Cache Viewer, you can add a shortcut to the application to your desktop. Simply select the application, right-click and select **Install Shortcuts**, or click the Install button, . A shortcut is then added to the desktop as shown in Figure 17.2.

Figure 17.2 A shortcut to Notepad Demo application.

You can then launch the Java Web Start application just as you would any native application.

Deploying Java Web Start Applications

This section describes the basics of deploying an application using Java Web Start. Deploying an application involves the following steps:

1. Setting up the Web server
2. Creating the JNLP file

3. Placing the application on the Web server
4. Creating the Web page

This section uses the Notepad example application to demonstrate Java Web Start technology. You can find all the source files for the Notepad application example in the `\demo\plugin\jfc\Notepad` directory within the JDK installation directory.

Setting Up the Web Server

Before you can deploy an application with Java Web Start over the Web, you must ensure that the Web server you are using can handle JNLP files.

Configure the Web server so that files with the `.jnlp` extension are set to the `application/x-java-jnlp-file` MIME type.

How you set the JNLP MIME type depends on the Web server you are using. For example, for the Apache Web server, you simply add the line:

```
application/x-java-jnlp-file JNLP
```

to the `mime.types` file.

For other Web servers, check the documentation for instructions on setting MIME types.

Creating the JNLP File

The key to running an application with Java Web Start is the Java Network Launching Protocol, or JNLP, file. The JNLP file is an XML file that contains elements and attributes that tell Java Web Start how to run the application.

An Example JNLP File

Following is the JNLP file for the Notepad demo:[6]

6. `docs/books/tutorialJWS/deployment/webstart/ex5/Notepad.jnlp`

```
<?xml version="1.0" encoding="utf-8"?>
<!-- JNLP File for Notepad -->

<jnlp spec="1.0+"
      codebase="http://java.sun.com/docs/books/
                tutorialJWS/deployment/webstart/ex5/"
      href="Notepad.jnlp">
  <information>
    <title>Notepad Demo</title>
    <vendor>
      The Java(tm) Tutorial: Sun Microsystems, Inc.
    </vendor>
    <description>Notepad Demo</description>
    <homepage href="http://java.sun.com/docs/books/
                tutorial/deployment/webstart/running.html"/>
    <description kind="short">
      ClickMeApp uses 3 custom classes plus several
      standard ones
    </description>
    <offline-allowed/>
  </information>
  <resources>
    <jar href="Notepad.jar"/>
   <j2se version="1.3+"
         href="http://java.sun.com/products/autodl/j2se"/>
  </resources>
  <application-desc main-class="Notepad"/>
</jnlp>
```

JNLP File Contents

Table 17.1 describes the elements and attributes in the sample JNLP file.

Note: This table does not include all possible contents of the JNLP file. For more information, see the Java Network Launching Protocol & API Specification (JSR-56).[7]

---

7. http://java.sun.com/products/javawebstart/download-spec.html

Table 17.1 Elements and Attributes of a JNLP File

Element	Attributes	Description	Since	Required
`jnlp`		This is the main xml element for a JNLP file. Everything is contained within the jnlp element.	1.0	yes
	`spec`	The `spec` attribute can be 1.0, 1.5.0, or 1.6.0, or can use the wildcards such as 1.0+. It denotes the minimum version of the JNLP Specification that this JNLP file can work with.	1.0	
	`codebase`	The `codebase` attribute specifies the base location for all relative URLs specified in href attributes in the JNLP file.	1.0	
	`href`	The `href` specifies the URL of the JNLP file itself.	1.0	
	`version`	The version of the application being launched, as well as the version of the JNLP file itself.	1.0	
`information`		The `information` element contains other elements that describe the application and its source.	1.0	yes
	`os`	Specifies the operating system for which this information element should be considered.	1.5.0	
	`arch`	Specifies the architecture for which this information element should be considered.	1.5.0	
	`platform`	Specifies the platform for which this information element should be considered.	1.5.0	
	`locale`	Specifies the locale for which this information element should be considered.	1.5.0	
`title`		The `title` element specifies the title of the application.	1.0	yes
`vendor`		The `vendor` element specifies the provider of the application.	1.0	yes
`homepage`		The homepage of the application.	1.0	

(continues)

Table 17.1 Elements and Attributes of a JNLP File *(Continued)*

Element	Attributes	Description	Since	Required
	href	A URL pointing to where more information on this application can be found.	1.0	yes
description		A short statement describing the application.	1.0	
	kind	An indicator as to what type of description this is; legal values are one-line, short, and tooltip.	1.0	
icon		Describes an icon that can be used to identify the application to the user.	1.0	
	href	A URL pointing to the icon file; may be in one of the following formats: gif, jpg, png, ico.	1.0	yes
	kind	Indicates the suggested use of the icon; can be default, selected, disabled, rollover, splash, or shortcut.	1.0	
	width	Can be used to indicate the resolution of the image.	1.0	
	height	Can be used to indicate the resolution of the image.	1.0	
	depth	Can be used to indicate the resolution of the image.	1.0	
offline-allowed		Indicates that this application can operate when the client system is disconnected from the network.	1.0	
shortcut		The shortcut element can be used to indicate an application's preferences for desktop integration.	1.5.0	
	online	Can be used to describe the application's preference for creating a shortcut to run online or offline.	1.5.0	
desktop		Can be used to indicate an application's preference for putting a shortcut on the user's desktop.	1.5.0	
menu		Can be used to indicate an application's preference for putting a menu item in the user's start menus.	1.5.0	

(continues)

Table 17.1 Elements and Attributes of a JNLP File *(Continued)*

Element	Attributes	Description	Since	Required
	sub-menu	Can be used to indicate an application's preference for where to place the menu item.	1.5.0	
association		Can be used to hint to the JNLP client that it wishes to be registered with the operating system as the primary handler of certain extensions and a certain mime-type.	1.5.0	
	extensions	Contains a list of file extensions (separated by spaces) that the application requests it be registered to handle.	1.5.0	
	mime-type	Contains the mime-type that the application requests it be registered to handle.	1.5.0	
related-content		Describes an additional piece of related content that may be integrated with the application.	1.5.0	
	href	A URL pointing to the related content.	1.5.0	yes
update		The update element is used to indicate the preferences for how application updates should be handled by the JNLP client.	1.6.0	
	check	Indicates the preference for when the JNLP client should check for updates. It can be always, timeout, or background.	1.6.0	
	policy	Indicates the preference for how the JNLP client should handle an application update when it is known that an update is available before the application is launched. It can be always, prompt-update, or prompt-run.	1.6.0	
security		This element can be used to request enhanced permissions.	1.0	
all-permissions		Requests that the application be run with all permissions.	1.0	

(continues)

Table 17.1 Elements and Attributes of a JNLP File *(Continued)*

Element	Attributes	Description	Since	Required
j2ee-application-client-permissions		Requests that the application be run with a permission set that meets the security specifications of the J2EE Application Client environment.	1.0	
resources		Describes all the resources that are needed for an application.	1.0	yes
	os	Specifies the operating system for which the resources element should be considered.	1.0	
	arch	Specifies the architecture for which the resources element should be considered.	1.0	
	locale	Specifies that the locales for which the resources element should be considered.		
java (or java se)		Specifies what version(s) of Java to run the application with.	1.6.0 (java)	
	version	Describes an ordered list of version ranges to use.	1.0	yes
	href	The URL denoting the supplier of this version of java and where it may be downloaded from.	1.0	
	java-vm-args	Indicates an additional set of standard and nonstandard virtual machine arguments that the application would prefer the JNLP client to use when launching Java.	1.0	
	initial-heap-size	Indicates the initial size of the Java heap.	1.0	
	max-heap-size	Indicates the maximum size of the Java heap.	1.0	
jar		Specifies a JAR file that is part of the application's classpath.	1.0	yes
	href	The URL of the JAR file.	1.0	yes
	version	The requested version of the JAR file. Requires using the version-based download protocol.	1.0	
	main	Indicates whether this jar contains the class containing the main method of the application.	1.0	

(continues)

Table 17.1 Elements and Attributes of a JNLP File *(Continued)*

Element	Attributes	Description	Since	Required
	download	Can be used to indicate that this jar may be downloaded lazily, or when needed.	1.0	
	size	Indicates the downloadable size of the JAR file in bytes.	1.0	
	part	Can be used to group resources together so they will be downloaded at the same time.	1.0	
nativelib		Specifies a JAR file that contains native libraries in its root directory.	1.0	
	href	The URL of the JAR file.	1.0	yes
	version	The requested version of the JAR file. Requires using the version-based download protocol.	1.0	
	download	Can be used to indicate this jar may be downloaded lazily.	1.0	
	size	Indicates the downloadable size of the JAR file in bytes.	1.0	
	part	Can be used to group resources together so they will be downloaded at the same time.	1.0	
extension		Contains pointer to an additional component-desc or installer-desc to be used with this application.	1.0	
	href	The URL to the additional extension JNLP file.	1.0	yes
	version	The version of the additional extension JNLP file.	1.0	
	name	The name of the additional extension JNLP file.	1.0	
ext-download		Can be used in an extension element to denote the parts contained in a component-extension.	1.0	
	ext-part	Describes the name of a part that can be expected to be found in the extension.	1.0	yes
	download	Can be used to indicate that this extension may be downloaded eagerly or lazily.	1.0	

(continues)

Table 17.1 Elements and Attributes of a JNLP File *(Continued)*

Element	Attributes	Description	Since	Required
	`part`	Denotes the name of a part in this JNLP file to include the extension in.	1.0	
`package`		Can be used to indicate to the JNLP client which packages are implemented in which JAR files.	1.0	
	`name`	Package name contained in the JAR files of the given part.	1.0	yes
	`part`	Part name containing the JAR files that include the given package name.	1.0	yes
	`recursive`	Can be used to indicate that all package names, beginning with the given name, can be found in the given part.	1.0	
`property`		Defines a system property that will be available through the `System.getProperty` and `System.getProperties` methods.	1.0	
	`name`	Name of the system property.	1.0	yes
	`value`	Value it will be set to.	1.0	yes
		Note: A JNLP file must contain one of `application-desc`, `applet-desc`, `component-desc`, or `installer-desc`.	1.0	yes
`application-desc`		Denotes this is the JNLP file for an application.	1.0	
	`main-class`	The name of the class containing the `public static void main(String[])` method of the application.	1.0	yes
`argument`		Each argument contains (in order) an additional argument to be passed to main.	1.0	
`applet-desc`		Denotes this is the JNLP file for an applet.	1.0	
	`main-class`	This is the name of the main applet class.	1.0	yes
	`documentbase`	The document base for the applet as a URL.	1.0	
	`name`	Name of the applet.	1.0	yes
	`width`	The width of the applet in pixels.	1.0	yes

(continues)

Table 17.1 Elements and Attributes of a JNLP File *(Continued)*

Element	Attributes	Description	Since	Required
	`height`	The height of the applet in pixels.	1.0	yes
`param`		A set of parameters that can be passed into the applet.	1.0	
	`name`	The name of this parameter.	1.0	yes
	`value`	The value of this parameter.	1.0	yes
`component-desc`		Denotes this is the JNLP file for a component extension.	1.0	
`installer-desc`		Denotes this is the JNLP file for an installed extension.	1.0	
	`main-class`	The name of the class containing the `public static void main(String[])` method of the installer.	1.0	yes

Encoding JNLP Files

Java Web Start supports encoding of JNLP files in any character encoding supported by the Java platform. For more information on character encoding in Java, see the Supported Encodings Guide.[8] To encode a JNLP file, specify an encoding in the XML prolog of that file. For example, the following line indicates that the JNLP file is encoded in UTF-16:

```
<?xml version="1.0" encoding="utf-16"?>
```

Note: The XML prolog itself must be UTF-8-encoded.

Placing the Application on the Web Server

The next step in deploying your application with Java Web Start is as simple as placing all the application's JAR files and the JNLP file on the Web server. You must ensure the JAR files are in the locations specified by the `href` attribute of the `jar` element in the JNLP file.

8. `docs/technotes/guides/intl/encoding.doc.html`

Creating the Web Page

Once you've completed the preceding steps, you are ready to write a Web page that gives users access to your application. Adding a link to your application in a Web page for users with Java Web Start already installed is simple; however, you must also design your Web page for users that might not have Java Web Start installed.

Adding the Basic Link to the JNLP File

In order to enable your users to launch the application from a Web page, you must include a link to the application's JNLP file from that Web page. To add this link, you use the standard HTML link syntax, with the `href` attribute specifying the location of the JNLP file:

```
<a href="Notepad.jnlp">Launch Notepad Application</a>
```

Assuming Java Web Start is installed on the client computer, when the user clicks this link, Java Web Start executes the application based on the instructions in the JNLP file.

Adding the Link When Java Web Start Is Not Installed

For users who might not have Java Web Start installed, you must write scripts in your Web page to:

1. Detect which browser the user has.
2. Detect whether Java Web Start is installed.
3. If Java Web Start is not installed, either auto-install it or direct the user to a download page.

For more information and sample scripts to use for these steps, see the Java Web Start Guide.

Developing Java Web Start Applications

For the most part, you develop applications to be deployed through Java Web Start just as you would develop stand-alone Java applications. However, there are some packaging considerations, which are described in the following sections.

Packaging the Application in JAR Files

To deploy an application with Java Web Start, you must package the application as one or more JAR files. In particular, you must package the application's files into one or more JAR files.

Note: Other resources such as images and property files can, if necessary, be outside of JAR files and retrieved using HTTP requests. However, storing resources in JAR files is preferred, because JAR files are cached on the local computer by Java Web Start.

If the application needs unrestricted access to the local system, all JAR files and entries must be signed. For more information, see the Java Web Start and Security section (page 538).

Reading Resources in a JAR File

Use the `getResource` method to read resources from a JAR file. For example, the following code example retrieves images from a JAR file:

```
// Get current classloader
ClassLoader cl = this.getClass().getClassLoader();
// Create icons
Icon saveIcon  = new
                 ImageIcon(cl.getResource("images/save.gif"));
Icon cutIcon   = new
                 ImageIcon(cl.getResource("images/cut.gif"));
```

The example assumes that the following entries exist in the JAR files for the application:

- `images/save.gif`
- `images/cut.gif`

Untrusted Applications

Unless you sign your application's JAR files, which requires users to accept your certificate, your application deployed through Java Web Start is untrusted. Untrusted applications have the following restrictions:

- The application cannot access the local disk.
- All JAR files for the application must be downloaded from the same server.
- The application can only make network connections to the server from which the JAR files were downloaded.
- A security manager cannot be removed or replaced.
- The application cannot use native libraries.
- The application has limited access to system properties. The application has read/write access to a set of system properties known to be secure and read-only access to the same set of properties as an applet.

For more information, see the Java Web Start and Security section (page 538).

Also, see the next section for information on using the special Java Web Start packages in your applications.

The JNLP API

The Java platform includes the JNLP API to enable you to provide additional information to applications deployed through Java Web Start.

The JNLP API is included in the `javax.jnlp` package, which is delivered in the `jnlp.jar` as part of the Java Development Kit version 6, in the `sample/jnlp/servlet` directory. The `javax.jnlp` package is also delivered in the `javaws.jar`, which is located in the JRE's `lib` directory.

Table 17.2 provides an overview of the main interfaces and classes in the `javax.jnlp` package. For more information, see the API documentation and the Java Web Start Guide.

Warning: Java Web Start warns users of the `javax.jnlp` interfaces and classes about the potential security risk of allowing an untrusted application to access the file system, use the system printer, use the system clipboard, or increase the disk space used by the `PersistenceService`.

Table 17.2 Interfaces and Classes in the `javax.jnlp` Package

Interface or Class	Description
`BasicService`	Provides methods for: • Determining the codebase of the application • Determining whether the application is online or not • Determining whether a Web browser is supported on the current platform and by the JNLP client • Opening a specific URL in the browser
`ClipboardService`	Provides methods for copying contents to and from the client system's clipboard. The `ClipboardService` interface works for applications running in a sandbox.
`DownloadService`	Provides the ability to control how the application's resources are cached.

(continues)

Table 17.2 Interfaces and Classes in the `javax.jnlp` Package *(Continued)*

Interface or Class	Description
`ExtendedService`	Provides additional support to the current JNLP API. It allows applications to open specific file(s) in the client's file system.
`FileContents`	Encapsulates the name and contents of a file. An object of this class is used by the `FileOpenService`, `FileSaveService`, and `PersistenceService` interfaces.
`FileOpenService`	Provides the ability for applications to open files on the local file system.
`FileSaveService`	Provides methods for exporting files to the local disk, even for applications that are running in the restricted execution environment. **Note:** This interface provides the same level of disk access to potentially untrusted Web-deployed applications that a Web browser provides for content it displays through its Save As dialog box.
`JNLPRandomAccessFile`	Supports reading from and writing to a random-access file. A random-access file behaves like a large array of bytes stored in the file system.
`PersistenceService`	Provides methods for storing data locally on the client system, even for applications that are running in a sandbox. **Note:** This service is similar to the cookie mechanism for HTML-based applications. Cookies allow a small amount of data to be stored locally on the client system. That data can be securely managed by the browser and can only be retrieved by HTML pages that originate from the same URL as the page that stored the data.
`PrintService`	Provides methods for access to printing, even for applications that are running in the restricted execution environment. **Note:** Starting with Java Web Start 5.0, you can use the Java Printing APIs, so there is no need to use this interface. If the application is running in a sandbox, Java Web Start opens a security dialog box asking the user for permission to print.
`SingleInstanceService`	Provides a set of methods for applications to register themselves as singletons, and to register listener(s) for handling arguments passed in from different instances of applications.

Java Web Start and Security

This section describes the basics of security for applications deployed through Java Web Start.

Java Web Start Security Basics

Applications launched with Java Web Start are, by default, run in a restricted environment, known as a *sandbox*. In this sandbox, Java Web Start:

- Protects users against malicious code that could affect local files
- Protects enterprises against code that could attempt to access or destroy data on networks

Unsigned JAR files launched by Java Web Start remain in this sandbox, meaning they cannot access local files or the network.

Signing JAR Files for Java Web Start Deployment

Java Web Start supports signed JAR files so that your application can work outside of the sandbox described above, enabling the application to access local files and the network.

Java Web Start verifies that the contents of the JAR file have not changed since it was signed. If verification of a digital signature fails, Java Web Start does not run the application.

When the user first runs an application as a signed JAR file, Java Web Start opens a dialog box displaying the application's origin based on the signer's certificate. The user can then make an informed decision regarding running the application.

For more information, see the Signing and Verifying JAR Files section (page 507).

Security and JNLP Files

For a signed JAR file to have access to the local file system and network, you must specify security settings in the JNLP file. The `security` element contains security settings for the application.

The following example provides the application with complete access to the client system if all of its JAR files are signed:

```
<security>
  <all-permissions/>
</security>
```

Dynamic Downloading of HTTPS Certificates

Java Web Start dynamically imports certificates as browsers typically do. To do this, Java Web Start sets its own `https` handler, using the `java.protocol.handler.pkgs` system properties, to initialize defaults for the `SSLSocketFactory`[9] and `HostnameVerifier`.[10] It sets the defaults with the methods `HttpsURLConnection.setDefaultSSLSocketFactory`[11] and `HttpsURLConnection.setDefaultHostnameVerifier`.

If your application uses these two methods, ensure that they are invoked after the Java Web Start initializes the `https` handler, otherwise your custom handler will be replaced by the Java Web Start default handler.

You can ensure that your own customized `SSLSocketFactory` and `HostnameVerifiter` are used by doing one of the following:

- Install your own `https` handler to replace the Java Web Start `https` handler. For more information, see the document *A New Era for Java Protocol Handlers*.[12]
- In your application, invoke `HttpsURLConnection.setDefaultSSLSocketFactory` or `HttpsURLConnection.setDefaultHostnameVerifier` only after the first `https URL` object is created, which executes the Java Web Start `https` handler initialization code first.

Common Java Web Start Problems

Problem: My browser shows the JNLP file for my application as plain text. Most likely, your Web server is not aware of the proper MIME type for JNLP files. See the Setting Up the Web Server section (page 525) for more information.

Furthermore, if you are using a proxy server, ensure that the update versions of the files are returned by updating the time stamp of the resources on the Web server such that the proxies will update their caches.

Problem: When I click on a link to a JNLP file with Internet Explorer and Java Web Start launches, I get the message "Could not load file/URL specified: C:\Documents and Settings\ . . . \application[1].jnlp". This problem only occurs with Internet Explorer. It is usually caused by a no-cache directive from the

9. `docs/api/javax/net/ssl/SSLSocketFactory.html`

10. `docs/api/javax/net/ssl/HostnameVerifier.html`

11. `docs/api/javax/net/ssl/HttpsURLConnection.html`

12. `http://java.sun.com/developer/onlineTraining/protocolhandlers/`

Web or proxy server, which causes Internet Explorer to not write the JNLP file to the local disk.

This frequently happens when you upgrade a Tomcat-based server, as later versions set the no-cache directive by default for any resource that is within a security constraint in the `web.xml` file. Try removing the relevant URI from the security constraint.

This problem can also occur because of a full cache or if the cache is turned off in Internet Explorer.

Problem: My browser seems to find the JNLP file, but Java Web Start says it can't find it. The most likely cause is that your browser and Java Web Start have different proxy settings. To modify Java Web Start proxy settings:

1. Open the Java Application Cache Viewer.
2. From the **Edit** menu, select **Preferences**. The Java Control Panel opens.
3. Click **Network Settings**. The **Network Settings** dialog box opens.
4. Select **Use proxy server**, enter the proxy server name and port number (typically 8080).
5. Click **OK**.

Questions and Exercises: Java Web Start

Questions

1. In a link that is to run a Java Web Start application, which file is specified as the `a` tag's `href` attribute?
2. Which MIME type must a Web server recognize in order for it to host Java Web Start applications?
3. In an application's `JNLP` file, which two elements must be specified within the `resources` element?
4. Which interface provides the ability to control how the Java Web Start application's resources are cached?
   a. `BasicService`
   b. `DownloadService`
   c. `PersistenceService`
   d. `ExtendedService`
5. True or False: Java Web Start applications run in a secure sandbox by default.

6. True or False: If a Java Web Start application is running in a secure sandbox, JAR files for the application can reside on different servers.
7. For a Java Web Start application to support operations outside of the secure sandbox, what must you do with its JAR files?

Exercises

1. Write the XML code you would add to a `JNLP` file in order to request that the application have complete access to the client system.
2. For a Java Web Start application, you have two icons, `one.gif` and `two.gif`, in the `images` directory in a JAR file. Write the application code you would use to access these images.

Answers

You can find answers to these Questions and Exercises at:

```
tutorial/deployment/webstart/QandE/answers.html
```

18

Applets

THIS chapter talks about the basics of applets, advantages of applets over applications, how to load applets in a Web page, how to convert applications to applets, and how applets work.

An applet is a special kind of Java program that a browser enabled with Java technology can download from the Internet and run. An applet is typically embedded inside a Web page and runs in the context of the browser. An applet must be a subclass of the `java.applet.Applet` class, which provides the standard interface between the applet and the browser environment.

Swing provides a special subclass of Applet, called `javax.swing.JApplet`, which should be used for all applets that use Swing components to construct their GUIs.

By calling certain methods, a browser manages an applet's life cycle if an applet is loaded in a Web page.

• Life Cycle of an Applet

Basically, there are four methods in the `Applet` class on which any applet is built:

`init` This method is intended for whatever initialization is needed for your applet. It is called after the param attributes of the applet tag.

`start` This method is automatically called after init method. It is also called whenever user returns to the page containing the applet after visiting other pages.

`stop` This method is automatically called whenever the user moves away from the page containing applets. You can use this method to stop an animation.

`destroy` This method is only called when the browser shuts down normally.

Thus, the applet can be initialized once and only once, started and stopped one or more times in its life, and destroyed once and only once.

For more information, please refer to The Life Cycle of an Applet section (page 547).

• When to Write Applets versus Applications

In the early days of Java, one of the critical advantages that Java applets had over Java applications was that applets could be easily deployed over the Web while Java applications required a more cumbersome installation process. Additionally, since applets are downloaded from the Internet, by default they have to run in a restricted security environment, called the "sandbox," to ensure they don't perform any destructive operations on the user's computer, such as reading/writing to the filesystem.

However, the introduction of Java Web Start (see Chapter 17) has made it possible for Java applications to also be easily deployed over the Web, as well as run in a secure environment. This means that the predominant difference between a Java applet and a Java application is that an applet runs in the context of a Web browser, being typically embedded within an HTML page, while a Java application runs stand-alone, outside the browser. Thus, applets are particularly well suited for providing functions in a Web page that require more interactivity or animation than HTML can provide, such as a graphical game, complex editing, or interactive data visualization. The end user is able to access the functionality without leaving the browser.

• Loading Applets in a Web Page

In order to load an applet in a Web page, you must specify the applet class with appropriate applet tags. A simple example is below:

```
<applet code=AppletWorld.class width="200" height="200">
</applet>
```

For development and testing purposes, you can run your applet using the lightweight `appletviewer` application that comes with the JDK. For example, if `AppletWorld.html` is the HTML file name, then you run the command as:

```
appletviewer AppletWorld.html
```

Once you know your applet runs within the `appletviewer`, it is important to test your applet running in a Web browser by loading the applet's Web page into the browser window. The browser can retrieve the class files either from the Internet or from the local working directory used during development. If you make changes to your applet's code while it is loaded in the browser, then you must recompile the applet and press the **Shift + Reload** button in the browser to load the new version.

This chapter is intended to get you started with applets and Java Plug-in, and it does not include all available documentation. For more information about applets, see the Java Plug-in Developer Guide.[1]

Getting Started with Applets

Run the HelloWorld applet[2] in the online tutorial or compile and run the applet yourself (Figure 18.1). It is a simple Java class that prints the string "Hello World" in small rectangle.

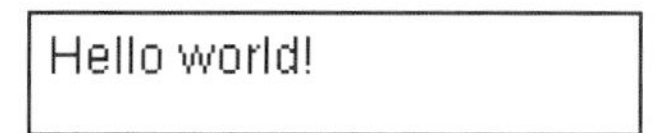

Figure 18.1 A screenshot of the HelloWorld applet.

Following is the source code for the HelloWorld applet:[3]

```
import javax.swing.JApplet;
import java.awt.Graphics;

public class HelloWorld extends JApplet {
  public void paint(Graphics g) {
    g.drawRect(0, 0,
               getSize().width - 1,
               getSize().height - 1);
    g.drawString("Hello world!", 5, 15);
  }
}
```

An applet such as this is typically managed and run by Java Plug-in. *Java Plug-in*, which is automatically included when you download the Java SE Runtime Environment (JRE), extends the functionality of a Web browser, allowing applets to be run under Sun's Java SE Runtime Environment (JRE) rather than the Java Runtime Environment that comes with the Web browser. It works with the Mozilla family of browsers and with Internet Explorer.

---

1. `docs/technotes/guides/plugin/developer_guide/contents.html`
2. `tutorial/deployment/applet/examples/helloWorld.jar`
3. `tutorial/deployment/applet/examples/HelloWorld.java`

• Converting Applications to Applets

An application is a stand-alone program consisting of at least one class with a `main` method. Applets differ significantly from applications. First, applets do not have a `main` method that is automatically called to begin the program. Instead, several methods are called at different points in the execution of an applet. The difference between Java applets and applications lies in how they are run. Applications are usually run by loading the application's main class file with a Java interpreter, such as the java tool in the JDK 6.

The basic steps to follow to convert an application program into an applet program are:

- You need to create a subclass of `java.applet.Applet` in which you override the `init` method to initialize your applet's resources the same way the `main` method initializes the application's resources.
- `init` might be called more than once and should be designed accordingly. Moreover, the top-level `Panel` needs to be added to the applet in `init`; usually it was added to a Frame in `main`. That's it!

You will understand how to convert an application program into an applet by going through a sample application program `SwingUI.java`[4] and its corresponding applet program.[5]

When you compare these two programs, you may come up with the following major differences between the two:

- The applet class is declared `public` so `appletviewer` can access it.
- The applet class descends from `Applet/JApplet`, and the application class descends from `Frame/JFrame`.
- The applet version has no `main` method.
- The application constructor is replaced in the applet by `start` and `init` methods.
- GUI components are added directly to the `Applet`, whereas in an application, GUI components are added to the content pane of its `JFrame` object.

Extending Applet or JApplet

The first bold line of the following listing begins a block that defines the `HelloWorld` class:

4. `tutorial/deployment/applet/SwingUI.java`
5. `tutorial/deployment/applet/ApptoAppl.java`

```
import javax.swing.JApplet;
import java.awt.Graphics;

public class HelloWorld extends JApplet {
  public void paint(Graphics g) {
    g.drawRect(0, 0,
               getSize().width - 1,
               getSize().height - 1);
    g.drawString("Hello world!", 5, 15);
  }
}
```

Applets inherit a great deal of functionality from the `Applet` or `JApplet` class, including the abilities to communicate with the browser and to present a graphical user interface (GUI) to the user.

An applet that will be using GUI components from Swing (Java's GUI toolkit) should extend the `javax.swing.JApplet` base class, which provides the best integration with Swing's GUI facilities.

`JApplet` provides the same "RootPane" top-level component structure as Swing's `JFrame` and `JDialog` components, whereas `Applet` provides just a simple panel. See *How to Use Root Panes*[6] for more details on how to utilize this feature.

An applet may extend `java.applet.Applet` when it makes no use of Swing's GUI components. This may be the case if the applet does all its own rendering using the Java graphics libraries (such as with graphing or gaming) and/or uses only AWT components.

The Life Cycle of an Applet

Run the `Simple` applet[7] (Figure 18.2).

initializing... starting...

Figure 18.2 A screenshot of the Simple applet.

The following is the source code for the `Simple`.[8] The `Simple` applet displays a descriptive string whenever it encounters a major milestone in its life, such as when the user first visits the page that the applet is on. The pages that follow use the `Simple` applet

6. `tutorial/uiswing/components/rootpane.html`

7. `tutorial/deployment/applet/examples/simple.jar`

8. `tutorial/deployment/applet/examples/Simple.java`

and build upon it to illustrate concepts that are common to many applets. If you find yourself baffled by the Java source code, you might want to go to Chapter 2 to learn about the language.

```
/*
 * Java SE 6 Version
 */

import java.applet.Applet;
import java.awt.Graphics;

// No need to extend JApplet, since we don't add
// any components; we just paint.
public class Simple extends Applet {

  StringBuffer buffer;

  public void init() {
    buffer = new StringBuffer();
    addItem("initializing... ");
  }

  public void start() {
    addItem("starting... ");
  }

  public void stop() {
    addItem("stopping... ");
  }

  public void destroy() {
    addItem("preparing for unloading...");
  }

  private void addItem(String newWord) {
    System.out.println(newWord);
    buffer.append(newWord);
    repaint();
  }

  public void paint(Graphics g) {
    // Draw a Rectangle around the applet's display area.
    g.drawRect(0, 0,
    getWidth() - 1,
    getHeight() - 1);

    // Draw the current string inside the rectangle.
    g.drawString(buffer.toString(), 5, 15);
  }
}
```

Note: In this example, we extend the `Applet` class, not the Swing `JApplet` class, as we do not need to add Swing components to this applet.

Loading the Applet

You should see "initializing . . . starting . . . " above, as the result of the applet being loaded. When an applet is loaded, here's what happens:

- An instance of the applet's controlling class (an `Applet` subclass) is created.
- The applet *initializes* itself.
- The applet *starts* running.

Leaving and Returning to the Applet's Page

When the user leaves the page—for example, to go to another page—the browser *stops* the applet. When the user returns to the page, the browser *starts* the applet.

Browser Note: Some browsers reload the applet when you return to its page. In at least one browser, a bug exists where an applet can initialize itself more than once without being reloaded.

Reloading the Applet

Some browsers let the user reload applets, which consists of unloading the applet and then loading it again. Before an applet is unloaded, it's given the chance to *stop* itself and then to perform a *final cleanup*, so that the applet can release any resources it holds. After that, the applet is unloaded and then loaded again, as described in the Loading the Applet section (page 549).

Try This: If your browser or other applet viewer lets you easily reload applets, reload the applet. Look at the Displaying Diagnostics to the Standard Output and Error Streams section (page 583) to see what happens when you reload the applet. (See the Displaying Short Status Strings section, page 561, for information about the standard output.) You should see "stopping . . . " and "preparing for unloading . . . " when the applet is unloaded. You can't see this in the applet GUI because the applet is unloaded before the text can be displayed. When the applet is reloaded, you should see "initializing . . . " and "starting . . . ", just like when you loaded the applet for the first time.

Quitting the Browser

When the user quits the browser (or whatever application is displaying the applet), the applet has the chance to *stop* itself and do *final cleanup* before the browser exits.

Summary

An applet can react to major events in the following ways:

- It can *initialize* itself.
- It can *start* running.
- It can *stop* running.
- It can perform a *final cleanup*, in preparation for being unloaded.

The next section describes the four applet methods that correspond to these four types of reactions.

Methods for Milestones

The `Simple` applet, like every other applet, features a subclass of the `Applet` class. The `Simple` class overrides four `Applet` methods so that it can respond to major events:

`init` To *initialize* the applet each time it's loaded (or reloaded).

`start` To *start* the applet's execution, such as when the applet is loaded or when the user revisits a page that contains the applet.

`stop` To *stop* the applet's execution, such as when the user leaves the applet's page or quits the browser.

`destroy` To perform a *final cleanup* in preparation for unloading.

Following is the interface for these methods:

```
public class Simple extends JApplet {
    . . .
    public void init() { . . . }
    public void start() { . . . }
    public void stop() { . . . }
    public void destroy() { . . . }
    . . .
}
```

The `init`, `start`, `stop`, and `destroy` methods are discussed and used throughout this tutorial. For more information, you can also refer to the `JApplet` API Specification.[9]

Overriding These Methods

Not every applet needs to override every one of these methods. Some very simple applets override none of them. For example, the "Hello World" applet (page 6) doesn't override any of these methods, since it doesn't do anything except draw itself.

The "Hello World" applet just displays a string once, using its `paint` method. (The `paint` method is described on page 552.) Most applets, however, do more.

The init Method

The `init` method is useful for one-time initialization that doesn't take very long. In general, the `init` method should contain the code that you would normally put into a constructor. The reason applets shouldn't usually have constructors is that an applet isn't guaranteed to have a full environment until its `init` method is called. For example, the `Applet` image-loading methods simply don't work inside of an applet constructor. The `init` method, on the other hand, is a great place to call the image-loading methods, since the methods return quickly.

Browser Note: Some browsers sometimes call the `init` method more than once after the applet has been loaded. See The Life Cycle of an Applet section (page 547) for more details.

The start Method

Every applet that does something after initialization (except in direct response to user actions) must override the `start` method. The `start` method either performs the applet's work or (more likely) starts up one or more threads to perform the work. You'll learn more about threads in the Threads in Applets section (page 585). You'll learn more about handling the events that represent user actions in the Methods for Drawing and Event Handling section (page 552).

The stop Method

Most applets that override `start` should also override the `stop` method. The `stop` method should suspend the applet's execution so that it doesn't take up system resources when the user isn't viewing the applet's page. For example, an applet that dis-

9. `docs/api/javax/swing/JApplet.html`

plays animation should stop trying to draw the animation when the user isn't looking at it.

The destroy Method

Many applets don't need to override the destroy method, since their stop method (which is called before destroy) does everything necessary to shut down the applet's execution. However, destroy is available for applets that need to release additional resources.

Note: You should keep implementations of the destroy method as short as possible, because there is no guarantee that this method will be completely executed. The Java Virtual Machine might exit before a long destroy method has completed.

Methods for Drawing and Event Handling

Using the paint Method

To draw the applet's representation within a browser page, you use the paint method.

For example, the Simple applet defines its onscreen appearance by overriding the paint method:

```
public void paint(Graphics g) {
  // Draw a Rectangle around the applet's display area.
  g.drawRect(0, 0,
    getWidth() - 1,
    getHeight() - 1);

  // Draw the current string inside the rectangle.
  g.drawString(buffer.toString(), 5, 15);
}
```

Applets inherit the paint method from the Abstract Window Toolkit (AWT) Container class.

Handling Events

Applets inherit a group of event-handling methods from the Container class.

The Container class defines several methods, such as processKeyEvent and processMouseEvent, for handling particular types of events, and then one catch-all method called processEvent.

To react to an event, an applet must override the appropriate event-specific method. For example, the following program, `SimpleClick`,[10] implements a `MouseListener` and overrides the `mouseClicked` method:

```
/*
 * Java(TM) SE 6 version.
 */

import java.awt.event.MouseListener;
import java.awt.event.MouseEvent;
import java.applet.Applet;
import java.awt.Graphics;

// No need to extend JApplet, since we don't add
// any components; we just paint.
public class SimpleClick extends Applet
    implements MouseListener {

  StringBuffer buffer;

  public void init() {
    addMouseListener(this);
    buffer = new StringBuffer();
    addItem("initializing... ");
  }

  public void start() {
    addItem("starting... ");
  }

  public void stop() {
    addItem("stopping... ");
  }

  public void destroy() {
    addItem("preparing for unloading...");
  }

  void addItem(String newWord) {
    System.out.println(newWord);
    buffer.append(newWord);
    repaint();
  }
```

10. `tutorial/deployment/applet/examples/SimpleClick.java`

```
    public void paint(Graphics g) {
      // Draw a Rectangle around the applet's display area.
      g.drawRect(0, 0,
                 getWidth() - 1,
                 getHeight() - 1);

      // Draw the current string inside the rectangle.
      g.drawString(buffer.toString(), 5, 15);
    }

    // The following empty methods could be removed
    // by implementing a MouseAdapter (usually done
    // using an inner class).
    public void mouseEntered(MouseEvent event) {
    }
    public void mouseExited(MouseEvent event) {
    }
    public void mousePressed(MouseEvent event) {
    }
    public void mouseReleased(MouseEvent event) {
    }

    public void mouseClicked(MouseEvent event) {
      addItem("click!... ");
    }
  }
```

Run the resulting applet[11] (Figure 18.3). When you click within its rectangle, it displays the word "click! . . . ".

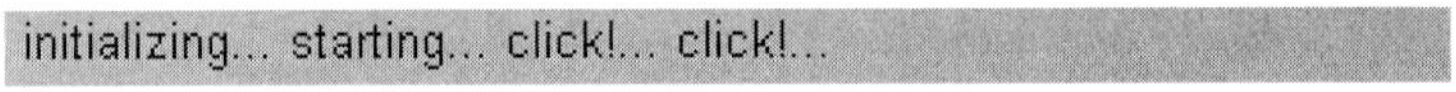

initializing... starting... click!... click!...

Figure 18.3 A screenshot of the SimpleClick applet.

Methods for Adding UI Components

The `Simple` applet's display code (implemented in its `paint` method) is flawed: It doesn't support scrolling. Once the text it displays reaches the end of the display rectangle, you can't see any new text. Figure 18.4 shows an example of the problem.

initializing... starting... stopping... starting... stopping... starting... stoppir

Figure 18.4 The output from the `Simple` applet demo showing the lack of scrolling.

11. `tutorial/deployment/applet/examples/simpleClick.jar`

The simplest cure for this problem is to use a pre-made user interface (UI) component that has the right behavior.

Note: This section glosses over many details. To really learn about using UI components, read *Creating a GUI with JFC/Swing*.[12]

Pre-Made UI Components

Swing supplies the following UI components (the class that implements each component is listed in parentheses):

- Buttons (`javax.swing.JButton`)
- Checkboxes (`javax.swing.JCheckBox`)
- Single-line text fields (`javax.swing.JTextField`)
- Larger text display and editing areas (`javax.swing.JTextArea`)
- Labels (`javax.swing.JLabel`)
- Lists (`javax.swing.JList`)
- Pop-ups (`javax.swing.Popup`)
- Scrollbars (`javax.swing.JScrollBar`)
- Sliders (`javax.swing.JSlider`)
- Drawing areas (`java.awt.Canvas`)
- Menus (`javax.swing.JMenu`, `javax.swing.JMenuBar`, `javax.swing.JMenuItem`, `javax.swing.JCheckBoxMenuItem`)
- Containers (`javax.swing.JPanel`, `javax.swing.JWindow`, and its subclasses)

Methods for Using UI Components in Applets

Because the `JApplet` class inherits from the AWT `Container` class, it's easy to add components to applets and to use layout managers to control the components' onscreen positions. Here are some of the `Container` methods an applet can use:

`add` Adds the specified `Component`.

`remove` Removes the specified `Component`.

`setLayout` Sets the layout manager.

---

12. `tutorial/uiswing/index.html`

Adding a Non-Editable Text Field to the Simple Applet

To make the `Simple` applet use a scrolling, non-editable text field, we can use the `JTextField` class. Here is the revised `ScrollingSimple class`:[13]

```
/*
 * Java(TM) SE 6 version.
 */

import javax.swing.JApplet;
import javax.swing.JTextField;
import javax.swing.SwingUtilities;

// Since we're adding a Swing component, we now need to
// extend JApplet. We need to be careful to access
// components only on the event-dispatching thread.
public class ScrollingSimple extends JApplet {

  JTextField field;

  public void init() {
    // Execute a job on the event-dispatching thread:
    // creating this applet's GUI.
    try {
        SwingUtilities.invokeAndWait(new Runnable() {
          public void run() {
            createGUI();
          }
        });
    } catch (Exception e) {
        System.err.println("createGUI didn't " +
                           "successfully complete");
    }
    addItem(false, "initializing... ");
  }

  private void createGUI() {
    // Create the text field and make it uneditable.
    field = new JTextField();
    field.setEditable(false);

    // Set the layout manager so that the text field will be
    // as wide as possible.
    setLayout(new java.awt.GridLayout(1,0));

    // Add the text field to the applet.
    add(field);
  }
```

13. `tutorial/deployment/applet/examples/ScrollingSimple.java`

```
public void start() {
  addItem(false, "starting... ");
}

public void stop() {
  addItem(false, "stopping... ");
}

public void destroy() {
  addItem(false, "preparing for unloading...");
  cleanUp();
}

private void cleanUp() {
  // Execute a job on the event-dispatching thread:
  // taking the text field out of this applet.
  try {
      SwingUtilities.invokeAndWait(new Runnable() {
        public void run() {
          remove(field);
        }
      });
  } catch (Exception e) {
      System.err.println("cleanUp didn't " +
                         "successfully complete");
  }
  field = null;
}

private void addItem(boolean alreadyInEDT, String newWord) {
  if (alreadyInEDT) {
      addItem(newWord);
  } else {
      final String word = newWord;
      // Execute a job on the event-dispatching thread:
      // invoking addItem(newWord).
      try {
          SwingUtilities.invokeAndWait(new Runnable() {
            public void run() {
              addItem(word);
            }
          });
      } catch (Exception e) {
          System.err.println("addItem didn't " +
                             "successfully complete");
      }
  }
}
```

```
    // Invoke this method ONLY from the event-dispatching thread.
    private void addItem(String newWord) {
      String t = field.getText();
      System.out.println(newWord);
      field.setText(t + newWord);
    }
  }
```

The `createGUI` method creates an uneditable text field (a `JTextField` instance). It sets the applet's layout manager to one that makes the text field as wide as possible (you can learn about layout managers in *Laying Out Components within a Container*[14]) and then adds the text field to the applet.

Run the resulting applet[15] (Figure 18.5).

initializing... starting...

Figure 18.5 A screenshot of the ScrollingSimple applet.

What Applets Can and Can't Do

This section gives an overview of both the restrictions applets face and the special capabilities they have. You will find more details in the Security Restrictions section (page 578).

Security Restrictions

Every browser implements security policies to keep applets from compromising system security. This section describes the security policies that current browsers adhere to. However, the implementation of the security policies differs from browser to browser. Also, security policies are subject to change. For example, if a browser is developed for use only in trusted environments, then its security policies will likely be much more lax than those described here.

Current browsers impose the following restrictions on any applet that is loaded over the network:

- An applet cannot load libraries or define native methods.
- It cannot ordinarily read or write files on the host that's executing it.
- It cannot make network connections except to the host that it came from.

---

14. `tutorial/uiswing/layout/index.html`

15. `tutorial/deployment/applet/examples/scrollingSimple.jar`

- It cannot start any program on the host that's executing it.
- It cannot read certain system properties.
- Windows that an applet brings up look different than windows that an application brings up.

Each browser has a `SecurityManager` object that implements its security policies. When a `SecurityManager` detects a violation, it throws a `SecurityException`. Your applet can catch this `SecurityException` and react appropriately.

Applet Capabilities

The `java.applet` package provides an API that gives applets some capabilities that applications do not have.

Here are some other things that current browers and other applet viewers let applets do:

- Applets can usually make network connections to the host they came from.
- Applets running within a Web browser can easily cause HTML documents to be displayed.
- Applets can invoke public methods of other applets on the same page.
- Applets that are loaded from the local file system (from a directory in the user's `CLASSPATH`) have none of the restrictions that applets loaded over the network do.

Taking Advantage of the Applet API

The applet API lets you take advantage of the close relationship that applets have with Web browsers. The API is provided by the `javax.swing.JApplet` class and the `java.applet.AppletContext` interface.

Applets can use these APIs to do the following:

- Be notified by the browser of milestones.
- Load data files specified relative to the URL of the applet or the page in which it is running.
- Display short status strings.
- Make the browser display a document.
- Find other applets running in the same page.
- Play sounds.
- Get parameters specified by the user in the `<APPLET>` tag.

This section discusses each of these topics in turn, except for the milestone methods (`init`, `start`, and so on), which are explained in the Methods for Milestones section (page 550). For information about how to use non-applet-specific APIs in an applet, see the Practical Considerations When Writing Applets section (page 578).

Finding and Loading Data Files

Whenever an applet needs to load some data from a file that's specified with a relative URL (a URL that doesn't completely specify the file's location), the applet usually uses either the code base or the document base to form the complete URL.

The code base, returned by the `JApplet` `getCodeBase` method, is a URL that specifies the directory from which the applet's classes were loaded.

The document base, returned by the `JApplet` `getDocumentBase` method, specifies the directory of the HTML page that contains the applet.

Unless the `<APPLET>` tag specifies a code base, both the code base and document base refer to the same directory on the same server.

Data that the applet might need, or needs to rely on as a backup, is usually specified relative to the code base. Data that the applet developer specifies, often by using parameters, is usually specified relative to the document base.

Note: For security reasons, browsers limit the URLs from which untrusted applets can read. For example, most browsers don't allow untrusted applets to use ".." to get to directories above the code base or document base. Also, since untrusted applets can't read files except those on the applet's originating host, the document base isn't generally useful if the document and the untrusted applet are on different servers.

The `JApplet` class defines convenient forms of image-loading and sound-loading methods that let you specify images and sounds relative to a base URL. For example, assume an applet is set up with one of the directory structures shown in Figure 18.6.

To create an `Image` object using the `a.png` image file under `imgDir`, the applet can use the following code:

```
Image image = getImage(getCodeBase(), "imgDir/a.png");
```

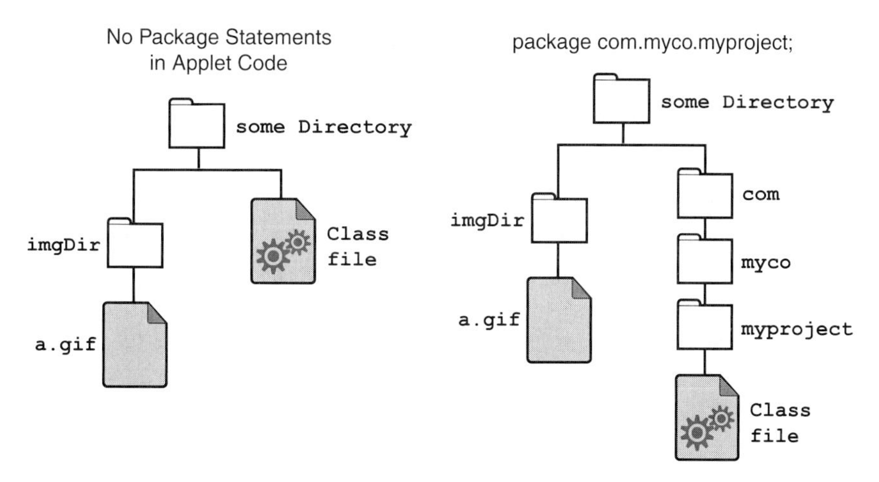

Figure 18.6 Two directory structures showing the image files and class files in separate locations, with different structures.

Displaying Short Status Strings

All browsers allow applets to display a short status string. All applets on the page, as well as the browser itself, share the same status line.

You should never put crucial information in the status line. If many users might need the information, it should instead be displayed within the applet area. If only a few sophisticated users might need the information, consider displaying the information on the standard output (see the Displaying Diagnostics to the Standard Output and Error Streams section, page 583).

The status line is not usually very prominent, and it can be overwritten by other applets or by the browser. For these reasons, it's best used for incidental, transitory information. For example, an applet that loads several image files might display the name of the image file it's currently loading.

Applets display status lines with the `showStatus`[16] method, inherited in the `JApplet` class from the `Applet` class.

Here's an example of its use:

```
showStatus("MyApplet: Loading image file " + file);
```

Note: Please don't put scrolling text in the status line. Browser users find such status line abuse highly annoying!

---

16. `docs/api/java/applet/Applet.html`

Displaying Documents in the Browser

Have you ever wanted an applet to display formatted HTML text? There's an easy way to do it: Ask the browser to display the text for you.

With the `AppletContext` `showDocument` methods, an applet can tell the browser which URL to show and in which browser window.

Here are the two forms of `showDocument`:

```
public void showDocument(java.net.URL url)
public void showDocument(java.net.URL url, String targetWindow)
```

The one-argument form of `showDocument` simply tells the browser to display the document at the specified URL, without specifying the window to display the document in.

> **Terminology Note:** In this discussion, *frame* refers not to a Swing `JFrame`, but to an HTML frame within a browser window.

The two-argument form of `showDocument` lets you specify which window or HTML frame to display the document in. The second argument can have the values listed below:

`"_blank"` Display the document in a new, nameless window.

`"windowName"` Display the document in a window named *`windowName`*. This window is created if necessary.

`"_self"` Display the document in the window and frame that contain the applet.

`"_parent"` Display the document in parent frame of the applet's frame. If the applet frame has no parent frame, this acts the same as `"_self"`.

`"_top"` Display the document in the top-level frame. If the applet's frame is the top-level frame, this acts the same as `"_self"`.

Run an applet[17] that lets you try every option of both forms of `showDocument` (Figure 18.7). The applet brings up a window that lets you type in a URL and choose any

Bring up URL window

Figure 18.7 A screenshot of the Bring up URL window applet.

17. `tutorial/deployment/applet/examples/showDocument.jar`

of the `showDocument` options (Figure 18.8). When you press **Return** or click the **Show document** button, the applet calls `showDocument`.

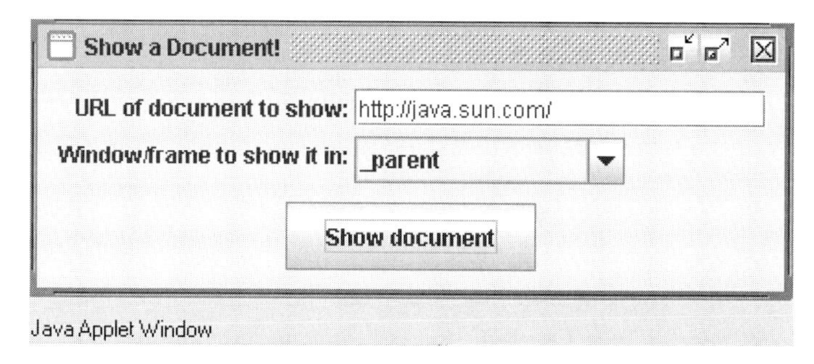

Figure 18.8 A screenshot of the ShowDocument applet.

Below is the applet code that calls `showDocument`:[18]

```
  ...// In an Applet subclass:
  urlWindow = new URLWindow(getAppletContext());
  ...
class URLWindow extends Frame {
  ...
  public URLWindow(AppletContext appletContext) {
    ...
    this.appletContext = appletContext;
    ...
  }
  ...
  public boolean action(Event event, Object o) {
    ...
    String urlString = /* user-entered string */;
    URL url = null;
    try {
        url = new URL(urlString);
    } catch (MalformedURLException e) {
        ...// Inform the user and return...
    }
    if (url != null) {
      if (/* user doesn't want to specify the window */) {
          appletContext.showDocument(url);
      } else {
          appletContext.showDocument(url,
            /* user-specified window */);
      }
    }
    ...
```

18. `tutorial/deployment/applet/examples/ShowDocument.java`

Sending Messages to Other Applets

Applets can find other applets and send messages to them, with the following security restrictions:

- Many browsers require that the applets originate from the same server.
- Many browsers further require that the applets originate from the same directory on the server (the same code base).
- The Java API requires that the applets be running on the same page, in the same browser window.

Note: Some browsers let applets invoke methods on other applets—even applets on different pages in the same browser—as long as all of the applets come from the same code base. This method of interapplet communication isn't supported by the Java API, so it's possible that it will not be supported by all browsers.

An applet can find another applet either by looking it up by name (using the `AppletContext getApplet` method) or by finding all the applets on the page (using the `AppletContext getApplets` method). Both methods, if successful, give the caller one or more `Applet` objects. Once the caller finds an `Applet` object, the caller can invoke methods on the object.

Finding an Applet by Name: The getApplet Method

The `getApplet` method looks through all of the applets on the current page to see if one of them has the specified name. If so, `getApplet` returns the applet's `Applet` object.

By default, an applet has no name. For an applet to have a name, one must be specified in the HTML code that adds the applet to a page. You can specify an applet's name in two ways:

- By specifying a `NAME` attribute within the applet's `<APPLET>` tag. For example:

```
<APPLET CODEBASE=example/ CODE=Sender.class
  WIDTH=450
  HEIGHT=200
  NAME="buddy">
...
</APPLET>
```

- By specifying a NAME parameter with a <PARAM> tag. For example:

```
<APPLET CODEBASE=example/ CODE=Receiver.class
  WIDTH=450
  HEIGHT=50>
<PARAM NAME="name" value="old pal">
...
</APPLET>
```

Browser Note: Although at least one browser enabled with Java technology conducts a case-sensitive search, the expected behavior is for the getApplet method to perform a case-*in*sensitive search. For example, getApplet("old pal") and getApplet("OLD PAL") should both find an applet named "Old Pal".

Two applets[19] illustrate lookup by name (Figures 18.9 and 18.10). The first, the Sender, looks up the second, the Receiver. When the Sender finds the Receiver, the Sender sends a message to the Receiver by invoking one of the Receiver's methods (passing the Sender's name as an argument). The Receiver reacts to this method call by changing its leftmost text string to "Received message from *sender-name*!".

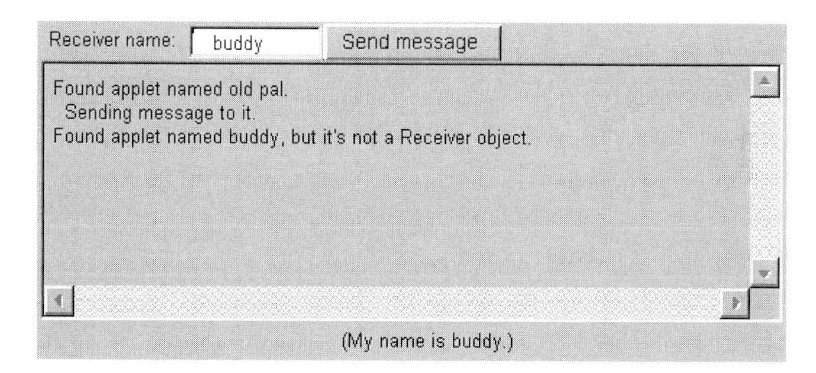

Figure 18.9 A screenshot of the Sender applet.

Figure 18.10 A screenshot of the Receiver applet.

19. tutorial/deployment/applet/examples/sender.jar

Try This: Click the **Send message** button of the first applet (the Sender). Some status information will appear in the Sender's window, and the Receiver will confirm (with its own status string) that it received a message, After you've read the Receiver status string, press the Receiver's **Clear** button to reset the Receiver. In the Sender's text field labeled "Receiver name:," type in **`buddy`** and press **Return**. Since "buddy" is the Sender's own name, the Sender will find an applet named buddy but won't send it a message, since it isn't a Receiver instance.

The code the Sender program[20] uses to look up and communicate with the Receiver is listed below. Code that you can use without change in your own applet is in **bold font**:

```
Applet receiver = null;
String receiverName = nameField.getText(); // Get name
                                           // to search for.
receiver = getAppletContext().getApplet(receiverName);
```

The Sender goes on to make sure that the Receiver was found and that it's an instance of the correct class (`Receiver`[21]). If all goes well, the Sender sends a message to the Receiver:

```
if (receiver != null) {
  // Use the instanceof operator to make sure the applet
  // we found is a Receiver object.
  if (!(receiver instanceof Receiver)) {
      status.appendText("Found applet named " +
                        receiverName + ", " +
                        "but it's not a Receiver object.\n");
  } else {
      status.appendText("Found applet named " +
                        receiverName + ".\n" +
                        " Sending message to it.\n");
      // Cast the receiver to be a Receiver object
      // (instead of just an Applet object) so that the
      // compiler will let us call a Receiver method.
      ((Receiver)receiver).processRequestFrom(myName);
  }
} ...
```

20. `tutorial/deployment/applet/examples/Sender.java`

21. `tutorial/deployment/applet/examples/Receiver.java`

From an applet's point of view, its name is stored in a parameter named `NAME`. It can get the value of the parameter using the `Applet getParameter` method. For example, Sender gets its own name with the following code:

```
myName = getParameter("NAME");
```

For more information on using `getParameter`, see the Writing the Code to Support Parameters section (page 573).

The example applets in this section perform one-way communication—from the Sender to the Receiver. If you want your receiver to be able to send messages to the sender, then you just need to have the sender give a reference to itself (`this`) to the receiver. For example:

```
((Receiver)receiver).startCommunicating(this);
```

Finding All the Applets on a Page: The getApplets Method

The `getApplets` method returns a list (an `Enumeration`,[22] to be precise) of all the applets on the page. For security reasons, many browsers and applet viewers implement `getApplets` so that it returns only those applets that originated from the same host as the applet calling `getApplets`. Run an applet that simply lists all the applets it can find on this page (Figure 18.11).[23]

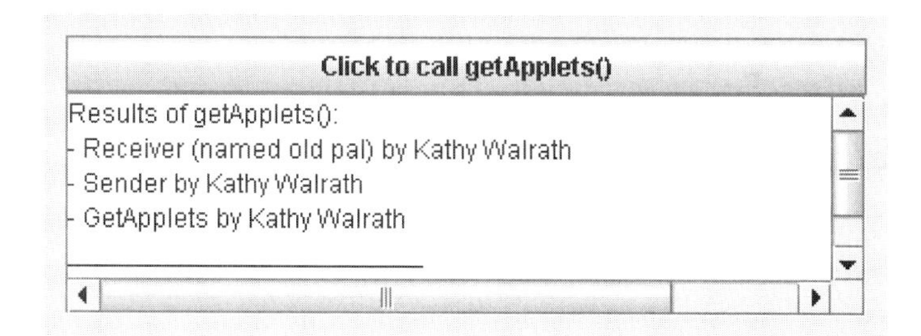

Figure 18.11 A screenshot of the GetApplets applet.

Below are the relevant parts of the method that calls `getApplets`:[24]

22. `docs/api/java/util/Enumeration.html`

23. `tutorial/deployment/applet/examples/getApplets.java`

24. `tutorial/deployment/applet/examples/GetApplets.java`

```
public void printApplets() {
  // Enumeration will contain all applets on this page
  // (including this one) that we can send messages to.
  Enumeration e = getAppletContext().getApplets();
  ...
  while (e.hasMoreElements()) {
    Applet applet = (Applet)e.nextElement();
    String info = ((Applet)applet).getAppletInfo();
    if (info != null) {
        textArea.appendText("- " + info + "\n");
    } else {
        textArea.appendText("- " +
                              applet.getClass().getName() + "\n");
    }
  }
  ...
}
```

Playing Sounds

The `JApplet` class in the Java Swing package (`javax.swing`) and the `AudioClip`[25] interface in the Java Applet package (`java.applet`) provide basic support for playing sounds. Currently, the Java API supports only one sound format: 8 bit, μ-law, 8000 Hz, one-channel, Sun ".au" files. You can create these on a Sun workstation using the `audiotool` application. You can convert files from other sound formats using an audio format conversion program.

Sound-Related Methods

Below are the sound-related `Applet` methods. The two-argument form of each method takes a base URL, which is usually returned by either `getDocumentBase` or `getCodeBase`, and the location of the sound file relative to the base URL:

`getAudioClip(URL), getAudioClip(URL, String)` Return an object that implements the `AudioClip` interface.

`play(URL),play(URL, String)` Play the `AudioClip` corresponding to the specified URL.

The `AudioClip` interface defines the following methods:

`loop` Starts playing the clip repeatedly.

`play` Plays the clip once.

`stop` Stops the clip. Works with both looping and one-time sounds.

25. `docs/api/java/applet/AudioClip.html`

An Example

Run an applet called SoundExample[26] that illustrates a few things about sound (Figure 18.12). Note that, for instructional purposes, the applet adds up to 10 seconds to the load time for each sound. If the sounds were larger or the user's connection slower than ours, these delays might be realistic.

Figure 18.12 A screenshot of the SoundExample applet.

The SoundExample applet provides an architecture for loading and playing multiple sounds in an applet. For this reason, it is more complex than necessary. Essentially, the sound loading and playing code boils down to this:

```
AudioClip onceClip, loopClip;
onceClip = applet.getAudioClip(getCodeBase(), "bark.au");
loopClip = applet.getAudioClip(getCodeBase(), "train.au");
onceClip.play();     // Play it once.
loopClip.loop();     // Start the sound loop.
loopClip.stop();     // Stop the sound loop.
```

Since there's nothing more annoying than an applet that continues to make noise after you've left its page, the SoundExample applet stops playing the continuously looping sound when the user leaves the page and resumes playing it when the user comes back. It does this by implementing its `stop` and `start` methods as follows:

```
public void stop() {
  // If one-time sound were long, we'd stop it here, too.
  // looping is a boolean instance variable that's initially
  // false. It's set to true when the "Start sound loop" button
  // is clicked and to false when the "Stop sound loop" or
  // "Reload sounds" button is clicked.
  if (looping) {
    loopClip.stop();    // Stop the sound loop.
  }
}
public void start() {
  if (looping) {
    loopClip.loop();    // Restart the sound loop.
  }
}
```

26. `tutorial/deployment/applet/examples/sound.jar`

The SoundExample applet features three classes:

- A `JApplet` subclass, `SoundExample`,[27] that controls the applet's execution.
- A `Hashtable` subclass, `SoundList`,[28] that holds `AudioClips`. This is overkill for this applet, but if you were to write an applet that used lots of sound files, a class like this would be useful.
- A `Thread` subclass, `SoundLoader`,[29] each instance of which loads an `AudioClip` in the background. During the applet's initialization, the applet preloads each sound by creating a `SoundLoader` for it.

Preloading the sounds in a background thread (with `SoundLoader`) improves the perceived performance by reducing the amount of time the user has to wait to be able to interact with the applet. It does this by reducing the amount of time spent in the `init` method. If you simply called `getAudioClip` in the applet's `init` method, it could take quite a while before `getAudioClip` returned, meaning that the applet couldn't perform the other statements in its `init` method, and that the applet's `start` wouldn't get called. (For this SoundExample applet, a delay in calling the `start` method doesn't matter.)

Another advantage of loading the sounds in a background thread is that it enables the applet to respond appropriately (and immediately) to user input that would normally cause a sound to play, even if that sound hasn't been loaded yet. If you simply use the `Applet play` method, for example, then the first time the user does something to make the applet play a particular sound, the applet's drawing and event handling are frozen while the sound is loaded. Instead, this applet detects that the sound hasn't been loaded yet and responds appropriately.

This example is discussed in more detail in the Threads in Applets: Examples section (page 586).

Defining and Using Applet Parameters

Parameters are to applets what command-line arguments are to applications. They allow the user to customize the applet's operation. By defining parameters, you can increase your applet's flexibility, making your applet work in multiple situations without recoding and recompiling it.

The next few sections discuss parameters from the applet programmer's point of view. To learn about the user view of parameters, see the Specifying Parameters section (page 575).

27. `tutorial/deployment/applet/examples/SoundExample.java`

28. `tutorial/deployment/applet/examples/SoundList.java`

29. `tutorial/deployment/applet/examples/SoundLoader.java`

Deciding Which Parameters to Support

This section guides you through the four questions you should ask as you implement parameters:

- What should the applet let the user configure?
- What should the parameters be named?
- What kind of value should each parameter take?
- What should the default value of each parameter be?

It ends with a discussion of the parameters defined in a sample `<APPLET>` tag.

What Should the Applet Let the User Configure?

The parameters your applet should support depend on what your applet does and on how flexible you want it to be. Applets that display images might have parameters to specify the image locations. Similarly, applets that play sounds might have parameters to specify the sounds.

Besides parameters that specify resource locations (such as image and sound files), applets sometimes provide parameters for specifying details of the applet's appearance or operation. For example, an animation applet might let the user specify the number of images shown per second. Or an applet might let the user change the strings the applet displays. Anything is possible.

What Should the Parameters Be Named?

Once you decide what parameters your applet will support, you need to figure out their names. Here are some typical parameter names:

SOURCE or SRC For a data file such as an image file.

***XXX*SOURCE (*for example*, IMAGESOURCE)** Used in applets that let the user specify more than one type of data file.

***XXX*S** For a parameter that takes a list of *XXX*s (where *XXX* might be `IMAGE`, again).

NAME Used *only* for an applet's name. Applet names are used for interapplet communication, as described in the Sending Messages to Other Applets section (page 564).

Clarity of names is more important than keeping the name length short. Do *not* use names of `<APPLET>` tag attributes, which are documented in the Using the `applet` Tag section (page 595).

Note: Although this tutorial usually refers to parameter names using ALL UPPERCASE, parameter names are case-insensitive. For example, `IMAGESOURCE` and `imageSource` both refer to the same parameter. Parameter *values*, on the other hand, are case-sensitive unless you take steps to interpret them otherwise, such as by using the `String` `toLowerCase` method before interpreting the parameter's value.

What Kind of Value Should Each Parameter Take?

Parameter values are all strings. Whether or not the user puts quotation marks around a parameter value, that value is passed to your applet as a string. However, your applet can interpret the string in many ways.

Applets typically interpret a parameter value as one of the following types:

- A URL
- An integer
- A floating-point number
- A boolean value—typically "true"/"false" or "yes"/"no"
- A string—for example, the string to use as a window title
- A list of any of the above

What Should the Default Value of Each Parameter Be?

Applets should attempt to provide useful default values for each parameter, so that the applet will execute even if the user doesn't specify a parameter or specifies it incorrectly. For example, an animation applet should provide a reasonable setting for the number of images it displays per second. This way, if the user doesn't specify the relevant parameter, the applet will still work well.

An Example: A Sample <APPLET> Tag

Here's what a typical `<APPLET>` tag looks like.

```
<APPLET CODE=SampleApplet.class CODEBASE=example
  WIDTH=350 HEIGHT=60>
<PARAM NAME=windowClass VALUE=BorderWindow>
<PARAM NAME=windowTitle VALUE="BorderLayout">
<PARAM NAME=buttonText
  VALUE="Click here to see a BorderLayout in action">
</APPLET>
```

When the user doesn't specify a value for a parameter, the applet uses a reasonable default value. For example, if the user doesn't specify the window's title, the applet uses the window's type as the title.

The next section shows you how to get parameter values from the user.

Writing the Code to Support Parameters

Applets use the `Applet getParameter` method to get user-specified values for applet parameters. The `getParameter` method is defined as follows:

```
public String getParameter(String name)
```

Your applet might need to convert the string that `getParameter` returns into another form, such as an integer. The `java.lang` package provides classes such as Integer that you can use to help with converting strings to primitive types. Here's an example of converting a parameter's value into an integer:

```
int requestedWidth = 0;
...
String windowWidthString = getParameter("WINDOWWIDTH");
if (windowWidthString != null) {
  try {
      requestedWidth = Integer.parseInt(windowWidthString);
  } catch (NumberFormatException e) {
      // Use default width.
  }
}
```

Note that if the user doesn't specify a value for the `WINDOWWIDTH` parameter, the above code uses a default value of 0, which the applet interprets as "use the window's natural size." It's important that you supply default values wherever possible.

Besides using the `getParameter` method to get values of applet-specific parameters, you can also use `getParameter` to get the values of attributes of the applet's `<APPLET>` tag. See the Using the `applet` Tag section (page 595) for a list of `<APPLET>` tag attributes.

Giving Information about Parameters

Now that you've provided all those nice parameters to the user, you need to help the user set the parameter values correctly. Of course, your applet's documentation should describe each parameter and give the user examples and hints about setting them. Your job doesn't stop there, though. You should also implement the `getParameterInfo` method so that it returns information about your applet's parameters. Browsers can use this information to help the user set your applet's parameter values.

Below is an example of implementing the getParameterInfo method:

```
public String[][] getParameterInfo() {
  String[][] info = {
    // Parameter Name  Kind of Value  Description
    {"imagesource",    "URL",         "a directory"},
    {"startup",        "URL",         "displayed at startup"},
    {"background",     "URL",         "displayed " +
                                          "as background"},
    {"startimage",     "int",         "start index"},
    {"endimage",       "int",         "end index"},
    {"namepattern",    "URL",         "used to generate " +
                                          "indexed names"},
    {"pause",          "int",         "milliseconds"},
    {"pauses",         "ints",        "milliseconds"},
    {"repeat",         "boolean",     "repeat or not"},
    {"positions",      "coordinates", "path"},
    {"soundsource",    "URL",         "audio directory"},
    {"soundtrack",     "URL",         "background music"},
    {"sounds",         "URLs",        "audio samples"},
  };
  return info;
}
```

As you can see, the getParameterInfo method must return an array of three-String arrays. In each three-String array, the first string is the parameter name. The second string gives the user a hint about what general kind of value the applet needs for the parameter. The third string describes the meaning of the parameter.

Using the APPLET Tag

This section tells you most of what you need to know to use the <APPLET> tag. It starts by showing you the tag's simplest form. It then discusses some of the most common additions to that simple form: the <PARAM> tag, alternate HTML code and text, the CODEBASE attribute, and the ARCHIVE attribute. For a detailed description of the <APPLET> tag, refer to the Using the applet Tag section (page 595).

You should already have seen the simplest form of the <APPLET> tag:

```
<APPLET CODE=AppletSubclass.class WIDTH=anInt HEIGHT=anInt>
</APPLET>
```

This tag tells the browser to load the applet whose Applet subclass is named *AppletSubclass*, displaying it in an area of the specified width and height.

Specifying Parameters

Some applets let the user customize the applet's configuration with parameters, as described in the Defining and Using Applet Parameters section (page 570). For example, AppletButton (an applet used throughout this tutorial to provide a button that brings up a window) allows the user to set the button's text by specifying the value of a parameter named BUTTONTEXT.

The developer provides the value of a parameter using a <PARAM> tag. The <PARAM> tags should appear just after the <APPLET> tag for the applet they affect:

```
<APPLET CODE=AppletSubclass.class WIDTH=anInt HEIGHT=anInt>
<PARAM NAME=parameter1Name VALUE=aValue>
<PARAM NAME=parameter2Name VALUE=anotherValue>
</APPLET>
```

Here's an example of the <PARAM> tag in use.

```
<APPLET CODE="Animator.class" WIDTH=460 HEIGHT=160>
<PARAM NAME="imageSource" VALUE="images/Beans">
<PARAM NAME="backgroundColor" VALUE="0xc0c0c0">
<PARAM NAME="endImage" VALUE=10>
<PARAM NAME="soundSource" VALUE="audio">
<PARAM NAME="soundtrack" VALUE="spacemusic.au">
<PARAM NAME="sounds"
  VALUE="1.au|2.au|3.au|4.au|5.au|6.au|7.au|8au|9.au|0.au">
<PARAM NAME="pause" VALUE=200>
. . .
</APPLET>
```

Specifying Alternate HTML Code and Text

Note the ellipsis points (". . .") in the previous HTML example. What did the example leave out? It omitted *alternate HTML code*-HTML code interpreted only by browsers that don't understand the <APPLET> tag. Alternate HTML code is any text that appears between the <APPLET> and </APPLET> tags, after any <PARAM> tags. Browsers enabled with Java technology ignore alternate HTML code.

To specify alternate text to browsers enabled with Java technology and other browsers that understand the <APPLET> tag, use the ALT attribute. If the browser can't display an applet for some reason, it can display the applet's ALT text.

We use alternate HTML code throughout the online version of this tutorial to tell readers about the applets they're missing. Often, the alternate HTML code includes one or more pictures of the applet. Here's the complete HTML code for the Animator example shown previously:

```
<APPLET CODE="Animator.class" WIDTH=460 HEIGHT=160
  ALT="If you could run this applet, you'd see some animation">
<PARAM NAME="imageSource" VALUE="images/Beans">
<PARAM NAME="backgroundColor" VALUE="0xc0c0c0">
<PARAM NAME="endImage" VALUE=10>
<PARAM NAME="soundSource" VALUE="audio">
<PARAM NAME="soundtrack" VALUE="spacemusic.au">
<PARAM NAME="sounds"
  VALUE="1.au|2.au|3.au|4.au|5.au|6.au|7.au|8au|9.au|0.au">
<PARAM NAME="pause" VALUE=200>
Your browser is completely ignoring the &lt;APPLET&gt; tag!
</APPLET>
```

A browser that doesn't understand the <APPLET> tag ignores everything in the previous HTML code except the line that starts with "Your". A browser that *does* understand the <APPLET> tag ignores everything on that line. If the applet-savvy browser can't run the applet, it might display the `ALT` text.

Specifying the Applet Directory

By default, a browser looks for an applet's class and archive files in the same directory as the HTML file that has the <APPLET> tag. (If the applet's class is in a package, then the browser uses the package name to construct a directory path underneath the HTML file's directory.) Sometimes, however, it's useful to put the applet's files somewhere else. You can use the `CODEBASE` attribute to tell the browser in which directory the applet's files are located:

```
<APPLET CODE=AppletSubclass.class CODEBASE=aURL
  WIDTH=anInt HEIGHT=anInt>
</APPLET>
```

If *aURL* is a relative URL, then it's interpreted relative to the HTML document's location. By making *aURL* an absolute URL, you can load an applet from just about anywhere—even from another HTTP server.

This book uses `CODEBASE="`*someDirectory/*`"` frequently, since we group the examples for each chapter in subdirectories. For example, here's the <APPLET> tag that includes the Simple applet in The Life Cycle of an Applet section (page 547):

```
<APPLET CODE=Simple.class CODEBASE="example/"
  WIDTH=500 HEIGHT=20>
</APPLET>
```

Figure 18.13 shows the location of the class file, relative to the HTML file, when `CODEBASE` is set to `"example/"`.

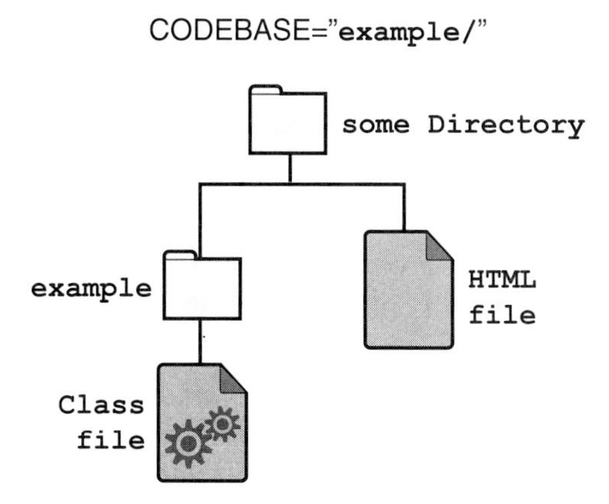

Figure 18.13 Location of the class file when `CODEBASE` is set to `"example/"`.

Figure 18.14 shows where the applet class can be if you specify an absolute URL for the value of `CODEBASE`.

CODEBASE="http://someServer/...someOtherDirectory/"

someDirectory

HTML file

someOtherDirectory (might be on another server)

Class file

Figure 18.14 Location of the class file when `CODEBASE` is set to an absolute URL.

Combining an Applet's Files into a Single File

If your applet has more than one file, you should consider providing an archive file that bundles the applet's files into a single file. Whether archive files make sense for your applet depends on several factors, including your applet's size, performance considerations, and the environment you expect your users to have.

Archive files reduce your applet's total download time. Much of the time saved comes from reducing the number of HTTP connections that the browser must make. Each HTTP connection can take several seconds to start. This means that for a multifile applet, connection time can dwarf transfer time. You can further reduce transfer time by compressing the files in your archive file.

If you specify one or more archive files, then the applet class loader looks for the archive files in the same directory that it would search for the applet class file. The applet class loader then looks for the applet's class files in the archive files. If a file isn't in the archive, then the applet class loader generally tries to load it in the browser just as it would if the archive file weren't present.

The standard Java archive format, called JAR, was introduced in JDK 1.1 and is based on the ZIP file format. You specify JAR files using the `ARCHIVE` attribute of the `<APPLET>` tag. You can specify multiple archive files by separating them with commas:

```
<APPLET CODE="AppletSubclass.class" ARCHIVE="file1, file2"
  WIDTH=anInt HEIGHT=anInt>
</APPLET>
```

Unfortunately, not all browsers understand the same archive format or use the same HTML code to specify the applet archive. Watch this page for the latest information about browser support for archives. To learn how to create a JAR file, see the Creating a JAR File section (page 490).

Other <APPLET> Tag Attributes

This section didn't discuss every attribute of the `<APPLET>` tag. Other attributes—which might seem familiar, since the `<IMG>` HTML tag uses them—include `ALIGN`, `VSPACE`, and `HSPACE`. The `<APPLET>` tag also allows you to load a serialized (saved) applet by specifying the `OBJECT` attribute instead of specifying a class file with `CODE`. Finally, you can name an applet using the `NAME` attribute. For a detailed description of the `<APPLET>` tag, see the Using the `applet` Tag section (page 595).

Practical Considerations When Writing Applets

The first two sections in this chapter discussed all of the applet-specific API. However, most applets rely on a lot of API that isn't specific to applets. This section gives you hints about using the Java API, covering the areas that are affected by applets' close relationships with browsers.

Security Restrictions

One of the main goals of the Java environment is to make browser users feel secure running any applet. To achieve this goal, we've started out conservatively, restricting capabilities perhaps more than necessary. As time passes, applets will probably get more and more abilities.

This section tells you about the current applet security restrictions, from the point of view of how they affect applet design. For more information on applet security, you should refer *Frequently Asked Questions—Applet Security.*[30]

Each applet viewer has a `SecurityManager` object that checks for applet security violations. When a `SecurityManager` detects a violation, it creates and throws a `SecurityException` object. Generally, the `SecurityException` constructor prints a warning message to the standard output. An applet can catch `SecurityExceptions` and react appropriately, such as by reassuring the user and by resorting to a "safer" (but less ideal) way of accomplishing the task.

Some applet viewers swallow some `SecurityExceptions`, so that the applet never gets the `SecurityException`. For example, the JDK Applet Viewer's implementation of the `AppletContext getApplet` and `getApplets` methods simply catches and ignores any `SecurityExceptions`. The user can see an error message in the standard output, but at least the applet gets a valid result from the methods. This makes some sense, since `getApplets` should be able to return any valid applets it finds, even if it encounters invalid ones. (The Applet Viewer considers an applet valid if it's loaded from the same host as the applet that's calling `getApplets`.)

To learn about security managers and the kinds of security violations they can check for, see The Security Manager section (page 455).

Existing applet viewers (including Web browsers) impose the following restrictions:

Applets cannot load libraries or define native methods. Applets can use only their own Java code and the Java API the applet viewer provides. At a minimum, each applet viewer must provide access to the API defined in the `java.*` packages.

An applet cannot ordinarily read or write files on the host that is executing it. The JDK Applet Viewer actually permits some user-specified exceptions to this rule, but older browsers generally do not. Applets in any applet viewer *can* read files specified with full URLs, instead of by a filename. A workaround for not being able to write files is to have the applet forward data to an application on the host the applet came from. This application can write the data files on its own host. See the Working with a Server-Side Application section (page 589) for more examples.

An applet cannot make network connections except to the host that it came from. The workaround for this restriction is to have the applet work with an application on the host it came from. The application can make its own connections anywhere on the network. See the Using a Server to Work Around Security Restrictions section (page 591) for an example.

---

30. `http://java.sun.com/sfaq/`

An applet cannot start any program on the host that is executing it. Again, an applet can work with a server-side application instead.

An applet cannot read certain system properties. See the Getting System Properties section (page 583) for more information.

Windows that an applet brings up look different than windows that an application brings up. You can identify the Applet window by the name "Java Applet Window," which is displayed at the bottom of the window. The application window would not have any name at its bottom. This helps the user distinguish applet windows from those of trusted applications.

Figures 18.15 and 18.16 show a window brought up by a program that can run either as an applet or as an application. Figure 18.15 shows what the window looks like when the program is run as an application on the Microsoft Windows platform. Figure 18.16 shows the window when the program runs as an applet on the Windows platform within the Mozilla browser.

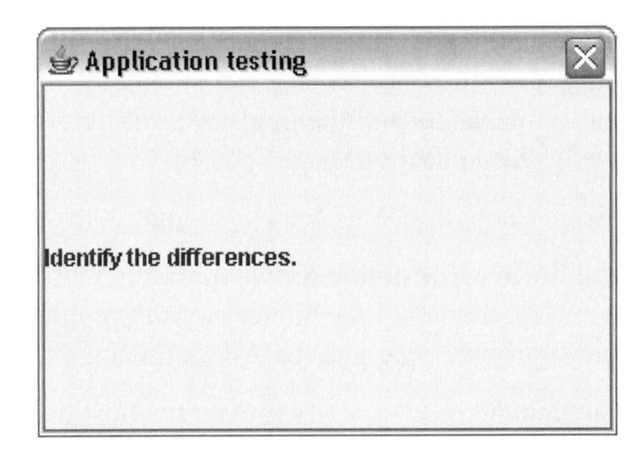

Figure 18.15 A program running as an application.

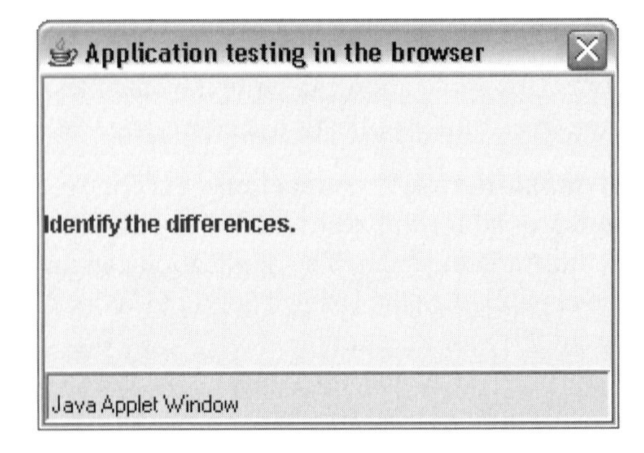

Figure 18.16 Same program running as an applet.

As you can see, the applet window has a label informing the user that it is running as an applet.

Creating a User Interface

Most applets have a graphical user interface (GUI). This is a natural consequence of the fact that each applet appears within a browser window. Because the `JApplet` class is a subclass of the `Applet` class, which is a subclass of the AWT `Panel` class and thus participates in the AWT event and drawing model, creating an applet's GUI is just as easy as creating an application's GUI. It's easier, actually, since the applet's window (the browser window) already exists.

In addition to its graphical UI, an applet can use several other UI types, depending on the kind of information it needs to give or get. Some applets play sounds, either to give the user feedback or to provide ambiance. Applets can get configuration information from the user through parameters that the applet defines. To give text information to the user, an applet can use its GUI, display a short status string (for text that's not crucial), or display to the standard output or standard error stream (for debugging purposes).

For information about sound, parameters, and status strings, see the Taking Advantage of the Applet API section (page 559).

Creating a GUI

This section discusses the few issues that are particular to applet GUIs. Some of the information in this section might not make sense until you've read the *Creating a GUI with JFC/Swing* and, in particular, the How to Make Applets section.[31] That trail discusses all the GUI concepts referred to in this section:

Applets appear in preexisting browser windows. This has two implications. First, unlike GUI-based applications, applets don't have to create a window in which to display themselves. They can, if they have a good reason, but they often just display themselves within the browser window. Second, depending on the browser implementation, your applet's components might not be shown unless your applet calls `validate` after adding components to itself. Fortunately, calling `validate` can't hurt.

The applet background color might not match the page color. By default, applets have a white background color. HTML pages, however, can have other background colors and can use background patterns. If the applet designer and page designer aren't careful, the applet's different background color can cause it to stick out on

31. `tutorial/uiswing/components/applet.html`

the page or cause noticeable flashing when the applet is drawn. One solution is to define an applet parameter that specifies the applet's background color. The `JApplet` class can use `JComponent`'s `setBackground` method to set the applet's background to the color specified in the Web page. Using the background color parameter, the page designer can choose an applet color that works well with the page colors. You've learned about parameters in the Defining and Using Applet Parameters section (page 570).

Each applet has a user-specified, predetermined size. The `<APPLET>` tag requires that the applet's width and height be specified. The Web designer can set an applet's size by pixels or by indicating a percentage of the browser window. Note that even if the amount of space is ideal for one platform, the platform-specific parts of the applet (such as buttons) might require a different amount of space on another platform. You can compensate by recommending that pages that include your applet specify a little more space than might be necessary, and by using flexible layouts, such as the `GridBagLayout` and `BorderLayout` classes, that adapt well to extra space.

Applets load images using the `Applet getImage` methods. The `Applet` class provides a convenient form of `getImage` that lets you specify a base URL as one argument, followed by a second argument that specifies the image file location, relative to the base URL. The `Applet getCodeBase` and `getDocumentBase` methods provide the base URLs that most applets use. Images that an applet always needs, or needs to rely on as a backup, are usually specified relative to where the applet's code was loaded from (the *code base*). Images that are specified by the applet user (often with parameters in the HTML file) are usually relative to the page that includes the applet (the *document base*).

Applet classes (and often the data files they use) are loaded over the network, which can be slow. Applets can do several things to decrease the perceived startup time. The `Applet` subclass can be a small one that immediately displays a status message. If some of the applet's classes or data aren't used right away, the applet can preload the classes or data in a background thread.

For example, the `AppletButton`[32] class `start` method launches a thread that gets the `Class`[33] object for the window the button brings up. The applet's main purpose in doing so is to make sure the class name that the user specified is valid. An added benefit is that getting the `Class` object forces the class file to be loaded before the class is instantiated. When the user requests that the window be created, the applet

32. `tutorial/uiswing/layout/example-swing/AppletButton.java`

33. `docs/api/java/lang/Class.html`

instantiates the window class much quicker than if the applet still had to load the window class file.

Displaying Diagnostics to the Standard Output and Error Streams

Displaying diagnostics to the standard output can be an invaluable tool when you're debugging an applet. Another time you'll see messages at the standard output is when an uncaught exception occurs in an applet. Applets also have the option of using the standard error stream.

Where exactly the standard output and error are displayed varies, depending on how the applet's viewer is implemented, what platform it's running on, and (sometimes) how you launch the browser or applet viewer. When you launch the Applet Viewer from a UNIX shell window, for example, strings displayed to the standard output and error appear in that shell window, unless you redirect the output. When you launch the Applet Viewer from an X Windows menu, the standard output and error go to the console window.

Applets display to the standard output stream using `System.out.print(String)` and `System.out.println(String)`. Displaying to the standard error stream is similar; just specify `System.err` instead of `System.out`. Here's an example of displaying to the standard output:

```
// Where instance variables are declared:
boolean DEBUG = true;
...
// Later, when we want to print some status:
if (DEBUG) {
  System.out.println("Called someMethod(" + x + "," + y + ")");
}
```

Note: Displaying to the standard output and error streams is relatively slow. If you have a timing-related problem, printing messages to either of these streams might not be helpful.

You should be sure to disable all debugging output before you release your applet.

Getting System Properties

To find out about the current working environment, applets can read system properties. System properties are key/value pairs that contain information such as the operating system that the applet is running under. System properties are covered in detail in the Properties section (page 443).

Applets can read some, but not all, system properties.

System Properties That Applets Can Read

Applets can read the system properties listed in Table 18.1.

Table 18.1 Valid System Properties

Key	Meaning
`"file.separator"`	File separator (for example, "/")
`"java.class.version"`	Java class version number
`"java.vendor"`	Java vendor-specific string
`"java.vendor.url"`	Java vendor URL
`"java.version"`	Java version number
`"line.separator"`	Line separator
`"os.arch"`	Operating system architecture
`"os.name"`	Operating system name
`"path.separator"`	Path separator (for example, ":")

To read a system property from within an applet, the applet uses the `System` class method `getProperty`. For example:

```
String newline = System.getProperty("line.separator");
```

Run an applet[34] which reads all of the properties available to all applets (Figure 18.17).

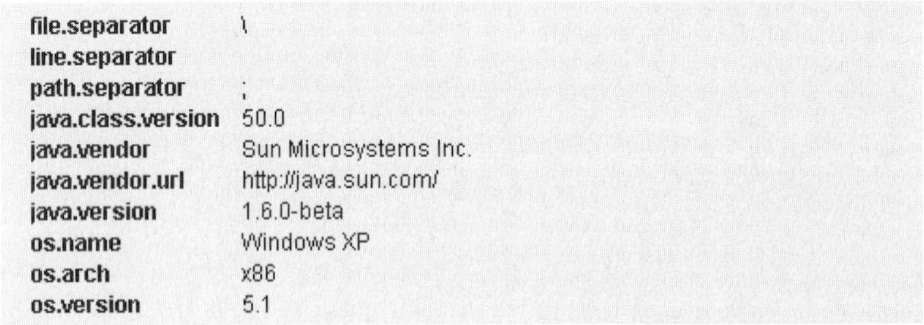

file.separator	\
line.separator	
path.separator	;
java.class.version	50.0
java.vendor	Sun Microsystems Inc.
java.vendor.url	http://java.sun.com/
java.version	1.6.0-beta
os.name	Windows XP
os.arch	x86
os.version	5.1

Figure 18.17 A screenshot of the GetOpenProperties applet.

You can find the source code in `GetOpenProperties.java`.[35]

---

34. `tutorial/deployment/applet/examples/properties.jar`

35. `tutorial/deployment/applet/examples/GetOpenProperties.java`

Forbidden System Properties

For security reasons, no existing browsers or applet viewers let applets read the system properties listed in Table 18.2.

Table 18.2 Forbidden System Properties

Key	Meaning
`"java.class.path"`	Java classpath
`"java.home"`	Java installation directory
`"user.dir"`	User's current working directory
`"user.home"`	User home directory
`"user.name"`	User account name

Threads in Applets

Note: This section assumes that you know what a thread is. If you don't, please read the Processes and Threads section (page 369) before reading this section.

Every applet can run in multiple threads. The applet's GUI is created on the event-dispatching thread. The threads that the major milestone methods—`init`, `start`, `stop`, and `destroy`—are called from depends on the application that's running the applet. But no application *ever* calls them from the event-handling thread.

Many browsers allocate a thread for each applet on a page, using that thread for all calls to the applet's major milestone methods. Some browsers allocate a thread group for each applet, so that it's easy to kill all the threads that belong to a particular applet. In any case, you're guaranteed that every thread created by any of an applet's major milestone methods belongs to the same thread group.

Run a `PrintThread` applet[36] (Figure 18.18). `PrintThread` is a modified version of `SimpleApplet` that prints the thread and thread group that its `init`, `start`, `stop`, `destroy`, and `update` methods are called from.[37]

As usual, to see the output for the methods such as `destroy` that are called during unloading, you need to look at the standard output. For standard output for an applet run in a browser, open the **Java Console** from the browser's **Tools** menu. See

---

36. `tutorial/deployment/applet/examples/threads.jar`

37. `tutorial/deployment/applet/examples/PrintThread.java`

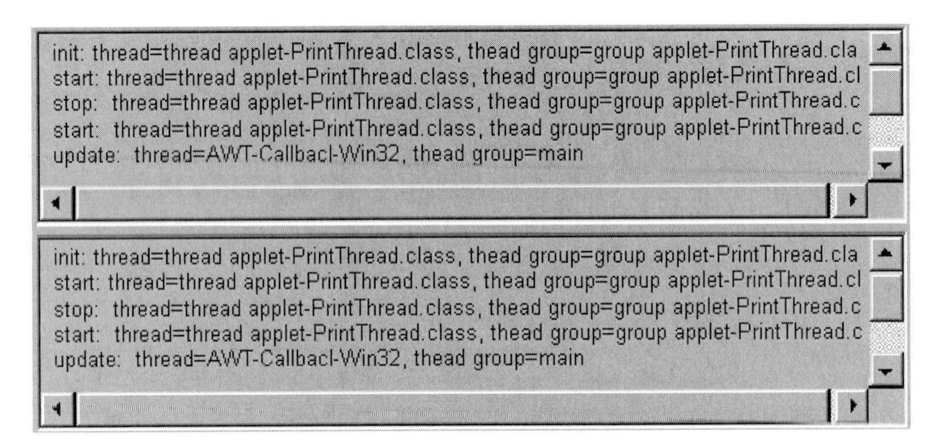

Figure 18.18 A screenshot of the PrintThread applet.

the Displaying Diagnostics to the Standard Output and Error Streams section (page 583) for information about the standard output stream.

So why would an applet need to create and use its own threads? Imagine an applet that performs some time-consuming initialization—loading images, for example—in its `init` method. The thread that invokes `init` cannot do anything else until `init` returns. In some browsers, this might mean that the browser can't display the applet or anything after it until the applet has finished initializing itself. So if the applet is at the top of the page, for example, then nothing would appear on the page until the applet has finished initializing itself.

Even in browsers that create a separate thread for each applet, it makes sense to put any time-consuming tasks into an applet-created thread, so that the applet can perform other tasks while it waits for the time-consuming ones to be completed.

Rule of Thumb: If an applet performs a time-consuming task, it should create and use its own thread to perform that task.

Applets typically perform two kinds of time-consuming tasks: tasks that they perform once and tasks that they perform repeatedly. The next section gives an example of both.

Threads in Applets: Examples

This section discusses two examples of using threads in applets. The first applet, AnimatorApplet, shows how to use a thread to perform repeated tasks. The second applet this page discusses, SoundExample, shows how to use threads for one-time initialization tasks. SoundExample is featured in the Playing Sounds section (page 568).

This section does not explain basic thread code. To learn about the Java implementation of threads, refer to the Defining and Starting a Thread section (page 371).

Using a Thread to Perform Repeated Tasks

An applet that performs the same task over and over again typically should have a thread with a `while` (or `do...while`) loop that performs the task. A typical example is an applet that performs timed animation, such as a movie player or a game. Animation applets need a thread that requests repaints at regular intervals. Another example is an applet that reads data supplied by a server-side application. (See the Using a Server to Work Around Security Restrictions section, page 591, for such an example.)

Applets typically create threads for repetitive tasks in the applet `start` method. Creating the thread there makes it easy for the applet to stop the thread when the user leaves the page. All you need to do is implement the `stop` method so that it stops the applet's thread. When the user returns to the applet's page, the `start` method is called again, and the applet can again create a thread to perform the repetitive task.

Below is `AnimatorApplet`'s implementation of the `start` and `stop` methods:

```
public void start() {
  if (frozen) {
      // Do nothing.  The user has requested that we
      // stop changing the image.
  } else {
      // Start animating!
      if (animatorThread == null) {
        animatorThread = new Thread(this);
      }
      animatorThread.start();
  }
}

public void stop() {
  animatorThread = null;
}
```

The `this` in `new Thread(this)` indicates that the applet provides the body of the thread. It does so by implementing the `java.lang.Runnable` interface, which requires the applet to provide a `run` method that forms the body of the thread. We'll discuss `AnimatorApplet`'s `run` method more a little later.

Notice that nowhere in the `AnimatorApplet` class is the `Thread stop` method called. This is because calling the `Thread stop` method is like clubbing the thread over the head. It's a drastic way to get the thread to stop what it's doing. Instead, you can write the thread's `run` method in such a way that the thread will gracefully exit when you tap it on the shoulder. This shoulder tap comes in the form of setting to null an instance variable of type `Thread`.

In AnimatorApplet, this instance variable is called animatorThread. The start method sets it to refer to the newly created Thread object. When the applet needs to kill the thread, it sets animatorThread to null. This kills the thread *not* by making it be garbage collected—it can't be garbage collected while it's runnable—but because at the top of its loop, the thread checks animatorThread, continuing or exiting depending on the value of animatorThread. Here's the relevant code:

```
public void run() {
  ...
  while (Thread.currentThread() == animatorThread) {
    ...// Display a frame of animation and then sleep.
  }
}
```

If animatorThread refers to the same thread as the currently executing thread, the thread continues executing. If, on the other hand, animatorThread is null, the thread exits. If animatorThread refers to *another* thread, then a race condition has occurred: start has been called so soon after stop (or this thread has taken such a long time in its loop) that start has created another thread before this thread reached the top of its while loop. Whatever the cause of the race condition, this thread should exit.

For more information about animation applets, see Threads in Applets, a section in *Creating a GUI with JFC/Swing*.

Using a Thread to Perform One-Time Initialization

If your applet needs to perform some initialization task that can take a while, you should consider ways of performing the initialization in a thread. For example, anything that requires making a network connection should generally be done in a background thread. Fortunately, GIF, PNG, and JPEG image loading is automatically done in the background using threads that you don't need to worry about.

Sound loading, unfortunately, is not guaranteed to be done in the background. In current implementations, the Applet getAudioClip methods don't return until they've loaded all the audio data. As a result, if you want to preload sounds, you might want to create one or more threads to do so.

Using a thread to perform a one-time initialization task for an applet is a variation of the classic producer/consumer scenario. The thread that performs the task is the producer, and the applet is the consumer. The Synchronization section (page 377) discusses how to use Java threads in a producer/consumer scenario.

SoundExample adheres closely to the model presented in Synchronizing Threads. Like the Synchronizing Threads example, SoundExample features three classes:[38]

- The producer: `SoundLoader`, a `Thread` subclass.
- The consumer: `SoundExample`, an `Applet` subclass. Unlike the Synchronizing Threads consumer example, `SoundExample` is not a `Thread`; it doesn't even implement the `Runnable` interface. However, the `SoundExample` instance methods are executed by at least two threads, depending on the application that executes the `SoundExample` applet.
- The storage object: `SoundList`, a `Hashtable` subclass. Unlike `CubbyHole` in the Synchronizing Threads example, `SoundList` can return null values if the sound data hasn't been stored yet. This makes sense for this applet because it needs to be able to react immediately to a user request to play the sound, even if the sound hasn't been loaded yet.

For more information on `SoundExample`, refer to the Playing Sounds section (page 568).

Working with a Server-Side Application

Applets, like other Java programs, can use the API defined in the `java.net` package to communicate across the network. The only difference is that, for security reasons, the only host an applet can communicate with is the host it was delivered from.

Note: Depending on the networking environment an applet is loaded into, and depending on the browser that runs the applet, an applet might not be able to communicate with its originating host. For example, browsers running on hosts inside firewalls often cannot get much information about the world outside the firewall. As a result, some browsers might not allow applet communication to hosts outside the firewall.

It's easy to find out which host an applet came from. Just use the `Applet getCodeBase` method and the `java.net.URL getHost` method, like this:

```
String host = getCodeBase().getHost();
```

Once you have the right host name, you can use all the networking code that is documented in the Custom Networking trail in the online tutorial.[39]

---

38. Refer to footnotes on page 570.

39. `tutorial/networking/index.html`

Note: Not all browsers support all networking code flawlessly. For example, one widely used browser compatible with Java technology doesn't support posting to a URL.

A Simple Network Client Applet

This section talks about the client to be an applet.[40] The client has been written not only to communicate with the host the applet came from, but also to have a graphical UI, and to have a loop so that it can get as many quotes as you like. You can run the applet by including it in a page with the following HTML code:

```
<APPLET CODE=QuoteClientApplet.class WIDTH=500 HEIGHT=100>
</APPLET>
```

The `quoteApplet.html` page[41] contains the above HTML code. By saving this page to a file on your local HTTP server, you can use it to communicate with the server-side application that will be running on the HTTP server. You must also save the compiled form of the applet to the same directory.

Before the applet can get quotes, you need to run the server on the host that the applet came from. You then need to note the number of the port that the server is listening on. After you enter this port number into the applet, it will hook up with the server and you'll be able to get one-line quotations. Below are detailed instructions, followed by pictures of the server and the applet in action:

1. Compile `QuoteServer.java`[42] and `QuoteServerThread.java`.[43] A text file (`one-liners.txt`[44]) should be in the same directory as the resulting class files.
2. On the computer that serves the applet class file (through HTTP), invoke the interpreter on the `QuoteServer` class. For example, if you view the applet's page with the URL **http://mymachine/quoteApplet.html**, then you need to run the server on the host named **mymachine**.
3. Record the port number that the quote server displays.
4. Enter this number into the applet's text field.
5. Press the **Send** button to request a quote from the server. You should see a quote appear in the text area.

40. `tutorial/deployment/applet/examples/QuoteClientApplet.java`
41. `tutorial/deployment/applet/examples/quoteApplet.html`
42. `tutorial/deployment/applet/examples/QuoteServer.java`
43. `tutorial/deployment/applet/examples/QuoteServerThread.java`
44. `tutorial/deployment/applet/examples/one-liners.txt`

Figure 18.19 shows a picture of the applet in action.

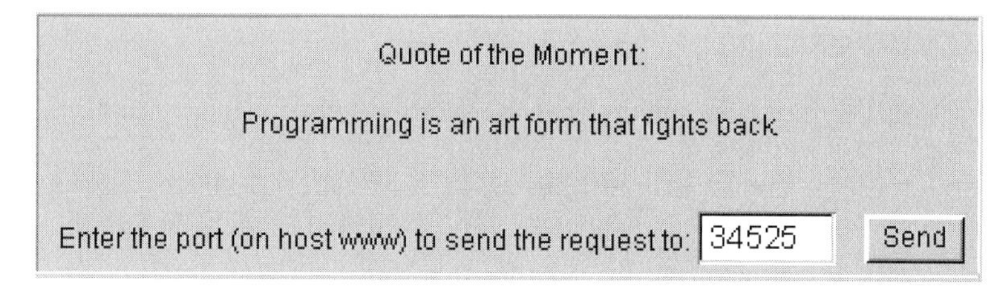

Figure 18.19 A screenshot of the QuoteServer applet.

Using a Server to Work Around Security Restrictions

As the What Applets Can and Can't Do section (page 558) explains, applets are subject to many security restrictions. For example, they can't perform file I/O, they can't make network connections except to their original host, and they can't start programs.

One way of working around these restrictions is to use a server application that executes on the applet's host. The server won't be able to get around every applet restriction, but it can make more things possible. For example, a server probably can't save files on the host the applet's running on, but it will be able to save files on the host the applet originated from.

This section features an example of a server that allows two applets to communicate with each other. The applets don't have to be running on the same page, in the same browser, or on the same computer. As long as the applets originate from the same computer, they can communicate through the server that's running on that originating computer. The example uses sockets, which are documented in All About Sockets.[45]

Here are the source files:

`TalkClientApplet.java`[46] The source file for the client applet. After you compile it, you can run it by including it in an HTML page with this tag:

```
<APPLET CODE=TalkClientApplet.class WIDTH=550 HEIGHT=200>
</APPLET>
```

The `talk.html` page[47] includes the above HTML code. After saving this page to a file on your local HTTP server, you can use it to communicate with the talk server.

45. `tutorial/networking/sockets/index.html`

46. `tutorial/deployment/applet/examples/TalkClientApplet.java`

47. `tutorial/deployment/applet/examples/talk.html`

TalkServer.java[48] **and TalkServerThread.java**[49] The source files for the server applet. After compiling both files, you can run the server on the applets' originating host by invoking the interpreter on the `TalkServer` class.

The instructions for running the server are just like those for the previous example (see the A Simple Network Client Applet section, page 590). Run the server on the applets' originating host, recording the port number that the applets should rendezvous on. Then initialize both applets (which can be running on different machines) to talk to the server port number. After this initialization is complete, type a string into each applet's text field. Then press the **Return** key to send the message to the other applet.

Here's the server in action:

```
www%  java TalkServer
TalkServer listening on rendezvous port: 36567
```

Figures 18.20 and 18.21 show pictures of the applets in action.

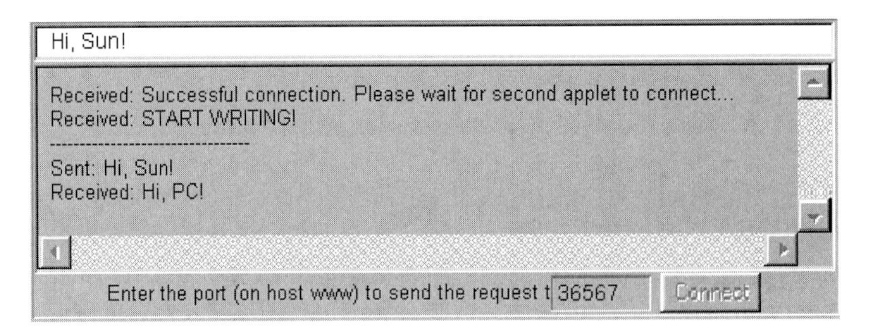

Figure 18.20 Sample talk output—machine #1.

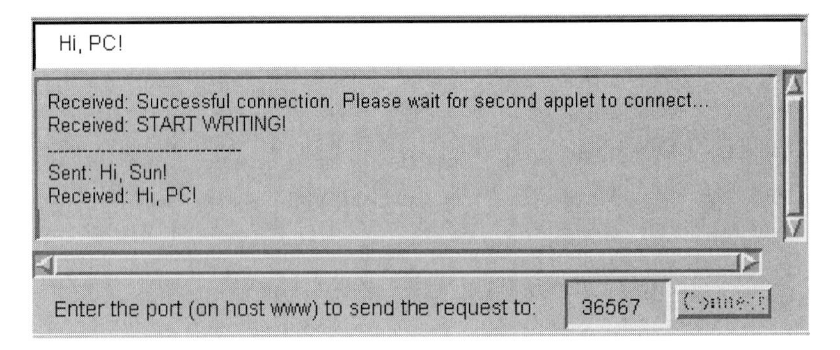

Figure 18.21 Sample talk output—machine #2.

48. `tutorial/deployment/applet/examples/TalkServer.java`

49. `tutorial/deployment/applet/examples/TalkServerThread.java`

Finishing an Applet

Before You Ship That Applet

Stop! Before you let the whole world know about your applet, make sure the answer to all of the following questions is **yes**:

1. **Have you removed or disabled debugging output?**

   Debugging output (generally created with `System.out.println`), while useful to you, is generally confusing or annoying to users. If you need to give textual feedback to the user, try to do it inside the applet's display area or in the status area at the bottom of the window. Information on using the status area is in the Displaying Short Status Strings section (page 561).

2. **Does the applet stop running when it's offscreen?**

   Most applets should not use CPU resources when the browser is iconified or is displaying a page that doesn't contain the applet. If your applet code doesn't launch any threads explicitly, then you're OK.

   If your applet code launches any threads, then unless you have a *really good* excuse not to, you should implement the `stop` method so that it stops and destroys (by setting to null) the threads you launched. For an example of implementing the `stop` method, see the Threads in Applets: Examples section (page 586).

3. **If the applet does something that might get annoying—play sounds or animation, for example—does it give the user a way of stopping the annoying behavior?**

   Be kind to your users. Give them a way to stop the applet in its tracks, without leaving the page. In an applet that otherwise doesn't respond to mouse clicks, you can do this by implementing the `mouseDown` method so that a mouse click suspends or resumes the annoying thread. For example:

   ```
   boolean frozen = false; // an instance variable

   public boolean mouseDown(Event e, int x, int y) {
     if (frozen) {
         frozen = false;
         start();
     } else {
         frozen = true;
         stop();
     }
     return true;
   }
   ```

The Perfectly Finished Applet

The previous section lists some of the ways you can avoid making your applet's users want to throttle you. This section tells you about some other ways that you can make dealing with your applet as pleasant as possible:

- **Make your applet as flexible as possible.**

  You can often define parameters that let your applet be used in a variety of situations without any rewriting. See the Defining and Using Applet Parameters section (page 570) for more information.

- **Make your applet accessible.**

  You can design your applet so that it is accessible to all. See the Swing chapter in the How to Support Assistive Technologies[50] section of the tutorial for more information.

- **Implement the `getParameterInfo` method.**

  Implementing this method now might make your applet easier to customize in the future. Currently, no browsers use this method. Soon, however, we expect browsers to use this method to help generate a GUI that allows the user to interactively set parameter values. See the Giving Information about Parameters section (page 573) for information on implementing `getParameterInfo`.

- **Implement the `getAppletInfo` method.**

  This method returns a short, informative string describing an applet. Although no browsers currently use this method, we expect them to in the future. Here's an example of implementing `getAppletInfo`:

  ```
  public String getAppletInfo() {
    return "GetApplets by Kathy Walrath";
  }
  ```

Deploying Applets

This section explains to HTML authors how and when to use the `applet`, `object`, and `embed` tags to add Java applets to Web pages, and provides guidelines for deploying applets on the Internet and Intranets and for use with different browsers.

50. tutorial/uiswing/misc/access.html

General Deployment Considerations

How you deploy an applet depends on whether users access the Web page through the Internet or an Intranet, and the type of browser they use. Note this information about your users, then follow the general guidelines below.

Deploying Applets on the Internet versus an Intranet

When deploying applets:

- Use the `applet` tag if the Web page is accessed through the Internet or if it is accessed through an Intranet in which people use different browsers.
- Use the `object` or `embed` tag if the Web page is accessed through an Intranet and you know which browser people use.

Deploying Applets for Specific Browsers

When deploying applets:

- For Internet Explorer only, use the `object` tag.
- For the Mozilla family of browsers only, use the `embed` tag.

If you must deploy an applet in a mixed-browser environment, follow the guidelines in the Deploying Applets in a Mixed-Browser Environment section (page 598).

Using the applet Tag

You use the `applet` tag to deploy applets to a multi-browser environment.

For complete details on the `applet` tag, read the W3 HTML specification.[51]

Note: The HTML specification states that the `applet` tag is deprecated and that you should use the `object` tag instead. However, the specification is vague about how browsers should implement the `object` tag to support Java applets, and browser support is currently inconsistent. It is therefore recommended that you continue to use the `applet` tag as a consistent way to deploy Java applets across browsers on all platforms.

---

51. `http://www.w3.org/TR/1999/REC-html401-19991224/`

Following is an example of the applet tag:

```
<applet code=Applet1.class width="200" height="200">
Your browser does not support the applet tag.
</applet>
```

For both Internet Explorer and the Mozilla family of browsers, if Java Plug-in is installed (version 1.3.1_01a or later) then the latest installed version of Java Plug-in is invoked to run the applet.

Note: You cannot use the applet tag to automatically download a JRE if one is not installed locally.

Using the object Tag

You use the object tag to deploy applets that are to be used only with Internet Explorer.

For complete details on the object tag, read the W3 HTML specification.

Following is an example of the object tag:

```
<OBJECT
  classid="clsid:8AD9C840-044E-11D1-B3E9-00805F499D93"
  width="200" height="200">
  <PARAM name="code" value="Applet1.class">
</OBJECT>
```

The classid Attribute

The classid attribute identifies which version of Java Plug-in to use.

The example shown below is the most commonly used form of the classid attribute. This example instructs Internet Explorer to use the latest installed version of Java Plug-in:

```
classid="clsid:8AD9C840-044E-11D1-B3E9-00805F499D93"
```

Following is an alternative form of the classid attribute:

```
classid="clsid:CAFEEFAC-xxxx-yyyy-zzzz-ABCDEFFEDCBA"
```

In this form, "xxxx", "yyyy", and "zzzz" are four-digit numbers that identify the specific version of Java Plug-in to be used.

For example, to use Java Plug-in version 1.6.0, you specify:

```
classid="clsid:CAFEEFAC-0016-0000-0000-ABCDEFFEDCBA"
```

The codebase Attribute

You use the optional `codebase` attribute to specify the location to download JRE from in case it is not installed on the system.

The codebase attribute has two forms:

codebase=<URL> With this form, if the JRE specified by the `classid` attribute is not installed locally, then the user is prompted to download the JRE from the URL specified.

codebase=<URL>#Version=major,minor,micro,update With this form, Java Plug-in compares the `classid` of the locally installed JRE with the required version of JRE, and if the required version is higher, prompts the user to download and install the newer version of the JRE.

Following is an example of how to use the `codebase` attribute to set up automatic downloads from the Sun Java Web site:

```
<object
  classid="clsid:8AD9C840-044E-11D1-B3E9-00805F499D93"
  width="200" height="200"
  codebase="http://java.sun.com/update/1.6.0/
    jinstall-6-windows-i586.cab#Version=6,0,0,99">
  <param name="code" value="Applet1.class">
</object>
```

Note: In this example, the `codebase=http://java.sun.com ...` line is broken for readability. In the actual HTML file it would be one long line.

Sun has packaged each version of the JRE installer in Microsoft cabinet (.cab) file format. You can view a list of these releases and the corresponding .cab file names.[52]

52. docs/technotes/guides/deployment/deployment-guide/autodl-files.html

Using the embed Tag

You use the `embed` tag to deploy applets that are to be used only with the Mozilla family of browsers.

Following is an example of the `embed` tag:

```
<embed code="Applet1.class"
  width="200" height="200"
  type="application/x-java-applet;version=1.6.0"
  pluginspage="http://java.sun.com/javase/downloads"/>
```

The `type` attribute can have one of two forms:

`type="application/x-java-applet;version=1.6.0"` With this form, the highest installed JRE that supports the MIME type

```
application/x-java-applet;version=1.6.0
```

is invoked to run the applet. If a JRE with a version number equal to or greater than the version number specified is installed locally, then that JRE is invoked. Otherwise the user is directed to the URL specified as the value of the `pluginspage` attribute and is prompted to download and install the required JRE.

`type="application/x-java-applet;jpi-version=1.6.0_01` With this form, a JRE with the exact version given by the the value of `jpi-version` (in this example, 1.6.0_01) is invoked to run the applet. Otherwise the user is directed to the URL specified as the value of the `pluginspage` attribute and is prompted to download and install the required JRE.

Deploying Applets in a Mixed-Browser Environment

You can deploy applets for users of both Internet Explorer and the Mozilla family of browsers in one of two ways:

- Through pure HTML
- Through JavaScript

Using Pure HTML

When using a pure HTML approach to deploy applets in a mixed-browser environment, note the following:

- **Internet Explorer**
  - Recognizes the `object` tag
  - Ignores the contents of the `comment` tag
- **Mozilla browsers**
  - Ignore an `object` tag with the `classid` attribute
  - Interpret the contents of the `comment` tag

Consider the following example code from an HTML page:

```
<object classid="clsid:CAFEEFAC-0016-0000-0000-ABCDEFFEDCBA"
  <param name="code" value="Applet1.class">
    <comment>
      <embed code="Applet1.class"
             type="application/x-java-applet;jpi-version=1.6">
        <noembed>
          No Java Support.
        </noembed>
      </embed>
    </comment>
</object>
```

Using JavaScript

Instead of using the pure HTML approach described above, you can use JavaScript to deploy applets in a mixed-browser environment.

Through JavaScript, you:

1. Detect the user's browser through the `appName` variable.
2. Use the `document.write()` method to write a tag based on the value of the `appName` variable:
   a. If the browser name equals "Netscape", write the `embed` tag.
   b. If the browser name equals "Microsoft Internet Explorer", write the `object` tag.

In the following example, the `document.write()` method outputs either an `embed` or `object` tag for each user "on the fly":

```
<html>
<script language="Javascript">

  var _app = navigator.appName;

  if (_app == 'Netscape') {
    document.write('<embed code="Applet1.class"',
      'width="200"',
      'height="200"',
      'type="application/x-java-applet;version=1.6">');
    }
  else if (_app == 'Microsoft Internet Explorer') {
    document.write('<OBJECT ',
      'classid="clsid:8AD9C840-044E-11D1-B3E9-00805F499D93"',
      'width="200"',
      'height="200">',
      '<PARAM name="code" value="Applet1.class">',
      '</OBJECT>');
    }
  else {
    document.write('<p>Sorry, unsupported browser.</p>');
    }

</script>
</html>
```

You can use the HTML Converter tool[53] to help with generating `object` and `embed` tags for mixed environments.

Solving Common Applet Problems

This section covers some common problems that you might encounter when writing Java applets. After each problem there is a list of possible solutions.

Problem: Applet Viewer says there is no `<APPLET>` tag on my HTML page, but it really is there.

- Check whether you have a closing applet tag: `</APPLET>`

Problem: I recompiled my applet, but my applet viewing application would not show the new version even though I told it to reload it.

- In many applet viewers (including browsers), reloading is not reliable. This is why we recommend that you simply use the JDK Applet Viewer, invoking it anew every time you change the applet.

53. `docs/technotes/guides/plugin/developer_guide/html_converter.html`

- If you get an old version of the applet, no matter what you do, make sure that you don't have an old copy of the applet in a directory in your `CLASSPATH`. See the Managing Source and Class Files section (page 191) for information about the `CLASSPATH` environment variable.

Problem: The background color of my applet causes the applet not to match or flicker when it is drawn on a page of a different color.

- You need to set the background color of the applet so that it works well with the page color. See the Creating a GUI section (page 581) for details.

Problem: The `Applet` `getImage` method doesn't work.

- Make sure you're calling `getImage` from the `init` method or a method that's called after `init`. The `getImage` method does not work when it is called from a constructor.

Problem: Now that I have copied my applet's class file onto my HTTP server, the applet doesn't work.

- Does your applet define more than one class? If so, make sure that the class file (*`ClassName`*`.class`) for each class is on the HTTP server. Even if all the classes are defined in one source file, the compiler produces one class file per class.
- Did you copy all the data files for your applet—image and sound files, for example—to the server?
- Make sure all the applet's class and data files can be read by everyone.
- Make sure the applet's class and data files weren't garbled during the transfer. One common source of trouble is using the ASCII mode of FTP (rather than the BINARY mode) to transfer files.

Problem: Applet is not loaded in my Web page. I see the error "java.lang.UnsupportedClassVersionError: Bad version number in .class file" in my Java Console.

- The problem is that the source for the applet is compiled with a newer version of Java than the one installed on your system. Which JRE version are you using? If it is not the latest version, make sure you install the latest Java SE Runtime Environment (JRE).[54]

Tip for Deployers: You can compile your applets with JDK 6 using compile time options as source –1.2 and target –1.2, so that you can run them with the older versions of JRE.

---

54. `http://java.sun.com/javase/downloads`

Questions and Exercises: Java Applets

Questions

1. Which classes can an applet extend?
2. How do you cause the applet GUI in the browser to be refreshed when data in it may have changed?
3. What do you use the `start()` method for?
4. True or false: An applet can make network connections to any host on the Internet.
5. How do you get the value of a parameter specified in the `APPLET` tag from within the applet's code?
6. True or false: An applet can run multiple threads.
7. Match the following tag names with the descriptions in the following lists:
   1) `EMBED` tag
   2) `APPLET` tag
   3) `OBJECT` tag

   a. Use to deploy applets to a multi-browser environment.
   b. Use to deploy applets that are to be used only with the Mozilla family of browsers.
   c. Use to deploy applets that are to be used only with Internet Explorer.

Exercises

1. For an applet using the `Exercise` class, write the `Applet` tag that sets the `ButtonName` parameter to `Save`.
2. Write the method to display an applet in the browser so that the contents are contained in a rectangle around the phrase "Exercise Applet." Have the applet be one pixel less than the size specified on the Web page and have the phrase start at the coordinates 5, 15.

Answers

You can find answers to these Questions and Exercises at:

`tutorial/deployment/applet/QandE/answers.html`

APPENDIX A

Java Language Keywords

TABLE A.1 contains a list of keywords in the Java language. These words are reserved—you cannot use any of these words as names in your programs. `true`, `false`, and `null` are not keywords but they are reserved words, so you cannot use them as names in your programs either.

Table A.1 Java Language Keywords

abstract	continue	for	new	switch
assert***	default	goto*	package	synchronized
boolean	do	if	private	this
break	double	implements	protected	throw
byte	else	import	public	throws
case	enum****	instanceof	return	transient
catch	extends	int	short	try
char	final	interface	static	void
class	finally	long	strictfp**	volatile
const*	float	native	super	whilex
* not used	** added in 1.2	*** added in 1.4	**** added in 5.0	

APPENDIX B

Preparation for Java Programming Language Certification

SUN Microsystems provides certification examinations for Solaris administrators and different types of Java programmers. Sun also offers training classes and practice exams for each type of certification.

Much of the material in this tutorial is pertinent to preparation for the examination to become a "Sun Certified Programmer for the Java Platform."

Some useful links are:

`http://www.sun.com/training/certification` An overview of all of the various certifications offered and their associated learning tools.

`http://www.sun.com/training/certification/java/index.html` Information specific to the certifications available for Java technologies.

`http://www.sun.com/training/certification/objectives` A table of links to the "Testing Objectives" for each Java certification exam—lists of what will be covered on the exams.

If you open the last link and select the Testing Objectives for the Sun Certified Programmer for the Java Platform, you will find a list of objectives that includes bulleted items in seven areas:

1. Declarations, Initialization, and Scoping
2. Flow Control
3. API Contents
4. Concurrency

5. OO Concepts
6. Collections/Generics
7. Fundamentals

In the text below, each of the bulleted items in each of the seven areas of the Testing Objectives for the Sun Certified Programmer for the Java Platform is quoted, followed by links to sections in this tutorial that include relevant material.

Disclaimer: This tutorial is not intended as a primer for the certification exam—it does not cover every subject to the depth that will be on the exam. The links below are presented so that you can use this tutorial as *one of many sources* for exam preparation.

Section 1: Declarations, Initialization and Scoping

Item 1

"Develop code that declares classes (including abstract and all forms of nested classes), interfaces, and enums, and includes the appropriate use of package and import statements (including static imports)."

- Declaring Classes (page 87)
- Abstract Methods and Classes (page 161)
- Nested Classes (page 122)
- Interfaces (page 139)
- Enum Types (page 128)
- Creating and Using PackagesCreating a Package (page 183)
- import statements, static imports: Using Package Members (page 187)

Item 2

"Develop code that declares an interface. Develop code that implements or extends one or more interfaces. Develop code that declares an abstract class. Develop code that extends an abstract class."

- Defining an Interface (page 142)
- Implementing an Interface (page 143)
- Abstract Methods and Classes (page 161)

Item 3

"Develop code that declares, initializes, and uses primitives, arrays, enums, and objects as static, instance, and local variables. Also, use legal identifiers for variable names."

- Primitive Data Types (page 45)
- Arrays (page 49)
- Enum Types (page 128)
- Understanding Instance and Class Members (page 112)
- Variables (page 43)
- Declaring Member Variables (page 88)

Item 4

"Develop code that declares both static and non-static methods, and—if appropriate—use method names that adhere to the JavaBeans naming standards. Also develop code that declares and uses a variable-length argument list."

- Understanding Instance and Class Members (page 112)
- Passing Information to a Method or a Constructor (page 93)

Item 5

"Given a code example, determine if a method is correctly overriding or overloading another method, and identify legal return values (including covariant returns), for the method."

- Overriding and Hiding Methods (page 152)
- Overloading: Defining Methods (page 90)
- Returning a Value from a Method (page 106)

Item 6

"Given a set of classes and superclasses, develop constructors for one or more of the classes. Given a class declaration, determine if a default constructor will be created, and if so, determine the behavior of that constructor. Given a nested or non-nested class listing, write code to instantiate the class."

- Providing Constructors for Your Classes (page 92)
- Using the Keyword `super` (page 154)

- Creating Objects (page 99)
- Nested Classes (page 122)

Section 2: Flow Control

Item 1

"Develop code that implements an `if` or `switch` statement; and identify legal argument types for these statements."

- The `if-then` and `if-then-else` Statements (page 69)
- The `switch` Statement (page 71)

Item 2

"Develop code that implements all forms of loops and iterators, including the use of `for`, the enhanced `for` loop (`for-each`), `do`, `while`, labels, `break`, and `continue`; and explain the values taken by loop counter variables during and after loop execution."

- The `for` Statement (page 75)
- The `while` and `do-while` Statements (page 74)
- Branching Statements (page 77)

Item 3

"Develop code that makes use of assertions, and distinguish appropriate from inappropriate use of assertions."

- assertion example: Questions and Exercises: Classes (page 119)

Item 4

"Develop code that makes use of exceptions and exception handling clauses (`try`, `catch`, `finally`), and declares methods and overriding methods that throw exceptions."

- Catching and Handling Exceptions (page 236)
- The `try` Block (page 238)
- The `catch` Blocks (page 239)
- The `finally` Block (page 240)
- Putting It All Together (page 241)

Item 5

"Recognize the effect of an exception arising at a specified point in a code fragment. Note that the exception may be a runtime exception, a checked exception, or an error."

- The Catch or Specify Requirement (page 235)
- Specifying the Exceptions Thrown by a Method (page 245)

Item 6

"Recognize situations that will result in any of the following being thrown: `ArrayIndexOutOfBoundsException`, `AssertionError`, `ClassCastException`, `IllegalArgumentException`, `IllegalStateException`, `NullPointerException`, `NumberFormatException`, `ExceptionInInitializerError`, `StackOverflowError`, or `NoClassDefFoundError`. Understand which of these are thrown by the virtual machine and recognize situations in which others should be thrown programatically."

- `ArrayIndexOutOfBoundsException`: Putting It All Together (page 241)
- `NullPointerException`: How to Throw Exceptions (page 246)
- `NumberFormatException`: Command-Line Arguments (page 448)
- `ClassCastException`, `IllegalStateException`: Object Ordering (page 328)
- `IllegalStateException`: The `Queue` Interface (page 316)
- `IllegalStateException`: The `List` Interface (page 306)

Section 3: API Contents

Item 1

"Develop code that uses the primitive wrapper classes (such as `Boolean`, `Character`, `Double`, `Integer`, etc.), and/or autoboxing & unboxing. Discuss the differences between the `String`, `StringBuilder`, and `StringBuffer` classes."

- The Numbers Classes (page 195)
- Characters (page 210)
- Strings (page 212)
- The `StringBuilder` Class (page 226)

Item 2

"Given a scenario involving navigating file systems, reading from files, or writing to files, develop the correct solution using the following classes (sometimes in combination), from `java.io`: `BufferedReader`, `BufferedWriter`, `File`, `FileReader`, `FileWriter`, and `PrintWriter`."

- `FileReader`, `FileWriter`: Character Streams (page 265)
- `BufferedReader`, `BufferedWriter`: Buffered Streams (page 269)
- `PrintWriter`: Formatting (page 272)
- `File`: File Objects (page 286)

Item 3

"Develop code that serializes and/or de-serializes objects using the following APIs from `java.io`: `DataInputStream`, `DataOutputStream`, `FileInputStream`, `FileOutputStream`, `ObjectInputStream`, `ObjectOutputStream`, and `Serializable`."

- Data Streams (page 279)
- Object Streams (page 282)

Item 4

"Use standard J2SE APIs in the `java.text` package to correctly format or parse dates, numbers, and currency values for a specific locale; and, given a scenario, determine the appropriate methods to use if you want to use the default locale or a specific locale. Describe the purpose and use of the `java.util.Locale` class."

Item 5

"Write code that uses standard J2SE APIs in the `java.util` and `java.util.regex` packages to format or parse strings or streams. For strings, write code that uses the `Pattern` and `Matcher` classes and the `String.split` method. Recognize and use regular expression patterns for matching (limited to: . (dot), * (star), + (plus), ?, `\d`, `\s`, `\w`, `[]`, `()`). The use of *, +, and ? will be limited to greedy quantifiers, and the parenthesis operator will only be used as a grouping mechanism, not for capturing content during matching. For streams, write code using the `Formatter` and `Scanner` classes and the `PrintWriter.format/printf` methods. Recognize and use formatting parameters (limited to: `%b`, `%c`, `%d`, `%f`, `%s`) in format strings."

- `String split` method: Manipulating Characters in a String (page 218)
- Methods of the `Pattern` Class (page 425)

- Methods of the `Matcher` Class (page 431)
- Scanning (page 270)
- Formatting (page 272)
- `PrintWriter`, formatting parameters: Formatting (page 272)
- formatting parameters: Formatting Numeric Print Output (page 198)

Section 4: Concurrency

Item 1

"Write code to define, instantiate, and start new threads using both `java.lang.Thread` and `java.lang.Runnable`."

- Defining and Starting a Thread (page 371)
- The `SimpleThreads` Example (page 375)

Item 2

"Recognize the states in which a thread can exist, and identify ways in which a thread can transition from one state to another."

Item 3

"Given a scenario, write code that makes appropriate use of object locking to protect static or instance variables from concurrent access problems."

- Thread Interference (page 377)
- Memory Consistency Errors (page 379)
- Synchronized Methods (page 380)
- Intrinsic Locks and Synchronization (page 381)
- Atomic Access (page 383)

Item 4

"Given a scenario, write code that makes appropriate use of `wait`, `notify`, or `notifyAll`."

- Guarded Blocks (page 386)

Section 5: OO Concepts

Item 1

"Develop code that implements tight encapsulation, loose coupling, and high cohesion in classes, and describe the benefits."

Item 2

"Given a scenario, develop code that demonstrates the use of polymorphism. Further, determine when casting will be necessary and recognize compiler vs. runtime errors related to object reference casting."

- Inheritance (page 147)

Item 3

"Explain the effect of modifiers on inheritance with respect to constructors, instance or static variables, and instance or static methods."

- Inheritance (page 147)
- Overriding and Hiding Methods (page 152)
- Using the Keyword `super` (page 154)

Item 4

"Given a scenario, develop code that declares and/or invokes overridden or overloaded methods and code that declares and/or invokes superclass, overridden, or overloaded constructors."

- Overriding and Hiding Methods (page 152)
- Defining Methods (page 90)
- Using the Keyword `super` (page 154)

Item 5

"Develop code that implements 'is-a' and/or 'has-a' relationships."

Section 6: Collections / Generics

Item 1

"Given a design scenario, determine which collection classes and/or interfaces should be used to properly implement that design, including the use of the `Comparable` interface."

• Object Ordering (page 328)

Item 2

"Distinguish between correct and incorrect overrides of corresponding `hashCode` and `equals` methods, and explain the difference between == and the `equals` method."

• `Object` as a Superclass (page 156)

Item 3

"Write code that uses the generic versions of the Collections API, in particular, the `Set`, `List`, and `Map` interfaces and implementation classes. Recognize the limitations of the non-generic `Collections` API and how to refactor code to use the generic versions."

• Generic Types (page 169)

Item 4

"Develop code that makes proper use of type parameters in class/interface declarations, instance variables, method arguments, and return types; and write generic methods or methods that make use of wildcard types and understand the similarities and differences between these two approaches."

• Declaring Classes (page 87)
• Defining an Interface (page 142)
• Passing Information to a Method or a Constructor (page 93)
• Returning a Value from a Method (page 106)
• Generic Types (page 169)
• Generic Methods and Constructors (page 172)
• Wildcards (page 177)

Item 5

"Use capabilities in the `java.util` package to write code to manipulate a list by sorting, performing a binary search, or converting the list to an array. Use capabilities in the `java.util` package to write code to manipulate an array by sorting, performing a binary search, or converting the array to a list. Use the `java.util.Comparator` and `java.lang.Comparable` interfaces to affect the sorting of lists and arrays. Furthermore, recognize the effect of the 'natural ordering' of primitive wrapper classes and `java.lang.String` on sorting."

- Algorithms (page 355)

Section 7: Fundamentals

Item 1

"Given a code example and a scenario, write code that uses the appropriate access modifiers, package declarations, and import statements to interact with (through access or inheritance) the code in the example."

- Controlling Access to Members of a Class (page 110)
- Using Package Members (page 187)

Item 2

"Given an example of a class and a command-line, determine the expected runtime behavior."

- Command-Line Arguments (page 448)
- Command-Line I/O Objects (page 452)

Item 3

"Determine the effect upon object references and primitive values when they are passed into methods that perform assignments or other modifying operations on the parameters."

- Passing Information to a Method or a Constructor (page 93)

Item 4

"Given a code example, recognize the point at which an object becomes eligible for garbage collection, and determine what is and is not guaranteed by the garbage collection system. Recognize the behaviors of `System.gc` and `finalization`."

- Using Objects (page 103)

Item 5

"Given the fully-qualified name of a class that is deployed inside and/or outside a JAR file, construct the appropriate directory structure for that class. Given a code example and a classpath, determine whether the classpath will allow the code to compile successfully."

- Managing Source and Class Files (page 191)

Item 6

"Write code that correctly applies the appropriate operators including assignment operators (limited to: =, +=, -=), arithmetic operators (limited to: +, -, *, /, %, ++, --), relational operators (limited to: <, <=, >, >=, ==, !=), the instanceof operator, logical operators (limited to: &, |, ^, !, &&, ||), and the conditional operator (? :), to produce a desired result. Write code that determines the equality of two objects or two primitives.

- Assignment, Arithmetic, and Unary Operators (page 56)
- Equality, Relational, and Conditional Operators (page 59)
- `Object` as a Superclass (page 156)
- Comparing Strings and Portions of Strings (page 224)

Index

Symbols

Numbers

A

F

K

L

M

N

Q

R

S

T

U

The Java Tutorial CD

THE *Java Tutorial* CD that accompanies this book is loaded with the latest Java SE software and documentation, including the content and code of this book. The solutions and answers (to the questions and exercises) are also included.

Product	Version	Notes
Java Platform, Standard Edition 6	Build 93	This bundle, originally released on `http://download.java.net/jdk6/`, includes the JRE, JDK, Java API spec, and the guide documentation.
The Java Tutorial	HTML. The August 4, 2006 build.	The latest tutorial is available on `http://java.sun.com/docs/books/tutorial/`. By the time of this printing, the entire tutorial will be updated to release 6.
The Troubleshooting Guide	The 5.0 version and an extract of the 6.0 version, distributed at JavaOne.	By the time of this printing, this guide will be updated to release 6 and available from the "Troubleshooting" link under "Sun Resources" at `http://java.sun.com/javase/index.jsp`.

The `README.html` file on the CD is the central HTML page that links you to all the contents. To view this page, use the **Open File** command or its equivalent in your Internet browser. On some platforms, you can simply double click on the HTML file to launch it in your browser.

The following resources offer useful information and help:

- The Sun Developer Network (SDN) offers free developer tools, newsletters, forums, and more. You can find it at `http://developers.sun.com/`.
- java.net includes technical forums, blogs, and early release of Java software. You can find it at `http://java.net/`.
- Official Java SE downloads are located at `http://java.sun.com/javase/downloads/`.